The United States and France: Civil War Diplomacy

by

LYNN M. CASE

and

WARREN F. SPENCER

UNIVERSITY OF PENNSYLVANIA PRESS

PHILADELPHIA

Copyright © 1970 by the Trustees of the University of Pennsylvania

Library of Congress Catalog Card Number 75–105108

SBN: 8122–7604–3

Printed in the United States of America

9.99

60334

The United States and France:
Civil War Diplomacy

In Grateful Tribute

to

ROY FRANKLIN NICHOLS
Inspiring Teacher and Patient Guide

PREFACE

One hundred and seven years have gone by since Franco-American relations began to be disturbed by the diplomatic problems of the Civil War. During this century there has been no attempt to deal in depth with the subject over the entire period and from the major documentary collections. The best scholarly work up to the present is Henry Blumenthal's chapter V (forty-seven pages) in his *Reappraisal of Franco-American relations, 1830–1870* (1959). This, of course, is a much condensed treatment, and the other studies were either contemporary propaganda pamphlets—like those of Cowell, Moreau, and George Bemis—or special studies, often limited to questions of international law or public opinion—such as those of C. F. Adams, Jr., Baxter, Harris, Case, West, Pratt, and Korolewicz-Carlton. In the meantime E. D. Adams and Ralph Lutz made full and definitive studies of England's and Germany's involvement in the crises of that war. It was for these reasons that the present authors began to explore the justification for a similar study devoted to France, and they became convinced that it deserved to be made and would reveal many important aspects of the diplomacy hitherto unknown or ignored.

The considerations leading to collaboration are understandable. One author, L. M. Case, has been pursuing for several years the preparation of a study of the diplomacy of Edouard Thouvenel, French foreign minister during the first half of the Civil War; and the other, W. F. Spencer, has been engaged in similar work on Thouvenel's successor, Drouyn de Lhuys. Consequently they were able to combine their specialized knowledge in the research and writing of this study and bring to it the great fund of new information revealed in many hitherto inaccessible and untapped sources. In the division of work Mr. Case has been responsible for chapters I through IX and Mr. Spencer for those from X through XVI, while both have collaborated closely

[vii]

in the preparation of the Preface, Introduction, conclusions, and Bibliography. It has been a pleasant and mutually helpful experience, and, it is hoped that impartiality may have been enhanced by the fact that both authors have lived and taught in the North and the South.

The authors wish to point out some deliberate emphases and restrictions in this study. Because of the pre-existence of Owsley's, Huntley's, and Callahan's studies on the diplomacy of the Confederacy, the present writers are emphasizing mainly France's relations with the United States. While this is logical because France did not recognize the independence of the Confederacy, the authors give adequate attention to the semi-official Franco-Confederate consultations wherever they are involved in the Franco-Union relations. Likewise, since the authors are primarily specialists in the history of France, this account will have a somewhat more French and European orientation in contrast to the American emphasis of so many histories of American diplomacy. As a final caveat, they wish to indicate that they have restricted their treatment of the Mexican expedition to the minimum. The diplomatic history of the Mexican intervention is a vast topic in itself. For reasons of limitations of size and for clarity they have had to attempt a concentration on the Civil War and have introduced only those aspects of the Mexican question which were obviously related to Civil War diplomacy.

On the other hand, in what relates directly to Franco-Union relations, they have tried not to stint. The archives of the world are now so fully accessible and the printed literature so exhaustively vast that they feel that a full-length and definitive history should now be written. Thus disputes and negotiations have been developed in considerable detail, and extracts from the most crucial and important documents have been quoted and often translated. To enliven the inimitable dialogues of the colorful characters in this drama, the authors have sometimes transformed indirect quotations into their original direct form. It is hoped that the present work will therefore be readable, enjoyable, and at the same time as nearly definitive, exhaustive, and impartial as possible.

During the several years in which the present authors have

been engaged in preparing this study, they have been the re-
cipients of so many kindnesses from so many institutions and
from personal as well as professional friends that space does not
allow them to recount in detail all the special favors shown them.
First of all, expressions of gratitude should be made to the University of Pennsylvania and to the Old Dominion College Edu-
cational Foundation for several grants of research funds, to the
American Philosophical Society for a summer research grant, and
to the Social Science Research Council for travel expenses
abroad. Among the archives and libraries to which they are
deeply indebted they wish to mention with special gratitude, in
the United States: the staffs of the Foreign Affairs Division of
the National Archives (especially the late Carl Lokke and Mrs.
Julia Carroll), of the Department of Special Collections of the
University of Rochester Library (especially Mrs. Margaret K.
Toth), of the Division of Manuscripts of the Library of Congress,
of the Manuscripts Division of the Princeton University Library,
of the Manuscripts Division of the New York Public Library, of
the American Philosophical Society Library, of the Van Pelt
Library of the University of Pennsylvania, of the Robert Morton
Hughes Library of Old Dominion College, and of the Ilah Dun-
lap Little Memorial Library of the University of Georgia; in
France, the staffs of the Archives du Ministère des Affaires étran-
gères (especially Messieurs Degros and Dethan), of the Archives
Nationales (especially the late Georges Bourgin, Mme d'Huart,
and Mme Gille), of the Archives de la Marine, of the Archives
Départementales de la Loire-Atlantique, of the Archives Dé-
partementales de l'Isère (especially M. Robert Avezou), of the
Bibliothèque Nationale (especially M. Albert Krebs), of the
Bibliothèque de la Sorbonne (especially Mme Spire), and of the
Bibliothèque de l'Institut; in Great Britain: the staffs of the Pub-
lic Records Office (especially Messrs. Timings and Blakiston), of
the National Register of Archives (especially Mr. Ellis, the
Misses Coates and Ranger, and Colonel White), and of the British
Museum Library and Manuscripts Division; in Austria: the
staff of the Haus-, Hof-, und Staatsarchiv; and in Sweden: the
staff of the Riksarkivet.

The richness of the collections of private papers makes the

x   THE UNITED STATES AND FRANCE

authors—for their kind permissions to use and to quote extracts—particularly grateful to the late Antoine Thouvenel and to M. Robert Heine (grandson and great-grandson of Edouard Thouvenel) for the Thouvenel Family Papers, to the late Duke of Gramont for the Gramont Papers, to Admiral of the Fleet the Earl of Mountbatten and Burma and the Broadlands Trust for the Palmerston Papers, to the Adams Trust for the microfilms of the Adams Papers, to Mr. Robert W. Messenger and Mrs. James Ireland for the Seward Papers, to Mrs. H. Emerson Tuttle for the Weed Papers, and to the Public Records Office for the Foreign Office papers.

Among their kind colleagues who have given them valuable advice and suggestions they would like to give sincere thanks to Professors Roy F. Nichols, Arthur P. Whitaker, Henry Blumenthal, Gabriel Kolko, Daniel W. Smith, the late Howard C. Perkins, Mrs. Frank L. Owsley, Dean Pierre Renouvin, Claude Fohlen, Father Guillaume de Bertier de Sauvigny, the late Georges Bourgin, the late Rembert W. Patrick, René Thalvard, and Mr. and Mrs. Jerome Stenger. There have also been, during these years, several research assistants whose loyal services must be gratefully acknowledged—Messrs. Raymond Lorantas, William Echard, Peter Rutkoff, and John Knapp—and many typists and copyists to whom warm thanks are also due—Mlles Germaine Depret-Bixio and Suzanne Lénault, Miss Sarah E. Calhoun, Mrs. Patricia F. Haines, and Miss Dorothy Disharoon. Last, but far from least, the wives of the authors have earned a special vote of thanks for the encouragement and patience that created the sustaining atmosphere in which all this effort could be carried forward. Thus, a multitude of staunch supporters, from around the whole wide circle of the Atlantic Community, have, without a clear awareness of it, combined in labor and kindnesses to make possible this recovered, and hence, enduring record of a decisive turning-point in transatlantic relations. With backward glance the authors wish to express their deep appreciation for all these helping hands and guiding thoughts.

Lynn M. Case   Warren F. Spencer
University of Pennsylvania   *University of Georgia*

CONTENTS

ABBREVIATIONS

AM   Archives de la Marine (Paris).

AMAE CP, MD   Archives du Ministère des Affaires étrangères (Paris).   Correspondance politique; Mémoires et Documents.

AN   Archives Nationales (Paris).

AN (M)   Archives Nationales (Paris).   Fonds de la Marine.

BFSP   Great Britain. *British and foreign state papers.*

BM   British Museum (London).   Manuscript Division.

CSDP   Confederate State Department Papers (Pickett Papers). Library of Congress (Washington).   Manuscript Division.

DDI   Italy.   *I documenti diplomatici italiani.*

FRUS   United States.   *Papers relating to the foreign affairs of the United States.*

HHSA PA   Haus-, Hof-, und Staatsarchiv (Vienna).   Politische Akten.

LQV   *Letters of Queen Victoria.*

NA   National Archives (Washington).

ORN   United States.   *Official records of the Union and Confederate navies.*

PRO FO   Public Record Office (London).   Foreign Office.

RCA LC   Russian Central Archives (photostats).   Library of Congress (Washington).

SDC   State Department Correspondence.   National Archives (Washington).

About the Notes
The notes will be found on pages 609–694. In the text, referential notes are indicated by superior numbers in roman type, explanatory notes by superior numbers in italics.   In the note section, headings at the top of each page indicate the pages of the text to which the notes refer.

The United States and France:
Civil War Diplomacy

INTRODUCTION*

The diplomatic repercussions of the American Civil War had wide and profound influences on the foreign relations of Europe and the Western Hemisphere. The war in the United States occurred during the same period as the unification of Italy, the Mexican expedition, the Polish insurrection of 1863, the Danish War of 1864, and menacing signs of an impending Austro-Prussian conflict. Furthermore, this Civil War raised a wide range of issues involving international law and practice: recognition of belligerence and independence, neutral rights, blockade, embargo, privateering, search and seizure, exequaturs for consuls, protection of foreign persons and property in belligerent countries, intervention, mediation, belligerent ships in neutral ports, neutral construction of belligerent ships, neutral supplies of contraband goods to belligerents, the floating of belligerent bonds in neutral countries, and the recruiting of crews for belligerent warships. Just five years before the outbreak of the American struggle, a Declaration of Paris, issued by the great powers and accepted by over forty states—not including the United States—had defined new international maritime law regarding blockades, privateering, and the treatment of neutral ships and goods on the high seas. This American war furnished the first occasion for the application of these new rules of the sea. There were sensational incidents such as the "Trent" affair, the Mexican expedition, the naval battles of the "Monitor" and "Merrimac" and of the "Alabama" and "Kearsarge," the escape of the CSS "Stonewall" from a French port, and the visit of the Russian fleet to Northern ports.

Beyond the purely diplomatic and legal aspects of the Civil War certain economic and social factors affected the international community. With the advent of the Industrial Revolution the

---

* The full citations of the sources and works mentioned in this chapter will be found in the bibliography at the end of this study.

peoples of the Western world were becoming more and more economically interdependent, a condition which this war brought home to those on both sides of the Atlantic. Without cotton from the South, there came a serious setback to the cotton industries of England and France; without the American market many French and British exporting industries suffered acutely. The shot fired at Fort Sumter, like that at Concord, was heard around the world, and its echoes reverberated in Europe down to the humble cottage and decaying slum, where to the usual poverty was added the misery of unemployment with concomitant deprivation, hunger, and the despair of crime, disease, drunkenness, and prostitution. If Cotton was King in the South, alas he wore a crown of thorns in France.

Along with the Industrial Revolution had come a new technology. The age of steam and steel had dawned, and this was one of the earliest wars in which all the current new technologies were brought into full use: mass production of weapons and war supplies, strategical use of railroads, military communications by telegraph, navies of ironclad steamships, gas and petroleum oil for lighting and fuel. French, Prussian, Austrian, and British observers swarmed over the theaters of operations, and a French warship watched at close range the encounters of the ironclad "Monitor" and "Merrimac." Detailed reports went home to the general staffs and admiralties, and feverish efforts were made to outdo rivals in armored ships and military railroads. Indeed, King Cotton was about to be toppled by Prince Steel.

Beyond all this, there was an ideological dimension. Like the shot from Sumter, so around the world went Lincoln's defiant words from Gettysburg—"We are now engaged in a great civil war, testing whether that nation, or any nation so conceived and so dedicated [in liberty and equality] can long endure." The youthful Republic of the Western World, torn, bleeding, and massively assailed, was trying hard to stay on its feet and hold its head high. Looking on from afar, the conservatives in Europe, monarchical and aristocratic in principle, saw in a Northern defeat the decline of republicanism, egalitarianism, and radicalism. They sympathized with the aristocratic Southern society and condoned slavery as its bulwark. In their subconscious minds land tenantry was not too far removed from slave labor. With a trace of inconsistency in their conservatism, these aristocrats appealed to the principle of nationalism in justifying the right of the South to its separate independence. On the other hand, the radical Liberals in England—the Cobdens and the Brights—and the liberal Orleanists, liberal Bonapartists, and republicans in France—Laboulaye, Broglie, Thouvenel, the Orleans princes, and Prince Napoleon—looked upon the North as the hope of liberal governments, whether monarchical or republican, the champion of human rights, the emancipator of slaves, and the crusader for American nationalism against parochial separatism.

. . . . . .
Humanity with all its fears,
With all the hopes of future years,
[Was] hanging breathless on [its] fate!

And yet—and how inexplicable it is—in spite of four long years of conflict and the weighty impingement of the war upon European diplomacy, in spite of its extensive bearing on international and maritime law, in spite of its technological transformation of warfare, in spite of the widespread economic disruption and suffering it caused, in spite of the fateful principles it endangered and rescued in the end, no one, after the passing of a hundred years, has written a comprehensive diplomatic history of the Civil War. To be sure, this war can boast an historical literature at least equal to that relating to any other episode in the national history of the United States, and its diplomatic history has been the subject of thousands of books and articles. In this study, restricted to relations with France alone, there are listed over four hundred items of printed collections, books, and articles; but each of these is restricted to some limited aspect, period, or area of the diplomatic history.* Among all of these items, outside of William H. Seward's own recollections of his diplomacy (*Diplomatic history* and *Seward at Washington*), there is only one which deals broadly with all the diplomacy of the United States during the war—Temple's sixty pages on the diplomacy of Seward in vol-

---

* Contemporary histories, in book or pamphlet form, of the 1860's and 1870's are not considered in this discussion.

ume VII of the series on *American secretaries of state and their diplomacy*.

Indeed, when it comes to overall diplomatic history, the Confederacy has outstripped the Union, because the South can boast of two respectable works: one by Callahan on the *Diplomatic history of the Southern Confederacy* and another by Owsley on *King Cotton diplomacy*. On Franco-Confederate relations Huntley published a dissertation in French in 1932, and Callahan did the same for Anglo-Confederate relations in 1899. There were also several articles of uneven value on Confederate diplomacy. Aldis (in 1879) was the first to use Slidell's official reports in the so-called Pickett Papers in an article on "Napoleon III and the Confederacy." Good, as far as it goes, it is based entirely on one source. Du Bose has a general article (1904) on Confederate diplomacy, and Spencer has one (1963) limited to Drouyn de Lhuys and the Confederate-Arman ironclads. However, both Spencer's article and Bigelow's earlier book (1888) on *France and the Confederate navy*, as well as Todd's dissertation (1941) on "Building the Confederate navy in Europe," transcend purely Confederate diplomacy and deal also with that of the United States. Bonham contributed a chapter in a Festschrift, and Gordon Wright an article, each dealing with the French consuls in the Confederacy; and Bonham's dissertation (1911) studied the *British consuls in the Confederacy*.

As far as the Civil War diplomacy of the Union is concerned, there are studies of relations with individual countries. The best known and one of the finest is E. D. Adams' *Great Britain and the American Civil War* (1925) in two volumes and now in a reprint edition (1959). Newton's two-volume biography of *Lord Lyons* (1913), based upon the Lyons papers, and his thirty-three pages on Anglo-American relations during the Civil War in the *Cambridge history of British foreign policy* (1923) preceded the Adams study. Then on Lord Lyons' opposite number in London, Charles Francis Adams, there are biographies by his son, Charles Francis Adams, Jr. (1900) and by Duberman (1961). Sixteen years ago a popular article by Belloff on "Great Britain and the American Civil War" appeared in *History* (1952). Of course, both Charles Francis Adamses, Senior and Junior, contributed a total of seven books and six articles on Anglo-Federal relations in this period.

On the German side we have Lutz's thorough study of *Die Beziehungen zwischen Deutschland und den Vereinigten Staaten während des Secessionskrieges* (1911) and his article on Schleiden's visit to Richmond (1917).

Curiously enough, Russia, which was so distant from the United States in space as well as in ideology, has enjoyed considerable study, perhaps because of the visit of her fleet. For Northern diplomacy Callahan contributed an article (1908) on "Russo-American relations during the American Civil War," and Woldman, in 1952, brought out *Lincoln and the Russians.* By utilizing Russian archival materials, both Golder and Adamov have given us scholarly articles of value—Golder's "The Russian fleet and the Civil War" (1915) and "The American Civil War in the eyes of a Russian diplomat [Stoeckl]" (1921); and Adamov's "Russia and the United States at the time of the Civil War" (1930).

While Germany and Russia were rather remote from the American crisis, Great Britain and France were in the very vortex of the storm. Thus it is understandable that Great Britain should have had a thorough coverage, by E. D. Adams, of her Civil War relations with the United States. Yet France's relations with the United States were equally important, not only because of her Mexican expedition, but also because of her concern for cotton, tobacco, wheat, exports, naval power, international law, and, of course, because of the "Trent" affair. Indeed, we see now that her action was decisive in the solution of the "Trent" dispute. In that case, as in all others, France worked closely with England, and they share in each other's diplomatic history.

Despite the important position of France respecting the Civil War and her close association with England, the historiography on her role, in contrast to that on Great Britain's, is woefully wanting and spotty. To be sure, twenty years after the war Teichmann, a German, wrote a combined study of *Englands und Frankreichs Stellung zum Burgerkriege;* but this had to be based on limited sources—published documents and self-vindicating memoirs—

and after all, France's role only occupied half of Teichmann's story. Other than this early German study there were only two partial and somewhat unsatisfactory monographic attempts to tell the Franco-Federal diplomatic story, both of them doctoral dissertations. Elliott Evans, in 1940, wrote a monograph on "Napoleon III and the American Civil War"; but the emphasis was on the ruler, and most of the sources were printed. The other doctoral effort, in 1951, by Korolewicz-Carlton, an American student at the Sorbonne, dealt with "Napoléon III, Thouvenel, et la guerre de Sécession." While using some archival sources available in Paris, for other countries this author had to rely heavily on the same questionable printed sources used by Teichmann sixty-six years before. The result was a disappointing amateur effort, which, at the same time, tended to concentrate on the interplay of the two men and ended with an erroneous conclusion—that Thouvenel's dismissal in October 1862 was due more to his disagreement with the emperor on the American question than to that on the Italian question. Moreover, it can be seen that, when Korolewicz' treatise ends, it has covered less than half of the Civil War.

For lack of an adequate full-length study of France and the Civil War, we have to fall back on two good one-chapter monographs: S. Bernstein's Chapter VIII in *Essays in political and intellectual history* (1955); and—the best of all the short treatments—Blumenthal's Chapter V in his *Reappraisal of Franco-American relations* (1959). Blumenthal should be highly commended for his wide use of unpublished official and private papers and for his skillful handling of the complicated issues within such a small compass, but forty-six pages is hardly sufficient for a history that required two volumes for a parallel study by E. D. Adams.

The rest of the historical literature on the French side is made up of short and fragmentary efforts on widely scattered topics. Lewis Einstein, a nonprofessional historian, in a short book and a shorter article, both in 1905—before the archives were open— wrote on the year 1861. W. R. West (1924), E. J. Pratt (1931), L. M. Case (1936), and Gavronsky (1964, 1966) contributed full-length books on French opinion; and Case has a few other articles covering France on the questions of secession, recognition, and the "Trent" affair.

On the war's economic repercussions in France there has also been sporadic and scattered research. The most thorough and scholarly of these economic investigations are Fohlen's work on *L'industrie textile au temps du Second Empire* (1956) and his article on the "Crise textile" (1953). Half of Case's book on *French opinion on the United States and Mexico* (1936) is devoted to the economic reports of the procureurs general during the war. While W. O. Henderson's article (1933) discusses "The cotton famine on the Continent," Pomeroy's (1943) studies "French substitutes for American cotton," and S. B. Thompson's book (1935) examines *Confederate purchases . . . abroad.*

One last category of these scattered and limited contributions is that of biographies of the leading French and American statesmen involved in the diplomacy. To Nicolay's and Hay's ten-volume *Lincoln* (1890) have been added more recently Randall's four-volume biography (1945-1955) and Monaghan's *Diplomat in carpet slippers* (1945). On the foreign ministers Sister O'Rourke has written a dissertation on Seward and international law (1963), and Van Deusen has contributed a classic biography of Seward (1967). On the French side Thouvenel's son, Louis, issued three volumes of his father's personal correspondence in *Le secret* (1889) and *Pages* (1903); while d'Harcourt in his *Quatre ministères* (1882) and Spencer in his more recent dissertation (1955) have shed new light on Drouyn de Lhuys. The diplomats in the field have come in for their share of attention with Carroll's dissertation on "Mercier in Washington" (1968), with Bigelow's own writings on his Paris assignments—*Confederate navy* (1888) and *Confederate loan* (1905)—with his son, Poultney's, two articles on Bigelow's relationship to Napoleon III and to Seward (1932), and with Clapp's laudatory study of Bigelow, uncharacteristically portrayed as the *Forgotten citizen* (1949). While secessionist Faulkner so far has only rated a thirteen-page article by McVeigh (1951), Slidell has been made the subject of biographical studies by Sears (1925), Dugan (1915), and Willson (1932). Of the unofficial envoys, Weed's biographer is Van Deusen (1947), and Archbishop Hughes enjoys the dubious luxury of four biographical studies between 1866 and 1947 by Andrews, Hassard, McGuire, and O'Daniel. Only Dayton and Montholon seem to be waiting for someone to rescue them from oblivion.

In spite of these incomplete and scattered studies on partial aspects of France's connection with the Civil War, France as a whole, likewise needs to be rescued from historical neglect. The task of writing a comprehensive history on France and the Civil War is therefore justified by the very fact of the nonexistence of such a history after the lapse of a century and is also encouraged by the present availability of an almost inexhaustible array of new sources, some in printed form and some in archival collections.

As far as printed official documents are concerned, the student of the Civil War is fortunate because its outbreak coincided with the inauguration by various governments of serial publications of their diplomatic documents. The British had been publishing their current selected diplomatic documents since 1801 in the form of *Parliamentary papers*, frequently referred to as *Blue books* and now as *Sessional papers* on microcards. France and the United States adopted this British practice, both in 1861, with Thouvenel's publication in France of the first volume of *Documents diplomatiques*, appropriately called *Livres jaunes*, and with Seward's issuance of the first volume of the *Papers relating to the foreign affairs of the United States*. In addition to these so-called "colored books" several countries republished annually their own and foreign documents for the use of their diplomats and consuls: the *British and foreign state papers* (since 1832), the French *Archives diplomatiques* (since 1861), and the German *Staatsarchiv* (since 1861). Thus the early contemporary historians of Civil War diplomacy had voluminous collections, however biased the material was by its justificatory selection.

Subsequently, in the late nineteenth and twentieth centuries, new material began to appear in print. In France, after the downfall of the Second Empire, some papers of Napoleon III were found in the Tuileries Palace and published as *Papiers sauvés* (1871) and *Papiers secrets* (1873), Thouvenel's *Pages* and *Secrets* were issued in 1903 and 1889, the journals of Prince

Napoleon's visit to the United States in 1933 and 1959, and the procureur reports on French opinion and economic conditions, edited by Case, in 1936. The American harvest was much greater because in the *Official records of the Union and Confederate navies* (1894-1927) historians obtained the official correspondence of Slidell and Mason, as well as of Mann, Yancey, and Rost; Nicolay and Hay brought out the first edition of Lincoln's works (twelve volumes in 1905); Basler issued a more recent supplement to Lincoln's papers (1953); Richardson edited the presidential *Messages and papers* (1896-1899) and the *Messages and papers of the Confederacy* (1905); and Rowland edited the papers of Jefferson Davis in 1923. There were also Baker's printed papers of Seward (1890), Senator Sumner's papers (1870-1883), and those of Archbishop Hughes (1865). On the English side (and always associated with France in the problems of the Civil War) there were the *Letters of Queen Victoria* (1908 and 1927), Martin's *Life* [and letters] *of the Prince Consort*, Ashley's *Life and correspondence of Viscount Palmerston* (1879), and Gooch's *Later correspondence of Lord John Russell* (1925). Further materials appear in the constant stream of memoirs: in France those of Prince Napoleon, Colonel Ferri-Pisani, Maurice Sand, and Baron Beyens; and in the United States those of Seward, Hay, Bigelow, Sumner, Chase, Bates, Welles, Browning, Hughes, Weed, Dr. Evans, and Bulloch. All of these printed papers of governments and statesmen are now available and would be richly rewarding for any future general diplomatic history of the Civil War or for the more restricted, but still neglected, Franco-American diplomatic history of the period.

Added to these printed collections are also the even more vast, richer, and, in most cases, still unused archival collections, both public and private. They have revealed, in many instances, the danger of relying too heavily on the highly selective printed governmental series, such as the *Livres jaunes* and the *Blue books*. While the British, French, and American archives of official diplomatic correspondence on the Civil War have been open to researchers since 1920, very few, except E. D. Adams researching the British story, have made exhaustive use of the correspondence of the foreign ministries abroad and of the state department in

Washington. Examples of the superficial use of these archives are those of Owsley and E. D. Adams. In the 1700 footnotes of his *King Cotton Diplomacy* Owsley cited the French foreign ministry archives only thirty-five times; and E. D. Adams, in spite of the close association of England and France in all their diplomacy relating to the Civil War, never used the French official foreign ministry archives at all. Korolewicz did use the foreign ministry archives, but in a hasty and partial manner and on a limited topic. Consequently the present authors, by trying to make full use of a large number of foreign ministry archives, found abundant new material to supplement the early governmental publications. Every volume of French archival correspondence with the United States and England, and at certain points also with Russia, was utilized for all the years between 1861 and 1866, including the consular reports. The same was true for the corresponding official diplomatic archives in England (in the Public Record Office) and in the United States (in the National Archives). Some use was also made of Hülsemann's reports from Washington in the Austrian Haus-, Hof-, und Staatsarchiv in Vienna and of Count Piper's reports from Washington in the Swedish Riksarkivet in Stockholm. The Russian correspondence of Baron Stoeckl (minister in Washington) to Gorchakov, now in photostat form, and the Schleiden reports to the Bremen senate, on microfilm, were both utilized by the authors in the Manuscript Division of the Library of Congress. Likewise in this same repository full use was made of the Confederate state department correspondence (sometimes called the "Pickett Papers"), now faithfully reproduced in the volumes of the *Official records of the Union and Confedrate navies*.

In connection with these official archives the authors would like to point out certain new groups of material which came to light. In the French foreign ministry archives were four boxes of manuscripts in a heretofore unused miscellaneous collection, designated in our references as "Fonds Divers. Guerre des Etats-Unis, 1861-1865." Here were found the communications from the Confederacy which would have been integrated with the regular "Correspondance politique" if the South had achieved its independence. Also in these boxes was the Anglo-French correspondence on maritime law. Neglected French naval records and documents (in the Archives de la Marine and in the Fonds du Ministère de la Marine in the Archives Nationales) were full of astonishing treasures, especially concerning warships in ports, construction of ironclads, and effectiveness of the blockade.

New material appearing in the National Archives of the United States was, first of all, the reports of Henry Sanford from Brussels in 1861 and 1862. Until Dayton assumed his post in Paris in May 1861, Seward relied on Sanford to explain to Thouvenel the views of the new Republican administration and to report on French government attitudes. Even after Dayton's arrival Sanford continued to proffer his unsolicited aid—so low did he rate Dayton and so high did he esteem himself. Yet, these reports have usually been overlooked because they were tucked away in the Belgian correspondence. Also quite often ignored was the correspondence between the French legation and the state department in Washington and in Paris the like correspondence between the American legation and the French foreign ministry. In the National Archives we find the Washington exchanges, which no longer exist in the French legation (now embassy) files because of the French legation fire in 1862, and also in the same repository we have on microfilm (Record Group 84) the Dayton-Thouvenel correspondence in Paris.

An even more abundant harvest of new manuscripts was gathered from new collections of private papers, whose availability is much more delayed than that of the governmental collections because there is no regular schedule of declassification. Proprietary families are often reluctant to permit the prying of historians or are heedless of the historical significance of their holdings. Eventually, however, after two or three generations of attic storage, very valuable sources of information emerge from sheltered concealment. Since World War II this has been particularly true of Civil War private materials. The most famous of all were the Lincoln papers of the Robert Todd Lincoln collection, deposited at the Manuscripts Division of the Library of Congress, opened to the public after 1950, and reproduced on microfilm for distribution. Likewise, the Adams Papers, including those of Charles Francis Adams, Sr., have been microfilmed and distributed regionally. Along with these came a host of other collections: the Seward and Weed papers at the University of Rochester Library; the Eustis papers of the secretary of Slidell, and the Mason papers in the Library of Congress; the George P. Marsh—minister to Italy—papers in the Library of the University of Vermont; the Sanford papers in Sanford, Florida; and the Bulloch letters in the Whittle papers in the Norfolk Public Library.

The discovery of new private papers in France almost equalled that in America. The new papers of Edouard Thouvenel was the biggest surprise of all. After Louis Thouvenel's publication of six volumes of his father's letters one had felt that everything of importance in his private correspondence had been revealed. But such was not the case. In 1870 the Germans had captured the main body of his private ministerial correspondence. These so-called Cerçay Papers were held, unused, by the Germans until the Versailles Treaty in 1919 compelled their restitution. Deposited in the Archives du Ministère des Affaires étrangères, Thouvenel's papers alone (mostly incoming) filled twenty-one fat manuscript volumes (AMAE MD, Papiers Thouvenel). Louis Thouvenel never had an opportunity to see or use them. But Louis Thouvenel's own collection of his father's papers had not been fully used in his six published volumes. Handed down to Louis' son, Antoine, thousands of unread letters had been reverently stowed away on wide, capacious closet shelves. When approached by Mr. Case, the elderly grandson generously permitted unrestricted research, even to the extent of contura reproduction of some of the most important items. M. Robert Heine, the present proprietary legatee, has been even more cooperative in allowing the full microfilming of the collection for deposit in the Archives Nationales as MI 192, consisting of about twenty-five microfilm rolls.

Included in these same restored Cerçay Papers were the private papers of Eugene Rouher, minister of commerce during the Civil War blockade and embargo. Five volumes of his papers, dealing mainly with foreign affairs, were deposited in the foreign ministry archives (AMAE MD); a larger quantity, dealing with Rouher's ministries of commerce, transportation, and public works, constitute the Fonds Rouher in the Archives Nationales. Several other French private collections have now become available: the Mercier papers at Château de Montaigne; the Billault papers in the Archives Départementales de la Loire-Atlantique in Nantes; the Gramont, La Valette, and Persigny papers in the Archives Nationales; and the Walewski papers in the AMAE.

The same new wealth of private papers for the Civil War period exists in England. The Royal Archives at Windsor Castle now permit research in the papers of Queen Victoria and Prince Albert. Other large and valuable private collections made available since 1925—after E. D. Adams' work—are: the Clarendon papers in the Bodleian Library, Oxford; the Russell and the Cowley papers in the Public Record Office; the Palmerston papers in the National Register of Archives and (for his letter-books) in the Manuscript Division of the British Museum; and the Gladstone papers, likewise in the British Museum.

To the authors of this work, therefore, the field of new unpublished and published sources was white for the harvest, and the neglect of the French side of the Civil War was a challenge to their historical instincts. As they approached their task and the treasures in those mountains of unmined gold, there were many questions to be put to these sources. Was the French story so significantly distinct from that of the British that it called for a separate telling? Did France follow a consistent or a fluctuating policy? Was there an appreciable difference between the policies of Thouvenel and Drouyn de Lhuys? Was Napoleon III consistently pro-Southern? What influences affected Napoleon III in his decisions?* Was it England which restrained France from forceful intervention or vice versa? Was Mercier pro-Southern or merely resigned to separation? Was the cotton famine the main factor in France's economic slump? Were there other kings besides King Cotton in the Civil War pack of cards? Did the Mexican expedition make France more hostile to the North or more accommodating? Was the French note on the

---

* On the many crucial diplomatic issues which arose, agonizing policy decisions had to be made in France, the United States, and England, to which references may be found in the Index under the heading "Policy decisions."

"Trent" affair as influential as Prince Albert's revision of the British note?

On the American side there were also many questions to raise. Was there more than meets the eye in Seward's proposal of a foreign war? Did naïve inexperience or astute calculation lie behind Seward's bluster and protests? Did the North have a good justification for protesting against French and British recognition of Southern belligerency? Did the Declaration of Paris of 1856 turn out to be much ado about nothing? Was the blockade really effective, or was its acceptance a deliberate tolerance by England? Was the cotton embargo an overall success? Did the Confederacy instigate the "Trent" affair or did it just come about by Wilkes's blundering? How did Franco-Union diplomacy articulate with the vagaries of military campaigns? Was emancipation a turning point in French sentiment toward the North? Was Seward accommodating toward the French presence in Mexico because of monarchy's incompatibility with the current Mexican mood? Taking a long backward look, do we conclude that the Civil War, in its overall effect, appreciably strengthened or weakened the Franco-American ties of friendship?

These are the questions which haunted the minds of the authors as they approached their tasks of research and writing. The fact that they now present this work answers the initial question in the affirmative. And in this study an attempt has been made to answer most of the other questions. Yet, questions and answers aside, a story has had to be told and has been told. The authors hope that it has been unfolded, in fact and in verdict, in the spirit of Lincoln and Napoleon III, "with malice toward none, with charity for all; with firmness in the right, as God [and the sources] give us to see the right."

However, the Civil War was not the first, nor yet the last, episode in the two centuries of Franco-American relations—nor, indeed, in the five centuries of the Atlantic Community. This conflict brought to those engulfed in it experience as well as disruption—experience in sharp but informative dialogue, in international law and practice, in mutual self-restraint. Hereafter the Atlantic peoples worked in closer harmony—arbitration, mediation, two alliances, comradeship-in-arms in two world wars for survival and freedom, and mutual economic help during the dark post-war years of recovery. And there are symbolic sentinels which stand guard over this oceanic heritage. On the western side, a French lady lifts her lamp beside a golden door; on the eastern side, white crosses, row on row, in the fields of that lady's war-torn land, mark the final resting places of Frenchmen, Dutchmen, and Belgians, of Yank and Rebel grandsons, and of Canadians and Britons, who gave their last full measure of devotion that that free intercontinental community might live. When storm clouds gather again, as gather they will in human affairs, there will be many "mystic chords of memory" to raise once more the chorus of Atlantic union. In those evil days, these authors hope that their story of three peoples and a war will have become embedded in those memories, evoking courage, loyalty, and a wise restraint.

Chapter I

SECESSION AND THE UNION

The news of the secession of South Carolina, which arrived in Paris on January 7, 1861,[1] was not the starting point of French concern over the issue of secession and the integrity of the American Union. The storm of civil war, soon to break over the North American continent, had been preceded for almost two years by the ominous roll of thunder and dark clouds on the horizon, amply alerting Frenchmen and their government to the dangers implicit in the situation for both sides of the Atlantic. Indeed, those who had read de Tocqueville's *De la démocratie en Amérique* had learned as early as 1835 about the sectional rivalries and growing weaknesses appearing in the American federal structure.[2] As the young republic spread across the continent into Texas, Oregon, and California, observers could not but wonder how soon it would fall apart from pure overextension if not from the more urgent problem of slavery in the new territories.[3] In the 1850's many in France read Mrs. Stowe's *Uncle Tom's Cabin* in translation as avidly as had people in the northern American states.[4] Some had been introduced to the larger ramifications of prospective disruption by Froebel's study in German of America and world viewpoints, published in 1859, in which he presented the possibility of a split United States producing two competing giants of greater danger to Europe than the then undivided republic.[5] Eugène de Sartiges, French minister in Washington in 1858, had also warned his government that separation would probably mean war; and his secretary of legation, Treilhard, in his absence, in early 1860 had pointed out to the French foreign minister that a civil war over secession would seriously disrupt the world balance of power whether union or disunion won out.[6] Then the diplomatic and press reports of the year 1860, dealing with the party conventions, the split in the Democratic Party, and the dire threats of Southern secession in case of a Lincoln victory naturally brought the impending crisis home to both French statesmen and the interested public.

Two Frenchmen in particular were to be especially concerned with this emerging American problem—Emperor Napoleon III and his foreign minister since January 1860, Edouard Thouvenel. All during the year 1860 they had been absorbed with other disturbing events in connection with the unification of Italy[7] and the European intervention in Syria.[8] Yet, in spite of these major concerns of French foreign policy, the emperor and his minister were forced to give attention to worsening American developments. Even without a civil war, the splitting of the United States into two confederations would be a serious matter for France. She counted on the American republic as a single great power to help offset the naval and commercial supremacy of Great Britain. Furthermore, the Northern states within the Union could help restrain the Southern states from aggressive expansionism in Latin America. A peaceful separation would not only disturb the balance of power but might also lead to Anglo-French rivalry, with each sponsoring one half of the disrupted union. If war should come, the situation might become even worse. France might lose her source of raw cotton and the market for her manufactured goods during and even after the period of hostilities. At worst she and England might be dragged in on opposite sides, and a general war might ensue wherein the other European powers might take advantage of France's overseas preoccupations. Thus it was that the harried emperor and foreign minister had to find time during this busy year to watch and deal with the looming American crisis.

In Search of Information

Lincoln had once said, in regard to the slavery question, "If we could first know where we are, and whither we are tending, we could better judge what to do, and how to do it." This, in a sense, was also the feeling of Napoleon III and Thouvenel. In the period of impending crisis—1860—they felt the need to acquire as much knowledge as possible about the American situation in order to cope with secession once it occurred. While the emperor was on vacation at Biarritz in the summer of that year, he had an opportunity to obtain new information from Professor W. F. Maury of the University of Virginia to whom he granted an interview of an hour.

> After having exhausted all the little information I could afford him [wrote Maury], draining me *à sec*, and leaving me, after all, under the impression that he knew more of all the subject on which he had examined me than I did myself, he turned with peculiar and undisguised eagerness to the Mexican question. . . . He knew the very number of guns *in the Morro*, the sums the United States had spent on the fortifications in Florida, the exports and imports of Galveston and Matamoras, in short everything which well-informed local agents could have reported to an experienced statesman eager for information. He examined me again on Texas and its population, the disposition of the French residents, the tendencies of the German colonists, the feeling on the Texas frontier. Twice I remember well he repeated: 'La Louisiane n'est-ce pas qu'elle est Française au fond?' . . . He insisted upon it that France must sooner or later have a *pied à terre* on the Florida coast for the purpose of protecting her commerce in the Gulf, for, he added, 'Nous ne voulons pas un autre Gibraltar de ce côté-là.' Finally, I think, he revolved in his mind the possibility of recovering a foothold in Louisiana. . . .[9]

After the emperor's return to Paris he found another opportunity to inform himself on the United States in an interview he granted to the American minister, Charles J. Faulkner, on October 8, 1860. Faulkner came to present a letter from President Buchanan, complimenting Count Sartiges on the occasion of his departure from his Washington post. Having received the letter, Napoleon then asked Faulkner to sit down and began, in the form of a friendly conversation, a most intensive interrogation about conditions existing in the United States and its relations with France. He wanted to know the extent of the territory, the population, the number of states in the Union, the growth of cities, the railroads, and harvests.

He was particularly curious to learn [Faulkner reported] the prospects of the completion of the Pacific railroad, its length and probable cost. . . . He said that during his brief visit to the United States [in 1837] he had been most deeply impressed with the energy, activity, and vitality which pervaded every class of society, and every department of business, so much so that when he returned to his country, it seemed to him that all Europe was asleep. . . .

He inquired about the age and health of the President; when his term of service would end; whether I would return to the United States after the 4th of March next; whether it was customary to change the diplomatic representatives with the change in administration; who were the candidates for the presidency; what were the distinctive points of principle or policy upon which they claimed the suffrage of their fellow-citizens; whether the Know Nothing Party still existed or exercised any influence upon the policy of the country.

Toward the end of the interview he asked, "What is the feeling of the people of the United States toward France?"

"They are of the most friendly character," Faulkner replied.

"I suppose so, as there is no point of collision between the two countries, rather everything in their past history and present relations tend to unite them in bonds of unity."

He ended the interview with a warm handshake and an expression of pleasure over what he had derived from the conversation.[10]

It is obvious that Napoleon III was an avid seeker after knowledge on all matters of interest. Beckles Willson gives us further interesting information on the emperor's thirst for American information:

He read [says Willson] the narratives of English and French travelers in America the moment they were published; he frequently quoted Stewart's *Travels in North America*, and the volumes of Basil Hall and Mrs. Trollope. Copies of the *Boston Transcript* and the New Orleans *Delta*, as well as the *Courrier des Etats-Unis* were often observed on his desk, with passages marked by his own hand; and evidence still more valid, he showed a familiarity with the published Congressional Debates which occasionally embarrassed a visiting American legislator.[11]

The emperor had an advantage over his minister because he knew English very well while Thouvenel knew only French. This helped the monarch both in conversations with Americans and his wider scope of reading. However, Thouvenel was as tireless as his master in seeking knowledge of American affairs in spite of his simultaneous preoccupation with Italy and Syria. He watched eagerly not only the press and the reports of his minister in Washington, Henri Mercier, but also the reports from his consuls. The consuls had been urged particularly to keep him informed on the secessionist activities in the South, and the foreign minister was most indignant because Belligny, the consul in Charleston, of all places, was not sending in any reports.

> I can not explain, Sir, [Thouvenel complained] your silence toward the department in the face of the grave events occurring in the United States. All your colleagues understood from the very first the interest that the emperor's government had in being informed as completely as possible on all the phases of the crisis through which the Union is going and their correspondence shows the care they are taking to satisfy [the government] on this matter. So I have reason to be astonished that you have been furnishing me directly none of the information that you are more especially in a position to gather in the post where you reside on the incidents which can aggravate the current complications. I do not doubt, Sir, that in the future you will keep in mind this warning that I regret having to send to you.[12]

To Mercier, on the other hand, he gave praise as an inducement to send full information. "I don't need to insist to you [he wrote] on the value I attach in fact to being carefully kept up-to-date on everything connected with the American crisis and of the various predictions which it elicits around you as well as in the principal American newspapers."[13]

The information kept pouring in with the arrival of every dispatch and every telegraphic news report. On Saturday, November 24th, came the news of the election of Lincoln and the consternation of the leaders of the slave states. In their anxiety to protect their slave property, said Mercier, they will break with

the Union. South Carolina has already called a special session
of her legislature to deliberate on secession. Buchanan seemed
to be perplexed about how he should proceed. A week later
another dispatch from Mercier told Thouvenel that Georgia
was the key state to watch because she would carry with her the
states of North Carolina, Florida, and Alabama, a large enough
group to form an independent state. There was a slump on the
stock market, and some banks had had to suspend payments. He
enclosed a resolution passed by a meeting of secessionists asking
the Emperor of the French to recognize a new Southern confederation. People in both the North and South believed that
France wanted the disruption of the Union. Mercier complained
that none of these people made any effort to consult him. On
December 11 the French minister in Washington suggested that,
in addition to the newly planned shipping line to New York, one
also should be inaugurated to New Orleans because a low tariff
would probably be enacted in the South. On Christmas Day
came the news of Buchanan's weak message to Congress in which
he denied the right of secession but also confessed the impossibility of the Federal government to prevent it by force. "Nine
out of ten congressmen whom I ask," affirmed Mercier, "express
the conviction that the Union can not survive the experience it is
undergoing."[14]

These were the items of bad news going across the desks of the
emperor and his foreign minister up to the time of the imperial
New Year's reception. On that occasion, after the usual ceremonies with the diplomatic corps, the emperor went around the
circle of envoys, speaking a few words to each. When he reached
Faulkner, he stopped for a much longer time. With the kindest
tone of voice he inquired: "What is the latest intelligence you
have from the United States? Is the situation as bad as the
papers describe them?"

"Like other nations, Sire, we have our troubles, which lose
none of their color as seen through the European press."

"Is it true, as reported," the emperor persisted "that some of
the states have separated from the general confederation?"

"At the date of my latest information," the American minister
replied, "no state has yet withdrawn from the confederacy.

Much excitement exists in a portion of the country, and extreme measures are being threatened by some few of the states; but such commotions are not unprecedented amongst a people so absolutely free and unrestrained as ours. Bound together by a strong sense of common interest, we have already passed in safety through some perilous crises in our history. Although the exasperation now is more than ordinarily bitter, yet, the experience of the past justifies the hope that the strength of the Union will be found equal to the severe strain upon it."

"I sincerely hope it may prove so," the emperor retorted, "and that you may long continue a united and prosperous people." He then moved on to the next diplomat in line.[15]

Faulkner was right about no news on a definitive secession, since that of South Carolina did not arrive until a week later. But also it must be remembered that he was a citizen of Virginia who hoped for negotiated concessions to the South and, as minister, was impelled to minimize abroad the embarrassments of the crisis. In the meantime more news came in from Washington. Mercier had had a long talk with Senator Benjamin—the future Confederate secretary of state—and Senator Slidell—the future Confederate envoy to France—who said that secession must move fast to succeed. They hoped that the strong sympathy for the South's position in the border states and in the North generally would enable them finally to reconstruct the Union without New England.[16] On January 18 came another fuller report from Mercier. The rabid Southerners wanted to have civil war to consolidate sentiment in the seceding states; but many Northerners, confident of their strength in such a war, wished to avoid hostilities because they feared that it would make impossible the salvage of the Union. The extremists on both sides seemed to be getting control; efforts at reconciliation were failing.[17]

Enclosed with this dispatch was a copy of Benjamin's speech in the senate. Here Thouvenel and Napoleon III could find the arguments for secession. Benjamin began by saying that all the Southern states would support South Carolina and follow her out of the Union. She had every right to leave. She joined the Union by a popularly elected convention, and she was leaving in the same way. Even Daniel Webster had said that a compact, broken by one party, could be repudiated by the other. The makers of the constitution had agreed that neither the senate nor the president could veto the decision of a state. South Carolina, as a sovereign state, had the sole right to determine whether the compact had been violated. Furthermore no troops could go against an insurrection in a state without the permission of the civilian authorities of that state. A South Carolinian is not committing treason because he is remaining loyal to his state. A civil war to subjugate the South would violate the constitution; a closing of the Southern ports by law would do the same. A blockade could only be applied if open war were declared. The Republicans, according to Benjamin, tried to remind secessionists of all the Union benefits they would lose. They would give us everything except our money and property. He urged finally that the South be allowed to depart in peace; but, if secession were resisted, he warned that Southerners would fight to the death. Loud applause from the galleries greeted this peroration.[18]

Thouvenel was very much impressed with this last report. "I read your no. 17 with particular interest," he wrote to Mercier. And on the face of the dispatch he had written in pencil. "This dispatch, which is very good, could be sent to all our big posts abroad for their information."[19]

On January 24 the French government received another report from its Washington legation in which Mercier predicted that all the cotton states would have seceded before Lincoln's inauguration. He agreed with General Cass, who had resigned because he wanted stronger action to hold the Southern forts and who affirmed that the Union can not be broken without a civil war and that, once a war comes, the Union can not be restored.[20]

Early Official Reactions

With all of this new information received since the New Year's reception, Napoleon III expressed his first views on the American dispute at a ball in the Tuileries on the evening of January 23. Having greeted Faulkner cordially, he remarked, "The civilized world looks with interest upon the issue of the events now in progress in the United States." "I hope that all causes of alienation between the two sections of the Confederacy may be speedily arranged to the satisfaction of all concerned." The minister thanked him for his deep interest and added that this was a deserved reciprocation for the sympathy which Americans had for France "on many occasions of historical importance."[21] Just as in the New Year's interviews, Faulkner seemed to be trying to remind the emperor that others besides the United States had had their own troubles.

During the rest of Buchanan's administration Napoleon III and Thouvenel received only the arguments of the secessionists. Faulkner, a secessionist himself, furnished them with no Unionist arguments against secession. Yet in this interim period it is interesting to see that the emperor, without Unionist prodding, was described by Faulkner himself on March 19, 1861 as hostile to secession.

> I have no hesitation in expressing it as my opinion founded upon frequent general interviews with the Emperor . . . that she [France] will be the last of the great states of Europe to give a hasty encouragement to the dismemberment of the Union. . . . He looks upon the dismemberment of the American Confederacy with no pleasure, but as a calamity to be deplored by every enlightened friend of human progress. And he would act not only in conflict with sentiments often expressed but in opposition to the well understood feelings of the French people, if he should precipitately adopt any step whatever tending to give force and efficacy to those movements of separation, so long as a reasonable hope remains that the Federal Authority can, or shall be, maintained over the seceding States.[22]

On the last of February, Thouvenel received a note from Mercier telling about having the three senators, Seward, Douglas, and Crittenden, for dinner and repeating their firm belief in the preservation of the Union. But the message still contained no Northern constitutional arguments, and Mercier also expressed his doubts about the survival of the old Union.[23] "At the present time," Thouvenel replied cautiously, "I can only follow attentively its [the crisis'] course and must . . . await a definitive outcome before sending you . . . instructions necessitated by any radical change in the constituional relations now existing between the Northern and Southern states of the Union."[24]

On the very day Thouvenel wrote this message, the Lincoln administration took office, and the new president's first inaugural address contained a succinct statement of the Unionist arguments. He guaranteed the protection of slavery in the slave states and the return of fugitive slaves. On secession he stated that the fundamental law of any sovereign national state never provided for its own termination, and the Constitution of the United States did not so provide in this case. Hence the Union was perpetual. It could not be abrogated by one party to the compact, but only by the mutual agreement of all. Historically the Union is older than the states. Therefore no state may lawfully get out of the Union. On his part he has taken an oath to preserve the Union and execute its laws. He intends to do so firmly but with all consideration to others, especially in this crisis. The regulation of slavery in the territories is not provided for in the constitution. It is then a matter for the majority to decide. An opposing minority can not leave the Union on that question. That would be a challenge to the democratic process and would encourage secession later even among and within seceded states. Secession in the end means anarchy. In brief these were the main arguments.

Two weeks later Thouvenel finally knew the Unionist side of the case as elaborated by the highest authority. The *Moniteur* reported the speech on March 18, and a dispatch from Mercier, received on March 22, also contained a copy.[25] On March 6 the new cabinet met and discussed foreign relations,[26] and on the 9th Seward sent out circular instructions to the major diplomatic posts abroad with the Unionist arguments and copies of the inaugural address, all of which were to be presented by our ministers to the governments where they resided.[27]

Faulkner must have received these instructions by the end of March, but he did not see Thouvenel until a fortnight later. This delay may have reflected his reluctance to present the Unionist point of view, although Thouvenel's own preoccupations may have contributed to a deferred appointment.[28] Whatever may have been the cause of the delay, they had a conference on Monday, April 15th The American minister handed Thouvenel a copy of the inaugural address and added: "I am instructed by the secretary of state to say to you that it embraced the views of the President of the United States upon the difficulties which now disturb the harmony of the American Union, and also an exposition of the general policy which it was the purpose of the government to pursue with a view to the preservation of the domestic peace and the maintenance of the Federal Union."

"Is there not," responded the French foreign minister, "some diversity of opinion in the cabinet of the president as to the proper mode of meeting the difficulties which now disturb the relations of the states and the general government?"

"On that point I have no information. Under our system the cabinet is but an advisory body; its opinions are entitled to weight, but do not necessarily compel the action of the president. The executive power is, by the constitution, vested exclusively in the president." Faulkner then went on to say, "I am further instructed to assure you that the President of the United States entertains a full confidence in the speedy restoration of the harmony and unity of the government by a firm, yet just and liberal policy, co-operating with the deliberate and loyal action of the American people."

"I am very pleased to receive this assurance," the minister replied.

Later on in the conversation Thouvenel came out positively in favor of the preservation of the Union when he said, "I believe that the maintenance of the Federal Union in its integrity is to be desired for the benefit of the people North and South, as well as for the interest of France. . . ."

Toward the end a more informal exchange of comments ensued.

"Do you think," Thouvenel inquired, "that force will be used to preserve the Union?" He may have known of the American minister's Southern sympathies and hoped to draw from him some counterarguments. If so, he succeeded.

Faulkner began to give the familiar line of the defeated American minority. "It is my personal opinion," he replied, careful not to appear to misrepresent Seward, "that force will not be used." (This was three days after the fall of Fort Sumter, but that was, of course, unknown in France.) "The government of the United States [he continued] is one of public opinion, and the constituion has a means to provide for a solution. But public opinion is against the use of force against the seceding states. So sincere is the deference felt in our country for the great principles of self-government, and so great was the respect for the action of the people when adopted under the imposing forms of state organizations and state sovereignty that I do not think the employment of force would be tolerated for a moment. The only solution of our difficulties will be found in such modifications of our constitutional compact as will invite the seceding states back into the Union, or the peaceable acquiescence in the assertion of their claim to a separate sovereignty."

Without necessarily agreeing with all of Faulkner's remarks, Thouvenel did say, in closing the interview, "Certainly the employment of force would be unwise and would tend further to rupture the Confederacy [i.e. the United States] by causing the remaining Southern states to make common cause with the states which have already taken action on the subject."[29]

Thus, even before the arrival of a minister representing the views of the new administration, Thouvenel knew the arguments of both sides, and he and the emperor were initially expressing sympathy for the integrity of the Union.

New Envoys for the Paris Legation

Owing to the distances between America and Europe—the crossing required from fifteen to twenty days—it took some time for a replacement for Faulkner to arrive. Indeed, Faulkner had requested his own recall and sent in his resignation to Secretary Black as early as January 14, 1861. Anticipating the secession of Virginia even at a time when the Unionists there seemed to be predominant, he appeared to be making his wish the father of his thought. At least he felt that his state could withdraw his allegiance from the Federal government. Even should Virginia remain in the Union, he wanted to quit anyway because "I am now made to feel too keenly in all the circles in which I move, the extent to which the national prestige of that once great and growing Republic has been impaired by those events which destroyed the unity of our People, and paralyzed the arm of our National Power."[30]   Again, after receiving news of the inauguration, he wrote the usual congratulations to the new secretary, William H. Seward, and boldly reminded him of his desire to resign by referring to his secessionist despatch no. 90 to Black.[31]

Seward did not have to be coaxed to accept Faulkner's resignation. Only the confusion and heavy work of establishing a new administration and the Atlantic distances delayed the fulfillment of the wishes of secretary and minister alike.   When Lincoln passed through New Jersey on February 21 on his way to Washington, he met William L. Dayton on the train and was so favorably impressed with him that he kept him in mind for a diplomatic post.[32]   At first the new president had thought of Dayton for the London legation and Fremont for Paris, possibly because of Fremont's French background.[33]   Seward, however, wanted Charles Francis Adams as the London choice, and Lincoln acquiesced, shifting Dayton, who knew no French, to the Paris legation.[34]   When Dayton insisted upon a month to close out urgent affairs at home before leaving for his post,[35] Seward decided to have Henry S. Sanford, minister-designate for Belgium, precede Dayton to Paris and make the urgent new contacts with the French government in order to counteract Faulkner and the emissaries who were rumored to be on their way from the Southern Confederacy.

Indeed, Sanford arrived in Paris in the evening of April 15—the very day on which Faulkner had got around to fulfilling Seward's instructions that he present the Northern side of the controversy. This new interim, or interloping, minister lost no time in making some private and diplomatic contacts.   The next morning he learned from one of Faulkner's friends that the retiring minister intended to adopt delaying tactics by staying on until Dayton's arrival.   Soon after that he went directly to Faulkner and showed him Seward's letter to Thouvenel concerning Sanford's mission.   In it Seward commended Sanford to Thouvenel and asked him to receive him and to listen to all that he had to say confidentially concerning his home government.[36] This, of course, caused some embarrassment to both men, but Sanford tried to explain that Seward had thought Faulkner wanted to leave as soon as his letter of recall had arrived. As a matter of fact, from what the American papers had said and from statements by members of his family at home, it was surmised that he might already have left his post. Faulkner showed no inclination to take the hint, and Sanford consequently requested that Faulkner obtain for him an interview with Thouvenel, promising not to present his letter of introduction until a subsequent interview to avoid embarrassing the retiring minister.

Faulkner arranged to have Sanford accompany him to Thouvenel's regular diplomatic reception on the next evening, Wednesday, April 17. A week before, Thouvenel had learned that Sanford was coming, but Mercier had said that he would probably be negotiating on the elimination of passports.[37] Now Thouvenel at least had a chance to meet him but made no move to invite him for an interview; and Sanford, knowing how punctilious the French minister was, refrained from broaching the subject. After the reception Faulkner continued to delay an arrangement of an interview for his rival colleague. But the latter kept busy in the meantime, applying to the grand chamberlain for an audience with the emperor and observing opinion. He met a diplomat who knew Thouvenel well and learned that the foreign minister had said: "The question of recognition causes us embarrassment. We care nothing for the political question of right in the matter and would do nothing were those the only concerns. But the commercial question, that's what troubles us." In other ministerial circles, however, Sanford learned, they generally believed in the right of secession and the finality of the breakup of the Union.[38]

Five days elapsed before Faulkner got around to presenting Sanford officially to Thouvenel on the 22nd. Then Sanford felt free to ask the foreign ministry for an interview, which was arranged for April 24.[39] This time he went alone, and the interview lasted forty-five minutes. The American envoy presented Seward's personal letter and went on to expound Seward's circular of March 9, defending the integrity of the Union, and read him Seward's instructions which dealt primarily with the non-recognition of the Confederate government and matters of the tariff and the collection of customs. After Sanford had read the circular containing a defense of the Northern position, Thouvenel replied with a fuller and more formal statement of the French attitude toward the secession issue:

> Our sentiments, in line with the traditional policy of France, brought us to regret profoundly the disagreements which split the United States. We consider ourselves to be interested in the integral maintenance of the North American Union [*Confédération*], and we sincerely desire to see reestablished the harmony which has unfortunately been disturbed. Far from contributing to a deplorable separation, from which we can expect no advantage, we should like to be able to ward it off. Feeling this way, we dread the effect of whatever might bring about armed conflict between the two parties [news of Ft. Sumter was still three days in the future]. The attitude of the central [border] states seems to us to counsel moderation. Any hostile act could make possible their rallying to the separated states, while time and reflection will lead them to realize the considerations, forgotten in a moment of frenzy, which require all the federated states to renew their bonds which unite them with a great and powerful government. I shall hold this same language [he added] with the representatives of the Montgomery government [Southern envoys], and I will neglect no effort to prove to them what we consider to be the principal and perhaps the only interest of all the states of North America.[40]

Sanford at the end of the interview was impressed by the fact that the French foreign minister "showed a much more precise knowledge of our country than I had anticipated from one who neither reads nor speaks the English language."[41] Thouvenel, for his part, sat down immediately and wrote a note to Seward, saying that it had been a pleasure to meet Mr. Sanford, whom he would be glad to see again on any occasion when he might have something to communicate.[42]

On May 12 Sanford saw the French minister again. This time

he tried to blame the South for the outburst of hostilities at Fort Sumter, and Thouvenel in reply reasserted his previous sympathetic statement: "Our feelings are all for the Union. I would look upon its dissolution as a great catastrophe, a blow to liberty and progress." Then he added a new dimension to France's attitude: "The emperor personally [he said] is deeply grieved at this war and its possible results . . . and he has told me that he would willingly offer his services in mediation if he thought they could be useful toward securing a peaceful termination of his unhappy difficulty." Then again, speaking for himself, he added: "The interests and the sympathies of France were both on the side of the Union." Twice during the conversation he reiterated his and the emperor's pro-Northern views. While Sanford said "he saw no way in which the emperor's good offices could be useful now" [after Fort Sumter], he was impressed by the foreign minister's information on the United States and by his sincerity. "Every remark breathed a desire for the preservation of the Union."[43] The "interim" minister had already had a confirmation of the emperor's favorable attitude from a friend who a week before had heard the emperor "express himself warmly in favor of the perpetuity of the Union in strong language of reprobation of the course of the secessionists."[44]

By May 22 Faulkner had said his official farewells and departed. Dayton had arrived on the 11th, and Robert M. Walsh, his secretary of legation, presented him to Thouvenel on the 16th. Here again the French minister spoke favorably for the Northern cause for himself and for the emperor.[45] He repeated the emperor's desire to use his good offices but explained that His Majesty had not officially tendered them for fear of rejection. Like Sanford, Dayton, through Walsh as an interpreter, thanked Thouvenel for the emperor's suggestion "but gave him no reason to suppose that such an offer at this time would be accepted."[46] When the emperor received Dayton and his credentials on May 19, he took occasion to repeat with such sincerity the same sympathies as Thouvenel, along with his offer of good offices, that Dayton was convinced that they were "a frank expression of his views on this subject."[47]

The Threat of a Foreign War

But the benevolence and friendly concern of the emperor and his minister were not entirely reciprocated in Washington. During the early crisis on secession Seward's truculence toward foreign countries went to the extreme of contemplating a war with France and other European powers in order to rally the South to the defense of the Union and distract attention from secession. For several months the new secretary had had the optimistic belief that the great majority in the South were Unionists, that the noise and excitement for secession came mainly from a few hot-headed leaders. In January 1861, before the Lincoln administration had come into office, Seward had made a speech before the New England Society in which he had said that if New York should be attacked by a foreign power, "all the hills of South Carolina would pour forth their population to the rescue." He cited Jefferson, a Virginian, who was supposed to have said that secession was inadmissible during a war with a foreign enemy.[48]   Early in March he noted that Governor Sam Houston, the great Texas hero, came out against the holding of a secession convention in his state. In many other Southern states he was in touch with Unionist leaders, such as John A. Gilmer of North Carolina and George W. Summers of Virgina, whom Lincoln called sarcastically Seward's "white crows."[49] Indeed, in the months of March and April, Seward tried to avoid a military showdown with the Confederates on the reenforcement of Fort Sumter and Fort Pickens until he could precipitate a foreign war, if necessary, to forestall secession. In a sense, he and the Secessionists would be competing for the Unionists in the South. If the fighting started over Fort Sumter, the Secessionists might win over the Southern Unionists to their side; if the fighting began by a war with England or France, Seward might attract the Southern Unionists and the majority of the South to the side of the Union. The Secessionists might then have the rug pulled out from under them.[50]   In a conversation with Lord Lyons, the British minister, on March 20, the secretary confided that he wanted to avoid civil war for the next three months because he saw a counterrevolution developing in the South; he saw signs of it already in Texas. He was contemplating cutting off Southern commerce for a while to make conditions bad and encourage the counterrevolution.[51]

The members of the diplomatic corps in Washington foresaw the danger of just such a trumped-up foreign war. As early as January 7, Lord Lyons was telling Lord John Russell, the British foreign secretary, "The temptation will be great for Lincoln's party, if they be not actually engaged in civil war, to endeavor to divert the public excitement to a Foreign Quarrel."[52] Schleiden, the envoy from Bremen, reported Seward as saying: "If the Lord would only give to the United States an excuse for a war with England, France, or Spain, that would be the best means of reestablishing internal peace."[53] A few days later Mercier was at dinner at the home of Senator Douglas, along with Senator Crittenden, Secretary Seward, and others. "These gentlemen," he reported, "all agreed in admitting that a good war might have been the best way to prolong the life of the Union."[54] Seward not only joined with this round-table opinion, but on later occasions he again hinted at a foreign war. To Schleiden he said, "Nothing would give so much pleasure as to see a European power interfere in favor of South Carolina—for then I should pitch into that European power, and South Carolina and the seceding states would soon join me in doing so."[55] To William Russell, the London *Times* correspondent, he threatened to break off relations with any European power which even unofficially received any Southern emissaries.[56] This remark may have been at about the time that Mercier heard that some-one had proposed in cabinet meeting that the French minister be handed his passports as soon as France admitted into one of her harbors a ship flying a Confederate flag.[57]

With all these threats and apprehensions in the Washington atmosphere, it is not surprising to learn that, in the midst of the pre-Fort Sumter debates, Seward actually made his famous confidential proposal of a foreign war to Lincoln. There were, at this time, only very flimsy pretexts for war. Santo Domingo had had a revolution, and its leaders had raised the old Spanish flag. Was Spain trying to regain some of her lost territory in America? Were England and France intending to intervene in

Mexico? Was Russia moving toward a recognition of the Confederacy? Seward submitted "Some Thoughts for the President's Consideration" appropriately, perhaps, on April Fool's Day. The changeover of administrations, with all the problems of new job appointments, he complained, had prevented the formulation of any definitive domestic or foreign policies. The secretary then proceeded to suggest a definite course of action at home and abroad.

For Foreign Nations

I would demand explanations from *Spain* and France categorically at once.

I would demand explanations from Britain and Russia and send agents into *Canada* and *Mexico* and *Central America* to raise a vigorous continental *spirit* of independence on this continent against European intervention.

And if satisfactory explanations are not received from Spain and France,

We would convene Congress and declare war against them.

Seward then volunteered his services to carry out vigorously whatever policy was agreed upon.[58]

Lincoln rightly did not take this communication as an April Fool joke, but gave it a firm, yet gentle, reply. On a warlike foreign policy he observed:

The news received yesterday in regard to St. Domingo certainly brings in a new item within range of our foreign policy; but up to that time we have been preparing circulars and instructions to ministers and the like, all in perfect harmony, without even a suggestion that we had no foreign policy.

As to devolving his duties on his secretary, he added:

I remark that if this must be done, I must do it. When a general line of policy is adopted, I apprehend there is no danger of its being changed without good reason, or continuing to be a subject of unnecessary debate; still upon points arising in its progress I wish, and I suppose I am entitled to have, the advice of all the Cabinet.[59]

The policy of a provoked foreign war was thus abruptly stopped for the moment, and Seward was put back in his place as one of several cabinet members. This is not to be the end of Seward's threats, however, as we shall see in the chapters on belligerency and maritime law; but for the moment France, unknowingly, had been spared a war crisis. Indeed, Seward, in his calm reaction to the reprimand, evinced a much more friendly attitude toward France than he did to his other intended victims. On the day following the president's rejection of his proposal the secretary of state sent a cordial and confidential note to Mercier, enclosing a protest he was sending to Spain regarding Santo Domingo. He hoped France would join the United States in this protest, since France had the same interest as they in the preservation of peace.[60] Although Mercier forwarded to his foreign ministry the American note to Spain, neither he nor Thouvenel seem to have made any response to this approach.[61]

While Seward may have momentarily assumed a more cordial attitude toward France after his proposal to Lincoln of April 1, a month later he singled France out for a public rebuff. In Thouvenel's conference with Faulkner of April 15 he had been incautious enough to inquire about cabinet dissensions in the new Lincoln administration. The French minister was probably eager to receive information, thought his inquiry to be informal, and hoped to gain some impartial opinion from an outgoing Southern sympathizer. But Faulkner dutifully or deliberately reported it to Seward and thereby set off one of the Sewardian explosions.

The American secretary received the dispatch on May 3 and immediately wrote out a sharp note of instruction for Dayton. He not only resented what appeared to be an intrusion by Thouvenel in domestic affairs, but he also saw an opportunity to gain some cheap public favor by a show of defiance to a European power. It would fit in with the mood of exasperation of the American public, but France would have to be the sacrificial lamb for this wartime ritual.

You may, therefore, recall that conversation to Mr. Thouvenel's memory, and then assure him explicitly that there is no difference of opinion whatever between the President and his constitutional advisers, or among those advisers themselves, concerning the policy that has been pursued, and which is now prosecuted by the administration in regard to the unhappy disturbances existing in the country. . . .

You cannot be too decided or too explicit in making known to the French government that there is not now, nor has there been, nor will there be any the least idea existing in this government of suffering a dissolution of this Union to take place in any way whatever.

. . . Tell Mr. Thouvenel, then, with the highest consideration and good feeling [!], that the thought of a dissolution of this Union, peaceably or by force, has never entered into the mind of any candid statesman here, and it is high time that it be dismissed by statesmen in Europe.[62]

This would have been provocative enough if it had been read or repeated to the French foreign minister, but what made it particularly obnoxious was that Seward published it two days later along with the full text of Faulkner's earlier dispatch of April 15. Thus all the diplomats of Washington and of the world could read and witness a verbal reprimand administered to the foreign minister of a great power. For Seward it would have the added advantage of intimidating those countries who might want to show friendliness to the Confederacy because it would imply that the United States would not shrink from a fight with outside powers. This impression, too, would confirm their earlier suspicions.[63]

Seward's appeal for the support of public opinion was successful. *The New York Times* praised it as "one of the ablest, most vigorous and admirable documents of our diplomacy." "This is language [it added] to which the American people will heartily and enthusiastically respond. The purpose it expresses is theirs, and they will see that it is carried out." On the New York stock market the quotations rose by two per cent at the resounding whacks of Seward's whiplash.[64]

What Seward won on the sidewalks and stock markets of New York he lost, however, along the Quai d'Orsay in Paris. Thouvenel must have seen the translation of Seward's note in the papers of May 23. He was not only angered by the secretary's haughty tone but also irritated to read in the papers a communication to him which had not yet even been presented. A stickler for proper diplomatic procedure, he would obviously be deeply offended. Mercier, however, had been so slow in reporting the incident that his report did not arrive until May 28. "All I can say on this subject," Mercier remarked, "is that probably Mr. Seward was speaking in this case much more to the public of the North than to the government of the emperor." Yet the French envoy went on to dispute Seward's braggart claims of the eventual victory of the North and the indestructibility of the Union. One of the principal capitalists of the United States had just told him that the restoration of the Union had become a chimera.[65]

Although Dayton received the instructions by May 21, he prudently delayed inaugurating his mission by transmitting such an undiplomatic communication. In the meantime he had arranged for a conference on the Convention of Paris for the afternoon of May 29, the very day following Thouvenel's receipt of Mercier's report of the note's publication. The American minister observed that Thouvenel seemed reserved and irritated during the conference, and, before it was over, the French foreign minister let him know how he felt. In the first place, he said, it had been partly an unofficial conversation with Mr. Faulkner. In the future it might be necessary to exercise some reserve in similar conversations with the minister of the United States. As to the idea of the dissolution of the Union being dismissed from the minds of the statesmen of Europe, Mr. Seward, of course, has his own opinions, but the statesmen of Europe must be permitted to have theirs too. This was an inauspicious beginning for Dayton's first serious negotiations, and he begged of Seward that his dispatches not be published at home. Publication would only cause him embarrassment and make him of little service to his country at his post.[66]

By the reports and enclosures from Mercier and the conferences with, and communications from, Sanford and Dayton, Thouvenel had by then heard the arguments, constitutional and political, of both sides on the question of secession. In the meantime, earlier in the month of May, he had also received a fifteen-page study from E. de Bellot des Minières, which was clearly pro-Southern on all the issues. Two pages were devoted to the impossibility of bringing the South back into the Union and to the justification of Southern secession.[67] However, the French foreign minister did not seem to be led too far in one direction or the other by these many conflicting arguments. His neutral stand on the question of secession is clearly expressed to Mejan, his consul in New Orleans and his momentarily designated agent to go to Montgomery on the question of French goods on belligerent ships. To Mejan he wrote: "The government of the emperor does not wish to express an opinion on the dispute itself. It is not for it to examine whether legitimate complaints and constitutional arguments justified or not the Southern states to separate from the rest of the confederation. These are questions of domestic law on which it no more wants to give an opinion than on the eventual outcome of the struggle now under way."[68]

French Opinion on Secession

Napoleon III and his foreign minister may have indicated a polite sympathy for the preservation of the American Union and may have refused to be swayed either way by the arguments on secession, but the French press, at least, did not refrain from discussing every aspect of the major issues. The two Confederate agents, William L. Yancey and Pierre A. Rost, writing back on June 1 to Hunter, their secretary of state, admitted that the Orleanists and Republicans in France were the most unsympathetic to the South.[69] This attitude was certainly true of their newspapers in the early months when the question of secession was uppermost. The *Journal des Débats*, the leading Orleanist daily, attacked the South on slavery and praised the superiority of the North with free labor. When secession was under way, the *Débats* hoped that the border states would remain loyal to the Union and that Unionists in the seceded states would rise up and insist on reunion. While the *Débats* recognized the concern of the South for its slave property and its opposition to a Northern high tariff, it rallied to the Northern cause largely on slavery. But this paper, along with most Frenchmen, could not understand the federation principle because of their own centralized system of government. Consequently it felt that secession was illegal and that no constitution would ever provide for its own dissolution. It agreed with Lincoln that a federal pact could not be broken without the mutal consent of all the members; this was supposed to be international practice with multilateral treaties. Later in October the *Débats* supported the Union with the argument that France needed a strong and united American republic to counter Britain's sea power.[70]

The next most important Orleanist organ was the semi-monthly magazine, *Revue des deux mondes*. It hoped the South could be brought back into the Union by blockade rather than by bloodshed because a bitter war would make reunion almost impossible. In November 1861 it bitterly criticized the South because, it said, it only fought to perpetuate slavery. It would not have been abused under the constitution because, if its senators had stayed in the senate, they could have prevented any oppression of the South. Their tariff complaint was unsound because the losses of war would be greater than any tariff burden. Like the *Débats* it felt that France had "a great interest in the maintenance of a power . . . which could contribute to the maintenance of maritime equilibrium."[71]

Most of the independent, liberal papers were also favorable to the Union cause. Even before South Carolina had seceded, F. Gaillardet wrote a long article in the *Presse*, one of these liberal, independent sheets, in which he saw the border state of Virginia as one which might call a convention of Southern states, not to decide on secession, but rather to formulate guarantees for the South so that secession could be abandoned. Peoples who seek independence always look to France for help, he boasted, but the South must understand that France could hardly support a slaveholding cause. This writer also brought up the question of Louisiana. If the original French settlers in that state, as well as in Arkansas and Missouri, lost their slaves by Federal act, France could protest because the Louisiana Purchase Treaty of 1803 guaranteed the property of the French inhabitants. Gaillardet doubted, however, that France would act to defend slave property. Faulkner, the Virginian and Secessionist representative of the United States at that time, interestingly enough sent a copy of this article to Washington and remarked that the *Presse*, although not even semiofficial, "rarely utters its opinion upon grave public questions without first being satisfied that its views are in accordance with those of the Imperial Government."[72] In the independent *Courrier du Dimanche*, Prévost-Paradol, while he realized the determination of the Southerners to protect their slave property, wrote completely in support of the North. The old Union, he felt, was "the involuntary and unfortunate instrument of the rest of the world" in the crusade against slavery.[73] The *Opinion Nationale*, liberal journal under the patronage of Prince Jerome Napoleon (cousin of the emperor and second in the line of succession), in commenting on the new slavery Confederation, said: "A retrograde faction which in the name of slavery throws a country into confusion can neither claim nor receive the esteem or sympathy of the free nations of the world."[74] In the early stages of the secession discussion even Faulkner was led to admit that "all [French papers] appear to evince a sincere wish to see the Federal Union maintained in its integrity."[75]

But this pro-Northern press sentiment may be misleading to Americans a century later because it is hard to tell how much these views were merely the sponsoring of a foreign liberal cause as an oblique attack on the authoritarian regime of Napoleon III. Under the very tight censorship of the empire's government the press could not effectively criticize its policies or advocate a more liberal and parliamentary regime. "But," West tells us, "upon American affairs they could offer praise of democracy. . . . Skillful writers . . . made great success in the method of indirect attack."[76] In response, the opposition public, La Gorce notes, "was accustomed to read between the lines; it completed phrases, carried ideas to logical conclusions; and marvelled that journalists could say so many things in spite of the censorship."[77] Under such circumstances the press could never be an accurate indication of real French sentiment on the American Civil War.

On the other hand most of the Imperial press appeared to be pro-Southern. In contrast to Southerner Faulkner's despairing conclusion that the French press was Unionist, Northerner Sanford deplored its secessionist tendencies. On his arrival in Paris he found "the tone and sentiment generally, here and in Belgium, seems to be that 'secession' is final and that, at any rate, the Confederate Government is entitled to belligerent rights." He begged that Seward send over special agents and supply Dayton with a secret fund to combat the trend against the Union cause.[78] When Sanford saw Thouvenel on April 24, he complained about the pro-Southern attitude of the press and the supposed government authorization of a new pro-Southern journal. Thouvenel denied the truth of the authorization story and then added, "The press in Paris, with few exceptions, has shown no sympathy with the revolution; on the contrary three or four of the principal journals have opposed it and in fact the general sentiment of the civilized world is opposed to the principle on which it is based." Sanford did not contradict him to his face but confided to Seward that "if the Parisian press is not in favor of the 'revolution,' the columns of some of the leading journals are open to articles favoring the Southern cause."[79] But here again Sanford may have been trying to make the situation look bad in order to obtain more support from Washington.

Thouvenel was wrong when he said that there were "few exceptions" in the general French press sympathy for the North. Almost the entire pro-government or Imperialist press showed sympathy for the South. The leading Imperialist journal, the *Constitutionnel*, from December 1860 until May 1861, had shown some sympathy for the North. It condemned slavery and the Fugitive Slave Law, criticized the South for seceding after a proper constitutional election had taken place, and opposed the right of slaveholders to take their slaves into the territories. However, with the arrival of the news of Fort Sumter and the outbreak of hostilities, the *Constitutionnel* assumed a pro-Southern attitude and maintained it for the rest of the war. The Northern crusade for Union rather than for emancipation left it cold. The North, it asserted, had deliberately invited disunion by electing Lincoln in defiance of the warnings of the South. After all, could the North deny the South the right to secede in the face of the dictum in the Declaration of Independence which proclaimed that "governments depend only upon the consent of the governed?" By September it was ridiculing democratic self-government, which disintegrated with its first major crisis, suppressing freedom and conducting a reign of terror. By December it was saying that France had no obligation of loyalty to the United States since they had seldom shown gratitude for French aid in the Revolutionary War.[80]

The *Pays*, another semiofficial newspaper, perhaps reflected Southern coaching from the sidelines when it argued that in 1826 and 1827 the North had defeated a proposal for compensated emancipation.[81] Since the United States was only a confederation, the states had every right to secede, and reunion would be impossible. The *Pays* argued that the founding fathers had not prohibited slavery, the constitution had left such local institutions to the jurisdiction of the states, and the past presidents and congresses had all respected this jurisdiction. As to the two sections of the country, the North was the industrial rival of France and monopolized the exchange of goods between France and the South, a service which could now be assumed by Paris along with the profits and commissions.[82]

Another Imperialist paper, the *Patrie*, not only thought the Union could not be restored but also predicted that its disruption might well lead to five republics of north, south, center, west, and Pacific coast. It felt that the right of secession was valid and a separation was to the best interests of Europe. Politically the United States, if reunited, would become a threat to Europe; and economically Europe could trade on better terms with a divided America.[83]

Yet one must remember that French press opinion is not necessarily public opinion, particularly was this true during the Second Empire, when the newspapers were so closely censored and so regularly bribed.[84] For a better indication of grass-roots opinion the emperor, himself, discounting the importance of the press and the legislature, used several polling procedures. The most important of these were surveys and reports by his procureurs general (similar to federal district attorneys) and by his prefects (corresponding to American state governors).[85] Also these reports gave a view of provincial opinion which was missed in the Paris press.

What is noticed at first in these reports is a natural lack of interest on the part of the man in the street. In Lorraine it was said that the Civil War "is too far off to exercise any influence on us."[86] It was the same in Franche-Comté where the war seemed too far away to attract much attention. Only the issue of slavery elicited some interest.[87] Even as late as January 1862 a report from Nîmes said that "the American war only impressed opinion when it affected commercial interests."[88] Out of the 112 reports received between April 1861 and January 1862 only 18 mentioned any kind of reaction to the American crisis.[89]

Nevertheless there were some opinions in the provinces about the issues of the war. In the first year three instances of anti-slavery sentiment were reported—from Agen, Nancy, and Besançon; but the report from Lyons in December 1861 said bluntly that "the slavery question seemed forgotten."[90] In only three instances were there expressions of sympathy for the North. In Alsace, the procureur reported, "From all sides I hear the wish expressed for the reestablishment of the Union and the triumph of the federal authority." In Lyons and Bescançon there were fears that a defeat of the North would remove a friendly navy.[91] Yet in only two instances do we have outright favoring of the South. In Agen toward the end of 1861 there was some rejoicing that the aggressive and presumptuous United States was receiving its just punishment. So "the South has on its side a satisfied resentment." Lyons at first seemed pro-South until later the prospect of the decline of the Northern navy shifted sympathies to the other side.[92] In Besançon and Nancy there was some concern about the blockade and a possible shortage of cotton, and in Marseilles there was worry about the export trade to the North and South. But this seemed to be the extent of business anxiety in public opinion. At Colmar, in Alsace, people even wanted the war to continue so as not to disturb the status quo of high prices for cotton of which they had made large purchases. They hoped England would not try to break the blockade.[93]

The Paris press, by showing a constant interest in the Civil War, was not reflecting the general French apathy shown by the administrative reports; but its divided opinions were to some extent duplicated in the provinces wherever any opinion was expressed. Yet even this divided press opinion was deceptive because it could not be determined to what extent the pro-Northern articles were oblique attacks on the regime or how much the pro-Southern sentiment in the press columns was the result of money subsidies. For the year 1861, when secession was the important subject of discussion, the expressions of opinion were not decisive in either direction and therefore could not have influenced the emperor or his foreign minister to any great degree.

Nevertheless we do see these two men showing an intense interest in the developing crisis, informing themselves avidly on all its aspects and stages, and taking a cautious and diplomatically correct stand in favor of the preservation of the Union, the only authority with which France had up to then conducted diplomatic relations. But the situation was not without its deep anxieties. Already the danger of a foreign war, perhaps against France, loomed in the bumptious and threatening attitude of Seward and in the common practice of sovereign states to precipitate an outside war when they must distract their people from domestic difficulties. Should France join England in a common front to exorcise a threat of war? Should France recognize the new Confederate States? Should she challenge the blockade in order to maintain her imports of Southern cotton? All of these were problems France had to face in the early months of the war.

Chapter II

RECOGNITION OF SOUTHERN BELLIGERENCY

When the people in a portion of the territory of a sovereign state raise the banner of revolt with the avowed intention of seeking separation and independence, their rebellion always poses in the world community the question of whether they should be recognized as a new separate sovereign state. Out of deference to the state against which the rebellion is aimed and because of uncertainty about the probable success of the rebellion, foreign countries are inclined to delay their decision on recognition for a considerable time. There may be also strategic, commercial, or ideological reasons which will defer or hasten such recognition. France did not recognize the new United States until nearly two years after its declaration of independence, and the United States itself delayed its formal recognition of the Latin American republics for more than a decade after the outbreak of their revolutions. Usually the *de jure* recognition of the sovereignty of a newly established state depends upon the successful establishment and maintenance of its independence, its effective control of the people in its territory, and its ability and willingness to carry out its international obligations in the world community. Yet, short of this recognition of sovereignty, the established sovereign states may find it necessary to recognize the insurrectionary force as a belligerent authority over a certain area in order to protect their nationals and fulfill their legal obligations as neutrals. This recognition of belligerency may be the prelude to a later full recognition of sovereign independence if the insurrection is successful.

[45]

Pre-War Considerations of Recognition

In the case of the Civil War in the United States the question was raised even before hostilities began because of the long initial period of threats of secession and President Buchanan's hesitancy to take any action in the early months of the actual process of secession. As soon as Lincoln's victory was confirmed, an unofficial meeting of Southern leaders issued a manifesto proclaiming the secession of South Carolina, Georgia, Alabama, Florida, and Mississippi and inviting Napoleon III to send a special agent to recognize their new confederation. Since there was a general belief, Mercier admitted, that France wanted the dissolution of the Union, he was surprised that none of these Southern gentlemen approached him on the subject.[1]

By the month of February 1861 there had been enough talk about recognition among the diplomats in Washington to allow Mercier to report that the usually reticent Lord Lyons admitted that England's recognition of Southern independence would not be long in coming. The British minister saw the future possibility of England being caught between a blockade of Southern ports and high tariffs in Northern ports. In such a situation England would have to take her own precautions.[2] The Russian minister, Baron Stoeckl, had also reported home that material interests would impel England and France to recognize the South, and Russia should follow their example.[3]

With the change in administration on March 4th Seward, the new secretary of state, took an even sterner attitude than had Black and sent circular instructions to the Federal agents abroad to warn against foreign intervention or the recognition of the new Confederate government.[4] On the other hand, to seek recognition the Confederate government dispatched to Europe its first mission, consisting of William L. Yancey, Pierre A. Rost, and A. Dudley Mann.[5] Reacting to the news of this mission, Seward tried to give an indirect warning to England and France through William Russell, the London *Times* correspondent. "The Southern commissioners who had been sent abroad," he admonished, "could not be received by the Government of any foreign power, officially or otherwise, even to hand in a document or to make a representation, without incurring the risk of breaking the relations with the United States."[6] At about the same time, on the evening of March 20, Seward was so concerned about recognition that he went over to the British legation to see Lyons. For the next three months, he said, he wanted to avoid a crisis because a counterrevolution against secession seemed to be developing in the South, particularly just then in Texas. For that reason, he went on, "it was most important that the new Confederacy should not in the meantime be recognized by any Foreign Power." "Do you know," he asked anxiously, "if Brazil or Peru are going to recognize the South?" Of course Lyons did not know, but, speaking for Great Britain, he said that she would not want to do anything that would prolong the quarrel. However, if the United States tried to stop such important British commerce as she had with the South, Lyons did not know what might happen. On this evening the usually blustering Seward was obviously worried. He listened calmly to Lyons' veiled threat and said more than once that he would like to take the British minister over to see the president.[7]

Because of the prevailing obsession with the question of recognition in the diplomatic corps and the state department and the imminence of the Southern commission's arrival in Europe, Mercier wanted to acquaint his government with his own views on recognition. Since the United States had attempted to recognize the Hungarian revolutionary government in 1848 before it had succeeded fully in establishing itself, he felt that Washington could not complain if European countries gave an early recognition to the Confederate States. If the quarrel ended in civil war, the conflict would severely hurt England's and France's trade with both the North and South. Consequently he wanted to see an early recognition of the Confederacy before hostilities began. His prescription was to put off recognition until the dissolution of the Union seemed inevitable. But then he and Lyons, authorized in advance in order to take advantage of the psychological moment, should proceed together to recognize the South and bring about a peaceful arrangement between the two rival governments.[8] At the same time he sounded out his British and Russian colleagues, who opposed the idea of stand-by instructions. Lyons thought the onus of recognition would then fall on him personally, and Stoeckl wanted to delay Russia's recognition in order to let England and France have the brunt of Northern anger.[9] However, Lyons, in contrast to Stoeckl, was favorable to simultaneous recognition whenever it should come.[10]

The matter of simultaneous recognition was closely related to a broader consideration of Franco-British general cooperation in relation to the impending civil war. As early as February 12, three weeks before Lincoln's inauguration, Lyons suggested to Russell the advisability of cooperation with France if it became necessary to resist the exclusion of foreign ships from Southern ports.[11] No doubt Lyons and Mercier had both already been discussing cooperation because the latter, in forewarning Thouvenel of the probable danger from privateering, added that in case of privateering "I suppose you would have no trouble in coming to an understanding with England on what to do."[12] Again at the end of the month he wrote that "the solidarity resulting from this [Anglo-French] entente would also create a means for weakening the bad impression produced in the North by the decision of the powers [for recognition] and prevent it from having a permanently adverse effect."[13]

With the usual two-weeks delay of news between America and Europe, France showed a corresponding delay in her reactions to the issue of recognition. The mid-November appeal of the secessionist leaders, in their unofficial meeting, for the emperor's recognition began to elicit comments in the Paris press during the first week of December 1860, long before South Carolina had actually seceded. Even the pro-Southern American minister, Faulkner, however, considered this appeal to be "fictitious" and thought the hostile reaction of the Paris press to be indicative of an antisecessionist attitude of the French government. However, Faulkner did not question Thouvenel about it because he thought the appeal was nothing but a hoax.[14] Even when he received Black's circular,[15] announcing the impending arrival of Yancey and Rost and objecting, in advance, to any notice being given them by France, Faulkner did not contact Thouvenel because he claimed he had not been instructed to do anything about it. Yet, pro-Southern as he was, the American minister gave as his opinion that "the Imperial Government is not yet prepared to look favorably upon the object of their mission."[16]

Nevertheless, as long as pro-Southern Faulkner was at his Paris post, the Northern effort against French recognition of the Confederacy was carried out in a half-hearted and evasive manner. Prodded by more vigorous instructions from Seward, Faulkner had an interview with Thouvenel on April 15 in which he deliberately tried to delay discussion until Dayton's arrival. Yet, even though Faulkner gave the French minister every excuse for silence, Thouvenel volunteered his first expression of an opinion on recognition on that occasion.

> No application has yet been made to me by the Confederate States, in any form, for the recognition of their independence. The French government is not in the habit of acting hastily upon such a question, as might be seen by its tardiness in recognizing the new Kingdom of Italy. . . . The government of the United States may rest well assured that no hasty or precipitate action will be taken on the subject by the Emperor. But . . . I am equally bound to say that the practice and usage of the present century has fully established the right of a *de facto* government to recognition when a proper case is made out for the decision of foreign powers.[17]

In the meantime Thouvenel had his ambassador in London, Count Flahault, sound out Russell on the British attitude toward the expected Confederate mission and its request for recognition. Russell's reply was rather cryptic and uncommunicative: "When the time comes, England will consult her own interests as to the reception she will give to their request." But Flahault guessed that the British would be swayed by their commercial interests. Right now slavery in the South was balanced off by the high tariff in the North.[18]

Four days after Thouvenel received this information from England, Sanford had his first long interview with the French foreign minister—April 24. After presenting Seward's arguments against secession, the American interim agent brought up the question of recognition and elicited an elaborate reply from the French foreign minister.

Up to this time [Thouvenel said] no support or recognition has been sought from my government by the revolutionary party in the Southern States. When they do ask for it, it will be time to consider what should be done, and it would be considered solely in view of commercial relations[19] and with deliberation. These men who are announced as on their way . . . will be received by me on their application, as respectable foreigners, as I have received Poles, Hungarians, and others, and I shall listen to what they have to say and will advise them to peace and harmony. . . . But the government at Washington is the last to have a right to complain of the recognition of a revolutionary government. It has made itself always conspicuous in recognizing revolutionary governments all over the world. It hastened to recognize that in Hungary which I think was not unlike the one in the Southern States. My Government and others with different principles may with reason object if the case were applied to them. . . . We have no intention of giving any aid or countenance to the revolution—we sincerely hope that all will be settled satisfactorily—but we can not bind ourselves for the future. We shall certainly not hasten to recognize any new government. Our policy is opposed to it. Even the new government in Italy has not been recognized by that of France. But during the struggle there, we have not suffered interruptions in our commercial relations. Our ships and our mail packets have gone backward and forward between French and Italian ports without our concerning ourselves as to what authorities ruled there. With respect to commerce with your country, it is important to the interests of our people that it should be undisturbed. England, however, is more interested than France in this question and we will look rather to her course to guide us in our policy. We will not act alone, nor precipitately.[20]

This admission by Thouvenel of France's following the lead of England introduces again the early stages of Anglo-French cooperation and consultation on American affairs. The origin of this policy seems to have been with Lyons and Mercier in Washington, for there is no suggestion of it on the European side until after Lyons' note of February 12 and Mercier's of March 1 had already been received—about February 27 and March 18 respectively. Almost immediately after Thouvenel received Mercier's advice on Anglo-French cooperation, a hint of Thouvenel's adoption of the suggestion came out in the official *Moniteur*. An article appeared there on March 19 which reported that England was insisting in Washington that any future blockade would have to be effective. Then the *Moniteur* added significantly that "we are assured that other powers are to make a similar declaration." Eleven days later Russell made a suggestion of collaboration to Thouvenel in which he pointed out the "advantages which would result from frank explanations between the two governments on every report and every alarm tending to disquiet Europe."[21] When Cowley saw Thouvenel on April 2, the latter said this coincided entirely with his own views.[22]

Yet Thouvenel was still wary about making suggestions to England as a part of these mutual consultations. To Flahault, on April 17, 1861, he revealed his suspicious and cautious approach.

> I have no opinion to express to you on that subject [recognition of the Confederacy]. I even want to avoid in our communications with the government of H.B.M. anything which might resemble a suggestion and be represented later as such in the diplomatic papers of the foreign office [*Blue books*]. With this in mind I have avoided taking this matter up with the English ambassador [Cowley], and you yourself will take no initiative on this with Lord John Russell. Nevertheless, I am interested in knowing the attitude of the London cabinet, and I shall be much obliged if you would inform me on this point if you find a favorable occasion to sound them out.[23]

Two days later Flahault did sound Russell out and received a response which matched Thouvenel's instructions in evasiveness—the cryptic remark that England would only consult her own interests.[24]

Despite this mutual distrust, however, Thouvenel did not hesitate to tell one of his close friends in the diplomatic corps that "whatsoever they did [on the recognition of the South] would be, of course, in accord with England."[25] And, Russell, for his part, did have Cowley tell Thouvenel later that, "in receiving the Southern envoys, he intended to treat them with the utmost reserve as long as circumstances permitted."[26] It was on receiving this information that Thouvenel was more positive to Sanford in saying that England's course in handling the recognition question would guide France in its policy.[27] On the other hand Russell was not too candid about this budding collaboration. While Lord Wodehouse, speaking for the cabinet in the House of Lords, was saying that the British government had not been in correspondence with any foreign government on the question of recognition,[28] Russell was telling Dallas, the American minister in England, "that there existed an understanding between this government and that of France which would lead both to take the same course as to recognition, whatever that course might be."[29]

Thus, before the first state had seceded and long before the outbreak of hostilities, statesmen on both sides of the Atlantic had already become concerned about the problem of recognition; and, on the initiative of Lyons and Mercier, England and France were already laying the foundations of their subsequent practice of consultations and collaboration.

Hostilities and Belligerency

The question of recognition took a turn in a different direction as soon as the American political quarrel moved from peaceful secession to open warfare. The shot fired upon Fort Sumter on April 12, 1861, resounded across the North and South and eventually, like its forerunner at Concord, reverberated around the world. Three days later Lincoln issued his proclamation calling up 75,000 men from the state militias "to suppress said [secessionist] combinations and to cause the laws to be duly executed."[30] The wording of the proclamation made it a measure against internal disorder rather than a declaration of war in the sense of international law. But President Davis's counter-proclamation for issuing letters of marque and reprisal to privateers to prey upon Northern commerce used the words "the law of nations and the usages of civilized warfare."[31] This was followed on April 19 by Lincoln's proclamation of a blockade

of the ports of the seceded states "in pursuance of the laws of the
United States and of the law of nations in such case provided."[32]
By the wording of the two above proclamations both contestants
were recognizing a state of war in the sense of international law;
and, besides, blockades and privateering were not legally permitted unless there was a state of war.[33] Lincoln, then, perhaps
unwittingly, was recognizing the Confederate States as a belligerent, however opposed he was to the granting of any form
of recognition to them. Foreign countries, therefore, would also
have to take cognizance of such a state of war; and, in order to
benefit from the rights of neutrals as granted in international
law, proclaim their own neutrality and thereby recognize the
South at least as a belligerent, although not necessarily as a
sovereign and independent state.

Paris first heard of the bombardment of Fort Sumter on April
27; six days later came the news of the proclamations on Southern
privateering and the Northern blockade.[34] Thouvenel immediately realized that these warlike measures involved the neutral
powers in questions of maritime law and the recognition of
Southern belligerency, but, as he had said in April, he would
follow England's lead in these matters.

In the meantime Russell had sought legal advice from the
attorney general, who, on May 3 advised him to consider this a
regular international war (*justum bellum*) but to recognize the
belligerency of the South only after it acknowledged the principles
of the Treaty of Paris of 1856.[35] Realizing that a great deal of
time would be required to obtain this Southern acknowledgment, the British foreign secretary evidently decided to recognize
Southern belligerency at once and proceed later with obtaining
the assurances. On May 6 he informed Lyons that England
thought the Southern states should be considered legally to be
belligerent and that he should so inform the Washington government.[36]

Then, turning to France, he informed Thouvenel, through
Cowley, of his decision on recognizing the South's belligerency
and enclosed a copy of his instructions to Lyons. "In making
known to M. Thouvenel the opinion of Her Majesty's Government on this point," Russell continued, "Your Excellency will

add that you are instructed to call the attention of the French Government to the bearing which this unfortunate contest threatens to lay on the rights and interests of the neutral nations." In conclusion he suggested the cooperation of England and France in getting both parties to acknowledge articles II and III of the Declaration of Paris.[37]   Cowley saw Thouvenel immediately on May 7, and the latter expressed himself as being in complete agreement with England's policy.[38]   Two days later Thouvenel suggested that England and France issue a declaration that they intended to abstain from all interference in the American conflict.[39]

While Russell had been consulting his law officers and formulating his policy of neutrality, Thouvenel during the first week of May had been having deliberations on the matter in the foreign ministry.   A committee of experts on international law and precedents was called together, and it finally presented a memorandum which would form the basis of French policy on neutrality and the recognition of Southern belligerency.[40]   With this in front of him the French foreign minister on May 11 set about the detailed formulation of his policy to Mercier.   First of all he reemphasized France's desire for the preservation of the Union and her genuine regret at the outbreak of hostilities. Then, taking up the problems of the neutral powers in the face of these hostilities, he stated France's position on Southern belligerency.

> The government of the emperor . . . has not departed from its resolution to adhere to the strictest impartiality in the midst of the impending struggle. . . . It is certain that, whether justified or not, a considerable portion of the American Union has set up a separate confederation and that this confederation, making use of all the resources and administrative facilities which she possesses, has placed at her head an unquestioned authority, which, by the regularity of its operation has all the appearance of a *de facto* government in the eyes of foreign powers. Therefore, one must recognize that under such conditions, and whatever may be our regrets for such a state of affairs, the government of the emperor can not consider the two contending parties in any other light than as two belligerents, employing

against each other the forces at their disposal, in conformity
with international law. . . . The cabinet of Washington will
understand that from that moment [proclaiming privateering
and blockade] the government of the emperor had to be concerned with her neutral position and with the duty of safeguarding, as it would in any ordinary war, the interests of her
own nationals.

Mercier was not only instructed to read this note to Seward,
but he was given a copy of the ministry committee's long memorandum containing its expert arguments in defense of France's
recognition of Southern belligerency. First of all, the memorandum cited several precedents, such as the revolting provinces of
the Netherlands, the new United States in 1776, the revolts of
the Spanish colonies in America, and the Greek revolution in
1827.

> It follows from these precedents [the memorandum con-
> tinued] that according to international law the status of bel-
> ligerent is a question of fact rather than of principle and that,
> to be called belligerent, it is enough that a portion of a people
> in revolt have possession of only enough force to create, in the
> eyes of neutrals, a doubt as to the final outcome. In such a case
> modern international law requires that foreign powers, without
> prejudice to the final results of the clash of forces, keep an atti-
> tude of impartiality toward the two contestants. Should this
> conduct be followed in the case of the events in the New World?
> Most certainly—and it should be recognized that it is perhaps
> more applicable there than elsewhere [in the above example]. . . .
> Is it possible to conclude that a break between the various
> states is in itself such an illegitimate act in the eyes of neutral
> powers that the powers emerging from this revolution should be
> treated outside the law of nations? Most certainly not—and on
> the general question the right of belligerency should be recog-
> nized as to both parties.[41]

The very next day, May 12, Thouvenel encountered the first
stubborn Northern arguments against the French recognition of
Southern belligerency and against the French collaboration
with England. The occasion was a long conversation with

Sanford in which the French minister had another opportunity to elaborate his recognition policy. Part of the lively dialogue went as follows:

> *Thouvenel:* [France] felt constrained, in view of the great commercial interests involved, to take measures in conjunction with England to meet a condition of things which imperilled those interests. It was decided that communications be addressed by England and France,[42] to the Government of the United States and would be forwarded this week, informing it that they had determined to consider the Confederate States as entitled to belligerent rights. We can not ignore the fact that a Government was established and was performing all the functions of Government over those States and with Armies in the field was making war at this moment upon the Government of the United States.[43] . . . I earnestly beg you to bear this fact in mind, that the position we feel constrained to take *vis-à-vis* the Insurrection . . . is solely for the protection of the Commercial interests involved. It has been urgently demanded by all the principal Chambers of Commerce of France. My Government has no desire to give any countenance to the Confederate States, but the contrary.
>
> *Sanford:* I have always believed this and my Government and our people have always counted upon the sympathies of France . . . but I can not avoid expressing the painful surprise I feel, and especially after so many warm expressions of interest for the perpetuity of the Union, at finding France following England in a policy the effect of which will be to encourage the Insurgents and prolong the struggle. You have only fifteen days since received news of the determination of the President to employ force to put down this Insurrection, and it seems to me it is due to a friendly power at least to wait the result of a trial of its strength and not precipitately to give a quasi-recognition to those seeking to overthrow the Government.[44] You must be aware that your two declarations will give great moral support to the Insurrection. It will be hailed by its Partisans as a first step to recognition and correspondingly weaken the cause of the Union and its Laws among its friends in the South. I am not surprised at the course of England; she is jealous of our increasing power. . . . But it is to be supposed that the very reasons which would be apt to influence her, would have a

directly contrary effect in France, whose policy, it seems to me, is to encourage the growth and development of a commercial power, the rival of England.

Thouvenel: Yes, you are right in regard to France. The policy of "Old" England might not favor the increase of power of the United States. You will remark that while the French communication commenced by expressing its regret at this unhappy condition of things in the United States and its hopes for the integrity of the Union, the English communication was silent on the subject. You have the popular sympathies here, however, and in fact throughout Europe on your side.

Sanford: This fact, if no other, is a reason for not precipitately joining England in a policy which [English] popular sentiment might compel a change in, for if aroused, as it might be, it will likely prove too strong for the Government now in majority solely by the votes of the Liberals. In any event this course or any other the two Powers may adopt . . . will not effect the result. It may tend to prolong the conflict and shedding of blood; but the determination of the Government of the United States and the unanimous sentiment of the North is that the Rebellion *shall be put down.* We have infinitely more at stake in property, commercial relations, etc. with the South than you. . . . It is a grievous disappointment to us to see France on the side of England adding to our embarrassment in this conflict—especially in this recognition of the right of a portion of our citizens in rebellion against the laws to issue letters of marque at the very outset of our struggle with them.

Thouvenel (with great earnestness): The fact of war is staring us in the face—French property and interests are to a large extent imperilled by it, and we need to adopt some course in respect to existing facts. [Referring indirectly to his committee's deliberations, he went on.] We have thoroughly investigated the subject [of letters of marque]—all the precedents favor the course we have adopted. [Thouvenel then cited again the American, Hispano-American, and Greek revolutions.][45]

Seward received the report of this conversation on May 29, 1861, at about the same time that he learned of England's proclamation of neutrality. Thus he knew of all the strong arguments and precedents in favor of the recognition of belligerency two weeks before his famous interviews with Lyons and Mercier on the subject. Likewise, however, Thouvenel had learned from Sanford what was going to be the North's reaction to such a policy.

The Proclamations of Neutrality

Two days later—May 14—England issued her Proclamation of Neutrality in the war between the United States and "the states styling themselves the Confederate States of America." British subjects would not be allowed to enlist on either side, to recruit others for enlistment, to equip or commission ships, or to change or increase equipment while temporarily in a British harbor. Severe penalties were to be imposed for violations of the proclamation.[46]

Although France and Britain were coordinating their American policy, Thouvenel did not issue a corresponding French declaration until almost a month later. Lyons suspected that this delay may have been designed to let the British carry the main brunt of American anger.[47] Yet this suspicion was unjustified since, unbeknown to Lyons, Thouvenel had already sent his instructions to Mercier and had also told Sanford of France's support of the British policy on belligerency. To the minister of marine he indicated that France had formulated a policy similar to England's only after considerable deliberation in the foreign ministry—referring to the advisory committee meetings—but, he added, "it could not proceed at this moment to an official announcement."[48]   Perhaps Russell, like Lyons, was also a little uneasy about the French delay and tried to remind Thouvenel by indirection of his desire for collaboration. To Cowley he wrote: "Before you come away it may be as well to say to Mr. Thouvenel that we wish to act in this American business entirely in accordance with France. You may communicate confidentially the account of my conversation with Mr. Adams. . . ."[49]

Thouvenel, for his part, was moving along in implementing his policy of belligerency recognition. In addition to his instructions to Mercier he sent instructions to all his consuls in the North and South to practice a strict neutrality between the two belligerents;[50] he asked Chasseloup-Laubat, the minister of marine, on May 18, to inform the naval ship commanders in the West Indies of the neutral rights of French ships in those waters;[51] and on May 24 he sent the same minister a copy of his draft of a declaration of neutrality for his opinion.[52] The naval minister replied a week later with his full approval, especially because the terms of the declaration followed closely the terminology of relevant French law.[53] Thouvenel also referred the draft to Rouher, minister of commerce, who likewise approved its terms.[54] He then sent it on to the emperor for his approval, and the emperor himself signed the official copy without alteration as of June 10, 1861.[55]

The declaration opened with a statement that France was determined to observe a "strict neutrality . . . between the government of the Union and the States which claim to form a separate confederation." Thus the declaration did not use the word "government" in connection with the South and said it "claimed" to be separate. Then the declaration based its provisions on French law.[56] No privateers or naval ships of either belligerent could enter or stay in French ports with captured prize for more than twenty-four hours, except under stress of storms. No captured prize could be sold in French ports. No Frenchman could arm or equip naval vessels or privateers of either party, or receive letters of marque from them, or enroll in their army or naval services, or do anything unneutral as defined by French or international law. Any violators would be punished according to French law and would not receive French protection against the punitive measures of the belligerents.[57]

It is significant, too, that Thouvenel tried to soften the impact of France's neutrality upon the North. Since he had already heard of Northern resentment over the British proclamation, he furnished Mercier with assuaging comment for the benefit of the Washington government. He was to tell Seward that French law required the issuance of the declaration as a regular procedure so that both belligerents could know what privileges they still enjoyed in French ports, which included one day's anchoring and the export of the present orders for arms.[58]

The reaction of the other maritime powers was favorable to the French declaration. Thouvenel had informed all their governments of the declaration, and Prussia had replied that it was going to take the same measures as France.[59]   In his notification to Great Britain he asked for clarification on the British rules for the sale of prize in British harbors, and Russell replied that it was prohibited as in the French declaration.[60].   On the same day Russell also reiterated Franco-British solidarity in an official note to Lyons—with a copy sent to Paris: "With reference to [your] observation . . . upon the advantage of it being known that Her Majesty's Government and that of the Emperor of the French are acting together, I have to say that Her Majesty's Government desire to act in concert with the French Government upon questions regarding America, and that hitherto there has been no difference of opinion between them."[61] Dayton's own reaction was also mostly favorable.   Although the French declaration put the Confederate ships "in the same category" as those of the Union, he pointed out that it had limited the South to the fullest extent entailed by her belligerent status, and without showing any sympathy for her cause.[62]

The Rost Mission to Paris

The three Confederate commissioners—Yancey, Rost, and Mann—arrived in London on April 15 and 29, 1861, just after the news of Fort Sumter had reached England, and on May 4 they had an informal interview with Russell.   The foreign secretary's remarks on recognition in this interview were:

> I can hold no official communication with the delegates of the Southern States.   However, when the question of recognition comes to be formally discussed, there are two points upon which enquiry must be made: First,—whether the body seeking recognition can maintain its position as an independent state; Secondly,—in what manner it is proposed to maintain relations with foreign states.[63]

A little later in May, Rost made a preliminary scouting trip to Paris, where he had an encouraging conversation with the pro-Southern Count de Morny—the illegitimate half-brother of the emperor and son of Flahault, the French ambassador in England.

The friendly count assured Rost that full recognition would come in time, and that Anglo-French cooperation on neutrality and belligerent rights actually benefitted the South.[64] Morny's closeness to the imperial family and government and the details in his remarks leave the impression that he had been present during some of the cabinet discussion of belligerency recognition and was expressing the views of the court, if not of the government.

By this time Thouvenel knew that he, too, would soon be faced by the problem of receiving one of the Southern commissioners, and he inquired about how Russell had received them. Flahault's reply was that Russell had received them unofficially but had stated that recognition was out of the question for the present. England was keeping her full freedom of action for the future and would make no promise about recognition.[65] The French foreign minister knew from earlier communications of Black and Seward, as relayed by Faulkner, Sanford, and Dayton, that there would be strong Northern objections to his seeing one of the Confederate representatives.[66] Any lingering doubts in his mind must have been dispelled by a dispatch he received from Mercier on June 8, with an enclosed letter from Seward to Mercier in which Seward had said:

> A defeated sectional party have taken appeal from the polls to arms. They are weaker in arms than they were at the polls. At the polls they contended for the overthrow of a political party; in arms they must fight for the overthrow of the country. France, we know, wishes us well, and she is of course careful for herself. *Let her avoid giving any countenance to treason* against this Government. Foreign intervention would ultimately drive the whole people of the United States to unanimity, but the sympathies which have so long existed between the United States and France would, in that case, perhaps forever cease.[67]

Mercier also enclosed a clipping from the *New York Herald*, which, supposedly under Seward's inspiration, threatened dire consequences in the event of foreign favors shown to the rebel states.[68]

Yet, in the face of these threats from Seward, Thouvenel was not to be deterred from seeing unofficially whomever he wished. Sometime during the next two weeks—June 8-19—he received Rost for an informal interview. Thouvenel's account of his own statements on this occasion mentioned that he had expressed regrets over the war, said flatly that France was not favorable to the dissolution of the Union, and hoped that the two belligerents would patch up their quarrel in the face of the harm to each other and to foreign countries from the warfare which might ensue. "I added that we could not, besides, under present circumstances, give the Montgomery government the least hope of being recognized by France."[69] According to Rost the French minister also said that the French consuls throughout the South had reported the unanimity of the Southern people in their support of the Confederate government and the lack of any slave disturbances.[70] In general Rost got no more satisfaction from Thouvenel than the three had obtained from Russell.

Now Thouvenel had to face the ire of Dayton and Seward. On June 19, shortly after Rost's unofficial interview, Dayton had a meeting with Thouvenel. The American minister had received instructions from Seward in more specific terms than those in Seward's letter to Mercier. Any French reception of Southern representatives—official or unofficial—would be "injurious to the dignity and honor of the United States" and, by prolonging the war, "destructive to the prosperity of this country and aimed at the overthrow of the government itself." Seward hoped this timely warning would save the North from taking any action. At the beginning of the interview Dayton read earlier instructions from Seward expressing appreciation for the emperor's and Thouvenel's sympathies and good wishes for the integrity of the United States—an auspicious as well as diplomatic way of initiating a discussion.

Having thus put Thouvenel in a pleasant mood, Dayton deftly launched upon the irritating *Patrie* article which linked France's recognition of the Kingdom of Italy with the eventual recognition of the South. This would have been disturbing enough to Dayton because the *Patrie* was a semiofficial organ, but two days later even the official *Moniteur* picked it up and quoted it.[71]

Thouvenel's reply was that the *Patrie* had ceased to be a semi-official paper ten days ago and did not reflect the government's views, but the republication of the article by the *Moniteur* was a silly mistake (*une sottise*) in its practice of reproducing passages from other papers. Walewski had been out of town for ten days, and there had not been the normal close scrutiny of the press. Thouvenel had at first suggested a repudiation of the article, but Walewski said it would give too much importance to the affair. It would be better for it to sink into obscurity by ignoring it. For reassurance Thouvenel added: "The French government has no sympathy whatever with the seceding States of the South. It has no idea of recognizing them as an independent power. If France did ever recognize them, it would be only after a successful survival over a long period of perhaps three or four years."

This trend of the discussion gave Dayton an opportunity to read Seward's note No. 10 with its threats about receiving Rost and recognizing Southern belligerency. The foreign minister immediately defended his interview with Rost.

> Mr. Rost [said Thouvenel] applied to me through a third party and not as a commissioner from the South. If he had done so, I should not have received him. He had been received by Lord John Russell, and I could not turn him out-of-doors. Besides, I received him because I felt it a duty to get all the information I could and obtain knowledge of facts in reference to matters of so much importance from all possible sources. For this purpose I have received all sorts of people. On the same day I received envoys from Garibaldi and the King of Naples. Besides, I wished to inform Mr. Rost of the inutility of now seeking from the French government a recognition of independence. . . .

In reply Dayton's expressions were much more mild than those in Seward's note.

> Although our Government [he said] protests and will protest against all intercourse, official or otherwise, with these Commissioners as prejudicial and injurious to us, yet I do not know (aside from a mere act of conference) that we can have a just

cause of complaint of an interview with such a result as that. . . .
Furthermore, our Government did not mean to deny that
principle of international law which authorized the recognition
of a de facto Government when its status has become fixed and
its power to sustain itself satisfactorily shown.

Dayton's tone was not in accord with Seward's instructions,
but he had already done his duty by reading Seward's note. In
his report to Seward he observed that "the whole conversation
was, on the part of Mr. Thouvenel, kind and free." "I think I
may say with some confidence that all of the effects of the agents
of the Confederates on this side of the Channel have thus far
been abortive. They have no encouragement to their hopes of
recognition—they have met with no success in their attempts
to negotiate a loan—I do not believe they have got any considerable supply of arms; and I think that we know substantially
what they have done and are attempting to do."[72]

Although Thouvenel in this conversation had boldly defied
Seward's threats[73] by acknowledging and defending his interview with Rost, he knew from this time on that he must tread
warily in American affairs and cooperate closely with England.
On the other hand Dayton could not avoid seeing some reason-
ableness in Thouvenel's arguments and therefore softened his
remarks about the interview. Beyond the reading of Seward's
note, nothing seems to have been said in the interview about
belligerency recognition, but that subject was to be much discussed in Seward's conversations in Washington.

Thunder Along the Potomac

It was on May 11 that Seward first received intimations of
France's policy toward recognition. In Sanford's report of his
first interview with Thouvenel he read that the French minister
would receive the Southern commissioners "as respectable
foreigners, as he had received Poles, Hungarians, and others."[74]
A week later Seward learned of Lord John Russell's remark to
Dallas that he would consent to see the Confederate commissioners unofficially and would work closely with France on recognition.[75] And again a few days later he read Russell's remarks

before parliament that England would try to preserve her neutrality by not treating Southern privateers as pirates.[76]

With each arriving report the temperature increased in the state department until there was a violent Sewardian explosion whose reverberations threw the diplomatic dovecotes into a fluttering fright. Lord Lyons reported that Seward was very angry on receiving the news that England and France had recognized the belligerency of the Confederate States and that he was sending a strongly worded dispatch to Adams.[77] This, in fact, was the famous note in which he ordered Adams to discontinue all contacts with the British government as long as it had any relations, official or unofficial, with the Confederate commissioners.[78] At about this same time Seward is thought to have inserted the hot editorial in the *New York Herald* in which it attributed to the Federal government a well-thought-out plan of decisive measures against any foreign government which gave aid and comfort to the insurgent states.[79]

It was in the midst of this excitement that Mercier received a note from Thouvenel recounting his conversation with Sanford and his decision to see the commissioners when they arrived. He instructed Mercier to read it to Seward and also deliver a personal message from Thouvenel to the secretary. The nervous state of Mercier and the diplomats at this time is revealed by Mercier's report back to Thouvenel.

> I should have liked to execute this order [he wrote] without losing a moment's time, but this is why I have not been able to up to now. Since Mr. Seward, wrought up by events, has abandoned his peace policy, he has felt it necessary to express extreme opinions in the opposite sense and to assume toward European powers an attitude full of arrogance of which his recent instructions to Mr. Dayton can, for example, give you some idea; no moment passes without his making, in the presence of the diplomatic corps, some extravagant remark which is quite in line with the language of the newspapers said to be under his influence. . . . Lord Lyons and I thought that, as long as he is in such a bad humor, it would be better, in order to avoid any chance of complications, to refrain as much as possible from any political conversation with him.

However, reflecting again on Thouvenel's orders to let the secretary know how France stood on the matter, Mercier decided to bring it up incidentally after a conversation he and Stoeckl were invited to have with Seward on some question concerning Japan.

> But [Mercier continued] the Japanese matter was hardly concluded when, in discussing something about one of his consular agents, he had such a disagreeable row with my colleague that, in order not to get involved with a similar one myself, I thought it better to put off the conversation to a time when he would be in a better mood. Finally, after two or three unsuccessful attempts to meet him, I decided . . . to have an extract made of your dispatch and to present it confidentially to his son, the assistant secretary of state, so that he could transmit it to him [Seward] and his colleagues until I could have a chance to discuss it with him myself.[80]

Word went around among the worried diplomats that efforts were exerted in the cabinet meeting of May 21 to quiet Seward down. This seemed confirmed by Schleiden, the envoy from Bremen, to whom Seward had said on the 24th that he no longer feared that it would come to a break with England.[81] But the secretary's correspondence after the cabinet meeting seems to belie this diplomatic wishful thinking. On May 23 he wrote his dispatch to Dayton (discussed above) in which he direly predicted the permanent alienation of American friendship toward France. In the same ugly mood he wrote to Thurlow Weed in New York: "The European phase is bad. But your apprehension that I may be too decisive alarms one more. Will you consent, or advise us to consent, that Adams and Dayton have audiences and compliments in the Ministers' Audience Chamber, and Toombs's emissaries have access to his bedroom?"[82]

A week later Seward drew up a formal dispatch for Dayton, which showed he was still using a peremptory tone in his communications. Here he dealt with both the reception of the commissioners and the recognition of Confederate belligerency.

> First [he wrote]. I desire that Mr. Thouvenel may be informed that this government cannot but regard any com-

munications . . . even though unofficial, with the insurrectionary movement in this country as exceptionable and injurious
to the dignity and honor of the United States. . . . Even an
unofficial reception . . . has a tendency to . . . encourage their
efforts to prosecute a civil war. . . . It is earnestly hoped that
this protest may be sufficient to relieve this government from
the necessity of any action on the unpleasant subject to which
it relates.

Secondly. The United States cannot for a moment allow
the French Government to rest under the delusive belief that
they will be content to have the Confederate States recognized
as a belligerent power by States with which this nation is in
amity. No consent of action by foreign states so recognizing
the insurgents can reconcile the United States to such a proceeding, whatever may be the consequences of resistance.[83]

While the frightened French minister was still avoiding a
personal encounter with Seward, he received Thouvenel's instructions of May 11 and 16, which told him to concert closely
with Lyons—who had similar instructions—but to read to Seward
the note affirming France's recognition of Southern belligerency
and asking for assurance on the United States' fulfillment of
articles II, III and IV of the Declaration of Paris on maritime
law (to be discussed in the next chapter). Likewise the French
and English ministers were to cooperate in contacting the
South indirectly on the same legal question.

Mercier immediately consulted Lyons on June 5, and the two
men were agreed that it would be dangerous to carry out these
instructions immediately. Seeing how angry Seward was over
England's proclamation of neutrality, they felt they must use a
great deal of caution because Seward did not always realize how
detrimental some of his remarks and actions were to friendly
diplomatic relations. Finally they decided that Mercier should
have a "preparatory" conversation with Seward before they
proceeded to a joint official interview.

Consequently Mercier, with fear and trembling, went to the
state department, probably on Thursday, June 6th, and began
by reading Thouvenel's instructions of May 16 in which his
foreign minister expressed his and the emperor's deep regrets

over the outbreak of civil war in the United States, repeated the emperor's offer of his good offices for a peaceful solution, and emphasized Napoleon III's preference for the preservation of the Union. "Of course [Thouvenel had added cautiously] this does not mean that we are making a definite mediation proposal to the Washington cabinet. This is neither an offer nor even a suggestion. All we mean is that they should know just what His Majesty's sentiments are."[84]

Seward listened carefully as Mercier read on, and, when he had finished, there was not much evidence that the secretary had been impressed by the expression of French friendship and good wishes. He said he had heard all of this from Dayton and had already declined the mediation offer. Europe, he emphasized, must not harbor any illusion that the dissolution of the Union was possible. What surprised him, he complained, was that the more autocratic powers of Russia, Austria, and Prussia were the first ones to express their sincere sympathies for the Union. Obviously England was not sympathetic or she would not have so quickly accepted belligerent status for the rebels. But "he had been shocked that France, whose interests were so different [from England's] had appeared disposed to let herself be dragged along in the same direction." It will not take long to put this revolution down, but its repression will be delayed by any moral support shown by the European powers. For its part "the Federal government, which is determined to perish rather than recognize the Southern Confederacy, will not suffer the Europeans to have relations with its present leaders, which would raise their prestige."

Mercier saw that the secretary was not in the proper mood for him to protest Seward's aspersions, but he did try to give some counterarguments. Since France wanted to preserve the United States' strong position, he observed, any grievances could easily be settled in a friendly manner. When England and France had the same grievances, they naturally acted together and were planning to do so in a few days. At this point Mercier gave Seward a copy of the foreign ministry memorandum containing the arguments in favor of France's recognition of the South's belligerency. This was just for Seward's information and was to be returned, but the French minister said he wanted the secretary to peruse it before they had their conference on neutral rights.

Seward thanked him and also asked for a copy of the note no. 8, which had been read first, so he could show it to the president. He said there was one point that impressed him in the note. The emperor seemed to be offering his mediation for the reestablishment of the Union, and then to have second thoughts about it [*d'y réfléchir*], while, from his Paris correspondence, he offered his mediation for an arrangement between the two parties.

Mercier said that he was not authorized to let him have any of these papers, but he would lend them to him and begged him not to compromise his position by making any use of them. The French minister also requested that they be returned the next day. But Seward kept them for over a week, much to Mercier's discomfort.

Out of this exploratory interview, however, Mercier and Lyons did gain some information. Seward was still very sensitive about any form of recognition and was still in a fighting mood. They would probably have no difficulty about Articles II and III (neutral ships and neutral goods), but contacting the South on these matters would probably cause trouble.[85] The important thing right then was to get Seward to accept frankly their belligerency recognition, and that was why Mercier had given him the committee's memorandum.[86]

It was not until a week later that Seward asked Baron Gerolt, the Prussian minister, to contact Lyons and ask him to come over to the state department. He told Gerolt that any security requested for English or French commerce could be easily guaranteed, but he would not tolerate a recognition of Southern belligerency.[87]

This was exactly the cue that Lyons and Mercier had been waiting for. Lyons admitted that he had "laid low for a time" and had not even seen the French minister for a week. But the next day they met and talked over their plans. Lyons said that, by asking him to come over, Seward was trying to drive a wedge between England and France. He guessed that the American secretary would like to accommodate himself to England's demands without acknowledging her belligerency recognition of the South and at the same time try to make it appear that France had not done so because she had not issued a proclamation. This would give him a good chance to play to the galleries by denouncing England and remaining silent toward France. The two ministers surmised that this explained why he had avoided France's initiation of talks on maritime law. For these reasons Lyons insisted that the next day they go together and face him firmly on the subject of the South's belligerent rights and use identical language.[88]

Mercier was therefore delegated to arrange an appointment for June 15. But Seward made such an effort to avoid a joint interview that this visit itself became a long interview. After the French minister asked for an appointment and inquired about Seward's thoughts on the two documents, the secretary said that a joint interview was unnecessary, since the Federal government always had and would observe Articles II and III on noncontraband goods. "We concede you what you want. If you officially announce belligerency recognition, you will provoke our opposition." Mercier wanted to know how the United States would handle depredations by Southern privateers. "Use retaliation," Seward replied. But the French minister said his country would have to maintain a neutral attitude. In the end the secretary said he thought that it was all being settled in Europe. Yet Mercier did not give up on the idea of a future joint interview and proceeded to consult Lyons.

They were relieved that they had the assurances on maritime law, but there remained the question of belligerency and contacts with the South. Yet the secretary seemed to put more emphasis on the form than the substance of the question. Finally they decided to go through with their plans and insist on the dreaded interview.[89]

Mercier and Lyons arrived at Seward's office at the same time late in the forenoon of June 15 and were announced.

> *Seward:* Who came first?
> *Clerk:* Lord Lyons, sir, but they say they want to see you together.

Seward (after a moment's pause): Show them into the assistant secretary's room, and I will come in presently.

The two ministers were led into Frederick Seward's office and exchanged greetings with him in a worried and distracted manner. Soon Seward entered, smiling and shaking his head.

> *Seward:* No, no, no. This will never do.
> *Lyons* (rising to greet him): True, it is unusual, but we are obeying our instructions.
> *Mercier:* . . . and at least you will allow us to state the object of our visit?
> *Seward:* No. We must start right about it, whatever it is. M. Mercier, will you do me the favor of coming to dine with me this evening? Then we can talk over your business at leisure. And if Lord Lyons will step into my room with me now, we will discuss what *he* has to say to me.
> *Mercier* (shrugging): If you refuse to see us together. . . .
> *Seward:* Certainly I do refuse to see you together, though I will see either of you separately with pleasure, here or elsewhere.[90]

Presumably, then, Lyons stepped in to Seward's office with the purpose of reading him his instructions on belligerency and maritime law and leaving him a copy. Seward asked permission to look at the document unofficially first to see whether he could receive it officially. Then on inspecting it, he declined to receive it or have it read. This was the affirmation of his policy of the "averted glance." He would not take notice of British or French statements about recognizing belligerency so long as they did not force an official document upon him or perform some act of which he had to take official notice. In the face of hostile public opinion in the North this seemed to him the only way to avoid a showdown with England. The secretary then said that he was instructing his minister in London to take up the negotiations on maritime law. Lyons therefore did not insist upon reading his instructions or following through with maritime law discussions. After all, he and Mercier had already received verbal assurances on the law questions. With this relaxation of the tension of the interview Lyons then informed Seward that

England would allow no disposition of prize in her ports. The secretary seemed pleased with this announcement and observed that it would be a deathblow to Southern privateering since France had adopted the same policy.[91]

Seward's conversation with Mercier opened by the secretary saying that he supposed that Mercier's instructions were similar to the ministry committee's memorandum. The French minister admitted they were somewhat similar, but his instructions, and not the memorandum, were what he was required to present. Thereupon Seward said, as he had with Lyons:

> I cannot receive from you a communication based upon the idea that the rebels are belligerent. I do not admit that circumstances have changed a thing in the relations of the Southern states and foreign powers. I will have no discussion with you on this subject, but I will send instructions to the American ministers in Paris and London to furnish M. Thouvenel and Lord John Russell all the necessary explanations on how the Federal government intends to guarantee your [neutral] rights.

Seward added that he would keep both men informed about these exchanges in their home capitals, and he would appreciate receiving unofficially their instructions, past and future. Mercier took the hint and gave his instructions to the secretary in an unofficial way.[92] Thus the policy of the "averted glance" was more than ever a pretense.

Then, in an unofficial conversation, the American secretary complained about the attempt to show an Anglo-French common front. He had no complaint against France because she had not issued a public proclamation of neutrality,[93] but he was much offended by the queen's proclamation, although he understood the public pressure which may have forced England to it. Again Mercier argued that the European powers were much less susceptible to joint proposals and did not make serious objections to such procedures. France had no ulterior designs behind these moves and wished for nothing better than a favorable outcome of present complications.

Of course, Mercier and Lyons consulted each other after this encounter.

Lord Lyons and I wondered [Mercier wrote Thouvenel] whether instead of giving in so easily to Mr. Seward's pretensions, we should have done better by insisting, as we had every right to do, that he receive our communications in the form prescribed by our instructions and that he make some sort of reply. But the more we thought about it, the more it seemed that we would have exposed ourselves unnecessarily to some new difficulty. In fact, Mr. Seward was in an embarrassing situation. Not only does he want to avoid any act that might raise Southern morale and to reserve for himself every means for minimizing the importance of the Anglo-French accord in the eyes of the public; but also, either rashly or out of consideration for his own personal position, he had begun by taking an excessively high tone toward Europe. Now he had difficulty to maintain this high and mighty attitude in the face of the cabinets' strong arguments,[94] or to soften it in the face of the special session of congress which will be very violent and relentless toward him. . . . So Mr. Seward must try to gain time. . . . He certainly does know our attitude; he subscribes to our demands; and his tone has clearly quieted down toward us. If he tries to divide England and France, Your Excellency is warned in advance and can thus easily counteract all his schemes.[95]

For his part Seward after these interviews, expressed his ideas on belligerency to Dayton for the benefit of the French government in two separate dispatches. The second one was quite succinct:

We wish to act singly and in good faith with the French Government. We understand, and continue to understand, that France does not concede belligerent rights to the insurgents in contravention of our sovereignty. [The news of the French declaration arrived the next day.] We shall insist that she does nothing adverse to our position, whatever may be *said* to the contrary. She has proposed to tell us that the Confederate states are entitled to belligerent rights. We have declined to hear it. We shall continue to regard France as respecting our Government throughout the whole country, until she *practically acts in violation of her friendly obligations* to us, as we understand them. . . . The responsibility for the next step remains with France and not with us.[96]

By the time the news of the French declaration of neutrality reached Seward, he had already vented most of his indignation, and, in this case, he reserved most of his rebuke for Dayton because the latter had taken the whole issue of belligerency with so much tolerance.

> You [Dayton] seem to have adopted the idea that the insurgents are necessarily a belligerent power because the British and French Governments have chosen in some of their public papers to say they are so, and, of course, the consequence that Great Britain and France are neutrals in regard to us because they have chosen to claim the position.
>
> . . . Our view is in the contrary. Neither Great Britain nor France, separately nor both together, can by any declaration they make, impair the sovereignty of the United States over the insurgents nor confer upon them any public rights whatever. . . . We do not admit, and we shall not admit even the fundamental statement you assume, namely, that Great Britain and France have recognized the insurgents as a belligerent party. True you say they have been so declared. We reply: Yes, but they have not been declared to us. . . . It must be not their declarations, but their actions that conclude the fact. That action does not yet appear, and we trust, for the sake of harmony with them and peace throughout the world, that it will not happen.[97]

Seward's sensitivity to the news of Thouvenel's reception of Rost was mollified by the diplomatic way in which the French foreign minister announced it. The latter told Mercier to recount to Seward how he had impressed upon Rost the fact that France regretted secession in the United States, that general French opinion was against the dissolution of the Union, and that he could not give the Montgomery Government the least hope of being recognized by France.[98] Mercier hastened to show this to Seward unofficially, who, on returning it, wrote: "I remit the instructions of your government which you had the goodness to leave informally for my perusal. Availing myself of your kind permission, I have made its contents known to the President, and it affords me great pleasure to say that he received the communication with very high satisfaction."[99] This is a far cry from his threat of breaking off relations if France and England received the commissioners. Indeed, Rost had been received in Thouvenel's "audience chamber" rather than his "bed chamber," and yet Seward expressed Lincoln's "very high satisfaction." And by his "averted glance" policy, the American secretary was accommodating himself even to the recognition of belligerency. Perhaps another reason for Seward's acceptance of the situation was the fact that Prussia, Spain, and The Netherlands were also proclaiming neutrality and thereby recognizing Southern belligerency.[100]   Lincoln, in his message of July 4 to the special session of congress, made no allusion to the recognition of belligerency or to the reception of Yancey and Rost. He merely remarked briefly that he was happy to say that the sovereignty and rights of the United States were now everywhere *practically* [italics mine] respected by foreign powers, and a general sympathy with the country is manifested throughout the world.[101]

Throughout this whole early episode involving recognition Seward was fighting a losing battle against accepted international law and practice. In spite of his protests and threats England and France recognized the belligerency of the South, proclaimed their neutrality, received the commissioners unofficially, and paraded their tighter collaboration. But there seemed to be necessity and design in Seward's madness. Necessity, because he felt the heat of public opinion from the aroused North against any sign of recognition of the South and because congress was soon to meet, an unknown quantity in the administration's experience. Design, because he must frighten the European countries with a threat of war to make them tread lightly in their relations with the Confederacy. There is no doubt that Seward learned a few lessons in law and diplomacy in the encounter, and by his "averted glance" and his transfer of attention to the questions of maritime law he tried to squirm out of an untenable position.

And yet, the seasoned diplomats of the old world, while they were vexed by Seward's inexperience, began to assume a more cautious attitude in order to humor this *enfant terrible* in the interests of peace. While the French and British envoys on the firing line trembled at the roar of Seward's cannon, their superiors at least huddled more closely and resolutely in order to present a united front. They all were obviously going to try to give as little offense as possible. Hence, Seward may have lost the battle on belligerency, but still might win the larger war on political recognition. Subsequent events would have to determine his degree of success or failure.

Chapter III

THE DECLARATION OF PARIS*

THE opening of hostilities at Fort Sumter and the proclamations of the Northern blockade and Southern privateering raised other questions of international law beyond neutrality and belligerency. Would the North institute an effective blockade? Would Europe treat the Southern privateers as pirates? Would the North and South give guarantees for the immunity of neutral noncontraband property at sea? Such speculations were in the minds of men on both sides of the Atlantic and led to complicated and only partially successful negotiations.

These negotiations dealt with the application of recently proclaimed maritime law at the Congress of Paris in 1856. Here seven of the powers attending the congress—France, England, Russia, Austria, Sardinia, Prussia, and Turkey—issued a declaration, on April 16, 1856, agreeing to the following four articles of maritime law: 1) privateers—private vessels authorized to prey on enemy shipping in wartime—were abolished; 2) enemy noncontraband goods on neutral ships were free from capture—free ships make free goods; 3) neutral noncontraband goods on an enemy ship were free from capture; and 4) a blockade to be legal must be effective—no paper blockades. Since privateering was outlawed in wars between these signatories, their privateers in such wars would be treated as pirates and hanged upon capture. At the same time all other sovereign states were invited to accede to the declaration; but they must agree to

---

* For reasons of clarity the question of maritime law has been separated from that of belligerency recognition, although they were sometimes treated simultaneously by the diplomats. Consequently some of the same instructions and interviews will be mentioned again in chapter III.

them in full and must promise never to sign a treaty on maritime law with another power without including all four of these articles. By 1861 about forty-three states had adhered to these provisions by an exchange of notes without the formality of treaties. Only the United States, among the larger maritime powers, withheld its assent.

When, in 1856, the powers had invited the United States to give its adherence, it had refused to accede unless *all* noncontraband private property at sea—including that category of enemy property—were free from capture and unless the restrictions on future negotiations were eliminated—Marcy amendment. Secretary Marcy had argued that the United States, as a weak naval power, had to rely on privateers in wartime unless all noncontraband private property at sea was immune. He also felt that restrictions on future negotiations were inconsistent with the sovereignty of the United States. France and Great Britain had taken no action on the Marcy amendment when, in 1857, the Buchanan administration discontinued the negotiations on the subject.[1]

The Reversal of American Policy

The Civil War, the first of maritime importance since 1856, was bound to turn attention to the declaration and to the United States's abstention. Three days before Lincoln's inauguration Mercier wrote home that, if war broke out, the American government would regret that it had not accepted the declaration because the South would arm privateers, and then France and England would have to decide what to do to protect their vast American coastal trade.[2]

Indeed, in late April 1861, Seward began to turn his attention to the question of adhering to the Declaration of Paris. Several things had happened since he came to office on March 4 to make him revert to this subject. President Davis on March 16 had sent his three commissioners (Yancey, Mann, and Rost) to Europe to seek recognition; President Lincoln had rejected Seward's foreign war idea on April 1; and the surrender of Fort Sumter had been followed by the Northern blockade—April 19—

and the Southern call for privateers—April 17. As Seward turned these events over in his mind, he must have been thinking along these lines. First of all, he seemed to be looking for a way to enlist the efforts of Europe to help crush Southern privateers by treating them as pirates. Already, he and Lincoln in their blockade proclamation had threatened Southern privateers with the "punishment of piracy,"[3] and in the reasons he gave for the United States's reversal of position on the declaration he mentioned "the bad resolution [of the South] to invite privateers to prey upon the peaceful commerce of the United States."[4] Secondly, he was certainly concerned about the possibility of France's and England's recognition of the South. If he could win their sympathies by adhering to the declaration right at the moment when they were fearing for their commerce in this new war, it might persuade them to delay recognition. To France he explained that he was prompted by "a sincere desire to co-operate with other progressive nations in the melioration of the rigors of maritime war" and "a desire to relieve France from any apprehension of danger to the lives and property of her people."[5] Having put France and England in a better mood by reassurances as to their neutral commerce and once having committed them to the execution of Southern privateers, he also shrewdly schemed that he could head off any recognition even of Southern belligerency. If they were resisting Southern privateers as lawless American marauders, they could not very well proclaim neutrality or give the Confederacy any international status. In a sense he frankly avowed this purpose when he told Dayton that "we expected to remove every cause that any foreign power could have for the recognition of the insurgents as a belligerent power."[6]

These seem to be the reasons for Seward's reversal of American policy and do not include the motive, attributed to him by Charles Francis Adams, Jr., of trying to precipitate a war with England and France as soon as they violated this new agreement by refusing to hang Southern privateers. Seward was to threaten war with England and France all during the period of the Civil War as a matter of tactics, but his genuine "foreign war" policy had been effectively torpedoed by Lincoln three weeks before he decided to favor the declaration. Besides, his offer went out to seven European states, and he certainly did not intend to engage them all in war along with the Confederacy.[7]

For all of these reasons the American secretary of state, three weeks before he learned of England's recognition of belligerency and long before Russell had made any proposal on maritime law, wrote instructions to our representatives in Europe on April 24, authorizing them to negotiate a convention with each country for the United States's adherence, without reservation, to the Declaration of Paris. The president, he said, still preferred the Marcy amendment and hoped it would eventually be universally accepted, but, because of war dangers in Europe (Denmark and Italy) and the insurrection in the United States, "prudence and humanity combine in persuading the President, under the circumstances, that it is wise to secure the lesser good offered by the Paris Congress, without waiting indefinitely in hope of obtaining the greater one. . . ."[8]

Anglo-French Concern for Maritime Law

The news of the fall of Fort Sumter arrived in London and Paris on April 27, and from that date onward Russell and Thouvenel on their part were concerned about the neutral status of their countries and about the protection of their commerce in case of a maritime war. This new situation was unique for England and France. For the last half-century they had not been neutrals at the same time; they had been either enemies, separate belligerents, or allied belligerents. Furthermore, this American Civil War would be the first large-scale war to test the new rules of the Declaration of Paris of 1856. Thus, at the same time that the two foreign ministers were considering the recognition of Southern belligerency, they were also concerned about American interpretations of international law and an Anglo-French common front to defend the maritime rights of neutrals.

After the arrival of the news of Davis' call for privateers Russell was asked in the house of commons on May 2 whether privateers under an unrecognized flag would be treated as pirates. The foreign secretary evaded the question by saying that the fleet was being strengthened in American waters but British policy was to try to keep out of the impending contest. On May 6, in reply to another question, Russell said that Southern privateers would not be considered as pirates because this would force Great Britain to take action against them and thus be unneutral.[9]

In the meantime the law officers had advised Russell that, since the Civil War was a regular war, international law would apply, and the belligerents should be persuaded to observe the Declaration of Paris concerning privateering and neutral goods.[10]

Then, since England and France had already adopted a policy of cooperation on the American crisis,[11] Russell wrote to Cowley with information and suggestions for Thouvenel. First he reviewed the recent American proclamations and the history of the United States's refusal to accede to the Declaration of Paris. He seemed to imply that privateering would have to be tolerated because of that article's earlier rejection by the United States and that the rule as to an effective blockade was already acknowledged by Americans. However, he felt that additional positive assurances should be obtained from both belligerents by France and England jointly on Articles II and III, dealing with neutral noncontraband property at sea.[12]

During this first week of May, Thouvenel, in the French foreign ministry, had been equally concerned with the American problem. By May 3 he knew of the blockade and the call for Southern privateers as well as Russell's first evasive statement in parliament. There is little doubt, therefore, that the question was brought up in the cabinet meeting of Saturday, May 4th. Perhaps at that time it may have been decided to have a committee of experts in the foreign ministry draw up advice on the international law involved. This committee no doubt met on May 6 and 7, and had preliminary advice for Thouvenel to use in the deliberations of the cabinet meeting of May 8, where the outlines of French policy were agreed upon.[13] The foreign minister also studied two articles in the London *Times* of the 7th and 8th devoted to a discussion of maritime law.[14]

With this background and preparation Thouvenel was ready for his interviews with Cowley, who came to see him first on May 7, about collaboration on Articles II and III in approaches

to both the North and South. The French foreign minister immediately indicated his complete agreement with Great Britain
on recognizing Southern belligerency and the two articles.[15]
On May 9, after the cabinet meeting of the 8th, the two men
had a longer conversation on the subject of maritime law. Here
Thouvenel indicated the deliberations which were going on in
the committee and cabinet when he said that the French government itself "had already been preoccupied with the same
questions . . . and after having examined them at some length
(*mûrement*), it had arrived at the same conclusions as the British
cabinet." "In looking over the precedents, it had been discovered that Great Britain, although treating letters of marque
as piracy at the commencement of the American war [1776],
had, after a time, recognized the belligerent rights of the States
in rebellion against her." Then the French foreign minister
went on to suggest that, since the Americans had always advocated the principles of Articles II and III, the British and French
ministers in Washington should solicit the North's official adherence to them and their consuls should try to obtain the same
from the South.[16] In anticipation of the future collaboration of
Mercier and Lyons in Washington, Thouvenel sent a copy of
his instructions to Mercier—for May 11—to the British, and on
the same day Russell sent a copy of his draft instructions to
Lyons—for May 18—to the French.[17]

It was in the spirit of these lofty attitudes that Thouvenel
completed his instructions of May 11 for Mercier. After deplor-
ing the divisions and hostilities in the United States and reaffirm-
ing France's determination to remain neutral, he underscored
France's concern for her neutral commerce, asked that Articles
II and III be observed by the United States, and requested
assurances that the United States would hold itself responsible
for any illegal conduct by Northern privateers. Then, in a
separate dispatch, he sent Mercier a copy of the memorandum
of the ministerial committee of experts "where you will find more
fully developed the arguments and considerations that you will
need to use in support of your instructions." The memorandum
insisted that, since a war now existed, it was necessary to have
the United States recognize Articles II and III on the immunity

of noncontraband enemy goods on neutral ships and of non-contraband neutral goods on enemy ships. It cited precedents of American recognition of these principles in treaties with Russia (1854) and the two Sicilies (1855) and in Marcy's statements in 1856.[18] In these instructions, it will be noticed, there was no attempt to get the United States to accede to the full Declaration of 1856. The right of privateering seemed to be acknowledged because the United States had not, prior to the opening of hostilities, agreed to its outlawry.

On the following day, May 12, Thouvenel had another opportunity to approach the United States through Sanford, who came for a long interview. In that part of the conversation which dealt with maritime law the French minister said that France and England were agreed in obtaining from both belligerents an acknowledgement of Articles II and III of the Paris declaration—immunity of noncontraband goods. Sanford assured him that the United States had always supported those principles, but he in turn expressed a fear of French interference with the blockade. Thouvenel said there would be no French objection to the blockade as long as it was enforced, but he still was not sure about whether France would allow Southern privateers to dispose of prize in her ports. A Confederate *merchant* ship would be admitted to a French port without objection to its flag just as was done in the case of similar Italian ships while the new Italian government still was not recognized. Likewise the French minister presumed that French citizens would not be allowed to enlist on privateers and concluded by saying: "All these questions will be treated in no spirit of encouragement to the enterprise that the 'Confederate States' have entered upon."[19] Except for the recognition of Southern belligerency, everything that Thouvenel said about maritime law and sympathy for the Union was favorable to the North in spirit and in tone.

At the same time the French foreign minister was having difficulty with the British approach. Cowley had shown Thouvenel a draft of the future British instructions to Lyons wherein "the French and English governments ask President Lincoln to adopt the [whole] declaration of the Congress of Paris of 1856." This was contrary to Russell's earlier suggestion of limiting the request just to Articles II and III. Thouvenel immediately pointed out his serious objections to this proposal. In the first place, since the United States had previously rejected Article I on privateering, it would look as if the two European powers were trying to take advantage of the rebellion to force that clause upon the North. In the second place, the South would probably refuse to agree to the abolition of privateering since, without a regular navy, it would have to rely on privateers. Hence if the North accepted and the South rejected Article I, France and England might have to treat Southern privateers as pirates and thus violate their professed neutrality. It would be better, Thouvenel felt, to limit their proposals as originally agreed, to the acceptance of Articles II and III.[20] Evidently Cowley telegraphed Russell about these reservations, and the latter replied the same day that he thanked Thouvenel for his cooperation on Articles II and III without saying whether he would limit himself to those two clauses.[21]

What now complicated the situation was the arrival on the morning of May 14 of Mercier's report of April 26 in which he said Seward was going to offer the acceptance of the whole Declaration of Paris. Thouvenel immediately sent the report over for the emperor to read[22] and urgently wrote to Flahault his further objections. Seward was obviously setting a trap to make the neutral powers treat the Southern privateers as pirates. If they accepted his proposal, they would have all sorts of difficulties and be put in a very "delicate" position. Consequently, he reiterated again his opinion that "we ought to limit ourselves to asking the belligerents to observe the second and third provisions proclaimed by the declaration of April 16." He would also like to authorize his consul at New Orleans to go to Montgomery to contact President Davis on accepting these two articles for the South.[23] Evidently he was not reassured by the cryptic noncommittal message from Russell.

On receiving these urgent dispatches, interspersed no doubt with telegrams, Flahault tried to see Russell but found he had left town because of his brother's death. He then sought Lord Palmerston and urged him to have the instructions to Lord Lyons limited to Articles II and III. The prime minister saw the point at once, and, after consulting his cabinet, agreed not to include privateering in the requests to the two belligerents.[24] Only the foresight and caution of Thouvenel had prevented Russell and the British cabinet from making an unwise approach to the two belligerents.

His instructions to Mercier were written before he heard from Flahault and told his Washington diplomat to concert with Lyons on Articles II and III and on the approach to the South. He enclosed his notes to Flahault and to the consul at New Orleans for guidance. In a postscript he added: "Just as I send this out I receive the inclosed telegram from Flahault. As I presumed, the English cabinet adopts completely the substance of the communication to be made to Washington and Montgomery."[25] Similar instructions were finally sent by Russell to Lyons on May 18 stressing Articles II and III and requesting assurances on the good behavior of Northern privateers. "You will endeavor (in concert with M. Mercier) to come to an agreement on the subject binding France, Great Britain, and the United States."[26]

On the same day that Lyons' instructions were finally sent out—May 18—Russell had his first interview with the new American minister, Charles Francis Adams, who, in line with his instructions, proposed a later interview to negotiate a convention for his country's adherence to the whole Declaration of Paris. Again Russell was typically vague and confusing:

> His Lordship [Adams reported] . . . expressed the willingness of Great Britain to negotiate; but he seemed to desire to leave the subject in the hands of Lord Lyons, to whom he intimated that he had already transmitted authority to assent to any modification of the only point in issue [Marcy Amendment?] which the government of the United States might prefer.

Adams' proposal was a clear fulfillment of Thouvenel's warning, and Russell seemed to be dodging it by being vague and assimilating it with his instructions to Lyons. Out of deference to Russell the United States minister quite properly dropped his negotiation until he should receive further instructions from Washington.[27]

The Washington Negotiations

There was thus an interlude of passing the ball back and forth across the Atlantic before the parties got down to real negotiations on the United States accession to the whole declaration. It was upon receipt of their instructions in early June that Mercier and Lyons began their consultations about initiating their joint negotiations with Seward, a part of which, dealing with belligerency, has already been discussed.[28] "I have just received your big packet dated May 16 [Mercier wrote privately to Thouvenel], and after having looked it all through, I shall try to carry out your orders to your greatest satisfaction. Circumstances require a great deal of circumspection and tact. I have not yet succeeded in plumbing the depths of American braggadocio."[29] Lyons received his instructions of May 18 on the next day, June 3. "M. Mercier and I had a conversation respecting these instructions a few hours after the dispatches containing them reached us," he wrote. They were convinced that the American explosion over the news of England's proclamation of neutrality required that they act closely together on maritime law.[30] Not only was Mercier frightened into "circumspection," but the entire diplomatic corps was atremble. Lyons wrote that "a sudden declaration of war by the United States against Great Britain appears to me by no means impossible." "I am very willing to let him [Mercier] take the lead in our communications about the Declaration of Paris." Likewise, the Austrian minister, Hülsemann, wrote home that "if by chance, in the interval from now until the assembling of congress, the masses and their leaders rightly or wrongly get the idea that France would come to the aid of the United States in a war with England, it would inevitably be declared before the end of July."[31]

It was therefore at this point that Mercier, in agreement with Lyons, went to see Seward in that preliminary interview of June 6 (already partially discussed in connection with belligerency recognition). On that occasion the French minister told Seward that "one of these days Lord Lyons and I shall have a communication to make to you on the subject of maritime rights." To prepare Seward for the later interview, he submitted to him unofficially the memorandum of the French ministry committee, to be retained only for one day. "When you [Seward] will have read it, we will talk about it and then we will take up the question of neutral rights."

Seward thanked him and said he would examine it carefully. As to maritime law, the memorandum showed that England and Spain, in the wars against their revolting colonies, had had to give up the policy of treating their privateers as pirates, thus indirectly recognizing their belligerency. "The principle of free ships make free goods should not seem to raise any difficulty, this doctrine having always been that of the United States." On Article III of the Paris declaration the experts said that recently the United States "had announced on several occasions in official statements the principle that neutral goods on an enemy ship were not subject to confiscation." Therefore France could expect to obtain adherence from the United States.

Actually Seward seemed to want to satisfy the two powers on maritime rights without having a formal interview. On June 8 he wrote Lyons, concerning the ship "Winifred," that this government [the United States] recognizes the right of the property of a *friendly* nation in the vessels of an *insurgent* [he avoids the words 'neutral' and 'belligerent'] to be exempted from condemnation." And Mercier concluded from this that "as far as neutral rights are concerned, I do not doubt that we will obtain a favorable reply."[32]

From all of this Mercier thought that there would be no difficulties on Articles II and III, but now the questions were how to obtain Northern acquiescence in contacts with the Southern authorities. Thus he and Lyons decided to concentrate on a joint interview on the belligerency questions, and Mercier went to see Seward on June 14 to arrange an appointment for the joint interview on the 15th. It was on this occasion that Seward tried very hard to avoid such a meeting. He told Mercier that the United States had always advocated the sense of Articles II and III, and therefore no interview was necessary. Besides, Adams and Dayton were already taking up with London and

Paris the adherence of the United States to the entire Declaration.[33]

Mercier insisted that their instructions required a joint interview, and one can imagine Seward's irritation in granting it for the following day. Thus it was under these unfavorable auspices that Lyons and Mercier presented themselves for the famous interview on the morning of June 15, and Seward had had plenty of time to plan his determined effort to hold separate interviews.[34] Mercier's experience was similar to Lyons', and we will let his account be the basis of the interviews. After Seward had asserted his policy of the "averted glance" on belligerency, the discussion turned to maritime law. The secretary said he knew from Mercier's earlier memorandum what France desired regarding questions of international law. He would not receive any note concerning belligerency, but he was having the law matters negotiated in Paris and London. Seward then promised to let them know what he wrote and asked them to tell him confidentially for his own personal use what instructions they had received on the question. In other words this suggested his unofficial receipt of the very documents he said he did not want to receive officially. They both took the hint and let him have their papers unofficially—still the "averted glance."[35]

To show that the question was getting a little confused, we have this additional account from Lyons.

> It appeared that he [Seward] conceived that the communication that we were discussing with him [Articles II and III] was a matter entirely distinct from his proposal to adhere to the Declaration of Paris. He seemed to have concluded, from a dispatch he had received from Mr. Adams, that your Lordship had authorized me to enter into a separate negotiation on the subject.
>
> I have this morning explained to Mr. Seward how the matter really stands. He said, in reply, that he thought he had reason to complain that the Governments of Europe had taken no notice of the offer he had made to them long ago, to adhere without reserve, to the Declaration of Paris. [He wanted to show that he had initiated this before the question of belligerency, had taken the initiative and had not been setting a

trap.] He had announced that he preferred the proposal of Mr. Marcy [freedom of all noncontraband property at sea]; but if that was not acceptable, he was ready to agree to the Declaration as it stood. He should now desire Mr. Adams to inform your Lordship that he was willing that the negotiations should be carried on either here or in London [alas, more confusion], without further delay.[36]

As a result of the interviews of June 15 and 17, Seward then took steps to pass the ball back to the European side of the Atlantic. His first new instruction went to Dayton on the 17th, relating his refusal to receive officially the French and English communications and the reason for his refusal—the question of the recognition of the belligerency of the South. The South could not be a belligerent because there was no war. There was only an insurrection in the process of being suppressed by the legally constituted government. He did recognize that there were hostilities involved and that foreign powers would be concerned about the safety of their commerce in the midst of these hostilities. In response to foreign concern about commerce on the Atlantic the United States had initiated as early as April 25 the negotiation of conventions with France and other foreign countries "to stipulate . . . our adhesion to the declaration of the congress of Paris as a whole and unmodified" if they still persisted in rejecting the Marcy amendment. "This was done . . . long before the date of the instruction which Mr. Mercier proposed to submit to us. We have ever since that time been waiting for the responses of foreign powers to this high and liberal demonstration on our part. We have, however, received no decisive answers on the subject from those powers."

He went on to say that the United States "have always when at war conceded the last three of these [Paris] rights to neutrals [neutral property immunity at sea and an effective blockade], *a fortiori* we could not when at peace deny them to friendly nations."[37]

> We are still ready [he concluded] to guarantee these rights, by convention with France, whenever she shall authorize either you or her minister here to enter into convention. There is no

reservation nor difficulty about their application to the present case. We hold all the citizens of the United States, loyal or disloyal, alike included by the law of nations and treaties. . . . What then does France claim of us that we do not accord to her? Nothing. What do we refuse to France by declining to receive the communication sent to us through the hands of Mr. Mercier? Nothing but the privilege of telling us that we are at war, when we maintain we are at peace, and that she is a neutral, when we prefer to recognize her as a friend.[38]

However much Seward concealed it, there must have remained the suspicion of foreign powers that he intended to have France and the other countries treat Southern privateers as pirates once the United States had renounced privateering (Article I) for both the North and South. The trap was there and was very probably intentional.

A similar note was dispatched to Adams two days later in which Seward noted that England was asking only for American acceptance of Articles II and III, while the United States had offered to accede to all four articles as early as April 25. Since Lyons did not seem authorized to negotiate a convention on the whole Declaration, he authorized Adams to undertake it in London.[39]

Lyons' final observations on the Washington side of the negotiations stressed the pressure of public opinion behind Seward and the necessity of Anglo-French cooperation in the whole affair. In a private and confidential letter to Russell the English minister expressed the fear that some incident might arouse Northern opinion to the point of forcing Seward into a war with Britain.[40]

European Negotiations: First Phase

From the last of June 1861 Dayton and Adams had to catch Seward's forward passes and carry the ball to an anticipated conclusion of a treaty by which the United States would accede to the whole Paris declaration.

Indeed, while Adams had stopped his negotiations after May 18, Dayton had gone ahead with his negotiations with Thouvenel during that same month. He had asked for a conference to initiate negotiations on May 24, and Thouvenel set May 29 as the day.[41] Sanford was on hand to help in these first negotiations and looked up for Dayton the meaning of the French laws and regulations in regard to neutrality. He thought that Dayton should obtain a clear understanding on French policy toward Southern privateers. Also most of the new Northern diplomats were stopping over in Paris on their way to their posts and joined in the preliminary preparations. Sanford said, "I find that all [these Northern diplomats] here have the same opinion that they had better try to secure the Marcy proposition if possible; if not, then to fall back upon the abrogation *pure et simple* of privateering" [i.e., the whole declaration without the Marcy amendment]. He was sanguine that England would accept the Marcy proposal in order to end Northern privateering, which in case of war would unleash over a thousand armed merchant ships against British shipping.[42]

Finally, at four o'clock on the afternoon of May 29, Dayton, with Sanford as interpreter, waited upon Thouvenel at the foreign ministry. Dayton evidently had been persuaded by Sanford and the other Northern visiting envoys that an attempt should first be made to obtain French acceptance of the Marcy amendment along with the Declaration of Paris.[43] His reasons were: 1) that Lincoln seemed to prefer that combination, 2) that this should be a quid pro quo for the United States's surrender of privateering, 3) that in 1856 both France and Russia had been willing to accept the Marcy amendment, and 4) Adams seemed to think that England would make the concession to obtain the accession of the United States to the privateering clause. Therefore the brief exchange on this negotiation, according to Dayton, went somewhat this way:

> I told him [Thouvenel] I was authorized to accept the four propositions adopted at the Congress of Paris in 1856, but with the desire expressed by the President that the provision should be added exempting private property afloat (unless contraband) from seizure and confiscation. I did not say, nor did he ask whether the four propositions would be accepted without

amendment. He said nothing could be done except by conference with the other powers; but if I would submit the proposition in writing, which I shall at once do, he will immediately address the other powers and we would probably receive an answer in ten or twelve days.[44]

Consequently, on May 31, Dayton sent a formal proposal to Thouvenel that the United States would be willing to sign a convention providing for its accession to the Paris declaration if the Marcy amendment were added to the first clause on privateering.[45]

There then ensued a long period of delay in which Dayton had an opportunity to rethink the prospects of the negotiation. In the first place he admitted his language difficulty when he said he thought Thouvenel meant he would consult the powers in ten or twelve days. It turned out that he meant he would consult his cabinet colleagues. Besides, Dayton began to sense that the European powers would understand that the Northern accession to the declaration would only apply to Northern privateers and not to Southern. "At least that is the view which I think is and will be taken of this question by England and France." Nevertheless, he did not worry about the delay caused by the request for the inclusion of the Marcy amendment because, he said, Adams had referred the matter to Washington. Dayton would therefore await further notification from Seward.[46]

It was not until June 10 that Thouvenel approached England on the matter of the Marcy amendment. Some of his thoughts, expressed to Flahault, turned to speculating whether exempting private property from capture would limit blockading to naval bases only. Some American papers were saying that the Marcy amendment would not be very fruitful if such property could be seized closer to shore by blockaders. Then he added toward the end: "We can expect the Washington cabinet to take advantage of us, by its agreement to abolish privateering, in asking us to apply it to the Southern States and to treat their privateers as pirates."[47]

Flahault then consulted Russell on the question of Article I, who replied that he would reject the Marcy amendment. To

Grey (his chargé in Paris) Russell explained that the Marcy amendment was disadvantageous to big naval and mercantile powers and would encourage a merchant disguise for war vessels. As to outlawing Southern privateers, that would be unneutral for England.[48]

Once Russell had heard of Dayton's offer to France, he surmised that Adams in the meantime had received instructions to make the same offer to England and supposed that was why Adams had asked for an interview for June 12. The foreign secretary promised Flahault that he would put Adams off by saying he had to consult the cabinet but in the end England would reject the Marcy amendment. Much to his astonishment, Adams said he had no instructions to propose the Marcy amendment, and this convinced Russell that Seward was trying to separate France from England. Writing to Grey in Paris, he remarked: "I trust that this effort will fail, and that the two Governments will continue to act together in this critical business."[49] Thouvenel, for his part, was very happy to learn of their complete agreement and of the mutual desire for a common front, especially in view of Seward's more threatening attitude and his apparent attempt to divide the two powers.[50]

It was three weeks after Dayton's initial proposal before Thouvenel gave any reply. It does not appear that he consulted any other power than England. After referring to the earlier negotiation on the Marcy amendment in 1857, he put off any French decision on the matter with the explanation that France would have to await an American proposal of the Marcy amendment to all signatories of the Declaration before she could negotiate.[51]

Dayton's reaction to this reply was to drop the negotiations for the time being, just as Adams had done in London. If Seward would acquiesce in the United States's adherence without the Marcy amendment, he himself was opposed and preferred the transfer of the negotiations to Washington.[52] After Dayton wrote this, he indicated in a postscript that he had just received Seward's instructions no. 19, telling him to have France negotiate with him, or through Mercier, on the unamended declaration just as it was. No doubt, clinging to the alternative suggestion of "through Mercier," he did not change his suggestion of a Washington negotiation and sent on his dispatch unaltered. Thus Dayton had completed the early phase of his negotiation and was referring the matter back to Washington just as Adams had done a month earlier. This helps to explain why, in the second phase of the European negotiations, Adams was active and Dayton was silent. Adams was to catch Seward's forward pass while Dayton was to fumble his.

European Negotiations: Second Phase

Such was the confusion over the transatlantic shifts in negotiations that, a week after Dayton had transferred his negotiations back to Washington, Adams was reopening in London his negotiations on the Declaration of Paris. This confused situation was caused by several of the principals in the negotiations. In the first place Seward's instructions of April 24 were vague on the Marcy amendment; secondly, Dayton took those vague instructions too seriously, probably on the prompting of Sanford; then Russell misled Adams by implying that Lyons was instructed to negotiate a convention on the whole declaration when actually he was only to obtain a favorable statement on Articles II and III; and finally Adams and Dayton did not consult sufficiently with each other.

Having received Seward's instructions of June 19, Adams wrote to Russell, complaining that he now learned that Lyons had no authorization to negotiate a convention and therefore asking that he be allowed an appointment to renew negotiation on the Declaration of Paris.[53] Russell arranged an interview for July 13 at 3:00 P.M. and defended himself by saying that Lyons had been authorized to come to an agreement on Articles II, III, and IV (not on Article I [privateering]), but not to sign a convention. He said that the fifty-six countries adhering to the declaration have done so by an exchange of notes.[54] Adams then proposed the draft treaty containing all four articles of the declaration. When Russell inquired why it could not be done by an exchange of notes, Adams explained that the American procedure of senate ratification required that the agreement be in the form of a convention. The foreign secretary agreed to consider it, obtained the cabinet's approval, and, because of the American minister's desire for haste, planned to sign the convention on July 16—only three days after Adams' proposal.[55]

It was at this point that Russell suddenly realized that he should, perhaps, consult France. The foreign secretary's impulse to move rapidly toward the signing is very strange when only six days before he had vowed to work with France if the negotiations were transferred to London and Paris. To Flahault he had confided a few days earlier that he thought it was an attempt on the part of Seward to divide England and France. "Lord John Russell," wrote Flahault, "is convinced that that is his aim, but he hopes that if Your Excellency [Thouvenel] shares this opinion, he [Seward] will have a hard time accomplishing it."[56] Yet, here was the foreign secretary already one day away from signing without consulting France and apparently without any reservation on Southern privateering. Finally on July 15, Russell merely told Flahault that he intended to sign "tomorrow" and "he supposed that Mr. Dayton will have similar instructions anyway." Surprised by this news, Flahault sent a hurried telegram to Thouvenel.[57]

On the next day Thouvenel called in Cowley and received a confirmation of Adams' move. Both of the men were perplexed because Adams was not insisting on the Marcy amendment as Dayton had in June and the United States was asking for a convention rather than for an exchange of notes. The French foreign minister then revealed that Dayton had not renewed the negotiations in Paris and also informed Russell through Flahault.[58]

The French ambassador in London was suspicious not only of Seward's attempt to divide the two European powers but also of his effort to get England and France to treat Southern privateers as pirates. This would violate their proclaimed neutrality. Flahault recalled Thouvenel's comment of two months before (May 14) that "President Lincoln's acquiescence in the declaration of . . . 1856 will have as effect to put the neutral nations in a delicate position." That was why Thouvenel had advised Russell to treat only on Articles II and III.[59] Consequently

Flahault had a long conversation with the befuddled and forgetful foreign secretary. He reminded Russell that they had finally limited their approach to the United States to just the two articles because the whole declaration would make France and England depart from their neutrality. That was probably why the United States was proposing the whole declaration now. Then the North and England and France would have to treat Southern privateers as pirates. Flahault therefore added that the two European maritime powers would have to make reservations to their acceptance of the new conventions and must work together on formulating them. Russell was much impressed with these arguments and remarked that he had already asked Cowley to consult France and was waiting to hear from him. The French ambassador urged him to delay for twenty-four hours until he could consult France. Russell agreed to this postponement. He said that Adams was in a great hurry, but he had not, and now would not, set a time for signing. Adams had told him, however, that Dayton had similar instructions.[60]

When Cowley went again to the foreign ministry and, in the absence of Thouvenel, talked with Billault, the latter said that France was not opposed to signing but felt that France and England should act along with the other signatories.[61] In reply Russell repeated that England wanted to work on this with France. He did not have any objection to a convention, if the American senate required it, but he would not sign unless Dayton also proposed a convention to France. He wanted to know what were the terms Dayton had proposed. France and England, in his opinion, did not have to consult the other signatories so long as the United States was making a similar proposal to them. Then he concluded with a significant statement on reservations: "It remains for me to notice that this convention can not in any way alter the Proclamations and other Instruments by which Great Britain and France have declared their intentions to treat the two Parties engaged in the Civil War in America as Belligerents. This declaration may be made verbally both to Mr. Adams and to Mr. Dayton."[62] At last Russell was heeding the warnings of Thouvenel and Flahault that Article

I on privateering would have to be qualified by a reservation in order to preserve Anglo-French neutrality.

Not knowing of Dayton's resolve to await confirmatory instructions before he reopened discussions on the Declaration of Paris, both the London and Paris governments were puzzled by his mysterious silence. Thouvenel was lying in wait for him at his regular diplomatic reception on Thursday, July 18, but was disappointed by Dayton's absence. He immediately telegraphed to England: "Mr. Dayton . . . did not attend and had not sent me any written communication in the sense of the proposal made by Mr. Adams to Lord John Russell."[63]

On the same day Russell gave a written reply to Adams in which he said he understood the reason for the United States desire for adherence by convention, and he would be glad to follow this procedure. But there was also the matter of the United States agreement with all the other signatories. A simultaneous signing with all of them would be difficult and conducive to long delays. He would be satisfied if the United States indicated that it was making overtures to all the signatories and if a simultaneous signing was arranged just with France. He did not bring up the question of reservations on Article I at this time, but he did send a copy of this to Cowley for Thouvenel.[64] This led Adams to write immediately to Dayton to ask whether he considered himself authorized to negotiate on the convention without the Marcy amendment or whether the whole thing must be delayed until new instructions were received from Washington.[65]

In the meantime Dayton was having a debate with Seward over whether to proceed with the negotiation. As early as June 12, before Thouvenel had rejected the Marcy amendment, Dayton had told Seward that "it is doubtful perhaps whether the other Powers will under the circumstances negotiate for the accession of the United States at this time to the treaty in question; but should they do so, it will be with the understanding, I take it, that it imposes no new duties upon them growing out of our domestic controversy."[66] In other words, Dayton was anticipating reservations by France and England which would permit privateering by the South. Seward did not like Dayton's anticipation of such a reservation and even talked frankly about it to Lyons. On July 6 he went over to the British legation to ask for a full list of the signatories to the Paris declaration. During the conversation he said he was trying to "disentangle a complication which had been produced by Mr. Dayton at Paris." Dayton was afraid France would not commit herself to something that would seem to interfere with her neutrality; but, said Seward, "if nothing was said on either side concerning this particular point, the accession of the United States might be given at once, and accepted, and the effect of it with regard to the States in revolt could be determined afterwards."[67] With these thoughts in mind Seward had already replied to Dayton that he was not to assume that foreign powers recognized Southern belligerency or that they would permit Southern privateers after signing a convention. The United States in concluding a treaty, he insisted, acts alike for its loyal and disloyal citizens and "shall expect . . . foreign nations to respect and observe the treaties so made." Dayton, like Seward, must ignore the belligerency recognitions and keep the attitude of the "averted glance."[68] Five days later Seward wrote Dayton again saying "you now see that by incorporating the Marcy amendment in your proposition you have encountered the very difficulty foreseen by us" [by delay causing the South to be treated differently than the North]. "We therefore expect you now to renew the proposition in the form originally prescribed" [without the Marcy amendment].[69]

In the face of Seward's peremptory instructions and Adams' queries Dayton finally did have to bestir himself again. His first reaction was to defend himself before Seward by saying that he had never thought of Seward using the "averted-glance" policy but that he did not think France would take offense at his official refusal to receive their notes. Dayton disagreed with Seward that France knew on what grounds United States adhesion would be made to the treaty. If it meant no recognition of Southern privateering, then France would probably insist that it appear in the text of the treaty and not be left to inference. The European press, Dayton added, was already talking about reservations on Southern privateering. As to Seward's complaint that he seemed to be accepting France's recognition of Southern belligerency, Dayton parried by saying he did not accept France's recognition of belligerency, but he did hesitate to make a treaty when France had proclaimed such a recognition. Such a course might bind the United States to forego privateering while the South would be allowed to use it as far as France and England were concerned.[70]

Having put his own views on record, Dayton, for the first time in his two months of residence in Paris, went to London on July 23 for consultation with Adams. The two ministers had a long conference on the morning of July 24. They compared their instructions and their action taken upon them. Dayton explained his reasons for hesitating to negotiate when European neutrality would seem to exempt Southern privateers. At least he would want to insist on the acceptance of the Marcy amendment, since Thouvenel had not specifically rejected it in his reply. Adams defended his opening of negotiations because of his clear instructions to do so. He had not insisted upon the Marcy amendment because Russell had said it was inadmissible to England. In the end Dayton agreed to start negotiations without demanding the Marcy amendment if Adams could get a written statement from Russell on his rejection of the amendment. Since Adams himself had had trouble with Russell's oral remarks, he could only agree with Dayton. On the following day Dayton left a letter with Adams, summarizing their conference and conclusions.[71]

Three days later Adams made a clever attempt to have Russell commit himself in writing on the rejection of the Marcy amendment. He told Russell that Dayton was ready to start negotiations in Paris if Russell thought the amendment was inadmissible to England. "But in order to remove all possibility of misconception between him and myself," wrote Adams "I have taken the liberty of recalling your Lordship's attention to the matter before it is too late." "Should there have been any essential error of fact on the main point, I trust your Lordship will do me the favor to set me right."[72] Russell replied two days later, stressing Adams' recollection that the Marcy amendment was inadmissible to England. "So far as I [Russell] am concerned this statement is perfectly correct." Here was exactly the assurance that Dayton wanted to justify himself before the senate over the dropping of the Marcy amendment. However, the Russell note initiated another complication anticipated by Dayton and inspired by Thouvenel: the foreign secretary hinted in his bumbling way at a reservation to the convention. He told Adams he was ready to go ahead with the convention simultaneously with France, but "I need scarcely add that on the part of Great Britain the engagement will be prospective, and will not invalidate anything already done."[73] On receiving this, Adams, curiously enough, claimed to be mystified by the last paragraph in spite of the frank talk Dayton had had with him. As he transmitted Russell's reply to Washington, he added, "I must frankly admit that I do not understand the meaning of the last paragraph."[74]

Before receiving the news of Russell's letter, Dayton began contacts with the French government. He saw Billault, in Thouvenel's absence, toward the end of July and apprised him that he would soon propose a convention to accept the Paris declaration without amendment. Billault said that the opposition to the amendment was elsewhere [England] and that "there would be no difficulty upon the part of France in treating in the form in which we proposed [by convention] . . . that the feeling of France toward the United States was such as made her always disposed to receive whatever came from us 'in good part.' "[75]

When Dayton received a copy of Russell's written rejection of the Marcy amendment, he was not at all mystified by the last paragraph. In his acknowledgment to Adams he said:

> You say you do not comprehend the drift of the last paragraph in Lord John's reply. I think I do . . . and I shall not be surprised if the meaning which he has purposely wrapped up in that general language should in the end, break off all negotiations. . . . Their comment . . . will be that it does not bind your disloyal citizens, recognized by us as a belligerent party. I long ago wrote Mr. Seward that these Powers would, in my judgment, either refuse to negotiate, or if they did negotiate, it would be with the understanding that it secured us no rights not already conceded and charged them with no duties

not heretofore acknowledged. It is advisable that we raise no question in advance in reference to this matter, but it is necessary that we know what they mean as we go along. . . .[76]

Thus both Dayton and Adams anticipated that reservations were going to be made, but both pretended they did not suspect any such Anglo-French maneuver. It is hard to understand Adams' mystification unless he maintained his pretense even toward Seward and Dayton. He was usually very shrewd in his diplomatic appraisals.

Finally after much delaying and consulting, and quite against his better judgment, Dayton made his formal negotiation proposal to Thouvenel on August 2, 1861. After reviewing all the earlier negotiations which sought in vain to add the Marcy amendment, he concluded that he had authorization to sign a treaty adhering to the Declaration without the amendment. He also enclosed a copy of the statement of Russell's willingness to negotiate in England. Both American envoys referred to their April instructions in order to emphasize that the United States initiation of negotiation had preceded the proclamations of neutrality and therefore had had no design of springing a trap on the privateering question.[77]

Thouvenel had been spending a week or two in his country home while Billault substituted in the ministry. He did not return until August 4, and consequently did not reply to Dayton until August 13.[78] In his communication he indicated his willingness to sign and asked to see Dayton's powers to negotiate. There was no mention of reservations.[79] Dayton furnished him with a copy of his powers on August 16,[80] and a conference seems to have been arranged for the 20th.

In the meantime the United States minister in Paris was trying to keep informed about the progress in London. Cowley had furnished Dayton a draft copy of the London version of the convention, and Dayton wanted the same from Adams to confirm it. Still looking for signs of reservations, he added that he requested "likewise a minute of any conversation or copy of any correspondence which may have passed upon the subject. . . ." Thouvenel, he said, seemed to think that Tuesday the 21st

(20th?) would be the day for the simultaneous signing, and Dayton also wanted this confirmed. He concluded: "I suspect that action upon this subject will after all have been more prompt than was anticipated at Washington." Seward in his last despatch had said "the President is not impatient about the negotiation."[81] Adams was perturbed by this last sentence because he had been hurrying the negotiations at the behest of Seward, and now the impatience had gone out of the home government. At least he acknowledged there was plenty of food for thought.[82]

And indeed there was much food for thought in the making, because Russell and Thouvenel had decided on written reservations to be presented as separate "declarations" to the conventions. After furnishing France a copy of the English version of the convention to be signed at London, Russell telegraphed Cowley a draft version of the reservation declaration which he was going to present to Adams.

> I propose [wired Russell] to give Mr. Adams in writing the following declaration: 'Lord Russell declares in the name of the Government of Her Majesty that the signature of the present Convention does not invalidate or alter in any way public acts to which Her Majesty's sanction has been already given.' If Thouvenel agrees, I will inform Mr. Adams beforehand. Will the 21st suit Thouvenel?[83]

But Thouvenel did not agree to this version, which no doubt seemed too vague as to what it should not apply to. So, probably he and Cowley drew up a new French text and its English translation, which read as follows:

> In affixing his signature to the Convention of this day between Her Majesty the Queen of Great Britain and Ireland, and the United States of America, Earl Russell declares by order of Her Majesty, that Her Majesty does not intend thereby to undertake any engagement, which shall have any bearing, direct or indirect, on the internal differences now prevailing in the United States.[84]

This revision was then sent back to Russell, who substituted the new version as his own and no doubt informed Thouvenel through Cowley. At any rate by August 16, Thouvenel informed Flahault: "I adhere to the declaration which Lord John Russell proposes to make to Mr. Adams."[85] As an extra precaution Thouvenel sent the revised text to Flahault for him to verify it again with Russell and to find out the manner in which it is to be presented. Chateaurenard, as French chargé in the absence of Flahault, saw Russell, who confirmed his acceptance of the new text. However, Thouvenel's query as to the manner (forme) made Russell realize that certain precautions should be taken. He was going to present the reservation in writing and ask Adams for a written acknowledgement of receipt. He would not go so far, though, as to ask Adams for a formal adherence to the reservation or for his signature of a protocol.[86]

Thus the two stages were set when Dayton called upon Thouvenel at noon on Tuesday, August 20, for the first negotiating session. Dayton believed, however, that the signing would come soon after "unless something shall occur altering the existing conditions of things"— revealing by these thoughts that he half expected some unacceptable reservations. And he was not disappointed. As soon as the discussion began, the French foreign minister handed Dayton an advance copy of the reservation declaration which would be presented at the formal signing of the convention.[87] According to Dayton's account the following conversation took place:

> *Thouvenel:* Both France and Great Britain have already announced that they will take no part in your domestic controversy, and we thought that a frank and open declaration in advance of the execution of the Convention might save difficulty and misconception hereafter. The provisions of the Treaty standing alone might bind England and France to pursue and punish the Privateers of the South as pirates. We are unwilling to do this and have already so declared. You can deal with these people as you choose, and we can only express our regrets on the score of humanity if you should deal with them as pirates, but we can not participate in such a course. Although England and France are anxious to have the adhesion of the United

States to the Declaration of Paris, we would rather dispense with it altogether than be drawn into your domestic controversy. You can take no just exception to this outside declaration, simultaneous with the execution of the Convention unless you intend we should be made parties to your controversy, and the very fact of our hesitation is an additional reason why we should insist upon making such contemporaneous declarations.

Dayton: I readily agree to the propriety of such a declaration being made in advance *if France and England do not mean to abide by the terms of the Treaty.* I have no reason to suppose that the United States desires to embroil your countries in our domestic difficulties [on the contrary]. . . . My instructions are to negotiate that Convention, and I have no authority to do anything or to listen to anything which would waive any rights or relieve from any obligation which might fairly arise from a just construction of its terms.

Thouvenel: I do not mean to alter its terms. It is not like an addition of other provisions to the terms of the Treaty itself.

Dayton: For the purpose intended, it is precisely the same as if the declarations you propose to make are to be incorporated into the Treaty itself. Its effect is to release you (without complaint on our part) from compliance with one of the admitted obligations of the Treaty. I shall consult with Mr. Adams and it is not improbable that we might feel ourselves under the necessity of referring again to our Government.

Thouvenel: That must be a question for you to determine.

Dayton: Any Declaration or action which looked to or recognized a difference or distinction between the North and the South was a matter upon which our Government is under the circumstances, peculiarly sensitive. We treat with foreign Governments for our whole country, North and South, and for all its citizens whether true men or rebels; and when we cannot so treat, we will cease to treat at all.

Thouvenel: I do not mean to contest your right to treat for the whole country and that is not the purpose of the outside declaration we propose to make, but, having heretofore adopted a course of strict neutrality, the declaration in question is right and proper to prevent misconception and controversy in the future.[88]

Having taken leave of the French minister, Dayton immediately informed Adams of the presentation of the reservation declaration ("just as I thought"), and suggested that they either refer the matter to Washington or sign with a declaration of their own "stating in substance that we have no power to admit and do not mean to admit that this outside declaration by Great Britain and France is to relieve them directly or indirectly from any obligation or duty which would otherwise devolve upon them in virtue of the Convention."[89]

Since the London negotiations were supposed to be almost simultaneous, Adams was going through a somewhat similar experience. Russell sent him on August 19 an advance copy of the reservation by messenger, which was received on the same day, even though Adams was on a tour of Warwick Castle. The Union envoy could not have been surprised but was annoyed by "another turn in the wheel of my singular negotiation." "This will render a thorough exposition of the whole indispensable."[90]

While Russell was waiting to hear from Adams, he had an interesting conversation with a Northern visitor, General Webb— a conversation which revealed how little store he put in Article I of the declaration and how England might have evaded it whenever she should become a belligerent. The general began by arguing that the United States was not a military nation and therefore in wartime depended upon volunteers. Privateers were comparable on sea to army volunteers on land. The United States would make privateers subject to naval rules and regulations and the laws of war.

> *Russell:* But did you say all this to the Emperor? [General Webb had just seen Napoleon III at Fontainebleau.]
>
> *Webb:* Aye, and more. I expressed my astonishment that *he* should have given [in 1856] his assent to a proposition so palpably designed to increase the naval supremacy of England, that *it was clearly of English origin*, no matter who brought it forward.
>
> *Russell:* And yet he did assent to it, and is in favor of it.
>
> *Webb:* My opinion is that he would hold us [Americans] in contempt and never forgive us, if we were to prove untrue to

ourselves and give England this great advantage over France as well as ourselves.

Russell: Altogether too much importance has been given to the subject, but as your present Government desire it, we will make the treaty, even if, as you say, it is certain to be rejected.

Webb: I hope not, because its rejection would only lead to other complications and discussions.

Russell: Not a bit of it. I am perfectly willing the treaty should be reached because I have long been of the opinion that no treaty stipulation would have been of any avail. War once commenced, you would only have to call your privateers 'volunteers of the navy' or some other equally appropriate term instead of 'privateers,' change somewhat the regulations with the name, and according to your own argument, they would become a part of your navy for the time being, and be respected accordingly by all the Powers. So we will give your administration the treaty they ask for, and they must then settle the matter with the Senate. They may accept it or reject it at their pleasure, for it would amount to nothing; but I rather like the manner in which you put to the Emperor the advantage conceded to us by the Paris Conference.[91]

A copy of the letter, relating the above conversation, must have been sent to Adams, but it did not make him more willing to accept the reservation declaration. Even though the North could thus have continued to have the benefit of disguised privateers, there was still the situation of the North being given adverse special treatment and of its acknowledging, in a sense, the recognition of Southern belligerency. Consequently, when Adams returned and also learned of Dayton's experience in Paris, he spent the entire day of Friday composing his reply to Russell. After giving a long recapitulation of the negotiations, he complained that such a reservation implied that the United States was trying to obtain a special benefit for itself instead of pursuing "a high purpose and a durable policy." "Rather than that such a record should be made, it were a thousand times better than the declaration remain unsigned forever." All three parties should sign on terms of perfect equality. Therefore, he said, he declined to fix a day for the signature of the convention, was referring the matter to his government, and was informing Dayton of his decision.[92]

At this point Dayton gave his definitive reply to Thouvenel's written communication. Following Adams' example, he gave a long account of the negotiations and detailed arguments on the interruption of the negotiations. Indeed, it seems as if both ministers were thinking as much of the future publication of their replies as they were of Seward's approval. In regard to the meaning of the French reservation Dayton said: "If the declaration . . . does not alter the obligations and duties which would otherwise devolve upon France . . . it is useless to make it; if it does . . . then I am not authorized to execute [it]." Like Adams, he denied that the United States was trying to involve Europe in its civil war by this convention. The United States had always been opposed to any form of foreign intervention in its domestic controversy. As to the maritime law involved, the United States had already adopted Articles II, III, and IV (goods on merchant ships and blockade). Thus the only point really concerned was Article I on privateering. On that the United States had always preferred to add the Marcy amendment, but the new administration, knowing the opposition [English] to it, had from the start been willing to accept Article I without the amendment. "But I can scarcely suppose it will assent to the execution of the convention . . . except upon terms of entire reciprocity and subject to no condition other than those existing between the original parties." He was, therefore, referring the entire negotiation back to his home government.[93]

Thouvenel's reply was not given until two weeks later, but in a friendly way he was anxious to explain carefully France's need to make the reservation and to assure the United States minister that he did not want this adversely to affect the friendly relations between the two countries. If the United States, he insisted, had accepted the Declaration of Paris before the Civil War, all the powers would have opposed Southern privateering; but, now that the war had broken out, France must make this exception while the war is still running its course in order to preserve her declared neutrality. "We also would sincerely regret the appearance of the least misunderstanding in our relations with the

United States not to make an effort to clarify them right away."[94]

Seward's first reaction to the reservations came as a result of Russell's evasive statement of July 31 in which the foreign secretary had said that Britain's engagement would be "prospective" and would not "invalidate anything already done." In this case the United States secretary was just as evasive as was the British. He looked upon Russell's statement as a "preliminary condition" or an "implied reservation" which the United States could not accept outside the regular terms of the treaty because the senate only ratifies what is specifically in the treaty. However, he took up the word "prospective" and pretended not to know what it meant because a treaty was alway prospective unless it was clearly stated to be retrospective in certain defined cases. As to "anything already done," he felt it would have to refer to something already done by the United States, or Great Britain, or the two jointly. Since he knew of nothing to which this could refer regarding the United States alone or jointly with Great Britain, then this must refer to something Great Britain had done. Following the policy of the "averted glance," Seward pretended that he could not guess what it was, asked Adams to clear this up completely before continuing with the negotiation, and also informed Dayton of this new delay.[95]

By the time these instructions had arrived in London and Paris, the crisis of the negotiations had come and passed. Seward received the reports on the interruption of negotiations on September 6 and made his long argumentative reply—again for the record—four days later. He began with a tiresome account of all the negotiation from 1856 to Thouvenel's new reservations. He then pointed out that the United States had been invited in 1856 to accede to the whole declaration; but now when it agreed to do so, it was required to acquiesce in a reservation which makes it an entirely different declaration, one which the other signatories have not had to accept. If France does not intend that the United States shall receive unequal treatment, then she must intend to exempt all revolutionary wars from the application of Article I. Since most nineteenth-century wars are revolutionary, this plan would cancel most of the good derived from

Article I. Indeed, this was now an inducement to revolution since revolutionary regimes would not be as harshly treated as regular sovereign states engaged in war. The United States, he reasserted, did not want to involve France in the Civil War and would not do so by France's signature to the convention. Seward's motives, he asserted, had been to make war more humane and to give assurances to French commerce. However, France seemed no longer worried about her commerce, since she declined the United States offer. He brought all of the above observations to a close with the words: ". . . the proposed declaration is inadmissible . . . and if insisted upon . . . you are instructed for the present to desist from further negotiation on the subject involved." Similar instructions were also sent to Adams in London.[96]

It was not until a month later that Dayton informed Thouvenel that the negotiations were broken off and inclosed Seward's instructions to explain the reasons for this action. Thouvenel merely acknowledged receipt and returned the Seward note with thanks. To Cowley, however, he did remark that "this only proved how right the two governments had been in making this declaration."[97] So came to an end a long and tortuous negotiation without a successful conclusion. However, in fact, France had obtained the Northern government's adherence to the last three of the four articles without its accession to the entire declaration, and she would not have undertaken the extra negotiation had not Seward persisted in it for his own devious purposes.

Charleston and Richmond Negotiations

While France and England had obtained the North's acknowledgment of Articles II, III, and IV without a formal accession to the whole Paris declaration, there still remained the problem of obtaining a similar statement from the South, the other recognized belligerent. The British law officers had advised Russell as early as May 4, 1861, that the South's adhesion to the Paris declaration should also be sought, and he promptly contacted France to propose a joint approach to both the Union and Con-

federate governments.[98]   Thouvenel expressed agreement with
Russell but felt it was only necessary to obtain a reaffirmation
from them both on Articles II and III.[99]   However, he went on
to suggest the method of approach: "He thought [Cowley re-
ported] a communication should be addressed to both parties
in as nearly as possible the same language, the consuls being made
the organs of communication with the Southern States."[100]   By
the end of the same week Thouvenel sent his instructions to
Mercier requesting the United States to reaffirm its adherence
to Articles II and III and reminding it that its privateers, if any,
should observe the same rules as its naval vessels.   Furthermore,
France would hold the United States responsible for any damages arising from unlawful acts of these privateers.   The significant passage came at the end: "The Cabinet of Washington will
not be surprised if we should feel obliged to require from both
belligerent parties the guaranties which you are instructed to
ask of it and if we therefore should also call upon the government
established at Montgomery to explain its position on this subject.   Please read this dispatch to Mr. Seward and send him a
copy."[101]

On the same day Russell sent Thouvenel a copy of his instructions to Lyons on maritime law and added: "It would be
necessary to address similar propositions to the organs of the
Southern Confederation either through their delegates in Europe,
or at Montgomery."[102]   The French foreign minister agreed but
stressed that they had better limit themselves to Articles II
and III.[103]

Thus, on May 16 Thouvenel wrote instructions to Mercier to
cooperate with Lyons on their approaches to the Northern and
Southern governments and to pass on Thouvenel's instructions
to the French consul in New Orleans, Mejan, who was to contact the Confederate authorities in Montgomery.   "Also, in this
regard [he wrote to Mercier], you will kindly consult with Lord
Lyons in order that you both may maintain, in our communications with the South, the same similarity as with those we will
have with the North.   I therefore authorize you to take measures
in this regard which will appear appropriate, and I am instructing Count Mejan to follow your recommendations."[104]

His inclosed instructions to Mejan began with an injunction to observe strict neutrality between the two sides in the war. As to maritime law Thouvenel explained France's desire for guarantees for neutral French property at sea in Articles II and III and stated that he was sure of such guarantees from the Lincoln administration. Then he requested Mejan to go to Montgomery and obtain similar assurances from the Confederate government and a promise that Southern privateers would obey the same regulations as ordinary naval vessels.[105] Russell's instructions to Lyons authorized the latter, after consultation with Mercier, to send similar instructions to the British consul at New Orleans or Charleston "to be communicated at Montgomery to the President of the so-styled Confederate States."[106]

By the time the two envoys in Washington had received their instructions to contact the South, Seward was at the height of his anger over the news of England's proclamation of neutrality. Both Mercier and Lyons were therefore very worried about what Seward's reaction would be when he learned of their intention to make contact with the South. "The great trouble [thought Lyons] will be the fuss which the Southern Government will make about receiving a communication from England and France. It will be a great advantage to have a discreet and able man like Mr. Bunch [British consul at Charleston] to employ in the South. I trust it may be possible to grant him some compensation for the risk and loss to which he is exposed by remaining there." Six days later (June 10) he was still worrying about this problem. It is going to be hard, he said, to make contact with the South. Probably he and Mercier could get passes from the Northern government, but it would be advisable not to appear to be personally connected with the affair. Lyons warned that the South would capitalize upon these contacts and the North would react adversely by withdrawing the exequaturs of any consuls involved. Only a firm Anglo-French stand could compel the North to acquiesce in some necessary European communications with Confederate authorities.[107] The experience of this seasoned diplomat caused him to foresee clearly the difficulties ahead, but first it seemed most important to him that by a firm common front France and England get Seward to acknowledge the justice of their recognition of Southern belligerency. Then he could have little objection to their contacts with Southern authorities on military or naval matters.

Thus it was that on June 6 Mercier ran interference for the Ango-French team by having his preparatory interview with Seward (see above). He read to the secretary Thouvenel's note expressing a desire for the preservation of the Union and offering France's good offices if any North-South negotiations could take place. While Seward seemed a little mollified by this friendly note, he rejected the idea of foreign mediation (which went beyond Thouvenel's intentions) and sensed in this suggestion the possibility of French approaches to the South. To prevent these contacts, he gave a guarded warning to Mercier that "the Federal government . . . would not suffer the powers to have contacts" with Confederate leaders. At this point Mercier deemed it unwise to pursue the matter further.[108]   Seward's heavy hand of intimidation was evidently having a good effect.

Eventually, nine days later, Mercier and Lyons did have their famous interviews with Seward on the recognition of Southern belligerency and maritime law. And it was on this occasion that Seward agreed to receive their notes unofficially but not officially—"the averted glance." Here he read France's open avowal of her intention to approach the Confederate government on maritime law and in his instructions to Dayton he took occasion to oppose such contacts. Seward asserted that any French dealings with the Confederacy, "indirect or unofficial," would be considered as an unfriendly act. Therefore he would not allow even the reading of any note which implied intentions to make such approaches.[109]   This was a note which Seward also read unofficially to Mercier and thus conveyed his threatening and blustering attitude, which was quite effective in making both France and England very cautious.

Lyons saw Seward on the day this dispatch was written, and Seward "commented with some bitterness" about France openly avowing the intention of negotiating with the Confederate government on the treatment of neutral vessels. The British minister expostulated that some intercourse with the South was absolutely necessary. To this Seward replied that it would then have to be without the North's knowledge, and so he could not receive a French note openly declaring such intentions. Lyons, playing Seward's own game, reminded him that the note had only been lent for his personal use and not officially communicated.[110] Seward evidently acquiesced in this kind of "averted glance" idea; but he protested against France's intentions in the above note to Dayton, and he even published that note at the end of the year—which could be called the "averted-glance" policy proclaimed from the house-tops.[111]

Lyons immediately rushed over to Mercier's residence to share with him the good news of a possibility of making contact with the South without angering Seward so long as they were discreet. The French minister suggested a cautious means. Instead of dealing directly with the Confederate government, they would have their consuls get in touch with the governor of the Southern state where they resided. It was always proper for a consul to consult with local authorities about the interests of his nationals. Then the governor could obtain the assurances from the Confederate government. Lyons liked the idea but wanted to use the consuls in Charleston rather than at Montgomery or Richmond (to which the Confederate government had been removed in late May). He had great confidence in the tact and skill of Robert Bunch, England's consul at Charleston, and Mercier saw no reason for not shifting the assignment from Mejan in New Orleans to M. de Belligny de Saint-Croix, French consul in Charleston.[112]

After this, however, there came a delay of about three weeks before instructions were sent to Charleston. The two main reasons for this postponement, Lyons said, were that he and Mercier wanted to see what Seward said to Dayton, because Lyons could not rely on a mere verbal statement, and secondly that Mercier wanted to use a ship of the French navy after the French admiral arrived. Finally the two letters of instruction were sent on July 5, 1861. Mercier sent on to Belligny a copy of Thouvenel's earlier instructions to Mejan and added his own admonition that the consul should try to approach President Davis through the governor of South Carolina in order to prevent the appearance of any recognition and coordinate his efforts with Bunch.[113]

It took two weeks more for Mercier's instructions to arrive in Charleston (July 19). Then Belligny and Bunch immediately consulted each other and held long conferences on just what they should do. There were several reasons why they did not want to work through Governor Pickens, but they mentioned only that he was staying at his plantation in the middle of the state and was not easily accessible. Therefore they agreed upon the alternative of using William Henry Trescott as their emissary. This was ill-advised in one sense because Trescott was not a local official to whom the consuls had a right to turn. As a private person he would be their agent dealing more or less directly with the Confederate government—a procedure which Mercier had wanted to avoid. There is no evidence that this adverse consideration ever entered into the deliberations of the consuls. They were evidently acquainted with Trescott, who was a former diplomat and recently had been assistant secretary of state under Buchanan, and they knew he was about to go to Richmond on private business, thus allaying suspicion about their purposes. Trescott agreed to undertake the mission, and they thoroughly briefed him on the inquiries to be made on maritime law and even gave him confidentially, a copy of Russell's instructions. Yet, as Trescott set out on July 20, Bunch was not sanguine about the results: "I fear they will not accept unconditionally."[114]

Trescott arrived in Richmond on July 22, only to find that Davis had gone to Manassas to survey the situation resulting from the battle of Bull Run. He therefore immediately took the road toward Manassas and at about half-way in his journey met Davis returning, and they came back together to Richmond. They arranged to have a conference on the matter on the 24th. While Davis did not refuse to discuss the matter, he did complain about the indirect approach. If the questions were so important, why did not the consuls come to see him in person? He claimed to be surprised and disappointed that the matter had not been taken up with his accredited commissioners in Europe. Nevertheless, a cabinet meeting was held, and the matter was referred to Robert Hunter, the new Confederate secretary of state. After a few days of deliberation he drew up a proposed resolution to be passed by the Confederate congress giving satisfaction on Articles II, III, and IV of the Paris declaration. On July 31, 1861, Bunch wrote Lyons: "Our agent writes: 'I think I have succeeded in doing what you wish, just as you wish; will be home at once.' " "My French colleague begs you to tell his chief" [Mercier].[115]

Trescott arrived back in Charleston on August 2. He reported on a plan of congressional resolutions to satisfy all France's and England's demands, which gratified very much both Belligny and Bunch. Then he presented several complaints from Davis and Hunter. Davis thought that their relations should be placed on a more regular and recognized footing and that, in reciprocity for his acknowledgment of maritime law, England and France should allow prizes to enter and be sold in their ports. To close their ports was more harmful to the South and therefore was not exactly neutral. Furthermore, they should make sure that the blockade was enforced or else ignore it and reopen their commerce with the South. Trescott said they hoped France would reconsider the opening of ports to privateers. To this Belligny countered by showing that the French rules went back to regulations made in 1681 under Louis XIV and by indicating how they were supported by the commentary of Valin, an authority on international law. "But it seems that my argument had no effect and his first impression was not changed." As an added gesture of good will Trescott gave them a copy of instructions given to privateers to assure that they would give proper treatment to neutral goods and vessels at sea. In a spirit of reciprocity the two consuls let Trescott read their draft reports, which they were going to hold up until they received word of the passage of the Confederate resolutions.

The Confederate congress passed the resolutions on August 13, and Davis promptly approved them. They provided for acceptance of Articles II, III, and IV of the Paris declaration, which gave guarantees to neutral goods and ships at sea and insisted on the legality of effective blockades only. But it specifically retained the right of using privateers in sea warfare.[116] Having received the notification of the passage of these resolutions, the consuls completed their reports to their home governments. Thereby France and England had received assurances in regard to maritime law from both the North and the South.[117]

The success of the Belligny-Bunch negotiation, however, would not lie in the passage of the resolution by the Confederate congress but rather in their ability to keep secret their contact with Davis. Of course Seward knew what they were up to, but he and they did not want the Northern public to know about it. It was here again that the supposedly "discreet" and "skillful" Bunch bungled the affair. Both he and the British business men in Charleston were very much upset by the blockade and its attendant interruption of commerce and communications. Therefore, when this first sign of British diplomatic relations with the Confederacy appeared, he could not resist the temptation of confiding the news, "on oath of secrecy," to one of his close British merchant friends—completely in violation of the repeated injunctions of Lyons and Mercier. He even seemed to imply that this approach was the first step leading to recognition. Since this British merchant's firm was likewise anxious about the trade interruption, he gleefully broke his "oath of secrecy" and told the whole story in a letter home.

But no harm would have been done because private mail communications from the South had been partly stopped by Federal regulations and their blockade enforcement. Yet Bunch's bungling overcame even this hurdle. Instead of consigning his own consular correspondence to the periodic visits of French or British naval ships, he gave his official pouch to another ex-British merchant—a naturalized American citizen of South Carolina—Mr. Robert Mure. Then he issued Mure a pass certifying that he was "a British merchant residing in Charleston" and allowed him to carry two hundred private letters with him outside the sealed diplomatic pouch, and one of these letters was the fatal one detailing the negotiations going on between Charleston and Richmond. While Mure was waiting in New York for a ship to England, he was apprehended on August 14 by the local police, who respected the seal on the diplomatic pouch but confiscated and read the private letters and arrested Mure. Now the fat was in the fire and Seward was furious, both at the fact that Bunch seemed to be encouraging the idea that this move was a step toward recognition and at the public revelation of something to which he wanted to apply his "averted glance." The American secretary sent on the diplomatic pouch intact and instructed Adams to demand the censure and removal of Bunch.

Russell, in his reply, openly admitted that England and France had instructed their consuls to contact the Confederate authorities on maritime law, a procedure which he defended as consistent with consular duties and necessary for the commercial interests of the two countries. He also complained that the interruption of postal service from Charleston by Federal orders violated a postal agreement with Great Britain and caused Bunch to use private messengers. Finally, however, he said that England by this incident only recognized the belligerency of the South but was not prepared to recognize it as an independent state. To these arguments Seward reiterated the view that he did not accept the belligerency of the South and would not acquiesce in any foreign negotiations with the insurgents. He regretted the interruption of the postal service which, caused by the insurrection, was beyond the control of the Federal government. However, he could not tolerate a violation of Federal regulations by a consul and therefore was forced to withdraw Bunch's exequatur. He had no complaint against Lyons; a new arrangement for naval vessels to pick up and leave consular correspondence in Southern ports would probably solve the problem; and he promised to grant an exequatur to any new acceptable consul. Russell protested and argued and Adams insisted and argued; but Bunch did lose his exequatur and, after considerable delay, left Charleston in February 1863.[118]

While the Bunch-Belligny negotiations were an example of the closest Anglo-French cooperation at every level of authority, they also provided an opportunity for Seward to try and separate the two powers. He did not ask for Belligny's removal nor did he withdraw the French consul's exequatur. As soon as Adams made his first request for the voluntary removal of Bunch, Russell began to hint to Thouvenel that he wanted French support.

He reminded his French counterpart that Belligny had had identical instructions and had carried them out in the same way as Bunch. "Indeed [Russell added] the first proposal for such an instruction seems to have been made by M. Thouvenel to your Excellency [Cowley] and is contained in a despatch of your Excellency, no. 684 of May 9."[119]

Thouvenel did not allow himself to take the hint at first, but he was anxious to know whether Seward was also angry with the French consul. He knew that the assignment had been shifted from New Orleans to Charleston, but he thought the consul in Charleston was Durand St. André because the latter has been sent as acting consul to relieve Belligny, who had been given permission to go home on leave. Actually Belligny delayed his departure in order to handle this delicate mission. Thouvenel now asked Mercier what had happened to the French consul.[120] In the meantime he confided to Cowley that Dayton had made no protest about Belligny's share in the affair.[121] While Russell may have been concerned over this different treatment meted out to the French consul, he felt relieved in the thought that, if Belligny was not blamed, then certainly Seward would not go so far as to send Lyons away.[122]

Information coming in sporadically from Lyons began to clear up some of the puzzle. When Mercier came back from his long American tour with Prince Napoleon and went to see Seward, he expected to be the butt of the secretary's rage. However, to his surprise, Seward was not very talkative and said nothing about the Bunch-Belligny affair.[123] At least this confirmed Dayton's silence in Paris, but it also worried Russell as to how he would be able to involve France in this aftermath of the joint mission. Lyons also explained to Russell that Belligny had gone on leave immediately after the Southern negotiation, and consequently "our position is unluckily not exactly the same with that of France."[124]

Thouvenel, as he began to see the difference between the English and the French positions, also began to take a more cautious stand on supporting England. Belligny's leave might be a way for France to evade Seward's wrath, and there was no use inviting trouble if Seward was trying to find ways to avoid it.

Furthermore, he began to sense Bunch's bungling of the affair when the news of Mure's arrest came out. This was confirmed when he obtained Mercier's more detailed account of the Mure episode. "The Cabinet of Washington [wrote Mercier] only got wind of it [Bunch-Belligny negotiations] through a letter seized on the person of a traveller, whose account of it was most inexact. It was only after these revelations that he [Seward] decided to ask London for the recall of the English consul at Charleston."[125] The Mure affair was clearly a British faux-pas for which France, thought Thouvenel, should not have to pay a penalty, especially if Seward was fair enough not to exact one. In the next report from Mercier, Thouvenel learned that Seward was even trying to find a way out for the British. Lyons had seen Seward on October 12 and the secretary apologized for all the trouble over Bunch but, he said, he had to take action when it came out in the open. Seward was having a lot of trouble in his dealing with the radicals and therefore had to react. Lyons showered him with arguments in which he underlined France's similar role in the affair. It was necessary that England and France have some means of making contact with the South in order to protect their subjects' persons and property. Such contacts were merely treating the South as a belligerent, not as an independent state. There was simply no other way out but for the United States to accept such contacts on war matters. Then Lyons dilated upon how small a matter it was, dealing with maritime law, and how the Confederate congress had passed the resolutions without any mention of the negotiations. Seward seemed to appreciate all these arguments and said he was searching for some subterfuge by which he could ease the North's relations with England. Perhaps England and France planned all this in May before they knew of the North's objections to belligerency recognition. Lyons' eyes lighted up, and he said both the English and French instructions were dated in May. Seward then asked for copies which he could use.[126] In Thouvenel's opinion there was no use stirring Seward up with French protests if he was already trying to find a way to smooth over his relations with England.

Evidently, however, Seward's idea was not to smooth things

over by any leniency toward Bunch. Since England would not dismiss him, Seward withdrew his exequatur. His leniency extended only to Lyons, who would not be given his passports. Loud and long were Lyons' protests about Bunch's treatment, all to no avail.

Then the British minister turned repeatedly to demands that France do something about it. No doubt Mercier heard these complaints many times but had no instructions to support Lyons. The British minister would have to get French action through Russell, and on October 14 he told Russell that "I think that France ought to take or make an opportunity of announcing as explicitly as we have done to the United States that she regards the South as a belligerent, and that she negotiated with the Southern government in concert with us."[127]

Russell, however, was becoming more and more convinced of Bunch's carelessness in the negotiation procedure[128] and did not feel free to insist too strongly to Thouvenel for support of Bunch. Indeed, he already knew what the French foreign minister's answer would be, for, in a conversation with Cowley, Thouvenel had laid the blame on Bunch's indiscretions and had stated flatly that France would do nothing unless Seward protested directly to France over her communicating (not negotiating) with the South.[129] But, at about the same time, Russell found a better way to approach the French: the South had just ordered all foreign property seized if the owners were living in the North. He wondered whether France would join England in protesting to the Confederate authorities. Because of Seward's susceptibilities he thought it would be wise to let him know in advance.[130]

Thouvenel replied by reminding Russell of the trouble caused by the Bunch-Belligny affair. While he had great confidence in Mercier and Lyons, he suggested that it might be better to take this matter up with the Southern commissioners in Europe, or they might have their consuls take it up with the local authorities who might be carrying out the confiscations.[131] Russell answered that, because of Bunch's loss of his exequatur, he did not favor using the consuls. To this Thouvenel retorted by saying that consuls always have the right to deal with local authorities and the Federal government would have no cause for complaint if the approach was on the local level. Bunch's loss of his exequatur, he said, was a purely British question on which he had no opinion to express. So far France had had no confiscation trouble, and, if Russell did not want to do anything right now, France was perfectly willing to let the matter drop for the present.[132]

At this point Russell suggested that he might use his consul in Richmond as the contact man with the Confederate government. Right away Thouvenel saw the danger in this and wrote in the margin of the dispatch: "I am not very sure about how such reasoning will stand up if the consuls at Richmond are made *de facto* diplomatic agents. I'll speak to Lord Cowley about it."[133] This led to Russell's agreement to use all the consuls locally and to Thouvenel's promise "that he will write the French consuls in the Southern States in the same sense as your [Russell's] instructions."[134] By this time the "Trent" affair was looming as a more important problem which thrust the consular question into the background.

Reflections

With the outbreak of war it is important for neutrals to have an understanding with the belligerents as to the rules of international law which will be applied. In our state system each separate sovereign state has the freedom to choose its own set of international rules. Therefore it was proper for England and France to seek statements from both the North and the South. Since the United States had not previously accepted the abolition of privateering, it was not feasible to expect the South to accept it at the beginning of a war; and consequently the Ango-French move naturally limited itself to obtaining a simple approval of Articles II and III only, on noncontraband goods at sea. This they received from the North by June 1861 and from the South in August. And these approvals should have ended the whole episode.

However, Seward had other objectives and motives which enlarged the scope of the whole affair and prolonged the negotiation over a period of nine months. As early as April 24, 1861, he had conceived the idea of negotiating United States acceptance of the whole Declaration of Paris without the Marcy amendment. There seems to be little doubt but what Thouvenel and Russell were right in suspecting a trap on the part of Seward. He had undoubtedly thought that he might forestall their recognition of Southern belligerency if they had already agreed to recognize *all* American privateers as pirates—Article I—and he would also then have the French and British fleets as auxiliaries in suppressing Southern privateers. When he could not prevent their recognition of Southern belligerency, he still strove to trap them into a position where they would have to violate their neutrality by warring on Southern privateers.

Such maneuvers were checkmated by England's quick proclamation of neutrality before Adams could arrive and by Thouvenel's early warning that reservations must accompany the acceptance of Northern adherence to the abolition of privateering. Seward's refusal to continue the negotiations after the presentation of the reservations is a clear indication of his ulterior motives. Although he could plead that the United States would be treated as an unequal under the reservations, he could not justify the argument that the reservations would give advantages to revolutionary governments everywhere, because revolutions against countries which had *previously* accepted Article I would not be allowed the benefit of reservations. At any rate he persisted in inviting an unequal treatment of his country by continuing the negotiations after the recognition of belligerency.

As to European contacts with the Confederate government, Seward was generally in the wrong. He could not very well object to their recognition of Southern belligerency when the United States was doing so time and again by blockading the South, by exchanging prisoners, and by sparing Southern privateer crews from the piracy penalty of death. Fenwick says, "It is now [1924] generally conceded by American writers that the position taken by the United States [on European recognition of belligerency] was an extreme one."[135] Certainly if the United States could deal with the belligerent South in the interest of its captured soldiers, it could not deny the same privilege to neutrals in the interest of their commerce. While Seward railed against European contacts with the South in order to appease war-excited opinion in the North, he realized the weakness of his position and would have allowed such limited contacts dealing with the laws of war if he could appear to be ignorant of them.

His policy of the "averted glance" was spoiled in this instance by Bunch's indiscretions and Mure's apprehension. Seward was quite justified in withdrawing Bunch's exequatur because of the unneutral opinion he expressed that the contact was the first step toward full recognition and because of Bunch's violation of Northern communications and passport regulations. Russell's eventual acquiescence in this punitive action against Bunch is a mute acknowledgment that there were at least three strikes against the consul. Nor could Thouvenel very well make an issue of it in the interest of Franco-British solidarity.

There is yet another valuable dimension to such negotiations and incidents. It gives a measure of the men involved. We have already considered some of Seward's ulterior motives. But in those aspects in which he was sincere he exhibited a lack of knowledge and experience in foreign relations and international law. On the other hand, as he felt his way along, he began to perceive that he could use this inexperience to frighten more experienced diplomats into a firm belief that he was rash enough to precipitate a foreign war and world revolution. While his bark was worse than his bite, he did rather successfully scare Lyons and Mercier and through them induce Russell and Thouvenel to adopt a caution which well bespoke their sincere desire for noninvolvement.

Russell was the one who took the initiative in starting the Franco-British negotiations on maritime law. But, except for this point in his favor, he was consistently clumsy in his handling of the affair. Thouvenel had to persuade him to limit the approach to Articles II and III, which he did not make clear to Adams in the first interview. Then, in spite of Thouvenel's early warning about the need for a reservation on Southern privateering, Russell went ahead with plans for a quick conclusion of an unrestricted treaty. It was only after fast footwork on the part of Thouvenel, Flahault, and Palmerston that they obtained England's cooperation on reservations. Even then Thouvenel had to rewrite Russell's initial formula to give it precision and clarity.

Of the three foreign ministers Thouvenel was by far the most experienced and competent. It was he who furnished the most cogent arguments to Seward. Likewise he was careful to leave the United States envoys with the feeling that he was sincerely sympathetic with their cause. As already mentioned, he originated the idea of reservations and phrased their final forms. At one point he slipped—when he planned to have his consul in New Orleans go directly to Montgomery to see President Davis. It was Mercier who rescued him from this error by transferring the negotiations to Charleston and trying to keep the contacts with the South on the local level. Thouvenel caught on to this quickly enough; and, when Russell again was in a fog on protests against Southern confiscations and proposed to have the Richmond consuls deal directly with the Confederate government, it was Thouvenel who reminded him that they would have trouble if they transformed their local Richmond consuls into *de facto* diplomatic agents. As usual, Russell eventually woke up and followed Thouvenel's advice by instructing all the consuls to act locally.

Adams was a model diplomat who kept his head, spoke seldom but firmly and to the point, and followed his instructions as literally as possible. On the other hand inexperienced Dayton, with his lack of knowledge of French, was a rather pitiful character. Dependent on Sanford for early guidance, he allowed himself to be persuaded to exceed his instructions by insisting at first on the Marcy amendment. This threw him entirely out of step with Adams and left an unjustified suspicion that Seward was trying to separate England and France by treating them differently. Yet, it was Dayton who saw, before Adams did, that reservations were in the offing. This prediction irritated Seward, who, in effect, told Dayton to stick to his knitting. Instinctively Dayton could see that the whole negotiation was futile, and he had the satisfaction of reminding both Adams and Seward "I told you so."

In Washington the British minister, Lord Lyons, resembled Adams in being quiet, cautious, firm, and correct. Since Northern opinion was more hostile to England than to France on neutrality, Lyons tried to lie low and let Mercier scout the positions of the explosive secretary of state. They were two very scared men, who scurried to their hiding places whenever the lion roared. On the other hand, as well-trained diplomats, they knew when to take advantage of an opening. They came to know how to work together and deal with Seward, and by official and private correspondence kept their home governments fully informed. Mercier's dispatches were less frequent and more delayed than those of Lyons.

On both sides of the Atlantic there was a great deal of pretended ignorance or innocence. Seward's "averted glance" was a game played by both sides in Washington for the benefit of Northern opinion. Certainly Seward offered the whole Paris declaration with a straight face, and the two foreign ministers pretended to welcome it unconditionally down to the last day. Both Adams and Dayton soon came to expect the reservations, but went ahead as if they did not, and expressed grieved surprise when they finally came. The best example of pretense was Russell's lecture to General Webb on how the privateer clause could be evaded, right at the time when he was about to sign the convention.

Such were the ways of the diplomats in a small comedy of errors. Yet it was not a case of much ado about nothing. France and England obtained their assurances on Articles II and III, and Seward won the closure of their ports against Southern prize. European intervention had so far been avoided to the satisfaction of all. But the evergrowing scarcity of cotton and of French exports was to raise new questions about another issue of international law, the blockade, which gave the diplomatic merry-go-round another whirl.

Chapter IV

THE BLOCKADE AND THE PORTS BILL

IT could almost be said that the diplomatic history of the American Civil War is a history of disputes in international law. So far the story of France's involvement in the war has dealt with recognition, belligerency, noncontraband property at sea, privateering, and the proposed Marcy amendment to the Declaration of Paris of 1856. The next issue to be discussed is the Northern blockade of the Southern ports—an issue whose evolution and disputes were going on simultaneously with those treated in previous chapters.

Premonitions of Strangulation

Coming events cast their shadows before them. Such indeed was the case with the Northern blockade and the Southern embargo of the Civil War. As a matter of fact the dire premonitions of the interruption of European trade with the cotton states of the South date from a time almost sixty-five years before Lincoln's first proclamation of the blockade. This fear of a denial of access to foreign raw materials was a common international phobia of the nineteenth and twentieth centuries. On the one hand, with the spread of the industrial revolution the whole world became one economy. On the other hand, the old system of separate national states—with their peacetime tariffs, prohibitions, immigration restrictions, currency controls, and sanitary regulations and with their wartime blockades, embargoes, seizures, litigations, and outright hostilities—tended to choke the free flow of trade in this world economy. The strangulation might be actual or anticipated, but in either case it was likely to induce a psychosis of frustration or desperation which contributed to aggressions and wars. It is partly for this reason that the industrial age has become the epoch of more frequent and more destructive world-wide wars. The Napoleonic Wars with their British orders in council, French imperial decrees, and American embargoes were harbingers of the new era. The desperation of have-not nations—such as Japan, Germany, and Italy—caught in the toils of this strangulation, tightened by depression, brought on internal fascism and external aggressions— the latest demonstration of the demoniacal impulses of a distraught world system. Only with the postwar return to sanity have a European common market and other trade relaxations and international forms of cooperation begun to make way against this greatest modern maladjustment.

One of the early signs of this modern world-wide economic interdependence was Europe's reliance upon raw cotton from the Southern states of the United States for its textile industries. By 1796, after the invention of Eli Whitney's cotton gin, American cotton had largely supplanted the inferior Indian cotton in England and France. Between 1840 and 1858 about eighty percent of England's cotton imports were from the South.[1] In 1820 France was importing fifty-five percent of her cotton from the South, and by 1860, ninety-three percent.[2] Such abject dependence on a foreign country for a vital raw material made both countries uneasy. After 1840 an extensive campaign was undertaken by British chambers of commerce, emancipation societies, and parliamentary committees to substitute Indian for American cotton in order to lessen this dependence. But it was all to no avail; the climate and conditions in India militated against any success. In 1851 John Chapman was writing that "the very singleness of that [cotton] source . . . [was] an element of danger; while the peculiar circumstances which affect that single source [danger of civil war or slave insurrection] greatly aggravate that danger." "Lancashire may any year be laid prostrate by causes from whose action she has no escape and over which she has no control."[3] Seven years later (1858) Henry Ashworth was still bemoaning "the dangers of our continued reliance upon the United States for so large a proportion of our cotton."[4] The French, too, were not blind to "the danger which this sole reliance [exclusivisme] represented."[5]

The South also was fully conscious of the great economic weapon in its hands. In 1855 David Christy published his famous book called *Cotton Is King* in which he saw the prospects of the South dictating its own terms for staying in the Union or successfully seceding therefrom because of the North's and Europe's dependence on Southern cotton. This became as popular a book in the South as *Uncle Tom's Cabin* was in the North. Senator Hammond of South Carolina, dramatizing in 1858 this exhilarating thought in a speech before the senate, exclaimed:

> Without firing a gun, without drawing a sword, should they make war on us, we could bring the whole world to our feet. . . . What would happen if no cotton was furnished for three years? . . . England would topple headlong and carry the whole civilized world with her, save the South. No, you dare not make war on cotton. No power dares make war on it. Cotton is king![6]

The feeling of Southern cockiness seemed to be borne out by a report by John Claiborne later in 1858. He had been sent to Europe by the pro-Southern Buchanan administration to make a study of the consumption of cotton in France. While he pointed out that France's cotton industry and her factory units were considerably smaller than the English ones, still he showed that that industry was a very important component of the total French economy. The cotton spinners and weavers together were making a 400 percent profit on cotton; they employed 275,000 workers; and, altogether, 700,000 people were dependent upon cotton for their livelihood. A reduction in cotton manufactures and a sharp increase in unemployment could push these restless and rebellious working people into open revolution. There was no consideration here of the additional suffering that might occur from an interruption of French exports to the United States in case of war.[7] With these confident views in mind at the beginning of the secession crisis, a Major Chase wrote an article boasting of the uslessness of a blockade of the South.

Such disastrous economic and political consequences in France and England would follow an interruption of Southern cotton exports, he predicted, that the British fleet would sweep away any attempted blockade. Indeed, he was sure France and England would not only break up the blockade but would not even allow the North to attack the South by land and thereby disrupt the cotton culture.[8]

With the election of Lincoln in November 1860 and the secession of South Carolina in December, speculation on a blockade changed to consideration of its actual possibility. Six weeks before Lincoln's inauguration Mercier was reporting the probability of a Northern blockade of Southern ports.[9] Right after Lincoln's inauguration the first cabinet meeting took place and considered the question of a blockade of the South.[10] During the discussion it was brought out that Southern cotton was the mainstay of the British and French economy and that British shipping interests were deeply involved. The evaluation of the subject was sober, and no decision was made or intended to be made in this exploratory session.[11] These discussions of the blockade and of the possible recognition of the Confederacy by European powers evidently went on in the cabinet meetings for the next two weeks with Seward apparently trying to discourage rash action on the blockade policy. Finally, on the evening of March 20, Seward himself went over to the British legation to sound out Lyons. He explained that he wanted to encourage the Unionists in the South by imposing a temporary blockade on the South and avoiding a premature recognition of the Confederacy by foreign powers. In this interim, he asked, could not England obtain her cotton from Northern ports? Lyons replied that the serious matter was the resulting scarcity of cotton and its increased price. England would be under heavy pressure to open the ports by legal means, and that might be by recognition. Seward's calm rejoinder was to suggest a talk with the president.[12]

While Seward did not take Lyons over to see Lincoln, he no doubt relayed the message to the cabinet. However, in the meantime, a stiffer tone seemed to be taken by Seward and the cabinet, perhaps because of the breakdown in the negotiations with the Southern representatives or because of the news of the

Southern diplomatic mission to Europe.[13]   At any rate, when Lyons invited the cabinet and several diplomats to a dinner on March 25, Seward was in one of his belligerent moods.   After an angry exchange with Mercier and Lyons over their consuls in the South he moved over to the question of trade with the South. Speaking in a loud voice, he threatened to confiscate any foreign ship leaving a Southern port without Federal clearance papers. He disputed Stoeckl's claim that this would be a blockade.   When Lyons gave his opinion that the closing of Southern ports might force England to recognize the South, Seward shouted: "Such recognition will mean war!   The whole world will be engulfed and revolution will be the harvest."   Lyons avoided any further exchange by turning his attention to some of his lady guests.   But Lyons and Mercier became more apprehensive about the imminence of a blockade and more than ever desirous of an Anglo-French common front.[14]

Mercier, in his report of these events, underlined the immense foreign commerce with the United States which would be interrupted by a war.   He felt sure that a blockade would be imposed as soon as hostilities began.   To give Thouvenel a good idea of the Southern commerce involved, Mercier sent him a brochure written by a Southerner and based upon official statistics.   Some allowance would have to be made for the prejudice of the author, but still it was an impressive picture.[15]

In the first week of April, Seward was blowing cold and hot again, as was characteristic of him.   It is sometimes hard to tell whether by these abrupt changes he showed a day to day uncertainty about his policy or whether he was doing this by design to frighten the European powers.   At least after his warlike April-Fool proposal had been turned down by Lincoln, he seemed much more reasonable.   At a dinner at the Russian legation he even promised that there would be no blockade and no forceful retention of the South in the Union.

This was a surprising about-face, but it only lasted a few days. When Stoeckl saw Seward again, it was at the British legation where Seward announced that there would be a blockade and Europe would have to put up with it.   Angered by this belligerence, Lyons retorted that England would get her cotton one way or another. Perhaps surprised by Lyons' uncharacteristically sharp rejoinder, Seward did not pursue the discussion further. Like two growling dogs, they seemed to be circling around and taking each other's measure.[16] In fact this was the state of things in Washington just before the Fort Sumter attack and the resulting proclamation of the blockade.

While all these pre-war anticipations of the blockade were making an appearance in America, France was already feeling the pinch of reduced sales of her usual exports to the United States. At the end of each quarter the French district attorneys (*procureurs généraux*) made detailed economic reports on their districts to the central government.[17] In those dealing with conditions during the last quarter of 1860, four months before the war, were a surprising number already noting a bad effect on exportations caused by the anticipated American conflict. In the Limoges district the luxury industries, such as carpets, gloves, flannels, and shoes, "fear especially a notable decrease of orders from America." In Lyons, the silk center of France, they reported that "manufacturing . . . would be very prosperous if it were not for the American crisis and the separation movements weighing on the United States." These same events were "paralyzing the velvet industry." In a special report from Lyons a month later we learn that "[silk] orders are no longer being filled and fabrics prepared for America are now being offered for sale here at a loss." "Silk prices have therefore quite naturally fallen."[18]

Three months later, but still before the outbreak of war or the imposition of the blockade, greater suffering was reported. In the Limoges district this time it was the china industry which complained. The Rochechouart china factories had to reduce operations "from lack of sufficient orders," and those of St. Yrieux attributed their slump "to the American crisis." In the Lyons silk industry "the American crisis has suspended almost completely the large orders which usually arrive at this time of the year from the United States . . . and form the principal basis of our operations." Unemployment was also increasing in the dyeing industries. In April, the city of Lyons was reporting the "disastrous effects" of the American crisis. "Not one order has arrived, and besides we could not fill orders for people who are about to plunge into the crippling experiences of civil war." Many silk and ribbon factories had closed down, and large numbers of workers were in misery. The government was already organizing relief and public works projects. In the Dijon district the glove industry of the department of Haute-Marne was in very bad straits because of the American situation.

> Already a third of the workers at Chaumont have been laid off [wrote the procureur general]. Others keep working only by the desperate efforts of the factory owners. All the output of these factories which formerly exported to North America find that since the separation in the United States the federal ports are closed, and not only have all orders been countermanded but even deliveries have been refused. This crisis is unprecedented, and unfortunately no one knows when it will end. One head of the best firms in Chaumont is about to close his workshops and turn out 400 workers, most of them heads of families, without any means of support.[19]

If such were the bad effects of the American dispute before France learned of Fort Sumter or the blockade, one can imagine the economic devastation that would come with four long years of conflict. So far the trouble was in the export industries; the cotton crisis was yet to come.

The French government was fully aware of the crisis in the export industries by the January reports. Summaries and extracts of the reports were often made for the emperor and his ministers. Likewise Thouvenel, on February 6, 1861, received Mercier's warning that a blockade might be used as a weapon against the South. Apprehensive of what might happen to French commerce, the government decided to reinforce its fleet in American waters by three additional ships of the line. At the same time they were hearing that England was seeking new areas for the production of raw cotton.[20] On March 19 the government also had its official paper, the *Moniteur*, report that England had already warned the Lincoln government that any blockade would have to be complete and effective. The article added significantly that "other governments are to make a similar declaration." [21]

On April 15 Thouvenel had received another Mercier report that a blockade was imminent from the statements Seward had been making, but he no doubt had not yet had a translation or read the Southern brochure on the South's economic strength and importance. However, when he had a long interview with Faulkner on the same day, he did not make any comment on France's commercial interests. It was, on the contrary, Faulkner who repeated his circular instructions and gave assurances for French interests.

> The President regrets [he said] that the events going on in the United States may be productive of some possible inconvenience to the people and subjects of France, but he is determined that those inconveniences shall be made as light and transient as possible and so far as it may rest with him, all strangers who may suffer any injury from them shall be indemnified.

Since there was as yet no news of hostilities or a blockade, both Thouvenel and Faulkner agreed that force would be an improper means to a solution of the difficulties. [22]

Thouvenel's first direct statement on his concern for French commerce was in his first conversation with Sanford, the Federal interim envoy, on April 24. In the early part of the interview Sanford did most of the talking—which came to him naturally. After repeating Faulkner's assurances about the North's solicitude for French citizens and their interests, Sanford went on to say that the trade difficulties would not last long unless Europe gave recognition, because the South would have to sell cotton to obtain credits. Northern purchases from France were more important than Southern cotton and would be permanently sacrificed by any French encouragement of the revolt. [23] He began to feel that Thouvenel was well informed on these matters and was agreeing with his observations. Continuing the conversation, Sanford indicated that United States ships would collect customs duties outside Southern ports, and any French evasion of this arrangement would amount to smuggling. Thouvenel was a little perplexed by this situation and lamely replied that

France would have to consult the other powers before determining her course of action.[24] The forty-five minute conversation ended with a discussion of the high Northern tariff, but Thouvenel could well have been convinced by that time (long before he knew of the blockade) that the looming commercial problems were going to be intricate and tricky and would require a cautious approach.

The Blockade Proclaimed and Conditionally Accepted

After all the anticipations, both in America and Europe, of a blockade and the interruption of trade in case of a civil war, no one was surprised when the Northern government proclaimed a blockade against Southern ports. On April 19, 1861, Lincoln issued a proclamation "to set on foot a blockade of the ports" of South Carolina, Georgia, Alabama, Florida, Mississippi, Louisiana, and Texas "in pursuance of the laws of the United States and of the law of nations in such case provided." Then later, on April 27, 1861, he proclaimed "an efficient blockade of the ports" of Virginia and North Carolina.[25] An examination of these proclamations will show that they provided for the blockading of the *ports* and not the entire coastline of these states. In the first proclamation the reference to "the law of nations" could well mean the North's acceptance of the requirement that the blockade be enforced and efficient because ever since 1780 the United States had accepted this definition of a legal blockade. In the second proclamation Lincoln actually used the word "efficient." It therefore seemed evident that the United States intended to conform with Article IV of the Declaration of Paris of 1856.

Even though the foreign powers might have understood these implications for what they seemed, they would want, as in the case of noncontraband property at sea, a clear statement from the United States government. Mercier and Lyons had been constantly in touch with each other on how to protect their commerce as much as possible from the effects of the blockade. In fact they "exhausted every possible means of opposition to the blockade"—all to no avail. On April 26, Mercier had not received an official notification with detailed regulations. And until he did he was not going to take any steps. He suspected that the blockade was imposed in the interest of New York City, which would lose its trade to Southern ports unless they were sealed up. Also Mercier suspected that the authorities chose the blockade rather than closing the ports by law in order to avoid international complications. On the next day—April 27—the French envoy received the official notification and, in acknowledging receipt, was careful to say that he considered it an advance notice (*simple avis*) and that the real institution would be when the United States had its ships on station before the ports.[26]

A week later, in a private letter to Thouvenel, Mercier gave his ideas on how the blockade problem should be handled. He was scornful of Ernest Baroche's[27] idea that France should tell the United States that their navy was not big enough to blockade such a long coastline and that therefore France would not recognize the legality of the blockade at all—"just like that" (*tout bonnement*).[28] Instead of this childish scheme Mercier proposed one only a degree less juvenile. He advised that, after coordinating it with Russell and, after assuring Dayton of France's desire to see the preservation of the Union, Thouvenel should tell Dayton that, in spite of the economic suffering involved, France would endure the blockade for a few months, but beyond that period would have to consider some countervailing action. While such a statement, said Mercier, would probably anger Seward, it would reassure the French cotton industry about its winter supply of raw cotton.[29]

As usual Mercier shared his thoughts with Lyons and received no encouragement from that quarter. The British minister thought that it would be better for England and France to formulate a joint policy and perhaps not acquiesce in the blockade at all.[30] As every issue arose, it always seemed wise to have Anglo-French cooperation. Hence it is not surprising that it persisted in varying degrees during the entire war.

While Thouvenel, in Paris, did not receive Mercier's last suggestions until about May 26, he knew as early as May 3 that a blockade had been proclaimed.[31] All his worst fears for the economic repercussions in France seemed about to be realized.

As has already been mentioned in the previous chapters, Thouvenel, during this week, had called together an advisory committee on international law and several conferences and cabinet meetings took place. They were watching closely England's reaction, and on the morning of May 7 he read in the *Moniteur* and Flahault's reports that Russell had said that the British would not recognize the blockade unless it was effective. The British secretary had not warned the Lincoln government of this, since the United States had long proclaimed the principle of an effective blockade.[32]   On that same day Cowley came to see Thouvenel in line with the coordination of English and French policy on neutrality and international law.   Among the many things they discussed, Cowley mentioned the imposition of a vigorous blockade by the North and the United States's earlier acknowledgment of Article IV of the Paris declaration (effective blockade).   In the end they seemed to agree that they only had to confirm the two belligerents' adherence to Articles II and III.[33]

Since there had already been such an adverse effect on the French export business just from the rumors of war, it is understandable that, once hostilities had started, the French government should be seriously concerned about its commerce.   Two days after the news of the blockade Napoleon III saw a friend of Sanford's—perhaps the emperor's dentist, Dr. Evans—and, after a strong expression of interest in the preservation of the Union and of condemnation of the secessionists, he "said it was of the highest importance to France that the interruption of commerce, likely to be caused by the war and the blockade of the Southern ports, should not be of long duration, and inquired with some show of anxiety whether, with this improving show of force and unanimity on the part of the North, peace was not likely soon to be restored."[34]   Thouvenel, in his first instructions to Mercier—before he had received the envoy's first report on the blockade—likewise expressed sympathy for the Union cause but added somewhat firmly: "I must, nevertheless, reserve the right of the emperor's government to consider also the interests it has to protect from that day onward when the nature of the accomplished facts forces such an obligation on it."   And again, further on, where he took notice of the imposition of the block-ade, he wanted to remind the United States that France must protect her neutral commerce in its rights under international law and also that the United States had acknowledged Article IV (effective blockade) in its reply in 1857 to the invitation to ad-here to the whole Declaration.   "I can not put in doubt that we may find President Lincoln disposed to accord to us today the guarantees that can be regarded as assured henceforth tacitly or expressly to all neutrals in time of war."[35]

On the following day Thouvenel had a long conversation with Sanford in part of which they discussed the blockade and com-merce:

> *Sanford:* You have doubtless observed that . . . it [the Union government] had been compelled to employ energetic measures of repression against the insurgents—among others that of blockading their ports—which, without any instructions on the subject [he had oral assurance from Seward before he left], I do not doubt the desire of my Government to make its effects as light as is possible on your commerce.   I presume there will be no disposition to rigorously enforce the Blockade upon vessels bonafide seeking egress to European ports loaded or loading in those ports.
> *Thouvenel:* I am very pleased to hear this because there are goods to the value of 14,000,000 fr. either on their way or ordered by our citizens from Southern ports.
> *Sanford:* Has your government received an official notification of the blockade?
> *Thouvenel:* No, not yet.
> *Sanford:* That is probably owing to the interruption of com-munications with Washington.
> *Thouvenel:* This condition of things in your country is causing us very great concern.   The interests of France involved in the trade with the United States are of great magnitude, and we have felt constrained, in view of the great commercial interests involved, to take measures in conjunction with England to meet a condition of things which imperil those interests. [Here he announced the decision to recognize Southern belligerency.]
> *Sanford* (later in the conversation): I will not for a moment presume that you intend to interfere with our blockade of

Southern ports and reducing refractory citizens to obedience to our laws.

Thouvenel: By no means. The blockade is an undoubted right. It will be respected when effective. There is no disposition to interfere with or impede the action of the Federal Government in this war.[36]

Thus, even before he had received an official notification of the blockade, Thouvenel had given a conditional acceptance of its imposition.

Five days after Dayton's arrival in Paris he had a meeting with Thouvenel (May 16) in which the foreign minister repeated most of the things he had said to Sanford, that is, that he would recognize an effective blockade, that he would like to know the United States stand on all principles of international law, and that he had not yet been officially notified of the blockade. Dayton promised he would try to get more specific information from his government on the questions of law and on May 24 sent Thouvenel copies of the two blockade proclamations.[37]

A subsequent study by Thouvenel evidently convinced him that the United States had previously stated its position clearly that it accepted the requirement of making the blockade effective. To Mercier and to the French consuls in America, he stated on June 7: "We also know that the intention of the belligerents is to conform to the rules established by the Congress of Paris concerning the blockade, which, consequently will only be recognized if it is effective." This he had repeated to Prussia a few days earlier.[38]

Having finally received the official notification from Dayton, Thouvenel took further steps to affirm his conditional acceptance of the blockade. In reply to a query from the minister of marine, Chasseloup-Laubat, as to whether the French government recognized the blockade of the Southern ports in the case of French goods in French ships, he stated: "Since the French government recognized the belligerency of the two parties, it must acknowledge the right of either to take whatever action it deems necessary against the other. Yes." When the minister of marine sent his orders out to the French fleet in American waters, he was even more specific:

The two fractions, today disunited, in the American confederation being considered as two belligerents, the government of the emperor recognizes their right to have recourse against each other to such blockade measures as they deem necessary, but only so long as the established blockades are effective. Consequently in case a sufficient force is maintained before the blockade ports to interdict access to them, our merchant ships, like those of other powers, ought to respect the blockade.[39]

Thus by June both France and England had announced in advance that they would accept the blockade if it was effective. But did it become effective?

The Effectiveness of the Blockade

The term "effective" is a qualitative judgment which must be made by some human institution or authority. The Congress of Paris, which agreed to Article IV of the Declaration, did not specify what was meant by effective; and subsequent international practice is "that a blockade does not cease to be a blockade because individual vessels may succeed in breaking it successfully, but that the blockade, to be legal, must present an actual danger to vessels attempting to evade it."[40] Capture, in other words, must be an ever-present danger, but not necessarily an invariable result. Yet, here again, there is need to make a qualitative value-judgment of whether the danger of capture is ever-present.

Then there is also the question of how much had to be blockaded in order to have effectiveness. Must every mile of the three thousand miles of coast line be patrolled? Some early European commentators thought so, and deemed it impossible; and therefore they claimed that the blockade could not be enforced. But Lincoln in his proclamation had referred only to "the ports" of these states, and generally it was recognized that these only would have to be patrolled. Yet there were 185 of these ports if you count every little fishing harbor, and no attempt was made to seal all of these. Actually there were only eight ports large enough for heavy trading in imports and exports—Norfolk, Wilmington, Charleston, Savannah, Mobile,

New Orleans, and Galveston—and the blockade could legally be limited to these ports if ships were merely challenged in front of them, since the blockade was officially inaugurated at the spot by the blockading ships and not by any government official in Washington. Fenwick says that "France and other continental states held that information of a blockade must be given to the vessel directly by the blockading fleet."[41] Hence in practice the blockade attempted to be effective mainly in front of these eight ports. But Norfolk was effectively blockaded by the same ships which kept the Chesapeake Bay open to Washington, Pensacola was guarded by Fort Pickens, New Orleans was captured in April 1862, Galveston temporarily in 1863, and Mobile in August 1864. As the war wore on, then, only four of the main ports remained to be blockaded in the usual way.

For the blockade patrol the United States at first had only three steamers at locations where they could be sent immediately. However, as ships were called in from service around the world and others in the navy yards had their routine repairs completed, there became available thirty-nine steamers and thirty-four sailing vessels. Eventually many more ships were built and others enlisted from the merchant fleets—even ferry boats—until at the height of the war there were six hundred ships patrolling the coasts or the high seas.[42] A few ships were on blockade patrol by the middle of May (one month after the proclamation), but generally it was three months before there was a semblance of blockading along the Atlantic.[43]

Historians themselves have disagreed on how effective this blockade was. Owsley, in his *King Cotton Diplomacy*, stressing the success of the small, shallow-draft blockade-runners, makes the most vociferous claim of its ineffectiveness. In 1861, he says, only one in ten of the blockade-runners were captured. "All the evidence in the way of testimony [he affirms] indicates that the blockade was no more effective in the Gulf than in the Atlantic. . . . The blockade during the first year of the war was almost nonexistent, and from that time on it was never able to stop more than one vessel out of four on the Atlantic Coast, even toward the last, and certainly no more than that on the Gulf Coast."[44] This is judging the blockade, however, by an absolute standard instead of by that of an "ever-present danger." Soley, on the other hand, insisted that the blockade was in the main effective.

> ... From the beginning [he argued], though the blockading force was then inconsiderable, the regular course of trade at the Southern ports was actually interrupted, neutrals for a time respecting the proclamation, or being satisfied to receive their warning and go elsewhere. . . . As to the legal efficiency of the blockade after the first six months, there can be no question; and by the end of the second year its stringency was such that only specially-adapted vessels could safely attempt to run it.[45]

Solely pointed out that 1,149 prizes were brought in, 210 of which were steamers; 355 ships were burned among which were 82 steamers—in all 1,504 ships of all classes. The total value amounted to thirty-one millions of dollars.[46]   To this Owsley would counter that most captured blockade-runners made five trips before capture.   Therefore if 1,500 were captured, a total of 7,500 violations were made—a record which he considered to mean inefficiency.[47]

Spears agreed with Soley.

> If the traffic [of blockade-runners] never ceased absolutely [he wrote], the constriction of the blockade was and is now mani-fest. It was so efficient that one can scarcely read of the effects produced by it in the South without tears.   One can believe that the blockade was a merciful as well as a just measure of war in that it shortened the struggle more than any other measure, and so saved many lives on both sides.[48]

Coulter, a Southerner, relying considerably on the Owsley point of view as to effectiveness, did give considerable credit to the blockade for the downfall of the South.   "Without a doubt," he wrote, "the blockade was one of the outstanding causes of the strangulation and ultimate collapse of the Confederacy; yet it was ineffective in the international law sense until almost the last months."[49]   Channing, a Northerner, takes a more favorable view of its effectiveness.

The blockade of the Confederate ports [he asserted] became stricter and stricter almost every month after the beginning of the year 1862. . . . The effectiveness of the blockade varied from time to time, owing to changes in commanders and of the necessity of using serviceable ships in other directions. It be-became so efficient, however, by 1862, that entirely new methods of breaking it [special blockade-runners] had to be adopted.[50]

Among the writers of diplomatic history Latané said that "the outcome [of the Civil War] was, in fact, due to the naval superiority of the North," and Bemis agreed that "the blockade was one of the great factors in the defeat of the Confederate cause." In commenting on Owsley's contrary arguments, Bemis retorted that "most of the vessels getting through were small craft, and . . . neutral vessels were not captured until after having first been warned away."[51]

Whatever the historians may say in retrospect about the effectiveness of the blockade, it is not so much what its effectiveness was as what contemporaries thought it was that counts in the human affairs involved. Decisions are made on information long before historians have a chance to confirm or invalidate it. For our purposes we are interested in the information given to France and England on the effectiveness of the blockade and their subsequent decisions.

Realizing the suffering which had already occurred in France even before the blockade, Thouvenel was naturally watching carefully to estimate the blockade's effectiveness. Also he was glancing at England out of the corner of his eye to observe any signs of her reaction. Once in August there came the rumor that the British admiral, Milne, had reported the blockade to be ineffective during the previous month. The French foreign minister immediately asked Russell about the report. His answer was that "no information of that nature has come to the English government, which is inclined, on the contrary, to consider the proclaimed blockade as being seriously enforced." Thouvenel was also watching the reports from his consuls and summarized the information he had received to the minister of commerce in these words: "According to the latest information received by me from the United States, this blockade was then

really effective especially for the ports of Virginia" [Norfolk].[52]
In September he began to receive more reports from his consuls.
From Charleston, St. André was writing, right after the Trescott
trip to Richmond, that mainly small coasting boats were coming
in.

> The South [he wrote] . . . has no navy to raise the blockade
> of her ports and suffers as a result because it used to import
> everything from abroad.   It is true that 51 ships have entered
> the port of Charleston and about 20 that of Wilmington since
> the proclamation of the blockade, but they did not bring any-
> thing in, because for the most part they were only in the coastal
> trade.   However, they must have forced the blockade; what they
> did, foreign ships could also try unless they think the blockade
> is effective.   The figures cited above prove that it is not al-
> ways. . . . It is then the foreign maritime commerce which
> really has the most occasion to complain about the measure
> adopted by President Lincoln for conquering the South.[53]

A fortnight later St. André is less favorable to the blockade's
effectiveness.   Two British ships and two Southern privateers
had run the blockade into Charleston.   Some had also entered
Georgia and Florida ports.   However, he added that the
Federal navy had made landings near Cape Hatteras and elsewhere which would deprive privateers of some of their ports for
prize.   Bunch was also writing home that "vessels of various
sizes enter and sail [from Charleston] almost at pleasure."[54]
   At this same time, too, Dayton was passing on to Thouvenel
the boast from Seward that "our blockade is rapidly becoming
perfect" and "even as it stands now, it sustains all the conditions
which a just interpretation of the law of nations require."[55]
This seemed to be confirmed by Rear Admiral Reynaud, commander of the French squadron.   He had just made a cruise
of the Atlantic blockaded coast and gave the following report:

> The large ports, such as Charleston and Savannah, while
> not blockaded as tightly as possible, nevertheless are effectively
> sealed off.   However, the smaller ports are not.   Sailing vessels
> patrol before them only a great way off.   From what I hear this

is also what is taking place in the Gulf of Mexico where, according to what Mr. Mejan was writing recently, the principal passes of the Mississippi are well guarded, but some schooners and small craft manage to get into the small neighboring ports. . . . In my opinion the blockade and patrolling will be almost impossible in winter.[56]

While there were qualifications in these reports, still most of them affirmed the effectiveness of the blockade where it counted — before the large ports of the South.

Later in the fall Thouvenel received more adverse news about the blockade. Montholon was reporting brisk blockade running to Havana and Jamaica. Belligny came home to Paris, saying that an effective blockade was impossible. At Charleston alone they would need eight ships. And Belligny's successor, St. André, repeated that the blockade was still ineffective at Charleston. On top of this came a communication from Rost, listing 400 ships which had evaded the blockade up to the end of August. Again this was confirmed by the British Commander, Lyons, who said in December that the blockade was not effective either at Charleston or Wilmington.[57]

But, if these later reports tended to make Thouvenel change his mind regarding the blockade, a report from Consul Paul on November 2 from the capital of the Confederacy must have made the minister return to the belief that the blockade was really being enforced. Paul said that the South needed army supplies from Europe but could not obtain them because of the blockade. "They are literally lacking everything"—weapons, cloth for uniforms, shoes, necessities for the civilian population. Because of a lack of manufactures in the South prices have risen 400 percent for manufactured goods. Goods produced at home were costing 200 percent more. Contrary to what Rost was reporting, Paul concluded:

> The leading business men here consider the blockade question as a vital one, and they watch the news from Europe with anxiety. They really can not continue the fight for long when they have at their disposition only a third of the resources available to the enemy. In the face of this ever-growing lack of

everything, the South is finding itself condemned to play a passive role.[58]

In spite of the small ships slipping through, the blockade must have seemed to be pinching hard if such conditions already existed after six months of enforcement.

Lyons, too, late in the autumn seemed to agree with Reynaud and Paul on the effectiveness of the blockade. In answer to a query from Russell, he reported:

> I am a good deal puzzled as to how I ought to answer your question whether I consider the Blockade effective. It is certainly by no means strict or vigorous along the immense stretch of coast to which it is supposed to apply [he overlooks that only ports, and not the whole coast, were blockaded]. I suppose the ships which run it successfully both in and out are more numerous than those which are intercepted. On the other hand it is very far from being a mere Paper Blockade. A great many vessels are captured; it is a most serious interruption of trade; and if it were as ineffective as Mr. Jefferson Davis says in his Message, he would not be so very anxious to get rid of it.[59]

Thus, during the summer and autumn of 1861 Thouvenel had reports on the blockade from many sources and the consensus of their opinions was that the blockade was somewhat effective. Were he and his government going now to accept it as effective or were they going to challenge it as insufficiently enforced and therefore illegal?

In the end the real decision was up to Napoleon III, and it was interesting to see what his attitude was at the beginning of his government's deliberations. This was shown by the emperor's conversation on August 1, 1861, with General James W. Webb, whom he had known during his exile in New York. The general had gone out to Fontainebleau at Napoleon's invitation, and the emperor made the cordial and intimate conversation one of those information fishing excursions, lasting nearly an hour. After he had pumped from his old friend all the information he could obtain on the issues involved as well as on the military and economic situation, he came around to the question of the blockade.

Napoleon (speaking in English): *You know* that all my sympathies are with you—only take care that the blockade is effective. I hope it is not true that you are going to neglect your blockade. That will be bad—that will embarrass me. I will be compelled to insist that it be—how do you term it?—effective.

Webb: We do not propose to neglect the blockade.

Napoleon: But have you extended the blockade on paper without providing a force to maintain it?

Webb: No. That is, we declare all the ports of the Rebels Blockaded; and we are sending all our own naval force, and using all the steamers suitable for the purpose, and building some 50 gunboats to enable us to make the blockade what it should be.

Napoleon: I am glad of it. I am glad of it. If you keep up the blockade according to what the law of nations requires, they [businessmen with complaints?] can not embarrass me. But I can not consent to any departure from the requirement on this head. Keep that matter right and all is well.

After some discussion of the question of closing the ports by law, the conversation continued.

Napoleon: Do not rest on that [closing the ports by law]. Do not cease to render your Blockade effective. That would embarrass me.

Webb: I do not believe that our government has any such intention. I am sure that, when I left home, its determination was to render it effective in the largest sense; and I doubt not they will carry that determination into effect. It believes in an enforced blockade because the United States has suffered so much from the opposite. . . .

Napoleon (toward the end of the interview): *You know,* all my sympathies are with you. I am pleased to learn the determination of the Government to bring the war to a close next winter. I am sure they can do it, but look well to your blockade. Our manufacturing interests in France have already felt great distress from the changed state of trade with America. You can, and should, bring the war to a speedy termination.

Webb: Of course, I do not consider myself at liberty to report this conversation to my Government but would feel gratified if I might repeat what relates directly to our public affairs.

Napoleon: You may do so.

Webb (trying to put more emphatic words in the emperor's mouth): But I want to do more.   I want your permission to say *from Your Majesty to our Government* that you sympathize with the United States, that you are most anxious to see the Rebellion put down and the quiet of the country restored, that you do not perceive how there can possibly arise any misunderstanding with France if we only render the blockade effective.

(Napoleon hesitated at this point, realizing that this was a statement of policy that ought to be elaborated with Thouvenel.)[60]

Webb (trying to overcome his hesitation): It would do good. England has offended our people, and we are all doubly anxious to be assured of the friendship of France.   Such a message would, if possible, stimulate the government to ever greater exertions to render the Blockade effective, and relieve Your Majesty from all possible embarrassment.

Napoleon (smiling good-naturedly): Well, have it your way.[61]

Here the emperor appeared to be so sympathetic to the United States that he wanted to avoid interfering with the blockade.   He did indicate that he was under pressure from business groups, and he only wanted an effective blockade to give him a good excuse for no action in the face of their importunities.

In the meantime, by mid-August, the emperor's foreign minister had come to the conclusion, from British naval reports and from France's own naval and consular reports, that the blockade had become effective.[62]   This opinion he boldly reasserted two months later to the Confederate commissioners themselves, to whom he had granted an unofficial interview.   According to their own account this was what he said:

> The French government watches with lively interest the contest between the two American governments, and there is an agreement between England and France to communicate to each other all facts and propositions which come to the knowledge of either. . . . As to the blockade the admirals of the English and French navies on the American coast are in close observance of it and have communicated to their governments that, although the blockade is not such as to seal up the ports

hermetically, it is yet not so ineffective as to authorize a protest against it.[63]

Thus by August, France had followed England in accepting the blockade as effective and continued to accept it throughout the war.

The Southern Ports Bill

As the weeks went by after the fall of Fort Sumter, the feeling in the North ran so high against the South both among the people and the men in congress and the administration that there was a wide search for every possible measure to punish the Southern states and force them back into the Union. The blockade had been proclaimed by almost reflex action; but, as the ships available for enforcement at first seemed few and much time would be required to get the blockade under way, many began to urge that the Southern ports be closed by law. As a sovereign state the United States had designated certain ports as ports of entry to which foreign commerce was limited because only in these were there customs officials. What a sovereign state may do it may also undo, and the Southern ports could be denied the right to be ports of entry.[64] This would prevent neutrals from entering but still require ships to intercept Confederate vessels, which would be very few in number. On the other hand, European statesmen were inclined to claim that the existence of a civil war compelled the substitution of international law for municipal law.

Just as the news of the fall of Fort Sumter was arriving in Washington, Lyons heard of this idea of closing the ports by law. He immediately branded this suggested measure as "a paper blockade of the worst kind." "It would," he wrote Russell, "certainly justify Great Britain and France in recognizing the Southern Confederacy and sending their fleets to force the United States to treat British and French vessels as neutrals in conformity with the law of nations." Again he advised firmness and cooperation with France.[65]

Mercier also had heard of this talk and reported that the North had given up the idea of closing ports by law in favor of a blockade in order to forestall a European recognition of the South.[66] It seems that threats of recognition may have sobered the more radical members of the cabinet. As the members of congress began to return to Washington for the opening of the special session—due to begin July 4—some of them told Lyons of their idea to propose a port bill. The British envoy told them emphatically that such a bill would get the United States into trouble with Europe because it would be a paper blockade.[67]

What at first was rumor became an official prediction when Seward mentioned it in despatches to France and England. In his famous threatening note to Adams of May 21 Lincoln had him justify a blockade "by our own laws" to suppress rebellion.[68] Here it would seem that Lincoln himself was thinking more in terms of an eventual port bill than was Seward. It was obviously under discussion in the cabinet. About a month later Seward came more directly to the point when he told Dayton that he reserved the right "to close such of our ports" as are in insurgent hands but would actually use the more "equitable" form of a blockade.[69]

As the date for the convening of congress—July 4—drew closer, Lyons was more and more confirmed in the belief that a port bill was going to be proposed and passed. "I hope [he wrote] France and England may be able without delay to come to a distinct agreement on the subject and be prepared to speak and act in strict concert in regard to it." He had tried to work with Mercier on the problem but ran into an attitude almost of incredulity on the part of the Frenchman. "M. Mercier [he complained] seems to me to think it so impossible that this government can run the risk of attempting to close the Southern ports otherwise than by regular Blockade, that I think he hardly gives due weight to the indications of such an intention, which are only too plain."[70]

In Europe the warnings of Mercier and Lyons induced immediate concern in Russell and Thouvenel. Russell called in Dallas on May 1 for a discussion of the subject, but the American minister pleaded ignorance and asked that he await C. F. Adams' arrival.[71] When Russell did see Adams on May 18, he did not inquire directly about a possible port bill but only discussed whether the blockade would cover the whole coast or just certain ports.[72] At the same time, however, he began to inquire of the law officers of the crown about the legality of the suggested port bill and to communicate to France extracts from Lyons reports.[73] Finally, in the last week of June, Russell told Adams that the law officers had affirmed the illegality of New Granada's closing rebel ports by decree and then mentioned slyly that he had heard rumors of the like intention in the United States against insurgent ports. Adams said he had heard of such threats in the previous session of congress, but he understood there were constitutional objections raised. "My own opinion was that the blockade would be persevered in, which would obviate all difficulty."[74]

In spite of such assurances, and perhaps because they were personal rather than official, Thouvenel took action against the proposed legislation before it was even enacted. In a dispatch to Mercier, sent on the very day congress assembled, Thouvenel said:

> I hesitate to believe ... that it [the Union government] thinks of going through with the idea of proposing to congress closing the Southern ports of entry by a law. To me it seems impossible that they would not understand that we could not accept such a measure, that ... we would be obliged to consider the closing of Southern ports by decree as substituting a paper blockade for an effective blockade, the latter of which being the only one that neutrals are required to respect.[75]

Thouvenel gave a copy of this to Cowley, which was transmitted through Russell to Lyons in Washington. With this enclosure went also Russell's instructions to Lyons to work in concert with Mercier. British law officers, he said, had advised that a port bill would violate the international law of effective blockade, even if the port holders were called insurgents.[76]

Yet these were not the only warnings France and England gave before the passage of the bill. On July 18, while on vacation, Thouvenel sent a more argumentative communication in which he showed that he expected the United States was going to abandon the blockade and substitute the port bill. This would mean that the North would seize foreign ships, destined for Southern ports, haphazardly without a genuine blockade before those ports. This, he said, would be a paper blockade against which both the United States and France have protested in the past. It was hard enough for France to endure the hardship of a legitimate blockade in the American Civil War without having to undergo the difficulties of an improper measure. Not only was an old principle of France involved, but Napoleon III had felt a particular responsibility to lead opposition to a paper blockade because of the universal condemnation of it at Paris in 1856 under his inspiration. Thouvenel, in closing, asked Mercier to concert with Lyons and decide on how much action they needed to take.[77] Russell, for his part, also sent a second note on July 19 in which he said Great Britain would continue to honor an effective blockade but not a paper blockade instituted by a law closing Southern ports. Such a measure would be considered "null and void," and England would not allow interference with her ships on the high seas under such a law. Lyons was to work with Mercier, "but at all events you will take care not to leave him [Seward] in ignorance of the decision of Her Majesty's Government."[78] Thouvenel and Russell exchanged copies of their respective notes in advance and approved of each other's instructions.[79]

Before any of these Anglo-French warnings could arrive, congress had assembled and a port bill had been proposed. Charles Sumner, chairman of the Senate's foreign relations committee, sponsored it in the upper house. The bill authorized (but did not compel) the president to take any necessary measures to collect custom duties in insurgent ports, to close insurgent ports as ports of entry, and (Article V) to open them to foreign commerce at his discretion. All of this was an optional authorization and not a requirement to the executive. During the deliberations Mercier had an interesting conversation with Sumner on the pending bill, in which Sumner argued that the port bill would merely reinforce the blockade.[80] But Mercier countered that foreign countries could not acknowledge penalties imposed on blockade-runners for violating this law. Secretary of the Navy Welles had also talked to another foreign diplomat recently and

admitted that the cabinet had in mind closing the ports by law
as a substitute for the blockade. In the light of all this, Mercier
begged for instructions, which, unknown to him, were already
on the way.[81]

Nevertheless, the new bill was passed in the second week of
July, and in the third week the first instructions were received
by the two envoys. Lyons was dubious about whether "the
new instructions . . . will enable us to do any good now" especially since they did not say anything definite about what
England and France would do.[82] Mercier, however, went immediately to see Seward about the bill on July 18 because it was
now a question of preventing the government from choosing to
take advantage of the optional authorization. He stated flatly
that France and England would recognize no blockade unless it
was effective. Seward did not make any statement about the
administration's plans, but merely thanked Mercier for his views
and asked him for a copy of that part of his instructions so that
he could present it to the president and the cabinet.

On the following day, the 19th, Seward asked Lyons to come
for an interview. On this occasion Seward was much less
reticent than he had been with Mercier in regard to the Port Bill.

> *Seward:* I am really not anxious to use the bill's authority, but
> I might be forced to it by the radicals, especially if England ir-
> ritated public opinion too much. You know on previous occa-
> sions I have had to take a very violent stand because of the
> very fact that I had to keep myself in the good graces of public
> opinion in order to remain in office and stave off the radicals.
> We intend to keep right on using the present blockade with
> ever increasing effectiveness. What do you think of the Port
> Bill?
>
> *Lyons:* I think I am now in a position to tell you that Great
> Britain will oppose it vigorously.
>
> *Seward:* M. Mercier has given me an extract from a dispatch
> from M. Thouvenel, and I would be most pleased if you could
> give me something of the same kind. I think these papers
> would be of great help to me when I have occasion to discuss
> this question with the president.

On the 20th Mercier went back to see Seward again, and the latter also explained to him apologetically the reason for his threatening tone of the last three months. But, as with Lyons, he gave the French envoy considerable assurances.

> No formal decision has yet been made, but you can rest assured that the difficulty will be avoided. For the time being the effective blockade will be maintained and the ships seized will be turned over to the proper authorities. I have a note to go to Mr. Dayton, which, I think, will give entire satisfaction to M. Thouvenel.

Both Mercier and Lyons accommodated Seward by giving him copies of extracts from their instructions, and they both felt very much relieved to receive even the provisional reassurances of Seward.[83]

The secretary of state then turned to the task of giving Adams and Dayton instructions on the Port Bill. Here the document— for he sent the same text to both—had to be more belligerent in tone than his oral conversations because it was designed for publication. The lengthy text went over again the differences in views between Great Britain (and France) and the United States on belligerency. Then, getting down to the subject, Seward said that the United States would not acquiesce in England's (France's) disregarding a closure of the ports. However, in subsequent passages, he hinted that the measures might not be put into effect.[84] There was only a partial reassurance in these words, but, taking into consideration his concern for his radical opposition, the European cabinets could have some cause for relief. At least that was the feeling of Prince Napoleon, to whom Seward read a copy of these instructions during his farewell call on August 10. "It is very reasonable," was the prince's comment. On this occasion Mercier had also had a chance to listen to the reading and gave his opinion to Thouvenel: "You will see in it that Mr. Seward is trying especially to dissuade [dégoûter] France and England from any act of intervention by frightening them concerning its future effects on their commercial interests."[85]

On the other side of the Atlantic the news of the passage and the actual terms of the Southern Ports Bill arrived in London on

July 26 and prompted Russell to communicate immediately with Thouvenel through Cowley. He termed the measure "a serious development" and wanted to move against it in concert with France.[86] Two days later Cowley had a long talk with Thouvenel about it. The French foreign minister felt he could only give his first impression because he wanted to have more information on it and more cabinet deliberations as to policy; but his first impression, while cautious, was rather positive and in the long run rather perceptive. He agreed with Russell that the law had "a very serious significance for neutrals" and in any case was in opposition to the statements they had sent to Washington.

> But I wonder [he said to Cowley] whether in practice it can have very appreciable results and whether it is of a nature to modify very greatly for neutral ships the present situation growing out of a state of war between the North and South. In fact it seems to me that the Union navy will not be able to collect customs duties on foreign ships unless it has forces enough to blockade the port of entry. And so an effective blockade remains in fact a necessity at the same time that the Union is claiming the right to establish a fictitious blockade. If the port of entry is not really closed by a sufficient force to interrupt access, neutral ships will enter without paying any duties. It is all right, certainly, to anticipate the occasion when the American navy might claim the right to check on the high seas whether a vessel has fulfilled the requirements of the bill. But this claim would be an obvious contradiction on the part of the United States, because, in insisting on obedience to the customs law in Southern ports in favor of the American treasury, they deny that the Confederate States are belligerents, and in submitting the neutral flag to visit and search [on the high seas] they are claiming a right that only a belligerent can assert.

Before ordering the French squadron to oppose the North's attempts to enforce the bill, Thouvenel thought, we should wait and see whether the Lincoln administration intended to put it into effect—since it was optional—and what effect Mercier's and Lyons' warning had, based upon their last instructions. In any case the European naval forces should have time to plan their proper action in the face of a variety of different circumstances which might arise, and they should not take action without first referring back to their governments. After all, they would very seldom be on the spot where visit and search or capture of their national vessels took place, and therefore their action would have to be one of reprisal in another form.

> The English government will no doubt feel that, before having recourse to this means, the two governments should have full knowledge of the definite facts in the case and a chance to weigh them carefully. It would be only after this that it would be wise to give our admirals instructions on how to act in opposing the pretensions of the American navy.[87]

Even though this was Thouvenel's first impression, it turned out to be a wise and prudent policy in the long run because we already know that Seward, under pressure from Mercier and Lyons, was trying to avoid the use of the law and promising to continue the effective blockade.

However, Cowley was unhappy about this cautious, wait-and-see policy. "I wish that the French were inclined to be more *bumptious*, as they seemed to be at first," he wrote to Russell. "I would at all times rather have the task of calming them, than of urging them on."[88] As a result of Cowley's discontent E. D. Adams, in his book on *Great Britain and the American Civil War*, left the impression that, throughout this Ports Bill incident, Thouvenel was uninformed, indifferent, vacillating, uncooperative, and timid. Furthermore, he claimed that England, rather than France, had raised the issue first.[89] From the whole account above we see that both France and England were constantly exchanging views on all the issues simultaneously and that, in the matter of the impending Ports Bill, Thouvenel's first instruction had gone out two days *before* Russell's. Indeed, Russell's instructions contained Thouvenel's as an enclosure. As to Cowley's discontent on July 28, we know now that on the *previous* day Russell had already recommended the same caution to the admiralty as Thouvenel did later to Cowley. Here are his very words.

I have now to signify to your Lordships [law commissioners of the admiralty] the Queen's command that Rear Admiral Milne shall be directed not to take any steps which might involve this country in hostilities with the U.S. of America without further instructions. It is very probable that the President of the U.S. upon receiving the communications already sent by the governments of Great Britain and France to Lord Lyons and M. Mercier may refrain from exercising the Powers entrusted to him by Congress. But at all events Her Majesty's government may expect some explanations and the friendly relations of Her Majesty and the United States are too important to be endangered by any chance collision or any premature action.[90]

Lord Cowley's face must have been a little red when he received this copy and saw that his own foreign secretary on the previous day had not been any more *bumptious* than Thouvenel. But this last message of Russell's also showed how wrong American and some French opinion was on England's desire to interfere against the North in the war. This indeed was a harbinger of England's rather subdued protest over the "Trent" Affair four months later.

When Thouvenel received a copy of Russell's instructions to the admiralty, he sent a copy on to his minister of marine and recommended the same policy for the French squadron. He also summarized his conversation with Cowley on a cautious approach.[91] On the following day he informed Russell that he approved of *England*'s cautious approach.[92]

Having reined in their respective navies, the two foreign ministers proceeded to exchange and to approve the texts of their notes to be sent to Washington,[93] urging that Lincoln not act upon the permissive powers in the Ports Bill. Both notes were sent on August 8. Thouvenel in his instructions to Mercier again used the friendly, persuasive approach. He approved Mercier's timely and categorical statement to Seward on the Ports Bill and hoped sincerely "that the Cabinet of Washington will persist in its wise attitude to which Mr. Seward seemed personally willing to conform." He also welcomed heartily "the assurances which the secretary of state of the Union repeated about devoting all his efforts to remain on peaceful and friendly terms with foreign governments."[94]   Russell's note was more blunt and to the point when he wrote Lyons that the Ports Bill would violate neutral rights, and he hoped that Lincoln would use his discretion by relying on the blockade.   Lyons was to read this to Seward and give him a copy; but, as an afterthought on the next day, Russell told Lyons to use his discretion about communicating it and keep in agreement with Mercier.[95]

Back in Washington, Lyons had had a very satisfactory conversation with Seward on the morning of August 16, eleven days before he or Mercier received their final instructions.   On this occasion Seward told him positively that there was no question of using the Ports Bill.   Either the envoys' earlier dispatches or the reenforcement of the British squadron had enabled Seward to restrain Lincoln and the cabinet.[96]

By this time Lyons was satisfied enough not to want to irritate Seward by raising the issue any more.   When he received his final protest instructions, he was very glad he had been given some discretion and told to consult with Mercier.   He could stall on doing anything by saying that Mercier was out of town.   Indeed, Mercier was absent for almost a month, travelling through the western states with Prince Napoleon, and all this time Lyons did nothing. Five times between August 27 and September 13 the British minister pleaded the absence of the French envoy. On the last occasion Lyons added that he did not think the matter urgent because Seward was not inclined to do anything about it anyway.[97]   Mercier's instructions were not mandatory as to seeing Seward, and no doubt on his return he easily persuaded Lyons to let the matter drop for the time being.[98]

Thus sputtered out the last legal and technical dispute over the blockade during the year 1861.   There was also to ensue, however, the practical discussion of how to obtain cotton, and, later the dispute over the stone fleet.   Both of these will be treated below.

Chapter V

THE FIRST YEAR OF THE
GREAT STRANGULATION

THE imposition of the blockade and its maintenance, as we have just seen, were the subjects of a great deal of diplomatic discussion. Now we must turn to the less legalistic and more economic and practical side to see how the tightening coils of trade constriction affected the relations between France and the United States. It was not just a question of the effects of the blockade, for there were many other restrictive factors at work. In the first place there was the Southern embargo of cotton which contributed as much to the cotton famine as did the blockade. Beyond that, is the fact that the cotton famine was itself only one of many factors contributing to the great strangulation. In some ways the export industries of France suffered as much as, or more than, did her cotton industries. In the first year there was a surplus of cotton in Europe, which gave a little slack to the severity of the cotton famine; but, as we have already seen in the preceding chapter, the luxury-exporting industries, such as silk, carpets, gloves, and china, were suffering from the impending crisis many months before the outbreak of the war. If the South could not, or would not, sell its cotton, it would not have credits abroad to buy luxury articles. If the North and South had to spend their substance on all the military expenditures of mutual slaughter, they would have to economize on the purchase of French luxury goods. Frenchmen themselves bought less of their own manufactured goods as business in general became worse; and, to top it off, England and other industrialized European countries, who likewise suffered from the cotton famine and the reduction of exports, also bought less French luxury goods. Thus began the fateful downward spiral so characteristic of the new worldwide economy under the old system of separate sovereign states. It just was not fair that two quarreling factions in far-off North America should cause all this suffering and disruption in a peaceful Europe; but fair or not, the misery came anyway, and no one found an effective political or diplomatic solution to the impasse. At least we begin to realize that the blockade and cotton were only a part of the picture.

The Deepening Depression

As far as the technical aspects of the blockade were concerned, France and England considered it effective after reading the reports of their consuls and ministers, as well as those of their admirals in American waters. But added to the blockade was the Southern embargo, which was inspired by the "King Cotton" philosophy of Christy and Senator Hammond. Their theory was that if the South withheld cotton, England and France would be forced to intervene, recognize the independence of the South, and break the blockade. This would lead either to an eventual victory of the South through her ability to import war supplies, or to a quick victory if the North went to war against France and England and was defeated by her three adversaries.

There were proposals of Confederate and state legislation to impose the embargo, but they never were enacted into law, perhaps because the Southern leaders wanted the blame for the cotton famine to fall upon the blockade. Yet, an effective extralegal embargo did exist during the first two years of the war. Southern newspapers all over the Confederacy urged the cotton growers to keep the cotton on their plantations or in storage in the interior of the country. Early in the war the Charleston *Mercury* proclaimed defiantly: "The cards are in our hands! and we intend to play them out to the bankruptcy of every cotton factory in Great Britain and France or the acknowledgment of our independence. . . . These countries do not seem yet to realize that the Confederate States are a power on earth—and the most important power to them the sun shines on."[1] Public opinion, however, hardly needed this press exhortation. Cotton planters and factors, alike, even at the price of severe temporary loss, were grimly determined to withhold their cotton. In this resolution they were aided in two ways. The Confederate and state governments made produce-loans, which transferred the cotton into government hands and compensated the planters, thus spreading the losses to the Southern public as a whole. In addition to this, local committees of public safety were organized, which watched out to see that there were no noncooperators, that no cotton was secretly loaded on blockade-runners, and that cotton was burned before it fell into the hands of the invading enemy. Owsley summed up the effort thus: "An embargo was supported widely the first year of the war. There was almost complete unanimity in the public press, and among the whole articulate southern population."[2]

The effectiveness of the embargo seemed to Owsley to be more unquestionable than that of the blockade.

> The impression created abroad [he wrote] was that there was during 1861 an air-tight embargo on cotton, and that it would be useless to attempt to come into the blockaded ports to obtain it. . . . The effectiveness of the embargo, during the year 1861 and far into the winter of 1862, was complete. It was as the English had supposed, just as near air-tight as human effort could make it. No embargo in history has been any more strict.

Yet, he added, "after the spring of 1862 the embargo was slowly relaxed until it completely ceased." Southerners were beginning to lose faith in "King Cotton," and they needed foreign exchange to buy war supplies. But by that time the blockade was becoming sufficiently effective to prevent Southern exports regardless of the changed Southern attitude.[3]

What effect, then, did the blockade and embargo have on the cotton industries of France during 1861 and early 1862? Fohlen's statistics on French importations of American cotton tell the story graphically.

1860	....	114,000 tons	1864	....	900 tons
1861	....	109,000	1865	....	2,900
1862	....	295	1866	....	43,200
1863	....	254			

The figure for 1861 is deceptive because it represents the heavy importations of the bumper crop of 1860 before hostilities began. The South should have started its embargo six months earlier. But there was hardship in France in 1861 as seen by the diminishing supply of raw cotton in Le Havre.

April	644,000 bales
October	187,000
December	141,000

Some of this decline was brought about by increased Northern purchases, since they could not buy directly from the South. Likewise French purchases of raw cotton from England rose.

1860	....	1,800 tons
1861	....	3,600
1862	....	24,300

The lines of trade became snarled as the nooses began to tighten.[4]

While this was the story of cotton imports and supply, it did not really represent the condition of the French cotton industries during the first year. There was such a surplus of raw cotton to begin with that manufacturing kept up most of the year. In western Normandy during the second quarter they were reporting that "the cotton industry [near Caen] is in a very prosperous condition, employing all available hands." Such was also the situation in other cotton regions of Nancy and Rouen. Only in the Haut-Rhin were there some manufacturers of fine cotton fabrics who suffered from a decline of sales.[5]

In the third quarter of 1861 mild early signs of suffering began to appear. In the Picardy region of Amiens it was said that "the Picard industries do not lack American cotton in any respect, it is sufficiently supplied with raw material, but [it] lacks American markets." In western Normandy in Falaise several cotton spinning factories were laying workers off. It was the same in Vire, Flers, and Ferté-Macé. Out in the Haut-Rhin they were beginning to discontinue the manufacture of the finer threads, but there were as yet no layoffs or wage reductions. In eastern Normandy, in the region of Rouen, profits were declining in the cotton industries; three factories had reduced production and dismissed 450 workers. At Le Havre they noticed the great decline of cotton imports and rightly attributed it to both the Southern embargo and the Northern blockade.[6]

At the end of 1861 the slump was much more noticeable. In the region of Douai the cotton industry was suffering from a 35 percent rise in cotton prices and a lack of American orders. In the Meuse department spinning activity was about normal, although one mill was running on three-quarter time and another had reduced piecework rates by one to ten centimes per meter of cotton sheeting. Near Paris, however, the cotton industry was running full-blast (*en pleine activité*). It was in the important cotton region of Normandy that the real pinch was beginning to be felt. In western Normandy, at Lisieux, one factory had closed down for lack of raw cotton, and at Falaise many workers had been laid off. It was hoped the unemployed might find work completing the Caen-Flers railroad line. In the more important region of Rouen, in eastern Normandy, the procureur gave statistical tables for the cotton industry.

	percent unemployed	percent partially unemployed
Spinning	14.5	17.7
Hand weaving	27	35.2
Calicoes	2.3	14.8
Dyeing	2.8	0
Bleaching	6.3	22.6

Here is a picture which caused real concern.[7]

But the exporting industries suffered more severely from the very beginning of the war (second quarter of 1861). In Montbéliard the clock and watch industry was declining and men were being laid off during the spring, and this trend continued during the rest of the year. In the Rouen region—eastern Normandy— by the winter of 1861-62, 55% of clock and watch workers were totally unemployed and 29% were partially unemployed—one to three days per week. The silk industry of Lyons was badly hit. In the autumn of 1861 there were 20,000 unemployed in silk fabrics and 30,000 in ribbons. This serious crisis continued all winter. There was a marked increase in prostitution as women workers, now unemployed, felt it necessary to find other means of support. Food relief was distributed, and work relief was organized for the construction of river levees (*terrassements*). In the districts of Riom and Nîmes the same crisis in silks existed. In Annenay alone 1200 workers were unemployed. The china-ware industry of Limoges by September 1861 had reduced working hours by half. During the winter one-fourth were working three-quarter time. High-grade woolens were another export casualty of the war. In eastern Normandy they exported to the United States 45,000 kilograms less in October 1861 than in October 1860, and 18,000 kilograms less in November 1861 than in the same month of 1860. Eight percent were totally unemployed and one percent partially. Similar crises of slightly varying degrees were registered in other exporting industries, such as glass, lace and embroideries, ship building and ship stores, hats, gloves, musical instruments, wines, and pins.[8]

Newspapers in 1861 and 1862 also gave nationwide statistics on the decline in exports. In the *Constitutionnel* appeared a comparison of exports to America between the first eight months of 1860 and the same period of 1861:

Linens .... 109,000 fr.
Silks .... 50,700,000 fr.
Silk floss .... 63,000 fr.
Worsteds .... 16,000,000 fr.
Cottons .... 2,600,000 fr.
Leather skins ..... 3,500,000 fr.
Leather goods ..... 3,900,000 fr.

The *Journal des Débats* gave another list for the full years 1860 and 1861 with the following losses in 1861:

Hats 1,600,000
Furniture........ 420,000 fr.
Wine.......... 18,000,000 litres[9]

Already, then, during the first nine months of hostilities French cotton and, especially, exporting industries were feeling a severe economic depression.

The Cry for Help

Here was the developing economic situation, but how did it translate itself into political pressure for relief from the American incubus? In the same procureur reports there were only two instances of demands for intervention to regain cotton and markets. The businessmen in Nancy were reported to be wondering whether England and France "will be forced to intervene under the pressure of imperious necessity," while those of Bordeaux were asking for "a solution, no matter what, that will open American ports to restore cotton deliveries to our markets and bring back to commercial transactions their former activity."[10] But, much more numerous than these suggestions of action were the demands for nonintervention and neutrality. The cotton manufacturers of the Haut-Rhin had loaded themselves up with high-priced cotton and did not want intervention which would flood the market with cheap cotton. Opinion in Douai did not want to join England "under any circumstance" to destroy her rival American navy, which was an auxiliary navy for France. Since this was also the period of the "Trent" affair, there were many demands for French neutrality in case of an Anglo-American war—these from Colmar, Lyons, Nancy, Rennes, and Riom.[11]

In spite of the relative silence of French business circles in the early months of the war, Thouvenel and his cabinet colleagues were keeping close watch of the ever-worsening business situation in France. Having seen the bad effects on the export industries of the mere rumors of war, Thouvenel remarked to a foreign diplomat: "The commercial question, that is what troubles us and is the important one for us, and it must govern our conduct."[12] In a later conversation with the French foreign minister, Sanford brought up the fact that France exported more to the North than to the South and therefore should not endanger her position with the North by any unfriendly policy (recognition). "On all these points [wrote Sanford] M. Thouvenel seemed to be well informed, assenting generally to my statements as to commerce, the course of trade, etc."[13]   Only two weeks later in another conversation with Sanford, Thouvenel announced France's recognition of Southern belligerency and based the decision upon the government's great concern for France's trade with the United States and the commercial interests involved.[14]

Dayton, on his arrival, heard indirectly that Persigny, the minister of interior, had exclaimed that France would have to have cotton by fall or break the blockade to get it.[15]   By August, after the Northern defeat at Bull Run, there was a great deal of press and private discussion about the future cotton supply and French exports, stemming from the general dismay over the prospect of a long war.

> If these countries get short of cotton [wrote Dayton] and we *are not ourselves in possession of the interior*, excuse enough will be made for breaking the blockade. The tone of the public press here indicates this; the private conversations of public men indicate it, and I may add, I have been reliably informed that the Emperor recently remarked . . . that the probabilities were that the work would be done to their hands by a second-rate power [Spain] without France or England having any trouble about it.[16]

It was early in this same month of August that Thouvenel's friend and colleague, Rouher, minister of commerce, began to receive strong protests from shippers over their experiences with the blockade. Unfamiliar with the laws of war and the unavoidable neutral suffering in time of maritime war, these French businessmen just could not understand why they should have to suffer when the North was only trying to hurt the South. They complained, too, that shipping insurance rates were going up. The company owning the ship "David" protested because it was forbidden entrance to New Orleans when it did not even know a blockade existed and because it was stopped again even in the Northern port of Philadelphia. A M. Morales, who owned a ship of American registry, complained because the Southern privateers threatened to burn ships when they could not sell them for prize. Another, a M. Pierre, owner of the ship "Regulus," protested because he had to go to New York instead of New Orleans when he had no advance word that there was a blockade. These numerous petitions demanded that the French government let them know about these developments earlier, that it protect their rights to go anywhere at any time, that, in effect then, it blast out the blockade as far as French ships were concerned.[17] Rouher was perturbed by these recurring complaints and no doubt discussed them with Thouvenel.

These protests, together with other unfavorable business reports, finally led Thouvenel to write Mercier a long private letter. While the original text seems to have been lost in the legation fire of 1862, we have Lyons' summary of it from what Mercier told him in Washington.

> He [Mercier] has given me, confidentially, an account of a private letter which he received during his tour with the Prince [Napoleon] from Monsieur Thouvenel. M. Thouvenel appears to have written that the question of procuring a supply of cotton for the French manufacturers during the winter was becoming extremely serious; that he was anxious to know whether the government of the United States had duly considered the influence which this must have on the course of the French government with regard to the American Civil War; that he wished Monsieur Mercier to state to him confidentially his ideas on the subject.[18]

While Mercier was still on tour, he wrote from Niagara Falls an equally long reply to Thouvenel on September 9. While travelling, he assured his superior, he had kept constantly in mind France's objective of finding a way to end the war so that she could restore her lost markets and end the cotton famine. It was his impression, from his travels, that Northern opinion was beginning to despair of saving the Union. There was more and more confusion in both thought and action, as shown by General Fremont's proclamation in Missouri for the confiscation and emancipation of captured enemy slaves and his repudiation by the Federal government. The United States had gone suddenly from a most prosperous situation to one almost approaching ruin.

So [Mercier continued] I was not astonished when one person, whose position puts him in contact with important politicians,[19] assured me that several among them today sighed for some pretext for an arrangement, and they could hardly wait for the time to come when France and England, pushed by their interest, would recognize the South and take a firm stand to obtain cotton come what may. Then, they said, the North could consider all chance of fighting as lost and could give up without shame. The person who spoke to me this way added: Not one public leader will dare make such a direct avowal, but I promise to give you written proofs that there are some, even in high places, who see no salvation for this country except by European intervention.

After a great deal of reflection on this information Mercier did not think the time was ripe for such an intervention until the masses felt the same way as these statesmen. For the moment they all wanted revenge for Bull Run, and the financiers supported the war effort. France should remain on the alert for an opportunity to help make peace but not until the next campaign had been lost or some other favorable development had intervened. Answering more directly Thouvenel's query, he advised that England and France must speak with one firm voice and that he and Lyons should have discretion to act at the right moment. If his independent action turned out to be unwise, he would not object to being disavowed. Finally Mercier suggested that Thouvenel send a note, with sweet words but an implied threat, describing the economic suffering in France and asking for some exceptional access to cotton through the blockade.[20]

While Thouvenel's letter and Mercier's reply were slowly and alternately crossing the ocean, the French foreign minister turned his attention to Rouher's petitioners. He had Rouher write him a formal letter on August 17, and then he made an official reply in which he showed all the action he had already taken to have the two belligerents observe international law in the treatment of French interests. However, as to the blockade, he continued:

The exercise of the right of blockade has as its natural consequence to prohibit to other powers their access to blockaded places. It is incontestable that these powers must suffer from this interruption imposed on their normal commercial relations, but they have no right to complain because they are only hit indirectly and there is no violation of their right of freedom of the seas, which they can claim as neutrals, where that freedom would make the legitimate military operations, allowed by international law, absolutely unworkable between belligerents.

So long as the blockade is enforced to the extent that it makes access a sure and certain danger, it is legal and must be observed.

These principles, accepted by all nations, seem to be completely unknown to the petitioners whose letters I have before me. They seem to think that their normal commercial relations ought not to suffer at all from a state of war in which their country does not participate nor admit that they must observe it in their later operations. Unfortunately it cannot be that way. If it is true that a belligerent cannot use against his enemy any procedure which will directly harm neutrals, it is none the less accepted that the latter always have to endure the indirect consequences of the disturbances growing out of the war from the moment it breaks out.

Another error of the petitioners is to believe that the blockade does not exist until it has been notified diplomatically and that it does not apply to neutral ships which have already left port before notification. A blockade is in force as soon as it is definitely established; a material result of a material fact, it does not need to be instituted in another way. It begins with the real investment, continues as long as that lasts, and ceases with it. It makes no difference whether the neutrals know it. If one of their boats approaches to enter a blockaded port, the belligerent has the right to turn it back. Generally a government informs the others of the blockading measures to which it is going to have recourse; but this notification, which is not absolutely required, has no value in itself; it is only a statement of a fact already existing and operating.

He then went on to show that, if a paper proclamation started the legality of the blockade, the blockade could or would be a paper blockade. In conclusion he suggested that Rouher let the various chambers of commerce know the principles of international law involved so they would not have such an exaggerated idea of what the government could do for them.[21]

Yet, while Thouvenel was trying to calm businessmen by telling them there was nothing to be done if the blockade was effective, he was already meditating what could be done to nullify its hardships. Before he had ever received Mercier's Niagara Falls letter, he wrote to Flahault: "They [the Northerners] have other cats to whip than just Mexicans, and it seems to me almost impossible that the cotton question in the next three months will not make it necessary for England and France to give attention to a vital interest for the prosperity and quiet of their industrial cities."[22]

The quiet of the working class was one of Napoleon III's great preoccupations. He tried to avoid the heavy-handed suppressions of his predecessor, Louis Philippe, and, to maintain control in a more constructive way, he undertook a big program of public works, including urban renewal, railroad-building, and land draining and clearing.[23] The greater the number of unemployed, the heavier were the burdens on the budget for work relief. Thus, it can be easily understood why he and Thouvenel were so anxious to end the Civil War in America and restore the cotton and export trade.

Finally, on about September 25, Mercier's "private and confidential" letter from Niagara Falls arrived at the Quai d'Orsay. Thouvenel perused it with keen interest and hurried it off for the emperor to read. Napoleon must have been equally impressed, especially at the suggestion of a trial appeal to the North and close collaboration with England, because in the margin of the letter he commented: "This letter might be very good to communicate to the English government. N." And Thouvenel immediately set to work to prepare a copy for England. He changed the salutation from "Mon cher ami" to "Mon cher ministre" and then marked those paragraphs to be copied, which concerned the political and military situation in America and Anglo-French cooperation to take a forceful stand on ending the war or opening the blockade. The part suggesting a trial note to be sent by Thouvenel was omitted.[24]

Yet it was to the trial note that Thouvenel next devoted himself for about a week and no doubt referred it to the cabinet and to the emperor at Saint-Cloud. Finally it was sent off to Mercier on October 3. It was one of those long, rambling, and analytical dispatches so characteristic of the diplomacy of that day, and especially of Thouvenel and Seward. The main ideas in it, however, were these:

> Today it is no longer possible to have any illusions about the duration of the struggle going on in the United States.
>
> . . . In the present state of the world, when industrial and commercial questions exercise a more noticeable influence every day on international relations, the general movement of trade transactions cannot be suddenly stopped with such an active, powerful, and rich people as those of the United States without its effects being immediately felt abroad. . . . It therefore happens that, by a combination of entirely special circumstances . . . the countries of Europe have more to suffer from an interruption of their normal relations with that country than with any other people whatever. What has taken place recently has already given us in France an opportunity to realize what a disturbance can be created here by even a temporary break in the earlier relations between the two countries.
>
> . . . The blockade of the Southern ports, by paralyzing all the current operations and by stopping all deliveries prepared here and in the United States, has from the outset seriously hurt numerous and important interests. And the present absolute interruption of postal communications with the seceded states increases still more the concern and would be enough by itself to put those of our numerous merchants who have business houses in the United States in the most disastrous situation.
>
> . . . I wish to speak . . . of those [disastrous effects] which result in the complete shutting off of cotton shipments. . . . It [cotton] is today so completely substituted for the numerous other [textile] materials for manufacture and consumption that there is nothing which can replace it when it is lacking. You know what are France's needs in this regard when she has a cloth production worth 700 million francs. Every year 400,000 bales from the United States arrive in our ports as a partial fulfillment of our requirements. . . . Our manufacturers in Alsace, Normandy, the Vosges, etc., can no longer obtain their

raw material, their production is stopped, and the very existence of a considerable population is involved. . . . These people require immediate relief. The crisis is just now beginning; our cotton supply is not yet exhausted. However, just the prospect of a supply shortage has brought on the first symptoms of a work slowdown.

. . . The government is right now besieged with complaints and petitions coming from the big commercial centers of France. We are approaching the time for new provisioning . . . and new protests will arise from all quarters, and it will not be long before they will consider government abstention as a denial of protection to interests which have a right to be protected.

. . . We would be happy if the cabinet of Washington could be led by its own reflexions to follow a policy which would easily bring it into an understanding with us . . . on an easing of the ordinary blockade rules so as to permit foreign provisions of such indispensable cotton. . . . The [port bill] against which we warned the Washington cabinet does, though, allow the president (in section V) to permit foreign trade.[25]

The foreign minister then proceeded to send a copy to England.[26]

The Seward Reaction

During the month and a half that Mercier was awaiting more definitive instructions from Thouvenel, he was sounding out the terrain at the British legation and the state department. On his return from Boston, where he bade farewell to Prince Napoleon, he went to see Lyons and had a long talk with him, telling him what he had reported to Thouvenel and his suggestion of a policy of a vigorous joint Anglo-French intervention. Then Mercier inquired whether England was not suffering more than France from the cotton famine. Lyons took a very unconcerned attitude. All he knew was what he read in the papers—in other words there were no urgent official instructions about it. "I do not . . . perceive that any great alarm is yet felt in England," he added. "He supposed English importers would scurry around and find other sources of cotton which would then free them in the future from their dependence on American cotton. Mercier was sure that, if the North captured Southern ports or voluntarily opened them by relaxing the blockade, the South would embargo cotton deliveries in order to force France and England to recognize them or break up the whole blockade. This seemed to be what Mercier wanted done, but Lyons would not encourage such an approach, saying that "since the present was not an opportune moment, we do not have to suggest any positive steps to our governments." The British envoy thought the North was stronger than did Mercier, but he agreed that the Southern embargo would spoil the chances of getting cotton. However, in the spirit of full cooperation Lyons showed his French colleague all the correspondence he had received from home during his absence from Washington.[27]

Mercier had gone over to see Seward on October 1, the day after his return. He and Lyons had previously agreed not to raise the Ports Bill question again or to irritate the secretary with minor questions. Thus he did not have much to talk about, and Seward reciprocated with minor chitchat. In the next day or two Lyons also saw Seward with the same results.[28] However, as if to forestall any requests for blockade relaxation, Seward sent a note to Mercier in which he said that foreign warships which were allowed to pass through the blockade must not carry passengers or mail except to consular authorities.[29] On the other hand, Seward and Chase (secretary of the treasury) let Lyons and Mercier know that the naval expedition, then on its way, would probably capture and open a Southern port so that cotton could be obtained from the newly harvested crop. But Mercier, who suspected that the port was New Orleans, was not as optimistic about access to cotton. He pointed out the determined and effective Southern embargo on cotton exports in order to compel European recognition and sensed a growing concern in Washington over European business pressures on governments.[30] With the harvesting of the 1861 cotton crop the battle with King Cotton was at its height, and European governments were already thinking about undermining the blockade or recognizing the South.

Seward was evidently worried about it. As a senator, he had heard the boastful speeches of Southerners proclaim King Cotton; now came the showdown. No wonder he had made an advance statement about opening a captured port. But in a conversation with Stoeckl he tried to appear very reassured. He had, he said, good news from Europe that nothing was to be feared from that quarter. The Russian minister disagreed and said he had heard that European countries were suffering from the cotton famine and that great unemployment in Paris was caused by the loss of trade. Seward insisted that England would never dare attack the United States and France cherished the Union too much to do it any harm. Stoeckl's observations after Seward had left were:

> These illusions, based on a bygone past, can cost the Americans dearly. I should add that the secretary of state only knows Europe through information received from Sanford. . . . This [fellow] is an adventurer and jack-of-all-trades and has been able somehow to gain Mr. Seward's confidence. The latter is alarmed or reassured according to the tone of his confidential agent's reports.[31]

It was just two days after Stoeckl saw Seward that Thouvenel's long note on opening the blockade arrived, on October 21. Mercier was delighted with it, for to him it "could not have been a better answer to the wish he had expressed recently." And he immediately shared its contents with Lyons and Stoeckl.[32] While waiting to see Seward, he sent on a report to Thouvenel in which he reiterated his belief that the South could not be conquered and that the cotton embargo would require recognition in exchange for deliveries of the new cotton. This Mercier still wanted at the opportune moment in cooperation with England.[33] Lyons, however, thought that Mercier was misinformed about the South through the prejudiced accounts of Sir James Ferguson and Robert Bourke, two British travellers in the Confederacy. Besides he still preferred the peaceful to the warlike approach on the blockade.[34]

Finally on October 24, Mercier acquainted Seward with his note on France's business straits and the opening of the blockade. Seward did not say much, but took a copy to show to the president and promised to see Mercier on the following day.[35] However, it was two days later, October 26, that Seward went over to the French legation to discuss the note with Mercier. It was obvious from the start that he was trying to bargain for the opening of the blockade for a withdrawal of France's recognition of Southern belligerency.

First of all Seward complained about Anglo-French co-operation when the interests of the two countries were so conflicting, and he hoped that England did not know about this note. Since the United States had learned to manage without this trade, she might not renew it after the war if a lasting resentment were aroused. It was already the European encouragement of the South which had prolonged the war.

Mercier here broke in to say that, while the emperor entertained only sincere "good wishes" for the Union, Mercier despaired of any possible reunion. Therefore, if there were no relief in sight for France's desperate situation, she would have to find some remedy. Could the secretary suggest some form of relief? Seward's vague reply was that, if the United States once again had France's moral support, he was sure cotton could be made available. But Mercier demanded to know how the North would obtain cotton and more precisely what he wanted France to do in return.

Here Seward was a prisoner of his own "averted glance" because he could not ask France to give up her recognition of belligerency when he refused to admit that he knew about it. But he had already thrown out the hint. Also he could not be sure of finding cotton in the face of the Southern embargo. The conversation gradually sputtered out with a few Sewardian boasts about twenty million resolute people winning out over ten million differing inhabitants.

Out of this long and exciting conversation Mercier noted several things. Seward would not have resort to a slave insurrection; he expected the Federal government to become strongly centralized; he was surprised and worried about Anglo-French co-operation; he counted on capturing a port and issuing licenses to trade; he might try to break Anglo-French cooperation by limiting his concessions to France; and he did not bristle at Mercier's lack of faith in the restoration of the Union.[36]

Seward reported the conversation to Dayton and admitted

that the cotton shortage presented a serious problem. An anticipated naval victory might solve the difficulty, he thought. In any case he was going to send a dispatch by a special messenger to help Dayton sound out France on her reciprocal concession.[37] It was evident that Seward was shifting the discussion to Paris where, perhaps, it would be less embarrassing to mention belligerency. In the next four days he worked on the long dispatch to Dayton which would be carried by the special messenger whom he had not yet chosen. This was the well-known instruction no. 75 whose terms would be revealed to Dayton and Thouvenel by the end of November.

The Weed-Hughes Missions

The special messenger of whom Seward spoke was to be Roman Catholic Archbishop John Hughes of New York City. The beginning of the plan for his special mission goes back at least to a request from Sanford in the month of May. Two weeks after his arrival in Paris he was begging Seward to send over special people who could promote the Union cause. "These green fellows who come over here to represent Uncle Sam [he wrote with his usual Sanfordian superiority] are for the most part here for the first time—are strangers in a strange land without acquaintances with people or language other than their mother tongue. Of what earthly use can they be at this juncture?"[38] This applied to Dayton as well as to others, and Seward's first attempted remedy was to send John Bigelow as consul general in Paris to devote himself more to Union public relations than to commercial affairs.[39]

Now that the battle with King Cotton was in full swing, he felt he needed to add to the informal public relations staff. At about the same time that Seward was dealing with Mercier's requests, he was trying to recruit some notable figures to go abroad. He asked Edward Everett, but he declined. The Episcopalian Bishop McIlvaine of Ohio agreed to go to England, but Seward wanted a Catholic clergyman to go to France. On about November 1 he called in Archbishop John Hughes of New York, a good friend of Seward's, but the cleric could not see how he could cancel some pressing engagements. While Seward stepped out of the room for a moment to confer with Count Gerolt of Prussia, Hughes talked earnestly with Thurlow Weed, a New York political leader and friend of the archbishop. The upshot was that Hughes agreed to go if Weed would accompany him. Weed consented, and on Seward's return Hughes accepted on that condition, a condition which did not arouse the enthusiasm of the secretary.[40] Seward had a long conversation with Hughes in which he outlined the importance of his job. He was to impress upon the French government and the emperor the need for France and England to maintain their impartiality in American affairs and the dangers of war, inevitable in case of intervention.[41] To inflate the self-importance of the archbishop, Seward added that he was going to confide to him an important message for Thouvenel and the emperor.

In his dispatch of October 26 to Dayton, Seward had not known who the special messenger would be, but on November 2 he revealed that it would be Archbishop Hughes. "As the Archbishop has the confidence of the President and myself, you may confer freely with him upon public affairs and may find his suggestions useful."[42] Then he turned to the preparation of his instructions to Hughes:

> You will repair to Paris; and will deliver to Mr. Dayton the dispatch herewith handed to you. You will on your way thither make yourself master of the contents thereof, by reading the copy which I confidently intrusted to you. You will confer with Mr. Dayton upon the subject; and explain to him verbally my views in desiring the fullest attainable knowledge of the disposition of the French Government, whether friendly or otherwise; and especially its views on the several questions set forth in my dispatch. At the same time you will be expected to do this in the most confidential manner, deferring in all cases to Mr. Dayton's judgment and acting as auxiliary to him only; as his cheerful consent, to the extent that he thinks your relations and associations in Paris, in Europe, may enable you to be useful. . . . While in Paris, you will study how, in co-operation with Mr. Dayton, you can promote healthful opinion concerning [our] great cause. . . .[43]

In another unusual move Seward went himself to New York and delivered his instructions to Hughes in person along with the secret instructions destined for Dayton and Thouvenel. Here there were further conferences with the three unofficial emissaries as to what they should endeavor to do abroad. These moves lead one to wonder why Seward took such precautions and used a special messenger for the first time in his communications with his ministers abroad. It certainly was not to flatter the vanity of the archbishop because he did not know who would be the bearer on the 26th when he announced to Dayton that he was going to use a special channel. It is more likely that he felt that this was a negotiation in which he might be able to split France from England. France's *quid pro quo* would be a rescinding of her recognition of the South's belligerency in return for an opening of the blockade. This would split her from England and force England to make the same concession in a separate negotiation in order to obtain the same benefit. Suspicious of British spy activities, especially on board a Cunard steamer, he was taking the precaution this time of forwarding his message to New York by hand and to Paris on the person of a venerable archbishop.

In the long run Hughes's partner, Weed, was to prove the most important of the three unofficial emissaries, but at the start he was rather shabbily treated by Seward, his fellow politician from New York. At the New York conference the secretary ungraciously observed that Mr. Weed was going voluntarily at his own expense. Mr. Minturn, a friend of Weed's, was angry at this remark and left the room. Later he gave Weed a check for $1000 and promised him more while he was in London.[44] Seward had not even furnished Weed a letter. Consequently Weed, while waiting for a later boat, wrote him the next day, after the archbishop had already gone on the "Africa," and asked if he should not also have letters of introduction. Otherwise was it advisable for him to go at all? Yet it was not fair to let the archbishop down after he had already departed. "If it is best that I should stay at home, say . . . and I will dismiss the whole matter and forget that it was even thought of."[45] Seward evidently abandoned his antagonistic whim and came to realize that he also needed this able contact man in the big fight that lay ahead. As a result he wired Weed immediately that letters would go to Dayton and would be there on Weed's arrival.[46] To Dayton he wrote:

> It is deemed important to the public interest that citizens of well-known high standing should visit Europe for the purpose of assisting to contradict the machinations of the agents of treason against the United States in that quarter. This opinion having been known to Thurlow Weed, Esq., of Albany, New York, the bearer of this communication, he has kindly offered his services, which, as he has the full confidence of both the President and myself, have been promptly and cheerfully accepted. It is not intended that he shall take part or interfere with your official proceedings.[47]

There were also letters to Adams, Russell, and Prince Napoleon.[48] A few days later Weed and Bishop McIlvaine left by another boat on a mission which was to involve combat with more than King Cotton. Just as they started out, the capture of Mason and Slidell, farther south off the coast of Cuba, was to precipitate another public relations battle abroad and was to greet them soon after their arrival in the form of the "Trent" affair.

Thouvenel between Hammer and Anvil

During the month and a half of waiting for a response from the United States on a proposed relaxation of the blockade, Thouvenel saw all the signs of a deteriorating economic situation in France. Rost and Yancey described conditions in early October as those of commercial and industrial depression, reduced government revenues from tobacco, unemployment, and labor unrest.[49] Thus "King Cotton" was beginning to press the fight right against Napoleon III's most sensitive spot—the turbulent working classes.

In addition to this a very poor harvest in wheat disturbed the food supply and government finance—all to the benefit of the Northern cause. Yancey and Rost admitted that the wheat deficiency amounted to the value of $200,000,000. Without the export of goods to the United States, France was having to use precious specie to make wheat purchases abroad. The price of

bread was going up, and this too was causing unrest. The Swedish minister reported that "the emperor returned to Saint-Cloud
and in the last two councils of ministers they have been giving
special attention to the economic and financial condition of the
country, which is in a bad way because of the American civil
war, the bad harvest, and the high price of bread."[50] One can
imagine Thouvenel's discomforture in these cabinet meetings
when all eyes turned to him to see what he was doing to ease the
situation.   Since Thouvenel in general held the line against the
pro-Southern sympathies of several of the other members of the
cabinet, at least he could feel some comfort in the fact that
"King Wheat" was beginning to loom on the horizon as an ally
against his foe "King Cotton."[51]

But it was not just the eyes of his cabinet colleagues which
were plaguing the French foreign minister in this moment of
crisis.   During the first two weeks of October there was a constant stream of manufacturers and delegations of chambers of
commerce to his office, all demanding that something be done
to open up trade again with the United States. Some wanted
mediation to end the war, others wanted recognition of the
South—that is, capitulation to "King Cotton"—still others
wanted intervention to break the "ineffective" blockade. Some
were urging a protection of their commercial interests in Mexico.[52] In addition to clamoring delegations there were also insistent petitions coming in from all parts of the country to
Thouvenel, to the emperor, and to the minister of commerce.
Bigelow wrote to Seward:

> The accounts from the manufacturing districts are already
> alarming. Petitions are already circulating through the princi-
> pal towns entreating the Emperor to endeavor to bring the
> American war to a close, as the continuation of it must be the
> ultimate ruin of various French industries. Several large firms
> at Marsey have been obliged to wind up during the last fort-
> night.[53]

The chambers of commerce of Lyons, Rouen, and Mulhouse
petitioned the emperor for "an immediate recognition of the
Confederate States, and the raising of the blockade."[54]

Finally Thouvenel's close friend and colleague, Rouher, the minister of commerce, under the pressure of these petitions sent the foreign minister an urgent letter. He expanded upon the severe suffering in the industries exporting silks, linens, cotton goods, leathers, and Paris variety articles. Also he described the crisis in cotton supply with increased prices and dwindling employment. Hours had been reduced one-sixth, and the workers were suffering most, just at the time when winter was coming on and public works were the hardest to undertake. Many companies were hesitating to load up with high-priced cotton because of the fear that the price would suddenly decline. As a parting shot he reminded Thouvenel: "It is for you to see what can be done to alleviate this situation."[55]

The foreign minister replied within a week. First of all, he reminded his colleague that he was not unaware of the serious economic situation in the country. He had already taken certain steps in urging the Washington government to do something to ease the situation. He enclosed his instructions to Mercier, which had expanded upon Thouvenel's concern for France's commercial plight. He had heard from Mercier, and the latter had already had a long talk with the Washington authorities. They were now awaiting a reply from Seward. In the meantime he had contacted England to see what they could do jointly about the situation, but England felt that we must be very cautious in dealing with the United States or they might lose more than they might gain. France did not have to act in the same way as England. "It is certain, however," he concluded, ". . . that we are also obliged to act with prudence if we wish to remain out of a conflict whose outcome cannot be foreseen, which does not allow us to discern yet to what side our real interests can make us lean positively."[56]

Indeed, this approach to England had been under way since October 3, when Thouvenel had sent a copy of his instructions for Mercier to Russell. The British cabinet had evidently taken it up on about October 17 along with petititions from their own manufacturers asking for the recognition of the South. As Thouvenel said, the decision was against any definite and hostile action at this time; and, as soon as the decision was made, Palmerston had an article published in the *Morning Post* which defended the English government on its wait-and-see policy.[57]

However, Thouvenel had some help from the French press in discouraging pressures in favor of intervention. Bigelow, whose job was to keep watch of the press and influence it wherever possible, wrote to Seward at this time that, because of France's dependence on American wheat, the press had let up on their anti-American tone. "I [Bigelow] have not read a single fling at the United States in any journal for a week, and two weeks ago I scarcely saw a journal without one. . . . At all events it does not look now [with the coming of the bad wheat crop] as if either England or France were likely to be in a condition voluntarily to make any enemies, especially on our side of the Atlantic." Yancey and Rost partially substantiated Bigelow by admitting that the Orleanist and "Red" Republican papers were pro-Northern. When the news came that Seward had defied European intervention by requesting the state governors to fortify their coasts, Bigelow said that "the press here observes a vigorous silence."[58]

Another aid for the Northern cause was Prince Napoleon, who had just returned from his American tour on October 11. He was received by the emperor at Compiègne where he was listened to with the greatest interest and where he strongly emphasized the probability of a Northern victory. During the following week he invited Dayton to the Palais Royal for dinner and on that occasion not only expressed his thanks for American hospitality but strongly supported the Northern cause.

> I not only wish success to the North in its present struggle [he said], but, I have no doubt at all but that it will be successful. I have no hesitation about expressing my opinion . . . anywhere and to anybody. . . . The communication printed in the London *Chronicle* [he said] . . . which assumed to give his views on conditions and prospects of the North as inferior to the South was without the least foundation. I have never made such a report to the emperor or so expressed myself to anybody.

His promise to spread the word in this critical hour was evidently fulfilled. Malakoff, the *New York Times* correspondent, reported that "Prince Napoleon declares to every one who wishes to hear him that 'the North is in the right and has all his sympathies; that the power, and the strength, and the greatness of the country lies in the North, and that the wicked and groundless rebellion must and will be subdued.' " This, Malakoff said, was making France and England delay any recognition of the South. Bigelow likewise reported back: "Prince Napoleon's words and hopes are all in favor of the North; he expects no speedy termination of the war but he says that America will emerge from the contest a great military power. My impression is that he advises an understanding between the French and American governments to be cultivated just so fast as the alienation of the American and English people increases." The prince's advocacy was particularly convincing, not only because of his high rank but also because he had made such a long and wide-ranging tour to both the North and South.

As a result of this princely testimony as well as of the wheat scarcity and the moderated tone of the press, Bigelow summed up the situation with considerable optimism. "France [he wrote], whatever may be the personal inclination of the Emperor, would not tolerate any 'transaction' with slavery. The French people have at last got hold of the true issue between the North and the South and now there is little or no feeling in favor of the South in any quarter."[59] Perhaps the pressures on Thouvenel from the industrial petitions had been eased by the attitudes of the other segments of the public; but, on the other hand, they had weakened his position in the face of Dayton and Seward when he should try to negotiate a relaxation of the blockade.

Having just experienced the hammer blows of French industry, Thouvenel now found himself on the hard, cold anvil of American resistance. After a two-weeks voyage Archbishop Hughes had arrived in Liverpool on November 20; and, although rather sick after such a trip at the advanced age of seventy, he proceeded to Paris on the next day. Two days were lost, however, as he tried to recover his strength before going to see Dayton. Finally, still somewhat shaky, he went to the legation on Saturday morning, the 23rd, and delivered Seward's dispatch to Dayton.   Here the cleric did not receive a very warm reception.

> He received me with great politeness [Hughes wrote].   After reading or glancing over his papers, some general remarks were made about matters and things, during which I could not help perceiving a certain amount of embarrassment on his part.   I understood it at a glance, and it was nothing more than what might have been expected under the circumstances. . . . Mr. Dayton took occasion to say, awkwardly a little in the manner of expressing it, that he did not feel disposed to introduce me to the Secretary of Foreign Affairs in this country.   I replied that I comprehended the delicacy of his position . . . that I could find abundant means to have an interview with him.[60]

Dayton did not give Hughes a chance to elaborate on Seward's views, and, treating him purely as a messenger, left no doubt that he was not going to have him share in the negotiations even by introducing him to Thouvenel.[61]

The American minister immediately announced to Thouvenel that he had just received an important dispatch by special messenger and would like an interview separate from the usual diplomatic reception day.   This the foreign minister granted for Monday, November 25.[62]   Four days before, Thouvenel had received a confidential personal note from Mercier about the dispatch of a special messenger, and another one from Montholon, consul in New York, identified the person as the archbishop and gave a detailed account of him.   Mercier had added that he thought Seward would try to explore Thouvenel's ideas and would not say more than what he had already said in Washington.[63]   For a moment Thouvenel was perhaps worried about the possibility that the New York archbishop was going to work up pro-Northern sentiment among the French bishops and create another pressure group to tie his hands in negotiations.   The clergy had given the government a great deal of trouble over the Roman question in the last legislative session, and the foreign minister did not want any new fuel to be added to the flames.   Consequently he had some investigations made as to Hughes's whereabouts and plans, and the first thing he seemed to talk about in the interview was the messenger rather than the message. As the archbishop related it: "He [Dayton] was quite surprised to find that Mr. Thouvenel was perfectly conversant with my movements—that . . . he knew everything about me." And then the French minister inquired anxiously: "How long is he going to remain in Paris? Does he intend to visit the provinces? Is he going to Rome?" While Dayton could not enlighten his questioner too much on these points, he saw he was going to have difficulty keeping the elderly clergyman in obscurity.

Then Dayton allowed the foreign minister to read a French translation of Seward's note. It was a long one and took much time; the first fourteen paragraphs were merely a repetition of the points in Thouvenel's previous note. Then, coming to Seward's reaction, he found that the secretary minimized the seriousness of the cotton famine in France. He felt that France was more in need of food [Northern wheat] and Northern purchases of French exports than of cotton imports. Next Seward dilated upon how the United States, France, and England formed one economic community, exchanging among each other raw materials, food, and manufactured goods. Virtually, the three nations [his note said], though politically divided, constitute only one great society or commonwealth. . . . Civil War in either country . . . retards the accustomed operating of industries in the other two countries." He went on to acknowledge commercial suffering from the Civil War but complained that it was the European powers who were prolonging the suffering by giving moral encouragement to the South. He did not say what it was, but was obviously referring to the recognition of Southern belligerency. These powers, he went on, would like to see a compromise which would divide the Union. But that would cause such disruption and resentment that the lines of interdependent trade would never be renewed. The United States was trying to use, in putting down the rebellion, only such means which would least harm the commerce of nations. That was why, so far, it was not making use of the powers to close the ports by decree. Likewise, while the blockade seemed necessary, the president still was considering seriously France's request for its relaxation. At this juncture Seward's opinion was that such a relaxation would weaken the North and help the South, especially if it had to be extended to all other foreign nations as well as France. He then complained that the French proposal did not specify the nature of Northern concessions, the type of products to be allowed through the blockade, or their quality, or the proportion among countries, or the period of time. There is no indication of what is to be used to pay the insurgent owners of cotton—whether gold, paper, luxury goods, or war supplies. "While these disadvantages to the United States are so manifestly probable," he continued, "Mr. Thouvenel does not favor us, except in the most general way, with any idea of the nature, form, or extent of the advantages which he supposes the United States are to acquire as equivalents for the concession." On the contrary, in the urgency of his plea lurked a threat of unfriendly action which would seem to belie all the concern for the Union's welfare which he had hitherto expressed. Seward could not conceive that European powers would intervene to come to the defense of slavery in a part of the United States. France had so far worked along with Great Britain, but on this question she had been so confidential in her approach that the Washington government did not know whether she was seeking a special concession or whether Washington could broach the subject to Great Britain as well.

Finally, Seward put several questions to Thouvenel: If the United States relaxed the blockade, would France continue to remain coldly indifferent toward the fate of the Union, or would she defend the cause of Union before other nations? Would the remaining blockade be challenged by France? Would France give shelter to Southern "pirates" in her ports? His replies to these queries would be given prompt consideration in Washington. Before closing his note, however, Seward suggested that the impending naval invasions of the coast might open ports without having to make special concessions. Yet, these questions revealed a desire for genuine concessions from the European side in return for the relaxation of the blockade and highlighted the problem of the status of the blockade if partial relaxation ensued.[64]

After a careful reading, Thouvenel replied that the note was

"of such a nature as to require reflection and mature consideration." Since it would also involve submitting Seward's ideas to
the emperor, he asked for a copy. However, Dayton hesitated
because he had not been authorized to leave a copy. Thouvenel
pointed out that he had not authorized Mercier to leave a copy
of his recent note either, and yet he saw that Seward had had a
full copy from the summary he gave in this note. He promised
not to make a copy of it but only to have it for reference as a
personal loan and not as an official submission, and Dayton
could hardly refuse in the face of these logical arguments. Yet
Thouvenel must have made a copy because he sent one on to
Mercier.

During the conversation Dayton brought up the possibility
that some ports would be opened by being captured, since news
had just arrived of successful landings at Port Royal. "Yes,"
Thouvenel remarked dubiously, "but will the South sell cotton
through these ports?"

"If it turned out that they would not," Dayton replied, "it is
something for which *we*, at all events, are not responsible."

"Yes, I suppose you are right. At any rate I hope I may be
able to have another conference with you at an early date."[65]

The French foreign minister confided to Mercier his first impressions of the note. He thought France was a better judge of
her own crisis than was Seward. Since France would have to
resort to some urgent action, it was up to the United States to
suggest a remedy in order to avoid this action. Thouvenel
claimed to be puzzled about how France could give any more
moral support to the North than she was already doing. The
French government had made public statements of sympathy for
the survival of the Union, and the French press had followed the
same line. Nevertheless, the French minister did not think they
could condone an ineffective blockade or a paper closure of ports
without violating international principles held in common by
both France and the United States. In all this he must have pretended not to take the hint about withdrawing belligerency
recognition.[66]

Dayton, in his reflections on the conversation, revealed a little more of the American anvil on which Thouvenel was placed. France, he said, needed bread and exports much more than cotton, and her statesmen realized that a Northern embargo on exported wheat or imported French goods would hurt them more than the lack of cotton. Therefore the American minister reassured Seward on the chance of France taking forceful action.[67]

The Suspension of the Cotton Negotiations

Only two days after Dayton's long conversation with Thouvenel the news of the "Trent" affair hit Paris like a bombshell. From that time on for a month and a half Thouvenel was too busy with cabinet meetings, conferences, and correspondence dealing with that Anglo-American war threat to be able to pursue very seriously the negotiations on cotton. Since Seward's note had revealed how complicated was the question of a relaxation of the blockade and how vulnerable was France's position, it may be that Thouvenel had lost interest in it anyway. Five days after the first conference—on November 30—Dayton wrote: "Mr. Thouvenel has not yet signified to me a desire for a further conference. . . . It is not improbable that the existing events of the last week may affect or modify in some way the views of the Government here."[68]

Finally on December 6, in the interview dealing mainly with the "Trent" affair, the French foreign minister did bring up the cotton negotiations. Handing back the copy of Seward's note, he remarked that France had not been asking for any special favor for herself in her request for open ports and would be bound by law to insist on an effective blockade. When Dayton asked if he had no further answers to give, Thouvenel replied that he did not know "whether or when" he would have anything to add. Dayton's impression was that nothing more would be done at least until after the "Trent" affair had been settled.[69]

Seward received this note on the Christmas day when the Washington cabinet was meeting to make its decision on the "Trent" affair. After the bigger question was settled, Seward wrote Dayton in regard to the cotton negotiation: "Important events roll on so rapidly, each crowding the other so entirely out of view, that this Government can see no reason to desire any further prosecution of the subject opened in those papers."[70] In France there seemed to be a like inclination to drop the matter because as late as January 20, 1862, Thouvenel was still reported to be silent on the question of opening ports even though Dayton was noting that the economic situation was getting worse and the suffering of the working classes in the industrial centers had become more acute.[71] The "Trent" affair may have been settled, but the problem of trade was becoming more prominent with the passing of time and was going to lead to a more menacing episode in the year 1862.

There is no doubt that France, from the start, was badly hit economically by the American Civil War.[72] In 1861 the pinch came particularly in the exporting industries and led Thouvenel to take Mercier's advice and make an exploratory approach to the United States on the relaxation of the blockade. By Seward's reply and other information the French foreign minister was rewarded for his exploratory efforts. He could see that the question of blockade relaxation was not a simple matter. What would it do to the sanctity of an effective blockade? Could France find a satisfactory concession to make for a favor granted— since the North had every legal right to have an effective blockade? Would not the rescinding of belligerent recognition be too great a price to pay and also encounter the refusal of England? After all, was it not the South's embargo more than the blockade that interrupted cotton? As to veiled threats to the United States, did they not merely evoke equally ominous threats from Washington of a Northern embargo of wheat and a prohibition of French goods, which would wreak more havoc than the temporary loss of cotton and the export markets? Alas, a wheat scarcity could not have come in a worse year for France. Thus for a time Thouvenel did not move beyond his initial exploratory query. He could tell his colleagues he had made an effort, but he would do better to wait to see how military events developed in America, how many ports were captured by the North, and how much cotton emerged from these ports. Now that England had been satisfied by the "Trent" decision of the

North, it would not be likely that she would soon join in a force-ful breaking of the blockade, and France certainly would not act alone. Hence the "Trent" affair also contributed to the trade impasse, and it is to the story of that affair that we must turn at this point.

Chapter VI
FRANCE AND THE "TRENT" AFFAIR

TO the questions of international law concerning the blockade and the Declaration of Paris was now added another involving search and seizure on the high seas, and raised by the Federal seizure of two Confederate diplomats, Mason and Slidell, on board the British ship "Trent" on November 8, 1861.

The Departure of Mason and Slidell

As early as March 16, even before hostilities had begun, President Davis had appointed William Yancey, Pierre Rost, and Dudly Mann as a roving Confederate commission to European countries to seek aid and recognition.[1] However, all during the summer months they had accomplished nothing in the direction of British and French recognition of Southern independence and had felt themselves snubbed by government circles in London. Also the Civil War now appeared as one of long duration and therefore required that the Confederacy have more permanent envoys to specific European capitals.[2] Consequently, in August, Davis decided to send James M. Mason and John Slidell to Great Britain and France respectively and to reassign the earlier commissioners.[3] In retrospect, because of attendant circumstances to be described below, one is also left with the suspicion that Confederate officials, in addition to their ostensible purpose for the double mission, had a secondary and ulterior objective of laying a trap deliberately to force England into war against the North by exposing this new mission to the possibility of Federal capture on a neutral British ship. The Confederate government allowed a month and a half to elapse between the announcement of the appointment of the commissioners and their departure, and no one made any attempt to keep the mission secret. "It was publicly and widely commented on by the Southern press," says E. D. Adams, "thereby arousing an excited apprehension in the North. . . ."[4] Both the French minister in Washington and the French consul in Charleston mentioned the new emissaries almost two weeks before their departure.[5] Therefore there were speculations on both sides of the ocean, well in advance of their sailing, as to the probabilities of their capture. In London, Lord Russell was consulting his advocate general in advance on the legal technicalities of visit and search in anticipation of possible trouble caused by the crossing,[6] while far away, in the harbor of Havana, Captain Wilkes of the U.S.S. "San Jacinto" was searching for legal justification for the seizure of these news-worthy diplomats.[7] Even Mason and Slidell themselves, complaining of their delayed departure from Charleston because of storms and a tighter blockade, admitted that "such sudden and unusual accessions to the blockade of the port made us infer . . . that our presence here and purpose had reached the enemy, and we were the cause of the unusual preparation we witnessed."[8]

Finally the two men ran the blockade in front of Charleston during the night of October 11–12 on the chartered ship "Theodora," and arrived in Havana on the 22nd.[9] While awaiting the British ship "Trent," Mason and Slidell made no secret of their voyage plans. Indeed, according to several accounts, they fraternized with the officers of the "San Jacinto," which was lying in wait in the harbor. Flahault, the French ambassador in London, reported this account, told to him by Lord Russell: "The 'San Jacinto' which had pursued them, had also arrived there [at Havana], and the envoys, thinking that they were perfectly safe, invited its officers to lunch, and on that occasion told them that, as they planned to take the English ship, they were free from any worries about arriving at their destination."[10] On the other hand Attorney General Bates heard from two different sources that, at a dinner on board the "San Jacinto," Mason and Slidell had made a deal with Captain Wilkes to capture them in just the way it took place.[11]

On November 7 the two men left Havana on board the

"Trent," and the next day the "San Jacinto" stopped the "Trent" in the Bahama Straits. Its boarding party removed the two emissaries and their secretaries from the ship, taking them back to the United States as prisoners. During the dramatic episode on board the "Trent" two lively scenes took place which tend to confirm suspicions. Lieutenant Fairfax from Virginia was one of the "San Jacinto" officers who had been a guest of the Slidells at Havana, and it was he who had the embarrassing task of making the seizure on the high seas. Flahault tells us further that "when Miss Slidell saw them [these officers] again on the deck of the ship, she lashed out at them and cried, 'You are spies, traitors, you have violated our hospitality, you only deserve to be scorned!' "[12] The second scene is described by the purser of the "Trent":

> A most heart-rending scene now took place between Mr. Slidell, his eldest daughter, a noble girl devoted to her father, and the Lieutenant. . . . With flashing eyes and quivering lips, she threw herself in the doorway of the cabin where her father was, resolved to defend him with her life, until, on the order given to the marines to advance, which they did with bayonets pointed at this poor defenseless girl, her father ended the painful scene by escaping from the cabin by a window, when he was immediately seized by the marines and hurried into the boat.[13]

However, subsequent reflection on this sensational incident suggests the possibility of a different interpretation. The two envoys, instead of hiding, came right forward on deck and identified themselves to the boarding officers. After a formal protest they willingly hurried below to pack their baggage, and it did not seem to take them long to do the repacking. When Miss Slidell's resistance seemed to be delaying the anticipated outcome, Slidell climbed out the cabin window in order to surrender himself to his would-be captors. On his journey to Boston on board the "San Jacinto," Mason wrote home to his wife, telling about the friendly and courteous treatment they were receiving from Captain Wilkes, who was even arranging for the forwarding of the letter. Then he added:

As to all questions arising from the circumstances attending our capture, it would not become me to discuss them here. . . . Of course there will be all sorts of conjecture in the newspapers concerning our capture and its consequences, but I have only to say, my dear wife, that you should not permit your mind to be affected by them, and draw no other inference from my silence concerning them. . . . I was never in better health in my life, and in no manner depressed. . . .[14]

Mrs. Slidell and her daughters, who went on to England, do not seem to have been as reticent. From London, Weed reported to Seward: "The females of the caged Traitors left the impression that the catching was voluntary. The secessionists in Paris were certainly jubilant over it."[15]

"Malakoff" of the *New York Times* confirmed Weed's impressions as far as the French public was concerned. In his article of December 20 he said that there was a general belief among Parisians that it was a secessionist plot to have the two emissaries captured on a British vessel. The French were saying that the sending of two more commissioners when the South already had three in Europe, their travel on a British ship, the publicity given to the mission, England's anticipation of impending trouble, and the elation, rather than indignation, of the Southerners in Paris over their arrest, all pointed to an ulterior motive behind the whole affair.[16]

When the news of the arrest broke in Washington, the Austrian minister, Hülsemann, echoed the suspicions current in the diplomatic corps in reporting that "Mr. Davis and his supporters had no doubt imagined that England and France would take advantage of the first pretext to assure the permanent destruction of the Union; and right now they still count on the consequences of the arrest of Slidell and Mason on board the English steamer."[17]

Indeed, the Southern reaction to the eventual release of the two men seemed to confirm this suspicion. Paul, the French consul in Richmond, wrote to Thouvenel:

The release of Messrs. Slidell and Mason has greatly upset [*consterné*] the South. The government of the Confederate States was hoping for a war between England and the United

States, and, as a consequence, the raising of the blockade. The outcome of the "Trent" affair had not been expected. They count now on later complications. According to the opinion of Mr. Jefferson Davis' cabinet, the English Government has not obtained all the satisfactions that it has a right to demand for the honor of its flag. Besides they complain about the way Lord Lyons treated their commissioners. . . . Their disappointment is complete and their pride is hurt.[18]

The same disappointment was openly avowed by Slidell in his later interview with Napoleon III in July 1862. When the emperor brought up the subject of the "Trent" affair, Slidell reported:

I took this occasion to say that I regretted not to have had an earlier opportunity of presenting on behalf of my wife and children my thanks for his friendly interposition, to which I mainly attributed my release, but that I had always regretted it, because if we had not been given up, it would have caused a war with England, which would have been of short duration, and whatever might have happened to myself, the result must have been advantageous to our cause.[19]

The Confederate government had good ostensible reasons for sending Mason and Slidell to Europe. However, since the main purpose of their missions was to obtain recognition by England and France and the raising of the blockade and since these could more surely be accomplished by an Anglo-American war, it seems reasonable to assume that Davis and his cabinet had thought of their envoys' travel on a British ship as an additional opportunity for attaining the desired goal. Furthermore, the evidence from the time of the two men's appointment to the aftermath of their release seems to confirm this assumption. In the early weeks of the "Trent" affair there was a great deal of suspicion that Seward had deliberately ordered the seizure in order to precipitate a war with England. When this suspicion was scotched by the North's release of the commissioners, it still seemed to have lingered on as a smoke-screen to obscure from later historians the more plausible suspicions of the Southern origins of the affair.

The Early French Reaction

After the seizure of Mason and Slidell the "Trent" had continued its voyage to St. Thomas, where most of its passengers, including Slidell's wife and daughters, transferred to the "La Plata," bound for England. It was not until the morning of November 27 that the latter vessel arrived at Southampton, from whence the news of the "Trent" affair spread very rapidly throughout England and the European continent.[20]

Thouvenel, the French foreign minister, received the news under very troubled circumstances. Having just returned to his duties after a siege of fever,[21] he had found himself beset with difficulties involving Italy, the papacy, an Austrian move into Herzegovina, as well as the North's withdrawal of the exequatur of the British consul at Charleston.[22] With these problems in his dispatch case he had had to travel that day forty-five miles to Compiègne to attend a cabinet meeting at the emperor's palace. In addition to all of this, when the sick and weary minister returned to the Quai d'Orsay late that evening,[23] he found a telegram awaiting him which was to give him many more headaches during the coming weeks. The message was from Flahault in London, sent at 6:20 P.M., and reported:

> The government of the queen has received the news that an English ship which was bringing to Paris and London the envoys of the States of South America [sic] has been stopped by a ship of the United States and that the two envoys have been seized and taken off. The British government has summoned the captain of the ship in order to obtain an exact account, and then plans to consult the law officers of the crown.[24]

To such a diplomatic expert as Thouvenel the implications of this incident were immediately recognized. Something of this sort might happen next to a neutral French ship. What would France do in such a case? The British lion would certainly roar at this brash twist of its tail; indeed, it might lead to an Anglo-American war. And this again involved France because France and England had agreed to act together in dealing with American affairs during this civil war.[25] Now France had to decide whether she would merely support the English position, or go as far as outright war against the United States, or offer mediation, or remain silent. Support to England at this time might also help to strengthen English reciprocal cooperation in the new Mexican venture, which had just been launched by France, England, and Spain. These and many other thoughts must have filled the French minister's mind as he left again for Compiègne the next day, November 28, to attend still another cabinet meeting, where this new topic intruded itself upon the agenda.[26]

What goes on in a French cabinet meeting can be inferred only in a fragmentary way. But we can surmise that Thouvenel discussed how the American seizure of Mason and Slidell violated the French concept of neutral rights. He probably recommended that France should write a note to defend her principles before such an incident occurred to a French vessel and that this note should carry on the policy of cooperation with Great Britain and make that country feel obligated to France—all without committing France to go to war. After some discussion and speculation on what the British reaction to the seizure would be, it was probably decided to approve the sending of a note. Discussion may also have extended to the contingency of England's recognition of the Confederacy. In that case there was a strong inclination in the cabinet to support England with a French recognition. Two days later Dayton reported:

> I have just learned from what would, under ordinary circumstances, be held good authority that Monsieur Persigny, Minister of Interior, informed the Marquis of Hertford at breakfast yesterday morning [November 29] that a Council of State[27] had been held on the preceding day (Thursday) at which it was resolved to *recognize* the Confederate Government.[28]

Yancey, Rost, and Mann—the three earlier Confederate commissioners—heard that "the opinion of the Emperor of the French and that of his Ministers is, that the affair of the *Trent* is a great outrage upon the British flag";[29] while Lord Cowley had information that the French "Minister of Marine seems . . . to be itching to take part with us."[30]

Not until later in the evening of the 29th, on his return from the second cabinet meeting at Compiègne, does Thouvenel reveal to us his feelings and those of the cabinet on the question of the "Trent." In an anxious private letter to Flahault he wrote:

> Everything else loses importance in the face of the ominous incident which has arisen in the relations of the United States and England. In order to know whether we will have to play, as a power interested in preserving neutral rights, a direct and active role, I must know how the law officers of the crown, and the English government itself, look upon the various questions involved in the halting of the "Trent," as well as in the seizing of the envoys of the Southern States. In any case, even should we look upon it only as an insult to the British flag—because of our [British and French] disagreement on the doctrines on the extent of the right of visit and on the definition of articles of contraband of war—still leave no doubt as to where we stand. In substance as well as in form we consider the Americans to be in the wrong, and our opinion, boldly expressed through our minister in Washington, to whom I will write next Thursday [December 5], will give moral support to Lord Lyons' instructions.[31]

Here we see that as early as one day after the arrival of the news the French cabinet had decided to support Britain in the "Trent" affair and to send a strong note of condemnation.

A week was to elapse before Thouvenel's courier would leave for New York, and during this interval he tried to inform himself as much as possible before writing his "Trent" note to Mercier in Washington. First of all, on November 30, he received full information from Flahault on the British decision and England's demands for satisfaction from the United States.

> He [Russell] authorized me [Flahault] to tell you that the law officers of the crown had declared that the way in which the captain of the American vessel had acted, in the affair of the ship "Trent," was contrary to international law and that, no matter how you stretch belligerent rights over neutrals, nothing authorized him to act the way he did. The English ministry, in yesterday's cabinet council, therefore decided to instruct

Lord Lyons to request Washington to release the seized persons immediately . . . and, further, to make an apology to the British government for the insult to the English flag. This decision was sent to the queen and approved by her. Lord Lyons will be ordered, in case all the demands are not met, to ask for his passports and leave Washington.

Lord Russell expressed great appreciation for the assurance I gave him that our minister in Washington [Mercier] would be instructed by you to give moral support to Lyons' demands.[32]

When Thouvenel saw Cowley for the first time after his return to Paris, he told him that "as far as my approbation has any value in the eyes of Her Majesty's Government, I highly approve [the British note]."[33]   In addition to Cowley, he also had a chance to talk with representatives of other maritime powers, all of whom agreed with him that Captain Wilkes had violated international law.[34]

The French foreign minister also heard disturbing rumors that the Northern government had deliberately ordered the seizure of Mason and Slidell in order to goad England into a war.   General Scott, who had just arrived in Paris, was reported to have said that he was present when the Washington cabinet decided on the action and that he had then been sent to France to make a Franco-American alliance against England.[35]   The falsity of this rumor, however, was revealed to Thouvenel by two other pieces of news which followed soon after.   A Reuters report, appearing in the London *Times* of December 2 and in the *Constitutionnel* of the 3rd, gave the first news that Wilkes had not been given instructions to seize the men.[36]   The second piece of evidence to contradict the rumor was a letter published by General Scott himself on December 4.   Bigelow, the American consul general in Paris, had been worried about the effect on French opinion of the "Trent" and the rumor about General Scott.   On hearing his defense of the Northern position, Garnier-Pagès urged him to put his arguments into an article for publication.   Instead of doing this, Bigelow hurried to see Thurlow Weed at his hotel, and these two public relations men hit upon the scheme of having General Scott himself sign a prefabricated letter.   While Weed rushed off to persuade Scott, Bigelow worked furiously on the composition of the letter. General Scott signed it that afternoon—probably November 29—and Bigelow had it immediately translated into French and published in the *Constitutionnel* and the *Universel* on December 4.[37] The letter which the French minister read that morning in the city papers contained the following reassuring passages:

> You were right in doubting the declaration imputed to me that the Cabinet at Washington had given orders to seize Messrs. Mason and Slidell, even under a neutral flag, for I am not aware that the Government has ever had that point under consideration. At the time of my leaving New York it was not known that the *San Jacinto* had returned to the American seas; and it was generally supposed that those persons had escaped to Cuba for the purpose of reembarking in the *Nashville*, in pursuit of which vessel the *James Adger* and other cruisers had been dispatched.
>
> I think I can satisfy you in a few words that you have no serious grounds for concern about our relations with England, if, as her rulers profess, she has no disposition to encourage the dissensions in America.
>
> . . . You may rest assured that an event so mutually disastrous as a war between England and America cannot occur without other and graver provocation than has yet been given by either nation.[38]

Although the reaction of the French press to the Scott letter came after the composition of the French note to the United States, there was a clear response in the press to the early news of the "Trent" affair during the five days preceding the note. The three notably pro-government papers—the *Constitutionnel*, the *Patrie*, and the *Pays*—were strongly hostile to the Northern action in the "Trent" case. The *Constitutionnel* thought that Mason and Slidell had just as much right to go to Europe to advocate the Confederate cause as Thurlow Weed, recently arrived, had to defend the Northern side and affirmed that Great Britain had international law on its side. If the affair is settled by an American concession, France will thus gain a British recognition of the Franco-American interpretation of international law; if war should come, France would get cotton and a Southern market for goods. Hence the *Constitutionnel* at this point did not seem very alarmed.[39] The *Patrie* on November 29 approved the British attitude and urged other maritime powers to support England in the affair. Mason and Slidell, according to this paper, had the right of asylum aboard a British ship. Wilkes could not commit such an act in the Bahama Channel any more than in the English Channel.[40] The *Pays* and the *Presse* were also sympathetic with the British position.[41] On the other hand the Orleanist *Journal des Débats* showed more sympathy for the Northern side in the dispute. At the first news it reserved its opinion; then on the following day it condemned the seizure while still maintaining its sympathy for the United States. On December 1 Louis Alloury, writing in the *Débats*, remarked regretfully that, whoever was to blame for the incident, it would weaken the just sympathies for the Northern cause. On the next day Xavier Raymond in the same *Débats* twitted England on changing her position on international law. "To repent was very fine and very virtuous, without doubt."[42] However, Forcade in the Orleanist *Revue des deux mondes* called Wilkes's action an "incomprehensible provocation" and feared a British recognition of the South and a breaking of the blockade.[43] Yet the more conservative and ultramontane *Correspondant* said that what Wilkes did might have been a mistake but not a crime and raised the question of the guilt of the English captain of the "Trent" who, in violation of the queen's proclamation of neutrality, allowed the transportation of Southern dispatches on his ship.[44] Nevertheless, in spite of these sympathetic expressions for the North, both John Bigelow and Thurlow Weed summed up the views of the French press and public with great pessimism. To Seward, Weed wrote that he was trying "to turn back the tide of opinion which is working so strongly against us."[45] Bigelow recorded later in his memoirs that the incident so demoralized the friends of the North that very few any longer expected the reconstitution of the Union.[46] Lord Cowley likewise confirmed these views on the French public's unfavorable reaction to the United States. In writing to Russell, he reported: "As far as I am able to form a judgment the public feeling of this country [France] is certainly with England in this awkward affair of the Trent, and I am happy to see that the calmness and decision evinced by Her Majesty's Government and the people of Great Britain . . . in demanding ample reparation of the insult offered our flag has made a great impression here."[47]

The French Note

Thouvenel's early decision to write a note supporting Great Britain was not changed by the information he had received by December 3rd. He agreed with the British law officers and the terms of the British note. The predominantly condemnatory sentiment of the French public against the North encouraged him to persist in his decision. Yet, he inclined to use discreet and moderate language toward the North because he began to sense that it might be reasonable in giving the British satisfaction. Wilkes's admission that he had acted without instructions from Washington and Scott's soothing letter to the same effect confirmed this hopeful prospect. No doubt on Friday, November 29, he began his usual consultations with advisers and legal councillors[48] on this thorny question,[49] and he may have left instructions on that day for a draft note to be drawn up by his staff over the weekend while he was away in the country.[50] On his return on Monday, December 2, he no doubt put the finishing touches on the draft because it was already completed on the morning of the third when he saw Lord Cowley and told him he approved the British note, a copy of which Flahault had sent him. "He informed me at the same time," the British ambassador reported, "that he was about to send for the Emperor's approbation a draft of instructions for M. Mercier." The French minister then read the draft to Cowley, and the latter expressed England's gratitude.[51] The emperor approved the note on the following day, and Thouvenel sent it to Mercier, as planned, by the courier of December 5.[52]

An interesting side-light on the conversation Thouvenel had with Cowley on the fifth was his revelation of Napoleon III's own statement of support for the British. "He showed me also [wrote Cowley] the Emperor's letter to him when H. M. [His Majesty] was informed of your [Russell's] intentions with regard to the United States. H. M. says that the measures of the British government have his entire approbation and that Thouvenel is to assure them of H. M.'s full sympathy to the end."[53]

Thouvenel's note to Mercier on the "Trent" affair was one of the most important statements made by France on the American Civil War and turned out to be crucial for the American decision (*see* below). For these reasons it seems appropriate that it should be here reproduced in full.

My dear Minister, the arrest of Messrs. Mason and Slidell, on board the English mail steamer "Trent" by an American cruiser, has produced in France, if not the same emotion as in England, at least an extreme astonishment and sensation. Public opinion has also been concerned about the legality and the consequences of such an act, and the impression made upon it has not been for one moment in doubt. The event appeared to it to be so much in violation of the ordinary rules of international law that it was led to lay the whole responsibility upon the commander of the "San Jacinto." We are not yet in a position to know whether that supposition is well founded or not, and the government of the emperor ever since then had also had to examine the question of the removal of the two passengers from the "Trent." The desire to prevent perhaps an imminent conflict between two powers for whom it is animated by equally friendly sentiments and the duty of protecting the rights of its own flag from any infringement and certain essential principles for the security of neutrals has, after careful consideration, convinced it that it could not, in this case, remain completely silent.

If, to our great regret, the cabinet of Washington was inclined to approve the conduct of the commander of the "San Jacinto," it would be either from considering Messrs. Mason and Slidell as enemies or as rebels. In both cases it would certainly be an unfortunate disregard of principles on which we have always found the United States to be in agreement with us.

In the first instance [as enemies] by what right might the American cruiser arrest Messrs. Mason and Slidell? The United States has agreed with us in a treaty concluded between the two countries that the flag covered enemy persons on board a ship unless it involved combattants actually in the service of the enemy. Messrs. Mason and Slidell were, therefore by virtue of this principle—for which we had never encountered any difficulty in inserting in our treaties of friendship and commerce— perfectly free under the neutral flag of England. Certainly it will not be claimed that they could be considered as contraband of war. What constitutes contraband of war is not precisely agreed upon, it is true, its limits are not absolutely the same for everybody, but as regards persons the special provisions found in the treaties dealing with combatants clearly define those who alone may be seized by belligerents. But, it is not necessary to prove that Messrs. Mason and Slidell could not be included in that category. There only remained, then, to justify their capture, the claim that they were bearers of official enemy dispatches. But it is here that it is necessary to recall a circumstance which dominates this whole affair and makes the conduct of the American cruiser unjustifiable. The "Trent" did not have as its destination any place belonging to either of the belligerents. It was taking its cargo and passengers to a neutral country, and furthermore it had taken them on board in a neutral country. If it could be claimed that under such circumstances a neutral flag did not completely cover the persons and goods it carried, then its immunity would be but an empty word: at any moment the commerce and navigation of third parties might have to suffer in their harmless or even indirect contacts with both belligerents. The latter would no longer just insist on a complete impartiality on the part of the neutral and forbid him any intervention in hostilities, they would instead impose on its freedom of trade and navigation restrictions whose legality modern international law has refused to accept. In other words we would be right back to the vexatious practices of earlier days against which no other power has protested more strongly than the United States.

If the cabinet of Washington saw the two arrested persons only as rebels to be rightly seized, this other question could not be decided any more readily in favor of the "San Jacinto's" commander's conduct. In such a case it would be a violation of the national territorial integrity of the country whose flag it flew and of the immunity from a foreign jurisdiction thereon. Certainly it is not necessary to recall the energy with which on all occasions the government of the United States has defended this immunity and the right of asylum which grows out of it.

Not wishing to enter into a more detailed discussion of the questions raised by the capture of Messrs. Mason and Slidell, I have said enough, I think, to prove that the cabinet of Washington cannot approve of the acts of the commander of the "San Jacinto" without violating principles whose respect all neutral powers are equally interested in assuring and without being inconsistent with its own conduct up to now. Under these circumstances, as we see it, there is obviously no reason for us to hesitate on what our decision will be. Lord Lyons is instructed to present the demands for satisfaction which the English government finds necessary to stipulate and which provide for the immediate release of the persons removed from the "Trent" and for the furnishing of explanations which will remove from the incident any character offensive to the British flag. The Federal government would be showing a just and lofty attitude if it deferred to these requests. One would search in vain to find in what interest, for what objective, it would risk provoking a rupture with Great Britain by a different attitude. For us who would see in this latter outcome a most deplorable complication of the difficulties against which the cabinet of Washington is already contending and a precedent of a nature to disturb all the powers outside the present conflict, we believe we are giving proof of our loyal friendship to the cabinet of Washington if, under these circumstances, we do not refrain from expressing our views.

I therefore invite you, Sir, to take the earliest occasion to have a frank talk on this with Mr. Seward, and, if he asks for it, to give him a copy of this despatch.[54]

Even before the courier left for the United States, Thouvenel sent a copy of this note to London to be read to Russell, and in the accompanying note to Flahault he reiterated his support of the British position:

. . . We saw with regret the trouble it [the incident] caused to Her Majesty's government and the complications it added to those already resulting from the American conflict. Besides, we could entertain no doubt nor feel any hesitation in our views on the question of right. To see it from the point of view of the cabinet in London, we have only to refer to our own traditions.[55] Guided also by a desire to contribute as much as we could to facilitating the settlement of this difficulty, we thought it would be useful to inform the cabinet of Washington without delay of the views we had on the conduct of the commander of the "San Jacinto" and to present to the secretary of state of the Union the reasons which, we thought, justified the rightful resentment of the English cabinet.[56]

European Reaction to the French Note

Flahault read the full text of Thouvenel's note to Russell on December 6, and the latter showed deep appreciation for the French support. "Neutral rights," he said, "could not have been defended more ably or more eloquently." "Please tell M. Thouvenel how much I and all the government of the queen are moved by the action which he was so kind to take and the support given us by the emperor's government in these circumstances."[57] At Russell's request a copy was later communicated to him and in turn shown to Palmerston. "He [Russell] and Lord Palmerston are both very moved by this mark of confidence," wrote Flahault, "[and] I have reason to believe that the principal purpose of their request [for a copy] was to read to the queen a dispatch which appeared to them to be peaceful."[58]

Later, when the full text of the note had been made public on about December 23, the British press's response was generally favorable. The London *Times* said that Thouvenel's note indicated an honorable way for the United States to get out of her difficult position, and the *Daily News* was glad that England now had an outside authority supporting her position and no longer only that of her own law officers.[59] Thurlow Weed thought he saw an appreciative reaction by the British public. Speaking of Seward's assurance to Russell that Wilkes had not been instructed to make the arrests, Weed wrote: "Your dispatch to Mr. Adams, with the dispatch of Mr. Thouvenel, has partly settled the English mind for peace."[60] There was, however, at least one loud dissenting voice from a David Urquhart, who sent in a letter to the editor of the *Free Press*. This gentleman was obviously an old-line supporter of Britain's earlier practice of manhandling neutrals in time of war. With this attitude he had objected to Britain's earlier acceptance of the Declaration of Paris of 1856, which he called "the Capitulations of Clarendon." He was therefore indignant over Thouvenel's letter because, on the matter of international law, it seemed to be aimed against England as much as against the United States. Indeed, he thought it seemed to be quite sympathetic to the Northern states. In a long and rambling discussion Urquhart endeavored to point out many errors and inconsistencies. "The document is stamped with so unworthy a character [he protested] as to bar its introduction into a discussion. [It is] an assembly of phrases inapposite and incoherent, and into which are introduced terms that are nonsensical and statements that are false."[61] This obscure opinion, however, seemed to remain in obscurity as far as any public reactions were concerned.

Charles Francis Adams, the American minister in London, did suggest a view not unrelated to Urquhart's. In commenting on the Thouvenel note, he expressed the feeling that France, consistent with her own view of neutral rights, was attempting to bind England to a more liberal international law for neutrals.[62]

While the English reaction seemed generally favorable, Thouvenel was anxious to elicit support from the continental maritime powers. It was with this purpose in mind that he prepared a circular for all his diplomatic agents, condemning Wilkes's action, supporting England, and enclosing a copy of his note to Mercier for their use in discussing the subject with the governments to which they were accredited.[63] The response was not invariably what Thouvenel was seeking. The Austrian reaction was so favorable that Rechberg, the foreign minister, wrote a similar note to the United States.[64]

The Prussian reaction was quite as sympathetic. Upon hearing La Tour d'Auvergne, the French ambassador, read the Thouvenel note, Count Bernstorff, the Prussian foreign minister, seemed favorably impressed and said that he would send a similar note to Washington. La Tour also noted that Prussian opinion reacted favorably and would no longer believe the gossip that France had wanted to take advantage of an Anglo-American war.[65]

While the Italian prime minister, Ricasoli, called the note "stupendous," he was careful not to write the United States before the decision on the two men was made. "If I did not protest officially against the violent act committed on the 'Trent,' " he explained to D'Azeglio in London, "it was out of modesty." "Now France had made that stupendous note, and it would not have been very dignified and, I think, not very effective to have tried to imitate her."[66]

The Russian reaction to the French note was not only less sympathetic than that of the other powers, but actually somewhat ungracious. Fournier, the French chargé, left a copy with Prince Gorchakov, the Russian foreign minister, for communication to Emperor Alexander II. After several days had passed, Fournier sounded Gorchakov out on the Russian views on the note, and to his amazement, elicited a most recriminatory response. The Russian foreign minister accused France of sacrificing the American navy for the benefit of her rival, England, just as France had helped abolish the Russian fleet in the Black Sea. Certainly, then, Russia would not send a similar note but would hold to her friendly counsels sent earlier to the United States.[67]

In a conversation Fournier had with Gorchakov four days later on the same subject the Russian minister said that England was so pleased with Thouvenel's note that she was trying to get Russia to write a similar one. However, Gorchakov did everything he could to preserve impartiality and to avoid England's importunities. "I am sought after everywhere I go, even at the theater, and I have to dodge these attacks by all sorts of little tricks." Then the prince read Fournier a memorandum on the "Trent" affair which had been drawn up for him but which he was going to keep confidential. Here was a long exposition of the Russian view of the international law involved. He cited the case of the "Diane" during the Crimean War in which England had done the same thing as Wilkes and had kept the Russian diplomat a prisoner during the rest of the war. He cited other cases in which Henry Wheaton and Sir William Scott, American and British authorities respectively on international law, had agreed that enemy dispatches were contraband no matter under what circumstances discovered. Gorchakov also alluded to a speech of the Duke of Broglie in the French chamber of peers in which he questioned that the deck of a ship could be treated in all cases the same as national territory. Therefore, he concluded, there are many interpretations, and Russia was not going to be drawn into the controversy. Brunnow, Russian ambassador in London, had written to Stoeckl, his counterpart in Washington, a private letter to appeal to the United States against going to war with England. Gorchakov approved that unofficial letter, but he was not going to write one himself.[68]

On receiving the report of Gorchakov's adverse reaction to the French note, Thouvenel defended his policy by saying that the purpose of the note was to uphold France's doctrine of neutral rights—which were also Russia's—to contribute to a peaceful settlement of the dispute, and to reaffirm France's concern for the future of the United States. "Nothing in this action [he added] . . . is to imply that we are not entirely determined in advance to observe a complete neutrality in the conflict which might break out."[69]

The publication of Thouvenel's note on December 24 aroused a tremendous amount of discussion in France. It crowded other news off the front pages and stepped up the excitement over the "Trent" affair in political, financial, and commercial circles. Yet, even "Malakoff" in *The New York Times* admitted that the comments were all one-sided, that is, favorable to the note. A few asked timidly whether this was not interference in the war and a gesture of sympathy for slavery, but soon these thoughts disappeared as the public became convinced that it was a "moral intervention on the side of a common principle violated."[70] The *Pays*, close to the ministry of interior, at first asked the question whether the note could be considered as a prelude to intervention or mediation, but concluded that it was more truly a declaration of principles on international law and reservation of France's future freedom of action.[71] Another government paper, the *Presse*, claimed that if a peaceful solution resulted, it would be due to the note.[72] But the opposition papers were almost equally favorable. The Orleanist *Débats* thought Thouvenel's arguments were much sounder than those of the British law officers, who seemed to put the emphasis on the technicality of not taking the "Trent" into port for adjudication. An article by Alloury expressed the hope that the United States would now disavow

Wilkes and release the Southern commissioners; while another by Camus warned that, if Britain went to war, it might cause a great increase in American sea power.[73] The republican *Siècle*, while approving Thouvenel's arguments, regretted that he had stated France's position so absolutely that she could not serve as arbitrator of a dispute which was particularly a proper subject for peaceful settlement.[74] Alfred Assolant, editor of the *Siècle*, published a humorous pamphlet *Cannoniers, à vos pièces* in which he criticized the "Trent" action of the United States, and the Count of Gasparin in another pamphlet *A word of peace in the Anglo-American conflict* took the same anti-North stand on the "Trent."[75] One neutral observer in Paris, Frederik Due, the Swedish minister, said that "public opinion received the note with lively approbation," and he himself praised it for its logic, moderation, and dignity. He noticed that Englishmen in Paris were boasting that the note had done more to cement the Anglo-French alliance than anything else.[76] Viewing the reaction of all Europe to this newly published note from his London observation post, Charles Francis Adams noted that "the harmony of sentiment on this subject is so general throughout all Europe as to have very much increased the confidence of the British ministry in their position."[77] If Thouvenel had been cautious in watching public reaction to the "Trent" affair before he sent his note, he must have been particularly gratified that Frenchmen of all political colors, Americans of the North and South, and Europeans of England and the Continent—with the exception of Gorchakov—seemed unanimous in praising and approving his statement of French policy.

The Question of French Arbitration

During the first week of December the air was full of suggestions of arbitration as soon as it was learned that Wilkes had acted without instructions. Many United States citizens, living in Europe and seeing the aroused attitude of the British government and public, were anxious to see an arbitration of the dispute in order not to have the British sea power join the Confederate cause. On December 4 Adams received a suggestion from George Fogg and Norman B. Judd, the United States ministers to Switzerland and Prussia, that the United States ask Napoleon III to arbitrate the "Trent" dispute.[78] Six days before this, when Baron Brunnow, the Russian ambassador, first saw Adams after the "Trent" news, he offered the services of himself and his government for the removal of obstacles to a settlement. Adams thanked him without committing himself in any way.[79] Later Adams did send on Fogg's and Judd's suggestion of arbitration to Seward, as they requested, but he again did not commit himself nor did he mention France as the proposed arbitrator.[80] Likewise Thurlow Weed, recently arrived in Paris, had the same thought when he wrote to Seward that "if other things fail, is not this, ultimately, a fit question for referral to a Friendly power?"[81] Weed and Bigelow were in such constant communication that it is not surprising that Bigelow should mention Napoleon III's arbitration two days later, although without enthusiasm.[82] While the French press had mentioned here and there the possibility of French mediation in general between the North and South, there was not widespread discussion in December about mediating between England and the United States. The *Pays* and the *Siècle* favored it, but the *Constitutionnel* was opposed.[83]

The question of arbitration, especially French arbitration, went beyond the conversational stage, however, and two diplomatic efforts were made to bring it about. One of these grew out of a conversation between Sanford and Talleyrand, the American and French ministers to Belgium. Both of these men had been in Paris at the end of November when the news of the "Trent" had arrived. Sanford, in his ubiquitous meddlesomeness,[84] was present during the composition of the Scott letter for which he seemed to claim credit. He also pretended to have influenced the French press on the "Trent" affair, the jobs which Bigelow claimed to have done. At any rate Sanford's arguments were those of Bigelow, Scott, and the *Constitutionnel* to the effect that the United States did not want a war with England and that the dispute, hanging on an error of procedure over not taking the ship in for adjudication, could easily be settled peaceably.[85] At the same time Talleyrand had busied himself at the French foreign ministry where the ideas of the French note were in the process of development. Returning to Brussels at almost the same time, Sanford sought out Talleyrand and repeated to him these arguments, and Talleyrand in turn gave the American his "personal" opinion that France might give some advice to the United States but would not join England in destroying a friendly power. It was at this point that Sanford inquired whether France could not offer her mediation. Talleyrand replied that this was going a little fast, but that there would probably be a lot of writing back and forth between London and Washington and at the proper time France might find an opportunity to mediate. That evening the French minister wrote the proposal to Thouvenel in a private letter and sent it by special messenger.[86] Somewhat apologetically Talleyrand tried to play down the importance of this suggestion. "I could not [he wrote] refuse to give you a brief account of our conversation." Thouvenel received the letter on December 4, before the cabinet meeting at the Tuileries on the 5th,[87] where the next stage of the "Trent" question was under serious consideration. The Swedish chargé has left us a detailed account of the cabinet deliberations.

> According to the information I have received [wrote Adelswärd], this council meeting to which the public attaches some importance because of the concern aroused by the Anglo-American dispute, was rather calm. The emperor asked his ministers for their advice on the attitude France should take in the complications to which this dispute could lead. Count Persigny came out strongly for an accord with England. But this opinion was opposed by M. Thouvenel, who insisted on absolute neutrality. He was supported by Count Morny and M. Billault. (The presidents of the senate and legislative body were both present.) The majority of the council shared the views of the minister of foreign affairs. The emperor, as is his custom in such circumstances, did not join the discussion.[88]

Evidently Thouvenel did not bring up Sanford's proposal of mediation, although he did stress neutrality in case of an outbreak of war. After all, he must have realized that his note, in condemning the position of the United States, precluded the impartiality required of a prospective mediator.[89] At any rate no mediation offer emerged from the Sanford-Talleyrand effort.[90]

While Sanford had been rather cautious and circuitous in his efforts to enlist French mediation, his reverend compatriot, Archbishop Hughes, had fewer inhibitions. The archbishop had come over with Weed and General Scott, but received a cold welcome at the United States legation. In spite of all sorts of hinting he could not obtain Dayton's assistance in arranging an interview with the emperor. Finally Hughes wrote directly to Napoleon III: "Sir, I wish to have the honor of a conversation with you," and received an invitation for the day before Christmas.[91] With quite officious self-importance he confided to Seward that on his own responsibility he would propose "that the Emperor of the French should act as arbitrator in the dispute . . . provided that they would agree on the one side and the other to submit the controversy to his friendly decision." "He will, unquestionably, be reserved on the subject, but at all events I shall write you my interpretation of the results."[92] Finally the great day came, and the emperor, the empress, and the little prince imperial gave him a very cordial reception. The interview lasted for over an hour. At an appropriate place in the conversation Hughes launched into his arbitration scheme.

> *Hughes:* I implore Your Majesty to use your good offices in preventing a rupture between England and America by the interposition of your kind and potent offices as mediator.
> *Napoleon III:* The United States, as you know, has all my best wishes. However, in this matter I can not act as arbitrator because, whilst it would be competent for me, if invited by the parties, to assume that office on questions of a material kind, such as deciding upon disputed boundaries, as things now stand, it is not a question of boundaries and the like, but it would be determining a *point of honor*, on which arbitration, between two such nations, would not be, perhaps, satisfactory to either.

This seemed to be a very firm and positive answer, and the archbishop did not press the point further. Indeed, Hughes thought the emperor's distinction to be "plausible enough."

Thus the direct approach for French arbitration also came to an end.[93]

Napoleon III was right in anticipating that England would oppose arbitration. There had been at first some inclinations by a few Englishmen to consider such a peaceful settlement. John Bright suggested arbitration to the United States on December 5; Cowley timidly mentioned it to Russell on the 9th, and on the same day a group of English Quakers asked that the dispute "be submitted to a competent tribunal of able jurists."[94] Russell's answer to Cowley's suggestion was a flat no,[95] and the London *Times*, in a tone of ridicule, rejected the Quaker suggestion by reference to Thouvenel's note:

> A few sanguine people, in the overweening pride of their benevolence, have been pressing us to refer the insult we have received to arbitration. Their prayers are answered [by the Thouvenel note] before they could have hoped for such a fruition. The arbitration has already been entertained, and the award has gone out contemporaneously with our demand.[96]

The "Trent" Affair in America

While Europe was waiting impatiently and apprehensively for news of the United States' reaction or response to the British note, a great deal was happening on the American scene. The news of the capture of Mason and Slidell had arrived in Washington late on November 15. Mercier had seen Seward on that day, and the latter mentioned that the two Southern commissioners had been captured. He did not elaborate because he did not yet have the details. This news did not greatly impress Mercier because it seemed to be just another affair between the two contending sides in the struggle. The blockading vessels may have caught them on a Confederate ship.[97] However, on the following day he heard that they had been removed from the British packet "Trent," and Mercier's concern over the Anglo-French common front therefore grew with the realization of the seriousness of the incident. Seward had not liked the appearance of Anglo-French solidarity. If circumstances of the Civil War led to American hostilities against England, he hoped to keep France neutral or persuade her to become an ally. It was a desire for protection against Seward's wiles that had led to the solidarity, and there were moments when the two powers suspected that he was deliberately trying to alienate them. Now the "Trent" affair might be another such attempt to isolate France from England. Alarmed by the cheering crowds in the street, Mercier left his warm fireside, wrapped himself in his great coat against the damp chill of a November day, and hurried directly to the British legation. Lord Lyons, the British minister with whom he had collaborated so loyally, had no more details than Mercier, but they both agreed that Captain Wilkes was in the wrong. Later in the day Chevalier Bertinatti of Italy, Baron von Gerolt of Prussia, and Baron Stoeckl of Russia, each came to call on Lyons, discussing the incident in restrained excitement and all agreeing that the United States action could not be justified.[98] Lyons told Mercier that he was not yet sure in his own mind about all the legal aspects of the question and that he was not going to do anything about it until he received instructions. If Seward said something to him, he would minimize its seriousness and refrain from discussion. "Besides, he deeply regretted an incident which involved his government without France, which he should like to avoid more than all else, or in backing down see its prestige suffer another and a serious setback."[99] After two days of reconnoitering, Mercier sat down and wrote a long dispatch to Thouvenel. He had heard rumors that the Washington government had ordered the seizure, but the cabinet was seriously split over the incident. Some say that the right of the United States is incontestable, that they should stand up to England, and that she will back down. Others, among them General McClellan, think that it would be folly to start a war with England right at a time when the war against the South might take a turn for the better. England might be looking for a pretext for war, and this would be playing into her hands. Public opinion, Mercier thought, might tip the scale between these two sides and would probably be on the side of defiance.[100] Both Lyons and Stoeckl also had heard that Seward had ordered the seizure without the knowledge of President Lincoln. "I'm afraid," Lyons wrote to Russell, "that he

[Seward] is not sorry to have a question with us like this, in which it is difficult for France to take part."[101]

In the meantime the French and British envoys learned that Captain Wilkes admitted that he had removed Mason and Slidell without orders from the government.[102] Lyons was trying to keep out of Seward's way, but Mercier saw the secretary of state on November 23, when the latter kept silent about the affair.[103] Seward noticed that Lyons was keeping silent, and he resolved not to open the discussion until the British did. However, Seward did inform the British that Wilkes had no orders to take the two commissioners from the "Trent."[104] Later Mercier and Lyons found out from one of their diplomatic colleagues that Seward had been very subdued in his remarks for some time. He seemed neither very fearful nor very hopeful. On one thing he did make a comment—how awful for the whole world would be an Anglo-American war. Significantly he mused on what France's role would be in such a war.[105] When news arrived on December 13, telling of the violently hostile reaction in England to the "Trent" affair,[106] Mercier learned of a burst of temper by Seward at a White House tea on Sunday, the 15th. Seward bustled into the room in a state of high excitement. He had gotten advance word, he announced, of a peremptory British note on its way, which accused the United States of a breach of international law and insisted on an apology and the return of the captured men to the British. The secretary added that, while this news was unofficial, Lyons would soon confirm it. Thereupon Senator Browning exclaimed that they ought to have it out with England. Again the next night at a ball at the Portuguese legation, the secretary, perhaps excited by considerable imbibing, became more belligerent in his remarks. Once more he expatiated upon the horrors of an Anglo-American war. "We will wrap the whole world in flames! No power so remote that will not feel the fire of our battle and be burned by our conflagration."[107] This outburst was presumably to frighten the powers, including France, into pressing England to reduce her demands or to avoid war by arbitration. "You are going to say," wrote Mercier to Thouvenel, "that the Americans are crazier than you thought, and you will be right." He went on to recount the belligerency of American public opinion and how disastrous such a war would be for the United States.[108]

Now all attention was turned to the anticipated British note. Mercier saw Seward just before the note arrived and was glad to report encouraging news to Lyons. Seward had said with conviction: "We won't have war; big countries like England and the United States don't make war just for fun [*par passion*]." He was sure he could prevent the war, and Mercier was convinced the secretary would do all he could to that end. Mercier and Lyons were still fearful of the effect of public opinion on Seward and the other members of the cabinet. They were encouraged by the more sober attitude of business circles, which Seward himself hoped would help give reason the upper hand over passion. In answer to Mercier's anxious queries Lyons said the British note had not yet arrived, but it should be there by tomorrow [the 19th].[109]

In fact the queen's messenger carrying the British note had landed in Boston on the 17th, was in Baltimore on the 18th, and there took a special train, arriving in Washington at eleven o'clock that same evening. Lyons had time to digest it, have it copied, and read the two accompanying private letters from Russell before he saw Seward on the afternoon of the 19th. On his return he kept Mercier informed.[110] Lyons had not presented the note but had just let Seward know in a friendly and informal way that England wanted the release of the men and an apology. Then he added tactfully that England preferred to have the American government make the suggestions itself. Seward appreciated this considerate approach but asked to know informally whether a time limit had been set. Lyons replied that he did not want to have an appearance of threatening, but, if Seward would take the information as confidential, he would say that the time limit was seven days. The secretary again showed his appreciation for this confidence and then asked two more favors: to let him have a copy, unofficially, to study and discuss with the president and to delay the official presentation until Saturday (two days later). To this Lyons agreed and on his return to the British legation he sent Seward a copy in a sealed envelope marked private and confidential. Seward had hardly completed the reading of the note when he left his office and went himself to the British legation. Here he told Lyons how pleased he was "that the Despatch was courteous and friendly, and not dictatorial or menacing." Now he needed badly to know one more thing: whether Lyons would be allowed to accept a preliminary reply asking for discussion beyond the seven-day period. Lyons said he could not accept such an answer and, upon Seward's further prodding, admitted, again confidentially, that he would have to ask for his passports. The secretary thanked him and said he would take the whole matter up with the president on Friday.[111]

The Agonizing Delay of the French Note

There was now nothing more to do until Saturday, the 21st. But Mercier all along had been talking with Lyons about whether he could give England support in this affair in line with their cooperative policy. Two things had stood in the way: Lyons' self-imposed silence before the arrival of the British note and Mercier's own lack of specific instructions from home. Now on the 19th Lyons was no longer silent and in one of Russell's private letters, which came in the same mail, was an indirect hint of France's attitude. Russell had written: "M. Thouvenel promises to send off a dispatch on Thursday next giving our cause moral support, so that you may as well keep the dispatch a day or two before you produce it, provided you ask at once for an interview with Seward."[112] Mercier was much relieved to see he would soon have instructions, and Lyons said he was glad to give Seward the advance copy of the British note because "it will give time for the Packet (which is indeed already due) to arrive with M. Thouvenel's dispatch."[113] Now Mercier could present his note on Saturday, on the same day as Lyons' official presentation.

As previously agreed, Lyons went on Saturday, the 21st, to make the official presentation of the British note. Once more Seward asked for more time by having the presentation delayed until Monday, the 23rd, and again Lyons was glad to agree because the French note had not yet arrived.[114] However, both

Lyons and Mercier were afraid that Seward and Lincoln were already drawing up the reply to England.[115] Unless France spoke now, it might be too late. Yet, Thouvenel's note still had not arrived. Finally, Mercier volunteered to go and speak plainly to Seward on the basis of what Russell had said in his private letter. The conversation took place on the same Saturday, December 21st; their dialogue went something like this:

> *Seward:* Do you think Lord Lyons' departure would necessarily be followed by war?
>
> *Mercier* (sensing that Seward hoped France would prevent war after a diplomatic break): It is difficult to doubt it in view of the immense preparations being made in England. A delay appears impossible. England has evidently made a decision which allows for no postponement of action. However much the government of the emperor might regret seeing an outbreak of a war with such fearful consequences, it could not blame the British cabinet for following a line of conduct which the French government would certainly follow in similar circumstances. But, as I must suppose, from what you told me recently, that you are inclined to go as far in the direction of reparation as is necessary to avoid war, I think you can count on the government of the emperor to do all that it can to make this decision less painful. As for me, if you think that I can be of some help, either in my conversations with senators or other influential people or in my attitudes, to explain or justify a decision favorable to a peaceful settlement, feel free to call on me.
>
> *Seward:* Have you received any specific instructions from your government on this subject?
>
> *Mercier:* No, sir, I have not, but I expect some immediately, and I have no doubt whatever what they will be.
>
> *Seward:* I am most appreciative of your kind offer, but let us wait and see what your instructions turn out to be. They may perhaps be different from what you suppose.

Mercier told Thouvenel he was sure that Seward was delaying the presentation of the British note until he had the French note.[116]

From all of this it seems that Seward did not need the French note to persuade himself to make a favorable response to England. It might help him to choose capitulation instead of further negotiation, but above all it would be needed to persuade the cabinet, the president, and the public to capitulate. Hearsay with them would not suffice, they would require documentary proof. All of them now—Lincoln, Seward, Lyons, and Mercier—were anxiously awaiting the diplomatic pouch from France.

Saturday, Sunday, and Monday went by, and still no French pouch arrived. "The packet is unfortunately so late," Lyons wrote Russell, "that M. Mercier will not receive the promised instructions from M. Thouvenel until tomorrow, but I cannot have again put off communicating your dispatch to Mr. Seward without an appearance of vacillation which would have been fatal."[117] Consequently the British minister went over to the state department on Monday, the 23rd, and made an official communication of Great Britain's demands.

By this time Lincoln already knew of its contents as well as of Mercier's support. On this same day someone—probably Senator Sumner—had also brought the president letters from Bright, Cobden, and Lyndhurst, all strong friends of the Union and all urging the United States to right the wrong promptly. The president replied that "peace will not be broken if England is not bent on war." He also promised to go over Seward's draft and remove any strong language such as he had used in his former despatches. These assurances, however, did not mean that Lincoln was yet prepared to go the whole way in the satisfaction of the British demands.[118]

Lyons and Mercier kept in close touch with each other as they awaited Thouvenel's note, and the British minister showed evident gratitude at Mercier's interview with Seward and its clear moral support of Britain. At first they had thought that a Sunday session (December 22) of the cabinet was a decisive one on the question. But Seward gave no sign of a decision in his interview with Lyons on the 23rd. Later the two envoys heard that the big session would be on the day before Christmas. This was true, but, unknown to them, Seward asked Lincoln for a further one-day postponement—"I shall then be ready."[119] It seemed that he was still hoping to receive the French note. This may be in part what Seward was referring to when he later wrote to Weed that "I have had to feel my way."[120]   But the note still did not come on the 24th, and Lyons and Mercier were in agony. "What the answer will be," Lyons thought, "depends very much upon the news which will be brought by the packet tomorrow." "If it convinces the people that it will be surrender or war, without any hope of a diversion in their favor by France, our terms will perhaps be complied with. If there is any hope left that there will be only a rupture of Diplomatic Relations, or that we shall accept the mediation of France, no concession will be made."[121]

The Cabinet Meeting

Unbeknown to the envoys, Christmas Day was the fateful day. The cabinet assembled in the White House at ten in the forenoon, and the session continued for four hours. First, Seward read the British note and its official demands, and then they proceeded to read letters from abroad to determine the attitude of Englishmen and Frenchmen. Lincoln invited Senator Sumner in to read letters from Bright and Cobden. Both letters showed that sentiment was all against the United States. Adams' report of December 6 seemed to have been read at this point, telling of the aroused feeling in England. The British thought the United States wanted war, and he expected relations to be broken off by the middle of January.[122] There was now little doubt about the attitude of England.

But what about France? Would France encourage the United States? Would this question split the solidarity of the Anglo-French front? Poor Seward, he still had no French note, but he did the best he could. First there was a private letter of December 2 from Thurlow Weed, which told not only of the rising hostility in England but which said "we can hpoe for nothing friendly from France."[123] Then came a more informative letter from John Bigelow, the American consul in Paris. He said that Frenchmen believed that the "Trent" action was ordered by the American cabinet. "It is universally regarded here by the press and people and government as a rude assault upon the dignity of a neutral nation, and the Emperor is said to have expressed his surprise." Bigelow had heard from La Guéronnière, a pamphlet writer for the emperor, that in case of war France would side with England but not go to war. The emperor, he surmised, would like to be free to act as mediator and to carry out plans for the Rhine while England was busy in America.[124] At least France would not help Seward to wage or to avoid a war. Bigelow and Weed both told how they had written and arranged the publication of General Scott's letter, which refuted the rumor that the American cabinet had planned the seizure. So then the Scott letter was considered. After that, Seward brought out a dispatch just received from William Dayton, American minister in Paris, which contained the direct and official statement from Thouvenel on December 6.

> Mr. Thouvenel [Dayton reported] said at once that the taking of Messrs. Slidell and Mason off a British Ship was the affair of England, not theirs, but he had no hesitation in saying that it was the opinion of the French Government that the act was a clear breach of international law; that the French Government could not permit the application of such a principle to their ships. He added that all the Foreign maritime Powers with which he had conferred agreed that the act was a violation of public law. He said furthermore that he had at once communicated these views to Mr. Mercier. . . . I thought it best to ask bluntly whether in the event of war with England we were to expect France to go beyond the expression of her opinion? He said, of course, it was not their affair; they would be spectators only, though not indifferent spectators; the moral force of their opinion would be against us.[125]

So at last they had a French official statement *before* Lincoln and his cabinet had made up their minds.

But this was not to be the only French official statement they would hear. Evidently the same boat from France which had brought in Bigelow's letter and Dayton's despatch had also finally brought the long-awaited instructions from Thouvenel.[126] Mercier received the note that morning, and after only a hasty reading he rushed to the state department to see Seward. Frederick Seward greeted him with the disappointing news that his father was in a cabinet meeting. Then Mercier, frantic with the realization that the decision was probably being made then and there without his note, urged the younger Seward to hurry and take it over to the meeting itself. Frederick, knowing that his father had been awaiting it for a long time, no doubt hastened across the lawn from the state department to the White House and handed the note in to the cabinet room.[127] When read to the cabinet members, the Thouvenel note confirmed what Dayton reported. But they saw that it also contained detailed arguments on international law and tactfully associated American principles with those of France in urging American compliance with British wishes. It was the best support for Seward's draft note among all the letters read.

Then Seward drew out his draft reply to England in which he made various weak arguments on international law, but claimed that the United States violated international law in the same way Britain had done it in earlier years. Therefore, to uphold American principles, he was releasing the commissioners and their secretaries to British authorities. The draft was read, considered, and argued. Attorney General Bates, representing the law, a cabinet member who had earlier favored Wilkes's action, now came to the defense of Seward's note. His later diary comments were that "the French government fully agrees with England that the seizure of Mason and Slidell, *as made* . . . was a breach of the law of nations." "And this appears by the instructions sent to Mr. Mercier, the minister here, who has furnished Mr. Seward with a copy." Bates went on to say that by Dayton's report and other private letters they knew that France was suffering from the lack of cotton caused by the blockade. She had no cotton or markets for exports. Therefore he feared that France would join England in the war, and he would agree with Seward's decision to avoid war by the release of the men.[128] Both Chase and Blair supported Seward; while Welles (Navy), Cameron (War), and Caleb B. Smith (Interior) were not yet convinced that such an extreme concession had to be made. Finally they decided to put the decision over for a day and meet again on the 26th. After the others had filed out, Lincoln showed he too had not been entirely convinced when he said to Seward: "Governor Seward, you will go on, of course, preparing your answer, which as I understand it, will state the reasons why they ought to be given up. Now I have in mind to try my hand at stating the reasons why they ought *not* to be given up. We will compare the points on each side." Seward willingly agreed.[129]

Mercier, most anxious to learn whether Seward had received his note and what the decision of the cabinet was, made it a point to see the secretary later in the afternoon. Seward thanked him for rushing the note over to him but did not comment on its contents. He merely told Mercier that no decision had yet been made and that, as soon as a decision was made, he would give him a most friendly reply.[130] This clearly refutes a later claim that Lincoln's mind had been made up before the receipt of Thouvenel's note.

Lincoln and the Two Notes

According to the American system the cabinet may deliberate, the secretary may advise, but the president decides. We must now turn to the evolution of Lincoln's ideas on the "Trent" affair. The president, like Seward, probably learned of the mere announcement of the seizure of Mason and Slidell on the afternoon of November 15.[131] By the 16th he no doubt had the details that the British ship "Trent" was involved, and that evening he remarked to Benson J. Lossing, an historian, and Elisha Whittlesy, comptroller of the treasury: "I fear the traitors will be white elephants. We must stick to American principles concerning the rights of neutrals. We fought Great Britain for insisting, by theory and practice, on the right to do precisely what Captain Wilkes has done. If Great Britain shall now protest against the act and demand their release, we must give them up, apologize for the act as a violation of our doctrine, and thus forever bind her over to keep the peace in relation to neutrals and so acknowledge that she has been wrong for sixty years."[132] Yet in his message to congress on December 3 Lincoln followed Seward's example by remaining silent on the "Trent" affair in his public statements.[133]

Then three weeks later the president heard of the first decision of the British law officers, which, according to *The New York Times*, seemed to say that the United States could seize Mason and Slidell on a British ship on the high seas.[134] This report was not entirely accurate because the law officers on November 12, 1861, had merely said that American naval officers could board and search a British mail packet on the high seas but could not take the commissioners off. They must seize the ship and bring it into port for adjudication. They had not been sure of the decision of a prize court.[135] Nevertheless, Lincoln knew only the inaccurate report as printed in *The New York Times*, which was brought to his attention by Mercier. On December 10 he remarked to Senator Browning that the British law officers justified the seizure of Mason and Slidell and so "there probably would be no trouble about it."[136] Yet, five days later the president's feeling of reassurance was demolished by telegraphic news that a British note was on its way demanding an apology and the release of the men. Senator Browning, who was at the White House when Seward brought in the news, remarked that he himself "didn't believe that the British have done so foolish a thing, but if she is determined to force a war upon us why so be it." He added with warmth, "We will fight her to the death."[137] Also this was the occasion when Seward seemed to have reacted angrily to this ominous news.[138]

At any rate Lincoln could have been somewhat upset by the difference between the supposed British demands and the law officers' advice and excited by the defiant spirit of Browning and Seward. So it was in this period of nervous uncertainty that he is reported to have said to an old treasury official, "Sir, I would sooner die than give them up." Whereupon his interlocuter replied: "Mr. President, your death would be a great loss, but the destruction of the United States would be a still more deplorable event."[139]

But Lincoln and his cabinet became more cautious as the British note neared its destination. At this point a cabinet meeting was called in which a preliminary discussion of the "Trent" affair was reported to have taken place. Here, it was said, they decided unanimously that no quarrel with England would interfere with the war against the Southern rebels. It was the latter who hoped for an Anglo-American war.[140] Then it was that Lyons, on the 19th, had given Seward a confidential and unofficial copy of the British note. The secretary must have then or the next day submitted this copy to the president because we find it (and not the final official copy) in the Lincoln Papers.[141]

Probably it was on December 20 that Lincoln began to write his unsigned draft of a note for Seward. As he read the British note, he also had in mind the recent news dispatches which spoke of French offers of mediation in England. On the 16th *The New York Times* had said: "We see it rumored that the Emperor of France has tendered his mediation in this instance. It is a case peculiarly fitted to such a mode of settlement, and we see no reason why, if offered, it should not be accepted." Then on the 19th it published a report that "the Paris *Temps* announces that Napoleon has tendered his services to the British government."[142] But in addition to these news reports the letters of Weed and Bright may have arrived by December 20, suggesting French arbitration of the dispute.[143] In his letter to Sumner, Bright proposed a strong American note of justification, coupled with suggestions of arbitration and an agreed revision of international law.[144]

The idea of arbitration, perhaps French arbitration, was therefore also in the air in Washington. It was not an original idea of Lincoln's, for he no doubt had these news reports and letters in his mind as he sat down to put his thoughts in writing. Thus some time on the 20th or 21st of December he found time to compose his draft dispatch. He would have Seward say that the British note "has been carefully considered by the President," who would like a chance to present the American side of the case in all of its various aspects, including legal points and precedents. He would also be willing to consider any further arguments from the British side. With all of these full statements of the case "the government of the United States will, if agreed to by Her Majesty's government, go to such friendly arbitration as is usual among nations, and will abide the award." Or he would leave it to England alone to determine the settlement, after examining the American case, if she does not exceed the terms of reparation in the British note, and if the decision shall determine the law for all such future cases.[145]

In the afternoon of December 21, Senator Browning went over to the White House for tea and had a long talk with the president on the "Trent" affair. The senator was in a much less belligerent mood than he had been on the previous Sunday.

> He [the president] told me that the dispatches from England had not been delivered by Lord Lyons, but were withheld for a few days at Mr. Seward's request, but that he had an inkling of what they were, and feared trouble. I told him I was anxious that a rupture should be avoided at present if it could be done without humiliation and dishonor, in which he expressed his full concurrence, and we both agreed that the question was easily susceptible of a pacific solution if England was at all disposed to act justly with us, and suggested that it was a proper case for arbitration. I also said that, as some of the rights of neutrals according to the principles of international law have long been in dispute between us and England, say to England to make her statement of what the law of nations is which shall govern this case, and all cases similarly circumstanced now, and forever thereafter, and we will agree to it. The President replied the same thought had occurred to his mind and that he had reduced the propositions to writing. He then took from his desk and read me a very able paper, which he intends, at a proper time, shall go as a letter from the Secretary of State to Lord Lyons (it now has that form) and in which both the foregoing propositions are stated with great force and clearness and very much more in detail than I have given them.[146]

It is quite possible, from Browning's account, that Sumner had shared his Bright letter with both gentlemen. At any rate it was evident that Lincoln's whole draft note had been completed by tea time on the 21st.

In the meantime Seward in seclusion had been working hard on his own note, which would release Mason and Slidell without arbitration. This was read to Lincoln in the cabinet meeting along with the letters from Bright, Cobden, Dayton, and Thouvenel. The president had listened to the arguments pro and con, and at the end had told Seward about his intention to draft a different reply.[147]   He did not reveal that he had already written the draft dispatch proposing arbitration rather than immediate release.

So during the remainder of the afternoon of Christmas—the cabinet meeting had adjourned at 2 o'clock—the president was reflecting on the question of his counterdispatch. Bright's and Cobden's letters were not new to Lincoln; Sumner had read them to him, and he had asked the senator to come in and read them to the cabinet. What had been new were the notes from Dayton and Thouvenel. Dayton had reported that Thouvenel said that France and all the maritime powers of Europe considered the "Trent" action to be a "clear breach of international law." In his famous note to Mercier, Thouvenel had stressed that the United States were violating their own principles and that "the federal government would be assuming a just and lofty attitude by acceding to these demands" of England.[148]   That these two notes were his main preoccupation is shown by his after-dinner talk with Browning that same evening. The president said he could not divulge what occurred in the cabinet meeting, but he did go on to talk about the one thing on his mind—the French note. It had arrived in the midst of the session, he revealed, and said "that the European powers were against us on the question of international law, and desired that we shall settle the controversy amicably." He then went on to mention the letters from Bright and Cobden.[149]

However, during that evening and the next morning, Lincoln, as one lawyer weighing the arguments of another (French) lawyer,[150] must have been more impressed by Thouvenel's two statements than by the suggestions of Bright. If France and all the powers already found the United States to be legally wrong, what good would be accomplished to submit the dispute to arbitration? It would be undignified to spin out arguments which were condemned in advance. Furthermore, to whom would they turn in seeking an arbitrator? All the powers had already taken sides against the United States.[151] France was the only one which could possibly be acceptable to both sides, and she had taken a strong initiative against the Federal government. Thus, as a result of the French note and declarations to

Dayton, the president's scheme for more diplomatic discussion and arbitration fell to the ground. He may have begun to feel, as had the London *Times*, that the French note had already handed down the arbitral award.[152]

On the next day, December 26, the cabinet reconvened. Again Seward read his reply. There were some regrets expressed around the cabinet table about the necessity of making such a complete capitulation to England. Several suggestions of phraseology were made by cabinet members, and accepted by Seward. The secretary waited for Lincoln to bring forth his counterproposal, but the president remained silent. Finally Seward's reply, full of weak and confusing legal arguments, yet releasing Mason and Slidell, and disavowing Captain Wilkes, was approved unanimously. When the rest were gone, Seward turned to Lincoln and remarked, "You thought you might frame an argument for the other side." The president smiled and shook his head. "I found I could not make an argument that would satisfy my own mind, and that proved to me your ground was the right one."[153]

Mercier and Lyons knew that this second day of cabinet deliberation was taking place on the 26th and thus were not surprised that no answer was forthcoming on that day. They received invitations to a dinner at Seward's for the 27th, which might be the occasion for an announcement. But, in fact, late in the afternoon of the 27th Lyons informed Mercier that he had been given advance notice that Mason and Slidell were to be released. There soon followed the two formal notes to Lyons and Mercier. With insufficient time to digest them, the two ministers had to rush off to the Seward dinner, which seemed to be designed as a public demonstration of the United States' good relations with foreign countries. "Mr. Seward gave a big dinner party this evening," reported the correspondent of *The New York Times*," at which were present Lord Lyons and other eminent diplomatists, and members of the Senate and House committees on Federal [sic] Relations." "This is a significant reunion, and needs no comment."[154] The decision and Seward's notes were still unannounced to the public, but after the dinner Seward took Senators Browning, Sumner, King, and Harris and

Representative Crittenden up to his room and read to them the British note, his reply to Lyons, his note to Adams, Thouvenel's note, and his reply to Mercier.[155] It must have been a very long reading session, but the secretary of state was evidently playing up the French note, as well as the British, before senators and congressmen.

The next day Mercier had a chance to read Seward's reply in a more leisurely fashion.

> I have submitted to the President [he wrote] the copy you were so good as to give me of a Despatch addressed to you on the 3d. of December instant. . . .
>
> Before receiving the paper, however, the President had decided upon the disposition to be made of the subject which has caused so much anxiety in Europe. That disposition of the subject . . . renders unnecessary any discussion of it in reply to the comments of M. Thouvenel. I am permitted, however, to say that M. Thouvenel has not been in error in supposing, first, that the Government of the United States has not acted in any spirit of disregard of the rights, or of the sensibilities, of the British nation, and that he is equally just in assuming that the United States would consistently vindicate, by their practice on this occasion, the character they have so long maintained as an advocate of the most liberal principles concerning the rights of neutral states in maritime war.
>
> . . . You will assure M. Thouvenel that this government appreciates as well the frankness of his explanations as the spirit of friendship and good will towards the United States in which they are expressed.
>
> It is a sincere pleasure for the United States to exchange assurances of friendship which had its origin in associations most sacred in the history of both countries.[156]

Mercier could not fail to be surprised at the most significant sentence in Seward's note, which declared that "before receiving the paper . . . the President had decided upon the disposition . . . of the subject." The fact that the president held cabinet meetings for two successive days on the subject would indicate to Mercier that Lincoln must have reserved his final decision until he saw the trend in the cabinet. Indeed, Seward had told the

French minister after the first day's meeting, and after the reading of the French note, that "nothing had yet been decided."[157] Lyons had been telling Mercier during those agonizing two days that he was less and less hopeful of a peaceful outcome. When the first good news had arrived, he confided to his French colleague that he "attributed this success . . . to your Excellency's [Thouvenel's] dispatch."[158] Mercier was a little more modest when he combined Thouvenel's note with what he thought were two other important considerations.

> It goes without saying [he wrote to Thouvenel] that I do not know exactly what could have taken place in the cabinet meeting, but I don't think I am mistaken in believing that nothing has contributed more to make his [Seward's] opinion prevail in favor of a peaceful settlement than the financial situation,[159] the hope for early successes in the South, and Your Excellency's dispatch.[160]

As we know now, and as Seward knew at the time, Lincoln had not come to a decision in his own mind before the receipt of the French note; and the dispatch had impressed him sufficiently to cause him to comment on it to Browning during the evening of the 25th. As a matter of fact Seward later told Lyons that "up to the morning of the 26th of December" no one in authority, except himself, was willing to surrender Mason and Slidell. He even told how Lincoln wanted to make an arbitration proposal first. Lyons' comment to Russell was:

> I don't think that Mr. Seward's present assertion quite tallies with that made in his note to M. Mercier, that surrender had been decided upon before M. Thouvenel's despatch was communicated to him; but, however that may be, the present assertion is, I believe, true. In fact I know that the note approving the surrender was sent to me as soon as possible after the surrender had been agreed upon in the cabinet and I did not receive it until the 27th.[161]

The American Reaction to the French Note

It was Seward's intention to announce the government's decision simultaneously with the publication of documents which would justify such a decision. The news and the texts of the documents were all set in type in the offices of the *National Intelligencer* on the night of December 27, but no telegraphic communication of them was allowed until the publication of the 28th.[162] There were five documents presented to the public: (1) Seward to Adams, November 30; (2) Russell to Lyons, November 30; (3) Seward to Lyons, December 26; (4) Thouvenel to Mercier, December 3 (in translation); (5) Seward to Mercier, December 27.[163] The first showed that England had been officially informed that Wilkes had taken the men without orders; the second revealed that England's note was mild and restrained; the third contained Seward's arguments aimed more at American opinion than at the experts on international law; the fourth, Thouvenel's note, was to convince the American public that the world was opposed to the "Trent" action and thought the United States were violating their own principles; and the fifth tried to deceive the American public by the impression that the French note arrived too late.

In spite of Seward's false denial of the timely arrival of the French note, it was obvious that he saw its value in gaining the approval of American opinion. It had been the fear of American opinion that had made the cabinet and the president hesitate to accept Seward's note on the 25th. It is likely that on reflection they saw the value of the French note in persuading American opinion to accept the surrender policy. On this point Mercier shrewdly observed that "Mr. Seward's haste in publishing it, rather proves the help he obtained from it and that which he still expects from it."[164] This value and use of the note is seen in the editorial of the *National Intelligencer*, the administration's favored paper. Here it probably was encouraged to say:

> It surely should give pause to all who may be disposed to challenging the propriety of the resolution to which the Administration has come, when they note that a contrary decision would leave us in opposition not only to the views of Great Britain, but also to those which the Government of France announces respecting the principles of public law involved in this transaction. The latter Government in making the declaration it does . . . is not open to the suspicion of being

animated by any unfriendly sentiment, or by the vindictive feelings which may be imputed to the British Government. . . . Least of all can the Government of France be supposed to act in subserviency to any consideration extrinsic to the international aspect of this case as one of public law important to all Maritime Powers, since we find M. Thouvenel merely anticipating from the tradition of our past history the determination to which our Government had come in advance of receiving the representations which the Government of France conceived itself called to make in the interest of the law of nations.[165]

The New York Times echoed these sentiments in its own editorial:

The lucid dispatch from Mr. Thouvenel . . . may be read with advantage by those who would learn the varying aspects the case presents when seen in the light of the public law of different nations.

. . . It would not be difficult to show that there are some positions of M. Thouvenel's reasoning that we can not agree with him in regarding as conclusive. . . . His judgment of the case is but an application of those doctrines of Neutral Right which France has long proclaimed and practiced. . . . While the policy of France and the United States has always accorded in seeking to establish the most liberal principles concerning the rights of most neutral States, there is not an entire agreement between the two nations concerning the application of those principles. . . .

. . . It [the note] shows conclusively that the conduct of the French Government in this international dispute . . . has been in the highest degree open, conciliatory, and pacific. . . . On the part of Napoleon III . . . there is nothing in his correspondence in the late unhappy difficulty that is not at once frank and friendly.[166]

On the floor of the house, however, Thaddeus Stevens attacked the French note:

The most unpleasant thing which I observed in this affair [declared Stevens] is the impertinent interference of France. Why should she intervene uninvited unless for the purpose of intimidation? The letter of M. Thouvenel is harsh and dictatorial. When we have settled our domestic affairs, it may be well to look into this holy alliance of these Powers and see how far their dictation is to control the conduct of nations.[167]

On the other hand, a week later Francis P. Blair, Jr. led a counterattack in the house by proposing a joint resolution of thanks to France for her kindly worded note. In the preamble to his resolution he summarized the French note, bringing out again that the United States had violated its own principles which had been in accord with France and the European powers. He called it an "arbitration in advance of the issue which was made by the British Government" and asserted that "the reclamation . . . was a proper interposition, considerately and kindly made. . . ." Therefore, it concluded: "Be it resolved . . . that Congress and the people of the United States are not insensible to the kindness which has animated the Government of France in its prompt and wise interposition. . . ."[168] This move was obviously to use the French dispatch as a defense of the administration's decision before public opinion. But Congressman Clement L. Vallandigham, a bitter foe of the administration, moved that the resolution be tabled and branded the French note as "an indication of hostility to the United States." The motion to table was voted down, showing at least an early and tentative approval by the house.[169] Blair's original motion was later made Joint Resolution No. 27 and referred to the house committee on foreign affairs,[170] from which it does not appear to have emerged.

Yet it was in the senate that the most dramatic notice was given to the French interposition. Senator Charles Sumner, chairman of the senate's foreign relations committee, had indicated that he would speak on the "Trent" affair on January 9, and, when the time came, the galleries were full, including most of the foreign diplomats.[171] At one point in his defense of the release of Mason and Slidell because they were not military personnel, Senator Sumner cited the French note: "M. Thouvenel . . . insists that the rebel emissaries, not being military persons actually in the service of the enemy, were not subject to seizure on board a neutral ship." Likewise on the question of dispatches he denied the right of the United States to seize the men or their dispatches. Then he added, "And here again we have the concurring testimony of continental Europe, and especially of the French Government in the recent letter of M. Thouvenel." And finally in his discussion of the immunity of neutral ships from capture he referred to the French foreign minister's dispatch as "remarkable for its brief but comprehensive treatment of all the questions involved in this controversy."

> I know not how others may feel [he continued], but I can not doubt that this communication, when rightly understood, will be gratefully accepted as a token of friendship for us, and also as a contribution to those maritime rights for which France and the United States, in times past, have done so much together. This eminent minister does not hesitate to declare that if the flag of a neutral can not completely cover persons and merchandise beneath it in a voyage between two neutral ports, then its immunity will be but a vain word.[172]

Mercier was among those in the galleries, and he reported that the speech was "listened to quietly with favorable attention; no one replied to it, and the question was dropped."[173]

Beyond the halls of congress Sumner's speech was widely read and favorably received.[174] Early in the "Trent" controversy Mercier had seen the value of French influence on American public opinion when he had offered his personal services to Seward on December 21. Now, after the presentation of the French note and the surrender decision he could write home that "we have especially helped them to make a necessary retreat," and four days later that "Mr. Seward is becoming the most tractable of men . . . he says he's very pleased with us and the tone of the Paris press."[175] A little later Mercier reported again that "numerous indications give me grounds for assuring Your Excellency that the way the government of the emperor proceeded was generally appreciated."[176]

Europe's Opinion on the Outcome

The European reaction to the American decision did not come until the second week in January 1862. Although Mercier's earliest announcement of the American settlement of the "Trent" affair did not arrive in Paris until January 10, the banking house of Jakob Rothschild received the first news on the 7th. Rothschild seems to have arranged for a quick means of getting the news so that he could buy securities on the market in anticipation of a rise. In this he appears to have been successful, even though the secret news leaked out during the day in the form of unconfirmed rumors.[177] The first substantiation of the rumor came the next day, the 8th, when the "City of Washington" arrived in Queenstown (Ireland) from whence telegraphic reports were sent to all parts of Europe. Strangely enough, Thouvenel, who was supposed to be at the diplomatic hub of Europe, does not seem to have heard any of the reports of the 7th.[178] At eleven o'clock on the evening of the 8th, during a ball at the Tuileries Palace, the emperor and empress were just coming forward to take part in a quadrille when some one brought His Majesty the first news of the American decision. He was so delighted that he turned to some Americans in a nearby group and remarked "that he almost felt that he could congratulate them on the favorable turn events had taken." Later in the evening, when the imperial couple was circling the hall to greet their guests, the empress stopped and spoke to one American lady whom she knew: "Ah, Madame . . . we have received such good news from America that I can with difficulty refrain from expressing all the pleasure it has afforded me."[179] However, in his letter to Cowley three days later Napoleon III was not so kindly disposed toward the United States: "From an English point of view [he wrote] I cannot help regretting the condescension of America. England will never find a more favorable occasion to abase the pride of the Americans or to establish her influence in the New World."[180]

Thouvenel had likewise heard the news on the evening of the 8th, but he considered it to be rumor until he received confirmation from London on the 9th.[181] He was writing to Mercier, approving his initial statement to Seward on December 21, on the day when the news of the American release of the Southern emissaries was received. He immediately added: "I do not want to await more detailed confirmation of this decision before congratulating the Federal government. We are happy to see an incident settled in this way, which otherwise might have led undoubtedly to a fearful collision between two powers friendly to France."[182] On the 10th Cowley said that Thouvenel had received a copy of Seward's reply to Mercier and had "expressed great satisfaction at the course pursued by the Government of Washington in surrendering the prisoners."[183] Five days later he sent, through Mercier, his official expression of gratification to the United States.

> You already know how much satisfaction the government of the emperor felt over it. It is a pleasure for me to see today that the communication which you presented in the cabinet of Washington was received in the same spirit of cordial frankness which inspired us in writing it and that the government of the emperor was not wrong in expecting to find the United States again taking the same stand with France as in earlier times in defending the same principles.[184]

Thouvenel was more consistent and sincere than the emperor in his favorable reaction to the United States' decision.

And there was an equally favorable response throughout France. For five days Dayton listened to French comments and concluded that the American action was "approved by everybody." "We have made character, not lost, by it."[185] This estimate is confirmed by Archbishop Hughes and Thurlow Weed, both in Paris at the time of the receipt of the news. The Catholic clergyman said it had turned sentiment in favor of the North and had appeared to Frenchmen not as a loss of dignity but as a magnanimous act for peace. Weed, in referring to Seward's letter to Lyons, remarked that "here [in Paris], as in London, the American side of the Trent correspondence is regarded as a Diplomatic achievement."[186] "Malakoff," reporting to *The New York Times*, found that Frenchmen were astonished at how coolly the Americans faced Britain's wrath and decided the matter on its merits. Five days later he stressed the French admiration of the statesmanship of Seward and Lincoln. "On every hand it is agreed that Mr. Seward has shown great ability in the treatment of the 'Trent' affair, and that he has fairly turned the tables against England. The subject is a matter of rejoicing from one end of Europe to the other—everywhere but in England."[187]

Of course the pro-Northern Paris papers praised the Washington decision. The republican *Siècle* called it an evidence of strength, not weakness; while the Orleanist *Journal des Débats* thought the American action was the only possible solution and expressed satisfaction that England had exposed herself to a proper condemnation of her own principles of international law.[188] In the Orleanist *Revue des deux mondes* E. Forcade praised the North for justifying the liberals in their faith that it would uphold their principles of international law. Now Forcade thought England and France should make it clear that they would not recognize the South.[189] The liberal *Presse* thought Seward's legal arguments were not the main reason for Mason's and Slidell's release; it was largely due to the desire of the United States to avoid a war with England.[190] The imperialist *Constitutionnel*, often critical of the Union, was gracious in its comments. "The Washington Government," it observed, "had done itself honor in the eyes of the civilized world by giving to England the satisfaction due to her." "The surrender of Messrs. Mason and Slidell is a victory of right, of moderation, and of good sense."[191] The hostile imperialist *Patrie* was not so generous. Its feeling was that, now the crisis was over, France, England, and the rest of Europe had better begin consideration of the recognition of the Confederacy.[192] Unfortunately, the good will that the United States seemed to have won in the French press by release of the Confederate envoys was partially lost a few days later by the news of the stone fleet, sunk in one of the channels leading to the Charleston harbor. Three of the imperialist papers—the *Moniteur*, *Constitutionnel*, and *Pays*—denounced the stone fleet affair as an act of vulgar barbarism.[193]

Not only did Frenchmen praise Lincoln's and Seward's decision, but Englishmen and Frenchmen alike tended to give Thouvenel's note the major credit for the result, in spite of Seward's disclaimer. At the same time—January 9—that Russell heard the news of the compliance of the United States with his demands, he received a note from Lyons telling of Mercier's presentation of the French note on the 25th. Lyons had added, "M. Mercier has, throughout, displayed great clarity and good will, and . . . excellent judgment in giving moral support to the demands of Her Majesty's Government."[194]   Thus, when Russell saw Flahault, the French ambassador, on the same day, he was most emphatic in crediting the French note with the diplomatic success.   He let Flahault read Lyons' dispatch and added that "your dispatch gave him [Lincoln] a golden bridge . . . for his retreat."[195]   Then the British foreign secretary asked that Thouvenel be thanked for his note and Mercier for his support in Washington.   "The course taken by the French Government in this affair was precisely that which was most useful to Her Majesty's Government.   Any other course, of doing more [threatening war] or less [silence] than had been done, might have been embarrassing."[196]   Flahault's account of this interview and his other conversations were more specific: "The principal members of the cabinet, Lord John Russell and Lord Palmerston among them, hastened to acknowledge that the opinion so clearly expressed in Your Excellency's dispatch to M. Mercier of last December 3rd has powerfully contributed to persuading the Union government to return the prisoners."[197]

Lord Cowley found an occasion to express England's gratitude directly to the emperor.   On January 11, Napoleon III had written the British ambassador: "I am glad that recent events have enabled me to give the English Government fresh proofs of my desire to march in step with it.   This is how I avenge myself for the contentions over Savoy.[198]   I am proud to have supported the English claims which were absolutely just; this enables me to side with you in peace as in war."[199]   No doubt feeling some embarrassment that the emperor mentioned his aid to England before Cowley had shown any appreciation for the aid, the British ambassador hastened to reply the next day.   "The Government of the Queen [he wrote] is very appreciative of the friendly support which it received from the Government of the Emperor in their difficulties with the United States, and I am instructed to assure M. Thouvenel of it.   Your Majesty's opinion, given as it was, spontaneously and without urging on our part, has powerfully contributed, we do not doubt, to the peaceful solution of that affair." [200]

Earl Russell's own party paper, *The Observer*, in rejoicing over the outcome of the affair, remarked that "the letter of M. Thouvenel is acknowledged by all to be perhaps the very best argument yet published in a succinct form against the illegality and violence of Captain Wilkes." [201]   However, the London *Times* went out of its way, in its first long editorial on the end of the "Trent" affair, to give France the credit for it.

> It would be ungracious to forget how much our cause has been strengthened by the approbation and good will of the other powers of Europe . . . Above all, the acknowledgements of Englishmen are due to the French Government. To the position taken by the Emperor from the outset of this discussion the Americans may, perhaps, owe it that they have not plunged into a mad and ruinous war. . . . The Imperial Government addressed to its Minister in Washington the remarkable dispatch dated the 3rd of December. . . . The good effects of this communication can not be doubted, nor are we inclined to underestimate its importance in causing Mr. Lincoln to yield to our just claims. . . . Had M. Thouvenel's note never been dispatched, the surrender of the four prisoners would, in all probability, have taken place. But, perhaps, this would not have been done with the same readiness, or until further steps had been taken by England to assert her rights, which would have embittered the animosity and humiliated the pride of a people whom she was unwilling to regard as enemies. By his good feeling and sound judgment the French Emperor has aided in bringing this dispute to a close. He has convinced the Americans from the first that they have no chance of engaging the sympathy or ambition of any European nation on their side. . . . [202]

Independent of the three parties involved in this dispute, the Italian minister in Washington, Bertinatti, was thoroughly convinced that Thouvenel's dispatch had "a notable, if not a decisive influence on the deliberations of the Washington cabinet." He added that "our glorious ally, Emperor Napoleon III, can rightly boast of having rendered an exceptional service to the United States as well as to the lovers of peace in general."[203]

If Englishmen and Italians were acknowledging French responsibility for the peaceful solution of the "Trent" affair, it is not surprising that Frenchmen should take credit for themselves. "Malakoff," *The New York Times* correspondent in Paris, said that "all the Frenchmen I have thus far met since the settlement of the Mason and Slidell affair attribute the result mainly to that [Thouvenel's] dispatch."[204] The Paris paper, the *Presse*, insisted that it was "to the circular of M. Thouvenel that the honor of the pacific termination of the difficulty provoked by the incident of the 'Trent' chiefly belongs." "No doubt the advice tendered by the Great Powers of Europe, and especially by the French Government, has powerfully acted on its [the Washington Cabinet's] mind."[205] Of the twenty-eight procureurs general in France, however, only one, from Bordeaux, reported any provincial opinion linking the French note to the American decision. "Impartial minds [in the Bordeaux district] once again acknowledge, in the decision taken by President Lincoln, the wise and pacifying political influence of France."[206] After this recognition and that of Mercier in Washington, Thouvenel might be forgiven if he too believed in the efficacy of his own note. To Benedetti he wrote, "You can easily guess that our success in Washington exceeds our hopes."[207] To Flahault he indicated more specifically that he thought his dispatch had done good for France in England and could be useful in America to ease the humiliation of public sentiment.[208] A month later the French lower house, the legislative body, echoed the general sentiment of the country and indirectly hinted at the effectiveness of the French note when it resolved:

> The legislative body highly approves Your Majesty for having, in this crisis and especially in the recent conflict between America and England, been concerned solely with obtaining respect for neutral rights. A government which takes right and justice as its invariable rule soon becomes the arbiter of the peace of the world.[209]

Although the French might have taken a selfish advantage of an Anglo-American war, they sincerely rejoiced in the peaceful outcome of the dispute, which at least preserved the American navy as a counterweight to the British. Looking back, Mercier observed that "We had the choice of three approaches: either to incite them to war; or to remain aloof; or to speak out as we did." To have encouraged the outbreak of war would have seriously compromised France in her relations with England, involved her with some responsibility toward the United States, and aroused the suspicions of Europe—all for an uncertain success. If France had remained aloof, it still "might have revealed . . . the tips of our ears." By sending the note, he felt, they had made England obligated to France in a dramatic way, apparent to the British public as well as to its leaders. "So then we made . . . the wisest and most honorable decision and in a perfect way."[210]   And in the same spirit he praised Seward, who "as soon as he saw the danger . . . took a firm stand to thwart it, and, without hesitating over a fear of losing popularity, which is very precious to him."[211]

A Proposed Conference on International Law

To many who had followed the controversy in all its stages the "Trent" affair seemed to be more than a diplomatic incident, to be in fact a great event in the development of international law. Superficially, to the uninitiated, it seemed as if England was modifying her previous high-handed attitude on the right of visit and search on the high seas. Now that England was the victim rather than the perpetrator of visit and search and was protesting as loudly as her erstwhile victims, these latter (most of the other powers) began to think that here was an opportunity to persuade England formally to adopt the rule that they had held against her.

Naturally it was first from the American side that the idea was broached with the prospect of obtaining some compensation for an American surrender to British demands. Bigelow, as publicity man in France for the Union cause, seemed to have proposed it first in Paris. On December 3 he wrote Seward, "I hope you may be able to secure the American doctrine on the rights of neutrals upon a durable basis in the negotiations, if so we can afford, as General Scott properly says in the letter he has written and is about publishing, to let the vagabonds go at large again."[212]   In fact Bigelow and Sanford had already prompted the *Constitutionnel*, in an article by F. Gaillardet, to put forward the plan to have England accept the American point on international law in return for the release of Mason and Slidell.[213] And it was Bigelow himself who had written General Scott's letter, which was published on December 4 and which contained a similar proposal. The general was persuaded to accept as his own the following passages:

> If under the circumstances England should deem it her duty, in the interest of civilization, to insist upon the restoration of the men . . . it will be from a conviction, without doubt, that the law of nations in regard to the rights of neutrals . . . requires a revision. . . . If England . . . is disposed to do her part in stripping war of half its horror, by accepting the policy long and persistently urged upon her by our government, and commended by every principle of justice and humanity, she will find no ground in the visit of the *Trent* for controversy with our Government. I am sure that the President and people of the United States would be but too happy to let these men go free. . . . if by it they could emancipate the commerce of the world.[214]

This letter was first published by the *Constitutionnel* and the *Universel* on the 4th,[215] but what was more significant was that the official *Moniteur* reproduced the whole letter on the 6th and added, in an editorial commentary, that it hoped a new doctrine in regard to the rights of neutrals might result from this event.[216] Then other Paris papers picked up the theme and pressed it before and after the news of the release.[217]   What was more, the *Moniteur* did seem to represent the emperor's own views. The correspondent of the London *Post* learned that both Napoleon III and Persigny were anxious for conciliation and "the *règlement* of the rights of neutrals."[218]   Whether this governmental interest came from cabinet discussion or individual inspiration,

Thouvenel also shared the hope of permanent benefit to international law. In a conversation with Prince Richard Metternich, the Austrian ambassador, he said he would like to have a conference of the powers to reaffirm the principles of international law of 1856 and tie England down to the generally agreed rules for neutrals.[219]

The news of this European interest in an English acknowledgment of a liberalized law in favor of neutrals arrived in the United States during the same week as the cabinet deliberations on the "Trent" affair. Seward received Bigelow's reports and suggestions along this line on the very day of the Christmas cabinet meeting. While the idea of a multilateral acceptance of England's supposed change of heart may have already been in Seward's mind, no doubt these reports from Bigelow and the news of Scott's letter at least confirmed Seward in following through with the suggestion. The whole burden of his arguments and reply to England was expressed in the words: "We are asked to do to the British nation just what we have always insisted all nations ought to do to us."[220] However, in his reply to Mercier of the following day the secretary of state was more specific when he stated: "The government of the United States will be happy if the occasion which has elicited this correspondence can be improved so as to secure a more definite agreement, upon the whole subject, by all maritime powers."[221]

This passage in Seward's letter to Mercier, a copy of which Thouvenel received on January 10, 1862, fitted in closely with the latter's ideas previously expressed to Metternich. In addition, the French press, of all shades of opinion, was crying for an international agreement. The democratic *Siècle* and the liberal imperialist *Opinion Nationale* stressed the need of a future international agreement just before Thouvenel received Seward's invitation.[222] But then came the telegraphic news that the *Journal de St. Pétersbourg*, as a reaction to the American decision, had published an editorial insisting that the "Trent" affair now become the point of departure for negotiations to bring about international recognition of common principles concerning the neutral flag and that England give the rest of the world solemn guaranties by signing a convention assuring universal respect for neutrals.[223]   This touched off a general press campaign in favor of an international conference to negotiate a convention. The official *Moniteur* published a summary of the St. Petersburg article with approval, and the imperialist *Presse* and *Journal du Havre* and the Orleanist *Journal des Débats* heartily echoed this approval.[224]   "Malakoff" reported that these sentiments were general throughout the French press.[225]

The whole question of a conference and a signed international convention came to a head in an hour and a half interview between Dayton and Thouvenel on January 24, when Dayton tried to carry out Seward's instructions on this matter. He urged the French foreign minister to call a conference which would commit Britain to the same principles of international law on search and seizure that had long been advocated by France and the United States. Dayton hoped that, on this occasion, France would propose the Marcy amendment which exempted from seizure all noncontraband private property on the seas. As an American contribution, he said, Seward would support the total abolition of blockades, including the present one, which will soon be superseded by the capture of Southern ports. In closing, Dayton warned that this was the last chance to have the United States favor the abolition of blockades, since henceforth it would become a leading naval power. Thouvenel seemed mildly interested in these propositions, but remarked that Great Britain, by her recent stand, had already committed herself to these principles. As to France's call of a conference, there should first be consultations among the powers and preliminary preparations by jurisconsults.[226]

There is no evidence, however, that Thouvenel ever took the initiative to consult England or the other powers on the conference proposal. A good explanation probably lies in the fact that just the day before—January 23—Lord John Russell had finally explained more fully England's stand on international law in the "Trent" dispute. It was in a note to Lyons refuting the loose and shaky legal arguments of Seward's note on the "Trent." Here the foreign secretary denied that it was Britain's view that a belligerent could capture neutral ships sailing between two neutral ports. Only in case the ultimate destination of the neutral ship was an enemy port could a belligerent, in the British view, capture it and confiscate its contraband cargo, not in the case of a neutral ship sailing between two neutral ports and clearly having no intention of stopping at an enemy port—as in the case of the "Trent."[227] This statement was quite in line with the French view and was communicated to Thouvenel during the last week of January.[228] While Russell's note seemed to indicate that no formal international act was necessary on the point of visit and search, a statement for the government in the house of lords by Lord Granville clearly rejected it. Taking cognizance of the press campaign, Granville said: "For the present we have no intention of participating in any congress or convention on the subject of international law concerning neutrals."[229] The French foreign minister, therefore, had neither a good pretext nor a good prospect for calling an international conference; and, furthermore, there seemed to be too much need for British support on other matters, such as the cotton scarcity and the Mexican expedition, to embarrass the English by a conference whose ostensible purpose would have been to compel them to reaffirm and sign what they had already accepted. Thus, at least for contemporaries, the discussion and controversy over the "Trent" affair gradually subsided.

The Historians on France and the "Trent" Affair

People living at the time of the Civil War may have lost interest in the "Trent" affair by the end of January 1862, since their attention was caught in the spring by other war events, such as the stone fleet in Charleston harbor; but the "Trent" affair was the subject of much treatment by historians in later years. It is interesting to note, however, that contemporaries were more aware of some matters involved in this affair than were later historians, who had the advantage of reading and studying at leisure the mass of material collected on the incident in subsequent years. As a matter of fact the "Trent" affair is a good illustration of how historians can sometimes be misled to neglect some important aspects of an historical event by a deliberate falsehood tucked away in their documentary materials.

In the first place the "Trent" affair was obviously a dispute between the United States and Great Britain, and not one primarily involving France. Therefore the attention of historians was turned to the English reaction, the English note, the Prince Consort's modulation of the tone of the note, Lord Lyons' handling of the negotiations, and Seward's famous reply to the British. To them France, Austria, and Russia seemed unimportant bystanders who could be relegated to the historical sidelines as they had been to the contemporary sidelines. In the second place there was Seward's false statement that Lincoln had made his decision before the arrival of the French note. Why, then, should any further notice be given to the role of France?

Consequently, in those histories where France is mentioned in connection with the "Trent" affair, her note is not credited with having any influence on the outcome of the dispute. In the only history—a most detailed one—of the "Trent" affair, by T. L. Harris, the French note is mentioned and quoted, but the author devotes his space to belittling Thouvenel's arguments without noticing the role it played in the negotiations and cabinet deliberations. A bare mention of the French note, without attributing much importance to it, is also characteristic of seven other detailed histories on the Civil War period.[230]

Yet, what is still more surprising is the fact that fourteen other treatments of the Civil War and of American diplomacy do not even mention the French note. This is particularly notable in the cases of such well-known authorities as J. G. Randall in his works on Lincoln, E. D. Adams in his two-volume study of *Great Britain and the American Civil War*, R. B. Mowat in his volume on American-British relations, Channing in his standard volume on the Civil War period, and H. W. Temple in his treatment of Seward in the series on the American secretaries of state.[231]

In only two cases—and both are French in origin—do the authors suggest the influence of France on the American decision to release Mason and Slidell. Pierre Renouvin in his *Relations internationales* said that "the French government joined in the British protest, and it was this assertion of Anglo-French solidarity which led Seward to give in." In this general work of synthesis Renouvin could not devote enough space to substantiate his general statement with detailed evidence, but it will be noticed that he suggests that Seward was the one who had to be persuaded rather than Lincoln and the cabinet. In the second French instance—actually an American's Sorbonne thesis—the author, Korolewicz-Carlton, gives credit to the French note but again does not give any evidence to convince the reader of this conclusion.[232]

In all this historical treatment of the past hundred years there is no notice given to Russell's and Thouvenel's intention to have the French note play an important role; no treatment of Mercier's, Lyons', and Seward's agonizing wait for the arrival of the one documentary piece which would turn the trick; no examination of the recollections of those who attended the fateful cabinet meetings; no scrutiny of the evolution of Lincoln's thought; no recognition of the use made of the French note by Seward to persuade the congress and the public; no extension of the search to the European side of the ocean where the impact of the French note on the United States seemed from afar to be incontrovertible. As a face-saving device Seward had denied the influence of the French note; and historians, evidently taking him at his word, were led unawares to ignore half of the "Trent" story.

Seward may have been responsible also—unwittingly—for the historians' heedless oversight of the possible Confederate inspiration of the "Trent" affair. From January 1861 right on to the end of the year Seward had played the role of a threatening war-monger either to counter civil war with foreign war or to forestall foreign intervention. Consequently in all Europe the first impression was that in the "Trent" affair the trouble-making Seward was trying again to provoke a war. Rumors flew and diplomatic comments shuttled back and forth between chancelleries about a Northern act of folly or desperation. But, when all of this was disproved by Wilkes's admission of sole responsibility and by Seward's release of the captives, the sighs of relief were so deep and the later distractions followed so fast that neither contemporaries nor later historians were inclined, after the fact, to put the shoe on the other and Southern foot where it more probably belonged. All the circumstantial evidence of contriving in Richmond, Charleston, Havana, and aboard the "Trent"—all the testimony in French and British circles and newspapers concerning Southern involvement—were quickly forgotten and not revived by later historians.

It is more excusable to overlook might-have-beens. The historians have too big a job already in treating of what happened without dealing with what almost happened. Yet, there are certain efforts which come to naught that are worthy of notice in themselves as reflections of the thinking of the actors on the scene. Such certainly were the efforts at arbitration before the dénouement and the attempts to hold a conference thereafter. Nowhere in all the literature on the period is there a discussion of the arbitration question. Nevertheless, Americans, Englishmen, Frenchmen, the press of all these countries, were full of the thoughts of arbitration; such important men as Lincoln, Adams, Napoleon III, Thouvenel, Cobden, Bright, Cowley, and Russell, and the lesser figures of Bigelow, Weed, Adams, Sanford, Talleyrand, and Hughes, at some point in their deliberations touched upon the idea of arbitration. Their thinking and their motivations on arbitration are revealing and add depth to the understanding of the contemporary scene.

Thus it was, also, with the urge to put England's protests on the "Trent" into a written acknowledgment of a new law on neutral rights. The shoe was on the other foot for England, and many wanted to tie it tight. Therefore public men and press correspondents began to agitate at first for a *quid pro quo* for the American liberation of the prisoners. Later, when the United States made the unilateral concession, the cry went up for a post-crisis conference to rewrite maritime law. Here again the thinking of Thouvenel, Seward, Lincoln, Dayton, Russell, and Granville as well as of the Russian and French presses are a matter of record. The suggestion of a conference revealed the weakness of Seward's arguments, the true position of England, and the post-crisis caution of France. Yet no historical account discusses the conference proposal and its rejection. There was no conference, to be sure, but there was a neglected story, and a story worth the telling.

The "Trent" affair, like a great organ concert piece, required the use of all the keys of all the keyboards and all the stops. The reflections, the basic attitudes and policies, the suspicions and designs of all the participants gave their undertones to the crisis. Conflicting themes of war or peace, victory or defeat, naval destruction or naval survival, intervention or nonintervention were sounded along with alternatives of cooperation or alienation, balance or imbalance of power. Certain episodes brought out the intricacies of international law and arbitration, blockade and armaments, while overtones were added by Canada and Mexico. All these myriad issues of the Civil War could be distinguished in the symphony of a two-month crisis. But this diplomatic crisis, although one of the most spectacular, had not been the first nor was it to be the last in this fratricidal war. France and Britain were to face many more before the great silence fell on Appomattox.

Chapter VII
THE PENDULUM OF
INTERVENTION THREATS

EVEN during the first year of the war the ugly head of European intervention had been raised. Mercier had hinted at it in his conversations with Seward on October 26, 1861, about the cotton crisis,[1] and the entire "Trent" affair had been heavy with the menace of British counteraction. Indeed Seward had been apprehensive that, with the peaceful settlement of the "Trent" dispute, "the next [crisis] would probably be a direct demonstration in Europe for recognition on account of the rigors of the blockade."[2] And Seward was not far wrong, as the events of 1862 would show.

The threat of European intervention could appear in many guises. There could be challenges to the efficacy of the blockade, heavy-handed attempts to obtain special exemptions to the blockade at certain ports, offers of mediation, suggestions of an armistice, and, most threatening of all, an outright recognition of the independence of the Confederate States. Any of the approaches might lead to a forceful intervention on the part of one or more European powers. To these various threats Seward could only counter with boasts of an early Federal triumph, or hints of special deals for access to cotton, or promises of opening captured ports along with demands that the recognition of belligerency be rescinded. *In extremis* he would even resort to counterthreats of a Northern wheat embargo or of a world-wide revolutionary war triggered by the United States declaring war on France and Great Britain. This extreme action would come only after an attempt to break the blockade or after a recognition of the South's independence. Nearly all these forms of threatened intervention or interposition were to appear in 1862.

[250]

The Stone Fleet

The excitement over the "Trent" affair had hardly subsided before all the maritime states were aroused over the Federal attempt to close a channel to the Charleston harbor by sinking twenty old whaling vessels[3] loaded with stones. The plan was known as soon as the Stone Fleet had left Northern ports. Both Mercier and Lyons reported its departure in late November,[4] and Russell in London was protesting the eventual deed a month later—December 20—on the very day the old ships were sunk outside Charleston. In anticipation of the sinking Russell not only characterized it a Northern admission of defeat, but also he condemned the action as "a plot against the commerce of nations" and "a project worthy only of the times of barbarism." This statement of condemnation was not only approved by Palmerston and the queen, but a copy of it was sent to Paris for Thouvenel's information.[5]

The news of the actual sinking of the stone ships reached Paris on about January 10 or 11, almost simultaneously with the news of the North's release of Mason and Slidell. While the French press praised the release, most of the newspapers denounced what they thought was the complete closing of Charleston's harbor. The French government's official newspaper, the *Moniteur*, was in the forefront of those criticizing the closure. On January 12 it denounced it as "an act of inhuman and barbarous revenge," and on January 22 it reproduced in full the London *Times*'s claim that a natural harbor, such as that of Charleston, is a place of refuge for international shipping and that the maritime powers had a right to remonstrate, or go even further (*pour ne pas dire plus*). Then it went on to cite the *Morning Herald*'s advocacy of Britain's breaking of the blockade. Other imperialist newspapers took the same attitude. The *Constitutionnel* also called the act "barbarous" and contrasted it with the behavior of the cultured Southerners who mingled with such ease in France's best social circles. The *Pays* denounced the Stone Fleet as "an act of vandalism and barbarity only worthy of the dark ages," and Grandguillot republished in pamphlet form his *Pays* articles on "The Recognition of the South." The *Patrie* went so far as to hint at the recognition of the South. On the other hand the opposition papers—the *Débats*, *Temps*, and *Opinion Nationale*—thought that the Stone Fleet was not a violation of international law and was more humane than the bombardment of the city and reminded their readers that the waging of a whole war to preserve the institution of slavery was even more inhuman than any one incident. As to opinion in general, "Malakoff" reported to *The New York Times* that "the opinion is growing that there would be an advantage to the separation of the Union," and the correspondent for the London *Morning Herald* declared that the North had lost sympathy because of the Stone Fleet.[6]

This kind of public reaction to the blocking of the Charleston harbor not only influenced the attitude of French governmental circles against the North but probably fortified a trend of thinking toward a breaking of the blockade. In the background was the concern over the cotton famine and unemployment, and now, added to that, was the feeling that the North's capitulation in the "Trent" affair was a sign of weakness and that the Stone Fleet in Charleston harbor was an admission that the cause was hopeless and a regular blockade could not be maintained. Should France therefore submit to any more economic suffering and acknowledge any longer the legality of the blockade just in order to humor the North's blind stubbornness? "Malakoff" reported that "the Cabinet and the Leglislative Bodies are much less sympathetic to the cause of the Union . . . than they were before the affair of the "Trent," and the correspondent for the London *Morning Herald* confirmed that there was a strong party in the legislative body in favor of recognition.[7] Weed's report to Seward on January 22 was probably the most ominous of all. In it he pointed out that the economic suffering in France, England, and Germany was attributed to the blockade. Since the North did not seem to be able to win and was unpopular because of the Morrill Tariff, the emperor was actually toying with the idea of hinting, in his speech from the throne,[8] as to recognition or breaking the blockade.[9] More specifically as to the attitude of Napoleon III, Prince Napoleon told Weed that "the Emperor had opened his ears to gross misrepresentations, and, to some extent was misinformed upon questions vital to America."[10] What alarmed Dayton and his Northern colleagues was the fact that Napoleon III was deliberately asking for information on American affairs as he prepared his annual legislative message.[11]

Dayton would have been even more alarmed had he known that the emperor's sole pro-Northern advisor, Thouvenel, was condemning the Stone Fleet. In his current instructions to Mercier (January 23) the foreign minister, from the facts he had at hand, denounced this "unprecedented" Federal action as a blow to international commercial interests, the permanent destruction of the port, a violation of international law, and an adverse influence on French public opinion. He did not want Mercier, like Lord Lyons, to make a formal protest, but to explain frankly France's attitude should an occasion arise. Not only did Mercier let Seward know of France's condemnation, but he left a translation of these instructions with the state department.[12]

Aware of the hostility in French circles and the emperor's search for information before delivering his annual message, Dayton and his Northern collaborators undertook a desperate campaign to head off the announcement of an adverse decision in the imperial speech. Dr. Thomas Evans, the American dentist serving the imperial family, saw Weed on January 21 and asked to be briefed on the Stone Fleet question, since he had an appointment with the emperor for the following day. We have some idea of Weed's coaching from Evans's conversation with the emperor on the 22nd. After asking for information about General McClellan, His Majesty launched into the question of Charleston harbor and conveniently opened the way for Evans, who said that the blocking was only temporary and that the harbor would even be improved after the war. Opportunities for refuge were available in nearby ports. By this exchange the good dentist felt reassured about the coming annual message and hurried back to inform Weed.[13]

Right at this point there came a new favorable development for the North in the form of a note (no. 97) from Seward in which he urged Dayton to repeat as often as possible the prospect of terminating the blockade as a result of the past and future naval successes against Southern ports. He also added that if England broke the blockade, it might end the resort to blockades for all time.[14] Dayton immediately showed the note to Weed, and they agreed that Dayton should see Thouvenel as soon as possible. Weed would see Morny, and Bigelow would visit Fould.[15]

Later that day Weed had a very satisfactory conversation with Morny, in which he reassured the count that Charleston harbor could be restored after the war, that the closing was no different from the powers' closing Dunkirk after 1713, and that the blockade might soon end at many ports anyway. Morny intimated that this news would be communicated to the emperor before his speech and urged the publication of these facts in the press.[16]

It was this demand for clarification that led Bigelow, the consul in charge of public relations, to begin the composition of a letter which he hoped would be published in the *Moniteur*. In this letter to the editor Bigelow said that the charge in the British papers that the Charleston harbor was permanently closed was erroneous. The United States had no intention of permanently closing the port. The stone ships closed only one channel that was barely nine feet deep at low tide. The ships had been sunk by removing plugs in the hulls, and they could easily be raised later on by inserting the plugs and floating the boats again. The port still had two other unblocked entrances. Then Bigelow pointed out the European precedents for blocking harbors: La Rochelle in 1628, the Scheldt and Antwerp in 1648, Dunkirk in 1713, Boulogne in 1814, Alexandria in 1807, and Sebastopol by the Russians in 1855. Of course, he went on, the United States and Europe were more enlightened now; and, if the powers want to abolish all blockading forever, the United States would be willing to join, even with the onus of being the last one to use a blockade. All of this was put together with the concurrence of Dayton and Weed and was to be taken to Morny for publication in the *Moniteur*.[17]

Finally on January 25, Dayton obtained his interview with Thouvenel which lasted for over an hour and a half. The early part of the conversation (discussed elsewhere) dealt with the question of a conference on international law as an outgrowth of the "Trent" affair and Dayton's suggestion of the international outlawing of all blockades. Thouvenel was impressed not only with the United States' desire to join such outlawry but also with their suggestion that the present blockade would soon be unnecessary. This led to a discussion of the Stone Fleet.

> *Thouvenel:* Recently we have been very much concerned over the permanent destruction of the Port of Charleston. I should be glad to hear what explanation you could give me of that proceeding. It made a most unfavorable impression against you all over Europe.
>
> *Dayton:* Although I have no specific instructions from my government, I must say that one of the principal objects of my visit was to correct erroneous impressions as to this matter. You realize that the only information we have is from the newspapers and my government has never declared its intention permanently to destroy that port. The temporary obstruction of one of its channels is, I believe, all that is sought. Had not stones been placed in the old hulks, sunk there to keep them down, we might as well have thrown chips into the sea; the very next gale would have swept them from their position. The bank on which they were placed is, I think, some five or six miles from Charleston, in the ocean, not in the mouth or bed of the river, and the depth there at high water is about eighteen feet and at low water about eleven feet only. . . . There will be no difficulty in removing them at a future day, if it is desirable to do so. Notice in this clipping from the Charleston *Mercury* where it scouts the idea of permanently closing the harbor. If newspaper reports were to be relied upon, I believe the South has itself sunk vessels, not only in the interior of the harbor, but in the Savannah river for the express purpose of keeping us out, and we have exercised only the same right as against them.
>
> *Thouvenel:* These explanations are most important. Has Mr. Adams explained this to Lord John Russell?
>
> *Dayton:* I know nothing about that, though it might be he has not. My suggestions are merely personal, volunteered, because Mr. Seward has not given me any authority to make such explanations. He never notices officially nor acts upon what

appears in the newspapers and probably never contemplated that the French or British governments would act upon information obtained from that source.

Thouvenel: It seems to me very important that the conduct of your government should be properly understood in this matter. Why hasn't it been explained through the French press?

Dayton: Personally I am forbidden by my instructions from writing anything for the press.

Thouvenel: That is understandable, but it should be done by others.

Dayton: It will eventually be done.

Dayton then drew out a map of the United States and showed the positions of the troops and the supposed plan of the spring campaign. Dayton explained that up to now the North had been largely making preparations, that Europe should give the United States a chance to show what they can do once they are mobilized. Thouvenel was always pleased with maps and detailed explanations, and at the end of the interview he promised to repeat the gist of the conversation to the emperor on Saturday evening.[18]

In the meantime Weed had had an interview with Prince Napoleon. The prince said that the emperor had recently been badly informed about America but that, since Thouvenel was "right," there was not too much to fear. The prince said he would see the emperor and do all he could on behalf of the North; and he, like Morny, invited Weed to come to him at any time in regard to American troubles.[19]

All these influences came to a focus when the French cabinet met at the Tuileries on Saturday evening, two days before the emperor's speech. At this time Thouvenel and Morny no doubt filled out the information which Dr. Evans and Prince Napoleon had already furnished the emperor. With the aid of the cabinet, including Thouvenel's prompting for the foreign policy sections, Napoleon III put the finishing touches on his address destined for the Monday ceremonies of the opening of parliament.[20]

With a lull in Italian and German affairs everybody concentrated upon the passage which the emperor would deliver on the American question. Would he finally come out for recognition and a denial of the validity of the blockade? Or would he continue his policy of patience and neutrality? As the emperor approached the paragraphs on foreign relations, he first mentioned his recognition of the new kingdom of Italy in June 1861. He did this, he said, "to contribute to the conciliation of two causes by sympathetic and disinterested counsels." Was this leading up to an announcement of a recognition of the South for similar reasons? Immediately he came to the American passage: "The civil war now ravaging America has come to compromise seriously our commercial interests. . . ."

"And so?" "Is he leading up to some action to stop it?" "Recognition, as in the case of Italy?" Only the pause of a breath, and yet these could well have been the thoughts which went racing through the minds of his listeners.

". . . However . . . as long as the rights of neutrals are respected, we ought to limit ourselves to praying ardently that these dissensions may soon come to an end."[21]

"There was a general murmur of satisfaction throughout the governmental bodies," was "Malakoff's" report to the *New York Times*. Bigelow told Seward that "the paragraph about the United States was received by the assembly with audible expressions of satisfaction." He also noted the implication that up to then the United States had not failed to respect the rights of neutrals. To Weed he remarked exultantly that "the friends of secession in Europe . . . are swearing at the Emperor this morning like pirates."[22]

In line with the usual practice a more detailed report on the state of the empire and on government policy, called *Exposé de la situation de l'Empire*, was published three days after the emperor's briefer address. In this long document the discussion of the American Civil War made no mention of the Stone Fleet nor of recognition. It was largely a survey of the last year's concern over the conflict and its economic effects on France. While it mentioned in passing France's willingness to use her good offices to bring an end to the war, the main passage reaffirmed France's neutrality. "The government of the emperor . . . had . . . only one line of conduct to follow: adherence to a strict neutrality."[23] Here, too, it appeared that the Union cause and the efforts of its agents in France had won out in this second crisis. Dayton's letter to Weed sums it up well: "I too believe that together at all events we did a good thing. Seward's dispatch too came in good time. The Secessionists here seemed to the last sure that a hostile policy would be announced in the Emperor's address and are of course proportionately disappointed."[24]

Slidell on the Scene

The Northern colony in Paris had hardly had time to breathe a sigh of relief over the emperor's speech when three days later their reassurance was threatened by the arrival of John Slidell on January 30. In touch with his predecessor, Pierre Rost, Slidell learned that Rost had an appointment with Thouvenel for the 31st, and Rost suggested that they go together. On second thought they decided against this procedure because the appointment had not included Slidell. However, the new commissioner asked Rost to inform the foreign minister of his arrival and of his desire to see him "in the mode which would be most acceptable to him."

During Rost's interview Thouvenel asked whether Slidell had arrived, and Rost took advantage of the query to say that the new commissioner would like an appointment. The foreign minister did not seem particularly enthusiastic about receiving the new envoy, saying he could not give an immediate answer and would have to consult the emperor. He did, however, advise that the request be made in writing. At one point in the interview Thouvenel was very explicit about the main subject of interest to Southerners—recognition: "I must say definitely [remarked Thouvenel] that the question of the recognition of the Confederate States can not now be entertained, nor am I prepared even to suggest the lapse of time or any circumstances which might hereafter render it a subject of conference with agents or representatives." On the other hand he seemed to give considerable importance to a list of ships which had run the blockade in both directions up to November 8, 1861.[25]

Slidell waited until after the weekend to send in his written request and was surprised and pleased to have an answer the same day with an appointment for February 7 at two o'clock, only eight days after his arrival.[26] He had decided, as a result of Rost's interview, not to raise the questions of recognition and the justification of secession which were prominent in his instructions; but, instead, to put his main emphasis on the blockade and the Stone Fleet.

Thouvenel received him courteously but rather coolly, not taking much initiative in keeping the conversation going. After a few exchanges on the "Trent" affair in which Slidell gave credit to Thouvenel's note for his release and admitted that he had preferred no release and a war between England and the United States, the Southern envoy explained that he would not bring up the question of recognition at this time. Consequently he proceeded with a discussion of Southern conditions, the blockade, and the Stone Fleet. Thouvenel then asked why so little cotton had come through if there had been so many blockaderunners. To this query Slidell had to admit that only small ships with light cargoes ventured through, a partial admission of an effective blockade which Thouvenel noted in silence. The Confederate agent then asked whether the powers had answered a reported British query by asserting that the blockade was ineffective. The French minister replied that he knew nothing about it. Not being able to keep the conversation going by himself, Slidell broke off the interview without waiting for Thouvenel's normal termination of such visits.[27]

The foreign minister's own description of the interview shows, however, that Slidell's assertion of Southern determination to resist to the end did have the effect of turning his mind again to the expedient of mediation. To Flahault he wrote:

> Mr. Slidell declared to me . . . that the determination of his compatriots was unshakable and that they would accept anything rather than reenter the Union. In the meantime the financial resources of the North are dwindling and a time will come, perhaps, when the idea of mediation will no longer be so objectionable to it. The big difficulty will be one of boundaries.[28]

In the meantime Slidell had an opportunity to meet other important members of the imperial administration. In regard to his two interviews with Count Persigny, the minister of interior, he said:

> He is with us heart and soul; he said that our cause was just, and that every dictate of humanity, the well established principles of international law, and the true policy of France called for our recognition and the declaration of the inefficiency of the blockade. He said that the Emperor entertained this opinion, but that he desired England to take the initiative. He said that Mr. Thouvenel's reserve and apparent coldness were habitual, arising partly from temperament and his diplomatic education, but still more from the restraints which his official position imposed. Mr. P. has invited me to call upon him frequently and his directed his huissier to admit me at any time.

After his visit to Jules Baroche, minister of justice, he wrote that "he is most decidedly favorable to our cause, and will exercise his influence, which is said to be great with the Emperor, to hasten our recognition." His interview with Achille Fould, the minister of finance, revealed that "he also was very cordial, and . . . his sympathies are decidedly with our Confederacy." Still later in the month he also saw Count Morny, the president of the lower house, and found him "decidedly favorable to our [Southern] cause."[29]

From all these interviews one may see that several important members of the cabinet—perhaps also Thouvenel and Napoleon III himself—were thinking in terms of mediation (semi-recognition), or recognition of independence, or blockade-breaking, any one of which would have been a form of intervention. Thus for the North the victory of the emperor's speech was already melting under the rays of Slidell's sun.

While in these early weeks the new Southern envoy did not have a formal audience with the emperor, he did have an unusual encounter with him at the Bouffe-Parisien Theater. Here Sophie Bricard, a native of the South, was to sing the leading role in *Florian*. When Slidell took his seat, he was greeted by a great deal of applause from his compatriots and French sympathizers.

The emperor later came and occupied the imperial box. At the end of Act II Slidell was invited to descend to the Green Room to congratulate Mlle Bricard. To his amazement he found the emperor there congratulating Offenbach and the whole company. When it came Mlle Bricard's turn to curtsy and the emperor had taken her hand, she, in her best stage dramatics, gestured toward Slidell and cried: "Over there, Sire, is the representative of my suffering country! The South is fighting for freedom. On my knees I supplicate Your Majesty. Give us the friendship of France!" Caught in this embarrassing situation, the emperor frowned and stepped back, but, in line with his usual graciousness, he calmly shook Slidell's hand and promptly left the room.[30]

But all this friendly encouragement to Southern supporters by cabinet members and the theater audience was cancelled out later in the month by British and French statements relating to intervention. Mann in London and Rost and Slidell in Paris had been attacking the efficacy of the blockade and presenting lists of ships successfully running it. These and British public protests against the acceptance of the blockade as legal had led Russell in January to inquire again of the law officers of the crown and of the admiralty regarding the effectiveness of the blockade at Charleston and Wilmington. Based on their advices he decided not to challenge the blockade of those ports even though some blockade-runners got through.

> Her Majesty's Government [he wrote to Lyons] . . . are of the opinion that the blockade is duly notified and also that a number of ships is stationed and remains at the entrance of the port, sufficient really to prevent access to it or to create an evident danger of entering or leaving it, and that these ships do not voluntarily permit ingress or egress, the fact that various ships may have successfully escaped through it (as in the particular instances here referred to) will not of itself prevent the Blockade from being an effective one by international Law.[31]

These diplomatic instructions were followed by public debates in parliament. When William Gregory, W. E. Forster, William S. Lindsay, and Lord Robert Cecil—later Lord Salisbury—

charged in the commons on March 7 that the blockade was illegal and that the South should be recognized, they were opposed
by Monckton Milnes, Sir Roundell Palmer, the solicitor general,
and eventually by an adverse vote in commons. Palmerston, as
prime minister, also approved the blockade.[32] Russell defended
the blockade in the lords five days later, using statistics and arguments furnished by Adams and Northern sympathizers. He
asserted that the United States were using 34 ships, 126 guns, and
10,000 men to seal off the ports, that the ships running the blockade were small coastal ones, that cotton is certainly not getting
exported, and that the South is suffering from lack of imports.
All of this, he concluded, shows that the blockade is effective.[33]

It was obvious that the British wanted a lenient interpretation
of an effective blockade as a precedent for them in future wars.
But it was also clear that the South's cotton embargo helped to
blunt their attack on the efficiency of the blockade. The absence of cotton imports in Europe was dramatic evidence which
the Confederates could not challenge without confessing their
own embargo.

All of these British debates and decisions did not go unnoticed
in Paris. France had accepted the blockade along with the
British in 1861 and certainly would not follow a different policy
now except for very serious reasons which did not appear in this
case. Thouvenel's query about the lack of Southern exports of
cotton revealed that he also inclined toward supporting the blockade in early February 1862. Likewise the French parliamentary
deliberations seemed to discourage recognition or blockade-
breaking. The paragraph on the Civil War in the senate's reply
to the emperor's speech was clearly pro-Northern.

> Like Your Majesty [the paragraph ran], it [the senate]
> recognized that the friendly relations of France and the United
> States required of the French cabinet a policy of neutrality on
> the substance of that distressing debate and that the struggle
> would be shorter to the extent that it is not complicated by
> foreign interference. But at the same time, the senate recognized
> your active vigilance in the internal measures you have ordered
> so that our workers will not suffer from too much unemploy-
> ment.[34]

In defending this paragraph in the senate, the government spokesman, Auguste Billault, made this official declaration:

> The emperor's policy is to be perfectly friendly to England. With its alliance . . . peace, the reciprocal good will of the two nations on both sides of the Channel, is a considerable guarantee for the peace and quiet of the world.
>
> . . . As to America, the fear of seeing sacrificed those old relations of friendship, those old memories which unite us to a people for whom our blood formerly served to cement their independence, that fear is not justified.
>
> . . . We have not ceased to show Americans our feeling of good friendship. Where has the honorable previous speaker found good reason to believe that this traditional policy of France should be sacrificed to certain selfish views at the very time when the British cabinet seems animated with the most conciliatory intentions toward the cabinet of Washington?
>
> . . . What is true is the friendship of the emperor for the United States, his sincere desire to see them return to peace, his inclination to cooperate as much as he can in that much to be desired reconciliation. But, as to doing anything which could be in contradiction to these sentiments, which are also those of France, the senate may rest assured, the emperor is not so disposed.[35]

These words not only were greeted by his hearers with loud applause, but they were deemed significant by all parties concerned. Thouvenel in his instructions to Mercier said:

> The language used, a few days ago, by M. Billault in the senate can not leave the least doubt in this regard [recognition]. Once more he stated that the attitude which the government of the emperor desires to maintain is one of benevolent neutrality. I had not thought to tell you about a conversation I had with Mr. Slidell because of its unimportance. I will say, however, now that I have the opportunity, that this conversation, which I could not refuse, had no other effect than to destroy any illusions which he may have harbored about our inclination to admit the definitive breakup of the Union.[36]

Dayton of course was exultant. "This speech," he remarked to Seward, "I am informed is universally regarded as closing for the

present all hopes on the part of the secessionists of France interfering to break the blockade."³⁷ This feeling must have been
nearly universal because even the two Confederate commissioners
were very discouraged. Mason declared:

> Monsieur B. it is said is the admitted exponent in the senate
> of the views of the Emperor, and thus spoke by authority. In
> this connection it would seem that the doctrines of Russell's
> letter [to Lyons] had been previously agreed on between the
> two Governments, nor could it well be otherwise, when we con-
> sider the entire accord existing between them. I submit it to
> you as the event of latest interest.³⁸

A month later Slidell was echoing in despair: "The sooner our
people know that we have nothing to expect from this side of
the water and that we must rely exclusively on our resources,
the better."³⁹

The pendulum had swung again from the high hopes of Slidell's
arrival and the fears described by Billault over toward the temporary advantage of the North and the South's deep dejection.
The big news of the month of March was to continue the swing
in the North's direction.

The "Monitor" and the "Merrimac"

The American Civil War interested Europeans not only because of its impact on their economies and the moral issue of
slavery but also because of the introduction of new methods of
warfare. French and English and Prussian officers followed one
another to the republic in the west to study carefully the new
large-scale use of the railroads, the telegraph, photography, and
the heavy artillery produced by the new metallurgy of the industrial revolution. In March 1862 came the navies' turn to
display how industries of iron and steel could fashion ironclad
ships and thereby unleash a worldwide revolution in naval
warfare.

It happened on the morning of March 8 when the Southern
frigate "Merrimac," reconstructed with heavy iron rails as plates
and five gun slits on each side, emerged from Norfolk into

Hampton Roads to wreak havoc upon the Union ships anchored farther out in the Roads. By evening two Union ships had been sunk, one beached, and the others driven under the protective guns of Fortress Monroe. On the following morning the "Merrimac" came out again, but this time it met its match in the form of the Northern "Monitor," which had just arrived from New York in the nick of time. This new challenger had an iron "cheese box" on an ironclad hull. Low in the water, it carried in its "cheese box" two revolving eleven-inch guns. The two ironclads began firing at each other from a distance, but they maneuvered closer and closer until, at times, they were only a few yards apart. The low-lying "Monitor" was less vulnerable and more maneuverable, and, in spite of its smaller size and fire power, brought the engagement to a draw, since the "Merrimac" had to return to base before low tide.

Just at the southern entrance to Hampton Roads the French frigate "Gassendi" had been lying at anchor. One of its assignments was to observe American naval warfare, and it had a veritable ringside seat as the only foreign professional observer on this occasion. On the second day, during the duel between the two ironclads, it even moved farther out into Hampton Roads in order to obtain a closer view. For some time there had been speculation in naval circles as to the effectiveness of ironclads in actual naval combat; and Captain Gautier, commander of the "Gassendi," realizing the significance of what he was witnessing and the value of this test of strength to his naval ministry, composed three successive reports—the last one perhaps the most detailed continuous account there is of the entire battle. He also sent an intelligence officer ashore to obtain more information about the designs and construction of the two ironclads. In the files of the French foreign ministry, along with the last report, are found a colored map showing the location and movements of all ships during the battle and colored designs of the "Monitor." However, as Captain Gautier closed his first tentative report, he had already come to a firm conclusion: "I can right now foresee," he wrote to Mercier, "how useless it will be for ordinary ships to try to fight against these new floating fortresses armed with rifled guns of nine and eleven inches in diameter, as those of the 'Merrimac' and of the 'Erickson.'"[40] In his final report to the minister of marine he declared:

> If the "Monitor" is a work of genius, the "Merrimac" is a work of desperation. Both have fully justified the opinions of their inventors, the latter by destroying at one fell blow two first-class frigates and two gunboats, the former by saving the rest of the American fleet anchored in Hampton Roads on March 9th.[41]

Mercier was so impressed with the accounts of this new type of combat that he urged that France send an officer specialized in ironclads to gather all possible data on the ships and the battle.[42]

The first news of the battle in Europe, arriving on March 25, was about the "Merrimac's" destructiveness on the first day.[43] This was followed by fuller accounts of the "Monitor" and the battle of the second day, and on March 30, Gautier's first account was received by Thouvenel. This engagement of the ironclads immediately created a sensation throughout Europe. Bigelow's first comments on the reaction showed the ramifications of the startling news:

> The devastating visit of the Merrimack in Hampton Roads on the 9th and 10th [sic] settled the fate of wooden vessels of war forever within one hour after the news arrived. The revelations of that day will be much more expensive to the other maritime powers than the day's damages were to us, for every dockyard will be put to its last resources in plating everything that carries a gun.
>
> The impression here is that peace will be restored by June— it is drivel of course not from American authorities but I presume from the French government who desire to quiet the public mind as much as possible in regard to trade and to encourage merchants to send in orders to the manufacturers.[44]

This reaction seemed based upon the "Merrimac's" performance and foresaw the breakup of the blockade by Southern ironclads. But the news of the "Monitor," following closely behind, caused great alarm in England and amusement in the French press as to what would have happened to the British fleet if

England had gone to war over the "Trent" affair.[45] This also obviously revealed that Frenchmen would not think of trying to break the Northern blockade at this time. Napoleon III was reported to have said that "it is now settled that there is no navy in the world that can make head against ironclad boats."[46] Bigelow"'s later observation was:

> That event had done more to re-establish us as a national power in Europe and inspire respect for our military resources than anything that has occurred since the rebellion. The Nations who were rejoicing in our weakness . . . two months ago . . . have suddenly discovered that the race is not always to the strong, and that it was the mercy of Providence rather than their own wisdom or sense of justice which prevented their being plunged into a war which in the natural course of things might have resulted in sinking half their navy before they would have heard of its arrival in our country.[47]

By the time that Captain Gautier's final report was in the hands of Chasseloup-Laubat, the minister of marine, he and the emperor were in conference over a more rapid modernizing of the French navy with ironclads. Napoleon ordered his minister to prepare a list of all French naval vessels which were worth the trouble of covering with iron. Two weeks later the minister was ordered to hasten the construction of armored naval batteries, and a month later four ironclad batteries with fourteen guns each were launched.[48]

England, the great naval power, was even more upset than France. Soon after the reports arrived in London, the debates over an ironclad navy began in parliament—March 29. In the session of commons on April 4 a speaker criticized the effort to build coastal gun emplacements and asked what the government had done on armored ships. In answer to a similar question in the lords, Palmerston replied that the government had previously been studying and experimenting on ironclads and by 1864 would have sixteen armored ships in service.[49] Even Austria sent two naval engineers to America to study both the "Monitor" and the "Merrimac" and the more recently constructed coastal defenses,[50] and the Italian government sent engineers to France,

England, and America to study ironclads and floating batteries. According to the *Moniteur* "this question of armored vessels seems to be preoccupying one after the other all the governments of Europe."[51]

And, as if to make matters worse for the Confederate cause, news began to arrive of Union victories in the capture of New Bern, Beaufort, Jacksonville, and St. Augustine, and in the battles of Pittsburg Landing and Island No. 10.[52] Dayton summed it up well concerning the connection of Hampton Roads and all these other Union victories in his dispatch of April 17:

> The change of conditions at home has produced a change, if possible, more striking abroad. There is little more said just now as to the validity of our blockade or the propriety of an early recognition of the south. The fight between the Monitor and the Merrimack has turned the attention of these maritime governments, and of England more especially, in another direction. They certainly appreciate more highly than heretofore the difficulty of shutting up distant ports with wooden ships. . . . With a powerful and disciplined army on foot, and a heavy iron-clad naval force at our command, the world will understand that our just rights are not to be trifled with.[53]

The Confederates in Paris had had a brief moment of rejoicing at the first news of the "Merrimac" unalloyed by the later accounts of the "Monitor," but the pendulum swung far out in the Northern direction as soon as the whole sensational story had been reported. The confrontation at Hampton Roads may have been a draw; but the Northern fleet had been saved. The South may have resurrected the old hull of the "Merrimac" with skillful improvisation, but she did not have the iron resources or the naval shipyards to out-produce the North in ironclads. More and better "Monitors" were on the ways and would soon be in service, and the whole growing Northern industrial complex stood ready to challenge any power in an ironclad race. These thoughts had two effects: one, to make Southern independence seem less likely and the other, to make any form of foreign intervention much too hazardous a venture.

Lindsay Rides the Pendulum

In spite of the Southern discouragement after the "Monitor"-"Merrimac" incident there was one man, William S. Lindsay, who made a bold effort in the month of April to obtain recognition for the Confederacy. Lindsay was said to be the largest shipowner in Great Britain, and, as such, he was anxious to end the Civil War and sympathetic with the Southern cause. As a natural advocate of free trade he disliked the new Northern high tariff, and, as a shipper, he suffered losses from the imposition of the blockade and the disruption of the cotton trade. This gentleman was also a member of parliament and had assisted in a minor capacity in the preparation of the Cobden trade treaty with France in 1860. Convinced that something must be done to break the log jam of war and interrupted trade and that a recognition of the South and the breaking of the "illegal" blockade were the ways to do it, he determined to go to France and urge Napoleon III to force England into joint action or to intervene by himself.

Lindsay arrived in Paris on April 8, at just about the time that Napoleon III was prodding the French navy to hurry the construction of ironclads. The next day he visited Cowley at the embassy and asked that he arrange for him an audience with the emperor in order to discuss with him some contemplated changes in the navigation laws. Knowing of Lindsay's role in the commercial treaty, Cowley made the request, and on the evening of April 10 the self-appointed envoy received a note from the emperor's secretary, Mocquard, asking him to come to the Tuileries at 1:00 P.M. on the 11th.

In the meantime Lindsay had had a conversation with Rouher, the minister of commerce, who was very much perturbed by the dwindling supply of cotton, the decline in exports, and the rising unemployment. The commerce minister felt sure that it was England which was preventing remedial action, because the emperor would not act without English collaboration. Rouher claimed that as early as the summer of 1861 and again in March 1862 France had made proposals to England for some form of joint action without any response from the English side.

At the appointed hour Lindsay was received very cordially by the emperor, who said he had looked forward to seeing him, since he had learned, through Thouvenel, of Lindsay's talk with Rouher. For a while Lindsay did discuss the French navigation laws as well as a scheme for a steamship line between Bordeaux and New Orleans. The mention of this city gave Lindsay a chance to shift the discussion to the Civil War. First of all he attacked the effectiveness of the blockade and furnished statistics on blockade-runners. Napoleon III agreed with him on its nonenforcement and claimed that Thouvenel had twice proposed to Cowley a joint action against the blockade without any response. Lindsay then suggested a joint recognition of the Confederacy. Following along this line, he said that the North could not reconquer the South, so the war was causing unnecessary bloodshed in America and suffering on both continents. Therefore it should be stopped by recognition and breaking the blockade. Rather inconsistently he slipped into his argument a complaint that the North could get all the war supplies it wanted while the South was "effectually cut off." The emperor did not catch him up on this, as the Englishman went on to emphasize that the North was not trying to abolish slavery at all.

Napoleon seemed to be in full agreement. He admitted that he had favored the preservation of the Union; but now that the cause of restoration was suffering so acutely from the war's senseless course, he would send a fleet to open New Orleans if England would. He advised Lindsay to ask Cowley's advice and return to the palace again on Sunday morning.[54]

With some excitement and an inflated ego Lindsay hurried over to Slidell's residence and reported this unique interview to him. To Slidell there was a return of hope, and the pendulum seemed to be swinging to his side. Then Lindsay went obediently to see Cowley at the embassy, where he told him about the two earlier feelers of the emperor and about the latter's desire now to intervene to obtain cotton because the Northern interruption of the cotton trade was a veritable interference in France's internal affairs. Upon being asked his opinion, to be relayed to the emperor, Cowley was very positive and outspoken. He denied that France had approached Great Britain on ending the blockade and expressed the opinion that the blockade was becoming even more effective than when England had first acquiesced in it.[55]

On Sunday, the 13th, Lindsay saw the emperor again and told him about his conversation with Cowley. The emperor reaffirmed his previous views and asked him to go back to England and tell Russell and Palmerston all that he had said. Also he would have Lindsay tell Disraeli and Lord Derby of his views, but not as coming from him because he did not want to have it appear that he was communicating with the opposition. Then he urged Lindsay to return to Paris for another interview to let him know Russell's views. "I do not want to be embarrassed by the forms and delays of diplomacy," the emperor concluded, "as I feel the necessity of immediate action."[56]

Cowley was irritated and disdainful of this clumsy, self-appointed mission of Lindsay's and suspected that the initiative was more Lindsay's than the emperor's. However, he went over immediately to see Thouvenel and asked him about the two notes sent to England. The French minister denied all knowledge of any such notes and declared they had never been sent. The two professional diplomats resented the activity of this amateur, and Thouvenel said he was going to take it up with the emperor on the next day—the 14th.[57] Thouvenel told Cowley that "he had endeavored to show both the Emperor and M. Rouher that to have recognized the independence of the South would not have brought cotton into the markets, while any interference with the blockade would probably have produced a collision." Still Thouvenel worried about the need for cotton. He wondered if the North could not open up just one neutral port.[58]

Napoleon III tried to soothe his irritated minister by saying that, from Rouher's urgent reports, he was alarmed over the cotton famine, felt something should be done, and was willing to have Lindsay pass the word along informally to Russell and Palmerston. This is how the emperor summed up his charge to Lindsay:

I can not, and will not, act without England. The official ground does not seem to be prepared enough so that my government could offer proposals to the minister of the queen. And, as they are the best judges of industrial interests which you are defending, you should go and see them. I will then learn confidentially of their opinion as they will come to know mine, and I will then see what will be possible to work out with the English government.[59]

On his return to England, Lindsay was rebuffed by Russell and Palmerston. The latter remained out of town, but Russell gave him a very curt refusal of an interview:

> As the Queen has an Ambassador in Paris and the Emperor an Ambassador in London, I think the best way for the two governments to communicate with each other is through the respective embassies. I shall always be ready to listen to any message which the Emperor might be pleased to send to the British Government either through Lord Cowley or Count de Flahault and to give such answers as the Cabinet might advise and the Queen approve.

Lindsay, in persisting for an interview, implied that the emperor wanted to have a confidential channel at this point. On this Russell held his ground by saying: "Lord Cowley and Count de Flahault can make the most confidential, as well as official communications."[60]

Thus, somewhat deflated, Lindsay returned to Paris on April 17 in the company of Mason to whom he confided that he had also seen Disraeli. The latter's reaction had been to suspect that Russell had made a nonintervention deal with Seward. On the 18th Lindsay had his third interview with the emperor to whom he recounted his rebuff in London. Napoleon appeared to be disappointed and disgruntled and complained that, in spite of his aid to England in the "Trent" affair, that country now seemed less disposed to act cordially with him. He also thought Disraeli's suspicion probably explained some of the strange recent attitudes of the English government.

> I think [the emperor continued] that the best course would be to make a friendly appeal to it [the Federal government], either alone or concurrently with England, to open the ports, but to

accompany the appeal with a proper demonstration of force on the Southern coasts, and should the appeal appear to his minister likely to be ineffectual, to back it with a declaration of his purpose not to respect the blockade. The taking of New Orleans, which I did not anticipate, may render it inexpedient to act. I will not decide at once, but will wait some days for further intelligence.

This time, however, Napoleon was a little more cautious and asked Lindsay to keep this interview confidential.[61]

Not only had Cowley and Thouvenel bristled at Lindsay's intrusion into the normal diplomatic channels, but Flahault showed undisguised resentment.

> I cannot conceal from you that this kind of relations are helpful to no one's position, not to the emperor's or to mine. If it should continue, I would see no other reason for it except the emperor's lack of confidence in me, either because I lack zeal or ability. . . . I should prefer a thousand times to cease to be His Majesty's representative in London than to continue to occupy this post after I no longer possess his entire confidence.[62]

Thouvenel probably tried to teach the emperor a lesson, and indirectly voice his own protest, by showing Flahault's letter to him.

> The emperor [Thouvenel wrote] charged me to tell you that it had never entered his mind an instant to do anything behind your back. His Majesty, *with that easy-going way you know so well*, allowed himself—excuse the word—to be exploited a little by his visitor. The latter profited by the occasion to try to exaggerate its importance, but *they* are enlightened today on his standing, and this little lesson can be very useful.[63]

Evidently Cowley had implied to Napoleon a similar dislike for this episode because the latter wrote him a personal note saying:

> I thank you for your note. I hope with you that our factories will soon have cotton. I have not been at all shocked that Lord Russell did not receive Mr. Lindsay. The latter had asked

my permission to report our conversation to the principal secretary of state, and I had given my consent and that's all there
is to it.[64]

As Slidell and Mason learned of Russell's inflexibility and
Napoleon III's retreat, their revived hopes began to sink again.
Then came a series of bad news reports: on April 23, that the
Confederates had been thrown back at Corinth, on April 24, that
Island No. 10 had fallen, on May 6, that Fort Pulaski near
Savannah had been captured.[65] Hotze, the Southern agent in
London, wrote in despair: "I have little hope of the initiative
either in raising the blockade or in recognition, being taken by
the Emperor."[66]

But the emperor had laid more stress upon the outcome of the
fighting around New Orleans, and all eyes were scanning the
news dispatches during April and May. Finally, the news
reached London on May 11 that New Orleans had been captured by Federal troops, and at about midnight Thouvenel received the following telegram from Flahault:

> Mr. Hammond [permanent undersecretary at the foreign
> office] informs me that M. Mercier wishes the government of
> the Emperor to be informed that Mr. Seward says that New
> Orleans has fallen; that postal service with the city is going to
> be re-established; and that he has informed Mr. Adams that
> the question of relaxing the blockade will be considered im
> mediately. But it would seem that they may intend to connect
> it with the withdrawal of recognition of belligerency.[67]

The next morning Russell told Flahault that the postal service to
New Orleans and a relaxation of the blockade were all to the
good, "but the Queen's cabinet has no intention of changing its
position relative to the two parties and . . . it would not reverse
its earlier decision of recognizing the belligerency of the Southern
states."[68] Thouvenel echoed this three days later when he said
that future military uncertainties did not justify departing from
a policy of strict neutrality.[69]

But the over-all effect of the fall of New Orleans was devastating to the Southern cause. "Malakoff" reported that "nothing that has occurred since the commencement of the war has made such an impression on the French as the fall of New Orleans." He pointed out that that city was thought of as a French town and was best known by Frenchmen except for New York. The news of its capture reverberated throughout the country.[70] When Thouvenel saw Slidell on May 14, he inquired right away about the future effects of the fall of New Orleans. The Confederate commissioner had to admit "that it was a heavy blow for us and would give the enemy command of the Mississippi and its tributaries, [and] enable him to harass and annoy our citizens living on navigable streams or in the immediate neighborhood."[71] This dejection spelled the full swing of the pendulum away from the high hopes reposed in Lindsay. Seward's demand for the withdrawal of belligerent rights to the Confederacy was an effective decoy which drew off the fire of intervention, especially in the light of the capture of Southern ports and the prospects of the relaxation of some of the blockade. Napoleon III confessed to Cowley: "I quite agree that nothing is to be done for the moment but to watch events."[72]

Mercier's Visit to Richmond

Victories by the North, however, did not entirely preclude all forms of intervention. They might discourage the rougher approaches of recognition and blockade-breaking; but, on the other hand, they might seem to pave the way for the mediation form of intervention. This would be on the theory that the North would be more willing to conciliate after victories than after defeats.

The news had arrived in Paris on March 6 of Federal victories in Kentucky and Tennessee, culminating in the fall of Fort Donelson.[73] Inspired by these developments, Thouvenel sent out mediation instructions on that very day:

> Today [he wrote to Mercier], especially in view of the recent successes obtained in Kentucky and Tennessee, the gains made by the Federal government are outstanding enough completely to satisfy its prestige.... Has not the time come for it at this point to examine, with all the calmness and moderation suit-

able to the present situation, whether the sole approach of coercion is really the best for curing past evils and still others to come. . . . Consequently we would regret, as far as we are concerned, not contributing, as far as it depends on us, to bring to the Federal government's attention the satisfaction Europe would feel in seeing it consider, itself, whether other ways than the continuation of the war would not contribute more efficaciously and under better conditions for everybody to a solution of the pending difficulties.

In doing this, Thouvenel explained, it would avoid many future evils for the United States and likewise end the ever-growing industrial and commercial slump in Europe. He then asked Mercier to take this up with Seward.[74] In a private letter to Mercier he was even more specific about an imminent mediation move. Speaking of Slidell, he wrote:

> The time may come, however, when his presence in Paris might be helpful if the North, feeling that its prestige had been saved, and seeing the difficulties of subjugating the South, came to the point of wanting to negotiate. Mr. Slidell then would be within reach of our counsels, and, without wishing to pronounce too soon the word mediation, our good offices would perhaps be useful. . . . Our industry is suffering horribly, and, for many reasons, the distress of our working classes do not leave us as cold as our neighbors [the English].

The minister continued to say that Dayton had told the emperor that the United States were very seriously concerned with this industrial situation and would soon obtain cotton for France. Thouvenel was curious to know whether this promise was based on predictions of an early triumph or on intentions of inaugurating a license system through the blockade.[75]

Mercier had received both of these communications by the end of March, and proceeded to have an interview with Seward. Before going to the state department he had decided not to discuss mediation or the means of getting cotton because the government was on the eve of important military and naval campaigns, the "Monitor" engagement had made the North feel less vulnerable to foreign navies, and the British government had just reaffirmed in parliament its recognition of an effective blockade. Consequently Mercier planned merely to repeat the sad story of the industrial plight of France in order to prepare the way for later talks on mediation or opening of ports. He had no sooner entered Seward's office, however, than the latter smoked him out and even inveigled the French minister into letting him read informally his latest instructions. Having barely glanced at the document, the secretary picked up two dispatches on his desk and said, "Look, here's my answer." Now it was Mercier's turn to read. The first document was Dayton's account of his conversation with the emperor in which the latter had stressed the bad industrial situation and the unemployment among French workmen and Dayton had given hopes of cotton being obtained after the capture of Mobile and New Orleans.[76] The second document, Seward's reply, spoke of the impending victories, minimized the likelihood that cotton would be destroyed, and then pressed the point that the emperor himself could help end the war swiftly and obtain cotton by withdrawing his recognition of Southern belligerency (no longer the "averted glance").[77] After an exchange of a few remarks they agreed to adjourn further discussion until the fall of New Orleans.[78]

Two weeks later the news had come of the fall of New Bern, Beaufort, and Jacksonville in North Carolina and Florida and of further victories at Shiloh and Pittsburg Landing in southern Tennessee. Now Seward, in another conversation with Mercier, was even more sanguine of an early reestablishment of the Union. The French envoy was so skeptical of the South caving in so easily that he remarked, more in a tone of musing, "I wish I could be as sure of it as you are." "It's just too bad I can't go down to Richmond and find out for myself what is the condition of things there."

"But go on down?" Seward exclaimed with what appeared to be genuine confidence. "Have one of your ships take you to Norfolk and I'll give you a pass. Your visit right at this time could have a very good effect and do us a real service."

Mercier was so surprised at this quick acceptance of his unpremeditated suggestion that he began to have qualms about the overall effect of such a visit. He told Seward he would have to think it over and would come back to let him know his decision. The more he thought it over, however, the more he believed that he ought to take up this offer. After all, a diplomat should take advantage of every opportunity for accurate information, and perhaps he could use the occasion to prepare the way in the South, as he was already doing in the North, for a future French or European mediation.

Having made up his mind, he went to see Lyons on April 10 and told him the whole story. Lyons shook his head and tried to dissuade Mercier because, going alone, he would appear to have abandoned his practice of cooperation with England. Mercier countered by saying that he could go back to Seward and say that he had consulted Lyons and that they were in accord. Besides, it would be absurd to lose a chance to obtain such valuable information and such possibilities of encouraging reconciliation just because of excessive cautiousness. The French envoy then even shared with Lyons his plans of what he would say to his Southern friends. He would tell them that their military situation looked desperate, and they could not look for any immediate recognition from European powers. Therefore should they not preferably make an armistice and negotiate terms with the North? Lyons advised him to add that the South could expect no alliance from any European power. At this point, too, Mercier suggested that Baron Stoeckl go with him, but Lyons did not like this at all. So Mercier, out of deference to his British colleague, dropped that idea.

About two days later the French minister returned to Seward, told him that he agreed to go, and revealed the sort of discouraging approach he was going to make to the Southerners. Seward not only approved Mercier's intended discourse but he added:

> You may also tell them that they have no spirit of vengeance to apprehend from me personally, and that they would be cordially welcomed back to their seats in the Senate, and to their due share of political influence. I have not said so to any other person, but I'll tell you that I am willing to risk my own political station and reputation in pursuing a conciliatory course towards the South, and I am ready to make this my policy and to stand or fall by it.[79]

Then Seward allowed Mercier to use the military telegraph to call the French frigate "Gassendi" from Norfolk to the Potomac to take him down to Norfolk. The French minister and his first secretary, Geoffroy, left Washington on April 14, were at Norfolk on the 15th, and arrived in Richmond on the 16th. Here Mercier immediately had a long talk with Judah P. Benjamin, the Confederate secretary of state and long-time friend from the days when he was senator in Washington. Benjamin thought that perhaps Mercier was being used by Seward to explore the situation but decided to carry along the game on Mercier's terms.

Mercier: I want you to know that I have come here with Mr. Seward's consent and knowledge. The purpose of this trip is none other than to verify for myself the real condition of things, and I come to ask your help in attaining it.

Benjamin: I will do that with great pleasure, and I am delighted that you can get down to the real truth, which from all I hear from the North, appears to me to be very little understood. I admit that I was somewhat mistaken in my predictions [made back in our Washington conversations]. I would never have believed that the war was to take on such proportions, that the North would show so much determination, and would so readily take a plunge toward bankruptcy. Also we have counted too much on Europe and the power of commercial interests [King Cotton]. Yet, however it may be, you will become convinced that we are determined to win our independence no matter what the cost. The people are unanimous on that. The have already suffered much, and they are willing to suffer a great deal more, if necessary, to attain their goal.

Mercier: Frankly, I must say that the capture of all your cities within reach of the [navy] is a matter of certainty. It is purely a question of weight of metal. As the North has undoubtedly a vast superiority of resources in iron and other materials for gunboats and artillery, I do not deem it possible for you to save any of your cities. Tell me what you think would be your government's course in such an event.

Benjamin: We don't deny that the Federals have vastly superior forces and possession of the sea, that they can in the long-run capture all our ports. But when they take our cities, they will only find women, old men, and children. All those able to bear arms will retire into the back country, out of range of gunboats. Before such resistance the North will have to give in. We remember that in the War for Independence the English at one time possessed almost all the coastal cities, and yet they lost. It will be the same this time. . . . Like the English, the Yankees are fighting today to save their power and riches, and we are fighting, like the Americans did, to win our independence.

Mercier: But before going to such extremities, if the North, as I think it is disposed, offered you serious guarantees, greater than you have ever asked of it, would you refuse to come to an agreement?

Benjamin: The time for such patching-up is passed! We don't think they are possible any more, and you will see that no one will any longer listen to such ideas. In fact we are two distinct peoples and each should have its separate existence. Our people today hate the Yankee as much as the French have always hated the English. . . . It has come to the point where the North must exterminate us or agree to separation.

Mercier: With numbers, money, and the sea against you, it is a very uphill fight.

Benjamin: Not as much as you suppose. [Here he gave a long discussion of the military situation and plans, showing that Shiloh was not a real Northern victory. Even if Richmond were lost, he said they would fight on from the interior.]

Mercier: But aren't you a little worried about your slaves?

Benjamin: Not a bit. As we retreat into the back country, we will take them with us, losing a few it's true, but we have to resign ourselves to that as with any property. As to getting them to revolt, if they try, they won't succeed. We're quite sure on that score.

Mercier: How and when do you ever expect the war to end? For you can not deny that the North is just as unanimous for the Union as you are for separation, and it is still far from being discouraged.

Benjamin: The war may still go on for a long time. However, we count on the financial exhaustion of the North. I admit to you that we don't understand how the government's credit has been maintained up to now.

Mercier: Are you really determined to burn your cotton and tobacco? And, if your ports are opened to commerce, do you believe your planters can resist the temptation of selling their crops to the brokers?

Benjamin: How can you suppose we won't burn cotton and tobacco? . . . Besides there's very little cotton in the cities. Only 600 bales in New Orleans. All this year's crop is still on the plantations where it is hard to get. Any planter who tried to sell would be exposed to the retaliation of his compatriots.

Benjamin then complained about the failure to recognize the South by the European powers and their acceptance of the blockade. He did not argue, however, when Mercier tried to explain the Franco-British point of view, but he did try to prove the ineffectiveness of the blockade. Mercier confessed later to Thouvenel that "I was a little embarrassed in trying to answer his arguments." He evaded the subject by saying it was a matter of international law and of multilateral consultations.

Mercier (in closing the interview): But how can anybody talk to either side? I dare not utter to you a single sentence that does not begin with the word independence, nor can I say a syllable to the other side on any basis other than the Union.

Benjamin (good-humoredly): Why should you say anything to either side? I know your good feeling for us, and we require no proof of it, but you know we are hot-blooded people, and we would not like to talk with anybody who entertained the idea of the possibility of our dishonoring ourselves by reuniting with a people for whom we feel unmitigated contempt as well as abhorrence.

Mercier and Geoffroy stayed for about three days, learning the same story from other Southern leaders. They could not see Mr. Botts, a well-known Unionist, because he was in jail, but Mercier talked with one of his business friends who said that people there were so terrified that they could not tell him the truth but that the people would welcome the Federals as liberators. This seemed to Mercier to be a very small voice against the Confederate chorus. His conclusion was that all attempts at pacification would have to await the outcome of the impending military engagements.[80]

The French envoy returned to Washington on April 24 and

saw both Lincoln and Seward. The president listened with interest but in silence. Seward, however, seemed disappointed over the recalcitrance of the Southern leaders, and he tried to pass it off by comparing it to the excitement during an election campaign and then the quiet which would follow. Mercier was not impressed because the whole secessionist furor had followed Lincoln's election.[81]

Mercier's trip to Richmond also caused a great deal of public comment in the North. In a conversation with Lyons, Seward said:

> I have had some difficulty in preventing M. Mercier's journey making an unfavorable impression on the public. With this view I have caused to be mentioned in the papers that M. Mercier has had a long interview with me on his return from Richmond. I have taken him to the President which also I shall put in the newspaper. Tonight I am to dine with M. Mercier to meet the captain of the French ship of war the "Gassendi" which has brought M. Mercier back. Tomorrow the President will pay a visit to that ship.[82]

Indeed, Seward had two statements published in the press[83] and not only had Lincoln visit the "Gassendi" but held an evening reception for the officers of the ship and had the ship refuel from American naval stores. "I like to think," wrote Mercier, "that all these demonstrations had, in part, their purpose to convince the public that my visit to Richmond could not have a motive contrary to the interests of the North."[84]

If there was some eyebrow-raising and speculation in the United States concerning the trip, there was downright consternation and flurried excitement in French and English circles. The news of Mercier's departure for Richmond arrived in Paris by telegraphic dispatch on the morning of April 29, saying that the purpose seemed to be in the interest of French tobacco. This was followed by a telegram from Russell who said the purpose was to bring the South back into the Union. The next day Thouvenel also heard from Flahault, who passed on Russell comments that Mercier had even invited Stoeckl to go along and Lyons was upset over this breakdown of Anglo-French solidarity.[85] Thouvenel, a stickler for proper procedures, was most concerned over the effect this unauthorized trip would have on Anglo-French cooperation. He wrote immediately to Flahault, for transmission to Russell, that "nothing had come to forewarn him of such a decision," that "in the absence of any information from him [Mercier], I can not doubt that he decided on this under the stress of the most serious considerations." He assured the English that he was reminding Mercier to continue a policy of collaboration with Lyons.[86] That very day Thouvenel sent out to Mercier the sharpest note ever found in their otherwise cordial correspondence.

> Having discovered nothing in your correspondence which could suggest such a step on your part [scolded Thouvenel], I was at first disposed to question the authenticity of the report. . . . Although I do not doubt for a minute that you were motivated in this case by the most serious considerations, you understand, Sir, that I am waiting with impatience for the information that you will not have failed to send me on the subject of the reason which prompted this grave decision. I am sure in advance that you will have taken every precaution so that your move would not be interpreted by anyone as an indication of a divergence of views between the emperor's government and the cabinet of London. In fact we have not ceased to think that an entente cordiale with England should be the basis of our policy toward the United States. You yourself have understood this policy too well and practiced it too wisely ever since the beginning of the American crisis for me not to be convinced that you will be careful in this instance to avoid anything which might cause any doubt about the continuance of this entente.[87]

Napoleon III was just as unhappy about it as Thouvenel. The latter may have had suspicions, as did the Confederate commissioners, that the emperor may have instructed Mercier behind the foreign minister's back. But Napoleon took pains to reassure his minister. "The emperor seemed very upset by M. Mercier's action," Thouvenel wrote to Flahault, "and I have again gained the certitude that His Majesty intends to do nothing in the United States without a complete accord with England." He would give Russell a copy of Mercier's report as soon as he received it.[88]

Four days later Thouvenel was much relieved to learn that Russell still believed that France would adhere to the two-power solidarity and saw nothing in this incident which would cause him to doubt it. However, the foreign secretary believed that, if Mercier had thought the matter through a little more, he would have given up the idea.[89] In the meantime Flahault had had a chance to sound out British opinion and had this reassuring report for the Quai d'Orsay:

> This action [the trip] does not arouse here any susceptibilities, does not cause any distrust, and it appears to me from the language of the newspapers and of those I hear around me, that neither the government nor opinion questions our firm desire to continue to march in complete accord with England on the American question.[90]

Thouvenel did not receive Mercier's first report on plans for the trip until four days after the English had the news, May 3. The French courier service was much slower than the English, and Mercier usually lacked punctuality in writing his dispatches. It was not until late on the 14th that the foreign minister received Mercier's long final report. In the meantime Slidell asked for an interview on the subject, which was granted for earlier on the 14th. Thouvenel seemed to be much more cordial and talkative than in his previous interview. He began right away with a question on the fall of New Orleans. This was the occasion when Slidell frankly admitted the disaster this meant for the South. As soon as he could, Slidell brought the conversation around to the Richmond visit. He asked for the same privilege to be informed about Mercier's visit to Richmond as Adams received regarding Lyons' activities in Washington. Thouvenel agreed completely, but said he had had no final report from Mercier. However, he shared Lyons' report with Slidell and promised to let him see Mercier's report when it arrived. They also talked about the question of mediation. Thouvenel asked what France could do in the face of the South's recalcitrance. In reply Slidell said the powers should recognize the South, and then she would be willing to accept an armistice for six months including the suspension of the blockade. Thouvenel asked what was to be done with the border states, and Slidell insisted on self-determination, which might lead at first to a separate confederation. The Southern emissary left with considerable encouragement that France might act after a few Southern victories during the summer.[91]

Mercier's report came that same evening—the 14th—and by Thouvenel's prompt reply we see his latest thoughts on mediation.

> The impressions which you brought back from your trip [he wrote Mercier] can only confirm us in the opinion to which our impartial examination of the situation had already led us. It is evident that, in the present state of things, future events can have a decisive influence on the outcome of the conflict, but without our knowing yet on which side this influence will be exerted. So it is not in the face of such an uncertainty that it would be a good time to abandon our attitude of strict neutrality for which circumstances have made it a requirement for us up to now.. More than ever it is best to wait before modifying, if at all, our line of conduct.[92]

Once again curiosity and hopes had been aroused among the Confederates on both sides of the ocean, this time by the fact of a French diplomat's journey to Richmond; and once again these hopes had been dashed by the Washington government's extreme cordiality toward the returning Mercier and the firm determination of France and England to wait a little longer for a more decisive trend in the military operations. The fall of New Orleans and the Confederate withdrawal at Shiloh were already pushing the pendulum again to the Union side, but they did not seem as decisive as the impending Richmond military confrontation would be. Thus a stillness brooded over the Western world as valiant men assembled in Virginia and anxious eyes watched from many shores.

Chapter VIII

OPENING SOUTHERN PORTS AND RETREAT BEFORE RICHMOND

France Requests Open Ports

DURING the intervening months of April, May, and June, while awaiting the impending clash of arms in Virginia, a great deal of attention was given, on both sides of the Atlantic, to the question of relaxing the severity of the blockade by opening some of the Southern ports to European trade. We have already seen that, in his instructions of early March, Thouvenel had been urging a North-South truce negotiation, possibly through France's good offices, not only to end the bloodshed in America but also to ease the industrial and commercial suffering in France.[1]

It was at this point that Emperor Napoleon III reentered the picture. As a result of his first interview with Slidell, the Confederates had gained the definite impression that the emperor "considered the disruption of the Union and of its rising navy as a great misfortune to France, and was of late inclined to hope that it might be reconstructed, and further that he would under no circumstances incur the enmity of the North by taking the lead in recognizing us."[2] No doubt this more cautious and pro-Northern attitude was caused by the news of the Northern victory at Fort Donelson, which had arrived in March.[3] It was in this mood that Napoleon III took the initiative in inviting Dayton for an interview at 2 P.M. on Tuesday, March 25. The emperor began the conversation by inquiring about the possibility of opening some Southern ports for the export of cotton since he saw no relief in sight by way of early termination of the war. He was also worried about the danger of cotton growers burning their own crops. Dayton followed the Seward line of predicting an early end of the war and discounting the seriousness of Southern threats to destroy cotton supplies. After these reassurances Dayton proceeded to read Seward's dispatch of February 27 (no. 118) in which he pointed out the difficulties of giving France special mail privileges with New Orleans. These would require granting the same benefits to all other countries and to all other blocked ports. Nevertheless, Seward said, he was giving the question his serious consideration and was wondering whether "the complaint cannot be removed in another and better way," i.e. by the capture of New Orleans. Then the Northern envoy went on to read Seward's dispatch of February 28 (no. 120) in which the secretary said that the Union government was already considering ways of opening trade with the interior of recaptured areas and that this study might now include "some alleviation of the rigors of the blockade." Seward then injected the issue of the withdrawal of the recognition of Southern belligerency.

> We could doubtless go much farther and faster in [this] direction . . . if we could have any reason to expect that concessions on our part would be met by a withdrawal on the part of the maritime nations of the belligerent privileges heretofore so unnecessarily conceded, as we conceive, to the insurgents.[4]

The emperor listened attentively to this reading, whereupon the following conversation took place:

> *Napoleon III:* Yes, I know your forces are on the way to New Orleans. Now, if you take the city, do you think they will then get a supply of cotton?
> *Dayton:* I have little doubt of it. Mr. Seward has always said that, when we take possession of the country in which the ports are located, the blockade will be removed, and when removed, I think that cotton to a considerable extent will come forward. The secretary, in the last paragraph of his second dispatch, raised the point about the withdrawal of the recognition of belligerency. In that regard we honestly believe that, if a Proclamation by France and England, withdrawing belligerent

rights from the Insurrectionists is made, the insurrection will collapse at once. It is the moral support only, which that concession has given them, that has sustained them so far. They have always looked to it as a first step towards their final recognition as an independent Power. If that concession is withdrawn, I believe, as an equivalent the blockade will be raised at an early day.

Napoleon III [sensing that some diplomatic horse-trading was involved here]: The concession of belligerent rights was made upon an understanding with England. Some legal questions were involved in it originally, and I will have to speak to M. Thouvenel about them.

Dayton: You will notice, Your Majesty, that the Confederate flag has been scarcely, if at all, seen in a port of France. They have almost no commerce on the ocean and scarcely the pretense of a Navy. The two vessels (Nashville and Sumter) which have alone been in European waters, have demeaned themselves as pirates rather than as Ships of War. A withdrawal of belligerent rights will, under these circumstances, take from the South no *material* advantage; it will only deprive them of the countenance and moral support of other nations.

Napoleon III: I must say frankly that, when the Insurrection broke out, and this concession of belligerent rights was made, I did not suppose the North would succeed. It was the general belief of Statesmen of Europe that the two sections would never come together again. This belief was probably the principal reason why this concession of belligerent rights was then granted. Even now, though, it is a large country and, for that reason, difficult to subdue.

Dayton: We do not have to seize hold of a man's entire body to control him. If we grasp firmly any sensitive extremities it is enough. You controlled Russia for the time being by taking possession of Sebastopol. I should like to have Your Majesty note how few ports there are in the South and how seizing and holding them will effectively exclude from the outer world the people of the interior whose entire surplus industry was devoted to raising articles for export. This advantage, in connection with the fact of the unquestionable existence of a large Union element in parts of the South, will bring them, I think, into the Union again.

Napoleon III: I'll think these matters over, but I hope in the meantime that something will be done by your government to relieve the difficulties here, growing out of the want of cotton.[5]

The clearest indication of Thouvenel's attitudes at this time is found in a long private report from Sanford, which has remained so far unpublished. On April 7 the news had arrived in Paris of the fall of New Bern, North Carolina, the imminent fall of Beaufort, and the capture of Jacksonville and St. Augustine in Florida. On the following day came the news of a Confederate defeat at Winchester and the (false) report of the Federal capture of the "Nashville." On the heels of all this good Northern news Sanford came to Paris from his post in Brussels on the afternoon of April 9. Learning that Thouvenel was having his regular diplomatic reception that evening, he hastened to the Quai d'Orsay and succeeded in having two long conversations with the foreign minister. Thouvenel greeted Sanford in the ante-chamber and began talking about American affairs before he entered the main reception hall.

> *Thouvenel:* I have just been reading about your important victories, and you know my wishes for the success of your cause, but above all for the early termination, one way or the other, of the war which is bearing heavily on us in France. We are nearly out of cotton, and cotton we *must have*.
>
> *Sanford:* You have to blame in part your own manufacturers who have speculated on late high prices and sold largely to go back to the United States. The stock here was at the beginning of the year unusually large, demand for fabrics was less, and to the want of cotton ought not, moreover, to be ascribed the distress among the working classes. The price of coarse cotton, which is nearly that of the raw material, is proof that it is rather a want of demand from consumers.
>
> *Thouvenel:* The amount sold abroad by our manufacturers is comparatively trifling, and the fact as regards stock in the country is that there is only supply at full employment of our mills to last into the month of May. This question of cotton supply is with us a grave question of the moment. Unless the war has an early termination, I can not say what grave complication may arise.
>
> *Sanford:* We are going on rapidly, shall soon be in possession

of New Orleans and I have little doubt that, e'er long, that important outlet will be open to the export of cotton.

Thouvenel: My reports are that the army, especially that of the Potomac, is in a high state of efficiency and I hope it will make rapid work with the enemy.

At this point the foreign minister had to give his attention to his other guests, but he renewed the conversation before Sanford departed.

Thouvenel: Our people are getting to be irritated and some of the communications I have received from the Chamber of Commerce are even menacing in their language. The United States government has, I think, unnecessarily stimulated this feeling by its rigorous refusal of communication with the South. For example, the merchants of New Orleans want to be allowed to make their commercial and monetary payments to France.

Sanford: Merchants are rarely satisfied with wars, but like all others have to submit to their necessity.

Thouvenel: Well, we are going to have to have cotton even if we are compelled to do something ourselves to obtain it.

Sanford: Well, what can you do about it? The intervention of all Europe can not make cotton grow. On the contrary it might destroy it. It can not hasten its export. The only intervention that can be useful, but which we do not want or need, would be in favor of the Union to help crush its enemies, who are pursuing their savage warfare not only to burning cities of their own people, but to destroying in their revengeful malice the very staple you need.

Thouvenel: I can not say what can be done or where best to do it. It may not be simply a question of policy abroad that we shall have to deal with but of public peace at home.

Baron Jacob Rothschild (who had joined them in the conversation): Of course I am in favor of the Northern cause. Yet I know not what you politicians may say about it, but I tell you as a businessman that this state of things can not continue long. I will admit to you that European intervention may not secure a bale of cotton, but here is a whole Continent in convulsion from this cause. When your patient is desperately sick, you try desperate remedies, even to blood-letting.

Sanford's report went on to say that during the reception he talked with Count Casablanca, a senator, who insisted that the distress came definitely from the scarcity of cotton and not so much from the lack of French exports or the Cobden Treaty. Such conditions, warned the senator, had led to popular revolutions in other periods of French history. Again, on the following day, Sanford had been riding in the Bois de Boulogne with Prince Murat when they met the emperor. They were both impressed with Napoleon's worried appearance. "He seems very much preoccupied and is very taciturn," the prince commented.[6]

For the whole month of April and in the early part of May, Seward was being bombarded by scare reports from Europe. On April 11, Weed was saying, "If possible, open ports, and let the enemy refuse the cotton." On the 15th Count Morny sent for Weed and opened the conversation by saying that, now that some ports had been captured, the North should allow trade with them to obtain cotton. Weed countered that France's and England's belligerency recognition had prolonged the war and caused the cotton famine, and therefore they should withdraw that recognition to help get cotton. Evading a reply to this proposition, the count described the economic desperation in France, suggested again the opening of ports in Federal hands, and urged that Weed acquaint Seward with the serious situation.[7]

Three Ports Are Opened

When Seward read this on April 30, there was no longer any question but what the heat was on. Yet, five days later came another urgent plea from Weed. Prince Napoleon, the North's best friend, was very troubled about the cotton famine, and Weed closed his message on a frantic note: "Depend upon it, this Government is in a tight place. Help as far and as fast as you can."[8] And still again two days later came another urgent appeal from Weed, apologizing for further importunities, but predicting "an outbreak, e'er long, from more than one Government for cotton." Then as a final argument he added: "If you [Seward] open some Cotton Ports, and the enemy refused to let Cotton out, the feeling here will then turn against the South."[9]

After reading Dayton's account of his conversation with Napoleon III and later Sanford's long talk with Thouvenel, Seward, on April 25, sent Sanford's letter over to Salmon P. Chase, the secretary of the treasury, with the following message scribbled at the bottom of the last sheet:

> Please read this letter carefully this evening, and call at the Department tomorrow morning. I incline to think that we may open three or four ports safely, this with restrictions, and thus pass through this last foreign peril without the South getting much aid or France (I fear) getting much cotton. If we should open three or four ports, we should probably be able to save all the great ones, and make a ground on which France might rescind her decree awarding belligerent rights. . . .[10]

At this point it seems that Seward was won over to the idea of trade concessions, but he still wanted to bargain regarding belligerent rights before opening any big ports—probably thinking of the future capture of New Orleans, Mobile, and Charleston. We have no evidence of a conversation with Chase or any cabinet deliberation. But, by the time the news of the capture of New Orleans had arrived—about April 28—Seward had evidently had enough chance to consult Lincoln and his cabinet colleagues to tell Dayton that the capture of New Orleans "will enable us, before another despatch day shall arrive, to restore the mails to that great commercial city."[11] By May 1 he had received Weed's report on Morny's warning and indicated that even more concessions to France were being considered. "The President . . . [Seward informed Dayton] is directing that measures be taken to mitigate the rigor of our blockade, with a view to the relief of France, whom we would not willingly see suffer unnecessarily by reason of the calamities that have befallen our country." While this statement seemed to imply something more than establishing mail communications, the secretary still harped on France's belligerency recognition, which had "aggravated and prolonged" the war and the cotton famine. A true neutrality—that is, withdrawal of that preliminary recognition—was what he expected.[12] The following week he was telling Dayton to have the emperor state publicly that the South should not expect any favor from him. "To bring the Emperor to this conviction is your [Dayton's] present urgent duty."[13]

Yet Seward did not wait for these concessions from France before he began to relax the blockade restrictions at New Orleans. A circular of May 2 announced only that "the mails are now allowed to pass to and from New Orleans and other [recovered] places." Military surveillance would still continue over these civilian communications.[14]

The news of other Northern victories began to come in during the first two weeks of May 1862. Corinth, Fort Macon, and Yorktown fell on May 2, Williamsburg on the 5th, and Norfolk on the 9th. Union troops were penetrating ever closer to Richmond in Virginia, and as far south as northern Mississippi in the Middle West. These events could have stiffened Seward's recalcitrance about opening the ports for European trade and have reenforced his demand for the withdrawal of belligerency recognition before any trade concessions would be granted. Indeed, Mercier's mood at this time indicated that the French might have yielded a little if the American secretary had pressed his point. The French envoy had gone to Yorktown soon after its fall and had come away with a strong impression of Southern weakness and dejection and Northern military strength and determination. In his report home he warned against antagonizing the North and suggested that, if France did not withdraw belligerency recognition, it should take other steps to humor the United States.[15]

In spite of the more favorable situation on the battlefields and in the French legation, Seward and Lincoln went beyond the mail service concession and proceeded to open Southern captured ports to other forms of trade without insisting first on the withdrawal of belligerent rights from the Confederacy.[16] Lacking any open avowal of motivation, the historian can only venture the opinion that the secretary of state did not expect to win out on the belligerency issue. He seemed to be using it largely as a parry against the threat of a European recognition of Southern independence. He may have thought that he would make the European powers feel so guilty or fearful for not having withdrawn belligerent rights that they would not venture toward the

opposite extreme of full recognition. Besides, by the time a re-
calcitrant demand might have been delivered to Europe, the
capricious fates of war might have reversed the favorable Northern military situation. A generous gesture of opening ports
might have a good effect in victory or in defeat.

Whatever were the principal motives inspiring the Lincoln
administration, Seward and Lincoln issued a proclamation opening the three ports of Beaufort, Port Royal, and New Orleans
to all trade except contraband of war.[16] Seward chose the two
unimportant ports of Beaufort and Port Royal; but he could
hardly omit New Orleans, considering its significance and its
ties with France.

Mercier had hurried to see Seward on April 28 to obtain confirmation of the fall of New Orleans and then had urged Lyons
to expedite a telegraphic message through London to Thouvenel.[17] It was probably this telegram from London which the
French foreign minister received on the evening of May 10, and
Adams had wired Dayton to the same effect on the 11th.[18] The
message not only confirmed the fall of New Orleans and the opening of French mail communications, but it said that the lifting
of the blockade before that city was under discussion. However,
this good news was blunted somewhat by the last sentence: "It
appears that Mr. Seward may be inclined to treat the question
of the modification of the blockade together with a renunciation
of the recognition of belligerent rights."[19]

The reaction of Russell and Thouvenel to this news would have
disappointed Seward if he had known it. On May 13, Thouvenel
learned of Russell's reaction.

> The principal secretary of state told me [wrote Flahault] that
> the government of the queen did not consider that there was
> any occasion to attach great importance to the capture of New
> Orleans by the Federals; that undoubtedly the re-establishment
> of postal communications and, especially, the plan to ease the
> blockade, if it is carried out, are looked upon by him as very fine;
> but that the cabinet of the queen did not intend to change in
> any way whatever its attitude toward the two parties, and that
> it would not reconsider its decision to grant belligerent rights
> to the Southern states.[20]

This news on New Orleans was arriving at the same time as Mercier's account of his visit to Richmond with its impression that the South would hold out to the bitter end. Hence Thouvenel's inclination was somewhat the same as that of Russell, and perhaps influenced by Russell. According to him future events in Virginia would be more decisive in modifying French policy. "It is therefore not in the presence of such uncertainty that it would be wise to abandon a position of strict neutrality which circumstances have so far imposed upon us." Besides, Thouvenel said he had heard nothing from Dayton about New Orleans, mail, trade, or belligerent rights, but he evidently already had his answer prepared on the last question. [21]

Four days after the arrival of the New Orleans news Slidell saw Thouvenel and repeated the South's determination to fight on. In response to this he reported Thouvenel's attitude as follows:

> He said that was the opinion of every one here. He seemed to regret the taking of New Orleans, and rather intimated that if it had not occurred and we were able to sustain ourselves at Corinth and in Virginia, we should soon have been recognized, and that decided successes in Corinth and in Virginia would lead to the same result. He repeated that France could not act without the concurrence of England. [22]

The news of the fall of New Orleans, accompanied as it was with reports of the Confederate burning of cotton, did not give Thouvenel much hope that the cotton famine would be eased. There had been similar reports of the burning of cotton when New Bern and Beaufort fell in North Carolina in April. When Dayton finally had a long conversation with Thouvenel on May 21, 1862, the French foreign minister had little to say about the opening of the blockade or hopes for the accessibility of cotton. Dayton read him Seward's note urging the withdrawal of France's recognition of Southern belligerent rights, and Thouvenel spent most of his time discussing this subject. He said that there seemed to be little doubt now but that the North had the power and resources to conquer the South. Yet the insurrection was so widespread that it would seem very difficult to bring the disaffected back to a loyalty to the Union. He foresaw tremendous problems in this regard. As to belligerent rights, the maritime powers had issued their neutrality proclamations out of concern for clashes with Southern naval vessels. Now that Southern ships were practically swept from the seas, the North suffered no disadvantage from those proclamations. Furthermore, the foreign minister contended that the withdrawal of belligerency recognition would not weaken the South's will because right now, by its harassment of Europeans by property confiscation, the South showed it did not particularly value the goodwill of Europe and was actually resentful toward France. Also he added:

> It would not be a handsome thing in a great government, at once upon the South being worsted, to withdraw a concession which had been made to them in their day of supposed strength. Aside from all political reasons I feel that such a proceeding would not be exactly worthy of France. The thing would not look well. Besides we can do nothing upon this subject without England. We have acted together and, although there has been no treaty to that effect, yet France considers herself bound by this understanding.

When Dayton brought up the argument that the Southern cotton embargo was the cause of the cotton famine and that the European belligerency recognition was the main reason for the continuing of the burning and non-planting of cotton, Thouvenel merely begged for more Northern efforts to obtain cotton. "In any case [he argued] the federal government would be serving its own interests if it made every effort and found the means to obtain cotton for the foreign market. On the basis of your own arguments you would deprive the South of one of the reasons you claim it has for influencing European governments."[23]

Reverses in Virginia

The eventual showdown in Virginia, for which European statesmen had been waiting came in the months of June and July of 1862. General McClellan had been permitted to make his thrust toward Richmond northwestward from Hampton

Roads instead of southeastward from Washington. Hence he had begun a penetration of Virginia from the mouths of the James and York rivers. Yorktown was secured by May 3, and Norfolk, where they found the "Merrimac" scuttled, was abandoned to the Unionists on May 10. Williamsburg fell on May 5, and then with the aid of naval gunboats McClellan went up the James and Chickahominy until, by the end of May, his troops were within five miles of Richmond. At this point the Confederates threatened Washington by having Jackson engage the Federals at Winchester and drive them across the Potomac at Harper's Ferry, thus pinning down McDowell's forces before that capital. Soon after this move General J. E. Johnston, defending Richmond, tried to blunt McClellan's invasion from the southeast by attacking his forces at Fair Oaks (or Seven Pines) south of the Chickahominy—May 31 to June 1. Successful on the first day, the Confederates had to withdraw on the second with a thousand more losses than those of the Federals. Johnston was wounded, and Lee was given the supreme command in Virginia. After considerable maneuvering and shifting of troops by both sides, Lee launched a series of attacks called the Seven Days Battle—June 26 to July 2. McClellan was forced to retreat from the Chickahominy area down to the James River at Harrison's Landing. From here he could have begun another stab at Richmond if General Halleck, his superior, had not ordered his army back in front of Washington. Thus the campaign in Virginia was a serious setback for the North in the eyes of the anxious Europeans.

On June 9 the *Moniteur* carried the first news of Jackson's victory at Winchester and of the Federal retreat northward across the Potomac. A few days later Thouvenel received Mercier's private report of panic in the North over the threat to Washington and Baltimore.[24] Even the news of this marginal reverse of the North seemed to set in motion a renewed consideration of mediation efforts. After reading the early *Moniteur* account of Winchester, and before receiving Mercier's letter, Thouvenel began to talk again about mediation. While Winchester did not change the Federal position much, he said, still the recent Northern successes had not seemed to undermine the determination of the South. French opinion was alarmed over the prospects of a protracted war. He wanted Mercier to be cautious and continue France's noninterventionist attitude. However, on the other hand, Thouvenel hoped his minister in Washington would use every opportunity to encourage the North toward a reconciliation policy, with which France would cooperate by offering her good offices "with alacrity."[25]

No doubt agitation in the French press had revived this Thouvenel flirtation with mediation. Both the *Constitutionnel* and the *Patrie* had begun again to hammer at the idea.[26] At the same time it led to a visit by Count Persigny, the minister of interior, to London to persuade England to agree to intervention. There is no evidence that he was instructed to do so by Napoleon III or Thouvenel; he may have done it on his own impulse.[27] This trip synchronized with a renewed flurry of mediation talk in London. Perhaps at the instigation of Persigny, Russell may have approached Palmerston to inquire about a mediation policy. In any case we have a letter from Palmerston to his foreign secretary after Persigny's arrival in which he said: "I may say that no Intention at present exists to offer Mediation. In fact it would be like offering to make it up between Sayers and Heenan [two rival boxers] after the Third Round."[28] On the same day Palmerston replied to Hopwood in parliament that "we [the British] have not received at present any proposal from France to offer mediation and no intention at present exists to offer it on our part."[29]

While Persigny's visit did not seem to lead to anything, the news of the Battle of Fair Oaks, where the North finally held its ground before Richmond, continued the attitude of suspense in Europe. The details of the battle were available to London and Paris by June 15. While it indicated an interruption of the North's progress, the report ended with McClellan's forces still five miles from Richmond.[30] On the 19th came news of the capture of Memphis, and on the 25th Thouvenel had Mercier's account of these events, in which he stated that, while the Confederates had successfully disengaged themselves from Fair Oaks, the fall of Memphis foreshadowed the imminent loss of the entire Mississippi.[31]

In these engagements the French government and press saw only a Southern withdrawal and the loss of Memphis—nothing to encourage an attempted mediation. In fact, because of this news and England's momentary rejection of mediation, the French government and press fell silent about mediation.[32] Slidell was "heart-sick" at the lack of conclusive victories. In a letter to Mason he wrote despondently: "I have seen enough since I have been here to be convinced that nothing that I can say or do will advance for a single day the action of this government, and I am very much inclined to resign." Indeed, while in this mood, Slidell began to look for a more retired and economical residence.[33]

Three weeks later, this temporary silence in France was suddenly broken by the arrival of the news of the Seven Days Battle and the Northern retreat to Harrison's Landing on the lower James River. On Thursday, July 10, the first news arrived reporting the Northern defeats of the first two days. Then on July 15 came the final news of McClellan's retreat to Harrison's Landing on the James, of the heavy losses on both sides, of the Northern suppression of the details of the disaster, and of Lincoln's call for 300,000 more volunteers.[34] This all seemed to indicate a great Northern disaster in this Virginia confrontation and to confirm anew the hopelessness of continuing the war for the reunion of the seceded states.

Slidell Sees the Emperor

Slidell, who had fallen into discouraged seclusion, quickly revived his spirits and began to think about renewing demands for recognition. In the meantime, too, this Confederate commissioner had received four dispatches of instructions from his government. One was an attack on the legality of the blockade accompanied by a list of over 100 vessels breaking the blockade. Benjamin claimed that the cotton famine was caused by Europe's acceptance of the ineffective blockade and offered to trade cotton for manufactured goods. The last dispatch claimed Shiloh as a victory but admitted the loss of Fort Pulaski in Georgia and Island No. 10 in the Mississippi. New Confederate ironclads, soon to be launched in the Mississippi, would promptly reverse the situation there. But it was instruction No. 3 which intrigued Slidell more than the others. Here Benjamin proposed a deal with France alone whereby the Confederacy would offer 12.5 million dollars of cotton in return for French war supplies which could enter Southern ports free of duty. Because of inflated prices in both countries France would realize a profit of about 100 million francs, which could serve as a subsidy to compensate for the naval action needed to break up the illegal blockade. There was also a plea that a quick recognition of the South would bring an early end to the war by discouraging the war spirit in the North.

Slidell was on the point of seeking out Count Persigny when the latter, recently returned from England, asked the Confederate envoy to call on him. Slidell confided in him the substance of his new instructions, and the interior minister urged him to go to Vichy during the following week to see the emperor and gave him a warm letter of introduction to General Fleury, aide-de-camp of Napoleon III.

Slidell arrived in Vichy on July 15 and the next morning applied to General Fleury for an audience with the emperor. Evidently Napoleon III had also been reading the newspapers and was ready again to consider the possibility of joint mediation or joint recognition along with Great Britain. Indeed, it is possible that he was behind the Persigny approach to Slidell. In any event he responded with an invitation to Slidell for that very afternoon at 2 o'clock. This conversation of July 16 is so revealing of the emperor's current attitude that much of it will be reproduced in full. After giving Slidell a very cordial reception and urging him to be seated, the emperor began a long statement of his own in French.

> I have just been reading last evening the press accounts of the defeat of the Federal armies before Richmond. Mr. Lincoln's call for 300,000 additional troops is evidence of his conviction of the desperate character of the struggle in which he has been engaged and of the great losses which the Federal forces have sustained. Although it was unquestionably for the interest of France that the United States should be a powerful and united

people to act as a *contrepoids* to the maritime power of England, yet my sympathies have always been with the South, whose people are struggling for the principle of self-government, of which I am a firm and consistent advocate. I have from the first seen the true character of the contest and considered the re-establishment of the Union impossible and final separation a mere question of time. The difficulty is to find a way to give effect to my sympathies. I have always desired to preserve the most friendly relations with England, and in so grave a matter I have not been willing to act without her co-operation. I have several times intimated my wish for action in your behalf, but have met with no favorable response. Besides, England has a deeper interest in the question than France. She wishes me to draw the chestnuts from the fire for her benefit. What are your views of the state of affairs and of what can be done to bring the war to a close? What is the size of your army?

Slidell was delighted with this show of sympathy and the imperial invitation to state his views. Beginning with a covert compliment to his imperial host by asking permission to speak in English,[35] he went on to discuss the military situation, stating that the South had about 350,000 under arms. They could have more men if they wanted them, but what they really needed were arms and clothing. The Northern troops were well supplied, clothed, and fed; but their units were often made up of foreign mercenaries, while the Southern soldiers were resident citizens. This made Southern soldiers better fighters, but their battle losses constituted a heavier blow to civilian morale.

At this point the Confederate commissioner complained bitterly about the European acquiescence in the paper blockade. It was really a violation of neutrality against the South, and France for the first time was failing to uphold this aspect of international law. At this point the emperor broke in, continuing the conversation in English:

I have committed a great error, which I now deeply regret. France should never have respected the blockade; the European powers should have recognized you last summer when your ports were in your possession and when you were menacing Washington. But what can now be done? To open the ports forcibly would be an act of war; mediation would, if offered, be refused and probably in insulting terms by the North; and mere recognition, while of little advantage to you, would probably involve me in a war.

Here Slidell interrupted to say that much of the Southern coast was not really blockaded now, and France could declare it open and enforce international law at these points by use of her navy. The North might bluster, but it would back down as it had done in the "Trent" affair. After all, Slidell said, he was sorry that England had not been drawn into the war by that affair because the war would have soon ended, and with a Southern victory.

Here the emperor remarked:

> I think you're right. I regret to say that England has not properly appreciated my friendly action in the affair of the "Trent." There are many reasons why I desire to be on the best of terms with her, but the policy of nations necessarily changes with circumstances, and I am consequently obliged to look forward to the possible contingency of not always having the same friendly relations as now exist.

This remark suggested the recent Anglo-French disagreement over the Mexican expedition, and Slidell used this as the occasion to offer the South's alliance with France against the Juarez government in Mexico.

> Although I have no instructions from my government in relation to the military expedition which Your Majesty has sent to Mexico, I do not hesitate to say that it will be regarded with no unfriendly eye by the Confederate States; they can have no other interest or desire than to see a respectable, responsible, and stable government established in that country. They are not animated by a spirit of political proselytism which so strongly characterizes the people from whom they have recently separated themselves, and confident that Your Majesty has no intention of imposing on Mexico any government not in accordance with the wishes of its inhabitants, they will feel quite indifferent as to its form. As the Lincoln Government was the

ally and protector of your enemy, Juarez, we can have no objection to make common cause with you against the common
enemy.

Then Slidell abruptly changed the subject with a question to
the emperor as to whether he had seen or heard from Count
Persigny recently. The ruler said no. The Southern commissioner thereupon described Benjamin's offer of cotton in return
for duty-free goods and war supplies from France. Napoleon
III seemed interested but asked, "How are you to get the
cotton?"

"Of course," Slidell replied, "that depends on Your Majesty."
"You will soon have a fleet in the neighborhood of our coasts
strong enough to keep it clear of every Federal cruiser." Here the
Southern envoy expanded upon the weakness of the Federal
navy and the ability of the French fleet to hold New York and
Boston at its mercy. He thought the emperor agreed. Slidell
also emphasized that the cotton proposal was limited to France
and not offered to England.

The long conversation then turned to the ever-recurring subject of recognition and mediation.

> *Napoleon III:* On the matter of recognition, a simple recog-
> nition would be of no value, and as to mediation, that would
> be refused by the North.
> *Slidell:* I agree with you as to mediation. If offered, it would
> be refused by the North, but would be accepted by us. Such
> acceptance and refusal will be of vast advantage to our cause
> and enlist the sympathies of the civilized world in our favor and
> afford sufficient reason for more potent intervention. But we
> do not ask for mediation, all we ask for is recognition. There
> is a large minority in the Northern States in favor of peace and
> separation, but a reign of terror exists which for the present
> stifles all expression of such opinions. The congressional elec-
> tions are approaching and the recognition would give the peace
> party courage to organize and perhaps place them in a majority.
> *Napoleon III:* I am pleased to see that there has been a great
> peace meeting in New York.
> *Slidell:* Recognition will at once bring out many similar
> demonstrations. Although we do not place ourselves on that

ground, the interests of humanity might be urged as calling on Europe and especially on you who exercise so potent an influence over the destinies of the world to put an end to a strife which is not only devastating the South and exhausting the North, but paralyzes the commerce and industry of Europe.

Napoleon III: What you say is true, but the policy of nations is controlled by their interest and not by their sentiments, and ought to be so.

Slidell: I fully admit your proposition, but the interests to be consulted should not be those of the hour. England seems to have abdicated the great part which she has been accustomed to play in the affairs of the world, and adopted a tortuous, selfish, and time-serving policy, which has only served to make all nations either her bitter enemies or her fair-weather friends. We, at first, had been well disposed toward England, but having for selfish ulterior purposes, to revive for her advantage the old exploded principles of blockade, and to secure the monopoly of cotton for her Indian colonies, given a false interpretation to the treaty of Paris, we shall never hereafter consider her our friend.

Napoleon III: I have already told you what I think of the blockade and as to the culture of cotton in India supplanting yours, I consider the idea entirely chimerical. If you do not give it to us, we cannot find it elsewhere.

Slidell: Your Majesty has now an opportunity of receiving a faithful ally, bound to you not only by the ties of gratitude, but by those more reliable ones of a common interest and congenial habits.

Napoleon III: Yes, you have many families of French descent in Louisiana who yet preserve their habits and languages.

Slidell: Your Majesty is right and I can give you an instance in my own family where French is habitually spoken.

Napoleon III: Do you anticipate no difficulty from your slaves? [The only mention he made of this subject.]

Slidell: They have never been more quiet and more respectful and no better evidence can be given of their being contented and happy.

Napoleon III: Do you expect that England will agree to coöperate with me in your recognition?

Slidell: Your Majesty of course must have much better means of information than I, but our friends in England are more hopeful now than they ever have been before, and our commissioner in London, for the first time since his arrival, wrote encouragingly. The motion of Mr. Lindsay recommending recognition will be brought up on Friday; and probably the debate will bring out Lord Palmerston with a declaration of purpose.

. . . .

Napoleon III: It is very singular that while you ask absolute recognition, Mr. Dayton is calling on me to retract my qualified recognition of you as belligerents. [The emperor was noticing Seward's counteroffensive.]

Slidell: Such a demand is another evidence of the insolence of the Washington Government.

Napoleon III: If France and England intervene, on what terms can a peace be made? The question of boundaries is a most difficult one. What will you do with the border States? You will not be willing to accept what the North, even if she submits to separation, will accord.[36]

Slidell's reply to this was a clever reliance on the emperor's principle of popular self-determination by suggesting plebiscites in the border states of Maryland, Missouri, and Kentucky. It is interesting that, while he thought all three would vote to go with the Confederacy, he claimed the natural boundaries of the Chesapeake, Potomac, and Ohio, which would not include Maryland or Delaware. Hearing all these strange geographical names, Napoleon remarked that he regretted he had no map at Vichy that they might trace the line.

The whole interview lasted only an hour, and it was Slidell rather than the emperor who brought it to an end in this exchange:

> *Slidell*: I have perhaps omitted to present some arguments which, if not new to you, are from a different point of view, but I have prepared a formal demand of recognition in which they are embodied, and I intend to present them to Mr. Thouvenel so soon as he shall return from England, and I will feel much obliged, if you see any reason to object to such a course as I propose, that you will intimate your wish.
>
> *Napoleon III*: I see no objection to your presenting your demand. I hope in the future there will be less difficulty in your seeing me than has heretofore existed.[37]

Thouvenel's Trip to London

While the emperor was at Vichy, closeted with Slidell, Thouvenel was in London, distributing the prizes won by Frenchmen at the International Exhibition of 1862. Prince Napoleon was supposed to have performed this function, but at the last moment he had had to hurry back to Paris because of the imminent confinement of Princess Clothilda. In the midst of problems involving the United States, Mexico, Serbia, and Italy—and with only two days of advance notice—Thouvenel had to rush off suddenly to London on July 9, accompanied by Herbet, his director of commercial affairs.[38] He performed his prize-awarding duties on July 11, had conversations with Palmerston and Russell during the ensuing week, took a trip out to the University of Oxford, and returned to Paris on the 20th.[39]

When the Paris papers learned of Thouvenel's departure, they mistakenly concluded that he was going to London to persuade the English government to bring the Civil War to an end by mediation.[40] What heightened these rumors was the arrival just at that same time of the news of McClellan's retreat in Virginia. This led Lindsay to plan to revive his motion in parliament, urging joint Anglo-French mediation between the two belligerents. Even in the light of the bad news, Thouvenel did not seem inclined to suggest any joint intervention at that moment, and it is unlikely, from what he wrote to his London ambassador, that he even brought up the subject during his London visit. He was still in England on July 18, however, and no doubt followed the news reports of the debates on Lindsay's motion which took place on that day in the commons. In defense of his motion Lindsay cited the recent Northern defeats and claimed that slavery was not an issue because the North was tolerating it in the border states. Gregory backed up his colleague with arguments on the distress in Lancashire caused by the cotton famine. But this latter argument was undermined by the silence of all the Lancashire members, save Hopwood. Then Palmerston took the floor to oppose the motion, saying that neither belligerent would accept mediation at this time, that parliament should not bind the government's hands by a resolution, and that the South's independence was not yet sufficiently assured to grant recognition. At this point Lindsay withdrew his motion.[41]

In Vichy the emperor had already read of the Northern reverses, had had a long interview with Slidell, and probably had heard from Persigny on his recent contacts with pro-Southern Englishmen. When he read in the *Moniteur* of July 19 that debate was about to take place in the house of commons, he must have finally decided he should make a formal and direct approach to the British government while Thouvenel was still there. He put it in the form of a telegraphic query: "Ask the English government if they don't think the time has come to recognize the South."[42]

The message arrived in cipher on the morning of the 20th, just after Thouvenel's departure from London. Flahault, the French ambassador, could not read it because he did not have Thouvenel's code book, and consequently he sent it back to Thouvenel in Paris. When Thouvenel received it on July 21—all decoded by his own office—he was at first afraid that it had been sent uncoded to London. Once reassured on that point, he used this occasion to formulate his opinion on recognition at this time. His official statement to Flahault was:

Although I am more and more inclined to doubt that the present conflict can end in any other way than with a definitive separation of the South from the North, and although the government of the emperor desires just as much as that of Her Britannic Majesty to see the time come when its good offices as well as those of Great Britain could be accepted in the United States and join in helping to re-establish peace, I agree completely with the opinion expressed in parliament by Lord Palmerston on the Lindsay motion. In the present state of affairs and given the present attitude of the belligerents between whom we would interpose our good offices, the latter had no chance of being received and therefore could not possibly hasten the end of the war. For the present it is obviously not the right time for us again to swerve from our policy of abstention and neutrality which we have observed up to now.[43]

In his private letter of the same day he revealed to Flahault some other considerations along the same line:

> The emperor's telegram, which you forwarded to me, and which I should have hesitated a great deal to use if I had received it in time, will have proved to you how correct I was in what I told you during my recent visit. [Thouvenel had evidently told Flahault about the emperor's desire to do something.] . . . The more I examine the question and the more I think of the financial difficulties and those of the Mexican expedition, the more I believe our haste in starting a conflict with the United States is unwise and dangerous. To me it seems impossible that the cabinet of Washington will not soon be brought around to realize the enormity of its sacrifices. But I think right now a foreign intervention would arouse the susceptibilities of the Northern masses to the point of committing some act of folly. [Seward's threats were having their effect.] Besides I could not conceive how we should be in more of a hurry than England or that we should risk to take on the sole burden of a job from which she would obtain the benefit and draw down upon us all the resentment which Americans now feel toward her. I am therefore most grateful to Lord Palmerston for his speech which backs up the moderating and delaying tactics which I am trying to have prevail here without being certain of succeeding in it much longer.[44]

We know therefore what Thouvenel's ideas were upon his return from London. He had been against hasty action before he left, and he was opposed to the sense of the emperor's telegram when he received it back in Paris. Therefore he turned immediately to the task of calming the emperor's impatience with the above arguments and with those of Palmerston, which had persuaded Lindsay himself to withdraw his motion.[45]

Thouvenel and Palmerston together may have convinced Napoleon III that there was no use in urging Britain to join in mediation. But it seems that the emperor was not entirely resigned to complete inaction, and it may have been he who insisted on approaching Russia with the question of joint mediation—not recognition. If Napoleon was the initiator of this then it is probable that his minister acquiesced, since it would humor his sovereign, prolong the delay, and quite certainly receive a negative reply. Thus it was that three days after the London trip the French foreign minister asked Fournier, the French chargé, to approach Gorchakov with the suggestion of a joint Anglo-French-Russian conciliation effort between the warring parties.[46]

The Russian reply came quickly and firmly. When Fournier saw Gorchakov on July 29, the Russian foreign minister started right off with a statement of warm support for the Northern cause and a restoration of the Union, along with deep regrets for the devastating war then going on. As to the French invitation, Gorchakov declared that he was in favor of conciliation but not in company with England, who was so heartily disliked by the North. Such a joint step would appear as a threat to the North, whereas Russia still favored reunion. In his subsequent report to Thouvenel, Fournier went on to explain, especially for the benefit of Napoleon, that Russia had no need to expose herself in this way. She had very little demand for cotton, and she had a privileged position in the eyes of the United States, being outside the European community and therefore not being the target of the common American antipathy for western Europe. "Both of them being young nations in the life of the civilized world, Russia and America have a special regard for each other which is never adversely affected because they have no points of conflict."[47] This Russian attitude was in line with what Gorchakov had said during the "Trent" affair.

Slidell Sees Thouvenel

While the Russian reply came to Thouvenel's assistance by moderating the emperor, the French minister had to face a renewed assault from Slidell. This Confederate commissioner had been squirming in inactivity for some time. After the news had come in mid-June of the minor Confederate successes at Winchester and Fair Oaks, Slidell and Mason had agreed that they would both simultaneously present demands to France and England for recognition. However, pro-Southern friends in England had advised delay, and the two envoys complied with their wishes, even though Slidell had already prepared his communication. But in July came the news of the sensational Southern Seven Days victory in Virginia and the emperor's benevolent interview of July 16. On that occasion Slidell had said he was planning to see the French foreign minister on his return from London. Consequently, on the very evening of Thouvenel's return—July 20—he requested an interview, which was granted for 7 o'clock, on Wednesday evening, the 23rd. Here again was a long session, in which Thouvenel learned for the first time about the Vichy interview of the previous week. After some preliminary talk about the London trip and the war situation in America, they proceeded with the main topics of the interview.

Slidell came to the point by announcing his and Mason's intentions of making official requests for recognition to both France and England. At first Thouvenel advised against such a premature attempt until the military situation was clearer. However, when, to his surprise, he learned from Slidell that the emperor had heard all the arguments for recognition and had seemed impressed, the foreign minister no longer discouraged the recognition request. He did interject the opinion that no one in France any longer believed in the possibility of the reunion of the North and South.

Toward the close of the interview Slidell asked permission to have the French consular bags carry his correspondence into Confederate ports. Thouvenel said that privilege was not even permitted to French subjects, but that after recognition such a service might be granted. When the Confederate representative handed him the note requesting recognition, the foreign minister said he would have it translated immediately and send a copy to the emperor. He himself would study the matter during his ten-day trip to Germany, but he could have no definite answer until his return. Thouvenel also requested a copy of the Confederate government's proposal on cotton and asked whether England had received similar proposals. To this Slidell replied in the negative, saying that even Mason did not yet know about it. Two days later he wrote to Benjamin, "I am more hopeful than I have been at any moment since my arrival in Europe."[48]

When the note had been translated, Thouvenel found in it all the detailed arguments justifying secession and French recognition. The Confederate communication went into the constitutional right to withdraw from the Union, the mistreatment of the South in the Union, the right of people to self-determination and self-defense. "They [the Confederate States] approach His Imperial Majesty with the more confidence, as he has lately championed this great cause in the recent Italian question." Slidell went on to show how large, rich, powerful, and enduring was the new Confederacy. Recognition would shorten the war and bring the cotton supply again. He felt that recognition was so much more to the interest of France than to that of Great Britain that France should consider it independently of England. France could have a privileged position in trade and in the access to Confederate raw materials, such as tobacco, sugar, naval stores, lumber, coal, and iron. An independent Confederacy would also bring a balance of power to North America and a friendly neighbor to the French in Mexico. As to the blockade, it was ineffectual and therefore illegal. Even if legal, it could not subdue the South—which was its justification—and so it should no longer continue as a practice damaging to third parties. The South will never return to the Union, and the North is only endeavoring to subjugate and conquer an unyielding people. "With what prospect of success let . . . the battles before Richmond of May 30 and 31 [Fair Oaks], the series of engagements from June 26 to July 2 [Seven Days Battle], the broken and flying columns of the grand army of the North seeking shelter on the banks of the James River under the protecting fire of their floating batteries, answer." In closing, the unrecognized envoy urged that French official channels of communication be open for all civilian use, French and Confederate, and enclosed a report on the large number of ships going through the unenforced blockade.[49]

We can see how little Thouvenel was impressed with these arguments and how resistant he was to any precipitate anti-North action by what he wrote to Flahault three days later. In that letter he cited Mercier's statement that the recognition of the South would mean war with the North and indicated that he had urged the emperor to postpone a decision until they both had returned to Paris. And then he added this significant passage: "I see with great satisfaction that, on this point as on others, we are in agreement, and I shall perhaps need your help in order to guard us from an adventure even more serious than the Mexican one."[50]

In the meantime, on July 24, Mason had submitted to the English government his arguments for recognition and asked for an interview. A week later he received a very formal note, worded in the third person, in which Russell promised to submit the question to the cabinet on August 2, but, as to the interview, the abrupt note concluded that "Lord Russell does not think any advantage will arise from the personal interview . . . and must therefore decline it." Promptly on August 2, after the cabinet meeting, Russell sent Mason a more courteous note in the first person in which he gave the cabinet decision. In this communication he refused to take sides on the constitutional question of secession and pointed out the conflicting predictions of North and South as to eventual victory. He felt that "the fluctuating events of the war" made it unwise to grant recognition at that time. Although Mason was naturally disappointed with these replies from Russell, he expressed a hope to Benjamin that if France gave an encouraging reply, "it may yet be that they [the British] may be dragged into an ungraceful reversal of their decision."[51]

France Evades Recognition

Mason and Slidell were both, therefore, awaiting Thouvenel's return from Germany for a French reply on the question of recognition. By August 20 no official note had been received from the Quai d'Orsay, but both the emperor and his foreign minister communicated with Slidell indirectly. On August 17 Morny called the Confederate commissioner for a long conference. He presented a M. Laubat, who had just come from America and seemed to have been briefed by someone to the effect that the North would let the South have any concessions she demanded if she would only agree to reunion. Slidell spurned this indignantly, and M. Laubat left the room. "When again alone with the duke [Slidell wrote] he expressed himself very warmly in favor of our cause; said that he had frequent conversations with the Emperor on the subject, who deeply regretted that circumstances would not permit him to act without the co-operation of England, but he hoped that the time was not distant when that difficulty would be removed."

Two days later a foreign ministry contact man was delegated by Thouvenel to tell the Confederate envoy that he "did not want to send an unmeaning reply to [his] demand for recognition; that at present he [Thouvenel] could make no other, that unless he [Slidell] insisted he would remain silent." Slidell then consulted Persigny, and on his advice decided to await more battle reports as well as the emperor's return from Chalons and Biarritz before asking for a reply to his recognition request.[52]

In a private letter to Mercier the French foreign minister expressed more directly and more fully his policy in the middle of the month of August.

> The deplorable crisis [he complained] that Italy is going through [Garibaldi threatening Rome from the south] absorbs all my attention this week, and, on top of that M. de Banneville [director of political affairs] is absent. So don't be surprised if you receive nothing [official] from us. What I do want to be sure to tell you, however, is that I am a great deal more reassured about our position and that our policy of waiting and inaction is finally considered as the only reasonable and practicable one right now. M. Slidell, again this time, has not gained anything by his effort, and I don't suppose that he will try it again soon. Nevertheless I ardently hope that a peace party may develop under the influence of events. What I should like to see, if one could make one's desires or dreams come true, would be the formation of two *federated confederations*— please excuse the barbarism. The North and South would make their own laws separately, and, even if they didn't guarantee them, they would promise to respect even their peculiar institutions reciprocally. They would have the same diplomatic service abroad and the same economic regime [tariffs]. We might explore the possibility of their having a small mixed senate for the sole purpose of proving the existence of a federation of two republics. As my pen runs along, I am giving you

my possibly absurd ideas, but if they are of any value, I leave
it to you to elaborate them as I also confer on you the absolute
right to criticize and change them. Anyway, if the hour for
real mediation or some unofficial action should ever strike, it
would be helpful to have a sketch of an arrangement in my
pocket.[53]

Indeed, this desire to have on hand some plan of solution to
the American question had led Thouvenel to ask his staff to work
one out in June, and he received a detailed plan on July 4, unsigned, but entitled "Note for the minister, the American question." It began by designating as logical a dividing boundary
line as possible between two independent republics of North and
South based upon a compromise between free and slave territory
and the military *uti posseditis* at the time of an armistice. This
border would run along a line defined by Chesapeake Bay, the
Potomac, Acquia Creek, the northern boundaries of the Virginia
counties of Culpepper, Madison, Rockingham, Pocahontas, and
Nicholas, up to the junction of the Gauley and Kanawha rivers,
then down the boundary between Virginia and Kentucky to the
northern border of Tennessee, and along that northern border
and the northern border of Arkansas. Thus northern Virginia
as well as all the border states would remain with the North.
"In order to get around another serious difficulty, that of
tariffs," the writer continued, "a tariff union with uniform tariff
rates could be proposed. M. Mercier has already suggested that
in Richmond, and although he met there a strong opposition to
this idea, once separation has been agreed to, one could hope that
the Americans themselves would recognize its necessity."

On other minor matters there should be agreement that the
Mississippi would have free navigation, that the South would
assume its proportionate part of the United States pre-war public
debt, that the South should pay for the federal properties of which
it had taken possession,[54] and that the North should agree to an
effective system for the return of fugitive slaves.[55] This plan no
doubt inspired Thouvenel's proposal, with his later addition of
a scheme similar to the eventual Austro-Hungarian dual monarchy of 1867 (joint senate and combined foreign service).

As was true in most world affairs, diplomatic policy depended upon the course of military campaigns. After the Federal victories in the West and along the Confederate coasts, especially at New Orleans, the North was able to open three ports to European trade—a rather empty gesture—but it did ease the pressure from the French and English governments and put the onus for the cotton famine upon the Confederates. Then, with the Northern setback in Virginia, came the emperor's and Lindsay's reopening of the questions of recognition and mediation. However, Palmerston, Russell, and Thouvenel were too cautious to abandon strict neutrality at this time. The Union still did not seem too seriously defeated; new recruits were rushing to the colors in the North, showing a stubborn will to fight; and the menace of a Federal ironclad navy still hung over the heads of restive Europeans. They would wait and watch a little longer before moving off dead center.

Chapter IX

EMANCIPATION AND THE OCTOBER INTERVENTION CRISIS

Slavery and Emancipation

BOTH French and British opinions were divided on the Civil War because of two liberal principles involved: the right of national self-determination of peoples and the human right of personal freedom. Those who put the emphasis on the first principle tended to be sympathetic to the South in its fight for national self-determination and independence; many who emphasized the second principle sympathized with the North because it was combatting the defenders of human slavery.

Yet the North in the first two years of the war gave very little encouragement to its European adherents. Secession meant the dissolution of the nation and caused a patriotic nationalist reaction in the North to save the Union. The Union, and not emancipation, became the war cry of 1861. In his first inaugural address Lincoln had devoted most of his time to defending the inviolability of the Union and attacking the principle of secession. On the other hand he had denied any intention of abolishing slavery. "I have no purpose [he had said in quoting a previous speech], directly or indirectly, to interfere with the institution of slavery in the States where it exists. I believe I have no lawful right to do so, and I have no inclination to do so."

This kind of appeal left Frenchmen cold. Patriotism is such a localized sentiment that Frenchmen could not be stirred by Lincoln's appeal to American patriotism, but they were very much disappointed by his turning his back on the universal sentiment for human freedom. Many friends of the Northern cause began to think that it made no difference which side won because slavery would be maintained in either case. When the suffering became intense during the cotton famine, it is not surprising that many pro-Northern as well as pro-Southern Frenchmen began to wonder whether the prolongation of the war was justified. Peace by separation seemed advisable and inevitable.

This trend pointed up the dilemma in which Lincoln and Seward found themselves. To retain the loyalty of the slaveholding border states (Delaware, Maryland, Kentucky, and Missouri), they should resist efforts to make the war an abolitionist crusade; but on the other hand to prevent France and England from intervening to stop the war and obtain cotton, they should strengthen the pro-Northern elements in those countries by making emancipation the war aim of the Northern cause. To escape this dilemma, the two Northern statesmen must maneuver cautiously during 1861 and early 1862. When General John Fremont, the Federal commander in Missouri, issued a proclamation in August 1861 confiscating the slaves of rebels, Lincoln had to annul the order and relieve him of his command. The same disavowal was issued when, in May 1862, General David Hunter, the Federal commander in the recaptured coastal area of Georgia and South Carolina, tried to liberate the slaves of those regions and enroll them in the Federal army.[1] However, when, early in 1862, Northern forces had overrun western Virginia, Kentucky, western Tennessee, and northern and central Missouri, the Lincoln administration no longer had to be quite so tender toward the slavery sentiments of the border states. Meantime, alarming reports were coming from Europe describing the suffering from the cotton famine and the threat of some form of intervention. These two factors, domestic and foreign, seemed to encourage a slight shift of emphasis from Union as the war aim to emancipation in order to mobilize pro-Northern opinion in France and England against intervention.

Thus there began to appear, early in 1862, a series of measures which moved in the direction of emancipation. On the legislative side this was made easier by the absence of congressmen from the seceded slave states. In February the president refused to commute the death sentence of the slave trader, Captain

Nathaniel P. Gordon, who became the first of such offenders to be hanged as a pirate. In April, Lincoln signed an antislave-trade treaty with England, and in July he signed a law to enforce it. Moreover, while the antislave-trade treaty was still being negotiated and debated, Lincoln sent to congress in March 1862 a proposed resolution in favor of gradual, voluntary, and compensated emancipation in the border slave states. In this proposal the Federal government was to contribute to the compensation. It may be significant that, in the message on this measure, the president said that "it is recommended in the hope that it would soon lead to important practical results." No doubt, one hoped for result was that the border states would adopt compensated emancipation, but Lincoln could also have had in mind and hoped that congress would have in mind the practical results in Europe as well. The house passed the resolution on March 10, and the senate followed with its approval three weeks later. In the same month of April 1862 the congress and the president enacted a law abolishing slavery in the District of Columbia, with compensation to the slave owners.[2]

As to the attitude of France and England on slavery, we have two strong testimonials at the beginning of 1862. The Northerners in Europe were always embarrassed by the Federal government's stress upon the Union issue over that of emancipation. Weed, who had been sent to Europe to influence opinion, wrote after the solution of the "Trent" controversy that the North's failure to make emancipation the purpose of the war antagonized the emperor more than the tariff. Prince Napoleon understood the situation, but not Morny.[3] A similiar report was given by Weed's Confederate competitor, Yancey, on his return to New Orleans. This fire-breathing secessionist had come back from Europe very dejected over the inflexible antislavery sentiment he found in Europe. When forced to speak before a group at the St. Charles Hotel he reported dolefully:

> I do not bring you glad tidings from over the sea. Queen Victoria is against us and so was Prince Albert. Gladstone we can manage, but the feeling against slavery in England is so strong that no public man there dares extend a hand to help us.

We have got to fight the Washington government alone. There is no government in Europe that dares help us in a struggle which can be suspected of having for its result, directly or indirectly, the fortification or perpetuation of slavery. Of this I am certain.[4]

The North as well as the South would take warning from such reports.

Later on, in March 1862, the debates in the French lower house—the legislative body—also revealed considerable anti-slavery sentiment. The small five-man Republican majority proposed an amendment to the address to the emperor—the traditional reply to his speech—in which they declared:

France should not interfere in the civil war which is devastating the Republic of the United States of America; but she declares loudly that her sympathies are all on the side of the States of the North, defender of the right and of humanity. She hopes that their victory will bring the abolition of slavery, and that by that action once more it will be proved that the most serious crises could not be harmful to the people who do not make a distinction between democracy and liberty.

While Ollivier defended this amendment, he consented to withdraw it in favor of one by Morin, a liberal Imperialist, which said in part: "The civil war devastating America brings with it a serious blow to our industry and commerce. We ardently hope that these dissensions will have an early end and that the great principle of the abolition of slavery may issue victorious from the fight undertaken in its behalf."

Morin defended this amendment by saying he would not take sides between the North and the South, but the legislative body should take sides with the abolition of slavery from whichever side it may come. The South might start gradual emancipation during the war, and this amendment might encourage her to do it. Slavery was the real cause of the war, he said, and not the tariff. The tariff had come after secession. The North said it only wanted to prevent the extension of slavery to the territories, but that was the death knell to slavery. If the North won, it would be grateful for the moral support of this amendment; if the South gained independence, it would be warned that it must do something about slavery in order to be admitted into the society of civilized states.

Granier de Cassagnac, a government supporter, spoke against the amendment because it was interference in the internal affairs of another government. The logical sequence to this would be a condemnation of the Spanish colonies, Brazil, and China. He favored the principle of emancipation but could not accept the amendment. Morin interrupted to point out that France was interfering in the internal affairs of Syria.

Granier was followed by the government's official spokesman, Billault, who, on the issue of slavery, had this to say: The French government was for abolition. France could only give advice to others. On the other hand France wanted peace and concord in the United States, and to agitate the big question which divided them was not a way to obtain peace and concord. He then asked for the rejection of the amendment, and the house soon after voted it down. But there was little doubt about the general sentiment of the legislature on the question of slavery and emancipation.[5]

Because of that ever-present fortnight of transoceanic delay the news of the United States' compensated emancipation began to trickle into France on March 21, 1862. First came the news of Lincoln's proposal to congress. Then on March 26 came the news of the house's approval, and on April 16 of the senate's favorable action on compensated emancipation in the District of Columbia. By April 24 Frenchmen knew that compulsory compensated emancipation for the Northern capital had been put into effect.[6]

The early reaction in Europe was favorable to Lincoln's proposal. The more liberal imperial papers hailed this first step toward the end of slavery. Prince Napoleon's *Opinion Nationale* said this proved their prediction that the war would solve the slavery problem. It did not think that the Southern states would emancipate voluntarily but that the border states might. The *Presse* hailed this first move as a turning point in the war and surmised that border-state emancipation might spread the move-

ment farther South. From now on, abolition was to be the purpose of the war. The *Presse* lauded Lincoln, referred to his
"House Divided" speech of 1858, and concluded that now finally
he was fulfilling it. The imperialist *Patrie*, however, denounced
this measure as a mere political maneuver which would not work
anyway. It reiterated its belief that slavery was not the cause
of the conflict. What is somewhat significant is the fact that the
imperial government's official organ, the *Moniteur*, for two days
in a row, reproduced the favorable reception given by London
papers to the news of compensated emancipation.[7] Dayton reported gleefully that this new measure had made "a most favorable impression on Europe." "It is almost universally looked
upon as the beginning of the end, and that is much, although the
end may be distant." During the long interview he had with
Napoleon III on March 25 the latter spoke of this emancipation
proposal, and Dayton thought that he "had been favorably impressed by it."[8]

This favorable trend for the Northern cause may have been
sensed by Lindsay, and in his interview with Napoleon III on
April 11 he took care to stress that emancipation was not a war
aim of the North. What it wanted was the subjugation of the
South and a high protective tariff. He cited Lincoln's inaugural
address, his reprimanding of confiscating generals, and the retention of slavery in the District of Columbia. He quoted the
emperor as saying that "he believed that this was a true statement
of the case."[9] This apparent change in the emperor's attitude
may be only the reflection of prejudiced wishful thinking on the
part of both Dayton and Lindsay; but when the news arrived on
April 24 of emancipation in the District of Columbia, it must
have scuttled one of Lindsay's arguments in the mind of the
emperor.[10] There seemed also to be a less favorable press reaction to compensated emancipation later in April. "Malakoff" in his news dispatch of April 18 reported some French
criticism. Thinking in terms of black and white—that the North
was all antislavery and the South all proslavery—many Frenchmen were astonished and disappointed that there was such a
large element in the Northern congress opposed even to compensated emancipation. Learning about border states, these French-

men believed these states should abolish slavery in self-defense, since they found themselves between the hammer and the anvil in the war. Some Frenchmen also began to doubt the genuineness of American republicanism if there were so many defenders of slavery in America and to despair of a strong central government when there were such deep local cultural and social differences.[11] That there was still a French governmental interest in keeping the emancipation side of the American conflict before its readers is seen in the fact that the *Moniteur* continued to publish details on it. On April 16 a delegation from the English and Foreign Anti-Slavery Society had come to the American London legation and read a resolution praising the steps toward emancipation, asking for more, and urging American enforcement of the new antislave-trade treaty. The *Moniteur* gave considerable space to this and to quotations from Adams's reply in which he said:

> The American nation has the desire, as far as it can be in conformity with all engagements contracted, to extend over the entire surface of the territory the happiness which comes from free institutions. . . . I have confidence that those who are the most profoundly interested in the question can in time have the means which are suggested to them, and that, as you say, it is by having the real cause of the conflict disappear that the reunion can be regained.[12]

Certainly, then, the French government was not trying to stir up its people to support an anti-Northern intervention. On the contrary, quite possibly it was trying to diminish French impatience over the cotton famine by creating more sympathy for the North.

No doubt the favorable effect of the early emancipation measures on European public opinion encouraged Lincoln and Seward to make further use of that issue as a counterweight to later threats of European intervention. Then, too, there was the rising demand of the abolitionists at home, reenforced by the converts to sterner measures as the war losses inspired more revengeful sentiments in the North. The congressional elections were approaching, and Lincoln needed to find as many supporters as possible. He could not expect to win the support of the peace Democrats, and so he might as well look to the abolitionists. The border states were not supporting his mild compensated emancipation, and he therefore had no alternative to offer to the abolitionists. When the setback came at Fair Oaks and defeat in the Seven Days Battle, he had to call for 300,000 more volunteers. A bigger appeal could be made for recruiting if the war took on the appearance of a crusade for Negro freedom as well as for union. After the Fair Oaks defeat Mercier wrote: "The most striking symptoms seem to indicate that, for the time being, there is no other alternative than separation or an emancipation war with all its horror and, perhaps, the permanent destruction of cotton culture. And yet, on the other hand, there are a thousand obstacles which stand in the way of both of these extreme solutions."[13]

But Secretary Chase and Senator Sumner were urging some form of general emancipation after the failure of the Virginia invasion. Sumner wanted a proclamation on July 4 to make that date doubly commemorative. Lincoln's reply showed that he was already thinking seriously about such an action: "I would do it if I were not afraid that half the officers would fling down their arms and three more States would rise." He would do it, too, no doubt to forestall the danger of European intervention after the news of the Virginia defeat arrived over there.

But Lincoln left us a statement of his own on the trend of his thinking in early July:

> It had got to midsummer, 1862. Things had gone . . . from bad to worse, until I felt that we had reached the end of our rope on the plan . . . we had been pursuing [the Virginia invasion]; that we must change our tactics, or lose the game. I now determined upon the adoption of the emancipation policy; and without consultation with, or the knowledge of the Cabinet, I prepared the original draft of the proclamation, and, after much anxious thought, called a Cabinet meeting upon the subject.[14]

Indeed, soon after McClellan's retreat in Virginia, the president went repeatedly to the cipher room of the military telegraph office of the war department. Here, finding he was almost alone because of restricted access by others, he began very secretly to draw up the first draft of a military proclamation of emancipation. A week later—July 13—he confided to Seward and Welles that he was working on such a proclamation; but it was not until July 22 that he submitted the question to the cabinet. He would make the final decision, he told the members of the cabinet, but he welcomed their comments. There was general approval of the principle; but Seward, for one, with an eye to both foreign and domestic reactions, objected to its issuance on the heels of a severe military setback. He had just been warning Europe that intervention might lead to slave insurrections and then no cotton at all. "Now," he argued, "foreign nations will intervene to prevent the abolition of slavery for the sake of cotton." ". . . We break up our relations with foreign nations and the production of cotton for sixty years." This argument seemed to point to a European hostility to emancipation instead of its devotion to it. But, farther along in the cabinet discussion he seemed willing to have the proclamation issued if it came on the heels of victory when it would make a better impression at home and abroad.

> It may be viewed [Seward thought] as the last measure of an exhausted government stretching forth her hand to Ethiopia, instead of Ethiopia stretching forth her hands to the government. It will be considered our last *shriek* on the retreat. Now, while I approve the measure, I suggest, Sir, that you postpone its issue until you can give it to the country supported by military success, instead of issuing it, as would be the case now, upon the greatest disaster of the war.

Lincoln was much impressed with this argument and told F. B. Carpenter, who painted the cabinet emancipation picture, that the wisdom of Seward's argument struck him "with great force." "The result was," he confessed, "that I put the draft of the proclamation aside, as you do a sketch of your picture, waiting for a victory."[15]

And so the first draft of the famous document was filed away, and a secretive silence was drawn around it for exactly two months.[16]   Indeed, Lincoln was not only silent but sometimes even misleading. To a delegation of Christian ministers presenting him resolutions from a mass meeting in the Bryan Hall in Chicago, resolutions which asked him to issue just such a proclamation, he gave many arguments against the idea. He personally favored emancipation, he said, but not under present circumstances. "What good would a document from me do?" Then he concluded: "I do not want to issue a document that the whole world will see must necessarily be inoperative, like the Pope's bull against the comet." And then on August 20 came an editorial blast from Horace Greeley, editor of the New York *Tribune*, who said a prayer of twenty million Americans rose to Lincoln to use his full power to bring slavery to an end. Again his famous reply to the editorial gave little sign that a proclamation was saved up for a sunny day. He merely told Greeley that the Union was the primary purpose of the war and that what he did or did not do about slavery was determined by whether it would help save the Union.[17] These statements hardly rallied the emancipationists at home or abroad, and it is puzzling that he deliberately answered Greeley's open letter when he could have kept silent until his proclamation was issued. Here he was momentarily antagonizing those whom he wished to win in a few weeks.

The Battle of Antietam

Lincoln, Seward, and the cabinet were thus waiting for some forward movement of the Union armies and a dramatic victory before anything further could be done about emancipation. However, the Army of the Potomac was not moving forward; quite the contrary, they were withdrawing toward Washington to consolidate its defense. What was worse, in the process of this concentration on Washington, General Pope's forces had been defeated at the second Battle of Bull Run on August 29. Again there was panic in Washington and in the cabinet apprehension because McClellan was again in command when the troops were in the vicinity of the capital.

To make matters even worse, General Lee, not McClellan,

was the one who made a forward movement of his Army of Northern Virginia. His plan was to march through Maryland, bring over the people of that state to the Confederate cause, obtain his needed supplies from that area, and then strike a blow at Harrisburg in Pennsylvania. If he won here and destroyed the railroad bridge which linked the West with the East, he might threaten Baltimore and Philadelphia. A thorough defeat of McClellan in this campaign might open the way for a peace based on separation or a Northern discouragement bring defeat to the Republicans in the fall congressional elections.

Lee did march rapidly through Maryland up to Hagerstown near the Pennsylvania line. But everything seemed to go against him. The Marylanders did not rally to the Confederate cause, nor would they sell him supplies Confederate currency was unacceptable, and food supplies and cattle were hurried away toward Pennsylvania. Then, to make matters worse, Lee's plan of campaign fell into the hands of McClellan, who was hurrying northward to checkmate the invaders. The two hostile forces finally met in battle on September 17 along Antietam Creek, near Sharpsburg, Maryland. Seventy-five thousand Union soldiers were pitted against fifty-one thousand Confederates. The outcome was the defeat of Lee and his withdrawal southward across the Potomac. Each side lost over eleven thousand men, hence the percentage loss of Lee was much higher. But, unfortunately, McClellan did not follow up his victory by a hot pursuit.[18]

Here was a victory which Lincoln might utilize for issuing his emancipation proclamation, but it was hardly striking enough to impress Americans or Europeans. After all, it was a negative success: the South was not being conquered, she had just been prevented from conquering a part of the North. Union losses had been heavy, McClellan had failed to pursue Lee's forces, and, indeed, two months later the Federal government relieved McClellan of his command, which did not signify a reward after a victory. Yet Lincoln now felt he must make this negative and indecisive battle the occasion for the proclamation. The Maryland campaign and the Antietam encounter might make France and England more convinced of the need for some form of intervention unless slavery were put into the scales against it.

Consequently, four days after the news of the Antietam "victory" the president brought up again before the cabinet the emancipation proposal. Now was "the time for acting," he said gravely. He had made a promise to himself and to his Maker that, as soon as the enemy was driven out of Maryland, he would issue a proclamation of emancipation. He then read his draft, article by article, with his own added comments. Blair was the only one to oppose it, purely on the grounds of its harmful political effects at home. All the others approved, even Chase. Seward wanted it to be understood that the freedom of the slaves would really be maintained in the long run.[19] Thus on September 23, 1862, the famous Emancipation Proclamation was published for the whole world to read. One of its paragraphs threw down the gauntlet both to the Secessionists and to Europe. ". . . That on the 1st day of January, A.D. 1863, all persons held as slaves within any State or designated part of a State the people whereof shall then be in rebellion against the United States shall be then, thenceforward, and forever free."[20]

The first European reaction to the Proclamation came from the European envoys in Washington. Mercier's earliest impression was that the proclamation was "so inconceivable and so serious" that he would postpone giving Thouvenel his opinion. Two days later he wrote that he thought its purpose was to make a desperate attempt to discourage European intervention. In spite of it Mercier urged a joint European mediation plan without stipulating separation or recognition but just basing it on the vague phrase of union. By his earlier correspondence the French envoy had been advocating the solution of political separation and economic union. Evidently he wanted to use the vague term of union as a devious approach to the economic union settlement. Finally, a week later, he reported at length on the Proclamation. He was puzzled because Lincoln had opposed emancipation to an abolitionist delegation just a week before the Proclamation. The final decision, to him, must have been a desperate one to obtain abolitionist votes in the coming elections, to help the recruiting of new volunteers, and to stave off European intervention. Mercier thought this desperate "last card" Lincoln was playing might cause him to lose the game rather than win it. The peace party would look upon it as a confirmation of their views, the troops of the border states might very well go over to the other side with all their weapons. There were even "encouraging" signs in the Army of the Potomac, probably meaning signs of war weariness as a result of Antietam and the Proclamation. McClellan was about to resign or be dismissed. As to the South, the proclamation would probably push it to ever more determined efforts. Therefore, the French minister wondered whether, in the face of possible slave insurrections to be added to the war, it would not be wise for the European powers to insist on a truce now and, failing this, to threaten to consult solely their own interests in the future. As far as Mercier was concerned, it seems as if the Emancipation Proclamation was having the opposite effect of impelling him to recommend European intervention rather than cautious abstention. The French minister reported that Seward had avoided any comment to him on the Proclamation. However, Mercier had seen Weed, who had returned from Europe, and urged upon him his plan of political separation and economic union, offering the emperor's good offices to bring about a truce. According to the Frenchman's report, Weed "appeared very impressed with my language on the subject, seemed very satisfied with it, and . . . said to one of his political friends that some good could come from this conversation."[21]

The British chargé d'affaires, William Stuart, thought Lincoln had forestalled the complaints of the sixteen governors meeting at Altoona, Pennsylvania, but he had also alienated the conservatives and surrendered himself to the radicals. As to the European effects, Stuart concluded that, since the Proclamation freed no slaves, its main purpose was to arouse European sympathy, but that its unintended result might be slave insurrections.[22]

France and the Emancipation Proclamation

It is interesting that even before the news of the proclamation had arrived in Paris, Dayton was gaining the impression that Thouvenel was favorable to the North on both issues—slavery and secession. The United States minister had an interview with

Thouvenel on September 12—three weeks before the news of the Proclamation arrived—in which they discussed the rumor that the South was making some kind of proposal as to the modification of slavery. On this subject Thouvenel did not give a direct reply but made a general statement that "you [Dayton] know well that my sympathies and my acts have been with you from the beginning." From the rest of this conversation and from previous ones Dayton gave these reassuring impressions to Seward: "I have always been satisfied that Mr. Thouvenel's views on these subjects [slavery and secession] were right. He knows and perfectly appreciates the fact that slavery lies at the basis of the insurrection. . . ."[23]

The news of the Emancipation Proclamation was in all the Sunday evening papers of Paris on October 5, and the first reaction was not favorable. While Bigelow was delighted that emancipation had been made an objective of the war, he recorded in his diary: "Exchange has gone up to 32 [cents to the franc] and gold is at 24¾. This is a bad sign and prevents my being as much encouraged by the news as I would like to be."[24] From this it would seem that the indecisive victory at Antietam and the Proclamation were both being interpreted momentarily as signs of Northern weakness.

A few days later Bigelow received a circular from Seward on the subject of the Emancipation Proclamation and, with some hesitation, had it published widely "to improve the effect of that document."[25] In the circular Seward had claimed Antietam as a victory and boasted that the Union army was now set for a new campaign, and on emancipation he had changed the Northern objectives from "Union and not abolition" to "Union and abolition."

> In the judgment of the President [the circular declared] the time has come for setting forth the great fact distinctly for the serious consideration of those [rebellious] States, and for giving them to understand that if they will persist in forcing upon the country a choice between the dissolution of this necessary and beneficent government or a relinquishment of the protection of slavery, it is the Union and not slavery that must be maintained and preserved. With this view the President has issued a procla-

mation in which he gives notice that slavery will be no longer recognized in any State which shall be found in armed rebellion on the first of January next. While good and wise men of all nations will confess that this is just and proper as a military proceeding for the relief of the country from a desolating and exhausting war, they will at the same time acknowledge the moderation and magnanimity [compensation to loyal citizens] with which the government proceeds in a transaction of such great solemnity and importance.[26]

Bigelow was the North's publicity agent and now reported that the Proclamation had been "emphatically commended" by the Orleanist *Débats*, and he felt that "it will find an echo throughout France . . . for France is unanimous for Emancipation and our cause will now daily grow in grace here as it grows in age."[27]

Sanford, who was again in Paris at this time, was also very gratified by emancipation. He claimed that the Proclamation had assured to the North the sympathies of the liberal parties in Europe. "It represents in France twelve million people whose will is respected because its revolutions are feared." Again in closing he said that "the Proclamation of the President works well over here" and that "it gives now a basis for our friends here to work upon and to appeal to the sympathies of civilized Europe."[28]

Like Bigelow, Dayton did not report an early favorable reaction to the Proclamation. Indeed, in his first comments on emancipation, he anticipated a hostile European press reaction. What was worse he prophesied: "You must not be surprised if another spasmodic effort for intervention is made, based upon the assumed ground of humanity but upon the real ground that emancipation may seriously injure the cause of the South, and will interfere for years to come, at least, with the production of cotton."[29] In this prediction the American minister was not far wrong, as subsequent events will show.

Sanford may have been right that the Emancipation Proclamation rallied more firmly the loyalty of twelve million French liberals to the Northern cause, but the opinion of the press, much of it inspired by a pro-Southern minister of the interior (Persigny), leaned heavily against the Proclamation. The *Constitutionnel* greeted it with ridicule because it would perpetuate slavery if the slave states laid down their arms.[30] The other important imperialist paper, the *Patrie*, attacked this type of emancipation along the same lines—that is, that it guaranteed slavery in loyal states and showed that the war had nothing to do with freedom.[31] The pro-government *France* was even more violent in its reaction. In its view the Proclamation came too late to convince the world or emancipate the slaves in the South. Lincoln might just as well have tried to free slaves in a foreign country or in the whole universe. It was a scheme for the wholesale butchery of defenseless women and children.[32] Another pro-Southern paper, the *Presse*, recognized that Lincoln had tried to compromise between two extremes. "Unfortunately, half-measures satisfy nobody." As to Seward's circular it remarked that "in place of a principle, it is only a bomb thrown into the midst of the population of the South."[33] The *Revue contemporaine* made the obvious observation that slavery was maintained where the Federal government had authority and abolished where it had none.[34] One provincial newspaper, the *Moniteur de la Côte d'Or* of Dijon, we know continued to heap scorn and criticism on the North after the Proclamation.[35]

While official inspiration encouraged the majority of the French press in attacks on the Proclamation, there was a considerable number of the liberal organs which praised the act in varying degrees. "Malakoff," in his report to the *New York Times*, affirmed that "the liberal press and public unanimously approve the Proclamation."[36] The Orleanist *Journal des Débats* in its early edition of October 9 greeted the news of the Proclamation with enthusiasm, saying it refuted those who said slavery had nothing to do with the war.[37] The democratic *Siècle* was disappointed that slavery had not been totally abolished, but thought that the Proclamation was one more step in that direction.[38] The Orleanist *Revue des deux mondes*, in its next number of October 15, gave this cautious approval of the measure: "It seems that Mr. Lincoln's proclamation ought to be the decisive blow or at least the last ordeal in this unfortunate conflict. Since it was necessary to have recourse to this extreme measure, we hope that it may be indeed the beginning of the definitive abolition of slavery."[39] In the provinces we know of at least one journal, the *Courrier du Bas-Rhin* of Colmar, which continued its support of the North in the period of the Proclamation.[40]

Just as the semi-official press was influenced by the pro-Southern sympathies of the minister of interior and of the cabinet, so were the procureurs general—imperial district attorneys—who had the job of reporting French public opinion. In reports of October 1862 and January 1863 the procureur general of Colmar, in Alsace, affirmed that popular support for the South increased. In the later report the procureur general observed that "the really monstrous proclamation by the Republicans of the North, which, by the very words of President Lincoln, carefully preserves slavery in their country while abolishing it in their neighbors', arouses indignation everywhere [in his district]."[41]   From Nancy, in Lorraine, came a similar report that "the North had the moral advantage of being antislavery, and yet it is far from winning sympathy."[42]   Similarly in Bordeaux, in spite of the Proclamation, "public sympathies indeed stand out distinctly in favor of the Southern provinces."[43]

On the other hand, in Dijon—in Burgundy—sentiment was evidently divided. Pro-government papers, like the *Moniteur de la Côte d'Or*, denounced those papers and individuals who sympathized with the North on the grounds of emancipation. The procureur general did not like this attitude because it "might hurt the feelings of those people with high ideals and make it appear that the opposition families [local Bourbonist and Orleanist families] were on the right side."[44]   Curiously enough, it was in one of the biggest cotton manufacturing centers, Rouen, that the Proclamation seems to have met a favorable reaction. "People now appear less desirous of intervention," wrote the procureur general.[45]

In general, it must be admitted, the initial impact of the Emancipation Proclamation on French public opinion was slight. If there was any appreciable influence, it may have been to confirm more strongly the pro-Northern sympathies already existing. Since one of the purposes of the Proclamation was to forestall European intervention, we should now turn to that question as it developed in the late summer of 1862.

The October Intervention Crisis

We have already seen that during the spring and early summer of 1862 there was still an inclination on the part of France and England to wait for further developments before moving officially toward mediation or recognition of the Confederacy. In spite of the Northern setback in Virginia there were such considerations as Northern victories in the Middle West and the opening of ports for cotton export, all of which called for caution before any serious departure was taken from a position of impartial neutrality. In the eyes of British and French leaders it was still too early to tell whether the North's cause was hopeless from a military point of view. There was also the obvious fact that, with three Southern ports open, it was the Southern embargo rather than the Northern blockade which was causing the cotton shortage. This situation, tied to the ominous threats of Seward, tended to restrain France and England a little longer.

During the period of late August and early September there were several reports indicating a French attitude of watchful waiting. Bigelow, in his official report of August 22, remarked the emperor's hesitancy in making up his mind on any policy toward America. "It is clear that he has lost pretty much all of the little faith he had in our ability to reduce the South to obedience, and he is now hovering over us, like the carrion crow over the body of the sinking traveler, waiting until we are too weak to resist his predatory instincts." As for French public opinion, Bigelow felt that, in spite of the hostility of the official and unofficial press, the public was so hostile to slavery that it would not permit any policy helpful to the South.[46]. On this same day Sanford had dinner with Thouvenel, where the talk ran much on the cotton famine. The foreign minister said to Sanford that, if the North can defeat the South, let it hurry up and do it, because the French economy can not long endure the strain. Everybody on this occasion assured him that there was not going to be any early intervention. Yet, in spite of these assurances, Sanford felt convinced "that something in the nature of intervention in the shape of remonstrance or offer of mediation is to be made later by several European powers" and that "there is an evident lying in wait for a more convenient season."[47]

These reports from the American consul in Paris and from the minister to Belgium were confirmed by the American minister to France, Dayton himself. The latter had had a conversation with Thouvenel on August 29 in which they had discussed the new possibilities of obtaining cotton. The French foreign minister was "all alive with interest" at the mention of cotton. "I hope it will come," he said, "not more for our sake *than for the sake of the United States.*" Dayton noted and underlined this veiled threat, but at the time he reminded Thouvenel that the reopened ports had, in the pre-war period, exported two-thirds of the cotton shipments. The French minister's plaintive reply to this was: "But it does not come!" This was just what Dayton was waiting for, and he gave him the quick answer, "That is no fault of ours, we have allowed it to come and have offered to guarantee its safe transit and shipment." At this point the American minister was surprised to learn that Thouvenel understood that the Federal authorities would only let Unionists trade in cotton and receive payment in foreign money. This Dayton flatly denied and showed Thouvenel the assurances from Seward and the orders issued permitting trade by all inhabitants in captured territory. Here Thouvenel's favor for the North and his reluctance to intervene revealed themselves because he begged Dayton to have this information published in the *Débats* or somewhere. The fact that Thouvenel mentioned the *Débats* in preference to the unofficial press revealed his rivalry with Persigny who was inspiring the unofficial press in favor of the South. Thouvenel was evidently not sure this pro-Northern news would be published in the imperial press. Yet he wanted the information to come out in a newspaper which was pro-Northern as he was.[48]

A few days later Dayton, writing to Seward, defended his reports of French nonintervention against the rumors of Confederates and visiting Northerners. He said that the Confederates, such as Slidell, deliberately circulated exaggerated and false reports in their own favor; and many private Northerners without having access to the French government or to Dayton's sources of information heard and circulated the most alarming rumors.

No doubt, having Sanford in mind, Dayton went on to complain bitterly that "even [American] officials transiently in Paris, who should know better, pick up these rumors, become excited, hurry first to the Legation, then write to the Department." All of this denunciation of rumors was prefatory to his final conclusion that "nothing has occurred here . . . to justify the belief that the Emperor intends to interfere with us."[49]

One event seemed to confirm Dayton's view of Napoleon III. On August 18 Chasseloup-Laubat, the French minister of marine, married in Paris the niece of the Confederate general, Beauregard. Usually this marriage would have been held in the imperial chapel with the court and the cabinet attending. In this case it was not held in the chapel, and the emperor and his court did not attend. According to Bigelow "the Emperor was unwilling to give too much prominence to an event which he supposed might be regarded with suspicion at Washington." At least the event suggested that Napoleon III was not at that time going to arouse the North with an official intervention if he refrained from arousing it over a much less important private wedding.[50]

One other reason for France's late-summer nonintervention was the absence of any British encouragement at that time. French policy had always been one of only moving in cooperation with the British, and the latter were still inclined to wait for the outcome of late-summer campaigns. Russell was inclined to wait until October for a final decision.[51] In the meantime the cabinet had gone off in all directions for the long summer vacation, and Russell was attending the queen on her continental journey. While Russell was accompanying the queen, he wrote Palmerston that "we must allow the President to spend his second batch of 600,000 men before we can hope that he and his democracy will listen to reason."[52] Taking this literally, they would then have to wait a lot longer than October.[53]

However, by September 10 the news began to arrive of the series of engagements southwest of Washington which was to be called the Second Battle of Bull Run (August 26–30). Mercier had sent Thouvenel short despatches speeded by telegraph, and the press dispatches on September 10 carried the news of some of the Federal misfortunes in that area.[54] Thouvenel's early reaction to the incomplete reports was to register a continued uncertainty about intervention because of the inconclusive military campaigns. He and the emperor both wanted to wait for more battles and the results of the congressional elections.[55]

Yet, in spite of this cautious attitude, he saw Dayton on the following day—September 12—and confidentially opened to him his personal ideas on the hopelessness of trying to bring the South back into the Union. These intimate thoughts of the French foreign minister were consigned by Dayton to a written memorandum. Thouvenel had begun by saying that his conversation was unofficial and his thoughts were those of a friend sympathetic to the Northern cause. He regretted, he said, that in the beginning the North had not let the Southern states go in peace because, after a year or two, they would have returned to a slightly modified union. But now that force has been used against them, "I think that the undertaking of conquering the South is almost superhuman . . . to me the undertaking seems impossible." Besides, he continued, the South is so large and extensive that you could not hold it down if you conquered it. It is not the nature of a democratic republic like yours to hold so many hostile people in subjection. Then Thouvenel proposed a weak confederation scheme in which the states would be paramount in domestic affairs but united for defense and foreign relations.

Here, of course, Thouvenel betrayed his lack of knowledge of American history because otherwise he would have known that the confederation form had been tried and deliberately abandoned. Likewise a stronger guarantee for slavery in the Southern states had been offered in 1860–1861 and rejected by the more fanatical secessionists. In this scheme, however, is revealed Thouvenel's—and France's—desire to see America strong in armed forces and in diplomacy to act as a counterweight to the power of the British Empire.

Dayton did not enter into a detailed argument on this occasion, but he did not let these personal views of Thouvenel go entirely unchallenged. He observed that such a scheme had hidden complications and had already failed in America's early history. Dayton, in his report to Seward, feared the effect of the news about the second defeat at Bull Run, but felt no rash decision would be made immediately.[56] The subsequent news to which Dayton referred also told of Washington being threatened, of Maryland being invaded by Southern forces, and of Baton Rouge being recaptured by the Confederates.[57]

Naturally these military developments had their effect on English as well as French leaders. Russell wired Cowley on September 13: "The whole Federal Army has fallen back behind the fortifications around Washington," and in a private note of the same day he instructed the latter to sound out Thouvenel privately on what could be done.[58] To Palmerston, Russell wrote: "It really looks as if he [Jackson] might end the war. In October the hour will be ripe for the Cabinet." Palmerston's reply was agreeable: "If this [the fall of Washington or Baltimore] should happen, would it not be time for us to consider whether in such a state of things England and France might not address the contending parties and recommend an arrangement upon the basis of separation." Russell was more specific in his reply when he suggested mediation and, if that were rejected by the North, recognition of the South.[59]

No doubt Cowley was somewhat surprised at Russell's conversion to intervention because the British government and Cowley and even Thouvenel had been trying to restrain the impatience and concern of Napoleon III. Yet, three days after receiving Russell's unofficial instructions, Cowley had a long conversation with Thouvenel in which he raised the possibility, in the light of recent military reverses, of England and France proposing mediation. In spite of Thouvenel's knowledge of the emperor's earlier desire to have England propose such a step, he tried to discourage Cowley and Russell. The French minister thought it would be much better to wait until the American election returns came in. If the peace party won out, Lincoln and Seward would probably be set aside. But until that time France and England might be running serious risks in their relations with the North by intervening in any way. Cowley, rather half-heartedly, suggested that if all the powers urged an armistice with a threat of recognition of the South if the armistice were rejected, this approach would carry a great deal of weight in the North.

Thouvenel was not at all sure. He pointed out that Russia would probably not cooperate. France had previously sounded out Russia and England and had received an almost scornful refusal. Besides, he added, public opinion in France is not as insistent on recognition as opinion may be in England.[60]

However, the Second Battle of Bull Run and Cowley's conversation had made Thouvenel begin to think about mediation. On the same day that Cowley was reporting his conversation with the French foreign minister, the latter was suggesting to Mercier that the recent defeats might have conditioned Northern opinion to support a mediation effort. He asked to be informed of every indication in this direction.[61]

As this letter was being written, the news arrived that the Confederate forces were moving northward to carry out the invasion of the border state of Maryland (the maneuver that was to lead to the Battle of Antietam). Not only did it seem as if the Southerners were carrying the war to the North, but it suggested that possibly the three important Northern cities of Washington, Baltimore, and Philadelphia were threatened.[62] From this time on, the French and the English were anxiously awaiting the outcome of this new development where the North rather than the South, was on the defensive.[63]

While Thouvenel was having Mercier search out the extent of peace opinion in the North, he seemed to be holding the line against any decisive action in Europe. Sanford learned through a friend that Thouvenel had said that nothing would be done on the American or Italian questions until the emperor's return, and then both questions would be taken up. On another occasion the French foreign minister told Cowley that "as soon as the Emperor came back the two governments ought to enter into serious consideration of the whole question."[64]

In contrast to Thouvenel's passive attitude, the English leaders were now actively planning for the consideration of mediation and eventually of recognition. Russell returned from the Continent, where he had been in attendance on Queen Victoria, and immediately began to write up a memorandum for action which was to be embodied in instructions to Cowley. What he suggested was that, in the interim before the cabinet meeting in mid-October, he would try to persuade Russia and France to join England. He would recommend to them and to the British cabinet an offer of mediation to both parties. If the North refused, the powers would recognize the South. The mediation would be on the basis of separation, and recognition would be accompanied by a declaration of neutrality.[65] Russell not only sent this plan to Palmerston and Gladstone, but he also outlined it to Victoria, who seemed favorable except that she thought that Austria should also be consulted. Russell assured her that all three powers would be consulted, but France first.[66] Palmerston's reaction to the memorandum was sympathetic. In his view the offer of mediation should be made to both sides and include pro-Northern Russia as one of the mediators to make it easier for the Union to accept. He wondered whether mediation would imply European recognition of the South. The outcome of the impending battle [Antietam] might be the determining factor.[67]

Not only were Russell and Palmerston discussing intervention between themselves, but Russell took pains to let the French know about it. When Chateaurenard, the French chargé, saw Russell on September 23, the foreign secretary seemed to want to keep the discussion going on American affairs even though Chateaurenard had said he had no recent information on the war from Paris. Consequently the French chargé took advantage of Russell's loquacity on the subject to ply him with a few questions, such as, whether the *Morning Post* article indicated an early British recognition of the Confederacy and at what moment it would come. Russell remained vague by saying that he and Palmerston had been recently discussing the matter and that a decision would at least await the American election results and further Southern victories. The French chargé gathered from this exchange that England would act only jointly with France and that the outcome of the impending battles would be the decisive factor. He also noted that the distress of the working classes in Lancashire and elsewhere was exceeding all relief efforts.[68]

Three days later, on September 27, the news from the battle front in Maryland began to arrive in Europe. It told the story of the Confederate invasion of Maryland and of the North's meeting them in mortal combat at Antietam. According to these early reports McClellan had not only stopped the invasion but had hurled it back over the Potomac. Later reports told of heavy losses on both sides but confirmed a decisive Northern victory. Washington and Baltimore were again safe.[69]

In the meantime, between Second Bull Run and Antietam, Seward had had a long interview with Mercier on September 7 in which the latter had told Seward confidentially, but frankly, that the Union could not be restored. In lieu of that impossible objective he suggested two confederacies, united for certain purposes. Seward replied, as usual, that the military situation was not as bad as it seemed, that a victory was expected soon, and that the present Northern government would not entertain from within or without any proposal that was predicated upon separation. Again the American secretary boasted of the size of the Northern army, the development of the navy, and the inexhaustible resources of the country. In reporting this conversation to Dayton, Seward told him to see Thouvenel and, without reading him the dispatch, at least to give him strong arguments along the lines of what he had said to Mercier.[70]

Dayton received these instructions before the news of the victory at Antietam and "for obvious reasons" waited for countervailing good news before seeking an interview with Thouvenel.[71] The French minister's absence from Paris further delayed the meeting until Thursday, October 2. Dayton said he had informed Seward of Thouvenel's personal views on the hopelessness of reunion. It was too early for a reply; but the American minister had received information about a Mercier-Seward discussion on the same subject, and consequently he already had Seward's views on this question. Since Thouvenel was anxious to learn the Federal government's reaction to his personal observations, Dayton had a good opportunity to communicate Seward's response without reading the dispatch itself. The long conversation which followed, being the last information received by Thouvenel and almost the last expression of his ideas on the American conflict, is particularly significant.

Dayton: Our government and people are firm in their determination to prosecute the war to its close. We have the men and the means, the Southern country is adjacent to our own, and not difficult of access from the North. We have command of the ports and water communications on the other three sides. It is pierced in its most settled ports by navigable rivers which we can and will command. Whatever may be the views of foreign statesmen, we do not doubt our ultimate success in suppressing the rebellion. One thing seems to us certain: the slave owners of the South must conquer the freemen of the North or we must conquer them.[72] There can be no division, no splitting of the country into two parts. Our rivers, our railways, all of our internal channels of communication seem to be cast by nature, or arranged by man, for *one* country only. . . . It is a question of national existence, it is life or death; and such a question, in our own councils at least, must be held paramount to all other considerations. Although foreign statesmen may look on passing events with a calmer eye and cooler judgment, our own statesmen from a nearer standpoint will see and weigh matters and things coming in aid of their views not obvious to those afar off. Particularly, they will better appreciate and understand the difficulties of any attempted compromise and the terrible but certain consequences which would follow disunion.

Thouvenel (nodding assent): There are doubtless difficulties in a settlement which foreign statesmen cannot appreciate readily as those at home, though, upon other questions, connected with this subject I think they are quite as competent to judge as yourselves; and, as we speak unofficially (you know my sympathies) I must say I no longer believe you can conquer the South. Further, I am confident that at this time there is not a reasonable statesman in Europe who believes you can succeed in carrying out your first conception [reunion]. Have you heard from Mr. Adams lately?

Dayton: No, I haven't.

Thouvenel: I think things look as if it will not be long before Great Britain will recognize the South. Have you had no advices to that effect?

Dayton (somewhat jarred by this sudden turn of the conversation): No, I have received none, but my general impressions are that there is no immediate probability of such an event.

Thouvenel (avoiding any revelation of Cowley's unofficial approach): I judge only from the pressure on the [British] government through the public journals, which originated in the distress of cotton interests. . . .

Dayton: Do they expect to get cotton by such recognition?

Thouvenel (merely shrugs his shoulders).

Dayton: In my judgment, the effect of such a course of action would be to deprive them of the little cotton which they now get. . . . There is much bad feeling between the American and English people, and, if Great Britain takes this course, we shall prepare ourselves for . . . the ultimate consequence. [Dayton was cleverly threatening France while appearing only to threaten Britain.] Fortunately for us . . . our war . . . left our merchant marine and our sailors almost untouched. On our coasts and in our ports . . . we would be found better prepared than at any past period in our history. . . . Should Great Britain attempt to interfere with us, the whole power of the country would be called into action and we would defend ourselves and our interests to the last extremity. What she would get from interference would not be equivalent to its costs.

The conversation then turned upon opening a "neutral" port for the export of cotton. Dayton said that New Orleans was already an open neutral port. Thouvenel said that because of U.S. Treasury regulations cotton would not come out to New Orleans from the plantations. To this the American minister replied that the regulations in question involved the coastal trade and not foreign trade. Later Dayton sent the foreign minister a copy of the regulations.

The reaction of these two men to this long conversation are significant. Dayton told Seward that Thouvenel's revelations that England was contemplating recognition of the South "was to me the alarming feature of the conversation." He also thought that France's loss of hope for the preservation of the Union might soon lead to recognition.[73]

Thouvenel, on the same day, wrote to Mercier his last reflections on the American problem before his dismissal, reflections growing out of this long conversation.

If . . . we are approaching the denouement, the situation still looks very confused from afar. M. Dayton, to whom I suppose, M. Seward sent a whiplash, has become just as positive as his boss, and says he is as sure as ever of the defeat of the South. I did not conceal that my opinion differed from his, and that my duty, especially as a friend of his government, required that I do not encourage his hopes too strongly. Besides, his worried look betrayed his blustering language. . . . Lord Russell has been back in London only a few days and I myself am awaiting the return of the emperor to Saint-Cloud to take up seriously the question of the United States. . . . Here we are very close to the American elections, and I wonder if we ought not to wait for the indications they could give before we decide on anything. If the recognition which would then be irrevocable, touched off the powder keg in the North and we were forced to do our share of fighting along with England, I admit to you that I would think a long while before doing it. Mexico, the American question, and on top of all that the affairs of Rome, that's really too much all at once. Adieu, my dear friend, I shall write you officially as soon as I have worked out something with the emperor.[74]

However much Thouvenel belittled the belligerent attitude of Dayton, he was evidently impressed by it. He wanted to wait for the election results, he did not want to add an American war to the Mexican one, he would wait also for the return of the emperor. By the time the emperor returned, both men had fuller reports of the Antietam victory and also saw some of the reaction to the news of the Emancipation Proclamation. Both of these events would seem to support the current cautious approach. However, in mid-October the American question was elbowed aside by the Italian question, and the latter caused Thouvenel's dismissal before American affairs could even be considered.

On the British side the news of Antietam was making Palmerston more cautious about adopting Russell's memorandum. On the eve of Antietam, Palmerston had been thinking of intervention before mid-October; but, two days after the first meager reports of the battle, he began to hesitate in a letter to Russell in which he admitted that the outcome of the Battle of Antietam required a further delay in British plans. If war was to result from recognition, it might be better to wait for the spring of 1863 when Canada would be open for the arrival of defense forces. If anything was done in the fall and winter of 1862, it might be merely to send a "friendly suggestion" to both parties that reunion seemed impossible and that they ought to negotiate peace on the basis of separation. He ended with clear signs of uncertainty: "The whole matter is full of difficulty, and can only be cleared up by some more decided events between the contending armies."[75]

While Palmerston was hesitating, other cabinet members were strongly opposing the Russell memorandum. Granville, after hearing of the Antietam victory of the North, wrote to Russell that he thought mediation was "premature," that parliament and opinion preferred neutrality to intervention and possible war. To Lord Stanley he said "it was a great mistake."[76]

Yet, in spite of the news of Antietam and the Emancipation Proclamation and almost in defiance of Palmerston's and Granville's opposition, Russell, on October 13, drew up for consideration by the cabinet a new version of his memorandum in the form of a prospective circular note to the powers. In this he argued that the South had shown she could successfully defend herself, that there seemed to be no Unionist elements in captured Southern areas, that the Emancipation Proclamation freed no slaves, North or South, and only encouraged servile insurrection. Therefore England should urge the great powers to propose a "suspension of arms" in order to weigh calmly "the advantages of peace."[77]

During the intervening ten days before the cabinet was supposed to meet, the more important members individually rejected the circular memorandum. Gladstone on October 7 in his famous Newcastle speech had irritated Palmerston by stating, without cabinet approval, that Jefferson Davis had created an army and was about to create a nation. Then, on October 14, Sir George Cornwall Lewis, war secretary, replied by a speech in Hereford both to Gladstone and Russell's proposed circular by saying that the outcome of the war was still "undecided." "Under such circumstances the time had not yet arrived when it would be asserted in accordance with established doctrines of international law that the independence of the Southern States had been established."[78] When Palmerston had Lord Clarendon, a Liberal at that time without an office appointment, consult Lord Derby, the leader of the opposition, on the matter, he received another hostile report. Derby was against recognition because it would not help the South or obtain a single bale of cotton; he was against mediation because the demands of the two sides were irreconcilable. Recognition was of no benefit to England unless she intended to break the blockade and precipitate a war with the North.[79]

Indeed, Lewis, in addition to his Hereford speech, wrote a countermemorandum against that of Russell. In this the war secretary argued that "looking at this philanthropic proposition [Russell's], we may doubt whether the chances of doing evil do not preponderate over the chances of doing good, whether it is not

'Better to endure the ills we have

Than fly to others that we know not of.' "[80]

This countermemorandum then elicited Clarendon's own criticism of Russell's proposal. To Lewis, Clarendon ridiculed Russell's memorandum and commended Lewis' paper, which probably had brought about the abandonment of the cabinet meeting. Russell had been heading for a Yankee insult or their demand for a detailed proposal. Clarendon thought that the South qualified for recognition but that British interests required the avoidance of war with the North.[81]

After learning of the criticism of respected colleagues in and out of the cabinet and after reading both memoranda, Palmerston wrote Russell that he agreed with Lewis that, after the Confederate setback, nothing should be done for the present. The two belligerents would still be as adamant as ever.[82] This letter showed, as did Thouvenel's to Mercier, that the military developments were crucial in the decisions on intervention and recognition.

As a result of this change in Palmerston's attitude a cabinet meeting was not called. Many of the cabinet members met with Russell on October 23, the day planned for an official meeting, but Palmerston was not there. They decided by informal conversation against any move toward English and European mediation or recognition and adjourned the question *sine die*.[83] When Adams saw Russell later on the same day, the latter assured him that "it was still their intention to adhere to the rule of perfect neutrality in the struggle, and to let it come to its natural end without the smallest interference, direct or otherwise."[84] This was a far cry from the tone of his memorandum.

It should be noted, too, that certain long-range considerations reenforced British caution after the Antietam victory of the North. England was very much concerned about her trade with the United States as well as about her world trade and shipping. With the realization of her vulnerability to the Northern iron-clads she was not going to precipitate a war with the Union for light and transient reasons. The English business classes, who had the right of suffrage, were more influential in pressing for nonintervention on account of these considerations than were her antislavery working classes, who were still disfranchised. And finally there were lurking dangers in Germany, Poland, Italy, and the Near East, which seemed to make it unwise for either Britain or France to be embroiled at this time in a sea and land war with a mobilized United States.[85]

Since French policy was closely tied to that of Great Britain as to any form of intervention, this English postponement of action prevented immediate French action. Also, France was very much absorbed with the Italian crisis in the aftermath of Garibaldi's setback at Aspromonte and had to turn attention momentarily away from the American question. On October 16, 1862 this Italian affair caused Thouvenel's dismissal, which in turn delayed any great departure from neutrality in the Civil War until his successor, Drouyn de Lhuys, could familiarize himself with the details of the question and with rapidly changing events in America.

Chapter X

JOINT MEDIATION, 1862: CAUSES AND EFFECTS

New Foreign Minister

THE new French minister of foreign affairs was no stranger to the Quai d'Orsay; indeed, Edouard Drouyn de Lhuys had been the first minister to occupy that now famous building.[1] He was to remain in office until 1866, and thus it fell to his lot to conduct affairs between France and the United States during the remainder of the Civil War. Although the emperor was always the final authority in determining French policy, Drouyn de Lhuys exercised no small voice in the decisions relating to American affairs and he maintained a steady hand on the day-to-day conduct of these affairs. Despite Drouyn's important position and influence, there is no thorough treatment of him as a man or as a diplomat.[2] He remains to the French as well as to the American reader, very much a name only.

He was, of course, a living and breathing human being. In 1862 he was a rotund, medium-height, fifty-seven-year old diplomat whose hair line had begun to recede and who wore graying sideburns ending in little tufts on his cheeks. Lethargic in temperament only to the point of even and deliberate movement he was mild-mannered unless unusually aroused; then he became explosive and subject to long moods of sulking. Drouyn had the ability to inspire love and awe in those who served him.[3] His linguistic and oratorical abilities were widely recognized, but differently received. His critics maintained that he was full of "pomp and phraseology,"[4] and his friends considered him a master of expression. Drouyn knew how to make this ability serve his purpose: he could talk at length on a particular subject and never convey any information or knowledge. When reporting a conversation to Secretary of State Seward, Dayton frequently had to qualify his account with such phrases as , "I think this is what he said," or "If I am not mistaken, this was his meaning."[5] Referring to this sometimes useful ability, the Austrian ambassador to France, Count Hübner, described Drouyn as speaking with a "fluency of languages and a profusion of words which serves equally to reveal and to conceal his thoughts, and which in either case is the despair of his interlocutor."[6]

Drouyn's whole life had been devoted to public service. He was born in 1805 during the rising tide of the first French empire, of an ancient Soissonais noble family.[7] Members of his family had enjoyed distinguished careers as magistrates and army officers. His father was a receiver general for the district of Melun during the Bourbon Restoration. After completing his schooling at the college of Louis-le-Grand and his law studies at the University of Paris in 1827, young Drouyn married the daughter of Count Saint-Criq, the minister of commerce. Drouyn's own public life began in 1831, only after the overthrow of the Bourbon regime. He served in the French embassies at Madrid and at the Hague until 1840. At that time he was appointed director of commercial affairs in the ministry of foreign affairs when he was only thirty-five years old.

But Drouyn de Lhuys could not remain satisfied with the foreign or domestic policy of the Orleanist Monarchy under the leadership of Premier Guizot. In 1845 Drouyn moved over to the opposition and became a telling critic of the government. During the anxious months of 1848 he served the revolution both as a national guardsman and as a member of the national assembly, where he was chairman of the foreign affairs committee. After the presidential elections in December 1848, Louis Napoleon made Drouyn de Lhuys his first minister for foreign affairs. Later he was ambassador to England and minister of foreign affairs again in 1851. With the establishment of the Second Empire Drouyn once again became foreign minister, serving from 1852 to May 1855 when he handled the difficult diplomacy relating to the recognition of the empire and to the Crimean War. When Drouyn de Lhuys once more entered the foreign minister's office at the Quai d'Orsay, he was a knowledgeable and experienced diplomat, numbering among his personal friends such statesmen as Earl Russell, Lord Cowley, Prince Gorchakov, and Count d'Oubril.

During this time Drouyn had been active in fields other than government service. For many years he was president of the Agricultural Society of France, devoting his spare energies to the introduction of scientific farming to France and the use of new crops and products. He was also a leader in the work of the Penal Colony of Mettray, an organization dedicated to the rehabilitation of youthful criminals through the teaching of agricultural skills. At the same time he was president of the international Society of Acclimatation, the European-wide membership of which included scientists, financiers, and royalty. These organizations, and the interests which motivated his participation in them, reveal Drouyn's sincere desire to serve and remain in close contact with the people. He was not, then, a statesmen removed from the realities of the bulk of Frenchmen.

Drouyn's work as a diplomat and as a friend of the people did not go unrewarded. A grand officer of the Legion of Honor he was a recipient of its highest award, the grand cross. The sovereigns of Tuscany and Portugal, as well as the sultan and Emperor Francis Joseph of Austria decorated him. But perhaps his most valued honor came to him late in life, after his official duties had been laid aside; and it came to him as a sign of the affection which the people of Paris had for him. He was appointed president of the "General Patriotic Subscription Committee of the Women of France" designed to raise money to pay the indemnity and thus free France of the German troops who were occupying the northern section of the country in accordance with the treaty imposed after the Franco-Prussian War of 1870–1871.[8] The fact that this honor would be bestowed upon him after the defeat of the Second Empire testifies to the esteem in which the people of France held Drouyn de Lhuys personally; they seemed to look upon him as something more than a former minister of Emperor Napoleon III.

Drouyn's diplomatic approach was based partly upon his personal inclinations. He was fundamentally a conservative, aligned in French politics with the Empress Eugenie, Count Walewski, and the clerical party.[9] But his devotion to the Roman Catholic Church did not exceed his patriotism, and his position was nearer that of a "liberal clerical."[10] This combination of mild clerical tendencies and devotion to the national interest, linked with his long years of diplomatic experience during the first half of the nineteenth century, created in Drouyn a traditional view towards international affairs. He believed in the distributive balance of power, wherein each great power would maintain a position of strength in relation to the other great powers and a sense of obligation to uphold the interests of the smaller states. In his eyes, the tendency of the Orleans Monarchy to accept the anti-French coalition of Russia, Prussia, and Austria was wrong and should be replaced by a French initiative to seek allies from among the powers. He therefore accepted the emperor's principle of a close association with Great Britain and added to it his own inclination toward an intimate partnership with Austria, whose interests in the Near East coincided with those of France and England. Implied in this theory, also, was the maintenance of a divided Germany. Drouyn described his views to the emperor in these words:

> The strength of France consists in this: It is the largest state of Europe composed of a single race, and the largest race forming a single state. Other races more numerous exist, but they are divided into several states; more vast states exist, but they are composed of different races.[11]

Drouyn felt that "France had had enough of colonial experiences in Algeria; her strength is in her well defined boundaries."[12] When this theory of the consolidated strength of France was translated to affairs affecting America, it became a policy opposing the French expedition to Mexico, and favoring the withdrawal of its troops as soon as the honor of the flag had been vindicated.[13] It also rejected the idea that American problems were France's concern, and it tended to make Drouyn nonpartisan on the issues of the Civil War. Indeed, if Drouyn's policy towards the American question after 1862 could be summarized by one word, that word would have to be neutrality. As his predecessor had done, Drouyn intended to maintain the French declaration of neutrality, even if this at times caused him diplomatic embarrassment.[14] His tightrope diplomacy aroused resentment and a lack of confidence in his sincerity in agents of both the North and the South. As the Confederate agent Slidell put it, Drouyn "is very far from being as decided as the Emperor in his views of the policy to be pursued in our affairs."[15]

To Drouyn de Lhuys this policy of neutrality made sense in two ways. First, he considered affairs in Europe too significant for France to be hampered by commitments and expenses in America; these important events closer to home demanded his full attention and France's complete resources. Drouyn realized that the problems raised by the proclamation of the Italian kingdom in 1861 and the program of unification which Bismarck was beginning in the Germanies would more immediately affect France's traditional position of power than would the events then unfolding across the Atlantic. Indeed, Drouyn frequently disregarded American affairs in order to concentrate on European matters.[16] Second, neither Drouyn nor any one else could be sure of the outcome of the Civil War. It was not unusual in the European experience for a segment of a country to break off and establish its independence; Belgium had done just that. If French policy favored one side to the detriment of the other, Drouyn anticipated that the outcome of the war might cause embarrassment for France. To the French foreign minister, then, neutrality towards the two American belligerents was at once the safest, most honest, and most necessary policy for France to continue to follow.

However, no statesman, be he chief of state or minister, is ever completely free to carry out his own policy. He is always limited by circumstances and by the people with whom he must work. In Drouyn's case he had to work with Napoleon III, with the diplomats of France in the United States, and with those of Great Britain, the United States, and the Confederacy in Paris. A knowledge of his relations with these individuals, and the circumstances in which they developed, tends to clarify Drouyn's role in the diplomacy between France and the Americans during the remainder of the Civil War.

The most important person with whom Drouyn had to deal

was, of course, the emperor, who had the final authority in French foreign relations. Napoleon III's policy toward the American war has traditionally been described as favoring the South because of his Mexican policy and the need for cotton for the spindles of France. He had also energetically maintained a policy of self-determination among the European peoples, as can be seen in his Rumanian and Italian policies and in his love of plebiscites. Consequently he could well see in the South's military and political successes the proof of a general desire for independence which elicited his sympathy. Yet his government in the long run maintained a real neutrality. The difference, then, must have resulted from counsel by his ministers and the circumstances of each situation as it arose. The personal relations between the new foreign minister and his emperor were very close. Drouyn considered Napoleon III as the best possible ruler for France and his type of government as necessary for the stability of France. He had a strong respect for the emperor, and even in the midst of a policy dispute, swore his allegiance to Napoleon.[17] Nonetheless, Drouyn pictured himself as maintaining an independent position; he had resigned from the foreign office in 1855 because of a policy difference with the emperor. Again, in 1859, when Napoleon asked him to reassume the office at the Quai d'Orsay, Drouyn declined and, referring to the Italian policy of Napoleon, added: "I cannot accept the direction of a policy the goals of which I condemn and the regrettable consequences of which I apprehend."[18] Drouyn's own concept of his freedom of action occasioned difficulties not only in the matter of his personal relations with the emperor, but in October 1862 it also raised for the first time in the Empire the question of ministerial responsibility. The dismissal of Thouvenel and the appointment of Drouyn reflected a change in the Italian policy of France. Drouyn insisted that he could not work in the same cabinet with the Duke of Persigny and asked that he also be replaced. When the more liberal, pro-Italian ministers heard of this they threatened to resign; a compromise was finally reached, but Drouyn was not fully satisfied with the solution.[19] Nonetheless, he informed Dayton that "Whatever was done in connection with the foreign affairs of France would be done through him and through him only"[20] and then almost immediately entered into negotiations in which he told Lord Cowley that "he was rather fulfilling a duty which the emperor had imposed on him, than undertaking a work from which he expected any successful result."[21]

The circumstances of his appointment and the differences between his words and his actions reveal the difficulties Drouyn de Lhuys had in trying to maintain his own integrity and serve Napoleon III at the same time. His relations with the emperor, then, while personally cordial, were frequently strained over policy. At times the two men were working in direct opposition to one another. No truly great policy can be expected to have emerged from this relationship.

One other man affected Drouyn's conduct of policy; he was Henri Mercier, the French minister in Washington. Mercier was somewhat pro-separatist in his own feelings.[22] This had two important implications. First, Seward never felt completely at ease with Mercier, and thus affairs were not as openly discussed as they might have been. But even more important, Mercier's dispatches to Drouyn, which were the chief source of information for the French foreign minister, were not objective; indeed, they seldom reflected the accomplishments of the Lincoln administration, but rather stressed its shortcomings and inadequacies. This informational deficiency frequently placed Drouyn at a disadvantage and made it all the more difficult for him to execute his policy of true neutrality.

Drouyn's advent to office, then, implied no immediate change from Thouvenel's American policy. It did bring to Napoleon III's counsels a strong-minded, experienced diplomat, determined to consolidate and maintain French power and prestige. In addition to the problems of the Italian question, Drouyn was confronted almost immediately with the emperor's determination to change the policy of neutrality towards the Americans.

Immediate Background to the Joint Mediation Note

While the British Cabinet was reaching its inconclusive consensus on American affairs, Drouyn de Lhuys interviewed the

Northern and Southern representatives in order to formulate his own views.

Dayton already knew Drouyn and considered him to be a "gentleman of the highest character" who was "universally recognized as one of the ablest statesmen in France." He was sure their personal relations would be "entirely agreeable" and he especially looked forward to working with Drouyn because of "his perfect knowledge of our language."[23] At their first meeting on October 21, Dayton left copies of several dispatches which he had previously submitted to Thouvenel. Promising that he would examine them "with care," Drouyn spoke of the "unhappy condition" prevailing in America as being a "great source of regret to France." "Since the American question is a great one," he continued, "I will endeavor to study it up as soon as possible." Although Dayton had learned nothing of Drouyn's views on the Civil War, he was favorably impressed with this "gentleman of fine manners" whose "appointment is very acceptable, I find, to the Corps Diplomatique."[24] To Secretary of State Seward these observations were "interesting and instructive."[25]

Although Drouyn had revealed little beyond good manners to Dayton, the interview did serve to stimulate his thinking on the American question. Fulfilling his promise to "study up" on the problem, Drouyn formulated his first ideas about France's relations to the Civil War. Despite Mercier's advice that the Northern separatist movement made the moment opportune for a "European demonstration in favor of the reestablishment of peace in the United States," Drouyn saw in Seward's notes "a strong indication that the United States Government will resist all foreign efforts at help as insulting to the dignity of the United States." He felt that before France could take any action he would need to be "more completely informed on the basis of things and on the true exigency of the situation." Even if some move should then prove to be justified, he felt that it would have to be a joint one with other European powers, preferably England and Russia. Drouyn was strongly opposed to France being the first or only one to abandon the policy of "reserve." He was, in effect, asking Mercier to check his sources and to send more precise information.[26] Then he turned to the Confederates for their ideas.

Informally granting John Slidell an unofficial interview on Sunday, October 26, Drouyn had his first meeting with the famed veteran of the "Trent" affair. The shrewd Southerner began by indicating his pleasure with Drouyn's appointment "since you have expressed your sympathy with the cause of the Confederate States." Unperturbed, Drouyn calmly replied: "I am not aware of having expressed my opinion on the subject; not having anticipated being called to the post I now occupy, I have not given the American question the attention it deserves; but I assure you that I will examine the problem carefully and with the most perfect impartiality. What are your views on the subject?"

Slidell, making special reference to his interview with the emperor, cited several incidents to show that England was not playing an open hand with France on the American situation. Mentioning his preoccupation with the Italian problems, Drouyn responded that he did not know precisely what steps Thouvenel might have already taken, but he was "quite sure that in some form or other the British government has been invited to act with France on the American question." When Slidell persisted on trying to show "how entirely divergent were the interests of France and England on the subject," Drouyn stated clearly: "There are grave objections to acting without England, and I do not see how they can well be gotten over." Promising to consult the emperor, the foreign minister concluded the interview without "saying anything that would indicate his personal views and feelings."[27]

With the information and impressions he had garnered from his interviews with Dayton and Slidell, Drouyn discussed the American issues with Napoleon III the next day. To his surprise he learned that the emperor was contemplating immediate action. Napoleon wanted a joint European proposal for a six-month truce in the American fighting, an idea which he discussed with the English ambassador on the same day.[28] After each had heard it from the emperor, Drouyn and Cowley, friends of long standing, discussed the project. "I now perceive a very great desire on the part of the Emperor to attempt to put an end to the war," Drouyn remarked. "But I am reluctant to pursue such a policy; it would be better to wait a little longer. The fruit hardly seems ripe." The two diplomats agreed that any action should await the results of the forthcoming elections in the United States. Even so, Drouyn feared that the European powers could not remain united, for he felt Russia would not consider a Northern refusal sufficient justification for recognizing the South as England and France probably would. Cowley agreed that Drouyn should unofficially query the czar's cabinet on this.[29]

Drouyn's views on the American question, then, began to take shape in late October, and hardly differed from Thouvenel's. Yet the emperor was going ahead with his own plans, apparently basing his action on the British inquiries in September. At the same time that Drouyn and Cowley were discussing the policy toward America, Napoleon and Slidell were holding their famous meeting of October 28, 1862. The emperor greeted Slidell warmly and asked about the situation in America. The Southerner painted a picture of Confederate strength and confidence in the outcome of the war, and tried, as he had with Drouyn de Lhuys, to show that France's interests were different from England's. He maintained that France could act alone because her modern navy would be such a threat to the North's shipping and to the poorly defended coasts that the Washington Government would not dare to undertake a war with "the first power of the world." Napoleon expressed his sympathies with the South, but added that affairs in Europe prevented him from taking any action without England's cooperation. "What would you think," the emperor continued, "of the joint mediation of France, England, and Russia? Would it, if proposed, be accepted by the two parties?" Slidell replied that he thought the North would accept it, but that he could not speak for his own government at this time. He softened the implications of the latter statement by adding that he had no confidence in the role to be played by Russia and England and that the South would be more happy with a proposal which would not allow France to be outvoted by the other two powers; but in any case, the South would gladly submit to Napoleon's "umpirage."

On the same day that his foreign minister had adjudged the fruit not to be ripe, the emperor said to Slidell:

> My own preference is for a proposition of an armistice of six months, with the Southern ports open to the commerce of the world. This would put a stop to the effusion of blood, and hostilities would probably never be resumed. We can urge it on the high grounds of humanity and the interests of the whole civilized world. If it be refused by the North, it will afford good reason for recognition and perhaps for more active intervention.

Slidell naturally approved such a course as "judicious and acceptable," but he expressed doubt that England would cooperate to the extent of recognizing the South. Napoleon reassured him, citing a letter from Belgian King Leopold, written while Queen Victoria was in Brussels, urging him to relieve the textile workers of Europe by ending the war; he further tried to allay the Southerner's doubts by assuring him that Thouvenel and Cowley had discussed the matter, even if unofficially. Slidell, reluctant to see French policy so closely tied to that of England, changed the subject, and the conversation soon ended in the same warm manner in which it had begun.[30] The Confederate commissioner had learned of the emperor's wishes at almost the same time as had Drouyn, and he had supported them with more fervor than had the French foreign minister.

Without further ado, the emperor moved swiftly to transform his plans into action. Within two days, Drouyn, despite his reluctance, composed and sent a note to England and Russia over his own signature, proposing that the three powers offer their mediation in the American war. Why did he consent to the note at this time?

Perhaps the simplest reason is the true one: as he told Cowley, the dispatch was sent "by the emperor's order."[31] Yet Drouyn was no lackey to do the emperor's bidding unthinkingly. In this case, he had been in office less than a fortnight and had been occupied with other affairs until just a few days prior to writing the letters. Undoubtedly, the policy had been decided upon by the emperor before Drouyn had taken up his duties; he learned of it the same day and in the same way the ambassador from

England heard it, and only one day prior to Slidell's knowledge of it. Other than his own evaluation of the diplomatic scene he had no specific reason to delay or change it. He could only reluctantly acquiesce in Napoleon's command.

But why did Napoleon choose that particular time to make his overture? Why had he not acted in September when Russell was ready to do so? Mercier in Washington had long been leading him to the policy of intervention, and there was no new information which he had not had at the earlier date. The consular reports had predicted Democratic victories in the oncoming Northern elections; but why did Napoleon act before the elections and too late for his action to affect those elections?

The answers cannot be certain. It is true that the Italian crisis had delayed French action and did not affect British policy. Presumably Napoleon knew that the abortive British cabinet meeting of October 23 had reached no firm decision concerning the American question. But the real reason more probably revolves around the internal conditions in France. This factor was slow in emerging from the diplomacy of the day, and even slower in emerging from the economic picture of France. Unemployment in the textile and certain export industries was growing. Confidential periodic reports from the procureurs general in the provinces during 1862 showed that the pressure of public opinion was one of the important factors originally influencing the emperor to initiate some sort of joint mediation late in that year. A great many of these reports complained about the suffering in French cotton and exporting industries caused by the Civil War. Thirteen of these reports urged immediate action by France, either alone or together with other powers, while only five advised neutrality and nonintervention. Significantly, too, they were almost unanimous in their sympathy toward the South. A few samples will suffice: (from Bordeaux) ". . . [as to] the intervention of France . . . never would an act of our policy be more popular in the Gironde than that of reopening the American markets to our ships"; (from Colmar) ". . . opinion demands more and more insistently a mediation by the European powers"; (from Douai) ". . . the immediate and personal interests of our industrial classes would make them welcome any plan of mediation"; (from Nancy) ". . . public opinion . . . by one of these sudden reversals . . . today wishes that a peaceful intervention of France and England may . . . bring an end to a hopeless conflict"; (from Rouen) "one thing is certain, they want the two governments of France and England to propose mediation."[32] The emperor paid a great deal of attention to these reports; on one occasion he told his cabinet, "I feel the pulse of France twice a day."[32a] Consequently it is not surprising that the economic situation and the pressure of public opinion should lead him to insist on the notes to England and Russia. Furthermore, the legislative body would convene in January, and the emperor undoubtedly was anticipating its complaints and preparing the way for relief appropriations. Drouyn's own involvement in the Italian question and his recent advent to office made it difficult for him to deny this effort to pacify the people.

The Mediation Note and the Replies

The identic note to London and St. Petersburg suggested that the three powers jointly propose a six-month truce to the two American belligerents, during which time all military acts would cease on land as well as sea. "Europe," Drouyn's dispatch began, "follows with a sad interest the struggle which has been going on for more than two years on the American continent." The sacrifices, energies, and courage of both parties have been displayed "only at the cost of innumerable calamities and of a prodigious shedding of blood." Then, referring to the forthcoming emancipation proclamation, he stated that to these effects of a civil war are to be "added fears of a servile war which would put the finishing touch on so many irreparable misfortunes."

Turning to the effects of the war upon Europe, he did not hesitate to refer to the textile industry:

> As a result of the close relations which the increasing exchanges have created among various regions of the globe Europe itself feels the consequences of a crisis which is preventing the growth of one of the most fertile sources of public wealth and

which is becoming, for the great centers of labor, the cause of a most painful situation.

Having brought the American situation into the international arena, Drouyn then stated that "friendly neutrality" was duty-bound "to seek a way to be helpful to the two parties, in aiding them to escape from a situation which, at the moment at least, seems hopeless."

"A sort of balance of forces," Drouyn claimed, had been maintained since the beginning of the war, with military operations giving no promise or "hope for either side very soon to have such a distinct advantage over the other so as to tip the balance decisively and speed the conclusion of peace." This combination of circumstances, Drouyn held, "presents the opportunity for an armistice," and "no strategic interest seems to stand in the way." Indeed, "favorable attitudes towards peace, beginning to appear in both the North and the South, could on the other hand facilitate any steps to recommend the idea of a truce."

> So the emperor thought that this would be a good occasion to offer the belligerents the cooperation and good offices of the maritime powers, and His Majesty has instructed me to make such a proposal to the Government of Her Britannic Majesty as well as to the Court of Russia. The three cabinets would approach Washington as well as the Confederate States for a six-month suspension of hostilities during which time any war-like act, direct or indirect, would temporarily cease on land and sea, and such truce could be subsequently extended if necessary.

Such a proposal would not imply on the part of the powers "any opinion on the origins or outcome of the dispute or any pressure on the negotiations which might hopefully follow." The powers would in no way prejudge the situation; their "role would consist solely in smoothing the way and of intervening only to the extent allowed by both parties."

Furthermore, should the effort prove to be unfruitful, the three powers would not have acted in vain, for "they would have fulfilled a duty to humanity more especially called for in a war where passions make so difficult any effort at direct negotiations between the two enemies." Even in failure the overtures "could encourage the trend of opinion toward conciliation and contribute thus in hastening" the arrival of peace.

> It is a mission assigned to neutrals by international law, while at the same time requiring a rigorous impartiality, and never would they have made a better use of their influence than in exercising it in trying to end a struggle that is causing so much suffering and compromising such important interests throughout the whole world.[33]

So the long expected and feared overture for European intervention in American affairs had finally come. Drouyn de Lhuys had carefully based his appeal upon the interests of humanity, the obligations of neutrality, and the industrial needs of Europe. The French had acted, and the English and Russian responses would determine the immediate course of events.

That October 23 had not settled the American question for England is abundantly clear from Earl Russell's correspondence. On October 26, before the French proposal arrived, he wrote that he felt that if the great powers were to offer their good offices, and this be rejected by the North, then "we should be fairly entitled to chuse our own time to recognize the Southern States." He thought the best time would be the following spring.[34] This feeling was shared by others. As Drouyn's proposal was en route to London, King Leopold was encouraging Russell to cooperate with the French. He wrote that to oppose Napoleon's suggestion would support those Frenchmen who wished the North well only as future enemies of England; it was important, then, to maintain the close relations with France which existed in the American question.[35]

Unofficially Russell knew of the French proposal on November 1, and he exchanged correspondence with Palmerston on it on the 2nd.[36] The latter raised questions concerning the North's rejection of such an armistice proposal, especially as pertained to the lifting of the blockade and the difficulty about slavery. At any rate, he thought that the matter should await the elections in the North. Russell, however, felt that the French suggestion could be amended so as to make the offer "more creditable to us in Europe" by asking for the terms on which peace could be re-established on two bases: first, the restoration of the Union, and if this should be impossible, then the basis of the separation of the states. The question of slavery would then be handled according to the type of reestablished peace.[37] Russell, still intent upon some form of intervention, seemed to welcome the French action.

French Ambassador Flahault officially presented the written note to Russell only on November 10, and the British cabinet discussed it the following two days. The decision was to reject the French invitation for joint action, but to do so in a way that would not offend the emperor.[38] During the discussions Sir George Lewis, secretary for war, suggested that inquiry be made at Washington to determine if that government would accept mediation, but this Russell refused, admitting that there was no chance for an affirmative answer from Washington. Lewis felt that in supporting the French motion, Russell's "principal motive was a fear of displeasing France. . . ." Gladstone, ardent supporter of intervention, felt that "Lord Russell rather turned tail."[39] The cabinet finally decided that the time was not now appropriate for any action and left to Earl Russell the duty of writing a reply to Paris. This decision was less a direct reaction to the French proposal than it was a continuation of the discussions which had been under way since mid-September; the divisions of issues and men were identical to those which had arisen over Russell's own mediation plans.[39a] Drouyn's note in effect had precipitated the British cabinet meeting which was originally called for October 23 and then postponed. And the reasons for the British rejection of the French proposal were the same as those which had defeated Russell's mediation plan: a divided cabinet, assurance that the United States would reject the offer, fear of possible war with the United States, and the success of Union arms at Antietam. The conviction in London, as in the rest of Europe, that the South could never be reconquered and that recognition would one day have to be given, colored the rejection with a tentative hue.

Russell paid tribute to Napoleon's humanitarian intentions, even recalling England's gratitude for his actions during the

"Trent" crisis. But he expressed doubt that Russia would join the act and asked "is the end proposed attainable at the present moment by the course suggested by the Government of France?" His answer was in the negative, but he softened this rejection by indicating that changes in the future might later allow for such cooperation.[40] By thus holding the door open to future action and by his wording, Russell attempted to avoid irritation in Paris.

Russell accomplished his purpose, for Drouyn de Lhuys spoke "with great satisfaction" of the friendly tone of London's response, and Cowley was certain that the English objections to the French proposal "had not produced any irritations in the mind of M. Drouyn de Lhuys."[41]

Drouyn's easy acceptance of the English response was also reflected in his exchanges with Russia. He apparently had unofficially queried St. Petersburg, for on October 29 Prince Gorchakov told United States Minister Taylor that soon Russia would be invited to join some sort of European action in American affairs. Although the prince assured Taylor of Russia's loyalty, he also warned that unless the United States managed soon to settle the conflict, the European powers could not long avoid intervention.[42] Drouyn's official invitation to joint action was answered without the delay which deliberation usually requires. On November 8 the French ambassador to St. Petersburg was informed that Russia did not want in any way to offend the United States and thus could not join England and France in an armistice proposal. At the same time the Russian minister in Washington was instructed not to take any stand with France and England, but to limit his efforts to approval of any agreement between the North and the South. If, however, in Stoeckl's judgment the real desire for peace should arrive, and needed only the support of a friendly power, then he should take action in concert with the other powers.[43] Indeed, on November 7 d'Oubril, Russian ambassador at Paris, had informed Drouyn of the essence of the Russian response. Gorchakov's note was similar to Russell's in that he refused Russian cooperation on the basis that the purpose of the armistice could not be achieved at this time and that such joint action would prejudice the future effectiveness of the European powers in seeking peace in America.[44]

The Note and Public Opinion

Meanwhile, rumors had been flying since October 30, some even suggesting that France proposed an armed intervention in the American war. The hopes of the Confederates in Europe were raised: John Slidell wrote, on October 31, that he had learned "from a perfectly reliable source" that Drouyn was preparing a letter instructing Mercier to tell Seward that unless the war soon ended, interests of humanity would lead to an intervention.[45] A few days later, at the time that Drouyn was learning the responses of England and Russia, Slidell wrote of the armistice proposal and expressed certitude that regardless of the responses, France would act alone.[46] In England, Confederate Commissioner James Mason anticipated recognition of the South as a result of the French act and said that Russia had already assented and thus England could hardly refuse.[47] The Confederate rumor mills were grinding fast, if not exceedingly fine.

The French newspapers joined the clamors of speculation. The Imperialist press, naturally, found in favor of the proposal: the *Constitutionnel* of November 10 expressed the hope that reason and humanity would prevail over passions and expected the proposal to lead to "a durable and serious settlement."[48] But the liberal papers took a different view. *La Presse*, maintaining that an armistice would help only the South and thus would set back the abolition of slavery, said that a peace made now "would be made on the backs of the Negroes."[49] The Orleanist *Journal des Débats* observed that a truce which opened the ports of the South would so obviously aid its military effort that it would never be accepted in the North, and was answered by the Republican *Siècle* which held that nevertheless, some form of armistice could be arranged which would avoid that objection. The *Constitutionnel* concluded the first phase of this press debate by appealing to the need for some relief to European industry and commerce.[50]

To quiet the rumors, or perhaps to give better guidance to press speculations, Drouyn published the text of his own October 30 dispatch in the *Moniteur* on November 13, and the English and Russian replies in the November 16 issue.[51] Drouyn apologized to Cowley for the early publication of the October 30 note, explaining that he had already been informed of the tenor of Russell's reply.[52] No one, other than Dayton, seems to have been offended by the publications. Drouyn himself revealed no perturbation that the answers were negative; he simply busied himself with publishing them as soon as possible. Indeed, his chief aim, it seems, was not to work for English and Russian compliance, but rather to inform the French public of its government's action.

Knowledge of the official documents stimulated the French press to further debate. The day after the October 30 dispatch had been published, the *Constitutionnel* remarked that the government is to be "felicitated, even if its efforts should remain without immediate results."[53] However, J.J. Weiss, writing in the *Journal des Débats*, had another view. Despite the "skill, the prudence, and good intentions" of M. Drouyn de Lhuys, he said, the very nature of the proposal makes it unacceptable to one or the other of the belligerents. Its publication was designed not to prepare the public for a coming mediation, but rather to "explain the conduct of the French government" in order to exonerate it from "a suspicion of partiality against the North."[54] In the same issue, Prévost-Paradol, a friend of the Union, condemned the government's act even more strongly. Saying that the United States had no moral obligation to furnish cotton to France, he analyzed the proposal as being so favorable to the South as to make recognition only a formal step, and that, he said, "is war with the North."[55] The *Siècle*, which had earlier favored some sort of mediation, now opposed one that would raise the blockade of the Southern ports. The *Revue des deux mondes* warned that such a proposal could easily lead to intervention.[56]

The procureur reports from the provinces (January and April 1863) were much more uniformly favorable to the mediation effort than was the Paris press. Every district except that of Mulhouse favored the effort, and this almost unanimous opinion was particularly bitter toward England and Russia for refusing to cooperate with France's mediation plan.[56a]

Thus the opinion expressed by the majority of the Paris press and by the provincial reports supported strongly the mediation efforts of the emperor and his foreign minister. The French press, if it had done nothing else, had given wide publicity to the government's effort to mediate the American war and to procure cotton for the French spindles. Even the opposition press had rendered a real service by pointing out the difficulty and possible pitfalls of such an action. The alacrity with which Drouyn had published the documents and the wide freedom of comment allowed the opposition press indicates that the favorable reaction was not unexpected by the emperor's government. Had this, perhaps, been the purpose of the whole affair?

Dayton's Protests

Diplomatic repercussions from the rumors and press debates came only from the United States. While England and Russia expressed understanding and sympathy with the French position and the Confederates enjoyed a brief rise of expectations, the United States presented a different story. In Washington, Secretary Seward received the news of the French proposal calmly, but with a renewed determination to resist. In Paris, William L. Dayton became agitated by the French action, especially by what he considered to be Drouyn's lack of veracity in discussing it.

The French foreign minister had tried to prepare the way in Washington. On the same day on which he sent the proposal to London and to St. Petersburg, he wrote to Mercier explaining the act. Should the joint action be taken, his minister was directed to discuss it with Seward in a calm and friendly manner. Its purpose, he said, was simply to suspend hostilities during the winter, when army movements were difficult anyway, to allow time to search for peaceful solutions to the war. The act in no way passed judgment on the origins or the nature of the conflict, nor did it suggest the solutions which might be reached.[57] On November 6 he sent copies of the London and St. Petersburg dispatches to Mercier, drawing his attention to the fact that there was no particular French interest in the proposal; France, he said, had simply asked the other two countries, also motivated by friendship with the United States, to join it in an action for peace.[58]

Drouyn's efforts in Washington had no effect on Dayton in Paris. Rumor's there led him to confront Drouyn with the specific question: "Circumstances are such as to induce me to ask you distinctly whether any action is in contemplation by France, or by France conjointly with other Powers, in reference to the condition of things in my country." Drouyn at first equivocated, stating that nothing had changed; but he did mention the rumor that France, England and Russia were jointly considering mediation to fulfill their wish to end the war, and that France reserved "the right to express this wish to the parties" if it thought "any good would grow out of it." He also maintained that any contemplated action would be something less than mediation. "What would be the consequences," Dayton asked, "if such an offer should be made and rejected?" "Nothing; we would be friends as before," Drouyn replied and stated that France had no intention of recognizing the South. "We do not think of intruding in your affairs in any way or intervening in any form; our intent can be comprised in the expression of a wish to be useful if it can be done with the assent of both parties." Dayton found this first conversation, on the whole, to be "very satisfactory,"[59] and Drouyn inferred from it that Dayton was most fearful "of the consequences which might result to Mr. Lincoln's government were the offer of mediation to be refused by them."[60] Further, Drouyn already knew that the Russian answer would be negative, so he anticipated no real diplomatic problem from the United States.

However, Dayton was having second thoughts about his conversation. He realized that the fact of the proposal alone implied criticism of the Union war policy and that if the United States should reject any joint proposal, as he was sure it would do, it would "place us in a false position before the world" and would "aid the Insurgents in their aim for recognition." Thinking back upon his conversation with Drouyn, Dayton recalled the implication that "now" was a more favorable time than heretofore to do something to bring the war to a close. "I am not exactly satisfied with what that *something* is, or may be, as Mr. Drouyn de Lhuys expressed himself only in . . . general

terms."[61]   These second thoughts and growing doubts were fed
by the rumors and press comments on the contemplated action,
and Dayton hurriedly sought another audience with Drouyn.
On November 12, the two men held a long and significant discussion.

This conversation served to clear the air concerning the French
proposals to England and Russia. The two men spoke directly
and candidly; they were able for the first time to take the measure
of each other and better evaluate the intentions of their respective governments. Dayton began the meeting by asking Drouyn
precisely what France's intentions were and just what the other
powers were conferring about. Drouyn replied that he would
answer frankly, and proceeded to read the October 30 dispatch.
He added that the powers had no desire to press their views upon
the United States nor to imply any consequences should the
Federal Government reject their offer.

Dayton felt that this proposal was a very different thing from
what he had understood in his last interview with Drouyn. He
regretted that the note had been sent because he was sure "it
could do no good and might do harm." Dayton then launched
into a forceful defense of the Union position. No truce would
ever be acceptable to both sides, he maintained, because the
South would insist upon separation and the North would insist
upon union. The North had expended immense effort and
monies to put a large army and navy into action and just when
the benefits of this were about to materialize the French proposal
would be the same as "asking us to disband our armies and let the
South go." Furthermore, the North had no obligation to furnish cotton to the European factories. Such shortages were "the
common but indirect result of every war." He then referred to
slavery: "It has long been a mystery to us how the Government
could get rid of slavery. Now, in the exercise of the war powers,
the favorable opportunity has occurred; I wonder if it would be
worthy of the great nations of the world, in this nineteenth century, to step in and prevent it." Drouyn hastily interjected: "I
am no friend of slavery!" But Dayton was now in full swing;
ignoring Drouyn's remark, he spread a large map on the desk
between the two men and pointed to the slave-holding states,

reciting the numbers of human beings still held in bondage. Then he placed his finger on Louisiana, Florida, and Texas, stating that the people of the *whole* United States had either paid large sums or fought wars for those territories, and we would never "yield them up without a death struggle; France, I am sure, would not!" With this the one-sided conversation ended. Dayton found it eminently less satisfactory than the previous one.[62]

Drouyn was impressed by Dayton's performance. The American's strong arguments, his obvious indignation at the French proposal, and his dissatisfaction at the less than frank manner of Drouyn at the previous meeting, led the French foreign minister to question the accuracy of the information upon which he had acted. As soon as he knew the nature of the English and Russian responses, Drouyn wrote to Mercier that Dayton's strong objections and Washington's responses really did not matter now, because the other two governments are determined to "maintain a role of absolute abstention," and France, too, would reassume "the passive attitude" it had previously held.[63] He told Dayton on the same day that England "had declined the proposition." "This, then," replied the American, "from what you have told me, I presume will end any further effort in the matter." Drouyn "presumed so" although he had not seen the emperor since the responses had arrived.[64]

Thus two days after Dayton's presentation, with the English and Russian rejections in hand, Drouyn was willing to consider the whole affair closed. He presented the French overture to both Washington and to Dayton, as resulting from traditional French regard for the United States, and in no way as a reflection upon the Federal government. This was quite different from Napoleon's own views which he had expressed to Slidell on October 28. Furthermore, Drouyn appeared to have been genuinely surprised at Dayton's vehement and prolonged protests of November 12 and really to question the validity of the information coming from the French agents in the United States.

In this connection, Dayton was determined to inform Drouyn fully of the situation in America, especially in regard to the number of slaves in the various Southern states and in regard to the military strength of the United States. He submitted a long memorandum to Drouyn concerning these matters, which he concluded by trying to show how hopeless it was for the South to try to obtain a victory.[65] These conversations and the long memorandum received the approval of Secretary Seward and of President Lincoln. Seward expressly and specifically agreed that Drouyn de Lhuys had been "less explicit than you [Dayton] had supposed" in the first meeting concerning the proposal for mediation. Seward appeared willing to forgive, but perhaps not to forget.[66]

While bringing this particular episode to a conclusion, Drouyn nonetheless informed Washington that France still stood ready to aid in the cause of peace whenever and however it could. Since the tripartite effort had failed, France "could not think of taking any action of this nature alone and spontaneously . . . but our dispositions have not changed and . . . it would not be in vain to appeal to us, should our good offices seem to be able to be invoked usefully." Mercier, he wrote, should inform Seward that France would always be ready to contribute to peace whether it should be in concert with England and Russia, with all the other powers of the world, or alone; but at the same time, he should refrain from mentioning the recent proposal for a truce.[67]

Mercier knew that whether or not he alluded to the recent effort, relations between him and Seward were bound to be affected. Seward was now sending him messages through the English minister, Lord Lyons, from whom he learned the secretary's reaction to the effort: "They have tried to concern themselves in our affairs without consulting us, and since no communication has been made to us, we have no response to give nor any opinion to express." While he approved of this policy, Mercier nevertheless feared that his personal relations with Seward were damaged, and did not quite know how to mend them. He could only suggest that he wait and talk to the members of the new congress.[68]

Dayton, too, was concerned about the effects of the French overture on England and Russia. It took a little over a month for him to arrive at some conclusions as to cause and effect. His first reflections in mid-November led him to conclude that one of the purposes of the French overture was "to satisfy the workmen and manufacturing interests of France" because the emperor is "anxious to do what he can to alleviate their distress." He noted the French tendency to blame the government for any deficiency, and this he judged is what made Napoleon "anxious, most anxious, for the forthcoming of cotton."[69] Further reflecting upon Drouyn's various comments, he stated that the foreign minister really could not be blamed because the emperor's policy "seems to have no fixed purpose but grows out of circumstances; it is the result of current events." Finally he realized that the truce suggestion would be without diplomatic effect, as Drouyn had said, *only* if "the object of the proposition was to quiet, as far as possible in France, the uneasy and dissatisfied feelings of certain parties towards the emperor; the dissatisfaction among the workmen is great."[70] Later, in a note to Adams in London, Dayton wrote, then scratched out this sentence: "The hope of *Cotton*—cotton by means fair or foul is the moving reason behind the mediation attempt."[71]

Although Dayton failed to consider that other statesmen, such as Russell and Gladstone in England, felt as Napoleon did concerning the value of an armistice proposal, he nonetheless seems to have hit upon the chief motive behind the act. Napoleon knew that unemployment was becoming a serious problem in France, and he had to show his people that he was making an effort to end the American war in order to reopen the best sources of cotton. And this more than anything else accounts for the particular timing of the October 30 overtures. Certainly the handling of the press debates on the proposal tends to confirm Dayton's conclusion.

The Effects of the Note

The diplomatic effects were harmful to future relations between France and the United States. No longer did Mercier in Washington enjoy Seward's confidence, nor Drouyn de Lhuys enjoy Dayton's confidence in Paris. Furthermore, the British rejection of the French proposal pleased Lincoln and Seward; the fact that the French government made the proposal, displeased them. "Whether we consider our own situation or that of France," Seward wrote, "nothing could seem more unreasonable than an actual intervention by the French Government in our affairs." Any such attempt by France, whether in the form of aid to the Confederate States or a dictation over Federal policy, would result, Seward wrote, in a great repugnance among the American people against France, and would in no way change the Federal government's determination to pursue the war to a victorious conclusion. Seward was too experienced a stateman now to invite trouble; he intended to act according to the message he had sent Mercier: "At the same time we must not rashly and unnecessarily incur an alienation from France, and we must avoid it if possible." He instructed Dayton, then, to avail himself of every occasion to show Drouyn de Lhuys the increasing tendency toward a better understanding between the United States and Great Britain, and "the interest France has of securing and fortifying that traditional friendship on the part of the United States, which is so important to France in maintaining the political equilibrium of Europe."[72] To show his own good intentions in this direction, Seward attempted again to make cotton available to the European powers.[73]

The efforts of the Confederate agents and Napoleon III's desire to prove to his people that he was not ignoring their plight had resulted in much diplomatic action, but in no actual intervention. England's decision to reject the French offer had been made primarily on the expedient basis that the moment was not the best for success in an intervention. Although France had suffered a loss of confidence in her dealings with the United States and future relations would be adversely affected by this overture, she had learned from England and Russia that they expected a more opportune moment to arise in the future. Most European statesmen seemed still to agree with the opinion expressed by Thouvenel in early October: "I must say, I no longer believe you can conquer the South; and further there is not a reasonable statesman in Europe who believes you can succeed in carrying out your first conception."[74] France, in Drouyn's words, remained ready when the opportunity of success again presented itself, to offer her good offices in the interest of peace. The question of intervention might be over for England,[75] but for France it remained a matter of timing. As the French need for cotton and the Northern dissatisfaction with the war increased, French efforts to mediate towards peace were to be revived.

Chapter XI

UNILATERAL MEDIATION, 1863

THROUGHOUT the year 1863 the French government made several peace overtures directly to Washington, and there were numerous designs inspired by individuals on both sides of the Atlantic. The French efforts to effect a cessation of hostilities in America were motivated more by domestic conditions in both France and the United States than by any truly diplomatic question. Indeed, as the events of the winter months of 1862 to 1863 unfurled, the proposal of October 1862 assumed the appearance of merely the first in a series of acts designed to reestablish peace. In France the chief motivating factor was an economic one; in America it was a political one. These situations created popular demands in France for peace and an apparent inclination in America towards peace. Under these conditions the French government resumed its search for a formula that would end the fighting.

The Economic Thrust in France

The demands in France for peace in America came from various provinces, but especially from the cotton manufacturing centers in the northeast, in Normandy, and in Alsace, and from the centers of the export industries in the east and south of France. Confederate officials counted on a shortage of cotton to force the European powers to intervene in the Civil War, or at least to seek relief for the anticipated shortage-created economic problems through some diplomatic action which would result in the recognition of the Confederacy. Their plan held great promise, but failed because of the surplus stores in European warehouses resulting from the bumper cotton crops of 1859 and 1860.[1]

374

Furthermore, the disruption which finally did come to the cotton industry was not due to a lack of cotton, but to its price; cotton goods were always on the French markets, but frequently woolen and linen goods were less expensive. The problem was not one of production, but of consumption.[2] Nonetheless, the conditions in the textile industry in France did come to play a large role in the diplomatic policy of that country during the winter months of 1862 to 1863, and even beyond. Depressed wages and unemployment were factors fully considered by the policy-makers at the Quai d'Orsay.

The beginning of the war found the cotton industry depressed even before the effects of the American blockade could have been felt. There was an exceptionally poor wheat harvest in France in 1861 and the price of bread was high. The workers found that a larger proportion of their wages was going for food than before, resulting in a reduced outlay for clothing and cloth products. As the procureur general of Rouen put it: "They cannot buy clothes when they are pushed to buy food."[3] This poor harvest coincided with the application of the terms of the Commercial Treaty of 1860, which permitted the entry of English goods at a greatly reduced tariff. Many small factories, unable to modernize and thereby meet the competition of British imports, had already closed, creating unemployment in several areas of France. But with the good harvests of 1862 and 1863, these factors played a lesser role in French industrial problems, and after the early fall of 1862, "the responsibility for the crisis rested solely upon cotton."[4]

The extent to which the cotton supply was a factor in the crisis may be seen from a glance at the following chart showing the cotton import figures for France.

	1861	1862	1863
Total Imports*	624,600	271,568	381,539
Imports from U.S.*	520,730	31,420	4,169
bales*			

After 1863, the total continued to rise until by 1865 it had reached the pre-war level, but the imports from the United States did not rise appreciably until 1866. Obviously, France was getting her raw cotton from other sources, primarily Egypt, Brazil, and India.[5] Just as obviously, this short supply created an employment crisis for the workers during the latter months of 1862 and throughout 1863.

Just how great was the crisis? To what extent did it cover France? The cotton industry centered in three areas of France: in the North in the districts of Lille, Roubaix, and Tourcoing; in Normandy around Rouen; and in Alsace in the Mulhouse district and throughout the Vosges mountains. The exact number of workers employed in the cotton industry is impossible to determine; many of the weavers were country people who also cultivated small land holdings and some of the spinners were part-time workers. The figure is probably something in the neighborhood of 400,000 operatives.[6] In general, the cotton industry in Alsace was least affected by the cotton shortage. That area produced high quality, fine cloth; its consumers were the wealthier class who could afford to pay the higher prices brought on by the blockade in America. Even so, there was widespread unemployment in October of 1863, due to overproduction; but this area was never hit as hard as the other ones.[7] Hardest hit was the far north. There the cotton product was a coarse cloth, bought primarily by the poorer classes who could not afford the higher prices.[8]

By November of 1862 the Paris press began to report the difficulties of the cotton industry and the attendant unemployment problem. The *Siècle* reported on November 17 that 100,000 were out of work, with the number increasing.[9] On December 27 the same paper presented this summary of the situation: the most severely hit area was the department of Seine-Inférieure, especially Yvetot and Rouen; at Dieppe there were 10,000 unemployed, while the figure was 14,000 for Le Havre. In the parish of Robertot, with a total population of 600 people, 460 weavers were without work. In the whole department, the paper claimed, there were 300,000 unemployed. The *Revue des deux mondes*, on January 1, 1863, gave the end of the year summary for that one department as 130,000 men out of work. Such an amount of unemployment would affect the lives of approximately 390,000 persons. The *Siècle* of December 27, 1862, describing the lot of these unfortunates, painted a picture of "half naked children who went about the country to beg soup or potatoes from the farmers." Such was the story reported by the Paris press, especially by the opposition's republican organs.

The government's own reports confirmed that while the newspapers' figures may have been high, unemployment at the end of 1862 was a real problem for many areas of France.[10] The situation persisted into 1863. The 8,000 cotton cloth workers in Vienne, for example, continued to be without work, and in Colmar and Belfort thirty-five per cent of the spindles and forty-one per cent of the looms were inactive. As of April, four-fifths of the 1,700 cotton workers in Besançon had no jobs. The situation, moreover, was worsening: new factory closings in 1863 increased the number of idle workers by over 250 in Belfort and by over 200 spinners in Nancy.[11]

Despite these reports, it was almost impossible for the government to draw a completely accurate picture of the unemployment situation, for just as it was difficult to arrive at the exact number of employees, so it was to know the exact number of unemployed. Since most of the workers were also farmers, they had a second job; do the above figures count these individuals as weavers or as peasants? Furthermore, do the figures include those without work at all, or those whose work was reduced to less than two days a week? Even the official figures do not make this clear. In any case, the numbers of unemployed in the Seine-Inférieure as reported by the press must have been an exaggeration. How could there have been 300,000 or even 130,000 men out of work, when the department's major industry, cotton, only employed 81,000 workers? On the other hand, if all unemployed (not just the cotton industry unemployed) is totaled, the accurate figure might approach 96,000. For all of France, as of April 15, 1863, the total number of unemployed was approximately 223,336; by February 23, 1864, this figure had been reduced to 174,052.[12] At the peak of the crisis, then, it can be seen that the total number of unemployed in France was slightly more than half the number of workers estimated to have been employed in the cotton industry.

Some general characteristics of the cotton crisis appear to have developed. The crisis displayed a definite heterogeneity with the differences evident regionally—Normandy was worse hit than Alsace—and within the industry—weaving was more affected than spinning, and handweaving than mechanical weaving— and in relation to the size of the enterprises—the small ones were the first and the more irreparably affected.[13] Without a doubt, "the most critical period was in the last months of 1862 and during the first three months of 1863."[14] It can also be concluded that the figures of unemployment given at the time were exaggerated; the crisis was not actually as desperate as the republican Paris press made it out to be.

But the importance of the cotton crisis on French diplomacy comes less from the situation as historical research reveals it actually to have been than from the situation as the people of the day thought it to be. To them it appeared desperate. How did the French react to this crisis? What were the solutions attempted? The French reacted much as any people in times of a national economic disaster. First, private charities attempted to relieve the situation. In November 1862 some citizens of Rouen formed a committee to raise money for the poor. It was federated with other local committees which were formed later, and by February 1863 a "National Charitable Committee" was created. Between December 1861 and July 1863 this group raised over a million francs to be distributed for the relief of the unemployed.[15] The Paris press urged the people of that city to contribute to the cause; but by January of 1863 only 234,000 francs had been subscribed.[16] It became necessary for the government to join the effort. Without mentioning the cotton problem, the government on March 3, 1862, had provided 2,000,000 francs for the minister of the interior to "support public works and to distribute among charitable institutions." In January of the next year, 5,000,000 francs were provided specifically for the relief of the cotton workers. This was to be used primarily to provide employment in public works, such as building roads and bridges and improving the navigation of rivers. Five months later, another 1,200,000 francs were appropriated. The government also sponsored a public subscription which by February had raised two and a half million francs for the relief of the unemployed.[17]   Thus by the end of the height of the crisis almost twelve million francs had been raised by both private and governmental means for the relief of the unemployed of the cotton industry.

Another method of dealing with the cotton crisis was also tried. As cotton goods had become more and more expensive, linen and woolen goods experienced a sharp increase in sales. This, naturally, demanded an increased production and thus more workers. In the north, many of the unemployed cotton workers found work in one or the other of these industries.[18]   The imperial family aided in the necessary relocation and retraining of these workers through the "Société du Prince Impérial."[19]   Many of the unemployed cotton workers migrated from their home areas to take jobs in other industries, such as the manufacture of locomotives and rail equipment.[20]   But, as is obvious from the figures above, these other industries could not absorb all the workers who were either without work or were put on greatly reduced hours of work.

Relief measures, retraining, job relocations, and new sources for cotton did not satisfy the immediate needs of the unemployed workingmen. Although labor as such accepted this severe unemployment with little or no organized protest, there were nevertheless some ugly feelings. In the urban industrial centers, where republicanism was always strong, anti-imperial feelings found expression. Perhaps it was one such expression which prodded Napoleon III's government into more active diplomacy in another attempt to end the economic crisis: On the walls of a Mulhouse building were printed these words: "Bread or Death. Vive la République!"[21]

The cotton-shortage problem definitely entered into the French effort at mediation in November 1862. Several of the procureur reports in July had stated that while manufacturing was still going on, the supply of cotton would be exhausted within a few months.[22]   As early as August, Dayton reported that at the mention of the word "cotton" Thouvenel "seemed all alive with interest," and a spirited discussion followed on possible ways by which cotton might be obtained through those American ports which had fulfilled this role prior to the war.[23]   After the failure of that effort, the French government encouraged an unofficial attempt to procure cotton. In November, the minister of commerce, Rouher, urged the Bank of France to lend money to a private company which was organized to negotiate with the State of Texas for the purchase of cotton through the Mexican port of Matamoras. Minister of Marine Chasseloup-Laubat wrote to Vice-Admiral Jurien, commander of French naval forces at Vera Cruz, asking him to facilitate the operation of removing the cotton from the Mexican port.[24] But the amount of cotton procured by such means was insufficient to meet the needs of the industry.

Meanwhile in Washington, Secretary of State Seward was worried lest the French and English need for the staple should lead those governments to some diplomatic action. After England's and Russia's refusal in November to join Napoleon's mediation attempt, Seward called Mercier and Lyons to ask for their comments on a plan he had devised for getting cotton to Europe. The American told the two diplomats that his government intended to send troops into the South to seize cotton, tobacco, and sugar and to transport these goods to Northern ports where they would be sold to European countries. Seward added that the Federal government intended to compensate the Southern planters for their crops. Apparently feeling satisfied that the Europeans would jump at this opportunity to get the raw materials for their factories, Seward asked for their comments. When neither man would venture an opinion, Seward, somewhat taken aback, proceeded to explain how this would be done:

> A large expedition, he said, under Generals Grant and McClennon would descend upon Vicksburg from the east and would attack it by land, while it would also be attacked by the fleet from the Mississippi; General Banks would occupy Louisiana with 70,000 men and completely control the course of the river. The planters, under the pressure of the use of such a force would know that they had nothing to fear from the Richmond government, and would consult their own interests. They will hurry to make the profits the offer will allow them.

Both Lyons and Mercier objected to the scheme because of the possibility that English and French property might be confiscated. Mercier concluded this initial interview with a parting remark: "I fear that these new regulations will induce the Southerners to burn their cotton, not to sell it."[25]

Drouyn de Lhuys approved Mercier's reserve and agreed that the plan would be more likely to lead to the burning of the crops than to the selling of them. Furthermore, he was sure that "foreign powers could not regard such a method as properly falling into their rights as neutrals."[26] On this basis he rejected the idea. Time and events proved Mercier and Drouyn to be correct; the Southern planters did burn their crops, and the scheme did not result in any quantity of cotton reaching European shores. Later Drouyn received a vivid description of the flaming fields from the French consul in New Orleans.[27]

An adverse effect on the cotton industry was not the only economic impact of the Civil War on France. The export trade was hit by the loss of the American markets. Commercial activity in Bordeaux seems to have particularly felt the lack of business as the general shipping volume declined.[28] "The interruption of exports to America" affected the manufacture of leather goods and of brushes in Bourges, of cotton cloth in Vienne, of musical instruments in Mirecourt, of hats in Agen and Aix, of perfume in Aix, and bore on the precious gem cutting industry in Besançon. Finally, America had served as the source of the raw materials used in the manufacture of glue and of pencils in Metz. In all of these areas, unemployment or the slow-down of activity was attributed to the war in America.[29]

The procurement of cotton and the reopening of the American markets remained a problem for the French government. The conditions which had prompted the French attempt to mediate the Civil War in October of 1862 still existed at the turn of the year; indeed, now they were intensified by the increasing unemployment in France. The only quick solution to the French problems was peace in America; did conditions there seem to permit any hope for peace?

The Political Thrust in America

The results of the November 1862 elections in the Union states exhibited a lively dissatisfaction with the Lincoln administration's conduct of the war. Some of the results, indeed, revealed a strong desire among a segment of the population for an end to the fighting. The people of the West elected many Democrats to office who openly favored peace rather than continued war. Even the populous states of the East reversed their Republican votes of 1860. Congress remained under Republican control only by a slender margin.[30] There were 102 "Republicans and Unconditional Unionists," 75 Democrats, and nine border-state men. Even more significant, the Republican majorities of 1860 in New York and Pennsylvania were replaced by sizable Democratic majorities. In the Western states of Ohio, Indiana, and Illinois the Democrats won overwhelming victories. Even in those states where the Republicans maintained their control, the margin was greatly reduced. Three reasons for these defeats at the polls were usually given: the large number of arbitrary arrests; the fear of an inundation of cheap Negro labor coming to the North and the West; and the lack of any significant military victories.[31]

These election returns reflected a strong peace feeling among the people of the Union, especially the Democrats of the West. Political leaders now fearlessly expressed this peace sentiment.

This public dissatisfaction could be traced in large part to the reaction to Lincoln's gradually emerging plan for abolition. This plan reached its final expression in the Emancipation Proclamation of January 1, 1863, but its provisions and temper were forecast by the terms of the acts abolishing slavery in the District of Columbia (April 16, 1862) and in the territories of the United States (June 19, 1862). Lincoln's plan was most vividly revealed, of course, in the Preliminary Emancipation Proclamation of September 22nd. Richard T. Merrick of Illinois, speaking in early December, said: "With the objectives announced in this proclamation as the avowed purpose of the war, the South cannot be subdued and ought not to be subdued." And former Governor John Reynolds of the same state, in a communication printed in the Columbus (Ohio) *Crisis*, wrote: "I am for peace under any plan or able readjustment the people will make. I think a reunion is the plan of readjustment; but in the name of God, no more bloodshed to gratify a religious fanaticism."[32] The next month, Congressman Clement L. Vallandigham, of Ohio, delivered on the floor of the House of Representatives what is considered the "keynote speech for the peace group."

> Sir, my judgment was made up, and expressed from the first. I learned it from Chatham: "My Lords, you cannot conquer America." And you have not conquered the South. You never will. It is not in the nature of things possible; much less under your auspices . . .
> . . . But why speak of ways or terms of reunion now? The will is yet wanting in both sections. . . . What then? Stop fighting. Make an armistice—no formal treaty.
> . . . Let time do his office—drying tears, dispelling sorrows, mellowing passion, and making herb and grass and tree to grow again upon the hundred battlefields of this terrible war.[33]

Beginning with the elections of 1862 and lasting into the summer of 1863, the Copperhead peace movement was at its height.[34] The strongest opposition to the war and to Lincoln's conduct of the war coincided with the greatest intensity of the cotton crisis in France.

The French minister in Washington and the French consuls in the various Northern cities all sent evaluations of the election results to the Quai d'Orsay. Furthermore, most of these comments arrived in France after its government had issued its call to England and Russia to join in a mediation of the American conflict. The effects of the elections and the growth of the Copperhead peace movement, then, relate to an effort subsequent to the October effort.

Anticipating the November election, Consul Forney in Philadelphia had predicted a Democratic victory in that state. He cited opposition to the draft and dissatisfaction with the conduct of the military campaigns as the chief reasons for what he termed a growing desire for the reestablishment of peace.[35] The same story came from Montholon in New York and from the Baltimore consulate. After the election, they indicated that the Democratic victories would add new impetus to the budding plea for peace. The relief of McClellan as commander of the Army of the Potomac on November 7 and the Union defeat at Fredericksburg on December 13 also contributed to the spread of public yearning for peace in the North. This information was arriving in the French foreign office during the months of November and December.[36] Mercier expressed all that these reports contained in early November:

> The elections which have just taken place and which were to choose a certain number of representatives to congress, of governors, and the members of the legislatures of several states, whose terms of office had ended, will be even more favorable to the Democrats than had been generally supposed. . . .
>
> The seeming result can be looked upon as a strong witness of a great change in opinion on the subject of the war. A few months ago the North put an unlimited confidence in the superiority of its forces; and those who doubted the possibility of quickly cutting the Gordian knot by the sword were in such a minority that they did not even dare to express their opinion, and moreover they could not make them without exposing themselves to the rigors of the administration. But lately, the lessons of experience have been severe and have borne their fruit. At the moment of the election, the question posed to the people was to know if the war must be pursued to the finish with territorial integrity as its exclusive object, must it end in complete servile insurrection, to the complete devastation of the South and to the ruin of its public liberties, or if it must be contained within the limits that the principles and rights of the Constitution impose upon it, and if the Union must not completely attain the objective. The movement of opinion which has just been produced, even though it be an expression of diverse hopes, seems to me to be definitive and, especially by its practical consequences, altogether in opposition to the policy of war to the end. . . .

Mercier then remarked that Lincoln was master of the army only until congress should meet; then he would have to deal with that body, containing a much larger number of Democrats. The

French minister summarized his views by concluding that ". . . this is the moment in which I see develop those conditions which I believe to be opportune for the government of the emperor to prepare some conciliatory act which would come to the aid of reestablishing peace."[37]

From Richmond, Drouyn learned that "the sympathies of the South for France and the emperor are manifested with sincerity and even warmth." Furthermore, the confidence of the South in its ability to maintain its independence, enhanced by the victory at Fredericksburg on December 13, placed the Confederate officials "in a position of desiring, and ardently desiring, an armistice."[38]

It was this kind of information and this kind of opinion which Drouyn received from across the Atlantic only shortly after having read Earl Russell's refusal to join in a mediation attempt. Russell had said that he had no information to indicate that the North was ready to accept the proposal and that England therefore declined to act until there was "a greater prospect than now exists of its being accepted by the two contending parties."[39] To Drouyn that greater prospect seemed to be materializing rapidly; to him the question was not closed with the English refusal.

Indeed, when Drouyn notified Dayton of the Russian and English refusals of the French suggestion, Dayton understood him to mean that further prosecution of such a project is prevented only "at present." The American minister was relieved, but he added the fervent hope that some military victory would quickly come to render impossible any such foreign intervention in the future. "Our delays, disasters, and constant changes have been such as to make our best friends abroad almost despair of our final success."[40]

The economic conditions in France and the political manifestations of dissatisfaction with the war in the United States convinced the French officials that the time was propitious for another effort to reestablish peace in America. The French situation demanded peace and the American situation seemed to permit it. Drouyn de Lhuys and the other cabinet members decided in late December 1862 to take action.

Peace Commission Proposal: January 1863

The origin of the January proposal dates from the time of the October suggestion of a three-power mediation. Two days before the official request was sent to England and Russia, Drouyn de Lhuys had expressed the "opinion that it would be better to wait a little longer." As he had said, "The fruit hardly seemed ripe."[41] He had not been irritated when the English refusal arrived on November 14; rather he was pleased with the friendly tone of Russell's note.[42] Instructing Mercier in Washington to convey the failure of the effort to Seward and at the same time to explain in "friendly and mild terms" that the emperor's offer of good offices "still stands,"[43] Drouyn's policy even then seemed to be one of waiting for the fruit to ripen.

According to the information he received during the following weeks, he considered the time of fruition to have arrived. Late in the month of December, conversations among various French cabinet members gradually led to a decision to make an effort once again to bring the fighting in America to an end. Before action should be taken, however, they decided to test the proposal on Confederate agent Slidell. On December 30, the Duke of Persigny, who maintained a close relationship with Slidell, asked the Southerner his opinion of a plan which would provide for representatives of both sides to meet on neutral territory while the armies continued to fight. Slidell replied that such a plan was impractical and might result in making impossible the recognition of the Confederate States.[44] But the wheels which grind out the policy notes of a great nation were already in motion. A draft was sent to the emperor in late December and was approved and returned to the foreign office by January 8, 1863. Drouyn made the final revisions and sent the note to Washington on January 9.

In this dispatch Drouyn de Lhuys explained that the French actions were motivated by the friendship which traditionally existed between France and the United States and that this friendship made it impossible for the French to ignore even the slightest possibility of bringing the fighting to an end. "We cannot view without profound regret this war which is more than a civil one, comparable to the most terrible destructions of the ancient republics, and whose disasters are multiplying in proportion to the resources and courage which each of the belligerent parties displays." Following this introductory implication that his Government was about to make another proposal, Drouyn reviewed the objections raised when the former attempt had been made. "I ask myself," he wrote, "if those efforts at the establishment of peace were truly premature?" Drouyn's answer was in the negative.

> We are not less ready, in our hope for peace, to take into account all the susceptibilities of national sentiment, and we do not contest the right of the Federal government to decline the help of the great maritime powers of Europe. But is this help the only means available to the Washington cabinet to hasten the end of the war? And, if it believes it must reject all foreign intervention, could it not honorably accept the thought of direct conversations with the authority which represents the Southern States?
>
> The Federal government does not despair, we know, of giving a more active impulse to the hostilities: the sacrifices have not exhausted its resources, much less its perseverance and its firmness. The length of the battle has not shaken its confidence in the ultimate success of its efforts. But the opening of conversations between the belligerent parties does not necessarily imply the immediate cessation of hostilities.

Drouyn then pointed out that the negotiations for peace do not always follow the suspension of arms; indeed, he said, "more often they precede the establishment of truces." He recalled that the negotiations for the conclusion of the war for American independence were conducted in just this fashion.

> Nothing, then, should prevent the government of the United States, without renouncing any advantages it believes able to attain by continuing the war, from entering into conversations with the Confederates of the South, in case they would show themselves so disposed. The representatives or commissioners of the two parties could assemble at such a point as they would judge convenient to designate, and which would be, for this purpose, declared neutral.

The reciprocal griefs would be examined in this meeting. They could substitute for the accusations mutually hurled at each other a discussion of the conflicting interests which divide them. They could seek by a regular and profound deliberation to determine if these interests are definitively irreconcilable, if the separation is an extremity which can no longer be avoided, or if the memories of a common existence, if the lines of nature which have made the North and South a single, federated state and have carried it to such a high degree of prosperity, are not stronger than the causes which have put arms in the hands of the two populations.

Such negotiations, Drouyn continued, would incite none of the objections raised against a European diplomatic intervention and would raise no hopes of an immediate armistice, but would by their very existence have a happy effect upon the movement of events. Drouyn asked why such a meeting, causing no inconvenience to Washington, would not receive the approval of the Federal government. France, having sought for herself in the mediation of the maritime powers no "vain ostentation of influence," would accept, "without feeling offended, the opening of negotiations which would lead the two peoples to discuss, without the aid of Europe, the solution to their differences." The foreign minister, in directing Mercier to suggest this procedure to the Washington cabinet, authorized him to leave a copy of the dispatch with Secretary Seward.[45]

This effort, then, was very different from the abortive one of October 1862; it was more like a friendly suggestion, unsolicited advice, than an international step of any sort. Although Slidell had been cool to the idea when Persigny spoke with him, the information directly from Richmond had indicated that the Confederate government would accept such a proposal if it were first accepted in Washington. Being of such an informal nature, the proposal seemed to the French unlikely to arouse serious difficulty with either of the two American governments. Even though its timing coincided with the apparently most opportune moment for peace in both the North and the South, and with the moment when peace would have been most beneficial to France, it was just as unlikely to lead to peace as it was to arouse serious difficulty. What, really, was the purpose in sending this particular note at this particular time? The answer emerged gradually as the note traveled slowly across the Atlantic Ocean. Indeed, even before the French suggestion was dispatched, the Paris newspapers began to hint at another effort to end the war. On January 8, reports were printed of a long interview between Napoleon III and William L. Dayton supposedly held on New Year's Day. They indicated that the emperor had recommended an armistice and that this was followed by a conversation between Drouyn de Lhuys and Dayton on January 6, presumably on the same subject. Dayton, in reporting these press comments, hastened to assure Seward that "there was not a word of truth in any of these reports."[46] Press rumors on the American situation continued to flourish: that the emperor had asked the British government if the battle of Fredericksburg had not changed its view in regard to mediation; that Napoleon had received Slidell in a long audience, presumably to discuss French action in America. On January 12, just after the emperor's opening speech to the legislative chambers, Dayton met Drouyn de Lhuys in the "Grand Hall of the Louvre," and there the two men chatted. Drouyn was careful to deny all of these press reports, and he thoughtfully apologized that they should ever have appeared.[47]

The press reports and the other rumors which accompanied them nevertheless disturbed Dayton, and he called on Drouyn in order to clarify them. In response to Dayton's question concerning a reported effort by France to mediate the war unilaterally, Drouyn answered candidly:

> This is not an effort to mediate. Indeed, it avoids the usual objections to a mediation because it proposes no interference of any kind by a foreign power in the American affairs, and it does not even suggest a cessation of hostilities pending the negotiation. Rather, like the negotiations for peace in 1783, between the United States and Great Britain, it permits everything to proceed as if no efforts for peace were being made.

He then explained the contents of the note of January 9.

Dayton admitted that such a note would arouse little objection in Washington, but added that when the time was ripe "the suggestion of so obvious a plan as the appointment of commissioners to treat with each other would be certain to come from within. . . . Such a suggestion from abroad, however well-intentioned, is unnecessary." The American diplomat then took the initiative in the conversation. "There is another objection to further action by France in this direction at the present. His Majesty's late overture to England and Russia, in connection with his war in Mexico, has occasioned some mistrust in the minds of our people, and further action on this subject is calculated to increase it. They do not like to see His Majesty's hand always in their business."

Drouyn de Lhuys revealed no offense at this. Instead, he rose slowly, extended his hand to Dayton, and with a friendly grasp, said, "But may we not do it thus?" Sitting again, he assured Dayton that France had no permanent designs on Mexico. "That war is a great annoyance to us," he said. "We want to leave Mexico as soon as we have obtained satisfaction there. As to the implication that we have any purpose or design on the United States in connection with our proceedings in Mexico, it is madness to think of it."[48]

This conversation did not satisfy Dayton, and he continued to seek the real reason for France's action. His mind was so occupied with the military implications of the diplomatic act that he completely overlooked the real reason for the French note. Internal problems such as unemployment, for the moment, did not occur to him; all he could think of was Mexico. If the French suggestion for conversations between the two belligerents was not for the sake of the Mexican intervention, then why should France be so interested in stopping the fighting in America?

Again the Paris press seemed to provide the answer. On January 20 the semiofficial *Constitutionnel* pointed out the advantage of a commission from the North and South which could discuss the terms of peace even while the war continued. The wording of the *Constitutionnel* article was too close to the wording of the January 9 dispatch and to the words used by Drouyn de Lhuys during their last meeting for Dayton to fail to realize the source of the article. Admitting that a foreign intervention might wound the pride of the American people, the *Constitutionnel* asked: "But could there not be other ways which might lead to a solution?" At other times in history ". . . we have seen the work of peace go forward simultaneously with the work of war." Through such commissioners, the states of the North and of the South "would make reciprocal concessions and bring about that reconciliation so desired. . . ."[49] This obvious preparation of the public for the publication of the January 9 note drew Dayton's attention to the press, and he studied it with care.

He noticed that the French press tended to concentrate on reprinting articles from the English papers. One such item in the *Moniteur* for January 27 especially attracted his attention. It emphasized the importance of a cessation of hostilities prior to the spring planting season, so that a good crop of cotton could be harvested. Other Paris papers carried articles of the same tone; and they all related this to the rumored effort of Drouyn de Lhuys to effect a commission of negotiators from both the belligerents to stop the fighting. After reading these accounts and pondering their meaning Dayton, some twelve days after his conversation with Drouyn, began to appreciate the real French motivation. This government wants, he concluded, to convince the people "that they are making every possible effort to relieve" their sufferings. Dayton, realistically now, remarked that he did not doubt their "profession of friendship to us, but their first regards are, of course, due to themselves."[50] Seeking further why the French thought that the time was ripe for such action, he remarked to Drouyn that the Federal government did not consider it proper for any foreign power to intervene in any way in its domestic affairs, that no time would ever be the right moment for such action, but that especially this moment was not right. Drouyn's response was that "we are advised from various sources (especially our consuls in every part of the country) that now is the favorable time for action in your affairs." Dayton felt reassured, at least, that the action had stemmed not from any remark or indication he had made, but from information coming from the American side of the Atlantic. "They believe themselves as well informed by their own agents as to the situation of things and the probabilities of the future as we are," he wrote, "and I am constrained to say that our prophesies have failed so often that it is evident that they now listen to them with much mistrust."[51]   By relating the French cotton needs to their agents' reports of American dissatisfaction, Dayton had belatedly put two and two together and had arrived at the correct answer. Obviously, his preoccupation with the new military situation in Mexico had temporarily blinded him to those French internal problems which he had so often previously recognized as the dynamic force in diplomacy.

The accuracy of Dayton's conclusion regarding the needs of France were confirmed when leaks of the French overture began to appear in the press on January 26.   The *Patrie* first mentioned it on that date, and other papers took up the theme.   Drouyn's dispatch of January 9 was published officially in the *Moniteur* on January 28, 1863, before it had reached Washington. The foreign minister excused it by referring to the necessity to nip unfounded rumors of French recognition of the Confederacy.[52]   This publication was timed, undoubtedly, to influence legislative and public opinion on the government's efforts to relieve the conditions of the unemployed cotton workers.[53]

Indeed, in his speech to the legislative chambers, the emperor had himself related the two problems of the American Civil War and of unemployment.

> The indirect revenues increase steadily by the simple fact of the growth and general prosperity, and the situation of the Empire would be flourishing if the war in America had not exhausted one of the most fruitful of our industries.
>
> The forced stagnation of the work has caused at several points misery worthy of all our solicitude, and a loan will be asked of you to help those who bear resignedly the effects of a misfortune which it is not in our power to prevent.   However, I have attempted to reach them on the other side of the Atlantic with advice inspired by sincere sympathy, but the great maritime powers not having thought themselves yet able to join me I have been obliged to postpone to a more propitious season the mediation which had for its object the checking of bloodshed and the prevention of the devastation of a country whose future should not be indifferent to us.[54]

His promise of future action was duly noted as the separate chambers discussed the address. The senate in its response regretted the failure of the mediation effort "all the more because, as a result of the disturbance that the secession has thrown in our commercial relations with America, stagnation of work has reached a distressing state in several manufacturing districts."[55] The legislative body, in its expression of concern over the Civil War, emphasized the violations of humanity caused by the war; but even this was placed beside the "interests" of France.[56] The press rumors and the ultimate publication on January 28 of the note of January 9 undoubtedly influenced these discussions which were being held in late January and early February. Dayton's conclusion that the note had been written for domestic consumption was more than confirmed by events.

The Paris news media on the whole received the proposal favorably.[57] The *Presse*, which had long advocated some sort of friendly mediation, said that this offer would receive the approval of all Europe. The *Débats*, which had opposed the previous suggestion of an armistice, supported the French note of January 9 because it was "a great step indeed towards the respect of the right the North represents and towards the prudent and wholly French policy which is alarmed at mediation." But this organ doubted that the move would lead to peace. Having been so concerned recently about the unemployment among the cotton workers, even the opposition press could not criticize the government for the suggestion of the formation of a peace commission.

While the French press and legislative body discussed unemployment and the government's latest attempt to end the war, and while the January 9 note was making an unusually slow journey across the Atlantic, a curious peace effort developed in America. This episode remained completely unofficial, but it did involve French Minister to Washington Henri Mercier, Secretary of State Seward, editor of the New York *Tribune* Horace Greeley, and the idea of French intervention in the war. It also involved a bizarre character named William Cornell Jewett, an adventurer and "peacemonger." The incident, perhaps best called the Jewett-Greeley affair,[58] tends to confirm the French belief that the political situation in the United States was conducive to a foreign mediation attempt.

Jewett, recently returned from Europe and convinced that only a French intervention could end the war, brought together the volatile editor and the pro-separatist French diplomat. This in itself was a tribute to his promotional abilities. Greeley, a strong abolitionist, had lost confidence in the Lincoln administration; now advocating mediation, he had specifically denied this role to Napoleon III, calling him the North's "one substantial enemy in Europe" and the "destroyer of the French republic."[59] Mercier considered Jewett to be a "bit of a fool" and doubted his ability to exert influence over Greeley. Yet, on Jewett's insistence, Greeley traveled to Washington specifically to visit Mercier and to discuss French mediation with him.

After a long discussion, Greeley agreed that the October proposal "in final form would have been an excellent act." He visited President Lincoln, Senator Sumner, and other leading Republicans before returning to New York City where he set to work in the *Tribune*, as Jewett put it, to "place France right."[60] Meanwhile Mercier also contacted Sumner and western Republican Congressmen from whom he concluded that mediation would be welcomed in the North if the spring military campaigns brought no victories. Jewett was working on the newly elected Democratic governor of New York, Horatio Seymour, and on James G. Bennett of the New York *Herald*. Thus President Lincoln, the governor of New York, and editors of two of the most powerful newspapers in the North were now involved in this affair.

The only fruit of this frenzied action, however, was a new attitude toward France in the *Tribune:* Napoleon III was now presented as the one ruler most in step with republicanism because he was "more popular with his people than any other European monarch"; as one who desired peace but did not equate it with disunion; and as a humanitarian. Refuting a *Herald* attack on Napoleon, Greeley claimed that those who opposed foreign mediation were giving "aid and comfort to the Rebels."[61] This sudden change in the *Tribune's* attitude toward France and its mediation tendencies was too abrupt to go unnoticed and in the current political atmosphere too dangerous to go unchecked. Seward turned to his close friend, Henry J. Raymond, editor of *The New York Times*, and planted an attack against Greeley and Mercier.[62] Raymond accused Greeley of entering "into personal negotiations with M. Mercier" to promote foreign mediation. Speculating whether Greeley was guilty of "violating the law by dealing with a representative of a foreign state," the *Times* stated that if this were so, then "the Emperor should be requested to recall Mercier at once."[63] Despite some typical sputterings in the *Tribune*, including a printed denial by Mercier,[64] Greeley could not satisfactorily answer Raymond's charges. Seward, without publicly taking an active role, had successfully thwarted this American-inspired effort to foster foreign mediation: the Jewett-Greeley affair had come to an end.

After administering a diplomatic wrist slap to Mercier, the secretary of state allowed the matter to drop. But the timing is significant. Seward proved to Mercier that the Lincoln government, despite the Copperhead movement and the recent elections, on the question of foreign mediation was still strong enough to defeat so powerful a force as Horace Greeley and his *Tribune*. On the day before he received the January 9 note, Mercier concluded that any "offer of mediation will be declined by the administration even despite the public sentiment. . . ."[65] What little hope the French may have had for their peace commission proposal was dashed upon the wreck of Jewett's "peacemongering." Within three days after Mercier delivered a copy of Drouyn's dispatch, Seward had composed his negative response.

He began his reply with the usual courtesies concerning the traditional friendship existing between the United States and France stating that the French proposal had "been considered with seriousness resulting from the reflection that the people of France are known to be faultless sharers with the American nation in the misfortunes and calamities of our unhappy civil war."[66] Thus, just as the dissatisfaction in the North had been considered by Drouyn de Lhuys and his colleagues in initiating the peace suggestion, so the economic difficulties in France were considered by Lincoln and Seward in rejecting those suggestions.

Seward then made more explicit the Union desire to continue the war, not for the sake of expanding hostilities, but for the one constant purpose of maintaining "the integrity of the country." He reviewed at length the military reconquests achieved by the Federal troops in such a relatively short time, and he tacitly acknowledged the divisions in the North by referring to the vastness of the "pure democracy" which necessarily "produces vehement as well as profound debate, with sharp collision of individual, local, and sectional interests, sentiments, and ambitions." Nevertheless, Seward maintained, it is "through such debates that the agreement of the nation upon any subject is habitually attained, and its resolution formed and its policy established." Furthermore, he claimed, even in the heat of this debate not one voice outside of the insurrectionaries themselves had been raised "in favor of foreign intervention, of mediation, of arbitration, or of compromise with the relinquishment of one acre of national domain, or the surrender of even one constitutional franchise." This sweeping statement was followed by the essence of Seward's response.

After repeating most of Drouyn's dispatch, Seward remarked that the suggestion stemmed undoubtedly from Napoleon's "benevolent desire for the immediate restoration of peace," and might seem to be feasible. But looked at from the point of view of the Federal government, it becomes nothing less than

> a proposition that while this Government is engaged in suppressing an armed insurrection with the purpose of maintaining the constitutional national authority and preserving the integrity of the country, it shall enter into diplomatic discussions with the insurgents upon the questions whether that authority shall not be renounced, and whether the country shall not be delivered over to discussion, to be quickly followed by war and increasing anarchy.

There is no reason to expect the insurgents, he continued, to be willing to negotiate on any basis other than separation; and the Union is as determined as ever to prevent separation. The people of the United States, he said, will do just as much as would the people of France or of Great Britain or of Switzerland or of any other European country to maintain their national existence.

Finally, Seward said that indeed a forum for the discussion of peace between the insurgents and the people of the United States already existed, and that was the Congress of the United States. Representatives from the loyal portion of the country were there, "fully empowered to confer, and seats also are vacant and waiting Senators and Representatives from the discontented party." This novel application of the powers of congress seemed to catch Seward's fancy, for he further maintained that congress could call a national convention to ratify its recommendations concerning any agreement it might make with the insurgents. To arrange a direct meeting as Drouyn had suggested, the secretary stated, would be to set aside and disregard an important part of the Constitution of the United States, "and so would be a pernicious example."

Seward's rejection of Drouyn's suggestion, then, was complete, yet not unfriendly. In hearing the dispatch, Drouyn said that "his suggestion . . . had been made in a kind spirit and he believed the reply to be in like spirit." "I am not disposed," he said, "to make the reply or its suggestions the subject of debate or argument." Indeed, he then dismissed the affair, and Dayton was unable to discern any further or ulterior motive.[67] The whole episode was apparently without success and without effect as far as peace was concerned. Yet, the proposal had been motivated by the economic conditions within France, coupled with reports from America that a strong desire for peace there just might result in success. The failure of attaining peace was less important than the effect of having tried to attain peace, for the legislative assemblies had voted the relief for the unemployed cotton workers and those workers had been assured that their government was attempting to achieve peace. The diplomatic and press flurry had, therefore, served the primary purpose of the French government and it had created no difficult diplomatic problems. Nonetheless, it was one more example of the French emperor's hand meddling in American affairs and, coupled with other incidents, formed a link in the long chain of French diplomatic intervention in the American Civil War. The next link in this chain was to arouse more serious diplomatic reaction from Washington and is known as the Lindsay-Roebuck affair.

Chapter XII

THE "AWKWARD" ROEBUCK AFFAIR

DESPITE the legislative body's relief appropriations and programs, the French economic difficulties persisted into the spring and summer of 1863 and the emperor still sought ways to alleviate them. If his recognition of the Confederate States could produce cotton for the French mills and markets for their export industries, Napoleon III would seize the opportunity to act. In the late spring initiative came from England which at first seemed to afford France the occasion for concerted action. Two members of the house of commons sought the emperor's aid to force the Palmerston government to extend full diplomatic recognition to the South. Unfortunately one of them, John A. Roebuck, indiscreetly revealed the contents of an unofficial conversation with Napoleon which led to a diplomatic crisis between France and the United States. This affair was played out before a backdrop of international developments which affected both its origin and its conclusion.[1]

International Background

Following the peace commission proposal there were two months of relative diplomatic quiet on the American question. During March and April the newly appointed General Joseph Hooker was amassing a new Federal Army of the Potomac, and Northern statesmen and commentators tended to await the results of his efforts. The French were concerned about the slow progress of General Forey's forces at Puebla, Mexico. But by far the chief preoccupation of Europe's diplomats was with the problem raised by the Polish insurrection and Napoleon III's response to it.

The diplomacy of the Polish insurrection is particularly pertinent to the Lindsay-Roebuck Affair because it contributed to an estrangement between France and England. At each stage of the Polish crisis, which lasted from February to November 1863, Earl Russell encouraged Drouyn de Lhuys to make forceful proposals; at each critical point, the English government refused to take the necessary steps to translate the proposed policy into action. This was particularly irksome to the French government because the Empire had found in the Polish people's cause at least one foreign event on which the various French factions were united. The Roman Catholics were solicitous of their coreligionists who had long been pressed between Protestant Prussia and Orthodox Russia, and the anticlerical French republicans were sympathetic to the Polish struggle against the Russian autocracy. Therefore, any strong action by the French government, short of war, would be cheered by all of France—a welcome change from the unpopular reactions to the Italian or Mexican policies. But when, in the long run, Napoleon's policies failed to achieve any real relief for the Polish people, public opinion tended to blame the French government.[2]

The Polish insurrection of 1863 was one in a series of revolts during the nineteenth century. It began when young Poles, reluctant to submit to severe military regulations imposed by Russia, took to the woods and formed guerrilla bands. The clashes between the guerrillas and the Russian army and especially the Russian reprisals against the civilian populations aroused the feelings of the rest of Europe. In addition to these humanitarian feelings, European governments considered the problem to be an international one because Poland's status had been determined by the Congress of Vienna in 1815. When in early 1863 Count Otto von Bismarck signed the Alvensleben Convention with Russia, Drouyn de Lhuys seized the opportunity to claim that this agreement, too, raised the question to the international level. Based on these positions, the French government took the diplomatic lead in attempting to moderate the Russian treatment of the Poles and to check Russian influence in eastern and central Europe.[3]

Drouyn's interest in the Polish question was primarily with the balance of power in Europe. Because of his strong belief in the need to consolidate French strength, this problem inevitably took precedence over such distant issues as the American Civil War. Both Confederate agent Slidell and American minister Dayton complained that they could not arrange an interview with the foreign minister because, as Dayton wrote, "The insurrection of Poland has driven American affairs out of view for the moment."[4] On two different occasions—February 21 and July 20—Drouyn proposed to England and Austria that identic notes of censure be sent to Russia; he suggested a treaty with Austria on March first and again on the 21st; and he urged the calling of a general conference on the question on June 17. Drouyn did cast his eye across the Atlantic long enough to invite the United States to join the three powers in their "efforts in behalf of the Polish people." When Seward refused, Drouyn was not disappointed; he had, he said, "made the application more as a matter of homage and respect than otherwise."[5] Drouyn was no more successful with the European diplomats. To every proposal he received refusals from either Earl Russell or Count Rechberg.[6]

These constant rebuffs strained relations between Paris and London at a time when their concerted action on the American question might have produced some positive results. Certainly the estrangement over the Polish question coincided with, and probably contributed to, their differences on the American question as revealed by the controversy over the Roebuck motion in the house of commons.

Although Drouyn was almost exclusively concerned with Poland, Emperor Napoleon III was very personally involved in the Mexican expedition, and this supported his interest in the American Civil War. French troops had been defeated at Puebla in May of 1862, and the emperor had responded by sending larger forces under General Forey during that summer. However, Forey's progress was slow; he invested the city of Puebla in January of 1863, but did not receive its capitulation until May 17, 1863. This news reached Paris only in early June. The French march to Mexico City was uneventful, and that city was occupied on June 10, 1863. The emperor learned of this achievement late in the month. While it is difficult to show that

Napoleon's involvement in Mexico had any direct or immediate impact on his attitude towards the Civil War, it did undoubtedly quicken his interest in the course of events north of the border. In February, before the fall of Puebla, he showed a lively interest in the McDougall resolution in the United States Senate,[7] and thereafter he became much more alert to the reports reaching Paris from America.

The news arriving from America in March and April led the emperor to think that some kind of foreign mediation might have an effect upon the American Civil War. Consul Shouchard in Boston wrote that the military reverses, the financial chaos, and the apparent political irresolution in Washington had undermined the confidence of the New Englanders in the power of the North to subdue the South by force of arms. He reported that "the great majority" thought that peace through compromise was infinitely better than a prolonged war to the finish, and he indicated that there was a growing wish in New England to secede from the Union. This message reached Paris in March; by the next month Shouchard had to reverse his opinion. He wrote of a revival of war feeling which he ascribed to the failure of the Democratic leaders to achieve any real results from their peace overtures.[8]   Both of these notes were considered in cabinet meetings; if nothing else, they revealed a divided and undetermined public opinion in New England.

From the Confederacy contradictory reports were also received. First Confederate Secretary of State Benjamin announced that the blockade of the Charleston port was lifted; within a few days he added the ports of Galveston and Sabine Pass.[9]   But within a month Alfred Paul, French consul at Richmond, wrote that "the economic and commercial crisis has suddenly assumed alarming proportions in the Southern States." High and continuously rising prices of food had reduced some families to one meal a day; other families were fleeing the city to camp in the surrounding countryside.[10]   In April, Paul sent a vivid description of the bread riots and of the shop pillaging in Richmond. He criticized the Confederate government for being "too weak" to take the necessary strong action to restore law and order.   But the Frenchman's sympathy went out especially to

Lee's troops at Fredericksburg who, he said, were reduced to a few ounces of meat and a bowl of gruel a day, and this, he added in Gallic fashion, "without coffee, without tea, without wine."[11] It was obvious to the French officials reading these messages, that public anxiety existed on both sides of the Potomac.

After he had discussed some of these reports, and while others were on their way across the ocean, Napoleon III on April 10 expressed to Lord Cowley, the British Ambassador to Paris, his perplexity over the English policy towards American affairs. "If Great Britain would recognize the Confederacy," he said, "cotton would become available." He implied that France, of course, would follow England's example. Later in the month he again discussed American problems with Cowley and seemed to be "anxious" concerning them.[12] Napoleon's anxiety was real enough. The unemployment crisis in France had not yet subsided, and his own efforts to affect the American war had ended in failure. He obviously, now, felt that he must defer to England for any initiative towards America. Indeed, about this same time Slidell inquired at the foreign ministry through his friend, if, in view of Northern failures at Vicksburg, Port Hudson, and Charleston, "the time had not arrived for reconsidering the question of recognition." After consulting Drouyn de Lhuys, Slidell's friend responded: "It is believed that every possible thing has been done here in your behalf—we must now await the action of England, and it is thought that you must aim all your efforts in that direction."[13]

Slidell's own status in Paris came under a cloud at this time. In late February, Drouyn had told him that it would no longer be appropriate for the two of them to meet officially at the Quai d'Orsay. He suggested that they communicate through Slidell's friend in the foreign ministry.[14] And in early March, Drouyn, under pressure from Dayton, said that if "every conversation or interview I have with Mr. Slidell is to be made the subject of newspaper remarks, then it will be necessary that I exercise some caution in relation thereto."[15] Yet the Confederate agent was not completely isolated from the French government. The issues of war and peace and of belligerency and neutrality made him a necessary contact for the French. The emperor's own first secretary was a valuable contact: in April the Count de Mocquard secretly informed Slidell of the arrival of a Confederate vessel at a French port. And the next month, Drouyn himself found it necessary to communicate with him. Learning of the Confederate practice of recruiting French nationals into the Southern army, Drouyn wrote on the margin of a dispatch: "See M. Slidell and address to him confidential and urgent protests."[16] Taking heart from these manifestations of his importance to the French government, Slidell vigorously renewed his efforts to drive a wedge between France and England in their American policies. He considered the moment particularly propitious because of the effects of the Polish problems and France's unique interests in Mexico.

The Confederate agent turned to a new tack in his attempt to motivate France separately from England. He approached Spain where a Confederate sympathizer, Serrano, was momentarily foreign minister. On May 22, 1863, while talking about another matter with Isturitz, the Spanish ambassador in Paris, Slidell urged closer relations between Spain and the Confederacy and probed for Spanish recognition in return for a guarantee of the safety of Cuba. The reply was fully expected: expression of sympathy but refusal to act unless in accord with England and France. Slidell then slyly suggested that "Spain and other continental powers might unite with France" to recognize the Confederate States and through the unity of action have nothing to fear more than "some characteristic ebullitions from Seward of Yankee bluster and vituperation." While the suggestion was well received by Isturitz, Serrano left office when the O'Donnell cabinet fell from power.[17] The Spanish refusal to take such action was sent in July by the new foreign minister, who refused to act without consulting England and France. A copy of the dispatch was given to Drouyn de Lhuys,[18] who thus gained full knowledge of Slidell's overtures to Spain.

The Erlanger Loan

Although his approach to Spain came to naught, Slidell continued to try to split French policy and action from that of

England. Indeed, he had supported the long-pending Erlanger loan more for its political possibilities than its economic ones. Confederate finances in Europe were never stable, and by midwinter of 1862–63 the agents had agreed to use cotton as a security for loans in Europe. Mason in England and the various officials in Richmond were not anxious to contract such an arrangement, but John Slidell pushed the issue on political grounds.[19] He had been approached in October 1862 by representatives of the well-established firm of Erlanger and Company. He had immediately accepted the proposal, even though the financial conditions were not favorable to his government, but, because of the delays in communication and objections from Mason and Benjamin, he had to postpone further action. Finally, Jules Beer went to Richmond as Erlanger's representative and after much negotiation arrived at a contract with the Confederate government. He found very little enthusiasm for the scheme in the Southern capital and had to agree to terms less favorable to his company than those originally accepted by Slidell. The contract, nonetheless, assured Erlanger and Company its funds regardless of the stock sales. The validity of the stocks was based upon ultimate Southern independence, as they were redeemable in cotton at any Southern port six months after the reestablishment of peace.

With the agreement authorized by a secret act of the Confederate congress, Beer returned to Europe in mid-February. The first bond sales went on the markets in London, Paris, Amsterdam, and Frankfort on March 19, 1863. At first the sales went so well that the issue was oversubscribed three times in London alone, and the Confederate agents were exultant. But a reaction soon set in, and the Southerners had to use proceeds from the first flurry of sales to prevent the quotations from completely collapsing. With the news of Gettysburg and Vicksburg the bottom fell out. Owsley calculates that of the original 7.5 million dollars, the Confederate agents realized only about 2.5 million for their operations. The Erlanger loan, then, was something less than a financial success.

How did it fare politically? Did it, as Slidell had predicted, win potent friends to the Southern cause? Writing from Richmond, Alfred Paul, the French consul, had anticipated the economic failure of the loan. Reporting accurately the terms of the loan, he expressed surprise that Erlanger or any other European financier would deal with the Richmond government because the Confederate "financial condition is in such a state of chaos."[20] His dispatch reached Paris on March 21, 1863, and a copy went immediately and confidentially to the department of finance.[21] Since the Erlanger terms provided that the cotton bonds could be redeemed six months after hostilities for cotton at six pence sterling, Paul kept his eye on Richmond's cotton acquisition. On March 10, 1863, he reported the amount and price paid from each state. It varied from Mississippi's 77,292 pounds at a price of ten cents per pound, to South Carolina's 3,224 pounds at nineteen and a half cents per pound.[22] The Confederate government, then, was paying an average of twelve cents a pound for cotton which it was obligated to sell at six cents a pound. Even when the difference between Confederate money and British sterling was allowed for, the government was bound to lose. Such knowledge among the French officials could hardly instill confidence in the Southern cause.

The Federal officials in Europe looked upon the early reports of the Erlanger loan as being "at least doubtful," as Dayton expressed it. However, thirty days later and just four days before the bonds were to be put on the open market, Dayton received information which led him to be "inclined to believe that arrangements have been made with the House of Erlanger & Co., Frankfort, for a loan to the Confederates." Dayton also reported that information from Frankfort indicated that the cotton security for the loan was, if possible, to be placed in the hands of the French consul in Richmond, in the hopes "of dragging the French government into a recognition of the affair and making its protection a kind of security for the loan." And finally, Dayton relayed a rumor that one of the participants in the loan was the "House of Fould & Co., Paris (one of whom is the son of the Minister of Finance)...."

Dayton hesitated to speak to Drouyn de Lhuys about these rumors. He felt sure that, even if the loan did go through, it would not be listed on the French Bourse because, as he understood, "no loan can be quoted there without the authority of this government."[23]

Dayton came close to being correct, because when the Confederates asked permission to list the Erlanger loan cotton bonds on the French Bourse, they encountered difficulty. The Minister of Finance, Achille Fould, whose relatives were the bankers, approved the request, but Drouyn de Lhuys had the final ministerial word since a foreign government was involved. Drouyn, recognizing that such official approval of the loan would give the United States legitimate reason to protest, denied the permission to "advertise the Erlanger Loan" on the French Bourse. However, Erlanger himself went to Napoleon III and made a personal plea. The emperor instructed his secretary to write a note to Drouyn de Lhuys, requesting that he grant an interview to Erlanger. Such pressure was sufficient. Once he learned of the emperor's direct interest, Drouyn permitted the quotation on the Bourse.[24] But as Dayton had anticipated, this was done reluctantly and, indeed, at the expense of some ministerial pride. It hardly won many friends in the process.

The day after the Erlanger loan bonds went on sale Dayton spoke to Drouyn de Lhuys about the rumor concerning the participation of the House of Fould. Drouyn's response was a quick negative: "Oh, I cannot believe that; the House of Fould is too prominent."[25] Dayton seemed satisfied. Seven days later he expressed with even more certainty the conviction that the loan was negotiated through Erlanger and quoted on the various exchanges "as a thin veil to cover the real transaction." Dayton had made inquiries as to the extent of French participation in the loan. He wanted to know if the French government or any individual had acted in such a way as to violate the French declaration of neutrality. He reported to Seward:

> I have been informed by parties here that little, if any, of this loan has been taken out of England and it is believed to have been taken there principally as a means of giving shape and a seeming security for claims against the Confederates already existing or contracted for. This is most probable. Some of our bankers and business men here believe the whole loan a pre-

tense and that nothing has been or will be advanced upon it. But the preceding suggestion is probably the true one.[26]

Although some debts in England were paid with Erlanger bonds,[27] there is no indication in the correspondence of those who planned and negotiated the loan that such was its principal purpose. Dayton, however, chose to believe this. Having received Seward's instruction to discuss the loan with Drouyn de Lhuys and having persuaded Seward to his own views concerning the loan,[28] Dayton had a long discussion with the French foreign minister.

He asked Drouyn about "the loan of eight millions of francs said to have been negotiated here in behalf of the rebels." Dayton was not asking if the loan had been negotiated; he knew it had, and he knew Drouyn de Lhuys knew it had. He wanted to discover, rather, to what extent the French government or its officials had been involved in it. Drouyn's answer was categorical: "I have heard nothing of it and I do not believe it. I can see no reason why an outsider, to whom no debt from the Confederates is due, should be willing to advance money anew on an engagement by the Confederates to deliver cotton at six pence sterling per pound at a seaport in the United States within six months after peace. When peace occurs, the purchase of cotton will be free and six pence sterling is rather beyond the price of cotton. The only inducement to advance money now would be to get cotton now, when it is so much needed, and this agreement does not seem to contemplate that." Drouyn's response confirmed Dayton's own conviction that the loan was made only to pay existing Confederate debts in England. Drouyn's pragmatic reference to the need for cotton "now" reflected the continuing French interest in their own textile industry; it was a statement of true self-interested neutrality.[29]

Dayton was completely satisfied with the conversation and did not again refer to the Erlanger loan. The loan, although cited on the Paris Bourse, caused hardly a ripple in the relations between Paris and Washington.[30] But it did serve to recall Drouyn's attention from the Polish problem to the American ones. The Roebuck affair was taking shape as the Erlanger Loan affair was receding from the diplomatic arena.

Roebuck's Motion and Interview with Napoleon

The "awkward Roebuck affair," as Napoleon III later called it, had its origins in late May 1863 at a meeting in England. With the Polish question temporarily quiescent, with the French expedition to Mexico making progress, even if slowly, with the Erlanger loan still healthy on the European exchanges, the Union failures at Vicksburg and the Confederate victory at Chancellorsville indicated to Southern sympathizers in parliament the appropriateness of acting to gain British recognition of the Confederate States. The same William S. Lindsay who had visited Napoleon III a year earlier to plead for the recognition of the South, and who had long been a close associate of Mason, invited him to meet with John A. Roebuck at Lindsay's country home near London. There the three discussed the merits and tactics of forcing the Palmerston government through parliamentary resolution to recognize the South.[31] Roebuck soon gave notice in the house of commons that he would submit a motion in favor of recognizing the Confederate States of America. This would have remained a purely British affair, except for the coincidence of circumstances and events in Paris.

John Slidell, continuing to act on the premise he had used in his correspondence with Spain, decided to ask for another meeting with Napoleon III. In his request dated June 8 but delivered to the emperor June 12 by Persigny, Slidell once again referred to the different interests of England and France in the American conflict: France, he said, needed two strong American republics to continue to challenge English mercantile and maritime power, while England was perfectly satisfied to see the war drag on in order to further weaken her competitors. The quickest way to end the hostilities would be for France and other continental powers to recognize the Confederacy. Obviously, Slidell put little trust in Roebuck's motion. But Napoleon III's attitude and the events which were transpiring in London forced Slidell to change tactics.

During the first few days of June 1863 British government officials, anticipating debate on Roebuck's motion, let it be known
that the government would oppose the motion on the grounds
that Napoleon III had changed his mind about recognizing the
South. Roebuck, smelling a typical Palmerstonian trick, hit
upon the bold idea of going to France, as Lindsay had done in
1862, to ask the emperor himself about this; he wrote to Lindsay
suggesting that the two of them make the trip. Meanwhile,
Slidell was notified that he would be granted an interview, and in
preparation he wrote Mason asking about the chances of success
for the Roebuck motion. Mason replied by sending a copy of
Roebuck's letter to Lindsay suggesting the trip to France.

When Slidell saw the emperor on June 18, he soon discovered
that, sympathetic though Napoleon might be, he was not going
to risk antagonizing the North without the protection of the
British navy—thus Slidell's argument for continental action
quickly fell to the ground. The Southern agent then returned to
joint Anglo-French action by raising the subject of the Roebuck
motion and the rumored response of the British ministers. He
asked Napoleon if it were true that he had changed his position;
the emperor denied that he had and authorized Slidell to so inform Roebuck and to do so on imperial authority. Slidell then
read portions of Roebuck's letter suggesting an interview with
Napoleon and asked if Napoleon would agree to see the two
members of parliament. The emperor replied that he "would be
pleased to converse with them on the subject of Mr. Roebuck's
motion." Warming to the topic and enjoying as always this
direct but unofficial diplomacy, Napoleon added: "I think that
I can do something better—make a direct proposition to England for joint recognition. This will effectually prevent Lord
Palmerston from misrepresenting my position and wishes on the
American Question." Thus spake the adventurer; but the careful ruler then added: "I shall bring the question before the cabinet meeting today; and if it should be decided not to make the
proposition now, I shall let you know in a day or two through
Mr. Mocquard what to say to Mr. Roebuck."[32]

The imperial ministers in the cabinet meeting of June 18
applied official brakes to Napoleon's headlong dash into dan-

gerous diplomacy. As his friend reported to Slidell, the emperor's suggestion "has been judged at this time inopportune." He continued:

> The ministers did agree to deny, as far as the British cabinet is concerned, the reports which falsely attribute to us sentiments and a policy less favorable for the South; to recall to them that on several occasions we have addressed to them propositions which they thought they should not accept; to declare that our feelings have not changed—quite the contrary; to state to them further that we shall be charmed to follow them up, and if they have any overtures to make to us in a like spirit to that which has inspired ours, we shall receive them with quite as much eagerness as pleasure. Baron Gros will receive instructions accordingly.
>
> The minister charges me to tell you that he will await you day after tomorrow, Sunday, between 10 and 11 o'clock in the morning.[33]

These decisions were exactly what the Confederate supporters in London wanted; however, Drouyn de Lhuys did not send such instructions to Baron Gros following the cabinet meeting. Not for four days—June 23—and only after Napoleon's interview with Roebuck and Lindsay, did the instructions go to Gros. Nonetheless, Mocquard, the emperor's secretary, sent Slidell a note dated June 21, in which he stated: "M. Drouyn de Lhuys has written to Baron Gros, our ambassador in London, to sound Lord John Russell on the question of the recognition of the South, and has authorized him to declare that the cabinet of the Tuileries is ready to discuss the subject."[34] Whether the emperor thought Drouyn had actually written to Gros is not clear; but it is clear that Slidell, Mason, Roebuck, and Lindsay thought the letter had been sent.

In the meantime, Slidell called upon Drouyn de Lhuys on Sunday, June 21. The foreign minister told Slidell, in as kind and candid a fashion as possible, why France could not extend official recognition to the Confederate States. Slidell chose to interpret the reason as being a "deep, and, as I think, a well-founded distrust of England"; his own words reflect his self-delusion:

Mr. Drouyn de Lhuys says, that were a direct proposition made and refused, as it probably would be, Earl Russell would communicate the correspondence to the Lincoln government; that it would produce great irritation and although it might not be followed by direct hostilities, would induce that government to encourage the departure of bands of volunteers for Mexico, thus aggravate the difficulties already very serious, with which Gen. Forey has to contend; that the encouragement would probably be so open as to compel the Emperor to declare war, a contingency which he desires to avoid and which England would aid in creating.[35]

The cabinet members had refused to suggest recognition of the Confederate States out of respect for Union influence in Mexico and fear of endangering their already precarious position in that country. Implicit in this decision is a clear lack of confidence in the Confederate ability to aid the Mexican designs of France. Thus while France obviously took advantage of the American Civil War to intervene in Mexico, that intervention did not tend to cause France to pursue a policy favorable to the South. Indeed, in this instance, France, following her own interests, had to avoid a pro-Southern act at least partially because of the Mexican adventure.

Although the cabinet had decided on June 18 to notify the English government that no change had taken place in its position towards recognizing the Confederacy, no such notice was sent until after the emperor had repeated his error of 1862 by meeting with the two Englishmen on June 22.[36] Exactly what was said to whom at this meeting is not clear. Basing his story upon the accounts rendered by Lindsay,[37] Owsley quotes the emperor as saying that he could not make a formal request to England because once before when he had done so, "that application was immediately transmitted to the United States Government, and I cannot help feeling the object of that proceeding was to create bad blood between me and the United States." He is reported also to have said: "I have just requested Baron Gros to ascertain whether England is prepared to coincide with my views in regard to recognition, to suggest any mode for proceeding for the recognition of the Southern States which I so desire." And finally, the emperor is supposed to have authorized Roebuck and Lindsay to deny in parliament that he had changed his views on the recognition of the Confederacy.[38] This account stresses three items which created diplomatic difficulties: the first two— concerning the implied betrayal by England and the instructions to Baron Gros—aroused parliamentary debate, raised questions of the veracity of English and French officials, even of Napoleon himself, and certainly contributed to the coolness already existing between the two governments over the Polish question. The third—reference to Napoleon's strong desire to extend recognition to the South—returned to haunt the relations between France and the United States. Since Roebuck and Lindsay were the ones who could profit, it is this version which was publicized at the time, both through Roebuck's debate in the house of commons and through the London press.

But there are other views. Napoleon III's American dentist, Dr. Thomas W. Evans, ever a watchdog for Union interests, reports a different story. Evans heard that Roebuck planned to speak in parliament about his conversation with the emperor; he went immediately to Fontainebleau and, in his own words:

> I saw the Emperor as soon as he had left his bed, and communicated to him what I had learned about Mr. Roebuck's intention. I asked him if anything in the conversation he had had with that very active member of Parliament could be construed into a promise to recognize the Southern Confederacy on certain conditions; and if Mr. Roebuck had his permission to make an announcement to that effect in the House of Commons. His majesty most unhesitatingly denied having given him any assurances or promises whatever. The conversation he said had been general and he should be greatly astonished if Roebuck were so to report the conversation that it could be considered as containing a promise or pledge on his part to act in relation to the matter conjointly with the British government.[39]

While Evans may not be the most reliable source, his account is the only one which reflects the emperor's own description of the meeting before the public blowup over Roebuck's statements in parliament. Evans, then, gives Napoleon's view of the conversation before Napoleon had to worry about American, British, or French reaction. What is striking is the similarity between this and his own later account.

Napoleon's own account was elicited by the debates in the English parliament. Roebuck, on June 30, after Russell's denial of any approach by the French, repeated essentially the points made by Lindsay: that Napoleon III hesitated to make a formal overture to the British government because he feared another betrayal to the United States; that he stood ready to recognize the South if England should do so; and that he had instructed Gros so to inform the British cabinet. This revelation by a member of parliament of the intimate details of an unofficial conversation held with the chief of a foreign state, caused gasps and exclamations of surprise and resentment throughout the chamber. It also had its repercussions in the press of London, Paris, and eventually of the United States. When Russell and his representatives in the house of commons continued to deny any kind of French overture on the subject of recognition of the Confederate States, Roebuck was made to look a fool and his motion was all but defeated. After another short debate on July 2, Roebuck formally withdrew the motion on July 13.

Fixing the Responsibilities

The charges and countercharges of the debates had raised questions of the veracity of the principle characters. What had actually transpired at the meeting between Napoleon and the two Englishmen? Had Drouyn de Lhuys actually instructed Gros to approach the British cabinet? If so, had Gros failed to do so, or had Russell or Palmerston lied about it? Even the statesmen involved did not know the answers to these questions, much less the press or the general public. Indeed, scholarship has not completely clarified the confusion.

In trying to answer the above questions, John Slidell tended to place the brunt of the blame on Drouyn de Lhuys, and he was partially correct but for the wrong reason. Slidell surmised that Drouyn, a "man of timid temperament, fond of little diplomatic finesses, and . . . very far from being as decided as the Emperor in his views of the policy to be pursued in our affairs," had not executed the emperor's orders in good faith.[40]   It is true that Drouyn disapproved Napoleon's personal diplomacy: to the Austrian ambassador, Drouyn revealed his "despair over the indiscretion committed by his Master";[41] to the English ambassador, Cowley, Drouyn acknowledged "that he disliked these unofficial communications as likely to lead to error."[42]   After the disastrous debate on June 30, Drouyn, "much annoyed with Roebuck's speech in the House of Commons," asked the emperor for an explanation.   According to Lord Cowley, this is Drouyn's account of the meeting between Napoleon III and Roebuck and Lindsay:

> These gentlemen had come to him and stated that there was an idea very prevalent in England that His Majesty was opposed to the recognition of the Southern States. His Majesty denied that this was the case, and was then requested by the two gentlemen to make a proposal to Her Majesty's Government having for its object that recognition. The Emperor declined taking this step observing that his former overtures had been refused, and had subjected him to mis-representation but that he was resolved not to separate from England on the American question, and that if a proposal of recognition came from thence he would probably not object to it.   He would desire that Baron Gros be instructed in this sense.[43]

As the controversy increased, Drouyn went to Fontainebleau on July 4 to discuss with the emperor the proper course of action. The two decided that the best way to answer Roebuck's statements and those of the British press was to offer an official explanation of the interview in the *Moniteur*.[44]   The next day the following notice appeared:

> The papers have reported an incident which took place during the sitting of the house of commons last Tuesday on the occasion of a motion by Mr. Roebuck.   A few explanations will suffice to dissipate the misunderstandings to which this incident gave rise.
> Messrs. Roebuck and Lindsay came to Fontainebleau so as to induce the emperor to take some official steps in London for the recognition of the Southern States, because, in their opinion,

this recognition would put to an end the strife which is staining the United States with blood.

The emperor expressed to them his desire to see peace re-established in those countries, but observed to them the proposal of mediation addressed to London in the month of October last not having been accepted by England, he did not feel called upon to make another before being assured of its acceptance; nevertheless the French ambassador at London would receive instructions to sound the intentions of Lord Palmerston on the subject and to let him understand that should the English cabinet believe that the recognition of the South would put an end to the war, the Emperor would be disposed to follow it, with that end in view.

Any impartial man will see by this simple explanation that the emperor did not seek, as certain of the press pretend, to influence the British parliament through the intervention of two of its members, and that everything was limited to frank explanations exchanged in an interview which the emperor had no reason whatever to refuse.[45]

While general in tone, this account closely follows the one which Dr. Evans had received earlier, and it is different from the one Napoleon had given to Slidell a few days earlier in one detail only. The emperor had mentioned to Slidell his suspicion that England had exploited the October 1862 proposal to create bad feeling between the United States and France.[46] On three separate occasions, Emperor Napoleon III had maintained in general terms that he had committed no indiscretion in the private talks with the two Englishmen. But the public would not let the matter drop, and Drouyn de Lhuys, anything but timid and subservient, continued his pressure on the emperor. Finally, on July 14, 1863, Napoleon wrote to Drouyn, again explaining the interview, but this time acknowledging at least an error in judgment:

My dear M. Drouyn de Lhuys:

I hasten to answer your letter on the subject of the awkward Roebuck affair (*la malencontreuse affaire Roebuck*). The conversation having taken place in English, it is very probable Mr. Roebuck misunderstood what I said to him; it was enough to make him understand that I could not address to the English Government an official proposition to recognize the South without first knowing its intentions, because the official act of the month of last October was not accepted, and it came back to me (which however I doubted) that the English Government boasted in Washington for having refused our offer of mediation. I added that having no motive of animosity against the United States, I did not want to put myself in the wrong with them without being sure of the help of England. There is the truth of it—I spoke to the misters Lindsay and Roebuck openly; I should have been more diplomatic.[47]

Indeed the emperor should have been more diplomatic! This last statement of Napoleon's view of what had transpired at the meeting tends to balance the views of Roebuck and Lindsay. While it is true that Napoleon erred in being too open with the Englishmen, it is even more true, as Drouyn had feared, that such unofficial and personal interviews could, and did, lead to error. The English ambassador, Cowley, had earlier expressed the belief that Roebuck's statements in commons resulted from a misunderstanding of Napoleon's English; even John Slidell accepted this view.[48]   At one point Cowley relates that when Lindsay and Roebuck asked if Napoleon's words on possible recognition of the Confederacy could be repeated, the emperor shrugged and said, "They are no secret." Thus the error which Drouyn had feared resulted not only from the Englishmen misunderstanding Napoleon's English, but also from their natural tendency to infer from his vague and ambiguous language just what they wanted to hear.

Exactly what transpired at the meeting between Napoleon III and Roebuck and Lindsay is probably accurately reported by each. In a conversation conducted in a language strange to the emperor, and in vague and ambiguous phrases, each participant interpreted through inference exactly what he wanted to carry away from the meeting. Roebuck and Lindsay were probably sincere in believing they could repeat what the emperor had said regarding the matters of recognizing the Confederacy, of the British government's misuse of the previous French proposal, and of the French government's official notification to the British.

At the same time, Napoleon was just as sincere in denying most of these items. But what of the matter of notifying the British cabinet? Did Napoleon III keep his word?

The record is not clear. Professor Owsley found only one such message, a telegram dated July 1, 1863. He concludes that there was a previous one of June 22, but he was unable to locate it in the French archives.[49]

The French archives are strangely uninformative as to this aspect of the Roebuck Affair. Lord Cowley and Drouyn de Lhuys, however, worked very closely and Cowley was well informed on the events and on the correspondence exchanged between Drouyn and Baron Gros. On June 26 Cowley conveyed to Lord Russell that Drouyn had directed Gros to correct the rumor in London that France had changed its position on recognizing the Confederacy, and that Gros had replied by stating that no such rumor existed. On July 7 Cowley states that "the correspondence with Gros was repeated."[50] Owsley seems to be correct, then, in assuming that the telegram of July 1 was the second message on the subject. But what of the first one? When was it sent? What, specifically, did it ask Gros to do?

Napoleon had volunteered to Slidell on June 18 to make an overture to England, but the French cabinet had refused to do so. It had, however, agreed to inform the British cabinet that France would not object to an overture from London to recognize the South. But no message was sent. On June 22, Napoleon met with Roebuck and Lindsay at Fontainebleau; the same day he wrote to Drouyn de Lhuys: "I wonder whether Baron Gros may not be instructed to state unofficially to Lord Palmerston that I am resolved on recognizing the independence of the Southern Provinces. We could not be compromised by such a declaration, and it might determine the British Government to take a step." Drouyn received the emperor's letter on June 23 and immediately sent the following telegram to Gros: "See Lord Palmerston and in the course of conversation give him to understand that the Emperor has no objection to recognize [sic] the independence of the South."[51]

Drouyn's first "instruction" to Baron Gros, then, differed basically from Napoleon's "instruction" to Drouyn. Instead of directing Gros to state unofficially that Napoleon was "resolved on recognizing" the Confederacy, Drouyn had instructed him, in "the course of conversation" to give Palmerston "to understand that the Emperor has no objection" to recognizing the South. The difference is fundamental; apparently Drouyn made the change without conferring with Napoleon and on the strength of the cabinet's decision of June 18. Napoleon had kept his word to Slidell and the Englishmen; Drouyn had fulfilled the cabinet's wishes.

Gros did not respond to the instruction until after the commons debate of June 30. Indeed, Napoleon's patience wore thin and after Roebuck's remarks and the British ministerial denial of receiving word from Paris, on July 1, 1863, he had Drouyn send a second telegram to Gros: "You were to have spoken unofficially (*officieusement*) to Lord Palmerston of the recognition of the Confederate States. When and how have you done this?"[52] The wording of this second telegram comes closer to the emperor's instruction to Drouyn than did the first one; Gros must have been surprised to receive so sharply worded a message. Yet Gros was more indignant toward the British government spokesman who had answered Roebuck by saying that Gros had specifically denied having any message to convey to the foreign office. Writing on July 1, before he received the above telegram, Gros summarized the debate of June 30, then added: "I regret the manner in which Sir G. Grey . . . spoke of my interview with Lord Russell; it seemed to imply that I had gone to the office of the Principal Secretary of State for the express purpose of saying to him that I had no communication on the subject of the recognition of the South." Gros had gone to Russell, he recalled to Drouyn, to discuss the Polish question, "and it is very likely," he wrote, "that I incidentally said to him that having no official communication to make to him on the recognition of the Southern States, I was personally persuaded that the emperor was disposed to recognize them."[53]

Gros seemed unperturbed that he had not more explicitly carried out the emperor's wishes; this was probably due to the mild tone of Drouyn's telegram of June 23. Drouyn, too, was unperturbed; this was probably due to the fact that the cabinet's wishes instead of the emperor's had been fulfilled.

Owsley concluded that:

> The shifting of the emphasis from the main point of the inter-
> view [between Russell and Gros] and from "no official communi-
> cation" to "none at all," on the part of the British Foreign
> Office, was primarily responsible for the "mess." If it was not
> outright lying, it was a case of superfine sophistry.[54]

Owsley, then, settled the question of veracity by exonerating the Confederates, Roebuck, Lindsay, and, reluctantly the French, for he "was amazed to catch this arch liar [Napoleon III] in a truth. . . ."[55] Blame beyond misunderstanding, Owsley placed in the British foreign office, especially upon Earl Russell. But Owsley was writing without benefit of Napoleon's letter to Drouyn on June 22 and Drouyn's first telegram to Gros on June 23. The correspondence reveals that while the British foreign office did change the emphasis, the basic change occurred in the French foreign ministry, as exemplified by the differences between Napoleon's letter to Drouyn on June 22 and Drouyn's telegram to Gros on June 23. The "mess" of the Roebuck affair was caused less by lies on either side of the Channel than by Drouyn de Lhuys' effort to enforce the French cabinet council's policy as opposed to the emperor's personal policy.

Diplomatic Reactions

The official policy of the French cabinet was determined primarily by the flow of events in America. Although news concerning Northern opposition to the war effort reached Paris during the spring months and news of Lee's movements toward Pennsylvania boosted the Confederate cause, the French ministers were respectful of Federal power and hesitant to arouse it against their own country. Indeed, they had already refused to make another overture to England out of fear of Federal influence in Mexico. And even though the emperor might not be concerned directly with United States Minister Dayton, Drouyn de Lhuys, fully conscious of Northern sensibilities, did have to deal with that gentleman and with the persistent and insistent notes coming from Seward. If the matter of the Erlanger loan caused hardly a ripple in the relations between Paris and Washington, the Roebuck affair, lashing against those diplomatic ties, almost burst them asunder.

Dayton first indicated his suspicions of French involvement in the Roebuck resolution even before the interview between the Englishmen and the emperor. Later an article in *La France* reported that the emperor had received Slidell in an interview, that the South celebrated France's victories in Mexico, that Roebuck and Lindsay had visited with Napoleon, and that Spain was negotiating with the Confederacy for recognition in exchange for guarantees regarding Cuba. The article concluded: "The cause of the Confederates gains new sympathies every day and their heroic resistance on the one side, on the other the impotence of the armies of the North prove that there is in them a people strongly organized, worthy in fact to be admitted among the independent states." This article was too much for Dayton; he hurried to Drouyn's office and asked "distinctly if any change in the policy of this government towards us is contemplated? Whether anything is in agitation?"

Drouyn, at first, blandly responded that he knew of nothing; but sensing Dayton's anxiety, he quickly added: "I have not seen the emperor for some days and I cannot therefore answer for what he has said and done. I am satisfied that he has seen Mr. Slidell here in Paris, and I believe that he has seen Misters Roebuck and Lindsay in Fontainebleau, but of this I cannot speak with certainty." Dayton pretended to accept Drouyn's explanation, but he was not satisfied. He speculated that the subject of the Slidell-Napoleon interview was Confederate approval of the French invasion of Mexico. He felt that he could not have confidence in what Drouyn said because of the "self-judging, governing and reticent power behind him." He then warned Secretary Seward not to underrate the danger of recognition of the Confederacy, because "these foreign governments do not believe it would be a just cause for war, nor that it would lead to it."[56]

Dayton had no reason to pursue the matter further until the news of the June 30 commons debate reached Paris. When he read what Roebuck said about Napoleon's views concerning American affairs, however, Dayton was greatly distressed, and he immediately sought an explanation from Drouyn de Lhuys. The French foreign minister expressed regret that Roebuck should have violated the confidences of "an unofficial and private conversation." He was certain that the emperor had not authorized Roebuck to communicate his views to the house of commons; Drouyn added that "in point of fact *no official communication of any kind* has recently passed on this subject between France and England." It is probable, Drouyn continued, that in the course of conversation the emperor had said that his views were unchanged and that he wished to act in concert with England on the subject of American affairs; but, the foreign minister repeated, contrary to Roebuck's statements nothing officially had been proposed to the British government. Drouyn knew, of course, that the messages he had sent were unofficial; perhaps more important, he knew that they had not contained the same proposals which the emperor had requested and to which Roebuck very likely was referring. So he could speak to the American with confidence and with a fairly clear conscience.

Dayton, however, pressed the point. Even if no official communication had been made, an authorized version of a private conversation assumed a "quasi-official character and is therefore the fair subject of inquiry and explanation," he insisted. Drouyn assented, but at great length once again denied that Napoleon could have possibly given Roebuck permission to reveal the private conversation. As Dayton was about to leave, Drouyn remarked that he wished for the termination of the American War and would welcome any suggestion from England that might accomplish it, but that he saw no way this could be done. "It certainly will not be brought to a close by a recognition of the South," Dayton replied; "such an act might extend and enlarge the war by drawing other nations into it." To this, Drouyn made no comment, and the interview ended.[57] Dayton remained anxious over the question of recognition. He knew only of the engagement at Gettysburg, but not of the outcome of the battle. "If Lee should take Pennsylvania and drive the government out of Washington," he wrote, "the effect would be immediate recognition from all of the European States."[58]

Dayton's anxiety over the military situation in America was no longer shared in Washington, for Lee's troops were now in retreat from Gettysburg and Grant's troops were consolidating their hold on Vicksburg. But because of the slowness of communications, Seward like Dayton was deeply concerned over the diplomatic developments. Fed by the news reports of Roebuck's speech and abruptly reminded of the French efforts in October 1862 and January 1863 to mediate the Civil War, Seward feared some precipitate action before the news of the Union victories could reach France. Helpless to prevent such action, Seward felt that he could only instruct Dayton as to the response he should make in view of recent military events. Not entrusting the instructions to the usual diplomatic dispatch system, Seward sent two letters by special messenger from Washington. The first, dated July 8, revealed his concern over the emperor's views as reported by Roebuck and as influenced by French interests in Mexico:

> The Government of the United States with unanimity unprecedented in its councils, has already inoffensively and with becoming respect, made known to the Emperor of the French that any new demonstration of activity by him prejudicial to the unity of the American people, will be necessarily regarded as unfriendly and will produce a strain upon the fraternal bonds that have for so long united the two countries. We should profoundly regret a proceeding that would be followed by such a consequence. We cannot think so unkindly of the Emperor of the French as to believe that his recent success in Mexico would influence his judgment upon a question so entirely independent of the merits of his war against that Republic, and at the same time so profoundly interesting to the United States.

Seward felt sure that any tendency by Napoleon III to take an action prejudicial to the United States would soon be neutralized by news of Gettysburg and Vicksburg. But what, in the meantime, should Dayton's response be?

If the emperor shall by any official act violate the sovereignty which you represent, *your functions will be suspended.* If he shall go further than to propose, either separately or in conjunction with any other power to again address the United States concerning their affairs, you will inform Mr. Drouyn de Lhuys that you have good reason to expect that they will not *in any case* be induced to depart from the course they have so distinctly indicated in regard to foreign intervention.[59]

This was the furthest Seward ever went during the Civil War period towards breaking diplomatic relations with France. He was prompted to take such a strong stand by Roebuck's speech, the French and Union military victories, and the lack of quick communications. Confident in victory, he was nonetheless anxious lest ignorance of the outcome of the battles should prompt France to take an unwise step.

By the same messenger, Seward sent a second note. He had received, he wrote, from good authority a report concerning certain remarks made by Baron Gros. The French ambassador to London was reported to have said that Napoleon III would soon renew his request to England to recognize the Confederate States, and this time if England should refuse, then he would proceed alone. Seward also reported that after the battle of Gettysburg and the fall of Vicksburg, Mercier had suggested that the French Government should notify the Richmond cabinet that the South could no longer expect recognition from it. These two developments led Seward to instruct Dayton to seek from Drouyn de Lhuys "an explanation of the policy of the Emperor in regard to the Civil War existing in the United States."[60]

Dayton received these dispatches after he had already been assured by Drouyn that no official communication had been made to England and after having received the news of the Union victories. Thus he felt there was no longer any urgency involved. Awaiting Drouyn's regular reception day, he took up the question of the Roebuck-Lindsay affair and French policy towards the American Civil War in the course of a normal conversation. Drouyn once again spoke at length on the former, reiterating essentially the same points he had made earlier. Dayton specifically elicited from Drouyn the statement that France would not act alone on American affairs. When questioned about the reported statements of Baron Gros, the foreign minister hardly let Dayton finish his accounting of them. Shaking his head violently, as if knowing what Dayton was about to say, Drouyn positively said, "Baron Gros never made such remarks; he never said anything of the kind either officially or unofficially, public or private." When Dayton queried Drouyn on the emperor's policy conerning America, the latter responded quite candidly: "He has none; he awaits events."

The two statesmen then discussed the recent military events in America. Drouyn fully understood the impact of the Union victories, especially of the capture of Vicksburg. Dayton left the conversation satisfied that France anticipated no move antipathetic to Union interests.[61]

Thus the serious crisis ended. Seward had learned that Roebuck's statements were not substantiated by the French as early as July 11; and he received an official explanation from Mercier some days later, but he remained anxious until late in the month.[62] Indeed, both Dayton and Seward brooded over the implications of Napoleon's statement to Roebuck as reflected in the *Moniteur* article of July 5. Seward made this the subject of a special dispatch which he ordered be read to Drouyn de Lhuys. When Dayton did so, Drouyn answered that any such discussion was purely "academic" since the affair was over; but the article had been a truthful one, reflecting what actually had been exchanged during the interview. That the emperor was not suggesting a new policy, Drouyn concluded, was borne out by the events.[63] On August 31 and September 8 Seward finally closed the books on the "awkward Roebuck affair" by acknowledging Dayton's dispatches and conveying the president's congratulations to Dayton for the superior manner in which he had handled the episode in Paris.[64]

From Richmond, the French cabinet learned the effect of the Union victories. Although the Southerners applaud the French victories in Mexico, Paul wrote, and look forward to a friendly neighbor, "these are the dreams of an unhappy people." Their former illusions have fallen. There is, he continued, popular dissatisfaction with the leaders, political unrest, especially in

North Carolina, an economic crisis resulting from the fall in the value of the dollar—and the only answer the Confederate government could make is higher taxes and a desperate rumor that Lee, despite his losses, will gather another army of 80,000 for still another invasion of Pennsylvania.[65] This is not information likely to instill confidence. Indeed, although there were diplomatic flurries concerning recognition through January 1865, there was never again a serious consideration of it by the emperor or his cabinet.

To Benjamin, Slidell, and Mason, the Roebuck resolution represented the anticlimax to their efforts to gain foreign diplomatic recognition—as Owsley states; to Napoleon III, mindful of Mexico and the textile crisis, the resolution offered another opportunity to probe for a positive act of recognition in conjunction with England. The potential was great, and it was real. To Drouyn de Lhuys, mindful of the Polish problem, the resolution created another irritating example of the emperor's proclivity for unofficial and distracting diplomacy. The foreign minister, by patient and careful work, managed to prevent lasting harm, but he had to rely on the French cabinet's decision and to support it over the emperor's desires. To Dayton and Seward, acutely aware of the French efforts to intervene in the war during the past months, Roebuck's actions and words created the most dangerous diplomatic threat to arise from Paris during the course of the Civil War. Dayton was convinced that, save for the fortunes of the battlefields, the European countries, led by France, would have extended official diplomatic recognition to the Confederate States. Seward, not aware of Drouyn's restraining hand on the French emperor, but confident in his own knowledge of the Union victories at Gettysburg and Vicksburg, established the conditions for breaking diplomatic relations with France.

If the battle of Antietam had been the moment of decision for the British cabinet and the Roebuck resolution was an anticlimax for the Southern cause, the Northern officials were not conscious of it. Never aware of the closeness of British-French action in the fall of 1862, Seward and Dayton were much more concerned in the summer of 1863. Had it been left to Napoleon III alone, their fears might well have been justified; but the French cabinet and the foreign minister followed a more cautious policy, and the deep fears of the Americans were really unwarranted. The issues raised by Roebuck's speech were actually settled on the American battlefields, and the diplomatic flurry remained simply, as Napoleon III named it, "the awkward Roebuck affair."

The French efforts in 1862–63 somehow to intervene in the American Civil War had come to an end. Perhaps they had served their purpose, for the domestic economic picture began to improve in the fall of 1863. New sources of cotton, retraining and job relocation, and a gradual decline in unemployment made unnecessary any future note like the one of January 9, 1863, or any unfortunate international "mess" like the Roebuck Affair. But the gigantic struggle in America had yet another two years to run and France continued to be diplomatically involved in its problems.

Chapter XIII

CONFEDERATE NAVAL
CONSTRUCTION IN FRANCE

EVEN before the French efforts to intervene in the American
conflict had come to an end in the Roebuck affair, another
facet of French neutral rights and obligations was developing.
This involved the complicated question of the construction of
ships for one of the belligerents in the shipyards of France, and it
raised the question of the limits of the French proclamation of
neutrality and of the application of French municipal laws in
sustaining that proclamation. It resulted from the Confederate
effort to create a navy in Europe in order to prey upon Northern
shipping and to destroy the Union blockade. The question became a real one in France for the first time in 1863, only after the
British government revealed its reluctance to allow the Confederates to use its large facilities for such a purpose.

Early in the war, Confederate Secretary of the Navy Stephen
R. Mallory realized that the newly formed country had neither
the natural resources nor the facilities to construct a navy capable
of performing the functions of forcing the blockade and of attacking the Northern maritime commerce.[1] He wanted an
ironclad navy of the type already built and used by England and
France. Since he understood the French government to be
friendly to the Confederate cause and expected its "recognition
of our independence at an early date," he sent Lieutenant James
H. North to France to either purchase the French frigate
"Gloire" or to contract for the construction of a similar vessel in
a French shipyard.[2] Naively he anticipated no difficulty in accomplishing this delicate mission.

North, unfortunately for Mallory, lacked the patience and audacity necessary to fulfill his task. Meeting with no immediate encouragement in France, he gave up and went to England to join forces with another Mallory agent, James D. Bulloch.[3] There Bulloch, a happier appointment, energetically and successfully set about his assignment of procuring munitions and ships for the Confederate navy. He contracted for twelve ships and put four of them into service, the most famous being the "Florida" and the "Alabama."[4] Working carefully within the bounds of the British Foreign Enlistments Act, Bulloch concentrated his efforts in England until the spring of 1863 when the controversy over the so-called Laird rams convinced him that the British government would prohibit their delivery.[5] By January 1863 he had concluded that "if we get money and I contract for other ships I should go to French builders." "The British Government will prevent iron ships leaving," he wrote two weeks later, "because their object is too evident for disguise." "Any other ships," he advised Mallory, "had better be built on the Continent, say, in France."[6] Thus the efficient Bulloch in 1863 turned to the country abandoned in 1861 by the ineffectual Lieutenant North. Exactly what advantage did he expect to find across the Channel?

Bulloch knew that the French proclamation of neutrality was more specific than the English one and that it forbade any French subject to cooperate in any manner whatever in the equipment or armament of a vessel-of-war for either belligerent. But the Confederates assumed that the "Executive Government of France was well nigh autocratic, and it was fully understood that whatever might be the declared policy, it might and could be modified in practice without any public notice or any formal appeal to the law courts to determine the meaning of specific statutes." And again, according to Bulloch, the Confederate officials felt that "in France everything might and probably would depend upon the secret purposes of the Chief of State, and the effect which the chances of success or defeat to the South might have upon him." The French endeavors in Mexico apparently played a large part in the belief of the Southerners that Napoleon III favored the South.[7] Once they felt doubt as to the British attitudes, they were ready to transfer the bulk of their operations across the channel; all they needed was some sign from France that the "secret purposes of the Chief of State" indeed would be served by allowing the Confederates to build ships in his country. That indication had come in an interview between Napoleon and John Slidell, the Confederate commissioner to France, as early as October 1862. It led eventually to the sale of the Laird rams to Bravay and Company and to the placing of orders for the construction of four wooden and two ironclad vessels in French shipyards. Indeed, during the year of 1863, France became the center of Confederate naval activities in Europe.

The Arman Contracts

Emperor Napoleon III had initially suggested that the Confederates build warships in France. In October 1862, when French industry was feeling the full effect of the American war and when the emperor was formulating his tripartite mediation plan,[8] he held a long conversation with John Slidell. The Southerner remarked that the strength of the two French ironclads, the "Gloire" and the "Normandie," was such that they "could enter without risk the harbors of New York and Boston and lay those cities under contribution." "Why have you not created a navy?" Napoleon asked, as if the thought had just occurred to him. "A few ships would inflict fatal injury on the Federal commerce, and with three or four powerful steamers you could open some of your ports." Visions of cotton bales passing through those ports obviously appealed to him. Slidell explained the Confederate naval procurements in England and the problems of manning and arming the ships. "If Your Majesty could give some kind of verbal assurance that your police will not observe too closely when we wish to put on board guns and men, we will gladly avail ourselves of it." But Napoleon's mind was racing beyond Slidell's suggestion; he was thinking of constructing the ships in France. After some hesitation, he asked: "Why do you not build them as for the Italian Government? I do not think it will be difficult, but I will consult the minister of marine about it."[9]

At that time Bulloch's work was going well in England and he felt no need to pursue the emperor's suggestion. But Slidell was fascinated by its possibilities and in late December asked Mocquard, Napoleon's private secretary, whether the emperor had yet consulted the marine minister. Within five days the secretary reported to Slidell that after consulting "some of his ministers" Napoleon "found greater difficulties in the matter than he had anticipated, and . . . for the present at least he cannot give any encouragement."[10]

This response should have warned Slidell that Napoleon was not as independent of his ministers as the Confederates assumed, and he probably would have concluded this except for a proposal made to him three days later by Mr. Lucien Arman. Slidell knew Arman as the largest ship builder in France and as a confidant of the emperor on naval matters; he must have been surprised, therefore, when so soon after Napoleon's discouragement Arman offered to build ironclad steamers for the Confederate government. Claiming he spoke "from authority," the Frenchman added: "There will be no difficulty in arming and equipping the ships." When Slidell spoke of financial problems, Arman again referred to Napoleon: "If the Emperor will let it be understood that he favors the negotiation of cotton bonds, I think that mode of payment might be acceptable."[11]

Slidell was faced with a dilemma. Despite the ministers' opinions, Arman, hinting strongly that he came directly from the emperor, offered to build, equip, and arm ironclads without difficulties. Surmising that the cabinet members objected because of the pending peace commissioner's proposal,[12] Slidell realized that the emperor was capable of acting through a personal and unofficial representative if he thought it would relieve France's economic problems. It was natural for the Southerner to attach great importance to Arman's conversation and to urge action on the strength of it. Indeed, it was the January conversation with Arman, not the October interview with the emperor which prompted the Confederates to transfer most of their naval activity from England to France.

Slidell easily persuaded Bulloch, who was beginning to experience problems with the English government over the Laird rams, to make the change. After a time-consuming correspondence with Richmond, the two Southern agents received permission to investigate the construction of ships in the French yards.[13] Two considerations occupied them the next several weeks: money and assurances. When the details of the Erlanger Loan were completed in mid-March, Bulloch met with Arman in Paris. His English problems fresh in his mind, Bulloch questioned the shipbuilder closely about the French neutrality law and the chances of getting the ships to sea fully equipped and armed. Arman assured him that Commerce Minister Rouher had told him that Napoleon was willing for him to construct the ships and put them to sea under the French flag for delivery to the Confederates. But Bulloch had been through this before; still skeptical, he asked what would happen when the United States minister protested to the foreign minister: would the ships still be delivered? Again Arman reassured him. Without saying he had consulted Drouyn de Lhuys, Arman said that he "had been informed" that so long as he applied to arm the ships according to law, the government would require no further evidence at any time. He intended to propose building the ships, he continued, for the China Sea trade and to justify the armament as the usual and necessary self-protection from the pirates of those waters. The emperor, he said, fully understood the details of these arrangements; there would be no difficulty with any of the executive departments with which he would have to deal.[14] Arman's whole tone implied not only that the emperor understood these plans, but that he fully approved them; certainly Slidell and Bulloch drew that inference from his remarks.

But Slidell still was not fully satisfied. Since their conversation in early January he had, in a sense, been checking on Arman. Taking advantage of an interview with Drouyn de Lhuys on February 22, he had asked about the Arman proposal to build ships for the South. The foreign minister had said that such an activity related more to the minister of marine or of commerce, and he advised Slidell to consult them. "It is better that I know nothing of it," Drouyn had said, "I am quite willing to close my eyes to it until some direct appeal is made to me."[15] In effect the foreign minister had said that he would assume an ignorance of

the Confederate activities—almost an "averted glance"—as long
as he could; but should the Federal authorities protest, he had
made no promise as to what action he might be obligated to
take. From the commerce minister he had received more
definite assurances. Rouher had said positively that "if we were
to build ships of war in French ports, we should be permitted to
arm and equip them and proceed to sea."[16] He did not, apparently, consult the minister of marine.

Thus, by mid-March when he and Bulloch were talking with
Arman, Slidell had no positive assurances from the emperor, only
a qualified promise from the foreign minister to ignore the matter
as long as possible, and a direct assurance only from the commerce minister. Arman's implications seemed to Slidell and
Bulloch to be sufficient evidence of the French intentions to
proceed with the arrangements. After Bulloch had seen for himself the construction facilities in the Bordeaux yards, a preliminary agreement was signed for the construction and arming of
four wooden frigates, or clippers, of the "Alabama" class.[17] But
before agreeing to a final contract, Slidell insisted on a direct approval from the emperor.

On March 28 Arman asked Napoleon if he would agree to
meet with Slidell in order to satisfy the Southerner's demand for
his direct approval, and thus remove the last obstacle to a final
contract. At first Napoleon was inclined to do so, but, according
to Arman, he then said that his assent to the contract should be
sufficient for the Southerners.[18] Progress on the ships and the
pressure of time forced Slidell to accept a final contract with
Arman on April 15; but, since he still lacked the imperial sanction, he stipulated that the contract would "take effect only when
assurances satisfactory to me are given that the ships will be allowed to leave the French ports armed and equipped."[19]

These persistent and tortuous efforts to gain the emperor's
personal authorization to arm the ships reflect both Bulloch's
costly experiences in England and Slidell's uncertainty and skepticism in regard to Arman. The emperor was proving to be more
difficult to pin down than any of the Confederates had anticipated. Arman had been confident, however; he had begun
work on the four clippers in April and by June "good progress

had been made."[20] French law required ministerial approval to arm the ships and accordingly on June 1, 1863, Arman sent his request to Minister of Marine Chasseloup-Laubat. He identified the ships as destined by "a foreign ship owner for service in the China Seas and the Pacific, between China, Japan, and San Francisco." He further justified the special armament, which he was seeking permission to install, by stating that the ships were designed for "eventual sale . . . to the governments of China and Japan."[21] The minister "willingly" authorized Arman to "put an armament of twelve to fourteen 30-pounder-cannon on the four wooden" vessels.[22] This seemed to the shipbuilder to be conclusive authorization and he immediately showed it to Slidell. "The letter of the minister of marine which you have shown me and of which you have left me a copy, authorizing the arming . . . of four steamers at Nantes and Bordeaux," Slidell answered, "is satisfactory, and I see no reason why the contract made with you . . . should not at once be put into execution."[23] So finally the Confederate Commissioner's doubt was stilled, and he authenticated the contract in early June when the four ships were half completed. His search for assurance ended with the marine minister's permission to arm the ships; he never did receive the emperor's direct approval for the scheme.

Nonetheless this encouraged the Confederates to take a further step in France. Bulloch had long considered their greatest naval need to be blockade-breaking ironclad steamers. The Erlanger Loan seemed to provide the necessary funds to build such ships and when Slidell managed another meeting with the emperor on June 18, 1863, he asked about the prospects of constructing ironclads in France. "I require only your verbal assurance that they shall be allowed to proceed to sea under the Confederate flag before entering into contracts," he told the ruler. "You may build the ships," Napoleon replied, "but it will be necessary that their destination be concealed."[24] With this qualified sanction, on July 16, 1863, Bulloch entered into a contract with Arman for the construction of two ironclad vessels, designed for river combat.[25]

By the middle of July 1863 the South had contracts for the construction of six ships of war, all handled by Arman, though two of the clippers were farmed out to Voruz in Nantes. They entered into these contracts in good faith that the French government would allow the ships to be armed and delivered to Confederate naval personnel. They based their conviction on the belief that the emperor could more easily circumvent French law than the British government could circumvent English law. They realized that success depended upon Napoleon's personal determination to control his ministers and this, they knew, depended upon the military and political situation at any given moment. The wooden vessels were contracted for before the Roebuck Affair, before the battles of Gettysburg and Vicksburg, and before the French occupation of Mexico City; the ironclads contract had been entered into before the news of those battles reached Europe. The Southerners therefore were still optimistic about their ultimate success. Yet they had received, in fact, only the weakest of assurances that the government or the emperor would allow the ships to be armed, equipped, and put to sea for the Confederate navy. Arman had told them that the emperor had approved, but the emperor really had given only his passive permission for the arming of ships to be used in the China seas. The most he said about the ironclads was that they could be built, but that their destination would have to be kept secret. The obvious implication in both cases was that if the real destination of the ships were to be discovered, then the French government might have to disavow their delivery, depending upon the military fortunes of the Confederacy and its own diplomatic needs. The foreign minister refused to take cognizance of any of the activity, and the minister of marine, as far as the records show, had never been consulted directly by the Confederates. Only the minister of commerce, whose department had the least to do with the enterprise, had given unqualified approbation to the building of ships in France. So it was really on the positive words of Arman and Rouher only that the Southerners undertook this ambitious scheme.

The first contract with Arman for the wooden ships specified the construction of four "Alabama" type ships, designed to cruise against the Northern shipping. They were to be slightly larger and faster than the "Alabama" and would be more heavily armed, with some iron armor on the sides. Since the contract called for delivery ten months after the date of signing, Arman was forced to arrange the construction of two of the ships in Nantes. Mr. J. Voruz, deputy from that city, was an eminent iron founder and engineer. He employed local shipbuilders to make the hulls, and his own firm undertook to construct the arms and gear for the ships. The construction of such ships was not in violation of any French law; even their armament was not unusual and required only a permit from the ministry of marine. The only question of illegality arose with their delivery to a belligerent. As long as the ultimate destination of the ships could be concealed, the government really would have no basis to prohibit their construction, arming, or sailing. This was exactly the method Arman followed in his application for permission to arm the vessels. Since Voruz actually manufactured the cannon in his iron foundry, in late July he sought and received permission to make the guns "which are to be placed on the four vessels that have been described to you by Mr. Arman in the letter he had the honor to write to you on the 1st of June last."[26]

The contract for the ironclad rams created a different situation. Since the ships were not to be armed, Arman felt that he did not need to apply to the government for permission of any kind. But the very nature of their construction and armor did create a possibility of their becoming suspect as they had in England. The ships were built to operate with a very shallow draft and to maneuver with ease. An innovation was that each had two sternposts permitting the use of two separate screw propellers, each operated by a different engine. Thus, by reversing the motion of the screws, the ship could be turned quickly. The largest gun was a 300-pounder of twelve tons, mounted in the forward turret and pointed in line with the keel; it had no lateral movement, and was to be aimed by maneuvering the whole ship with the two separately operated screws. This had the advantage, according to Bulloch, of presenting the smallest possible target to the enemy. Each ship also had a projecting prow which made them "very formidable as rams." All of the guns for the rams were being made in England at the Elswick Works of Sir William

Armstrong.   The plan was to deliver the guns at a rendezvous point somewhere at sea, as had been done with the "Alabama."[27]

By the end of July 1863, then, the Confederate agents in Europe had entered into two contracts with Arman for the construction of a formidable naval squadron consisting of four fast and heavily armed cruisers and two powerful ironclad steamers. These vessels, they anticipated, would serve not only to sweep the United States merchant marine off the seas and to force the United States navy to lift the blockade of the Southern ports, but would also serve "to strike severe and telling blows upon the Northern seaboard."[28]   Faced with the obstruction of the British government, the Southern agents had transferred their activities to France during the time when the French government was concerned about unemployment and growing involvement in Mexico.   The apparent readiness of Napoleon to acquiesce in their activities gave the agents false hopes that the Arman contracts would provide the Confederacy with the naval power to defend their shores and to open their ports to European shipping. This, they expected, would assure them of official diplomatic recognition and of victory in the war.   Their success depended upon secrecy in France and a favorable military situation in America.   Unfortunately for the Confederacy, neither lasted as long as it took to build the ships.

Federal Protests

The Confederate agents in Europe could do little about the military situation in America.   It fell to them, then, to concentrate on building the warships and on preventing leaks of the ships' true ownership and ultimate function.   But the necessary precautions were not taken until it was too late.   Indeed, Bulloch seems to have visited Bordeaux openly in order to inspect the ships under construction.

Inevitably rumors spread.   So persistent were they by early September that Captain Hore, the British naval attaché in Paris, decided to visit Bordeaux to see "the vessels building for the CSA."   Hore was received warmly by Arman and was shown around the yard.   He saw the two clippers, now named the

"Yeddo" and the "Osacca," which, he reported, "are said to be building for a company about to open a line of steamers between Japan and some of the ports in the East." He also saw the two ironclad steamers. "M. Arman told me, with a smile, that they are for the Pasha of Egypt, but that the orders were given by the late pasha." These two ships, now appropriately named the "Cheops" and the "Sphinx," were formidable crafts, ordered by Captain Bulloch of the Confederate navy, Hore concluded.[29] So impressed was the British officer, and so strong were rumors of other ships being built on Confederate order, that he later made another trip to Le Havre and to Harfleur to investigate. But he reported no Southern shipbuilding activities in that area.[30] It is unfortunate that Captain Hore did not go to Nantes and leave a disinterested report on the two clipper ships there.

Federal agents became aware of the rumors. John Bigelow, the Federal consul general in Paris, had heard through "wholly irresponsible sources, usually needy Confederate refugees" that "Confederates were building warships in France." But his consuls in the shipbuilding ports had been unable to confirm the reports, and, by early September, Bigelow "had ceased to attach much importance to them."[31] But he was soon to be shocked out of his complacency.

Ironically, on September 9, the very day Arman was showing Captain Hore around his shipyard in Bordeaux and was smilingly referring to the pasha's orders for the two ironclads, a timid Frenchman hesitantly entered the Paris office of William L. Dayton, the United States minister. Much to Dayton's surprise, the Frenchman, a clerk in Voruz's office in Nantes named Trémont,[32] offered written evidence that warships were then being built in Bordeaux and Nantes for the Confederates. Citing dimensions, costs, nature of the turrets, and other details, Trémont stated that the ships would be completed in about three months. The authority to construct these ships, he said, had been obtained from the French government with "fraudulent representations," and so he felt confident that if the evidence he offered were to be submitted to the proper officials the construction would be stopped. Finally, he asked for nothing in return until full success had been achieved in preventing the delivery of the ships to the Confederates.[33]

Impressed by Trémont's knowledge of detail and by his apparent sincerity, Dayton was tempted to enter immediately into an agreement with the stranger. But he "thought it better, under the circumstances, to have nothing to do with the preliminary arrangements" and referred Trémont to Bigelow. Should he make use of the evidence, he wanted to be able to say that the matter had been brought to his attention by the consul and "not by virtue of any direct communication between myself and parties who, if their story be true, must be acting treacherously in some way to their employers."[34] And so he wrote a note for Trémont to take to Bigelow, recommending "the bearer and his statement" to the consul.[35]

The next day, Thursday, September 10, Bigelow received Trémont. The Frenchman casually asked if the consul had heard rumors of the Confederate shipbuilding activities in France. When Bigelow replied just as casually that he no longer attached much importance to them, Trémont proceeded to recite the details which had so interested Dayton. When he mentioned that the builders had already received the government's approval for the ships, Bigelow interrupted to inquire, then, how any kind of proof "could change the destiny of the ships." Trémont responded, much as he had the day before, that the authorization appeared "to have been procured through false representation."

"Of course what you state is of grave importance to my government if it can be substantiated, but none at all without proofs which cannot be disputed or explained away," Bigelow interjected. "What kind of proofs can you furnish?"

"Original documents," Trémont calmly responded; "and, what is more, I will engage that, with my proofs in hand, you can effectually secure the arrests of the ships." He immediately handed to Bigelow a certified copy of Chasseloup-Laubat's June 6 authorization to arm the clippers, and some half-dozen original letters and papers, which proved to Bigelow's satisfaction the essential truth of all that Trémont had said.[36] The Frenchman left the papers with Bigelow and said that he would return in two days with even more data showing the tie-in between the builder and the Confederates.

Although he was almost overwhelmed by the potential importance of Trémont's information, Bigelow managed nonetheless to bargain with him on the compensation the United States government would pay. Trémont, admitting that his efforts involved some expense and inconvenience, asked for 20,000 francs upon the prevention of the ships' delivery to the Confederates. This seemed to be an arrangement highly favorable to the United States since it would have no expense at all unless and until the ships were definitely denied to the South. But Bigelow still bargained until Trémont accepted the figure of 15,000. Even so, Bigelow expressed the hope of reducing the amount by another 5,000 francs.[37]

The documents finally produced by Trémont, and submitted to the French government, were ten in number. They included three letters exchanged between Arman and Voruz and between Voruz father and son in which the ships were referred to as being built "for the account of the Confederate States"; one letter between Voruz and Blakely of England concerning the manufacture of the cannon for the ironclads; the exchange between Arman and Chasseloup-Laubat requesting and granting the authorization to arm the clippers; the exchange (three letters) between Voruz and Chasseloup-Laubat on the same subject; and a letter from Voruz to the minister of commerce requesting permission to arm the ironclads for Blakeley.[38] These papers definitely and incontrovertibly identified the clippers as being built for the Confederates and not for the China Sea trade as claimed by Arman; they identified the ironclads as being ordered by the Confederates and not by the pasha of Egypt, as claimed by Arman; and they revealed that the arming of the ironclads was being handled by the French builders. Finally, the documents showed, on the face, that the French government's approval for the arming of the vessels had been based upon false information. Thus, although Bigelow claims to have suspected official complicity from the very beginning,[39] there was no evidence in the Trémont papers to show that the French government had in any way violated its neutral obligations. The evidence did conclusively prove that Arman had fraudulently obtained permission to arm the clippers and did intend to violate the provision of the French proclamation of June 10, 1861, which prohibited any Frenchman from helping or cooperating "in any manner whatsoever to equip or arm a ship or a privateer" of either belligerent.

Doubtless Trémont had acted to reveal the situation on the assumption that no French official was in any way involved. Dayton, at first, seems to have been of the same opinion, and he followed this line in all of his correspondence with Drouyn de Lhuys and Chasseloup-Laubat. The diplomatic position of the United States in the face of the Confederate naval construction question was set by the contents of the original Trémont papers; it was that certain French individuals were conspiring with Southern agents illegally to construct, equip, and arm warships which would go to sea directly from French ports against Federal merchant shipping and naval units, and that this conspiracy involved fraudulently obtained authority so to arm and deliver the ships into the hands of the Confederates. Even after it later became evident that certain French officials were involved in the plan, the Union diplomats maintained this attitude. The same view was adopted by Drouyn de Lhuys and Chasseloup-Laubat in their exchanges with Dayton and Bigelow. The subsequent diplomacy was based upon a collective "averted glance."

After Bigelow and Trémont had conducted their business, Dayton called upon Drouyn de Lhuys on September 18. Referring to the evidence gathered from Trémont, he claimed that the Confederates were building "at least four, if not five, warships . . . in the shipyards of Bordeaux and Nantes." "I am greatly surprised," Drouyn responded; "I had no knowledge of anything of the kind." He assured Dayton that his government would maintain its neutrality, requested copies of the original papers, and said that he would at once investigate the facts and the French legislation bearing upon them. "Thank you for calling this matter to my attention so promptly," he concluded. "I fully recognize the importance of it, and I will let you know what will be done."[40]

Was Drouyn just acting or was he really surprised? Dayton

"had no doubt" that the foreign minister was genuinely shocked by the contents of the papers.[41] Of course, at that time Dayton had no indication of any French official complicity, and he was not looking for any particular reaction by Drouyn. It is entirely possible that Drouyn did not know the extent of the shipbuilding program. He had, according to all records, last spoken to anyone about it seven months earlier and then in a negative way, making it clear that he did not want to know about any such activity in France. Nothing had happened since that would have required his knowledge or action. It is quite credible, then, that Drouyn was honestly surprised that Arman was building four or five ships for the South, that he had received Chasseloup-Laubat's permission to arm them in France, and that Arman had so openly requested this permission by misrepresentations to the minister of marine. It is almost certain that he had "no knowledge of anything of the kind" on such a large scale going on at Bordeaux and Nantes.

Dayton, however, was not confident that the documents would produce the desired results. Lee had been turned back at Gettysburg and the Mississippi had been cut at Vicksburg; but this was balanced by the French occupation of Mexico City and sponsorship of Maximilian. In Dayton's thinking the likelihood of French recognition of the Richmond government had not appreciably decreased during the summer of 1863. Napoleon III's mediation suggestion of the previous October, his unilateral act of January 9, 1863, and the Roebuck affair were still fresh in Dayton's mind. He realistically concluded his account of the interview with Drouyn with this evaluation:

> It seems to me that their action on this subject is likely to afford a pretty good test of their future intentions. As to what the law may be it does not, I apprehend, much matter: if they mean that good relations with our country shall be preserved, they will stop the building of those ships, or, at least, the arming and delivery of them; if they mean to break with us they will let them go on.[42]

Confederate Captain Bulloch, when he heard of the Federal protests, adopted much the same view. "The construction of the ships will not be interferred with, but whether they will be allowed to leave France or not will depend upon the position of affairs in America at the time of their completion." Should the Southern cause be in the ascendancy, he said, then the departure of the ships would be connived at; but if the Union should prosper, "the affair of the 'Confederate ships' will be turned over to the responsible Ministers of the Empire, who will justify their claim to American gratitude by a strict enforcement of the neutrality of France."[43] And Consul General Bigelow, some twenty-five years later, stated that "it was fear of us, not respect for his obligations either as a neutral or as a friend, which made [Napoleon III] abandon Arman and his associates." Evaluating the diplomacy, Bigelow claimed that Napoleon's "course towards us from the beginning to the end of the plot was deliberately and systematically treacherous, and his ministers allowed themselves to be made his pliant instruments."[44] Thus from the beginning of the diplomatic phase of the naval construction project, agents of both belligerents surmised that the fate of the ships would be determined by the battles fought by the boys in blue and gray rather than by French law or by French ministerial will. They were nearly correct; but they all overlooked the most decisive factor—the French involvement in Mexico and the foreign minister's determination to maintain a strict neutrality in the Civil War because of that involvement.

Drouyn's mention of French legislation and his request for copies of the documents caused Dayton to push his scribes and to research the law. On September 22 he presented copies of the documents to Drouyn. After having summarized them and having indicated their collective importance, Dayton revealed the results of his legal researches. Citing sections of the neutrality proclamation, Dayton effectively showed that Arman's action was in violation of the proclamation and that under its own law, France was obliged to prosecute such violators according to particular articles of the penal code. Noting that the French government had been induced "by the extraordinary misrepresentation as to the purpose and destination of these ships" to authorize their arming, and recalling the escape of the "Alabama" from the British authorities, Dayton directed Drouyn's attention to the "danger of the shipment of these arms and projectiles" to the Confederates in defiance of French law and the wishes of the government. On the basis of the documents, the laws, and the real and present danger of the surreptitious delivery of the arms, Dayton requested that the French government take certain specific actions:

> I respectfully ask that the authorization to provide the said ships with an armament, heretofore granted by the Minister of Marine, be withdrawn and that the manufacture of arms and projectiles, hereinbefore referred to, be stayed or, where the fabrication of the same be completed, that their delivery be prevented, and that such other proceedings be taken by the French Government as it may deem most advisable to prevent the further construction and delivery of said vessels.[45]

Three days after Dayton submitted the documents and his demands, Drouyn sent them to Chasseloup-Laubat with a long letter of his own. After summarizing Dayton's letter, Drouyn expressed his own opinions and called for an immediate investigation. His interdepartmental note contains the seeds of a ministerial squabble and of Drouyn's assertion of his control over the affair.

> I recommend this affair to your examination, my dear colleague, in a very special manner. Mr. Dayton has succeeded, as you see, in procuring the most positive proofs of the facts on which he bases his claims, and we could not deny [*nous ne saurions nous dissimuler*] that in presenting them he is justified in appealing to the terms of our declaration of June 10, 1861.
>
> I must regret, moreover, that your department did not earlier deem it proper to consult with that of foreign affairs at the time it had to respond to the requests of M. Arman. This is the procedure the department of war takes each time there is a question of sending arms to a foreign country, since political considerations could force us, in certain circumstances, to refuse the requested authorization. Now it will not escape you that this consultation is much more urgent when there is a question of the delivery of materials as important as those whose nature and destination are so clearly established in the present case.

And, in his own handwriting, Drouyn added this postscript: "The gravity and urgency of this claim, my dear colleague, must not escape your attention."[46]

The letter reveals much about the Confederate belief that the French officials had approved the construction of their warships, about Bigelow's later claim of French treachery, and about the ability of a French minister, given the proper circumstances, to take over the conduct of a matter in which the emperor had a personal interest. The letter was not, like many diplomatic messages, designed for publication in order to placate public opinion or to justify the government's position on some issue; rather, it was an interdepartmental memorandum with no ulterior goal. Apparently Drouyn was one government official who knew nothing of the Confederate attempt to construct a navy in French shipyards. When he learned of that attempt, he considered the Federal claim to be justified, the plot to be a violation of the proclamation of neutrality, and the situation to be grave and urgent.

But the real test of Drouyn's sincerity was the success of his actions. Since shipbuilding was a slow process there was no need for immediate success. The fact is that ultimately no ship was delivered to the Confederates from a French port; the only one they did gain possession of was acquired through a third power and by chicanery, and furthermore was acquired too late to participate in the war. And this delay was almost exclusively the work of Drouyn de Lhuys.

Chasseloup-Laubat, out of town when Drouyn's letter reached his department, did not respond for over a fortnight. Meanwhile, Dayton continued to gather more evidence and to press Drouyn for an answer. On October 8 he presented five more letters including copies of the Arman-Bulloch contract of July 16 and letters detailing arrangements about payments and armaments manufacture. At the same time Drouyn told him that the minister of marine "entirely agreed with him that no violation of the neutrality of France should be permitted." And, Drouyn added, "You might be assured that it will not be." Dayton persisted: "In a matter of such importance I do not like to have it rest upon my report or recollection of a conversation merely; I should like you to put your answer in reference to these vessels in writing. Furthermore, I should like you to state to me not general principles only, but please apply them to this particular case, and let me know what the government will do in respect to these vessels now being built at Bordeaux and Nantes." Drouyn promised that he would "cheerfully" do so at an early date. Dayton was concerned because he had heard that the construction was progressing rapidly and that the Confederates promised more money if that would hurry the completion. They had already spent, Dayton understood, some three million francs on the ships.[47]   In Washington, Seward and Lincoln anxiously awaited the French reply, and Seward halted the passage of a large quantity of French-owned tobacco through the blockade at Hampton Roads as a lever to a prompt and favorable reply from Paris.[48]

Drouyn immediately sent Dayton's new evidence to the marine ministry, and accompanied it with this note to Chasseloup-Laubat: "Dayton insists and we cannot deny that it is within his right to have a prompt answer. I attach great importance, as you know, to the most prompt answer possible."[49]   Certainly the foreign minister was acting in the spirit of his conversations with Dayton; indeed, he seems to have been as anxious as Dayton, Seward, and Lincoln for the explanations from Chasseloup-Laubat.

Finally, the marine minister returned to Paris and prepared his answer to Drouyn. He explained the grant of his authorization to Arman to arm the clippers just as Arman had expected him to. The request, he wrote, was for permission to arm commercial ships designed for use in the China Seas, and "I could not, upon such a declaration and knowing besides that the vessels of commerce which navigate the waters in question ought always to be furnished with a certain armament in view of the numerous pirates which infest them, I could not, I say, answer negatively to the request of Mr. Arman." So far, so good for Arman's— and perhaps even Napoleon's—plan. But Chasseloup-Laubat continued:

Upon the whole my Department has only conformed in this circumstance to its precedents. It could only trust to the declaration of Messrs. Arman and Voruz, and it could not be responsible for the unlawful operations which might be undertaken. I am going however to call forth from Messrs. Arman and Voruz explanations upon the facts of which you have spoken to me, and you may rest assured, my dear colleague, that the Department of Marine will continue, as it has done up to the present day, to do everything which shall be necessary according to the wish of the Emperor, and conformably to the Declaration of this Government, in order that the most strict neutrality be observed in that which concerns the war which desolates America at this moment.[50]

The answer amounted to an explanation of the marine ministry's routine response to what it apparently considered to be a routine application by Arman. Chasseloup-Laubat further explained to Drouyn that, since the request for arming the ship involved no foreign government, he had not felt it necessary to consult the foreign ministry. Had arms for a foreign navy been requested, he said, he certainly would have "come to an understanding" with the foreign minister.[51] So Chasseloup-Laubat made only one concession to the implications of the Trémont papers: he would call for "explanations" from Arman and Voruz.

Drouyn de Lhuys seemed highly pleased with Chasseloup-Laubat's letter. But Dayton soon let him know that "explanations" from the shipbuilders would not satisfy the United States. "I think it is due the United States as a friendly power," he said, "that the authorizations be promptly withdrawn." "But," Drouyn responded, "this letter from the Minister of Marine is a promise to do just that. He has agreed with me that a strict neutrality must be maintained, and since the arming of these vessels for the purpose indicated in the documents would be a clear violation of neutrality, then he must withdraw the authorization which was granted as a result of the misrepresentations submitted by the builders." Dayton's answer reflected the urgency he felt: "The intended action on this question is too important to be left to inference; I beg an explicit answer as to what will be done in reference to this authorization and to these vessels." As if to back up his claim for immediate action, for the third time Dayton left documentary evidence which implicated the builders with the Confederates. This was a letter from Arman to Confederate naval officer Maury concerning the building of still another ironclad. Drouyn seemed to think that Dayton was too importunate, but offered to pass on to the marine minister Dayton's request for a more explicit reply.[52] He was as good as his word. On the same day apparently just following this conversation, Drouyn sent the Arman-to-Maury letter to Chasseloup-Laubat, noting that it showed even more connections between the shipbuilders and the Confederates. He also repeated Dayton's strong request that the arming authorization be withdrawn immediately. Drouyn concluded this short letter with an almost curt comment: "It seems impossible to me, my dear colleague, that we cannot satisfy this request when it is supported by such precise information as that which the United States minister makes known to us."[53]

The shipbuilders sent their "explanations" to Chasseloup-Laubat on October 16, but the letters were not received in the department of marine until October 18 and 20. This made little difference because they revealed nothing new. Arman, unaware of the contents of the Trémont papers, denied any wrong doing and still claimed that the four clipper ships were destined for the China seas. He protested his perfect right, under the law of July 12, 1847, to complete the ships and announced it as his intention to fulfill his contractual responsibilities. He did state that he had no intention to arm the ironclads.[54] Voruz made much the same claims regarding his work. He further denounced the person—apparently still unsure of his identity—who claimed to have proof that the ships were being built for the Confederacy.[55] These letters indicate that neither of the shipbuilders fully realized the seriousness of the situation. Arman apparently thought that the plan of action he had outlined to Bulloch the previous summer was still adequate. He seemed fully confident that he could deliver the armed clippers and the unarmed ironclads on schedule to the Southerners.

But this confidence was soon broken. On October 19, Drouyn de Lhuys and Chasseloup-Laubat met and agreed on their course of action. They determined, although Arman claimed he had a right to build the ships, that under article ten of the July 12, 1847 ordinance the government could prevent their construction. But the two ministers were less interested in their construction than in their arming, and they agreed to withdraw the authorization granted to Voruz to manufacture the arms for the clippers. Chasseloup-Laubat further agreed to submit to the foreign minister on the question of the departure of the ships. When completed, the ships could leave the ports only with Drouyn's permission and only with "the usual papers, properly authenticated." They equivocated, however, in regard to the ironclads. Since Arman did not intend to arm them, the ministers expressed no objections to their construction.[56] The next day in a conversation Drouyn told Dayton of these decisions—making no mention of the ironclads—and promised to send him copies of all the pertinent orders. On October 22 Drouyn informed Washington directly of the steps he was taking in the matter, and at the same time sent this letter to Dayton:

> I have the honor to announce to you, as a sequence of my letter of the fifteenth of this month, that the minister of marine has just notified M. Voruz of the withdrawal of the authorization which he had obtained for the armament of four vessels in course of construction at Nantes and Bordeaux. Notice [of the withdrawal of the authorization] has also been given to M. Arman whose attention, at the same time, has been called to the responsibility which he might incur by acts in opposition to our declaration of 10th June 1861. These measures testify, Sir, to the scrupulous care which the Government of the Emperor brings to the observance of the rules of a strict neutrality. It is in order to give your Government a new proof of our dispositions in this respect that we have not hesitated to take into consideration the information the authenticity of which you have affirmed to me.[57]

Dayton, although noting that the letter was something less than the promised copies of the orders, was nonetheless satisfied with Drouyn's actions. In Washington, Seward, who had been apprehensive throughout October, was pleased to receive the news. The president was satisfied and Seward called the act which revoked the license to arm the ships "a wise and just proceeding, equally honorable to France and loyal to the relations existing between that country and the United States." Mercier assured Drouyn de Lhuys that "all disquietude had been dispelled."[58]

Arman's confidence in the approval he had previously received from the emperor seems to have been severely shaken by Chasseloup-Laubat's new orders. By the tenth of November he stopped all work on the ships, and his yards, the Federal consul reported, were quiet. Not a man was to be seen at work there.[59]

But Drouyn de Lhuys was not confident that the ships would be detained. Lord Cowley, the British ambassador, aware that the construction of the ships was being protested by the United States and knowing that his own government was facing the same problem, had frequently prodded the French foreign minister for information. But not until November 3 did Drouyn talk. He then told Cowley of the Trémont papers and of the decisions he had made in regard to prohibiting the arming of the ships. Cowley felt that it was "evident from Drouyn de Lhuys' language that Chasseloup-Laubat will allow these ships to proceed to sea if it is possible," since "according to the law of France he cannot prevent an unarmed ship, built for a foreigner, from leaving the dock in which she was constructed." When Cowley asked if a ship "furnished with a ram would be considered unarmed," Drouyn replied: "I would rather not entertain this question until it is forced upon me."[60] Obviously Drouyn did not consider the matter closed; he also was reluctant to face up to the diplomatic implications which the new technology of naval architecture was creating. Cowley's inferences from Drouyn's language also suggest that the foreign minister believed that Chasseloup-Laubat was somehow involved in the original scheme to deliver the armed clippers to the Confederates. At any rate, as of his discussion with Cowley, Drouyn could be sure only that the clippers would not be armed in France; he was not sure that he could prevent their delivery, unarmed, to the Confederates. And he refused to even consider the ironclads until forced to do so. In other words, although the construction may have temporarily stopped, the ultimate fate of the vessels still rested upon the effectiveness of Confederate pressures and of Federal protests.

John Slidell did not long delay in applying the pressure. On November 6 he wrote a note directly to Napoleon III. His wording, made choppy by cypher, reveals his dependence upon the emperor as opposed to the ministers:

> The confident assertions of agents of the Washington Government and certain remarks made at ministries of foreign affairs and marine lead undersigned to apprehend that, without consulting your Majesty, orders may be given that will interfere with the completion and armament of ships of war now being constructed at Bordeaux and Nantes for the Government of the Confederate States. The undersigned has the most entire confidence that your Majesty, being made aware of the possibility of such interference, will take the necessary steps to prevent it. The undersigned has no access to the minister of marine and does not feel authorized to state to the minister of foreign affairs the circumstances under which the construction of these ships was commenced.[61]

Slidell's reference to the orders which "may" be given reflects that he did not possess full information on the actions taken by Drouyn and by Chasseloup-Laubat. His reluctance "to state to the minister of foreign affairs the circumstances under which the construction of these ships was commenced" confirms again that Drouyn had not been privy to the Arman plot. Apparently, as of November 6, Drouyn was still unaware of Napoleon's involvement in Arman's original misrepresentations. If so, such innocence did not last long. The day after Slidell's note reached the emperor, Drouyn, not Napoleon, responded by inviting Slidell to call upon him on the ninth. Napoleon, faithful to his promise and probably unaware of all the incriminating evidence contained in the Trémont papers, had instructed Drouyn to discuss the matter with Slidell

This interview had a profound effect upon the foreign minister. In his dealings with Chasseloup-Laubat he had been able to assert his position over the marine minister; but on November 9 he learned, apparently for the first time, the full extent of Napoleon III's involvement in the Confederate naval construction program. At first, Drouyn took "a rather high tone" with Slidell. Undoubtedly with the memory of the Roebuck interview still fresh in his mind, he told the Southerner that whatever had passed between him and the emperor was confidential. "France will not be forced into a war by indirection," he continued. "When we are prepared to act, we will do so openly; peace with the North will not be jeopardized on an accessory and unimportant point, such as the building of one or two vessels. We are bound by our declaration of neutrality." But Slidell refused to be silenced. He gave Drouyn a detailed account of the whole affair, saying that the idea had originated with the emperor and was carried out not only "with his knowledge and approbation but at his invitation." The emperor's role was so confidential, he continued, that "it was not to be communicated but to a few necessary persons." Slidell then played his trump card: This secretiveness "does not deprive me of the right to invoke, as I do, an adherence to promises which were given long after the neutrality declaration." Calmly, then, Slidell had put the matter squarely on the point of the emperor's honor. How could Drouyn, without knowing more of Napoleon's desires, without securing more official support for his own policy of neutrality, continue to berate the Southerner? His tone changed, and he spoke more softly. Indeed, Slidell was impressed, "and took leave of him satisfied that the builders would not be interfered with."[62] The Confederate's pressure diplomacy appeared to have worked.

A few days later, Slidell held a less satisfying conversation with Chasseloup-Laubat. Drawing a broad line of distinction between the clippers and the ironclads, the minister of marine suggested that with care the former could probably be put to sea, if unarmed. But, despite his October 19 agreement with Drouyn, he said that the rams were so obviously constructed for warlike purposes that to allow them to go to sea, even without cannon, would violate French neutrality and would amount to "an overt act of hostility" against the United States.[63] He was reflecting, no doubt, Napoleon III's original admonition to Slidell that the ships' "destination be concealed." But Drouyn de Lhuys made no mention to Dayton of this disposition of the question of the rams; indeed, he seems to have been awaiting some future developments concerning these novel warships.

Slidell's confidence in the emperor concerning the clippers was misplaced because he had not reckoned with the determination of the Federal agents nor the tenacity of Drouyn de Lhuys. John Bigelow, not content with Dayton's diplomatic protests to Drouyn, early consulted Pierre Antoine Berryer, an outstanding French lawyer and the leader of the opposition in the legislative body. A legitimist, Berryer was a consistent critic of Napoleon's Mexican policy and its apparent pro-South corollary. Bigelow sought Berryer's advice regarding legal action against Arman and Voruz. The lawyer agreed that the steamers should not be allowed to leave the ports; but he added that if the government decided to extend recognition to the Confederate States, then a court action would avail nothing because the judges would decide according to the government's dictate.[64] Dayton, however, doubted the wisdom of any court action because such an action would have to be brought by the French government.[65] Berryer submitted an elaborate brief to Bigelow in which he claimed that "all persons engaged on those vessels at Bordeaux and Nantes are responsible to the criminal laws of France." He cautioned that before a suit could be instituted against Arman personally, permission would have to be requested and received from the legislative body. Dayton felt that such a suit was unwise because he could not be sure of the result. Accordingly, Bigelow dropped the idea.[66] But his time and effort had been well spent, and proved to be of immense value later when the whole affair was publicized.

Drouyn de Lhuys, too, pressed on in his effort to enforce French neutrality. Despite his conversation with Slidell, he called in the two builders and personally told them that unless they furnished him with the clearest evidence that they had sold the ships to some other *bona fide* government, they would not be permitted to go on with their work. He willingly passed on to Chasseloup-Laubat Dayton's complaint that work on the vessels had been resumed even without proofs of such sales.[67] By the end of December, Drouyn reported to Dayton that Arman was seeking some other purchaser for the ships. Under these circumstances, he said, he felt that he could not stop construction of the vessels; but he did promise that he could and would prevent their arming and delivery to the Confederates.[68] Dayton was satisfied for the time being, but he maintained through his consular agents a strict surveillance of the shipyards, and through Bigelow an open avenue to Berryer for legal counsel.

Secretary of State Seward approved Dayton's constant "remonstrances with Drouyn de Lhuys" and added some pressure of his own. He instructed his minister in Paris to tell Drouyn de Lhuys that there could no longer be any doubt as to the purpose of the ships and that if France allowed the ships to leave it would, actually, be allowing the enemy to make war on the United States directly from French ports. He further stipulated that in the view of the United States government the Southern agents had a deliberate design to involve the United States and France in a war. Unless something was done by the French government, Seward concluded, the people of the United States could not but entertain strong anti-French feelings. Drouyn asked that a copy of this dispatch be left with him.[69] With Seward's warning words before him, Drouyn drew up a memorandum on the Bordeaux and Nantes ships. He was preparing to win support within the French government. At a council meeting on January 26, 1864, he received approval of his proposal for handling the ships according to the obligations of French laws. The arrangements were the same as those he had agreed to on October 19, 1863, with Chasseloup-Laubat.[70] Despite the knowledge of Napoleon III's personal interest in the ships, of which he had learned from Slidell on November 9, by the end of January Drouyn de Lhuys had gained the cabinet's approval of his handling of the affair, and he had secured his department's control over the ships.[71]

Thus, the Federal protests had succeeded within five months in preventing the armament of the clipper ships, but they had not succeeded in halting their construction. Drouyn had promised that the ships would not be delivered to the Confederates, and he had gained decisive control over them despite the emperor's personal interest. But because of the continued construction of the clippers, the ambivalence regarding the ironclads, and the constant rumors of sailing dates, the shipbuilding remained a lively diplomatic problem throughout 1864.

Rumors of Sailings

Rumors concerning the completion and sailing of the ships abounded throughout the year.[72] They served no purpose except to confuse the diplomatic picture. From all the distracting details three distinct developments emerge which had bearing upon the ultimate determination of the issue. First, the appearance of the CSS "Georgia" off the coast of France—in conjunction with the rumored sailing of one of the clippers—prompted Drouyn to issue his strongest statement of neutrality; then a Federal effort to coerce the French government into decisive action by publicizing the construction of the ships backfired and forced Drouyn to delay his stern orders to Arman; this, finally, led to the sale of the ships to other governments causing mutual suspicion and, eventually, the surreptitious delivery of one ironclad to the Confederates. These matters were being negotiated and discussed while excessive use of French ports by belligerents was forcing France to adopt new regulations on that subject; while efforts were being made to ship tobacco out of Virginia; and while the French were becoming more deeply involved in Mexico through their sponsorship of Maximilian. The time lapse required to exchange dispatches between Paris and Washington, and the ever-present rumors, coupled with the real, interacting problems, created a most tangled and involved diplomatic picture.

The Federal protests based on the Trémont documents had produced the French government's order that unless the Arman ships became the property of a neutral state, they could not put to sea. By January 1864 the Confederate agents realized that despite Arman's original assurances they might well lose all the vessels, and Slidell, Mason, Commodore Barron, and Bulloch met in Paris to determine future policy. They decided since Napoleon had "fully assented to the arming and departure of the corvettes," that they would retain title to the clipper ships in the hope that a change in the general situation would allow them later to be commissioned as Confederate warships; and since Napoleon had "consented only to the building of the iron-clads" but not to "their sailing unless their destination could be concealed," the Southern agents decided to authorize their sale.[73] Slidell and his friends relied on the imperial promise in their efforts to salvage at least some of the ships.

Arman immediately agreed, and "hastened to propose" the rams' sale "to those governments with which I am already in contact," and he offered the wooden clippers as well as the iron-clads.[74] Both the Italian government and emperor-designate Maximilian inspected and rejected them.[75] The shipbuilder then turned to Denmark. Since the Schleswig-Holstein problem had led to hostilities between Denmark and Prussia on February 1, 1864, he found in neutral Sweden a sympathetic banker who was willing to buy them and then sell them to the Danish government. Arman offered to let Drouyn read his contract, but so sure was the foreign minister of its validity that in a moment of misplaced trust he declined to do so. Everyone involved, even Bulloch, assumed the sale was to the Swedish government. When Dayton checked, the Swedish foreign minister naturally denied the existence of a contract between Arman and his government, and Dayton quickly passed copies of this correspondence to Drouyn.[76] But by the time the French foreign minister learned that Arman had misled him, other events had changed the picture. As of late March, Drouyn still thought the ships had been sold to a neutral government, and he assured Dayton that the six ships "would certainly be disposed of to neutral countries."[77]

Drouyn fervently wanted the ships sold to neutrals because at that moment Maximilian was preparing to sail to his new country. The foreign minister called Chasseloup-Laubat's "most serious attention" to the need "to avoid all acts which would in the eyes of the United States constitute serious and founded complaints" because they could create a situation fraught with dangers and unfortunate consequences "if it should adversely affect the enterprise which we pursue in Mexico."[78] The opinions which Dayton and Bulloch had expressed separately when the Trémont papers were first given to Drouyn were apparently justified, but for a reason neither had anticipated. It was not the fortune of war in America as such, nor the whim of the emperor, that led the French government to prohibit the delivery of the ships to the Confederates—rather it was the deepening French involvement in Mexico. Confederate Navy Secretary Mallory, not appreciating this, considered the decision to sell the ships as a "sudden prostration of well grounded hopes." "Among all the bitter experiences of the war," he wrote, "this disappointment stands prominently forth, presenting as it does among other considerations, a violation of faith, which challenged, and received our confidence."[79] In retrospect, Mallory's disappointment and frustration has a peculiarly ironic twist because he, like others both North and South, had expected the French involvement in Mexico to lead to a more active French support of the Southern cause.

That it did not is confirmed by another incident relating to the Bordeaux ships. The Confederate cruiser "Georgia" appeared off a French harbor in February and received a stern warning forbidding her to stay for more than twenty-four hours. Although indicating his intention to comply with the regulation, the skipper kept his ship just off the French coast until late April.[80] This led the Union officials, despite the French assurances of the clippers' sale to neutrals, to suspect that the "Georgia" was waiting to transfer men and munitions to one of the Bordeaux ships. Dayton expressed his distrust of Arman who, he thought, would "by chicanery or prevarication of any kind" try to deliver his ships to the Confederates.[81] Actually, in this case he was wrong in his evaluation of the man and the situation. The "Georgia," condemned by the Confederate high command, was waiting to transfer her own guns and personnel to the CSS "Rappahannock," lying in the Calais harbor. Eventually this plan was foiled by the French, and the "Georgia" was sold without being able to move her equipment to any other vessel.[82]

Dayton's complaints and the "Georgia's" hovering elicited from Drouyn de Lhuys the clearest statement of his position on neutrality; in it are to be found overtones of the Mexican affair and of Drouyn's desire to remain strictly neutral in accordance with the French declaration of neutrality. Recalling this declaration to Chasseloup-Laubat, Drouyn wrote:

In order to conform to this obligation we have denied MM. Arman and Voruz the use of a certain authorization which we had thought to be able to grant to them without inconvenience. I do not return to that affair because the ships they at first intended to deliver to the Confederate government have since received other destinations; but I must inform you of new facts which will not be less contrary to our neutrality if we tolerate them.

Stating that the "Georgia" was waiting to arm the clippers, Drouyn described the many seamen who claimed to be assigned to the "Georgia" as actually awaiting the launching of one of the clippers which, rumor had it, was to take place the next day. He continued his letter:

> This information was communicated to me by the legation of the United States which confirms its correctness, and we cannot, then, fail to take it into account. The American agents exercize, as you know, a most active surveillance on all acts in which they can uncover a practical deviation from a strict neutrality. You know, at the same time, my dear colleague, how the feelings in the United States have been manifested so unfavorably towards us: the recent vote of the senate in Washington against the recognition of the Mexican empire is a significant indication. I need not insist on the high political interest which the emperor's government holds in the present circumstances to avoid exciting this hostile tendency on the other side of the Atlantic. The most grave embarrassments could result for us and, consequently, we must try to prevent them, as much as possible, by giving to the Federal government no basis for complaint, no plausible pretext for its more violent recriminations against our attitude and our so-called ulterior motives. But the facts which I am calling to your attention inevitably provoke lively attacks against our loyalty, if we conceal them by our tolerance, when the authenticity of information furnished to us by the United States legation cannot be contested. I call, then, my dear count and dear colleague, your most serious attention to the whole situation which I have had the honor to indicate to you, and to the urgency of adopting the most proper measures to place beyond all question the responsibility of the emperor's government.[83]

The marginalia indicates that Chasseloup-Laubat immediately took measures to stop construction of the ships at Nantes (in Voruz's yards) and to force the "Georgia" to adhere to the time limits set by French law. Although the "known facts" in this instance were not accurate, Drouyn's most revealing words were "our attitude and our so-called ulterior motives." It is as if he said: "We have tried to fool the Federals so far, but from now on we must not try this; we must act straight-forwardly and without prevarication." It is at the same time an admission of past deception and a promise of future honesty. Drouyn, the author of this future policy, indicated that France could no longer tolerate chicanery for the sake of the emperor's whim.

As of late April, then, the question of Confederate naval construction in France seemed to have been settled. Arman was actively seeking purchasers for all of the ships; the Confederates on both sides of the ocean were convinced the ships were lost to them; and the French foreign minister, because of Mexico, was determined to follow a policy of strict neutrality toward both belligerents, the emperor's wishes notwithstanding. Had the North let matters lie, the episode would have ended with the bona-fide sale of the ships to foreign governments; but Bigelow's aggressive activity and Dayton's fear of false sales would soon cast the problem in a new light and would give it new life.

Bigelow, the former newspaper man, felt that publicity would prevent any connivance by the French officials at delivery of the ships into the hands of the Confederates. He first attempted, in January, to circumvent the government press control by arming Berryer with copies of the Trémont papers to use in a debate on an amendment which Arman announced he would offer to the section on American affairs in the emperor's speech from the throne. Since parliamentary debates were reported in the press, Bigelow would have secured the desired publicity without in any way implicating the United States. To Dayton, the possibility seemed too good to be true—and he was right. Arman, possibly learning of Berryer's intentions, withdrew his notice of amendment and no discussion of the American war took place. Bigelow was disheartened and Secretary of State Seward called the withdrawal a "sad disappointment."[84] Such an exposé in

January probably would have helped Drouyn de Lhuys in his efforts to enforce a strict neutrality. Once the plan failed, however, and once Drouyn had gained the support he needed from the cabinet, any further publicity would threaten to reveal the emperor's personal role in the shipbuilding program and could hurt the Northern cause.

Thinking of the ships' uninterrupted construction, and frustrated by his failure to publicize the Trémont documents, Bigelow made another attempt to pressure the French government. He had often inspired pro-Union articles in opposition newspapers and his contacts with *Opinion Nationale* had been especially fruitful. In late April he gave Georges Guéroult, the senior editor and a member of the legislative body, the Trémont papers "to be used on his double responsibility as journalist and deputy, and his alone."[85] Impressed by the evidence, Guéroult had his chief writer on American affairs, A. Malespine, write an article which was entitled "The Southern Privateers" and accused Arman of constructing the ships in violation of French law. Before publication, Guéroult showed the article to both Arman and Rouher, threatening to print it unless they could show him incontestable proof that the ships were not destined for the South. Since neither man could, or would, give the proof, he published Malespine's piece in the April 30 issue of his paper.[86] The article was very strong, and it aroused immediate government protest. Minister of Interior Paul Boudet "scolded Guéroult for devoting so much space in his paper to the prejudice of the shipbuilding industry of France," and forbade him to present any further discussion of the matter in the press. Arman, he said, had threatened to enter suit against the government if the ships were interfered with.[87] Not realizing the implications, Bigelow was beside himself with joy. The article "fell like a bomb on the Corps Législatif," he wrote. "Malespine is doing well; he has earned a year's pay in the last month."[88]

In his enthusiasm Bigelow urged Seward to use more force against the French government to assure a favorable decision concerning the ships. This elicited a clear statement from Seward concerning his policy toward France in general and the ships in particular. It was as important as Drouyn's earlier note on neutrality:

> I regret that you think my course towards the French Government is too conciliatory and courteous. If our armies succeed as we hope, we shall have no conflict with France or with any foreign Power. So long as our success in repressing the slavery faction at home is doubted abroad, we shall be in danger of war with some one of the Maritime Powers upon some sudden provocation. If we escape war with all, my courtesy to France will have done no harm. If we shall at last, through unavoidable delay here, fall under the calamity of a foreign war, it will then have come soon enough; and we shall be none the less able to meet it for all the prudence we practised in trying to delay and, if possible, to avert it. I think, with deference to your opinion, which I always hold in great respect, that, with our land and naval forces in Louisiana retreating before the rebels instead of marching towards Mexico, this is not the most suitable time we could choose for offering idle menaces to the Emperor of France.[89]

Thus while Drouyn de Lhuys worried about Mexico, Seward worried about the progress of the Civil War. Both men realistically checked more active members of their governments and insisted upon concentrating upon these essentials. It was fortunate that, at a critical moment in the shipbuilding question, both men saw the best interests of their countries to lie in mild and conciliatory policies towards each other. But Bigelow's joy over the impact of Malespine's article was unabated. He did not see it as a mixed blessing, with a twofold effect upon the French ministers.

The first result of the article was a debate in the legislative body during which Jules Favre acted as the questioner. Rouher, now minister of state, armed with documents from the marine ministry, managed to answer Favre without revealing Napoleon's role in the matter.[90] John Slidell was surprised and disgusted. "The keynote now," he wrote, "evidently is to cajole the North until Maximilian is recognized at Washington."[91] Bigelow's joy seemed justified.

But below the surface another reaction was developing. The ministers were taking Arman's threatened suit against the government seriously because if the question got to the courts, Napoleon's complicity might appear. Not only did Boudet prevent the press from discussing the issue of the ships, but Drouyn de Lhuys and Chasseloup-Laubat temporarily, at least, assumed a hard line towards Dayton. Three days after the Malespine article had appeared, Drouyn de Lhuys told Dayton that "Arman had recently seen him" and insisted on his right to send the clippers to sea even if he had to do it "in the Courts of Justice." The Federal minister expressed little concern because "we can without difficulty" prove Arman's handwriting on the Trémont documents.[92] But Dayton had missed Drouyn's point: the French government did not intend to push Arman to the point of a hearing.

His ability to frighten the ministers gave Arman confidence. For the first time since he had understood the seriousness of the government's intentions, he began to think of getting at least some of the ships into Southern hands. He suggested to Slidell that by a false sale to Sweden one ironclad and two clippers could be transferred to the Confederates on the high seas.[93] Such renewed confidence sprang only from the impact of the threatened law suit. Slidell and Bulloch were more optimistic than they had been since January when they had agreed to sell the ironclads. Bigelow's journalistic coup had, indeed, backfired.

Arman, however, consistently proving to be his own worst enemy, soon lost the leverage the threatened court suit had provided. Dayton's proof that the shipbuilder had not entered into a contract with the Swedish government reached the marine ministry about May 1. A mix-up, which confused everyone, arose from the fact that Arman's contract, if indeed there was one, was with a Swedish banker, not the government. Both Drouyn de Lhuys and Chasseloup-Laubat for months had assumed that Arman was selling the ships to a neutral government; they now felt that their trust had been betrayed. Chasseloup-Laubat drafted a notice on May 1, 1864, informing Arman that since his claim to have sold the ironclads to Sweden had been proven false, the ships would not be permitted to take to the sea "unless and until Drouyn de Lhuys is otherwise satisfied."[94] But he did not send it until May 20, obviously waiting for the threat of a law suit to cool and until he had stronger evidence against Arman.

Meanwhile, the marine minister was gathering information on the clipper ships which presented a more delicate situation than the ironclads. Unlike the latter, which were considered warships by their very design, the clippers, unarmed, could legitimately be represented as commercial vessels. As such, the French government had no real right to dictate as to their sale. Chasseloup-Laubat had received reports from a local engineer of the marine department and two affidavits from the builders testifying to the purely commercial characteristics of the clippers.[95] These reports were in his hands when the Malespine article appeared and when Arman's threat seems to have so influenced him and Drouyn. But in May, after learning about the so-called Swedish contracts, Chasseloup-Laubat sent a Captain Pierre from his own office to inspect the ships. The captain's report proved to be the last weapon needed by Drouyn de Lhuys finally to force the sale of the ships to neutrals. The four clippers, the captain wrote, have special rooms for ammunition, facilities designed for cannon implacements, and deck hatches too small for cargo. They are "veritable ships of war, and good ones"; they could not "be used as commercial ships without extensive alterations."[96] This was the first evidence that the wooden ships, by their design and structure, could be considered warships. Drouyn de Lhuys and Chasseloup-Laubat felt that they had enough proof, now, to act against all six vessels. Accordingly, on May 20, 1864, Chasseloup-Laubat sent his draft of May 1 to Arman in Bordeaux and to the two builders in Nantes.

The minister of marine informed Arman of the proof which Drouyn had submitted to him that there was no contract with Sweden, reminded him of the October warning that he stood in grave danger of violating the provisions of the neutrality proclamation, and stated that in consequence Drouyn had called his "attention anew to the construction and destination" of the ships being built at Bordeaux. Referring to Arman's two clipper ships, the marine minister continued:

Today I let you know that under no pretext will I allow the vessels to be armed . . . until you have proved satisfactorily to the department of foreign affairs the sale which has been made by you to a foreign government. I gave the most positive orders to the maritime authorities to prevent the fitting out of the vessels in question until his excellency, Mr. Drouyn de Lhuys, notifies me to the contrary.[97]

The letters sent to Nantes on the same date were just as specific. Chasseloup-Laubat, using almost the exact terms of Captain Pierre in his report, said to each builder that there could be "no doubt as to the nature of the vessel." "The ship," he continued, "is a regular corvette of war, evidently made with a view to fighting, and . . . is suitable for no other purpose than that of war."

To employ her in commercial enterprises, he concluded, it would become necessary to change her internal arrangements, to make a hold and hatches for lading, and to alter and make anew the berth deck, to adapt it to the requirements of a packet boat service, taking passengers. Under such circumstances, I must tell you, gentlemen, that I will not let the rolls of the "San Francisco" ["Shanghai"] be opened, nor allow this vessel to leave in the condition in which she now actually is unless it can be plainly shown that she has been ceded to a foreign government, and that you shall have proved clearly to the department of foreign affairs the regularity of the sale.[98]

Thus the fate of the ships was sealed. They were not allowed to be equipped or to make trial runs until the foreign minister was satisfied that they had actually been sold to foreign and neutral countries. In regard to the ironclads the government's right to interfere so forcibly was clear; but it was only after Captain Pierre's report which placed the clippers in the same category— warships by architectual design, regardless of actual cannon aboard—that the government interfered as to them. Drouyn de Lhuys as of May 20, 1864, was in undisputed control of the ships, and since he had so clearly enunciated the compelling reasons why France must practice a true neutrality, the Confederacy had lost all chance of building a navy in France.

But the principals in the drama did not know the author; they were unaware that the last scenes had already been written and so they still played their roles with vigor and determination. Arman, scorning the mere ministers, went directly to the emperor to register complaint. Much to his surprise the emperor "rated him severely, threatened imprisonment, ordered him to sell the ships at once, bona-fide, and said, if this was not done, he would have them seized and taken to Rochefort."[99] Drouyn had done his work well; the builders could do nothing but sell the ships.

The ships built at Nantes caused no further diplomatic problems after Chasseloup-Laubat's notice of May 20. Voruz, the financially responsible contractor for the ships, went about the task of selling the vessels in a business-like manner. He settled his accounts quickly and equitably with Bulloch, who had nothing but praise for him.[100] The original contact for the purchase of the "San Francisco" and the "Shanghai" was made by Seward in Washington. Mr. F. L. Barreda, Peruvian minister resident in Washington, approached the secretary of state at first to coordinate his activities with the Federal agents in Europe to avoid any mistake that the Peruvian purchases might be for the Confederacy. This act in itself speaks well for the vigilance and effectiveness of the Union watchdogs in England and France. Eventually introduced to Voruz, in December Barreda informed the United States legation in Paris that he had completed the purchase of the two ships.[101]

Arman, however, was another story. He had four ships to sell—the "Cheops" and the "Sphinx," both ironclads, and the two clippers, the "Yeddo" and the "Osacca." Ultimately he sold three of them to Prussia and the remaining one, the "Sphinx," he managed to get into the hands of the Confederates as the "Stonewall." Even the three he sold, however, caused diplomatic problems because Arman resorted to indirect and underhanded procedures to deliver the ships to Prussia which at that time was a belligerent in the Danish war. These procedures aroused Dayton's suspicions, and he protested and threatened at every move Arman made.

Arman's contract with Prussia, signed on May 25, 1864, designated Goll and Company of Amsterdam as the purchaser.[102] Drouyn stipulated that the vessels could sail provided they were unarmed and left under the French flag.[103] Dayton, fearing that the ships might still fall into Confederate hands, sent a strong protest to Drouyn which elicited a sharp rejoinder. "If we wished to help the South," Drouyn wrote, "we assuredly would not do it in this petty, indirect way, but we would acknowledge them at once. That would do them a substantial service—it would give them a position and standing among nations. But this petty mode of proceeding with a view to help the South would be unworthy of a great nation like France."[104] Aroused now, he wrote to Washington to assure Seward that the sale of the ships was valid and that no harm could result to the United States by their departures from France. His country's responsibility ended with the delivery of the ships into neutral hands; any action the new owner might take could not be accounted to France. The secretary of state refused to accept Drouyn's arguments, but in a friendly tone he conceded that "the French government has taken proper care to guard against the vessels being used to make war on the United States."[105] Seward seemed to sense Drouyn's irritation with Dayton's constant bickering, and tried to soothe it.

Then Arman played directly into Dayton's hands. Instead of delivering his first ship to Amsterdam, he sailed it directly to Bremerhaven. Drouyn was furious because it was as much a violation of French law to sell the ship to Prussia—a belligerent in the Danish war—as it would have been to sell it to the Confederacy. After detaining Arman's other ships until the Prussian-Danish war was "almost over and peace made," Drouyn released them to Prussia.[106] Arman's violation of French neutrality placed Drouyn de Lhuys and Chasseloup-Laubat in an awkward position when Dayton, backed now by three powerful Federal warships,[107] warned that the two clippers still at Nantes would be subject to capture by the Union vessels should they leave the harbor. Drouyn, resignedly, sent the letter to Chasseloup-Laubat for action. The marine minister, his temper short, stated that the ships "under a French flag, manned by Frenchmen, are still French," and he threatened to allow the trial runs under the protection of French naval ironclads.[108] Apparently enjoying this controversy between the other two men, Drouyn passed Chasseloup-Laubat's letter to Dayton and settled back to await the reply. The Northern minister, diplomatically, chose to accept the note as France's guarantee that the Nantes ships would not be allowed to fall into Southern hands.[109] When the trial runs were permitted, Dayton ordered the Federal ships not to interfere.[110] At some cost to ministerial tempers, he had made quite clear the Federal determination to prevent the Confederates from gaining possession of the clippers.

All but one of the ships were delivered honestly to some other government. Arman's surreptitious means of delivery had only served to arouse tempers; it had not succeeded in getting a ship to the Confederates. Indeed, Bulloch had performed the sad and discouraging task in early August of travelling to Paris to sign the final sales contracts with Arman.[111] The Confederates could spend the rest of the year only in recriminations, blaming Trémont's treachery and Washington's "vast organized system of espionage," and in laments of the Federals' perjured informers and their practice of theft and forgery.[112] Actually, they should have blamed the determination of Drouyn de Lhuys—concerned as he was as to the Mexican policy of his emperor—to maintain a truly neutral position towards the American Civil War. For it was his assumption of control over the ships in Bordeaux and Nantes and his enforcement of a simple, self-interested neutrality which spelled disaster for the Confederate hopes of lifting the blockade and attacking Northern coastal cities. Because of him the French government had fulfilled its neutral obligations and had circumvented the emperor's original plan of helping the Confederate States construct a navy in France. But even Drouyn, watchful as he was, could not prevent the delivery of one ironclad to the Confederates.

The CSS "Stonewall"

When Captain Bulloch signed his release contract with Arman in August, he understood that the ironclads were sold, one each to Prussia and Denmark. Indeed, Bulloch's agent, Captain Eugene Tessier, frequently visited the shipyards during the autumn and reported that a Danish naval officer was supervising the completion of the ironclad known as the "Sphinx," and making some drastic changes which would not please Bulloch. The Danish war ended with an overwhelming Prussian victory, and Arman, in early October, anticipating that Denmark would no longer want or need the ship, offered in some way to deliver it to the Confederates. But Bulloch refused because the ship was still in an unfinished condition and because he thought the sale to Denmark was complete and bona-fide. Furthermore, since it was still under French jurisdiction, he saw no way of safely getting it to sea in Confederate hands.[113]

Arman's arrangement with Denmark was not straightforward. Because of the war, he planned to make a false delivery to a Swedish banker, a Mr. de Torneshjehn, who would then transfer the ship to Denmark. When he applied for permission to deliver the ship to Sweden, Drouyn de Lhuys instituted a thorough investigation, checking by telegraph with Copenhagen and speaking with the Danish minister in Paris. He learned that the ship was in fact consigned to the Danish government, but, since the Danish War was now over, he had no objections to the arrangement. He gave his approval for the ship to leave France, under the French flag and with a French crew, for delivery to Mr. de Torneshjehn.[114]

The ship left Bordeaux on October 15, 1864, as the "Staerkodder" and plowed her slow way northward into the rough waters of the English Channel and the North Sea. Although cleared for the Swedish port of Helsingborg,[115] she went directly to Copenhagen. There, after several trial runs, the Danish authorities rejected the ship primarily on the basis of the late delivery. In early November the Danish government notified Drouyn de Lhuys by telegraph that its "dealings with Arman were at an end." The foreign minister passed this ambiguous message to the marine minister with the penned question: "To what does this refer? Please send me information."[116] But there was no answer. Not knowing whether Denmark had ended its dealings with Arman by accepting the ship or by rejecting it, and hearing no more of the affair, Drouyn seems to have forgotten this obscure and misleading message. But it is certain, at least, that as of early November the French officials thought the ship was safely delivered into Danish hands, and that they had no sure information that Denmark had rejected the ship. It is also certain that the Confederate agents considered the ship to be out of their reach. For a month or so the "Sphinx," alias the "Staerkodder," remained in Copenhagen unclaimed by anyone.

Arman, meanwhile, became concerned lest he lose his large investment in the vessel. He protested the Danish decision, though not vigorously, and considered an offer from the Prussian government. Since the "Cheops," already purchased by Prussia, was still in the shipyards at Bordeaux,[117] it is most likely that Prussia simply suggested the earlier delivery of the "Sphinx" instead of the later delivery of the "Cheops." This would still leave Arman with one ironclad on his hands, so he returned to his first customer, the Confederate States. Henri A. de Rivière, an Arman agent, proposed to Bulloch once again that the ship be delivered to the Confederates. Bulloch, considering this time that the vessel was "clear of the French interference" and knowing that "the purchasers were desirous to annul their bargain," on December 16, 1864, entered into an agreement with Rivière to accept delivery of the ship.[118] Briefly, the two stipulated that Rivière would go to Copenhagen and engage a Danish crew to sail the ship as if to return it to Bordeaux. But by prearrangement the ironclad would rendezvous with a vessel dispatched by Bulloch bringing men, supplies, and munition. An exchange of crews would give the South possession of the ironclad at sea. Upon evidence of the successful conclusion of the operation, Bulloch would pay Rivière a commission of 375,000 francs. Realizing the difficulties of arranging the details of this plan and the delicacy of executing it, Bulloch entered into the task with his usual vigor and thoroughness. The ownership of the vessel still remained clouded. Rivière did not sell the ship to Bulloch; he merely acted as a delivery agent. Apparently, Arman had never completed the transfer of ownership to Denmark, or he had already accepted it back. The Bulloch-Rivière agreement made only one reference to Arman; it provided that "coal, provisions, and other stores necessary for the voyage to the rendezvous" would be paid for "in final settlement with Mr. Arman."[119] Bulloch considered himself to be entering into new arrangements with the shipbuilder, not continuing the original ones. He had

not considered the ship to have been constantly in French ownership because he thought it was important that the "vessel was
clear of French interference."

Bulloch asked Barron in Paris to appoint a captain for the vessel and he himself went to England to arrange for a rendezvous
ship. Barron selected Captain Thomas Jefferson Page and authorized him, upon assuming command of the vessel, to "commission her as a Confederate States man-of-war and proceed on
a cruise against the commerce of the United States, and in the
performance of other duties appertaining to the office of a national ship." He then suggested the raising of the blockade at
Wilmington, N.C., the interception of the California steamers,
a "dash at the New England ports and commerce," and a "few
days cruising on the banks to inflict severe injury on the fisheries
of the United States."[120] Such were Southern expectations of
this one vessel! While Barron was expressing these hopes in the
form of orders, Bulloch was busy securing the English-owned
"City of Richmond" which was loaded to run the blockade at
Wilmington under the command of Hunter Davidson, a commander in the Confederate Navy. The owners agreed to delay
their trip in order to cooperate in Bulloch's enterprise. All that
was needed now was careful maintenance of secrecy and complete coordination between the various participants.

Rivière and Page were both in Copenhagen with the ship, and
by pre-arranged code they informed Bulloch of their preparations. Bulloch was carefully assembling a crew from the officers
in France and from the seamen who returned to Europe from
the captured CSS "Florida," now temporarily assigned to the
"Rappahannock" in Calais. His biggest worry was that the
Federal agents would get word of the operation and in some way
disrupt it. Indeed, Bulloch claimed severe "difficulties resulting
from want of prudence and from indiscretions" on the part of
compatriots who had somehow heard of the movement. One
night in a Paris railway station he met several young Confederate
naval officers who knew of the plan and who asked to be assigned
to the ship. This, he said, "forced me to make a partial confes-
sion in order that I might warn them to secrecy and caution."
His own clerk, from whom Bulloch had been careful to keep all

information, somehow had learned of the ironclad; and by a letter from Lieutenant Shyrock, Bulloch discovered "that the affair is very generally talked about in Paris." All this, he felt, had served to bring the USS "Niagara" to Dover and "spies . . . to Calais to tamper with the men on board the "Rappahannock."[121] But his fears were groundless. If the Confederate community was talking, the Union community was not listening. The "Niagara" had been sent to European waters as the result of a much earlier decision, and the Federal agents reported nothing of the Rivière plot.

Indeed, plans went smoothly. Telegrams sped between Copenhagen and London in words that spoke of buying and selling teakwood, but told of the movement of ships.[122] Finally, all was ready and the "Sphinx," alias the "Staerkodder," and now named the "Olinde" sailed from Copenhagen on January 7, 1865, with a Danish crew and captain and with Page and Rivière as passengers. The winter was severe, and the seas were high. The small ironclad, built for the smooth waters of rivers and coastal bays, had to put in at Elsinore, Denmark, and again at Kristiansand, Norway. She reached Nieuediep on January 20 where, by Bullock's careful planning, Lieutenant F. W. Carter had arranged for coaling. The "City of Richmond" sailed towards the rendezvous heavily loaded with men, munitions, and provisions for the ironclad, all in addition to the cargo for Wilmington. The two ships fought the storm-tossed seas; the heavy "Olinde" failed to rise with the swells, but rather went through the waves, "diving and coming up after the fashion of a porpoise."[123] The "City of Richmond," buffeted by the Channel winds and high seas, had to take refuge in Cherbourg to wait out the storm. Despite this, they did finally make their rendezvous in unguarded French waters just off Belles Isle, in the roads of Palais near the island of Houat. There, a third ship, the "Expéditif," from St. Nazaire, joined them with coal. She took off Rivière and the Danish seamen and departed. Page welcomed his crew aboard from the "City of Richmond," transferred provisions and munitions to the ironclad, and ordered the men to clean the filthy ship.[124] Finally, Page commissioned the ship the CSS "Stonewall," a name suggested by Bulloch as one "not inconsistent with her character and one which will appeal to the feelings and sympathies of our people at home."[125] For two days the ships remained in French waters, inevitably drawing attention and diplomatic comment to themselves.

In the morass of his detailed planning, Bulloch made one decision which is baffling; he selected a rendezvous point within French territorial waters. Earlier he had expressed relief that the ship in Copenhagen was "clear of French interference," and he had carefully removed the officers and men from France to England. Why, then, did he direct them back into the very jurisdiction he had so joyfully escaped? Why did he risk the vigilance of the Federal spies who, he claimed, had been aroused by loose Confederate talk? He not once anticipated disclosure or difficulty from this source. There seems no compelling reason for selecting the particular meeting place except that it was isolated and not under the direct surveillance of French maritime authorities. But there were other isolated and protected spots along the European coasts. Perhaps he had thought it necessary because the Danish captain had been hired to take the ship back to Bordeaux. The decision almost escaped repercussion because the Federal agents actually did not learn of the ships' presence until the day of their sailing. The only miscarriage of plans was that the "Expéditif" failed to return with additional coal. On January 28, the two vessels steamed away from Houat island, out of French territorial waters, and into the Bay of Biscay. All went well at first, the two ships travelling within sight of one another at about nine knots. But the next morning the seas began to rise, and as severe a storm as Commander Davidson had ever seen anywhere in the world swamped the ironclad, which again failed to ride the swells; indeed, the sea "seemed at times to cover her from knightshead to taffrail."[126] Running low on coal, Page headed his ship toward Spain. Having sprung a leak one day out, she limped in to the harbor of La Coruña on February 2, 1864. The younger officers aboard the "Stonewall" found the voyage to be unpleasant and the vessel to be not only unseaworthy but unequal to the tasks assigned to her. They described the trip in these words:

We left Belles Isles on the 28th January, standing across the Bay of Biscay with a comparatively smooth sea, going 8 to 9 knots. That night it came on to blow, and we put into this port [La Coruña, Spain] and anchored Feb. 2nd.

On the first day out, notwithstanding the favorable weather, it was observed that with a speed of 8 or 9 knots, the water would have flooded the forward turrets had the port been opened for exercise; and consequently, the berthdeck, forward shellroom and forward magazine would have been also flooded by the water pouring through the ammunition scuttles.

With a top-gallant breeze, her decks and turrets were flooded, and since they both leak, her quarters, both for men and officers, were rendered wholly unfit to be occupied.

This was not all. The watch officers were convinced that she could carry coal enough for only five days steaming, that she did not respond to her sails, and more important, they were convinced "of the impracticality of using her guns, or even of exercising them, except under more favorable circumstances than we have reason to expect." The ship, they maintained, even if she were to reach the American coast, "would not be in condition to accomplish anything nearly adequate to the slight chances of success attending the efforts of making the passage." Finally, they urged Commodore Barron, "before permitting her again to proceed to sea," to order "an inquiry into the real and true condition."[127]

So extensive were her needs that she transferred to the larger facilities across the bay at El Ferrol and remained there until March 24. During that time the Federal agents, who learned of the "Stonewall's" existence only because of the activity at Houat Island, were able to bring both diplomatic and naval pressure against her, and thus to delay her journey.

John Bigelow, chargé d'affaires since Dayton's death in November, received his first information about the "Stonewall" in the early afternoon of January 28 through the Danish consul at Nantes, after she had already cleared French waters.[128] Checking with his own consul, Bigelow thought that there were two warships, and submitted a note to Drouyn de Lhuys, calling attention to this alleged violation of French neutrality.[129] The next day he went personally to Chasseloup-Laubat, who professed complete ignorance about any such ships, explaining that the place under question was remote and not under surveillance of the usual naval forces. Thinking the intruding ships were still there, he said there was nothing he could do about them because no government guns could reach the point. "But," he continued, "Arman has deceived me twice before and he might easily try again. I will telegraph at once for information."[130] The marine minister, however, delayed the investigation until he heard from the foreign minister. On January 31, three days after the Bigelow-Chasseloup-Laubat conversation, Drouyn sent a copy of Bigelow's January 28 note to Chasseloup-Laubat with a request for information. Only then did the maritime minister telegraph his officials for information concerning the identity and movements of the ships. The maritime agents at Belle Isle, Nantes, St. Nazaire, and Auray took depositions from the crew of the "Expéditif" and others, and reported to the ministry. Chasseloup-Laubat was thus able to identify the vessels and to reconstruct their movements.[131] But this took time, and Bigelow was impatient.

His conversation with Chasseloup-Laubat had centered around the question of the ownership of the ironclad. The French minister claimed it was Danish, which relieved France of all responsibility for its actions. Bigelow immediately contacted the Danish legation and satisfied himself that the ship had never been accepted, much less paid for, by the Danish government; Arman, he concluded, had remained the owner and in complete control of the vessel.[132] But Bigelow never did learn of the false sale to the Swedish banker. At any rate, he wrote a second note to Drouyn and personally handed it to him on February 2. The foreign minister, accepting the note, refused to enter into a discussion because, he said, he had to await Chasseloup-Laubat's report.[133] So far, Bigelow had made little headway with the French officials.

Two days later he received a telegram from the United States chargé in Madrid, Horatio Perry, informing him that the "Stonewall" had entered La Coruña harbor. On Sunday morning, prompted by another message from Perry, Bigelow called upon Drouyn at the Quai d'Orsay. Happy to find him in, he immediately informed him that the ship was now at El Ferrol and asked Drouyn to request the Spanish government to detain it. The foreign minister rather laconically replied that he had not yet received the marine department's report and so could not really discuss the matter. "Why don't you go to the minister of marine's office to see about the report," Drouyn suggested. Obediently Bigelow drove his carriage across to Chasseloup-Laubat's department. The minister of marine joined in the spirit of the game, saying that the report was about to be sent to the foreign minister and indicating that if Bigelow called upon Drouyn at two o'clock he could get his answer. But when he arrived back at the foreign ministry Bigelow was told Drouyn had gone out for a ride! The American was furious. He had allowed himself to be treated like an errand boy and had been able to talk to no one. He had to content himself with writing another note to Drouyn de Lhuys, reiterating his request that France act through the Spanish government to detain the vessel.[134] Thus another day passed.

On February 7, having received the maritime report, Drouyn finally answered Bigelow's letters. The report did identify the "Olinde" as the "Sphinx," one of Arman's ironclads. Drouyn was determined to maintain the policy of neutrality which he had previously imposed on the Confederate naval construction program. As he saw the present case, if he admitted that the "Stonewall" entered Confederate service directly from French ownership and while it was within French territorial waters, that policy would be demolished. Taking the line first suggested by Chasseloup-Laubat, Drouyn insisted that the previous October he had taken particular care to assure himself that Arman's sale of the vessel to Denmark was real and final. He found nothing in the marine report to change his conclusion, he wrote to Bigelow, and he could not question the shipbuilder because Arman was in Berlin. As far as the French government was concerned then, the vessel had been Danish before it was commissioned as the "Stonewall" and France thus had no control over it nor responsibility for it. He advised Bigelow to direct his requests to Copenhagen or directly to Madrid. All the French government could do was to punish the St. Nazaire suppliers for having helped to increase the ship's fighting potential. He was happy to inform Bigelow, he concluded, that the marine minister's report was being sent to the minister of justice for his action.[135] By establishing Danish ownership of the vessel, Drouyn hoped to sustain his own policy of neutrality and to protect France against charges of responsibility for any future destruction the "Stonewall" might perpetrate against the United States. Drouyn seemed completely confident, furthermore, of the soundness of this position; later events justified this confidence.

After receiving Drouyn's note, Bigelow determined to let Seward handle the question of responsibility; he now concentrated on trying to prevent the ironclad from reaching American waters. Acting on a suggestion from Drouyn de Lhuys, Bigelow decided to send the available Federal warships to watch over the "Stonewall" and if possible to detain her. After much difficulty and some frustration, he reached Captain Thomas Craven of the USS "Niagara" and ordered him to El Ferrol. The "Niagara" arrived in the Spanish port on February 14, and a few days later the USS "Sacramento" joined her. Meanwhile, Perry had been active in Spain and had prevailed on that government to halt the repair work in progress on the "Stonewall." As of February 9, Bigelow judged that the Southern ironclad would be in El Ferrol for another season and he concluded that the attitude of the French government was of little importance.[136]

He was almost correct. Captain Page was not in complete disagreement with his watch officers. He gave "a bad account of the ship" to Bulloch and accused all who "were concerned with her outfitting and delivery [to] have been guilty of neglect, deception and cheating." Page asked that Arman send someone to El Ferrol who knew the ship to direct her repairs; Rivière, it appeared, had taken the only set of designs with him when he left her at Houat. Echoing his younger officers, Page wrote: "We cannot cruise and I know not into what port she can enter. . . ." Despondently, he decided to go to Paris for a conference with Slidell and Barron. Bulloch saw no reason for the trip because he was sending Tessier and an experienced engineer to El Ferrol to direct the repair work; he strongly criticized the skipper for leaving his ship when she needed him.[137] The Confederates, in their frustration, were falling out. Bigelow heard of Page's trip to Paris and vainly urged Drouyn to arrest him.[138]

Drouyn de Lhuys had become much annoyed with Arman because of the way he had helped the Confederates gain possession of the ship. He summoned the shipbuilder, now returned from Berlin, and severely censured him.[139] In this frame of mind, on February 16, Drouyn held a final discussion with Bigelow on the "Stonewall." The American was in a happier mood. Feeling safe with two United States warships at El Ferrol, knowing the ship needed extensive repairs, and reassured by Page's hurried trip to Paris, Bigelow relaxed and talked easily with Drouyn. The Federal chargé said that he was less interested now in the question of the nationality of the "Stonewall"; he asked Drouyn's intercession at Madrid only as a friendly gesture on the part of France to prevent the ship from preying upon United States commerce. Had the two diplomats known the ship as well as the Confederate naval officers did, they would have realized there was little danger of this. But Drouyn was highly pleased with Bigelow's comment; it took France off the hook of potential reponsibility, and he, too, relaxed and talked freely. He told Bigelow that at Madrid, Mercier, now French ambassador there, had let the Spanish government know that the detention of the "Stonewall" would not be unpleasant to him. Surprised, Bigelow remarked that "M. Mercier left upon the mind of our chargé at Madrid a different impression." "Of course he did," Drouyn replied, "it was his duty to do so, for he had no instructions which authorized him to act otherwise." From this Bigelow understood that Mercier "had considered himself instructed" to detain the vessel as long as possible without compromising his government with Spain, Denmark, or the United States; he was most happy with Drouyn's attitude and tone, and was convinced that the French foreign minister would soon take further action to prevent the "Stonewall" from going to sea.[140]

Bigelow had underestimated Drouyn's powers of diplomatic persuasion. The Frenchman did not intend to take direct action, but, with the Maximilian regime still unsecured in Mexico and with the Northern noose of Sherman and Grant drawing ever tighter around the Confederate nerve center of Petersburg and Richmond, Drouyn did want the American to think that France would act favorably whenever she could. He had taken the care to write to Washington in friendly terms as early as February 9, inclosing for Seward a copy of his February 7 note to Bigelow. After a discussion with Seward about the "Stonewall," Geofroy, the French chargé in Washington, was convinced that the secretary of state was "no longer very concerned with it." Indeed, Geofroy was right. With Sherman moving through the Carolinas and the most vital Confederate ports closed by capture, the Washington officials were less interested in resolving a diplomatic technicality than they were in preparing for the diplomacy of peace. As of March 11, 1865, when the "Stonewall" was still in El Ferrol, Seward informed his representatives in Europe that President Lincoln had directed him "on this occasion not to pursue further the question of ultimate accountability on the part of any foreign State, for what has been done or what has happened or whatever yet may happen in connection with the 'Stonewall'."[141] There was no need for any further diplomatic action. All of Bigelow's anxieties and accusations had produced no diplomatic change; Drouyn's policy of French neutrality, despite the acquisition of the ironclad by the South, remained unquestioned by Washington. The "Stonewall" had steamed across the seas, causing little more than a ripple in Paris-Washington relations.

Yet the diplomatic exchanges had not been for naught. The French marine report and Drouyn's correspondence with Chasseloup-Laubat and with Bigelow, in conjunction with the Confederate comments, prove conclusively that the French government had sincerely thought the sale of the ironclad to Denmark was real and final. The correspondence reveals, too, that Bigelow accepted Drouyn's sincerity despite his various demands; his charges of bad faith came only much later. But most important, it shows that although Napoleon III may have encouraged the initiation of Confederate naval construction in France, the French government did not participate in nor facilitate the delivery of the "Stonewall" to the Confederacy. Indeed, exasperated with Arman's activities, Drouyn had taken unofficial action in Madrid to detain the vessel at El Ferrol and had suggested that the Federal warships be sent to watch over her.

The diplomatic correspondence also highlights a characteristic of the "Stonewall" herself which has been strangely overlooked. Despite the modern technology of Arman's yards which had produced her, she was too finely designed. Basically the ship had very poor fighting qualities. It is true that the Confederate chiefs—Bulloch, Barron, Slidell—made her out to be a one-ship ultimate weapon that singlehanded could raise the blockade, lay waste to the North, and save the South from defeat. These men almost had to hold that opinion because otherwise all hope was gone. But the Confederate officers who served aboard her were not so sanguine. After wallowing in European waters, they would have laughed at the irony in Barron's orders to make a "dash at the New England ports"; and they knew better than any others that the "Stonewall" could not carry enough coal to cruise on the "banks to inflict injuries on the fisheries of the United States." They also knew that the 300-pounder in the forward turret, with no lateral movement, was useless in all but the smoothest of seas. Captain Page twice refused to do battle with the "Niagara" when the seas were just a bit rough.[142]   But on smooth waters, Captain Craven of the "Niagara" declined Page's challenge. Why? It seems he believed his own country's diplomatic agents. Dayton and Bigelow, strangers to the needs of a fighting ship, had emphasized only the "Stonewall's" strongest qualities—her armor and her powerful cannon. Craven read their reports and refused to do battle when he should have; he suffered through two courts-martial for his gullibility. After the "Stonewall" had arrived in American waters too late to participate in the war, another Union officer expressed an opinion about her. Acting Rear Admiral S. W. Godon had not read the diplomatic reports but he was "not very much impressed with her power," and judged that the " 'Canonicus' would have crushed her," and "the 'Monadnock' could have taken her beyond a doubt."[143] The "Stonewall" passed quickly through the American and into the Japanese navy where she remained on active duty for thirty years. The last American to comment on her, found her in Japan "in 1908, peacefully rusting away."[144]   Yet the legend of her invincibility has outlived the opinions held by the sailors who served aboard her.

Because the Civil War was almost over, the "Stonewall" affair was militarily "much ado about nothing." Perhaps it was just as well because the little ship could never have lived up to Confederate expectations.

The Confederate effort to construct a navy, such as Secretary of the Navy Mallory had envisioned at the beginning of the war, failed both in England and in France. At first the Confederates, encouraged by the acknowledgement of their belligerent status, depended too much on an early diplomatic recognition; then they resorted to circumvention of the declared neutrality of the two chief maritime powers, without fully realizing, it seems, that they needed favored, not neutral, treatment. Their efforts did raise several new questions of neutral obligations. Does a neutral government have a right to prevent a legitimate businessman from constructing and delivering to a belligerent government an unarmed vessel? Yes, the British government decided, if that ship is armed by the neutral country and enters directly into combat, as did the "Alabama." Does a neutral government have the right to declare a vessel, without guns, to be a warship by virtue of its architectural design alone? Perhaps so, the British government decided in the case of the Laird rams; but rather than risk a court test the government timorously purchased the ships for its own use. The French, on the other hand, answered by directing the builder on threat of governmental seizure to sell the ships to a foreign neutral government. And this decision applied not only to the ironclad rams whose war-making qualities were obvious, but also to those clippers which were designed to serve as merchantmen and whose war-making characteristics were limited to such things as the size of the hatches and the location of crews' quarters. The French had gone further than the British in defining neutral obligations as they pertained to ship construction for belligerents. These decisions were reached over a long period of time and were forged between the heat of diplomatic remonstrances and the incontrovertible results on the battlefields.

One of Mallory's first acts had been to authorize Lieutenant

North to buy or construct an ironclad in France; how ironic that such a ship finally did arrive off the Southern coast from France almost exactly thirty days after Lee's surrender at Appomattox. But the interval in France had seen some hard decisions, reached by realistic statesmen sometimes in spite of the dreams of their emperor. Drouyn de Lhuys, supported by the hobbling complexities of the French involvement in Mexico, and with a sharp eye on the fortunes of battle in America and another on the more important events in Europe—the Italian question, the Polish insurrection, and the Danish War—seized control of the Confederate naval construction program and imposed a self-interested neutrality. If Lieutenant North, Captain Bulloch, and Commodore Barron failed in their quest to construct a navy, it was less the result of their errors than of Drouyn de Lhuys' determination to enforce French neutrality. By early 1863 he had determined that the only way he could balance the overextension of French power in Mexico, Asia, and Europe was to accommodate the United States through a truly neutral treatment of both belligerents. Drouyn, hampered at times by Napoleon III, nonetheless applied the same formula to other problems of neutrality during the war years.

Chapter XIV

PROBLEMS OF NEUTRALITY: SHIPS AND HARBORS

WHILE some exchanges between Paris and Washington related to matters of high diplomacy such as mediation and recognition of the Confederacy, others proceeded on a lower level, leading to consideration of the rights of belligerents and neutrals viewed solely within the framework of international law. Of all the major European powers, France had a unique complication in its relations with the United States because each was a belligerent in a separate war and thus enjoyed the rights of neutrals separately. As events developed, questions pertaining to the American Civil War were of more importance than those pertaining to the Franco-Mexican War, but one nonetheless affected the other and this dual aspect implicitly or explicitly dominated the diplomatic exchanges between the two governments.

Incidents falling into this lesser category mainly concerned the maritime problems of belligerent ships in neutral harbors and the movement of goods between belligerent and neutral states. There were some serious affairs in which international law was discussed and occasionally changed; there were some humorous affairs in which officials of one country were bribed to perform their constitutional duties. But large or small, serious or humorous, these problems consumed the time and effort of diplomats and affected the mutual posture taken by the United States and France. The neutrality problems raised by belligerents' use of French ports proved to be one of the most consistent and irritating diplomatic issues of the Civil War period.

The implications of the Declaration of Neutrality in 1861 were far-reaching. France recognized the belligerent rights of the Confederacy, which the North officially and diplomatically refused to do; it recognized the efficacy of the Northern blockade of the Southern ports, which the Confederacy refused to do. Furthermore, France wanted to sustain the principles of the 1856 Declaration of Paris, which bound neither the North nor the South. The diplomatic problems implicit in this situation did not materialize until 1863, after the Confederacy had secured some vessels and needed the use of French ports. French municipal law—as opposed to international law—was very similar to that of England. Belligerent ships would be allowed in French ports and granted the use of the facilities only on the humanitarian condition that the ship was in need of repair to make it seaworthy and on the further condition that its armaments and personnel were not in any way increased during its stay in the port. France, unlike the other European countries, did not ban coal as a contraband of war; thus her ports were particularly attractive to belligerent ships in need of fuel. The law, however, did forbid any French citizen from serving on a belligerent vessel. All of these points were to be raised and sorely tested in 1863. Since the commanders of the United States ships had access to Northern ports, they did not as frequently request the use of French facilities as did the Confederate skippers. Without home ports, after sailing the seas for months, the Southern ships frequently had recourse to the repair and revictualling facilities to be found in France. Since the United States did not recognize these vessels as legitimate ships of war, the Northern diplomatic agents maintained constant vigilance at the ports and made recurrent complaints to the French minister of foreign affairs, Drouyn de Lhuys.

The Federal claim that all Confederate vessels were pirates was weakened when Congress authorized President Lincoln to issue letters of marque for the creation of privateers. Concerned for the safety of their commerce, the English discussed this threat with France and elicited an early statement from Drouyn de Lhuys on the belligerent right to use privateers. Secure in the knowledge that the congressional act was aimed at England,

Drouyn maintained that since the United States had not signed the Paris Declaration of 1856 she had every right to use privateers. But he hedged when asked if France would accept such a privateer as a regular vessel of war.[1] Although Lincoln refrained from exercising the power, the questions raised forced Drouyn de Lhuys to make a decision related to one aspect of a neutral's obligation toward belligerent vessels. Soon he would be forced to render decisions on other basic maritime questions, such as the legal status of Confederate cruisers, rules regulating belligerent use of French harbors and port facilities, and regulations controlling belligerent recruiting in French ports.

These basic questions were raised and settled largely as a result of incidents surrounding three Confederate ships: the "Florida," which put into the port of Brest in August of 1863 after many months of cruising, seeking repairs which she badly needed; the "Georgia," which put into Cherbourg in October, just in time to fan the flames of the controversy over the "Florida"; and the "Rappahannock," a vessel recently acquired from the British, which put into Calais later in November, seeking to refurbish and convert from a worn-out dispatch vessel into an armed cruiser. These incidents were further complicated by the activities—at the Arman and Voruz yards in Bordeaux and Nantes—which came to the attention of the Federal authorities in September 1863. Although all these problems interacted, the diplomats tended to treat them one at a time.

The Incident of the CCS "Florida"

On August 23, 1863, a large three-masted steamer, armed and flying the battle flag of the Confederate States, appeared off the harbor of Brest. Excitement spread through the populace as they recognized the battle flag, but concern arose among officials. The maritime prefect, having no experience in handling such a ship, wired Minister of the Marine Chasseloup-Laubat for instructions. Should he receive the ship as a recognized, legitimate vessel, or as an unofficial pirate? The minister responded that he should treat it as he would a vessel of any other country, but should make no specific commitments. As soon as he could consult the foreign minister, said the minister of marine, he would send further details.[2] Thus the problem of the "Florida" was placed immediately in the hands of the foreign minister and became a diplomatic question before the ship even entered the port of Brest.

The vessel under question was indeed an important one. Its career began on the banks of the Mersey River, in a shipyard in Liverpool, England. She was the first of the raiders acquired there by the Confederates. Unarmed when she left English waters, she went to Bermuda and there received some arms, a Confederate commander, and a new commission as the "Florida" of the Confederate States Navy. The skipper, Captain J. N. Maffitt, was dissatisfied with the armament and decided to risk the Northern blockade of Mobile, Alabama, in order better to arm and outfit the ship. After a daring escape from that Southern port, Maffitt guided the "Florida" on her equally daring career as a raider. Within eight months she had destroyed some thirty-six ships of the Northern merchant fleet. Time and effort took their toll of the "Florida" and by mid-August she was in need of rest. Being unable to enter a Southern port, Maffitt sought refuge in Brest. His arrival there was a surprise to both Captain Bulloch and to John Slidell.[3] The diplomatic problem had been considered by neither the French nor the Confederate agents in Europe. To the Federal agents in Europe the treatment which this notorious vessel would receive at the hands of the French was of primary importance. They wanted to prevent any help which might put the ship back into action. The French, for the first time, had to define their obligations as a neutral nation. The question was real and it was delicate.

While Drouyn de Lhuys was considering the case, he allowed certain minor concessions to the "Florida." Within a few days Maffitt was permitted to enter the harbor after unloading the ship's powder, and he was granted the right to receive commercial repairs. But Drouyn warned that the activities must "stay within the limits of neutrality," and he ordered a delay on all final decisions until he had determined the "form" that such arrangements should take.[4]

Drouyn had the advice of both William L. Dayton, the United

States minister to Paris, and of John Slidell. The former went to the Quai d'Orsay as soon as he learned of the ship's arrival, on August 24, but discovered that Drouyn would be out of town for a week. The next day he protested in writing: he stipulated that the "Florida" should not be permitted help of any sort; but, acknowledging the implications of the French recognition of Confederate belligerency, he insisted that should help be rendered, it should be limited to the narrowest possible interpretation. For instance, he wrote, the "Florida" had sailed all the way from Bermuda; obviously, if she could sail across the ocean without benefit of steam she did not need coal to make her seaworthy.[5] But Drouyn also consulted Slidell, and on September 3, 1863, he sent his decision to Chasseloup-Laubat. In a long letter filled with references to international law and to France's obligations under her declaration of neutrality of 1861, Drouyn rendered the following opinion: Since the "Florida" had no prize of war, she could stay in Brest until the repairs needed to make her seaworthy were completed; a ship being entitled to have all its normal facilities repaired, work on her steam equipment was included, even though she had sailed to Brest from Bermuda; the ship, however, could not be improved while in a French port—merely put back into working order according to her original state; and finally, since France had never considered coal to be a contraband of war, the "Florida" could be recoaled.[6] This letter reflected a decision completely in keeping with the obligations of a neutral and showed no favoritism to either side. Had it not been for later demands from both sides and for some legal proceedings inspired partially by the Federal agents in Paris, the incident would have ended with the ship's proper repairs and departure from Brest.

Captain Maffitt wanted more than the repairs which would make the "Florida" seaworthy. "Since leaving Mobile," he wrote to Bulloch, "we have been under a constant pressure, without a friendly port in which to overhaul or give ordinary attention to the engines." In addition, the shaft needed repair, copper needed replacing, and a blower was needed to "get steam with the bad coal we are often obliged to put up with."[7] Such repairs fell into the category approved by Drouyn. But Maffitt also needed repairs to his armament. The local customs authorities gave permission for Maffitt to land the ship's small arms for repair by a local gunsmith on the condition that they be not increased in quantity; but they refused permission to land the gun carriages to have them overhauled. How the work on the small arms was justified is not clear. Either Dayton did not get word of this, or he despaired of preventing it, for he does not mention it. Neither do the French archives contain references to it. If true, such work came close to violating the restrictions of neutrality. But there was an even more serious violation: according to Bulloch two gun carriages were made at Nantes and delivered later to the "Florida" at Belle Isle.[8] It is obvious from this that the Confederates exploited every opportunity to go beyond the neutral hospitality of the French.

A Brest merchant, one Mr. Menier, almost immediately entered two suits against the "Florida": the first for goods lost aboard one of her victims and the other for the cost of delay created when the "Florida" had forced one of his own ships, the "Bremontier," to detour in order to take aboard survivors. On September 2, 1863, Menier obtained a provisional order from the civil courts to seize the "Florida."[9] Dayton, sensing the possibility of using this legal suit as a means of keeping the ship off the high seas, sent Consul General Bigelow to Brest to investigate and to advise the litigant.[10] The suit did pose two significant questions of international law which forced the French government to make policy decisions concerning Confederate ships which it had so far avoided. The matter of the lost goods involved a clause of the 1856 Declaration of Paris which stipulated that neutral goods even under an enemy flag were not subject to capture by a belligerent; the forced detour of the "Bremontier" was a civil matter which could be brought only against an individual, not a sovereign state. Drouyn de Lhuys was charged with making these decisions for France,[11] and he had to decide whether a judicial decision should be allowed to establish a possible precedent relating to French policy towards a nonsignatory to the Paris declaration and, even more urgently, to determine official French designation of the character of Confederate ships.

Since neither belligerent was bound by the Paris declaration, they had little interest in the first case, and Drouyn, "anxious to avoid any precedent with regard to Maritime Law," easily prevented the issue from reaching trial.[12] The second case, involving classification of Confederate ships, was another matter. In Brest, Bigelow and Menier entered a suit for a 100,000 francs damage against Captain Maffitt on the legal assumption that the "Florida" was a privateer, citing the *Moniteur* of September 4, which had announced the arrival of "Le corsaire sous pavillon Confédéré le 'Florida'."[13] Unless the French government changed the "corsaire"—privateer—designation, not only would the suit be permissible in a civil court, but a precedent in French municipal law concerning all ships under the Confederate flag would be established. While Drouyn pondered the problem, George Eustis, acting in Slidell's absence, presented reasons for changing the ship's designation. The Union officials, perhaps too confident, failed at this time to submit the views of their government. Drouyn learned from Eustis's letter that the "Florida" was a "Confederate war steamer, forming part of the Navy of the Confederate States," which was outfitted in a Confederate port and whose officers were "regularly commissioned officers of that Government. . . ." In summary, Drouyn read, the ship is "in every respect a regular man-of-war, and not a privateer."[14] With no evidence to the contrary, and in view of France's recognition of Confederate belligerent rights, Drouyn felt compelled to change the status of the "Florida." He inserted in the *Moniteur* of September 16 a notice stating that the ship was not a privateer, but was a regular warship forming "part of the navy of the Confederate States,"[15] and later, attaching a copy of Eustis's letter, he notified Chasseloup-Laubat that Menier would have to withdraw his civil suit because such "private demands cannot be made against a regular navy vessel."[16] Thus, while the action could have been anticipated, the French extension of full naval status to Confederate ships actually resulted from Menier's civil damages suit, from Eustis's arguments and from the Federal failure to present a counterview. Henceforth, Confederate ships would receive the same treatment as the vessels of any nation with which France was at peace, including access to all port facilities and government shipyards, subject only to the French neutrality regulations. After Drouyn's decision concerning the "Florida," the North had no grounds to object when a Southern ship was received in a French port.

Even though this decision was important to the Confederates because they had no access to their own ports, it was not without frustrations. Captain Bulloch attested to both the importance and the frustration when, years later, he wrote that the "Florida" would have completed her repairs "within a few weeks" if she could have gone to any of the large British building yards and "there have done the work openly and in the ordinary commercial way."

> But, he continued, the constant peril of being stopped by an alleged violation of neutrality, the necessary applications of official personages on every small matter of detail, the hesitations, references to Paris, and general circumlocution, caused a great loss of time and a large increase in expenditure.[17]

The Confederates, while appreciating the use of French facilities, nonetheless lamented the enforcement of French neutrality. The frustrations extended even into the Quai d'Orsay because the Federals belatedly and constantly complained that the Confederates received favored and unneutral treatment.

Still another question of belligerent maritime rights was raised by the "Florida"—that of belligerent recruiting in neutral ports. Many crew enlistments had expired during the long cruise, and Captain Maffitt released seventy-five men upon his arrival in Brest. Arranging transportation for them to England, Maffitt carefully submitted affidavits to the French authorities, stating that he was "compelled to discharge" them, without, however, giving the compelling reason.[18] The recruiting problem centered upon whether the men were released voluntarily; if so, their replacement would not fall under the seaworthy or "act of God" clause of neutral practices. Further, when replacement was permitted, the question of the recruit's nationality and whereabouts became topics of controversy. Neither of these matters was covered by international law or practice.[19] In this case Dayton forced the French cabinet of ministers to make a decision, then he had to watch helplessly, but suspiciously, while the Confederates filled the "Florida's" crew.

When Dayton first heard of the seventy-five men leaving Brest, he thought they were being reassigned to the ironclads in England and contented himself by warning Seward.[20] But his agents soon furnished more accurate information, and on October 1 he protested to Drouyn that the "Florida" was recruiting sailors in England who would be shipped aboard in Brest which, he said, would be a clear violation of French neutrality.[21] Dayton also claimed that the men had been released voluntarily, submitting a letter from Maffitt to Bulloch which had somehow come into his possession. If this were so, he continued, the seaworthy principle should not apply in their replacement. Drouyn, who as yet had no other information on the subject, dismissed Dayton by remarking that the "neutrality of France will be maintained." "My whole purpose," he said, "is to settle the questions upon proper principles of international law."[22]

Drouyn had already sought the information he needed, and on October 21 received the Brest maritime prefect's report. The "Florida's" captain, the report stated, planned "to replace the men by the recruiting method generally used by ships whereby special agents, called 'agents pour équipager,' furnish on request of departing captains whether from this or other ports, foreign sailors who were abandoned or who deserted ships of their nationality." By this means, the report continued, Captain Barney, Maffitt's successor, could get the number of men he needed, "choosing naturally from among those of Confederate States origin." Barney "would not think . . . of recruiting in England."[23] Armed with Captain Maffitt's earlier affidavits and with this report, Drouyn submitted the question of Confederate recruiting to the cabinet of ministers.[24] From these documents the ministers concluded that the release of the men had not been voluntary, that indeed the enlistments had expired, and that the seventy-five sailors should be replaced in order to return the ship to its normal seaworthy condition. Noting from the Brest report that the Southerners had specifically denied any intent to recruit French nationals, and since the neutrality proclamation was silent on belligerent recruiting of non-French nationals in French ports, the cabinet concluded that the replacements could be enrolled in a French port. The ministers were particularly impressed by the maritime prefect's statement that the sailors, wherever possible, would be of "Confederate States origin." In keeping with the neutrality proclamation, the ministers stipulated that the "Florida" could depart with no more persons aboard than she had had upon her arrival.

Dayton protested this decision to allow Confederate recruiting in a French port as being unneutral and bad law. Drouyn replied calmly: "The council of ministers, who had unanimously arrived at the decision, did not consider it to be a bad one, and most of them are lawyers."[25] Despite further efforts, Dayton could not shake the French decision.

In practice, Dayton was nearer the truth than all the lawyers in the council. Although Captain Barney "would not think . . . of recruiting in England," that is precisely what the Southerners did. Needing English-speaking seamen and finding few, if any, in Brest, Confederate agents enlisted them across the Channel and forwarded them in small groups to Calais and other French ports, and thence to Brest by train. Since they had not submitted this method for French approval, they tried to be as unobtrusive as possible. Even so, Federal officials became suspicious of the unusual groups of nautical looking men, but they could not prove that they were enlisted for the "Florida."[26] John Slidell apparently smoothed the way for these sailors by making special arrangements with Chasseloup-Laubat.[27] The marine minister obviously agreed to overlook the source of the replacements and to allow them aboard the ship without raising any further question. If this was so, Chasseloup-Laubat had applied in a very flexible manner a tightly considered policy of the French government. But it would have been almost impossible to prevent the movement of sailors of various nationalities to the various French ports. Confederate recruitment continued throughout the war, and they were able to get a crew as late as January 1865 when they manned and armed the "Stonewall" off Belle Isle. Under Drouyn's direction, the French government had officially adopted a policy of strict neutrality in relation to recruiting naval personnel for belligerent vessels. The fact that it was practically unenforceable made it easy for individual members of the French government to circumvent it; but that was not the intent nor the policy: officially France was neutral in this as in other questions.

To all diplomatic excitement and concern caused by the "Florida's" presence in Brest, the sudden appearance of the United States ship "Kearsarge" soon added tension and uncertainty. The officials did not relish this direct confrontation between the enemy warships. Dayton had early requested sufficient naval strength to block the "Florida's" departure, but Secretary Wells had ruled that he could not spare the necessary ships.[28] Since the "Kearsarge" was already in European waters, Wells placed it under Dayton's control, and the minister ordered the skipper, Captain John A. Winslow, to sail to Brest, where he arrived on September 18. Winslow assured the port authority that he fully understood the twenty-four hour rule and would adhere to all the French rules of neutrality; he was in port, he said, only to recoal and reprovision his stores.[29] Although this work was completed by October 1 and Dayton reported that *the ship would not be detained "for any essential reason,"*[30] the "Kearsarge" remained in the harbor, just across from the "Florida." The presence of the two enemy ships aroused fear that French neutrality might be violated by a battle within territorial waters, and this led directly to a change in the rules on belligerent use of French ports.

The prefect at Brest immediately assumed the task of keeping the ships separated. By October 15, when both ships were ready to sail, the tension was reaching the breaking point.[31] Noticing that the "Kearsarge" maintained a head of steam, the prefect feared that Winslow was merely awaiting the "Florida's" departure and intending to follow immediately. He informed the marine minister of this possible violation of the twenty-four hour rule, and in turn Drouyn convinced Dayton that the "Kearsarge" should drop its steam. Denying any intention to follow the "Florida," Winslow stated that he used the steam only to forge metal and to condense seawater.[32] So tense was the situation that the prefect established a small watchship over the "Kearsarge."

For fifteen days the delicate situation persisted, then the

"Kearsarge" appeared to end it by sailing from the harbor on October 31. The prefect's relief, however, was short-lived because the "Kearsarge" returned on November 11. Three more times, the Northern ship was to leave and return to the harbor: out on December 5, in on December 11; out on December 29, and in again almost immediately; out again on January 16, 1864.[33] This activity greatly agitated the prefect. In order to assure peace, since both the "Florida" and the "Kearsarge" were in the Brest anchorage, on December 28 he sent the French corvette "Louis XIV" to station itself between the two ships. The almost constant movement of the "Kearsarge" caused the French ship much inconvenience and the prefect considered it to be "intolerable." On several of its short trips the Federal vessel "hovered" near St. Mathieu Isle which necessitated reconnaissance cruises by the "Louis XIV." Finally Chasseloup-Laubat complained to Drouyn de Lhuys about the "Kearsarge's" actions and asked him to take it up with Dayton.[34] But by that time the Northern vessel had quit the port, and the "Florida" finally had a chance to slip out on February 10, 1864.[35] The affair so disgruntled Chasseloup-Laubat that he suggested to Drouyn that the French adopt the English rules as to use of a port, namely that a belligerent vessel could use the same port only twice within one month.[36] Drouyn concurred in the need for a change, but insisted that the French word their regulation simply "that a belligerent ship may not use a French port as the center of its cruise." When the "Kearsarge" returned to Brest on February 18, the prefect so notified Winslow and added that the rule was in effect as of February 2, 1864.[37] The "Kearsarge," by its overzealous surveillance of the "Florida," had forced another clarification in the French rules of neutrality.

It is surprising that with all this activity, the "Kearsarge" did not prevent the "Florida" from sailing and resuming its depredations of Northern shipping. Why had it watched so carefully, then permitted the Confederate raider to escape? The answer, perhaps, is to be found in some exaggerated Northern spy reports. On January 22, 1864, Dayton submitted to Drouyn affidavits to the effect that the "Florida" and the "Rappahannock," at Calais, were arming from England with the intent to attack the "Kearsarge." This was denied immediately by the Brest prefect. Furthermore, the CSS "Georgia" had arrived at Cherbourg on October 28, just two days before the "Kearsarge" first quit Brest. The United States ship now had three ports to watch, and she divided her time accordingly, using Brest as a base of operations.[38] After the escape of the "Florida," the U.S. consul at Brest wrote that the presence of the "Kearsarge" had not been useless because she had "kept the 'Florida' at ancre [sic] for several months and this is something."[39] Partially concerned for his own safety and obligated to divide his efforts among three ports, Captain Winslow had allowed the prize to slip through his fingers.

While the "Kearsarge" occupied the prefect's attention with its antics, Dayton—belatedly—distracted Drouyn's attention with questions of the "legality" of the French hospitality to the "Florida." The United States minister raised questions as to the status of the "Florida"—whether she was a privateer or a regular ship of war—and as to the applicability of the Declaration of Paris of 1856, especially as it was first applied during the Crimean War. Exactly why Dayton had failed to submit these arguments in September, when Drouyn de Lhuys had been in the process of making his decision concerning the status of the "Florida," is not clear. Perhaps his 1861 negotiations on the Declaration of Paris had convinced him of the futility of trying to apply article one—outlawing of privateers—to the Southern ships.[40] But now, in October, Richard Cobden, the famous liberal and pro-Northern Englishman, suggested that to protest the treatment extended to the "Florida," the Federal agents should assume the Anglo-French position of 1854 which had preceded the actual adoption of the Paris declaration. Cobden knew that Drouyn de Lhuys had been instrumental in urging England to modify her traditional maritime practices towards neutrals and that he had stipulated that the new, more lenient rules should be in force only for the duration of the Crimean War.[41] Pursuant to the agreement, the two maritime powers issued a joint note asking the neutrals to refrain from aiding privateers. It was to this note that Cobden referred: he was curious, he wrote, "to know what answer the French government would now make if its own former language was quoted against the course now being taken at Brest in repairing . . . the 'Florida.' "[42]

The idea intrigued both Bigelow and Dayton, and when the latter raised the point with the French foreign minister, Drouyn also exhibited a lively interest. Reminding Dayton that he, himself, must have conducted the correspondence, he promised to "stand faithfully to its doctrines."[43] As the weeks passed and Drouyn made no move, Cobden again prodded the Northern diplomats. He found a copy of the 1854 dispatch and sent it to Bigelow with a long letter outlining the approach and even the language Dayton should use to prove that the "Florida" was nothing more than a privateer.[44] Cobden's suggestion ignored the 1861 negotiations over this very issue, in which his own government, as well as France, had refused the United States adherence to the Paris declaration precisely because it forced them into an unneutral position towards Confederate ships. But he put his advice on a high moral plane, suggesting that France was obligated to act on a level superior to the narrow technical one of the 1861 decisions.

Acting on Cobden's suggestion, Dayton composed a long letter to Drouyn. It was well organized, powerfully worded, and telling in its effect. Dayton borrowed heavily from the Englishman: he confronted Drouyn with his own words of some nine years earlier; he pointed out the emptiness of a statement of international law unless it is practiced by the powers who state it; and he described the Confederate cruisers as lawless marauders which refused to fight the Union warships. He even borrowed some of Cobdens very phrases, but by and large the strong, and sometime colorful wording was Dayton's. He called the 1861 French neutrality proclamation an "unhappy decree which gave the Rebels who did not own a ship of war or command a single fort, the rights of an ocean belligerent." Encouraged by foreign powers, Dayton maintained, the Confederates built ships "whose acknowledged mission is not to fight, but to rob, to burn, and to fly." To call such ships, which "have never sought a foe or fired a gun against an armed enemy," vessels of war was, he continued, a misnomer.

Manned by foreign seamen, armed by foreign guns, entering no home port, and waiting no juridical condemnation of prizes, they have already devastated and destroyed our commerce to an extent, as compared with their number, beyond anything known in the records of privateering.

To allow such vessels "while yet reeking with the smoke of their burned victims" to enter neutral ports because they are blocked from their own "is to make of their acknowledged weakness a source of strength." During the Crimean War the United States, in accordance with the Anglo-French 1854 note, had refrained from equipping and victualling Russian privateers. Dayton then asked:

Whether the reception of the "Florida" in the port of Brest, the repairs permitted, the supplies furnished, and the permission to renew her crew to the extent of the seventy-five men whose time, it is said, had expired, are not violations of the *spirit* of that action commended for acceptance in this dispatch to the Government of the United States.[45]

Drouyn was impressed by the logic, first suggested by Cobden, and by Dayton's powerful language. He could not soon clear his mind of the Confederate cruisers "reeking with the smoke of their burned victims" nor long admire those ships whose mission was "not to fight, but to rob, to burn, and to fly" and whose "conduct stamps them as piratical." And Drouyn must have been impressed with the moral force of Dayton's position for he did not make his usual legalistic answer. He could have said, for instance, that, having recognized the belligerent status of the Confederacy, France had no choice but to recognize also any privateer or commissioned ship of the South; that his own ideas of 1854 had been rejected by the United States in 1856; and that since Great Britain and France had been unable to approve United States adherence to the Declaration of Paris in 1861, after hostilities had begun, France now, in 1863, had neither legal nor moral obligations to enforce the 1854 ideas. But he did not say these things; instead he quietly went to work to strengthen the rules governing treatment of belligerent ships in French harbors.

Drouyn made no effort formally to respond, and Dayton did little to prod him.[46] Almost three months later, when Drouyn was considering the new rules for the harbors, Dayton asked if he had seen his note concerning the Crimean War policy laid down by England and France. With a smile, the foreign minister answered: "Yes, I have; that dispatch went very far!" Dayton, noting that Drouyn's smile indicated an unwillingness to discuss the issues, let the matter drop.[47] Actually, the strong note, coupled with the increased use of the French ports, had already brought the French officials to reassess their rules governing the treatment of belligerent vessels. But the fact that the reassessment eventually produced stricter rules against the Confederates flowed more from France's deeper involvement in Mexico than from Dayton's efforts.

Drouyn had begun to look into the French regulations in early December. He learned from Chasseloup-Laubat that under current rules belligerent ships had every right to use French harbors and facilities to make themselves seaworthy, but they could not in any way increase their armament.[48] The next day, in conversation with Dayton, Drouyn stated that "this recent and constant use of the French ports by the Confederates cannot have resulted from accident; it is intended to compromise this Government." Dayton naturally agreed, and Drouyn spiritedly continued: "We will not be compromised; we mean to be neutral. If there were any person to whom I could properly address myself, I would give him to understand that their action in this respect is disagreeable."[49] Early the next month, after the USS "Kearsarge" had begun its frequent trips in and out of Brest, Chasseloup-Laubat indicated that the declaration of neutrality of 1861 was not specific enough to guide the French officials. Recent belligerent use of French ports had given rise to claims that France was not acting in a neutral fashion. Especially, the minister of marine continued, did the case of ships of both belligerents in the same port simultaneously cause difficulties. He again called Drouyn's attention to the English rules and suggested that the French adopt similar ones.[50] The discussion reached the cabinet council level on January 26 when Drouyn presented a summary of the "French legislation on the matter of neutrality." He pointed out that the French policy differed from the English and American ones: while the latter two allowed trade in war contraband, France flatly forbade it. He went back to a treaty of 1681 to show that France was obligated to enforce what he called the "twenty-four hour clause," and he noted other laws which forbade Frenchmen from accepting a commission as a privateer from either belligerent, or from taking arms with either side. French laws did permit the manufacture of arms under license from the minister of war, but their export was prohibited by a decree of 1860. Sale of merchant, or unarmed, ships to foreigners was permitted, but the manufacture of arms for merchant ships was permissible only by a special license from the minister of war. In summary, Drouyn concluded that the government had sufficient power by law to prevent the armament of a ship in one of her ports, but it could not prevent the sailing of an unarmed ship; only a special decree of intervention could do this.[51]

High French officials were concerned about the charges of partiality and about the problems of maintaining a strict neutrality in the face of heavy activity in French ports. Complaints of unneutral treatment came from Dayton and the Union officials in France, who claimed that the Confederate ships, which in their opinion deserved treatment only as pirates, were in reality receiving favored services, and this concern of the French resulted more from the protests of the United States than from the increased activity. But why should such charges particularly concern the French government? Drouyn indicated the answer while talking with Dayton two days after the council meeting. Without in any way alluding to French obligations as a neutral, or even attempting to correct Dayton's use of the term "pirate," Drouyn simply "referred to the inconvenience or 'scrapes' as he termed them in which their recognizing of the South as a belligerent without acknowledging the government itself had involved them, and he took the occasion to say that they would be more cautious as to how they took this half-way position in the future." Dayton seized the opening to suggest that France could, then, do much worse than to "change this position, not by going on, but by coming back." Drouyn replied, "There is little probability of our going on; the Emperor has very highly appreciated the conduct and loyalty of your government in respect to Mexican affairs." In reassuring him of the U.S. nonintervention policy, Dayton referred to a dispatch containing the state department orders to General Banks when he was at Brownsville, Texas. Drouyn showed great interest in this document, because, as he said, "It has been reported to us in Mexico that the movement of your troops to the Western boundary of Texas was a 'deep laid scheme' to interfere in Mexico. I have told the Emperor that I do not believe this, and if you have any paper of the kind you referred to I would be greatly obliged if you would permit me to show it to the Emperor as a justification of my expressed opinion and position."[52] Later, in February, he spelled out to Chasse-loup-Laubat his fear of a United States intervention in Mexico. Summarizing a dispatch he had received from Seward which contrasted the difference between the Union's observance of neutrality in Mexico and France's in the Civil War, Drouyn stated that the United States had been more honorable than France. He concluded that the dispatch was of such a nature as to elicit "the most serious attention of the Government of the Emperor." Furthermore, he went on:

> The care of my responsibility obliges me to provoke anew all your solicitude on this subject and to ask you to adopt, if need be, measures of surveillance which seem to you to be opportune to avoid all acts which would, in the eyes of the United States, constitute serious and founded complaints. I hasten, then, to indicate to you the critical character of this situation and I need not belabor the dangers which it could create and the consequences which it could lead to if it should adversely affect the enterprise which we pursue in Mexico.[53]

It was the concern over Mexico, then, which led the French to adopt stricter measures toward Confederate ships in their ports and ultimately to prevent the warships constructed at Bordeaux and Nantes from falling into the Confederate hands and to prohibit the sailing of the "Rappahannock" from the harbor of Calais. Although Slidell and the other Southern agents expected the French-Mexican policy to lead to recognition of the

Confederate States, that policy acted in quite the opposite direction. Repeatedly the French government's official action became less permissive toward the South in order to avoid pushing
the North into intervention in Mexico.

In this particular case, the new rules adopted in relation to
belligerent vessels in French ports were published on February 5.
They were, in effect, a restatement of the principles already in
force: no belligerent vessel could stay in a French port any
longer than twenty-four hours, unless forced there by bad weather
or to repair its equipment necessary for safety in navigation; no
such ship could increase its armaments; such a ship must leave
the port within twenty-four hours after the completion of its
repairs, except in the case where ships of both belligerents are in
the same port simultaneously, whereupon all the ships of one
belligerent must leave at least twenty-four hours prior to any
ship of the other. These rules placed France more in line with
England, except that coal was allowed as a necessity for all
steam vessels. But more important were the instructions which
Chasseloup-Laubat distributed with the new rules:

> The continuation of the war having led the belligerents to
> carry naval hostilities into waters bordering upon neutral
> European states, and having led them to seek in our ports the
> means of repairing and revictualling, the Government of the
> Emperor judges it useful to recall to you once again the rules
> to observe for maintaining its neutrality, in accordance with
> public law and with the traditions of the French navy, and to
> determine, in consequence, the treatment which must be applied,
> without distinction of flag, to neutral ships.[54]

Drouyn had personally approved the wording of this, and the
emperor had approved the ideas expressed.[55] To make the rules
more explicit and to insist upon their impartial application, then,
was a decision reached by all the French ministers and approved
by the emperor. But it was Drouyn de Lhuys who pointed out
to them that the Mexican venture necessitated a strictly enforced
code of neutrality in order to prevent intervention there by the
United States. His brand of neutrality was highly pragmatic,
but it was a real neutrality to be strictly adhered to, not to be

used as a sham cover for favored treatment of one or the other of the belligerents. Perhaps the incident which best illustrates Drouyn's determination and ability to enforce this kind of neutrality was the case of the CSS "Rappahannock."

The Case of the CSS "Rappahannock"

The "Rappahannock" was unique among the Confederate vessels which sought refuge in a French port, or which were constructed in one. She was, as events turned out, almost an inactive ship once she entered the harbor of Calais. There was never a question of her having preyed upon Northern shipping, nor of her armaments being increased; there was no dramatic moment when a Frenchman revealed her true identity, as Trémont did for the ironclads at Nantes, nor any direct confrontation with a warship of the North, such as that between the "Florida" and the "Kearsarge." Nonetheless, her presence in Calais and the activity of the Southern naval officers did raise important questions of the rights of belligerents and the obligations of a neutral. The Northerners doubted that she had any rights as a belligerent because of her helpless condition when she entered the harbor, and they protested that she was being used as a Confederate naval personnel depot. The French reaction to these protests clearly reveals the foreign minister's role in circumventing the emperor's personal policy, and in maintaining French neutrality.

The "Rappahannock" was acquired by the Southerners in September 1863 when Commander M. F. Maury, the famous oceanographer, purchased a surplus English naval dispatch boat, the "Victor."[56] While repairs were being made on the ship, Commander Maury, fearing the British government might detain her, suddenly ordered her put to sea. At night, in the English Channel, Confederate naval officers boarded and renamed her the "Rappahannock." One day out of Sheerness, England, on November 27, 1863, she put into Calais claiming distress. So hurried had been the flight that she had no name painted on her side and some twenty carpenters who had been making repairs in England were still aboard. Indeed, her new commanding officer could not even produce the ship's papers to

the port authorities, claiming he had had to throw them over-
board to prevent their capture by the enemy. Shortly after her
arrival, about forty sailors from England were signed aboard as
crew. At first all the facilities of the port of Calais were available
to the ship, as they would have been for any vessel in distress.
Upon her arrival she had no armaments and the repair work
done was actually necessary to make her seaworthy. High rank-
ing Confederates and other "important people had come from
Paris to inspect her and several naval officers were aboard." So
obvious was her distress that despite the circumstances, she was
allowed the repair facilities of the port.[57]

But such an unusual ship, attracting the attention of so many
sailors and Confederate officials and naval officers, could not
long escape the interest of the Federal agents. Within a week of
her entrance, Dayton had sufficient evidence to present a complaint to Drouyn de Lhuys, and so thorough was the evidence
that this first letter expressed what was the essence of the Union
position throughout the remainder of the incident. Submitting
supporting affidavits from Federal agents in England, Dayton
accurately described the purchase, condition, and movement
of the ship. He claimed that the case of this vessel—which had
left England and having entered Calais voluntarily—was dis-
tinguishable from either the "Florida" or the "Georgia" and
could not claim "act of God" rights in the neutral port. Furthermore, he continued, the Confederates planned to repair, equip,
and arm her to cruise against Northern commerce. "On this
statement of facts no argument is necessary to show that permission from the French authorities to carry out her purposes would
be a violation of neutrality."[58] In the following months he sent
further reports and affidavits on Southern activities and movements related to the "Rappahannock" in and around Calais.[59]

From reporting Confederate activities, Dayton quickly moved
into aggressive protests. The United States, he said, would hold
France "justly responsible for all damages done" by the "Rappahannock." "Is it not desirable," he asked Drouyn, "to avoid, if
possible, all fair ground for future reclamation?"[60] Throughout
December and January Dayton was dismayed by the moderate
action taken by the French government.[61] Finally, in early

February he took his strongest stand. Even though the "Rappahannock" might not be arming in Calais, as he now admitted,
she was otherwise repaired and equipped, and would be armed
at sea by a ship from England. "If this be true (and it is probable) the effect upon the public mind of my country and the view
taken of it by my government must be obvious." To allow this
Confederate cruiser to be equipped in one neutral port and
armed from another is a direct participation "in a principal
wrong." The ports of England and France would become "the
base of military operations against us," a situation which the
United States government would never accept. He concluded by
repeating his earlier threat, this time in more official terms:
"And I now, with great respect, give formal notice that reclamation will be made in due time for all damages which shall be done
by the 'Rappahannock' to our commerce in case she be permitted, under the circumstances, to go to sea."[62]

Drouyn had reacted to Dayton's complaints. In December he
sent the latter's reports to the marine minister and insisted that
France must not make its facilities available to the Confederates
so to augment their aggressive powers. He wanted the "Rappahannock" to leave French waters immediately. Chasseloup-
Laubat agreed; since the vessel arrived unarmed, he said, she
must either leave at once or, if armed, she will be prohibited from
leaving at all.[63] A marine official in Calais indicated that Dayton's information was exaggerated, and Drouyn at that time contented himself by ordering that the ship be allowed to use only
those facilities necessary to make her seaworthy. He assured
Dayton that she would leave the harbor as soon as she was fit.[64]
At the same time he reiterated to Chasseloup-Laubat that French
soil must not be used by the Confederates to plan their aggressions, and that with the recurrent belligerent use of their ports,
"French neutrality must be more closely guarded than ever."[65]
Not until Dayton's formal notice of future damage claims, however, did Drouyn become anxious about the "Rappahannock."

On February 4, 1864, when Drouyn was revising French regulations concerning belligerent use of ports, he held a long discussion with Dayton on the "Rappahannock" case. "You send me
big words," Drouyn greeted Dayton. "Yes, but I send you no

unkind ones," was the reply. After some further serious talk, Drouyn for the first time admitted that the ship had not entered the harbor out of distress, despite her distressful condition.[66] As a direct result of this conversation, Drouyn de Lhuys[67] and Chasseloup-Laubat[68] instructed the Calais officials to permit the "Rappahannock" to leave only upon the express orders of the marine minister. Aroused by Dayton's protests and threats, convinced by the facts that the ship should enjoy none of the usual belligerent privileges, Drouyn now seized control of the affair: "The matter and all the papers are in the hands of Drouyn de Lhuys," Chasseloup-Laubat said.[69] Drouyn directed that the Calais port officials "take all measures necessary so that the 'Rappahannock' cannot leave the port," and stationed a French naval vessel at the harbor entrance to prevent the converted Southern vessel from leaving.[70] Dayton had done his job well and it was now the turn of the Confederates to complain.

John Slidell first requested Drouyn de Lhuys to release the vessel, but he received no reply from the foreign minister. From Chasseloup-Laubat, he received only a lecture: You have taken so long to make your repairs, the marine minister said in effect, that the ship and its condition upon entering the harbor have come to the attention of the Federal authorities; I can no longer shut my eyes to the violations of French neutrality.[71] Desperate now, the Confederates relieved the vessel's commander, and the new one determined either to get the ship to sea or to abandon her. Slidell admitted that "the affair of the 'Rappahannock' had been a series of blunders from the very commencement," and both the old and new commanders complained constantly that the repair work was of poor quality and the ship would never contribute anything to the war potential of the Confederacy.[72] As Drouyn continued to ignore Slidell's notes, the Confederates became more and more alarmed. Captain Bulloch considered the "Rappahannock" to be very embarrassing just at the time he needed the French government's good will in the Arman ship episode. He wanted to try to force the ship's release, but he was afraid of offending France. "Is it not possible to represent the situation," he asked plaintively, "in such a manner as while [sic] the facts and embarrassing circumstances should be clearly exposed, no threat should be conveyed?"[73]   Slidell tried to do just this, but his several attempts to arrange meetings with Drouyn were in vain.[74]   Unable even to talk to the foreign minister, the Confederates felt there was nothing they could do to force the release of the ship.

In despair they finally decided to strike their colors and to abandon the "Rappahannock."[75]   Lieutenant-Commanding Fauntleroy warned the Calais authorities that unless the ship were released by May 16, 1864, he would abandon her. Much to the surprise and consternation of the Southern officials, this threat did not alarm the French. When the deadline arrived, the port authorities calmly ordered the ship to be sold to pay the costs of docking.[76]   But before this could be carried through, Drouyn provided the Confederates with a way out of their dilemma by submitting the whole question of the "Rappahannock" to a consultative committee of the claims department (*contentieu*), headed by Raymond Théodore Troplong, president of the senate. Slidell, expecting an early decision favorable to the Confederacy, immediately ordered Lieutenant Fauntleroy not to relinquish command of the ship, and the situation returned to the *status quo*. What Slidell did not know was that Troplong despite his known pro-Southern feelings, was unable to act immediately because Drouyn had directed that no decision should be reached until after the adjournment of the legislative body.[77] The case was to drag on until the end of the war, although Dayton was so confident that he released the United States naval vessel from guard duty outside Calais.[78]   When Lieutenant Fauntleroy prepared to abandon ship, he drew up a list of the officers and crew of the "Rappahannock" as of May 16, 1864. As compared to the thirty-five men who had brought the vessel into the harbor in November 1863, there were now one hundred and seventeen seamen aboard her.[79] This increase in personnel verifies the Federal claim that the Confederates were using the ship as a personnel depot and that the ship's fighting potential had, indeed, been enhanced during her stay in the French port.

As time passed, Slidell became agitated over his inability to elicit any response from Drouyn de Lhuys. Turning to Chasseloup-Laubat once again he sought aid in getting the ship released. But the marine minister, saying that "it was altogether a very unfortunate affair," indicated that it had led to a more rigorous policy in regard to the Arman ships. Besides, he said, "the question has long since passed from me to the Minister for Foreign Affairs—I am in no degree responsible for the delays . . . As regards all this matter, I am entirely under the control of the Minister of Foreign Affairs."[80]

Denied official contacts within the French government, Slidell had to turn to the only other method he, as an agent for an unrecognized government, could use: the backstairs diplomacy so appealing to Napoleon III's sense of adventure. Here he was to meet greater success. He sought first that long-time associate of the emperor whose pro-Confederate sympathies were well known.

> Am I expecting too much, my dear Duc de Persigny, when I express the hope that your great and well merited influence will be exercised to obtain, if not redress for what I consider a flagrant wrong, at least some explanations which will relieve me from the humiliations of finding my remonstrances systematically unnoticed by the Minister of Foreign Affairs?[81]

He also approached the emperor's half-brother, the Duke of Morny, asking him to speak to Napoleon in behalf of the Southern effort to salvage some benefit from the ship lying at Calais. These endeavors were successful in producing a note from Napoleon III to Slidell which indicated that orders had been given to release the "Rappahannock." Slidell was elated, but despaired as days passed and no release orders reached Lieutenant Fauntleroy. Seeking an explanation, he again visited Chasseloup-Laubat, who knew nothing of the promised order and was surprised, even impressed, to learn of the differences existing between the emperor and the foreign minister.[82]

How deep were these differences? What had the foreign minister been doing while he ignored the emperor's order? He had busied himself by drawing up a "Rapport à l'Empereur sur l'affaire du Rappahannock."[83] This report was lengthy and thorough, and it clearly expressed Drouyn's concept of the responsibility of French neutrality:

> Sire: The decision to allow the "Rappahannock" to leave the port of Calais seems to me badly founded in law and dangerous in fact. I ask Your Majesty to permit me to justify this opinion:
>
> There are three points to consider in the affair of the "Rappahannock":
>
> 1. The character of the ship and its material condition at the moment when it entered Calais;
> 2. The nature of the repairs and the help which it has received in this port.
>
> These two points established, it then becomes a question of establishing in the 3rd place if, and in what measure, the asylum and help given by us to the ship are in contravention with our declaration of neutrality.

Drouyn then quoted the dispatches from Calais and from the various investigative commissions to show that the ship was not seaworthy when it entered the port, but that it could now take to the sea in perfect safety, and that the crew had been implemented to over eighty. Drouyn asked and answered two questions: Was the recruiting of the personnel in violation of French neutrality? Undoubtedly, it was. Did humanity demand that the repairs necessary for the safety of the men aboard be made? "Truthfully, this could not be sustained." After summarizing more documents, Drouyn concluded:

> As to the Federal Government . . . we cannot allow the "Rappahannock" to leave without violating our declaration of neutrality. In effect, we have one of two choices: either our good faith has been abused and then we are doubly in the right to retain it, or we were aware of the facts, and then the departure of the ship assumes the character of an act of partiality or even of hostility.
>
> As to the Confederates, the situation is not less delicate. All that they have done, has been seen, known, authorized by us. To forbid them to leave, at the most, would cause them harm which they know [*dont ils entendent*] and for which they have the right to hold us responsible.
>
> In such situations, when one does not want to denounce them by political considerations, by reason of state, it seems that there is only one means of solution:

Between two inconveniences, choose the lesser: now, it is certain that a refusal of permission to leave resolves itself, as far as we are concerned, into a question of claims for damages on which discussions can be held, while the departure would have much more grave consequences and would lead to war between France and the United States.

This analysis and Drouyn's strong conclusion were made solely in the interest of France. He appealed to the emperor, not on the basis of adherence to neutrality, but on the choice of the lesser of the two inconveniences. His reference to a possible war between France and the United States, in view of his constant concern over Mexico, must have conveyed to the emperor the delicacy of the question of Northern intervention in Mexican affairs. It was a strong note, based upon purely pragmatic considerations, designed to strike the emperor in his weakest spot: Mexico. That the recommendation, in this case, did in fact comply with French neutral obligations may not have been accidental; certainly Drouyn had revealed himself throughout the various controversies as in favor of a strictly nonpartisan policy.

But even this appeal did not convince the emperor. Obviously, Slidell's friends had been at work. From Vichy, where he was vacationing, Napoleon III summoned Drouyn and specifically ordered him to release the "Rappahannock."[84] The foreign minister, realizing that logic had failed, now resorted to more subtle means of preventing the escape of the ship. He gave permission for it to leave Calais, but only in the same condition as when it entered; and this, he specified, applied to the armaments and to the number of personnel aboard.[85] This meant that the French government would consider the "Rappahannock" as it did any other naval vessel of a belligerent and that all of Dayton's arguments to the contrary were being disregarded. Drouyn accepted this knowing that the order, although not strictly contradicting the emperor's directive, in effect prevented the ship from sailing, for such a large vessel could hardly sail with only thirty-five men aboard. True to his pragmatic approach to the affair, Drouyn was satisfied. When Slidell made a special plea to allow more men unofficially aboard the ship,

Drouyn took the question to a cabinet meeting on July 27, over which the empress presided. For the council of ministers to "unofficially" allow its own law to be so grossly violated was too much; Drouyn prevailed, and the council refused Slidell's request.[86] Thus the ship would have to leave, if at all, with a crew of thirty-five instead of the hundred which was needed for proper handling. Lieutenant Fauntleroy, the commander of the "Rappahannock," refused to sail under such conditions,[87] and the ship remained in the harbor for the duration of the war. As late as March 1865, when he was asked about the incident, Drouyn replied that the ship had violated French laws of neutrality and because of this he was determined it should never leave Calais under the Confederate flag. Despite the efforts of others, he said with a smug smile, "You see that the 'Rappahannock' is still at Calais."[88]

Drouyn was entitled to a feeling of smugness because almost alone among French officials, and against the efforts of such powerful individuals as Persigny and de Morny, Drouyn had assumed the direction of affairs, had persuaded the emperor—or had circumvented him—and had detained the vessel. His own brand of neutrality had prevailed. His achievement had resulted from his conviction that France must act in such a way as to, first, prevent a retaliatory intervention in Mexico by the United States, and, second, present a clean record to both belligerents so that regardless of the outcome of the war, France would not have created an enemy across the seas. It was this conviction that led to Drouyn's confident, though risky, opposition to such strong men. Revealing just how little he truly understood the matter, Slidell commented: "In this question the Minister for Foreign Affairs manifested throughout ill-will and bad faith. I attribute this to timidity, for strange as it may seem, the fact is patent, that Mr. Dayton has managed to convince him that the Lincoln Government is prepared to go to war with France. . . ."[89] Slidell was in error: it was not a timid man who reversed his emperor's policy. But the conflict between the two Frenchmen—the emperor and the minister of foreign affairs—caused misunderstanding and created distrust among both the Union and the Confederate officials. The conflict presented two

French policies to the Americans: one, the unofficial, personal policy of Napoleon III; the other, the official, governmental policy as determined by Drouyn de Lhuys. From Slidell's point of view, there was bad faith and ill-will; from Dayton's point of view, there was too much vacillation and indecision. Perhaps Dayton described the diplomatic consequences of the "Rappahannock" incident as well as the ship herself when he said: "The vessel is a miserable affair at best."[90]

The "Alabama"–"Kearsarge" Battle

One of the chief French objectives in issuing the rules for port officials to follow towards belligerents was to avoid a clash in French waters between ships of the two hostile powers. The danger existed whenever a ship of one power remained in a port for any appreciable length of time, because then the other government could send a vessel to challenge it upon its departure. This had been the purpose of the twenty-four hour rule. Yet the year's labor—the new rules designed to keep the two belligerents apart, the long hours of careful observation by the French port authorities, the many diplomatic conferences, and even the cabinet meetings—all culminated in the summer of 1864 in one of the great naval encounters of the war: the hour and a half running duel between the CSS "Alabama" and the USS "Kearsarge," fought within full view of the crowds who watched from the ramparts of Cherbourg. The story has been told many times,[91] but never within the context of French diplomacy and the Civil War.

The "Alabama" was an English-built Confederate ship which under the command of Captain Raphael Semmes had spent two years as the most successful raider in the Confederate service. Her reputation—infamous or glamorous, depending on the allegiance—preceded her to port. When she arrived in Cherbourg on June 11, 1864, after her long cruise, she needed a thorough refitting. Semmes hoped to use the imperial shipyards for the work. However, within three days the USS "Kearsarge" appeared just outside the three-mile limit, obviously awaiting the "Alabama's" departure. Captain Semmes, claiming that such a maneuver was an insult to his flag, notified Captain Winslow of his intention to forego the repairs on the "Alabama" and to come out to challenge the "Kearsarge." Word spread through the small port city and even reached Paris. Hundreds of people lined the shores, climbed to roof tops, balanced on the quays, to watch the two ships clash. Sentiment seemed to run in favor of Semmes for his courage in going out to do battle before the repairs were completed. On June 19, on the eve of relinquishing command of the raider,[92] that dauntless captain sailed the "Alabama" beyond the French territorial limits and the two ships locked in combat. The result was a sensational spectacle for the viewers, and a tragedy for the participants, especially for the men of the "Alabama." Superior marksmanship and fresh powder eventually took its toll, and the famous "Alabama" sank in ten fathoms of water about five miles off Cherbourg. The survivors were picked up by boats from the "Kearsarge," by a British yacht, the "Deerhound," and small French boats which were in the area. The marauding career of one Southern vessel was finally ended.

While the sailors fought, and some died, what were the diplomats doing? Did the battle affect official relations among the three governments? Were the officials involved in the affair at all? Yes, and intimately so. As soon as Dayton had learned of the "Alabama's" arrival, he had telegraphed Captain Winslow, who was in Flushing, and had requested from Washington more Federal ships, urging that the government "not delay until the rebel ship was out of harbor, as it had done on other occasions." He also immediately complained to Drouyn de Lhuys, claiming that the Southern raider should not be allowed within the harbor and pointing out that the Confederates were using French ports to create bad feeling between France and the United States.[93] Drouyn seemed to agree, and he kept in close touch with the minister of the marine. That harried official sent copies of his exchanges with the marine prefect of Cherbourg so that Drouyn knew what was taking place almost minute by minute.

Semmes' first request had been to put his ship in a French navy dry dock for repair; but before the French officials responded, the "Kearsarge" appeared and Semmes withdrew the request. He asked, merely, for permission to buy coal from a commercial provider, and this was granted. Captain Winslow then sent word that he wanted to transfer forty-five Union prisoners known to be aboard the "Alabama." But Chasseloup-Laubat, considering this to amount to an augmentation of the "Kearsarge's" crew, refused. So delicate was the situation and so sensitive was Chasseloup-Laubat to Drouyn's control of government policy that he concluded this letter with the almost pitiful remark: "I trust my department is fulfilling the intentions of the emperor."[94] As of June 15, then, the situation permitted by the French authorities was this: the "Alabama" was in port, being recoaled; the "Kearsarge" was standing just three miles off port, in communication with the Union consul. Dayton was in error when he reported to Seward that Semmes was ordered by the French to leave Cherbourg;[95] there is no doubt that Semmes chose to leave in order to challenge the "Kearsarge."

Drouyn de Lhuys made an effort to prevent the battle, at least to prevent it from taking place so close to French territory. Chasseloup-Laubat reported that although the "Kearsarge" was three miles off shore, it was still within cannon shot of the French coast; he found this situation intolerable and suggested that perhaps Dayton would order the "Kearsarge" to leave.[96] Drouyn agreed and informed Dayton that a battle was "shaping up in the face of France and at a distance from our coast within reach of the guns used on shipboard these days." The reason for the old three-mile rule, he said, no longer existed. "A fight on or about such a distance from our coast would be offensive to the dignity of France, and we will not permit it." He implied that a French naval vessel would escort the "Alabama" past the "Kearsarge." Dayton said that he knew of no limit other than the three-mile one, but that out of respect for the French request he would ask Winslow to sail further off if this would not put him at a disadvantage. He sent his son to Cherbourg with a letter to that effect, and the port authority allowed him to communicate with the "Kearsarge."[97] Chasseloup-Laubat then directed the marine prefect that, as long as the "Kearsarge" stayed outside the three-mile limit, there was nothing that could be done. When the "Alabama" leaves, he continued, escort it to the territorial water limits only.[98] Winslow did sail farther out, to a distance of about seven miles. The battle itself started with the "Kearsarge" sailing towards the shore, and the force of the battle took the two ships to within five miles of the shore. Thus, it is possible that, except for the diplomats' actions, the battle could have ended within the territorial waters of France. They could not prevent the clash from taking place.

On the day of the battle John Slidell went to Fontainebleau, where the emperor was staying, to protest what he thought was the order for the "Alabama" to leave Cherbourg. There he encountered Persigny and Prince Murat, who acted as his messengers to the emperor while they were all at the races. Before the news of the battle arrived, Napoleon twice denied that the French had forced the "Alabama" to leave the harbor.[99] But Slidell had aroused the emperor's concern, and, when the full details began to arrive, Napoleon sent a telegram to Chasseloup-Laubat: "I would strongly regret the catastrophe of the 'Alabama' if, as is said, we forced it to leave; I hope that this is not true. Why was not one of our ships ready to help the victims, whoever they were?"[100] The marine minister responded immediately that it was not true that "we forced the 'Alabama' to leave." He requested permission to go to Cherbourg, but the emperor instead ordered him to "come to lunch tomorrow; leave by the 9:00 o'clock train."[101] Whatever the two men discussed at luncheon, there were no recriminations. The minister actually received the thanks of both captains and of Dayton for the care extended to the wounded.[102]

The diplomatic repercussions of the naval engagement were recorded in a conversation between John Slidell and Drouyn de Lhuys on the next day. Slidell had precipitated the meeting by sending word that he considered the loss of the "Alabama" to be a direct result "of her unfriendly reception by the authorities at Cherbourg acting under instructions from Paris"; he now wanted to know in what manner the Confederate flag would hereafter be treated by the French. Drouyn opened the conversation by expressing his regret at the loss of the ship. Slidell counterattacked: he felt the loss of the ship to be the direct result of the refusal to allow the ship to enter the military basin, for if permission had been given, Semmes would not have felt honorably compelled to seek the fight with the "Kearsarge." Drouyn replied that the ship had been allowed to enter the port, though he did not say the permission extended to the military facilities, which indeed it did not. But the Southerner was now determined to carry the discussion further: all the frustrations of the delays suffered by the "Florida," of the impending loss of the Arman ships, of the entanglements of the "Rappahannock" burst forth in a whimpering complaint: "I said that I regretted to be obliged to say that I had observed for some months past a growing disposition to treat my government with scant courtesy, and that even the neutrality which the Emperor had proclaimed was not observed toward us." Drouyn's own difficulties in trying to maintain a strict neutrality caused him, "with some appearance of temper," to interrupt and say that "this was a question he would not permit himself to discuss."

> The government had decided to observe the strictest neutrality, he continued, and believed that they had done so, but that the best evidence of the fact was the constant complaint of Mr. Dayton of the partiality shown toward the Confederacy; that while the Emperor had the warmest sympathies with the Confederate cause, sympathies which were freely avowed, he was determined not to be drawn by indirection into a conflict with the Northern Government; that if such a conflict were to come it must be in pursuance of a policy openly declared and where no fault could justly be attributed to him.

Slidell wisely suggested that they abandon a "subject which was as disagreeable to me as to him."

The Southern agent then asked Drouyn about the "Rappahannock," whose fate was still in the hands of the Troplong committee; he said that the ship "had been detained without cause for four months, and that as I could not obtain a written response to my various communications on that subject, I hoped now to have a verbal one." Drouyn answered casually that he had not responded to Slidell's letters because he had no conclusive answer to give, but that he had asked the president of the senate for an early report and would inform Slidell as soon as he received it.

Slidell's deep sense of frustration and uselessness appeared in language and attitude when he inquired about the ironclads which Arman was building. Here he was really asking about the future of Southern hopes in France:

> I said I was about to ask a question, and that if he found it indiscreet it should be considered as not made. Had the sentiments of the Emperor become, from any cause, less kindly (*moins bienviellants*) toward the Confederacy? That I was quite at a loss to imagine any such cause, but that in relation to the ships we had been induced to build by his suggestions and for which we had expended large sums of money, raised with great inconvenience and sacrifice, we had been treated with extreme harshness. It was difficult to account for such a change of policy, if there was no corresponding change of feeling.

The Southerner failed to understand that his backstairs arrangements with the emperor were invalid; he felt the weakness, but he could not accept the fact that the French government, in what Drouyn would call "matters of state," could not indulge the emperor's whims. And so Slidell in an almost pitiful manner asked the above question—a question which indiscreetly revealed his own ignorance and weakness. Referring to the emperor's suggestions which had induced the Confederates to undertake the building of the Arman ships, Drouyn smiled and replied: "That is a matter of which I am of course ignorant; but I can assure you the feeling of the Emperor is unchanged. He is, as he always has been, prepared to recognize your Government, but he will not act alone."[103] Drouyn refrained from adding that it was he who refused to encourage the emperor to recognize the Confederacy.

The "Alabama"–"Kearsarge" battle had brought to a head the whole question of French neutrality towards the maritime rights of the Confederate States of America as a recognized belligerent. As Slidell left Drouyn's office, he must have walked with a dejected step and a sense of defeat. When the "Alabama" sank into the waters off Cherbourg, with her went the Confederate hopes of creating a navy in the French shipyards and of using the French port facilities to sustain those few raiders left upon the high seas. The history of the Arman ships and the "Rappa-hannock" had yet to evolve; but the policies were determined and the course was set. The questions of neutrality with regard to ships and harbors had been answered; French action would follow the strictest sort of impartiality; the Confederates, needing favoritism to survive, were already defeated. The man most responsible for setting that course was Edouard Drouyn de Lhuys, for it was his policy, based upon law and French interest, and proclaimed and hammered out in council meetings, which pre-vailed over the emperor's whispered suggestions and backstage actions. And, in the long run, his most potent ally in thus in-directly defeating the naval hopes of the South had been the influence of French interests in Mexico and French concern over Northern intervention there.

Problems concerning ships and harbors flowed from incidents occurring exclusively on the French side of the Atlantic. But the double relationship of neutrality and belligerency existing between France and the United States raised other questions originating almost entirely on the American continent. The movement of goods, whether contraband or free, created diplo-matic issues which affected the mutual postures of both govern-ments.

Chapter XV

PROBLEMS OF NEUTRALITY: MOVEMENT OF GOODS

THE movement of goods between neutrals and belligerents during wartime has long been a major issue in international relations. Belligerent powers claim the right to forbid neutrals from sending any goods which might enhance the enemy's military power; these are called contraband and include such items as arms and munitions. Other neutral products—free goods—may be sent to belligerents unless their transit is blocked by military operations. Although states have attempted to regulate this commerce by such international acts as the Declaration of Paris in 1856, in practice the traffic is controlled in accordance with military strength and national policy. During the Civil War, Paris and Washington dealt at length with both types: the contraband goods were arms moving primarily from the United States into Mexico for France's enemy, Juarez; the free goods were large quantities of French-owned Virginia tobacco held behind the Federal naval blockade. Both issues were involved with larger national policies and thus received the attention of high-level diplomacy.

Arms for Juarez

The matter of a belligerent arming itself through a neutral is always a serious problem, whether the arms are large ships of war, such as the Confederates tried to obtain in England and France, or small side arms. However, most governments make little issue of the traffic in small arms; they simply try to discover and arrest the movement.

In respect to its war in Mexico, the French government was well aware that Juarez had to arm his troops with foreign-made guns. The officials concerned themselves chiefly with preventing delivery of the weapons and did not generally raise diplomatic questions. As early as January 8, 1863, for instance, Drouyn de Lhuys warned the French consul in New York and the marine minister that "700 cases of arms bought in Belgium for the Mexican government" had been sent to New York for reshipment to Juarez. He instructed the consul to prevent the reshipment, and he noted to Chasseloup-Laubat that the vast amount of the traffic in arms for the North and for the South, as well as for Juarez, made investigations extremely difficult.[1] He did not demand that the United States take action; indeed, he did not even inform Seward of the shipment. He depended simply on action at the customs level in New York City, once the French consul had indicated the ultimate destination of the shipment.

On another occasion, much later, Drouyn asked the British government to prevent the sailing of the ship "Sea Queen," which was at the Vic Docks in London loaded with 800 tons of arms for Juarez. Russell answered that the vessel would have to violate English enlistment laws before the government could act. He suggested, however, that France could capture her upon the high seas if she carried contraband of war.[2] Such correspondence on the highest diplomatic level was infrequent and was always brief.

Drouyn used secret agents to inform him of arms purchases for Juarez. When a certain Mr. Schoffner volunteered to give information on shipments originating in England and destined for Mexico, Drouyn asked the French ambassador there to check on this individual. Baron Gros responded that the person in question "is at the moment very embarrassed and seeks to borrow money at a very high rate of interest." But even more important, "he is intimately tied in with the Mexican General Zirman who, sponsored by Mr. Adams, sends arms to the Mexicans." He concluded that Schoffner probably would be willing to betray Zirman for the money he would receive.[3] Whether the information came from Schoffner is not clear; but Drouyn did learn of activities in England from a secret agent.

According to one "confidential" and unsigned report, several "Yankee" agents were involved in buying arms for Juarez, though there was no proof of United States government participation. The report stated that M.B.H. Howell had an account of 100,000 pounds in the American banking house of Pickersgill and Company and that Howell and a certain Mr. Spencer were planting rumors that the United States had decided to oppose the French in Mexico. Furthermore, the report stated that a Mexican general had been sent to England to purchase arms, drawing upon the money in the Pickersgill Bank. Finally the report contained copies of letters which showed that a ship was leaving with arms for Matamoras.[4] With this information in hand, Drouyn reacted very strongly when he heard that the U.S. minister to England, Charles Francis Adams, had written a letter to facilitate the shipment of arms to Juarez.

This was one occasion when an arms movement did attract the attention and efforts of the diplomats and did become an incident which involved extended diplomatic exchanges between governments. The sequence of events can be stated quickly: Two men, the above-mentioned General Zirman for whom Mr. Schoffner worked and the "Yankee" agent, M.B.H. Howell, approached Adams asking for help. They had, they said, a cargo of goods for the Mexican republicans to be delivered to Matamoras on the Mexican side of the Rio Grande. The Federal naval blockade was so effective that they could not get insurance; but a letter guaranteeing the ship safe passage through the United States naval blockade would, they felt, enable them to get the coverage they required. They promised to show it to the underwriters confidentially in order to avoid publicity. Adams agreed, and wrote the letter; but at Lloyds the letter was posted and was soon published in the London press. Adams had addressed the letter to Commodore Dupont of the Union navy, stipulating that he gave it "with pleasure" and asking for free passage, including freedom from search.[5]

The action implied affronts to both England and France. Since the ship involved was an English one, Russell felt that "Adams showed favoritism to certain English shippers at the expense of others." He called it a "most extraordinary thing."[6]

But the greater affront was to France. Gros, informing Drouyn of the incident, assumed that the ship's cargo was munitions for Juarez. Drouyn spoke with Cowley about the affair in Paris where the publication of the letter had "excited observations." He told Cowley "in language savoring more of scorn than anger, that he proposed speaking to Mr. Dayton and writing to M. Mercier respecting the jurisdiction so impertinently assumed by Mr. Adams." And a few days later Cowley heard that "Dayton got a good dressing out over Mr. Adams' safe conducts."[7]

Though Drouyn did not actually dress out Dayton, he did summon him for a conference. He had, he said, made a "grave and serious complaint against Adams' letter." The cargo was munitions for Juarez and Adams had known it; furthermore Adams had written that it "gives him pleasure to distinguish this adventure of sending a shipload of arms to our enemies . . . to kill us with." Dayton strove to moderate the emotional reaction to this letter. There was nothing in any dispatch he had seen which indicated that Adams knew the shipment to be munitions; Adams had not intended, he was sure, to offend the French; since Matamoras was not under French blockade, Adams probably had not considered at all that he might be doing anything to arouse French sensibilities. But finally Dayton had to admit that if Adams had known the shipment to contain arms, then the letter was a grave error. The conversation led to a general discussion of the problem of supplying arms and materials for the belligerents in Mexico. Drouyn contrasted Adams' act with that of the Federal government, which forbade the export of mules, free labor, and even timber to the French in Mexico. Even when Dayton showed Drouyn correspondence in which the republican Mexican representative in Washington complained of unfair treatment because wagons had been sent to the French, but some 37,000 muskets for the republicans were interdicted, Drouyn refused to concede the point. After further discussion, he gave Dayton a written statement of his observations on the letter, and remarked that "France has no interest in Mexico besides asserting her just claims . . . , obtaining payment of the debt due with the expenses of the invasion and vindicating by victory the honor of her flag; we do not intend to colonize in Mexico or to obtain

Sonora or any other section permanently. . . ."[8]   Drouyn's note really said nothing else, except it asked that the Washington government disavow Adams' act.

This strong reaction to a relatively small shipment of arms—particularly in light of the agent's report—reflects France's constant fear that known Northern sympathy for Juarez and his republican form of government might lead the United States to intervene actively in that war.   Drouyn felt it was essential to separate Adams' act from official Federal policy, and it was thus that he so insistently asked for a specific disavowal by Washington.

While Drouyn's note and Dayton's account of the interview were crossing the Atlantic, correspondence between Paris and London actually settled the affair to Drouyn's satisfaction.   Both men had sent copies of the note to London.   Gros's reply was to summarize a public letter Adams had published in which he denied any intent to wound England.[9]   And Adams replied to Dayton disclaiming "all hostility to the French Government and all the unfriendly motives attributed to him" in Drouyn's memorandum.[10]   Drouyn was pleased to learn of Adams' repentance and was ready therefore to accept Seward's explanation and apology.   The explanation was a long one, but Seward seemed to have appreciated what was the chief sore point for France. He began by expressing gratitude for Drouyn's assurances concerning the French interests in Mexico, and he reasserted the United States policy of strict neutrality in the Mexican war, though acknowledging the real and close interest of the Federal government in Mexican affairs.   Seward also acknowledged Drouyn's good will in suggesting that the attitude expressed in Adams' letter was not that of the Washington cabinet and that Washington had had no previous knowledge of the affair.   Seward then explained Adams's conduct, disclaiming any desire or intent by Adams to offend France.   He concluded with the disavowal Drouyn wanted to hear:

> You will consequently say to Mr. Drouyn de Lhuys that, having taken the President's instructions upon the subject, I am of the opinion that the giving of the paper complained of to Zirman and Howell was in effect an unfriendly act towards France,

which was not in harmony with the sentiments and policy of this Government, and which it therefore views with disfavor and with regret, while it regards the proceeding on the part of Mr. Adams as having been one of inadvertence, and not of design or motive injurious to France.[11]

When Dayton had finished reading those words to Drouyn, the French foreign minister said he was much gratified by their contents and immediately added as respects the Adams letter, "let it be forgotten." Dayton concluded then that "we may consider this little diplomatic disturbance as something passed and gone."[12]

And so the episode concluded. The two countries had exchanged valuable assurances as to their respective intentions in Mexico. Drouyn consistently held that France should not attempt to establish herself permanently in Mexico, and Seward consistently held that the United States had no intention of intervening there. As long as these mutually satisfactory policies could be maintained, the two powers would avoid conflict over Mexico, and that is what Drouyn wanted. Indeed, this objective had largely shaped his policies relating to Confederate belligerent rights in France.

French agents in America kept a constant watch to assure that the public sentiment for Juarez did not lead to action detrimental to French interests in Mexcio. After Union forces captured New Orleans, that port was a potential outlet for aid to Juarez, and French Consul Fauconnet remained especially alert for any danger signs. In the spring of 1864 he reported the formation of a secret club for the "purpose of obtaining funds and purchasing arms for the Juarez party in Mexico," with a membership of Mexican refugees and Federal army officers. According to reports, he said, the club loaded munitions aboard United States ships ostensibly for Union troops in Texas, but actually for the Juarez forces in Matamoras. Fauconnet associated this club with the Defenders of the Monroe Doctrine, a public organization which held open meetings. It used any possible propaganda to convert people to its views. Among its members was Governor Hahn of Louisiana, who in a public speech "was not afraid to mention this doctrine by name, and to propose that Federal and Southern troops join together to chase the French and Maximilian out of Mexico."[13]   Two days after receiving this message Drouyn wrote to Washington—repeating much of Fauconnet's language—asking for an explanation.[14]   Seward assured the French that the governor was not a member of the Defenders; indeed, the organization was a harmless society designed to apply moral pressure on the United States government to enforce the Monroe Doctrine, but not to violate any law or the policy of neutrality.   But neither Geofroy, the French chargé at Washington, nor Fauconnet accepted Seward's explanation. Keeping a close watch, they caused six ships carrying munitions and supplies to Juarez to be stopped at the mouth of the Mississippi River.   Seward now had to change his story; although he still claimed the society was without influence, he acknowledged that a Union colonel and a general had been transferred from New Orleans.   Furthermore, the army had had the group under surveillance since April 30 and had found that its purpose was to enlist men and obtain arms and supplies for demonstrations in Mexico and elsewhere in South America.   He felt, however, that the persons involved were more interested in furthering "their own ambitions, personal projects, and fortunes, than interfering in the affairs of Mexico or any other nation."   When he received this information, Drouyn congratulated his agents and said the measures taken by Seward confirmed that the matter was well handled and that the materials for Juarez had been stopped.[15]   But France continued to keep watch on pro-Juarez activities in New Orleans, just as Union officials were vigilant in Bordeaux against Confederate activities.

Another center of strong sentiment for Juarez was the West Coast city of San Francisco.   The Mexican republicans found it easy to run ships down the coast to Pacific ports in the west of Mexico, usually Acapulco and Mazatlan.   French Consul Cazotte discovered that the Federal officials were effective in enforcing the ban against sending arms to either belligerent in Mexico as long as he located the munitions and specifically demanded action.   The latter years of the war found Cazotte frantically probing in hotel cellars and in the harbor area of San

Francisco, locating suspicious caches of arms, calling in the Federal officials, and hurriedly sending the count of confiscated munitions to Paris. He found 2,500 rifles in the basement of the St. Nicolas Hotel; he found a ship load of arms in the vessel "Constitution," but was unable to prevent it from sailing; he found 2,000 rifles in the office of the newspaper *Voz de Mejico*; he managed to get a ship—loaded and ready to leave—detained by the collector of customs and held under the guns of Alcatraz Island fortress.[16] But perhaps the most interesting episode occurred in early April 1864. Cazotte learned of a load of munitions aboard the steamer "John L. Stephens." He sought the proper authorities to prevent the departure of the ship and with the aid of the U. S. customs collector and the San Francisco chief of police, the contraband was confiscated. But Cazotte realized that the elected local officials, in the face of the strong pro-Juarez sentiment, needed some incentive beyond their oath to uphold the laws of the United States:

> In this country everything has its price, and if the armaments continue, as a result of the present situation in Mexico, I will be able to stop them only by means of "gratifications" at the right moment to certain officials, and especially the chief of police, who seems devoted to us. I dare, then, to propose to Your Excellence, that if Chief Burke should continue to make important seizures of arms and of contraband of war, to be so good as to put at my disposition funds for unforseen events; because 'where there is a will there is a way,' and I do not believe those whom I employ in these affairs will be very happy with pretty words.

In the margin, Drouyn wrote in his own hand: "Open a credit of 3,000 francs to the account of the consul at San Francisco." In another handwriting there appears: "Director of Accounts answered M. Cazotte concerning the opening of a credit of 3,000 francs, 24 May 1864."[17] With this reinforcement Cazotte continued his stringent watch, and the Federal and local officials continued their faithful enforcement of the United States laws concerning neutrality in the Mexican War. But they were not bashful about the encouragement from Paris. Indeed, Chief

Burke sent his thanks to Drouyn de Lhuys for the $200![18]   With this kind of honesty, Cazotte's job was easy.

Drouyn was so pleased with Cazotte's work that, in an unusual gesture, he conveyed his compliments in the official correspondence. Nonetheless, he also warned the French war and the navy departments to establish and maintain a close watch on the Mexican west coast, especially near Mazatlan.[19]   Despite all this counteractivity, Drouyn knew that munitions still reached Juarez' troops.

Recruiting for Mexican service was at first a coin with two sides. The initial mention of trying to get men for service in Mexico referred to a French effort in New York. In October 1862 General Forey of the French expeditionary forces sent an agent to recruit from among the French citizens, but French minister to Washington, Mercier, stopped him. Learning that he could not recruit in Canada either, he gave up. No other effort was made by the French to recruit in North America.[20] During the middle years of the Civil War, the United States effectively prohibited any recruiting for Juarez, and Drouyn acknowledged this with appreciation.[21]   It was not until near the end of the war that Juarez' agents became active in the United States. In early May 1865 the new French vice consul in New York City, Louis Borg, noted that Romero, the Mexican republican minister in Washington, claimed that the Federal government had a positive interest in aiding the Juarez regime and reported that a General Ortega was active in New York procuring men and arms to help Juarez. The Mexicans counted on the end of the war to make available many more men and arms for Juarez. General Grant, it was rumored, had approved of a plan to send men immediately to the aid of the Mexican republic.[22]   The real intent of the United States would then be tested. With the war ended, the Washington government would have no ulterior motive in enforcing its neutrality laws; would it truly adhere to those laws now that it had nothing to expect from France in return? That question troubled the French, and they increased their vigilance.

As events turned out, the United States did loyally adhere to neutrality. Although Mexican agents were active in New York and throughout the South, they were completely unsuccessful in organizing large expeditions, primarily because of a lack of funds and the alertness of the French and Union officials. One such agent established three recruiting stations in New York—all located in saloons. Borg bribed prospective recruits and gathered sufficient evidence to prevent the sailing of the ships, but never had to use it because the recruits refused to chance such an uncertain undertaking: they had not been paid and they lacked confidence in an activity which was opposed by the government. Cazotte, in San Francisco, was able to prevent the sailing of a large group of men for Juarez's forces. And Acting Secretary of State Hunter showed French chargé Geofroy his orders to the U. S. Army commander in Tennessee and to General Sheridan, on his way to assume command in Texas. Sheridan was ordered to patrol the Rio Grande very carefully, specifically to prevent soldiers from joining Juarez in Mexico. All the officials, including the French, recognized that the United States government could not prevent individuals, especially ex-Confederate soldiers, from slipping into Mexico to join the forces of Juarez. Taken altogether, the French officials throughout the United States were well satisfied that the Federal government effectively enforced its neutrality laws in relation to the enlistment of large groups for service in Mexico.[23] The matter was never the subject of an official dispatch from Drouyn de Lhuys.

The problem of arms and soldiers for Juarez, then, never became a major issue between the Paris and Washington governments. While Paris felt anxiety towards the end of the war concerning at least increased American aid to Juarez, it took no action and based no policy on this contingency. Certainly, it never complained to Washington in any major case, and its own Mexican policy appears to have developed independently of United States actions, though it was well aware of the desire of the people and the government to have the French evacuate Mexico.

French Tobacco

The French attempt to move government-owned tobacco through the Federal blockade affords an insight into the wartime diplomacy of the two American belligerent powers. The episode, beginning as only a complicated commercial operation, developed into a double-edged diplomatic weapon: the South used it to test the Federal blockade, and the North used it to counter the early French policy towards Confederate naval activities in France. It involved two informal understandings between Great Britain and France and an informal convention between the United States and France. The diplomats escalated this minor transaction into such a major, persisting problem that, in the exhilarating moment of victory, Secretary Seward, in a joking way, listed it as the most pressing issue existing between Washington and Paris.

The principal French official acting in this matter was Alfred Paul, the consul at Richmond. He was one of a corps of seventeen French consuls in the United States, seven of whom were assigned to cities now in the Confederacy. Although the consul general was in New York City, Paul assumed the leadership of those in the South because he was in the capital city. Indeed, both the Confederate and French governments tended at times to treat him as a chargé d'affaires. While the consuls in the Northern states made many political reports of which almost all were unfavorable to the Lincoln administration,[24] those in the Southern cities tended to limit their reports and activities to commercial problems and to the protection of French nationals.[25] Paul was the exception because he and Confederate Secretary of State Judah P. Benjamin held frequent discussions on political, military, and social affairs, and he faithfully reported these conversations to the Quai d'Orsay. Close to the Confederate nerve center, Alfred Paul saw the true condition of affairs and early concluded that the South could not possibly win the war. He stands alone among all the French consuls in predicting that manpower and economic shortages eventually would bring the South to its knees.[26]

The particular issue raised by the diplomats involved two quantities of tobacco which were purchased and paid for in late March and early April 1861, just before and after the blockade announcement. Paul acting as agent for the Régie Impériale, the French state tobacco monopoly,[27] had purchased some

7,000 hogsheads of tobacco, and the New York firm of August Belmont and Company had purchased about 2,200 hogsheads for the Paris branch of the Rothschilds.[28]   After an unsuccessful effort to confiscate the Rothschild tobacco, the Confederate government allowed Paul to store all of the tobacco as neutral property.[29]

In January 1863 Drouyn de Lhuys instructed Paul to try to get permission to send all of the tobacco to France.   Paul approached Benjamin, and received his hesitant permission to ship the tobacco through the deep water port of Richmond, City Point, Virginia, on the James River.   But when he consulted the Federal government, Paul received permission to ship the tobacco through the blockade only at Savannah, Georgia.   With the two American governments working at such cross-purposes, Paul was unable to move the tobacco at all.[30] In June he made one of his frequent trips through the battle lines to Washington to confer with the consul general and French minister Henri Mercier on measures for safeguarding the tobacco.

Because the Confederacy imposed certain restrictions on his correspondence, Paul remained in Washington until the middle of July.   He utilized the time to convince Mercier that the value of the tobacco and the amount of the Confederate tax to be imposed in 1864 justified another effort to remove the tobacco. Prodded by the consul, Mercier did reopen the question with Seward.   This second effort convinced the secretary of state that the tobacco was sufficiently important to the French to warrant his attention, and he consulted his cabinet colleagues.   He suggested that the United States could buy French good will if they allowed the tobacco to leave from the James River, through the Hampton Roads blockade.   Such a concession to a sovereign government was quite different from one to a private individual, he argued.   Since the tobacco belonged to the French government and had been purchased prior to the establishment of the blockade, the United States could permit its shipment without prejudicing the validity of the blockade. But Gideon Welles, the secretary of the navy, disagreed and vigorously contested Seward's proposal.   Welles stated that the principle was the same with governments as with individuals, that if the blockade were lifted for one government, it would have to be lifted for all, and that, besides, since the French sympathies were with the South, it did not "pain or grieve" him that they were so highly taxed by the "Rebels." When Seward reiterated that the tobacco had been bought and paid for prior to the blockade, Welles responded that "the rules of the blockade ought not . . . to be relaxed for their benefit."[31] Seward eventually prevailed on Lincoln to grant the permission, but this was achieved at the cost of Welles's good will. Seward also had to impose a special restriction on the final approval: the free passage through Virginia waters was granted only as a special exemption concerning the proper interests of a neutral government and not the private commercial interests of a nation. In order for this to be understood, acknowledgement and specific approval must be obtained from the government of Great Britain as the largest neutral maritime power.[32] The French consul now had his second chance to remove the tobacco.

While Paul made the return trip through the lines to Richmond, Drouyn de Lhuys in Paris wasted no time in seeking British acceptance for the removal of the tobacco. Baron Gros, French ambassador in London, asked Earl Russell, the foreign secretary, for his approval on July 28; three days later Russell agreed, for this one occasion, that the tobacco should pass the blockade, and he promised that his government would not ask for a similar favor.[33] Drouyn then immediately informed Mercier and Paul of Russell's satisfactory answer and added the hope that "the removal would proceed without delay."[34]

Paul echoed this hope, but matters were not to proceed so smoothly. For most of the summer Paul was incapacitated by yellow fever, and the Richmond summer heat was conducive to neither recovery nor activity. Nevertheless, he did manage to request from Benjamin permission to remove the tobacco through Virginia waters. Paul promised that it would be shipped directly from City Point to France. Benjamin's response was in appearance a complex but sincere approval:

> You propose that this tobacco be shipped directly from the port of Richmond; that it be sent on neutral vessels; that all the

shipping documents, both of the vessels and of the cargoes, shall show that the clearances are from Richmond, from which port the shipments are to be made directly for France; and finally that you pledge yourself that the vessels shall not touch nor stop at any port, bay, or point whatever belonging to the territory of our enemy.

After clarifying the last condition to include "our own ports now temporarily in [the enemy's] possession, such as Norfolk, Hampton Roads, etc.," Benjamin granted the permission on the further condition that the ships would not "take any papers nor clearances signed by the enemy. . . ."[35]   Benjamin's language was technically an assertion of Confederate sovereignty; it said, in effect, the government of the Confederate States of America was establishing all the conditions under which maritime activities could be conducted in territory it claimed as well as in territory it actually controlled.

But Benjamin was aiming at more than a mere statement of sovereignty: he was aiming at no less than "an abandonment of the blockade by the United States."   His active mind had jumped from a consideration of the removal of the tobacco to the ever-present King Cotton.   Why not sell cotton to the French government and arrange for its export in the same fashion as the tobacco?   "It seems difficult to discover any reason that the United States could give for refusing to consent that France should export the cotton belonging to the Government any more than the tobacco"; and if the French government, why not the English government?

> The shipment of this tobacco has doubtless been agreed to by the English Government but in point of principle it cannot be denied that the consent of the United States to the passage of this merchandise through the blockading forces is an absolute abandonment of the blockade to the world at large, and as soon as the first vessel passes through under this permission, not a vessel or cargo can properly be condemned in a Federal prize court if the facts be known.[36]

Benjamin was thinking along the very lines which Welles had followed against Seward, and the Confederate permission to remove the tobacco was but the first step in an anticipated series of steps designed to break the blockade by legalistic rather than military means. But Paul did not suspect this and was satisfied with the permission. Everything seemed to be in order to carry out the operation so as to create as little difficulty as possible with Richmond or Washington.

In September, still weak from fever, Paul made the arduous overland trip to New York. There he assigned the French naval vessel "Tisaphone" to accompany freighters which he hired to go to City Point for the tobacco.[37] But another delay was already forming in Washington.

With matters apparently well under control, Mercier, who had also been in New York, went to Newport for a rest at the seashore. Hardly had he had time to relax when an urgent telegram from Seward recalled him to Washington. As he rode the train southward, his harried mind wandered over the various possible reasons for this sudden summons. He decided that it must have something to do with Mexico: after all, the French had only recently announced their intention of supporting Maximilian as emperor of that ancient land; perhaps the president and his cabinet had determined to take a strong line against the establishment of a monarchy in the neighboring country. As the train rocked toward the capital, the September heat became more and more oppressive; Mercier imagined the worst, and, by the time he arrived in Washington, he fully expected to be asked to leave the country. Imagine his relief, then, when Seward told him that the summons was to inform him that the free passage of the tobacco out of Virginia waters would have to be denied.[38]

Unable to shake Mexico from his mind, Mercier asked if the denial were in retaliation for French action there; both Seward and Lincoln, whom he saw, insisted in very friendly terms that Mexico was not a consideration, but neither would give a reason. Mercier was perplexed; he knew only that the tobacco could not be shipped, but he did not know why.[39] Paul, just as perplexed, dismissed his ships and returned to Richmond despondently.[40]

What had caused the new attitude in Washington? Just as the French in America were making final arrangements for the removal of the tobacco, Americans in France were inadvertently upsetting those arrangements. On August 24 the Confederate cruiser "Florida" sailed into the French harbor of Brest. William L. Dayton, the United States minister in Paris, immediately protested its reception by the French authorities and reported this move to Seward, who received the dispatch on September 8.[41] At first he must not have realized its full import, for it was some six days before he called Mercier from Newport. He did not want to explain his actions to Mercier because he was not sure how the French would react to the Federal protests and he wanted to await developments. At any rate, he would withhold the tobacco until matters became clarified.

Another issue shortly arose which further complicated the picture. On September 24 Seward received for the first time proof of the construction of the Confederate ironclads at Bordeaux and Nantes.[42] This information confirmed his determination to refuse all favors to the French until they gave evidence of suppressing such extensive Confederate naval activity. Although Seward in Washington related these various events, Dayton in Paris did not see the connection. On October 19 Drouyn de Lhuys questioned Dayton about the order revoking the permission to export the tobacco. This was the first Dayton had heard of the project, and he did not understand that Seward was using it as a lever in the "Florida" case and in the Confederate ship construction question. Drouyn told Dayton that the revocation had been made because of the necessity of getting England's promise not to hold it as a precedent, and that since he had "gone to the trouble of getting the assent of the British government to this act," he hoped Seward would yet "as a favor permit the export." Recognizing that this was something Seward could grant or withhold at his pleasure, the French government, Drouyn concluded, "attached to the concession a certain importance." Having learned from Drouyn that the tobacco had been purchased and paid for before the war, Dayton wrote Seward that "it would seem there could be little objection, under the circumstances, to permitting its export."[43] By his reference to the "certain importance" the French government attached to the export of the tobacco, Drouyn had informed Seward, without saying as much to Dayton, that expeditious action on the tobacco might result in favorable French action on the Confederate ships.

On the same day that he received the report of Drouyn's conversation about the tobacco, Seward learned that Drouyn de Lhuys had instructed the French ministry of marine to withdraw permission to arm the ships being built at Bordeaux and Nantes.[44] Elated in this justification of his arguments against Welles, Seward immediately called in Mercier and told him that the administration was "very grateful" for this action and that "all disquietness was dispelled."[45] He considered it "a wise and just proceeding, equally honorable to France, and loyal to the relations existing between that country and the United States."[46] The American secretary of state then wrote to his minister in Paris that although the permission to allow the exportation of tobacco through the blockade had been an "act of liberality" on his part, the treatment of the "Florida" and the news concerning the ships being constructed at Bordeaux and Nantes had changed matters; that now "the subject will again be considered by the President in view of the very prompt and honorable proceedings of the Imperial Government in arresting the armaments in the French ports, and Mr. Mercier will be informed of the decision."[47] On the same day Lincoln issued an executive order outlining the conditions under which the exportation of tobacco belonging to foreign governments could be licensed.[48]

Seward obviously felt that his action on the tobacco had affected the French decision to withhold armaments from the Confederate ships under construction. Drouyn confirmed this when he expressed his appreciation for the permission to continue with the removal of the tobacco.[49] Although Seward's action had caused a delay in the export of the tobacco, it had also shrewdly conveyed to the French the seriousness of the Federal protests against the Confederate navy's activity in the French ports.

The executive order provided the means for a third attempt to remove the tobacco. Upon receiving a copy of the order, Napoleon III, through his private secretary, asked John Slidell to urge the Confederate government to cooperate in the tobacco export.[50] In Washington, Seward and Mercier drew up an "Informal Convention" designed to establish the regulations under which "the exportation of certain tobacco from within limits under blockade shall be governed."[51] Besides the expected provisions—the convention stipulated that the tobacco was "purchased and paid for prior to the 4th of March 1861"—it prohibited communication "with any soever," and it provided for the enlistment of forty laborers at Norfolk. The convention was to be valid for five months from the date of signing, which was November 23, 1863. This agreement was to be the controlling document throughout the episode.

Cut off from communication with Washington and Paris, Paul was waiting impatiently in Richmond. His anxiety about the tobacco and the tax soon to be imposed upon it grew with each passing week. His relief was great, when the French navy steam corvette "Grenade" arrived at City Point with the news that the "affair of the Régie tobacco was terminating at Washington and that [Paul] was awaited in the North to make the final necessary arrangements." Because of higher level diplomatic developments, from which he was largely removed, he had been given a third opportunity to ship the tobacco. He quickly boarded the ship and arrived in Washington by December 15, 1863.

On the way to Washington, the ship stopped at Fortress Monroe, and Paul called upon its commander, General Benjamin Butler. The general gave him a copy of the convention, and Paul's heart sank as he read article two stipulating that only the tobacco purchased prior to March 4, 1861, could be exported; but he thought that it must have been a slip of the pen and said nothing about it to Butler. Much to his dismay, he learned in Washington that the pen had not slipped, and he had to inform Mercier that he had not had a single hogshead of tobacco on March 4, 1861. Mercier, who had acted in good faith, and Drouyn de Lhuys in Paris, who had also acted in good faith, were shocked at the new turn of events. Paul, too, had acted in good faith, thinking Mercier had known the date of the purchase, and he was disheartened at the early failure of this new effort. With a heavy heart and with little hope he drew up a new report on the tobacco, and Mercier undertook to negotiate a new convention. The government in Washington showed little desire to hasten into a new agreement, and Paul went to New York "without having any illusion on the probability of a success."[52]

As Paul remained in New York, Mercier began a long trip to France. He was being reassigned, but while in Paris he was to present the details of the tobacco problem to Drouyn. The new negotiations obviously would be drawn out and transferred from Washington to Paris. Nevertheless, Paul seemed happy to be away from Richmond and "found it convenient to await the settlement of the negotiations" in New York City.[53]

Seward wasted no time in transferring the responsibility for further decisions on the tobacco from Washington to Paris. With Mercier in France, he felt matters could proceed more easily there. While he suspected Mercier's personal affinity for the South, he remarked that it would be unfair to "expect greater loyalty from a foreign minister than was exhibited by the Cabinet of Mr. Buchanan." Seward wrote that Mercier "bears with him the respect and good wishes of this government" and commended him to Dayton's "kind and respectful consideration."[54] His words for Paul were not so kind. Unhappy over the false starts and delays and the time spent on the matter of the tobacco, Seward at this point tended to blame Paul. He wrote that it was only after the signing of the convention that Paul "for the first time discovered, or at least made known the fact" that the tobacco had not been purchased prior to the stipulated date. Even so, if France desired to obtain England's assent not to consider the removal of the tobacco purchased after the announcement of the blockade as a precedent for her own commerce, then the president would reconsider the "case in the same spirit of liberality and comity towards France which has governed the proceedings of this Government."[55]

Drouyn de Lhuys was delighted with this attitude and found no fault with Seward's actions. Indeed, he tended to blame his own officials for the trouble because they had not informed him of the exact date of the purchase.[56] So sure were the French that the British would raise no objection to the new circumstances that they detailed a naval vessel to be at Paul's disposal for use in removing the tobacco even before they officially queried London.[57] At the same time, Paul was writing from New York that if the British assent could be obtained, it looked as if all the tobacco would be allowed to be exported.[58] On February 9 Earl Russell gave his assent to the exportation of the tobacco, though it had been purchased after the blockade had been proclaimed. He asserted that England would not consider the case a precedent for her own commerce.[59]

On March 7, 1864, an executive order authorized the French to remove not more than seven thousand hogsheads of tobacco through the blockade in Virginia waters, provided "it is the same tobacco respecting the exportation of which application was originally made by the French Government."[60] This order served only as an amendment to the original convention; all other articles of that convention remained in force, including the deadline of five months from the previous November 23. Paul, as the active French agent, then would have only from March 7 to April 23, 1864, to hire the ships, see to the loading, and actually clear Hampton Roads with the tobacco.

Given the complications and the frustrations already involved in this affair, this appears to be an unusually lenient attitude and action on the part of the United States government. Why did Seward follow this policy? The answer lies not in any specific event, but rather in the general state of affairs at the time. The arguments he had used earlier with Welles were still valid. At the moment, no specific problem disrupted the pleasant relations which had been created by France's decisive action in regard to the Confederate ships being built at Bordeaux and Nantes. But Federal troops had won no important victory since Vicksburg and Gettysburg, and the foreign opinion that the South could maintain its independence remained unchanged. Indeed, Dayton remarked to Seward that without substantial military victories and with Archduke Maximilian slated to become emperor of Mexico, the chances for full diplomatic recognition of the Confederacy by France seemed to be nearer reality.[61] If the permission to export the tobacco would help maintain a friendly feeling in Paris, then Seward could see nothing wrong in granting it. Besides, the affair would cost the United States nothing in money, nor diplomacy, nor military position.

In New York, Alfred Paul was almost beside himself with joy.

The Federal government had decided to permit him to remove all tobacco concerned in the original request, and since he had not acquired any other, Paul happily wrote that "this left nothing to be desired." He was in a hurry to get the tobacco out before the summer campaign began.[62] Excitedly Paul undertook the arrangement of the many details necessary to complete the removal of the tobacco. The prospect of actual accomplishment seemed to overwhelm him and to cause him to doubt his ability to execute the maneuver. As if reassuring himself, he wrote: "The execution of this important operation is now seriously undertaken, and I will do all that is required of me, Sir, for it to have a successful ending." He felt a sense of his own importance and of the pressure of time: "On the eve of my departure, at the moment when the last arrangements of this affair leave me not a minute during the day and force me to write the present dispatch during the night, I do not believe I can do better than to send you a copy . . . of the itinerary I am going to follow on my return to Richmond." Paul went from New York to Washington to leave copies of his latest plans. While there he asked Seward about the time limit set for the removal of the tobacco. He was worried that the operations might not be completed by the deadline of April 23; but Seward told him that this was unimportant. Then he boarded the "Tisaphone" in Baltimore. He stopped at Norfolk and Fortress Monroe, where he entered into a final understanding with General Butler. Because he had not communicated with the Confederate government since leaving Richmond in December, Paul knew that Benjamin was ignorant of the convention and of the delay caused by the purchase date of the tobacco. He felt that the airtight arrangements were necessary to preclude the possibility of the Confederate government changing its decision.[63]

The "Tisaphone" was now joined by the "Grenade," and by two British freighters which Paul had chartered in New York, the "Bidwell" and the "Miller."[64] The four ships proceeded to City Point and there loading began. The work was performed by sailors from the "Tisaphone" and progress was good. Paul was careful to take Commander Marivault, captain of the "Tisa-

phone," into Richmond to meet Benjamin and other officials.
All was going well, Paul felt, and he had no real worries.

But the appearance of the French naval vessels and their
freighters caused Seward some embarrassment, which necessitated his enforcing the convention's time limit. In his absence
from Washington, both Secretary of War Stanton and Welles
objected strongly to President Lincoln upon learning that the
foreign ships were at last beginning to remove the tobacco.
Lincoln refused to discuss the matter with Welles and summoned
Seward from New York.[65] On his return, as he had promised
Paul, Seward at first was willing to extend the time limit for the
tobacco operations, even entering into a correspondence for that
purpose with Louis de Geofroy, the French chargé d'affaires in
Washington. But the arguments of Stanton and Welles soon
prevailed and Seward had to give in; the date originally set for
the completion of the removal of the tobacco, April 23, he said,
could not be extended. He instructed Dayton "to state confidentially to Mr. Drouyn de Lhuys, that operations against the
insurgents in Virginia are contemplated with which the prosecution of the French undertaking for the removal of the tobacco
in Richmond would be incompatible. This suspension is made
for that reason and that only."[66] Paul's pet project was about
to meet another, and this time fatal, delay.

With only 150 hogsheads of tobacco loaded on the "Bidwell,"
Paul received a curt notice from General Butler to return with
all the ships to Hampton Roads because the time limit for the
operations had expired. Recalling Seward's casual remark that
the exact time was unimportant, Paul assumed that Butler's summons was the result of a misunderstanding, and he felt sure he
would be able to return to City Point and complete the loading
operations.

He visited Benjamin to explain this interruption in the loading
procedures. The Confederate secretary of state was concerned
lest the sovereign rights of the Confederacy might be violated
in the port clearance procedure of the loaded ship. Fearing
that his pet project concerning future exports might be compromised, he extracted a promise from Paul that the ships would
clear only from a Confederate port and would sail directly to

France. Paul assured him that he would return for the rest of the tobacco and that the whole trip was necessitated only because of a misunderstanding in the time limit clause of the convention. Having never heard of this convention, Benjamin immediately asked to see a copy of it. Paul promised to bring one back from Fortress Monroe and took his leave.

The two French naval ships and the two freighters proceeded down the river in a strange procession. The partially loaded "Bidwell" was towed by a steam corvette, but the other freighter managed to maneuver with its sails and the current. Paul had a premonition of the real reason for this summons, for as the tobacco parade went by, the shores suddenly became alive with artillery fire. When an occasional musket ball flew over the ships, Paul at first thought he was under fire; but as the intensity of the firing increased he realized that the major artillery barrage presaged further military action. Being acquainted with the slow-moving techniques of General Butler, however, he still hoped to be able to return to City Point and complete the loading operations.

He halted his strange parade several miles up river from Fortress Monroe and sent an officer to General Butler to explain that he could not further descend the James River because of mechanical failure of the "Tisaphone," hoping by this ruse to facilitate his return to Richmond. However, the officer brought a message from Geofroy which Butler had kept for five days without delivering it. For the first time Paul was officially informed that the military operations would prevent the return to complete the loading. He saw that this placed him in a very bad light with Benjamin because he would be unable to keep his promise that the ships would clear only from a Confederate controlled port. Furthermore, he recognized this as another frustration in his attempt to remove the tobacco.

Nevertheless the French consul persisted. He requested from Butler permission to send the "Bidwell" up river so it could clear from Richmond, but the general refused. All that was left to him was to dismiss the "Miller," now not needed, and to try to send the "Bidwell" to sea without touching upon a Northern port. The best he could do was to send her to Norfolk, under French flag, have her report to the French vice-consul there and obtain from him the clearance she should have received from Richmond; she was not to report to the Federal customs house in Norfolk. This done, Paul returned to City Point in the "Tisaphone" and reported to Benjamin.

The suspension of the exportation of the tobacco was taken in stride by Drouyn de Lhuys. He said that the fault was "partly their own, inasmuch as they had been guilty of unnecessary delay" in sending the vessels.[67] He did, however, take care to state "clearly" to Seward that, although military operations did interrupt the removal of the tobacco, the permission granted should remain in force and the operation should be resumed as soon as possible.[68] But he did not press the issue.

Paul, on the other hand, felt very deeply about the suspension of the removal operations. He could not understand why at Washington the explanation given was the approaching military operations and in Fortress Monroe it was the expiration of the time limit. "What to think of all this?—It does not seem appropriate to me that I should express my frank opinion in this regard." It is obvious that Paul blamed Butler not only for interrupting the removal operations, but especially for placing him in an embarrassing position vis-à-vis the Confederate government.[69]

Paul's difficulty arose from Benjamin's objections to the wording of certain articles of the convention of November 23, 1863, between France and the United States, and over the circumstances of the sailing of the "Bidwell." Benjamin saw in these a violation of the sovereignty of the Confederate States, and he questioned the French consul closely on all points.[70] By the convention, Benjamin said, France recognized "the pretentions of the United States to a control over neutral vessels and their crews" while in Confederate ports, and the convention was especially objectionable in that it provided for recruiting and using forty enemy aliens in a Confederate port. "Until the obstacle interposed by the objectionable convention" should be removed, no French vessel could be allowed to take on cargo in any Confederate port.

Paul answered these comments as best he could in his embarrassing position. He stated that neither he nor his superiors had intended in any way to derogate the "dignity or the moral or the material interests" of the Confederacy. As to the use of "enemy aliens," he himself had insisted on that clause in order to avoid offense to the Confederacy; he meant by it to employ *workers*, not *enemies*, in Norfolk; but this was a moot point anyway because the work had been done by French sailors from the "Tisaphone." His astute handling of the clearance of the "Bidwell" through the French vice-consul in Norfolk satisfied Benjamin on that point. The Southerner closed the exchange by reiterating the Confederate resentment over the fact that the convention had been entered into at all. It reflected, he said, the French acceptance of the United States' assertion of the right "to exercise powers of government in our territory, and [it] is a concession of their pretentions that we are not independent of their control"; the Confederacy could never accept this nor could it forget the French role in making the convention. Paul did not respond to this letter, and although neither man was satisfied, they both allowed the matter to drop. Benjamin had, reluctantly, to give up his idea of "forcing an abandonment of the blockade." The question of Confederate *de facto* sovereignty had been raised, then dropped. In any case, it was not this which had prevented the exportation of the tobacco; it was simply the necessities of military operations.

As the Union forces tightened their grip around Richmond in 1865, Paul's movements to and from Washington were restricted.[71] His only responsibility for the remaining tobacco now was to insure its proper storage and protection in Richmond. He placed special agents in guard over it and tried to get Benjamin's promise to assure the safety of the Rothschild tobacco as well as that belonging to the Régie Impériale. But Benjamin replied that if "France had not recognized the blockade, Rothschild could have gotten his tobacco long ago." Thus the fate of the banker's investment was sealed, because Confederate law required that all goods, especially cotton and tobacco, should be destroyed rather than permitted to fall into Federal hands. The Régie tobacco, being property of the French government, was not subject to this law.[72] Paul wrote that he could only wait "until the Federal

troops either withdraw from their advanced position along the
James River or until they enter the city of Richmond."[73]

February and March faded into April, and the event which
Paul had awaited arrived: the Federal troops occupied the city of
Richmond. His description of this momentous event and his
concurrent concern for the tobacco throw light upon the whole
diplomatic problem.

> The evacuation of Richmond is an accomplished fact. Al-
> though long foreseen, evidently it took place sooner than any-
> one expected. It cannot be attributed to any lack of food sup-
> plies, but rather to military operations which broke Lee's lines
> in two principal places. It was Sunday morning, the 2nd of this
> month, that this reverse was confirmed and announced to the
> Richmond government by a telegraphic dispatch from General
> Lee which surprised everyone. Mr. Jefferson Davis was in
> church when this shaking news was communicated to him.
> General Lee expressed little remaining hope to retake the lost
> positions and advised the president to leave that same night with
> all members of his cabinet.
>
> The news spread rapidly throughout the city. Within a few
> hours the greatest confusion reigned in the streets, within the
> ministries, and in public places.[74]

Secretary of State Benjamin summoned Paul to his office about
two o'clock that afternoon. Paul found him "extremely agitated,
his hands shaking, trying to do and say everything at once." He
was preparing to leave at five o'clock with the president and the
other cabinet members, "except the secretary of war who was
to leave Richmond the next day by horseback." Benjamin
greeted the consul and said, "I have nothing particular to say to
you, but I wanted to shake your hand before my departure."
His voice trembled as he continued, "We are going to Danville.
I hope that the railroad will not have been captured at the
Burkesville junction and that we will be able to pass through.
General Lee insists on the immediate evacuation of the city by
the government. It is simply a measure of prudence. I hope
that we will return in a few weeks."

Paul was shocked at the last sentence. "Really?" he asked,

watching the secretary closely to ascertain whether he had said this from a persisting illusion or from a lack of candor. "Do you think you will be able to return?"

"Yes," was Benjamin's answer.

"And the army, will it evacuate tonight?" asked Paul.

Although all well informed people had been assured for an hour that it would, the secretary of state replied, "I am not yet sure." Paul left the office with a feeling of sympathy for the man with whom he had so long dealt on diplomatic matters.

But his sympathy did not blind him to his duty. He went directly to the headquarters of General Richard S. Ewell to seek protection for the tobacco from the pillaging mobs that were beginning to gather. Ewell was cooperative: "My dear consul, speak to the provost marshal before he disappears; he will put a detail at your disposal."

> I got into my carriage in order to go to the agents who were watching over the tobacco and to give them final instructions. I also had to chase about after the provost marshal who, for his part, was giving his last orders everywhere. I met him in the city. He wrote in chalk on the panel of my carriage, the order which put at my disposal a guard detail, composed however of only thirty-eight men.
>
> Once all these formalities were accomplished, I returned to my home quite late and quite exhausted. The city was in a state of indescribable consternation. The silence which precedes great events was terrifying. I threw myself on my bed to take a little rest. In the middle of the night the Confederate military authorities set fire to the [Rothschild] tobacco before leaving the city, obeying the order to leave nothing not in flames. Towards four o'clock in the morning the Confederate troops left the area of Richmond.

As the Union soldiers entered the city, Paul was one person who was happy to see them. He rushed to the headquarters of General Weitzel, "to pay him a visit," and incidentally to ask for a small detail to guard his home and a larger one for "the surveillance and very efficacious protection of the warehouse containing the tobacco belonging to the Régie Impériale." All this the Union general granted in a very courteous and generous manner.

Seward's prediction that "Richmond is like to undergo a change of condition that may affect tobacco as well as other things there" had almost but not quite come true. Due to the French consul's ardent devotion to duty (or to tobacco), the title to the Régie tobacco was not changed by the Union capture of the city. Paul would yet have his chance to export the tobacco.

So persistent a problem had this become that when a spontaneous Washington street celebration resulted from the news of the capture of Richmond, Seward could not refrain from mentioning it.[75] The crowd had gathered in front of the Patent Office and someone suggested that the people "should take a line of march to the War Department." They immediately "proceeded with orderly and well measured steps up F Street to the Department of State." In front of the War and State Department building they heard telegraphic dispatches from the battle front and Secretary of War Stanton spoke to them. Then Secretary of State Seward spoke with the "peculiar felicity of style for which he is so remarkable." With his abundant hair blowing in the breezes, Seward raised his voice: "I thank my fellow citizens," he said, "for the honor they do me by calling to congratulate me on the fall of Richmond. I am now about writing my foreign dispatches. What shall I tell the Emperor of China?" With each country, Seward earned the applause and cheers of the crowd. When he came to England, he spoke of the cheaper cotton the English merchants could now procure; he would remind Lord Russell, he said, that this had been a war "for freedom and national independence, and the rights of human nature, and not a war for empire; and, if Great Britain should only be just to the United States, Canada will remain undisturbed by us so long as she prefers the authority of the noble queen to voluntary incorporation in the United States."

The crowd answered by cheers and exclamations of "that's the talk!" and "You are right!"

Amidst the cheering of the crowd, the secretary asked, "What shall I say to the Emperor of the French?" The answer was immediate: "To get out of Mexico!" But Seward had other things than Mexico on his mind: "I shall say to the Emperor of the French that he can go tomorrow to Richmond and get his tobacco so long held under blockade there, provided the rebels have not used it up!" The crowd laughed and cheered. Had Alfred Paul heard, he too would have cheered.

The effort to remove the tobacco through the Federal blockade was over, but it had raised several important questions and had influenced larger diplomatic maneuverings. The Confederate secretary of state had granted permission to export the tobacco with the hope that it would provide a means to invalidate legally the Federal blockade on government-owned goods. The Union secretary of state had used the tobacco episode as a lever to apply pressure against favorable treatment of Confederate ships in French ports and to prevent the arming of ships constructed in France. While Benjamin had failed to realize his potentially far-reaching change in international practice, Seward had succeeded in his efforts to moderate French actions concerning Confederate ships. The French tobacco in Richmond thus played an important role in the diplomacy of the Civil War.

For Paul and his precious tobacco, the Washington cheers indicated that the war was over. But the end of hostilities brought larger diplomatic problems and more momentous events than the removal of a certain quantity of tobacco from Richmond. The fortunes of the battlefields and the international postures of great powers would bear on the final cessation of hostilities.

Chapter XVI

THE CESSATION OF HOSTILITIES

THE end of the Civil War in America would have particular significance to the French because of their war in Mexico: the double relationship of neutrality and belligerency which Paris shared with Washington would be reduced to a single relationship of French belligerency and American neutrality. This prospect alerted the French to watch for all possible indications of a cessation of hostilities; they were particularly concerned that a negotiated peace might bring a combined military action against their forces in Mexico, or that an overwhelming victory by the North might lead Northern public opinion to demand a full-scale land and sea attack against the French south of the Rio Grande. In either case, therefore, the French government would be affected; its officials scrutinized every event to determine if a meaningful trend toward peace might be developing. The first to claim that he saw such a trend was the emperor himself. From the moment, he said, "that the plan of campaign arranged between Grant and Sherman was reported to me, I saw by the maps that it was the beginning of the end."[1]

General Grant was appointed by President Lincoln as general in chief of the United States Armies on March 9, 1864. He chose to make his headquarters with the Union Army of the Potomac, still under the command of General Meade, and to intrust the direction of the Armies of the West to General Sherman. For the first time, in the spring of 1864, the Union armies were under a single military command. As Grant's army crossed the Rapidan River and, in the face of Lee's murderous resistance, slid southeastward through the Wilderness, and as Sherman's troops left Chattanooga for Atlanta, the strategy of a giant pincers against the heartland of the South became apparent to any expert map reader. Napoleon III, a serious student of warfare, leaning over the maps in the Tuileries, could easily have foreseen that the Confederacy would not be able to defend itself much longer.

Whether the emperor and his ministers actually saw the coming end of the war so soon or so clearly cannot be certain. But a change of attitude in French diplomacy towards Richmond and Washington dates from the spring of 1864. With the exception of a mild flurry, during the ensuing summer, of diplomatic rumors that France would extend official recognition to the Confederacy, the policies of France were increasingly governed by a growing expectation of peace. The rumors of recognition were inspired by the unexpectedly slow progress of Grant and Sherman and by the political controversies surrounding the upcoming presidential elections in the North. After Sherman's capture of Atlanta and after Lincoln's re-election, French diplomacy seemed to become a waiting game—a game filled with suspense, anticipation, and some fear. The diplomats watched, as if fascinated, the slow march of Sherman to the coast, the tightening grip of Grant around Petersburg and Richmond; they feared the possible outcome of the Hampton Roads Conference; and they extended congratulations at the fall of Richmond and expressed shock and condolences at the assassination of Lincoln. But they moved slowly, while they put their own house in order and they quibbled over the rights of neutrals, before they officially recognized the end of hostilities in the summer of 1865.

Throughout this period, Federal diplomats acted with a marvelous restraint in view of the military victory they were sure would come. Secretary of State Seward, William L. Dayton, and his successor as U. S. minister to Paris, John Bigelow, sensitively respected the French rights and demands. They ignored the weak gestures toward recognition of the Confederacy in the summer of 1864; they hastened to reassure the Quai d'Orsay of unchanged policy after the Hampton Roads Conference; and they reasserted the neutrality of the United States at the moment of the fall of Richmond. The tragedy of Lincoln's death and of

Seward's wounds tended to immobilize the Federal diplomatic machinery temporarily; but the first task Seward assumed upon his return to work was to seek French recognition of the end of hostilities, and this he coupled with reassurances of continued neutrality in Mexico, even sending to Paris a copy of Sheridan's orders as that hero assumed command of the Union troops along the Rio Grande. If national ambitions, self-interest, and military strength ever appeared to be ready to ignite into war, they did so between France and the United States at the end of the Civil War; but if ever understanding and restrained diplomacy avoided war, this occurred between these two countries at this time.

Changing Attitudes

The single factor contributing most to changing the French attitude toward the American Civil War was her deepening involvement in Mexico. When France first entered Mexico, Secretary Seward protested but wisely made no threats. He received in turn a French promise that they intended no permanent aggrandisement in the Western Hemisphere, and the two governments reached a *modus vivendi* as of the summer of 1862. Tied down by the Civil War, Seward accepted at face value the French explanations of their actions in Mexico. His government, he wrote, "regards the conflict as a war involving claims by France which Mexico has failed to adjust . . ., and it avoids intervention between the two belligerents."[2]

Archduke Maximilian's acceptance of the Mexican throne in the fall of 1863, however, necessitated a reevaluation of the established *modus vivendi*. Seward refused to be drawn into this new stage of Mexican affairs even when Drouyn de Lhuys stated that the withdrawal of French troops would be hastened by Federal recognition of Maximilian. Mercier, in Paris en route to his new post in Madrid, freely spoke of the friction created by the Mexican question,[3] and Dayton was sure that while Napoleon III would not militarily intervene in the Civil War, his sympathies now were "in favor of the rebels." At the same time, Dayton felt that Napoleon really wanted only to get Maximilian to

Mexico and his own troops out.[4] Seward, meanwhile, relying
on Corwin's reports from Mexico, became convinced that a
monarchy could never be established successfully there and,
despite congressional pressure, saw no need for any Federal action against France or Maximilian.[5] He did protest to Paris
that in sending Maximilian to Mexico, France departed "very
materially from the assurances" it had previousy given.[6] Thus
the United States position in regard to Mexico was to remain one
of patient protest and of increasing pressure as the Civil War drew
to a conclusion. Basically, this unsteady arrangement prevailed
until the end of the war, and even until the French decision to
withdraw their troops in 1866.[7]

From the French side, Drouyn de Lhuys fully appreciated the
unsteady balance existing between Paris and Washington. In
principle opposed to any French involvement overseas, and in
particular averse to the Mexican venture,[8] Drouyn worked hard
to maintain a reciprocal neutrality towards the Civil War and
to avoid a confrontation over Mexico. After the fiasco of the
Roebuck affair and the Union victories of Gettysburg and Vicksburg, Drouyn constantly used the French vulnerability in Mexico
to prevail upon his emperor and his government colleagues to
maintain that neutrality and to avoid that confrontation. His
success was not always complete; events often forced him into
positions which he did not like and from which he had to withdraw with care. One such event was the arrival of Maximilian
in Mexico City in June 1864.

The months between Maximilian's election and his departure
for Mexico were filled with speculations and rumors. As early
as September 1863 Drouyn de Lhuys acknowledged French support for the archduke, while insisting that the French troops
would soon leave. He implied his own disapproval of the whole
affair, saying that since it had been in progress when he had returned to office he now only could "carry out the wishes of the
emperor."[9] At the same time in Austria the Hapsburg family
was attempting to work out Maximilian's relation to the Austrian
throne should he go to Mexico. While Mexican agents were actively trying to persuade the Austrian imperial family of the advantages to Maximilian, others were pointing out the disadvan-

tages. Journals "close to the U. S. legation" developed the theme that the Mexican population would be hostile to the French and that "the election of the Archduke would be a trap."[10] From Vienna to Paris the rumor spread that Maximilian conditioned his acceptance upon the prior recognition of the Confederacy by France.[11] Paris queried London about recognizing the South, and Lord Palmerston responded that, unless they were willing to force the blockade, such diplomatic action would be useless.[12] Drouyn, in one of his rare interviews with Slidell, reflected warmth towards the South, but told him that Lord Palmerston considered a diplomatic move impractical,[13] and Slidell knew that France would not act unilaterally. These rumors and weak diplomatic feelers, stemming from Maximilian's election to the Mexican throne, preceded his acceptance and his preparations for the trip across the Atlantic.

Part of the preparations were made during a week-long visit to Paris in March 1864. Busy arranging a loan to support his Mexican venture, Maximilian had no time to interview petitioning diplomats. John Slidell, trying to rationalize the snub, blamed a most improbable rumor. Mercier, he wrote, brought word from Lincoln that Maximilian would receive quick recognition from Washington provided he would avoid all negotiation with the Confederacy.[14] Dayton at the same time worried lest Maximilian recognize the South, indicating that he knew nothing about any such Lincoln message. Both Drouyn de Lhuys and Napoleon III assured him that "the Archduke while here never spoke . . . of recognizing the South."[15] In truth, the matter had been settled by Palmerston's refusal prior to the archduke's trip, but so strong were the rumors that the agents of both North and South were willing to credit the most unlikely.

Although nothing more than rumors resulted from Archduke Maximilian's visit to Paris, the Northern diplomats were compelled to take a long look at their possible future relations with France and Mexico. Dayton was pessimistic. He felt sure the Mexican policy would lead to French recognition of the South, and he saw no relief by way of military success with "battles gained and battles lost, but ending in nothing decisive." He was "heartsick of this question."[16] Later when he heard that the

French Mexican loan had been approved, he was certain that the South would be recognized because he saw "nothing in the present condition of things in Mexico to justify the hope that the Republicans can successfully meet the invading forces of France." Although the United States could tip the balance by intervening, Dayton insisted that "we cannot under existing circumstances afford a war with France for the quixotic purpose of helping Mexico."[17] In Washington, Seward, taking a harder look, refused to see such a dark picture. Specifically trying to shake off Dayton's discontent, the secretary predicted that Maximilian would have enough of insurgents in Mexico without extending his "guardianship to insurgents here," and that Napoleon could hardly "enlarge his responsibilities concerning American politics" while the Mexican question remained unsettled.[18] Thus Washington saw the Mexican developments as still a standoff: France was too tied down there to take any action in the South, and the United States was too tied down by its own struggle to take any action in Mexico.

As events began to converge in the summer of 1864, the question of French recognition of the Confederacy was raised for the final time. Maximilian and Carlotta landed on Mexican soil at Vera Cruz, in May, and moved on to Mexico City, where they arrived on June 12, 1864. At about the same time, the furious battle between the "Alabama" and the "Kearsarge" took place off Cherbourg; and Drouyn de Lhuys, on June 8, assured Dayton of the French determination to maintain a "strict neutrality," and the next month wrote his "Report to the Emperor on the Affair of the 'Rappahannock'."[19] In the Federal Union political affairs in preparation for the November presidential elections dominated the scene. Lincoln was nominated by the Baltimore Convention of the Union Party in early June, and the move to replace him began within the Greeley faction of the Republicans. The Peace Democrats seemed to control the machinery for their convention, still to come. Finally, the summer military campaigns appeared to be indecisive: Grant was checked by Lee at Cold Harbor, Early, active in the Shenandoah Valley, was soon to threaten Washington, and Sherman was stalled before Atlanta.

Consul Paul was writing from Virginia that he found the "Government of the South very confident, full of hope for the next campaign. ..." "It is believed," he said, "that Richmond will hold out." Furthermore, he added, "General Lee's army is in the best of condition," being composed of from seventy-five to eighty thousand men. Supplies in Virginia were complete, with everything arriving there from all over the South; the supply "has almost doubled in the last three months." But Paul also warned that inflation had continued to the point where paper money was worthless and that the military situation imposed upon the South conditions requiring "unheard of efforts to bring about success which moreover would have a very grave importance at the time of the elections in the North."[20] Such a mixed report on the state of affairs in the Confederacy hardly inspired confidence in its chances for independence, but neither did it reflect discouragement.

During the summer of 1864 European affairs demanded the primary attention of Drouyn de Lhuys. He was in the last stages of negotiating the September Convention with Italy,[21] hoping to settle the problem which had occasioned his return to office. Simultaneously since mid-April he had been deeply involved in the London Conference which had been called to negotiate an end to the war being fought by Prussia and Austria against Denmark over the Schleswig-Holstein duchies. As Maximilian arrived in Mexico City and Greeley began the move to replace Lincoln on the Republican ticket, Drouyn was seriously contemplating war against Prussia.[22] These European problems, so close to home, obviously assumed more immediacy to the Quai d'Orsay than did transatlantic ones.

In Paris, then, the foreign minister exercised extreme care in American affairs, even leading the cabinet council to pro-Union decisions at the moment Maximilian was ascending his throne in Mexico. In Washington, the president and his secretary of state were fighting for their political lives while their armies were fighting indecisive battles in the field. Such a concentration of various factors had not occurred simultaneously before during the Civil War. It was no time for diplomatic action by any party concerned.

In this unlikely climate rumors of another French effort to mediate the Civil War made the rounds of European capitals. John Slidell wrote on June 2, 1864, that Mason had learned through a friend that "Lord Palmerston had intimated a disposition not to oppose a motion tending toward an offer of mediation," and that Palmerston had received two messages from Napoleon indicating a desire "to act in American affairs." Upon such flimsy information were the rumors based. Slidell asked his friend in the French foreign ministry concerning the messages said to have been sent by the emperor to Palmerston. The response carried Drouyn's denial of any knowledge of such messages; but even the foreign minister did not deny their existence. The lack of such overtures to Drouyn was confirmed a few days later by Dayton, who further expressed his own doubt of their existence.[23] The Franco-British correspondence brings no such effort to light; if any exchange between Napoleon and Palmerston occurred it must have been personal and unofficial. The only reference to diplomatic action towards the United States was in correspondence between Montholon, currently French minister to Mexico City and soon to be minister to Washington, and Geofroy, currently French chargé d'affaires in Washington. Montholon inquired from Mexico City concerning the best "fashion in which the notification of the advent of the Emperor Maximilian should be received" in Washington. Geofroy replied that the "moment was badly chosen for such a communication because of the approaching election," and advised Montholon to delay any such action until the winter; even then he could not predict a favorable response by the Washington government. Informed of this exchange, Drouyn de Lhuys fully approved Geofroy's suggestion to wait.[24] How different was this reported French effort from the bold suggestion in October 1862 of a tripartite mediation, or from the unilateral offer of good offices on January 9, 1863. That the diplomats should be disturbed by such rumors reflects the toll on nerves which the long war years had exacted.

Only Seward, in the seat of the war-torn Washington government, in the midst of a critical political struggle, and Drouyn de Lhuys, conducting a foreign policy constantly subject to the whims of an unpredictable emperor, were calm and unexcited. Drouyn said, simply, "Wait." Seward, on the other hand, stood fast in his confidence in the Union cause. To the early rumors of the mediation effort, Seward wrote Dayton: If they be true, "You will then inform Mr. Drouyn de Lhuys that the United States adhere to their determination, heretofore announced, namely, to be exclusive of all foreign nations, the arbiter of its [sic] own rights and duties in the present civil war." Later, after some reflection, he wrote that he did not anticipate any trouble with France because "European questions have become too critical to allow active hostilities against us at the present." He further stated that the Civil War was approaching an end and he was sure it had developed "martial forces here which are sufficient to arrest the attention of statesmen, however unwillingly, in foreign countries." And, finally, as the battle of Atlanta was in progress, he wrote that should any action be taken by France, then Dayton was to express himself "not doubtfully in the sense in which I have written."[25] But Drouyn's admonition was being heeded, and no suggestion of a mediation attempt was made.

Indeed, French diplomatic activity towards the Americas seems to have been suspended during the remaining months of the year. August and September were months of intense political maneuvering in the United States. The Democratic Convention, meeting in Chicago in late August, nominated General George B. McClellan as candidate for the presidency, but only after he had stated his strong belief in the Union. August also saw a strong but unsuccessful effort by some Republicans to force Lincoln from the race and to nominate another, a peace candidate. And September, after Hood's evacuation of Atlanta on the second, saw General Frémont withdraw as a candidate of the disaffected radicals.[26] While details of this confusing American game were reaching France, so were details of the peace efforts of Horace Greeley in Niagara and of the Jaquess-Gilmore mission to Richmond.[27] Such a profusion of contradictory information was underscored by reports reaching Paris from its own agents in America. In mid-August, consul to New York Boilleau's analysis described in detail the separatist tendencies in various parts of the former United States. Referring to the West's independence movement, Boilleau concluded: ". . . it is not a question only . . . of preventing the division of the United States into two republics, one in the North and one in the South, because this first separation, should it come about, would inevitably lead to others, and the United States would be exposed, more and more, to falling into the condition of most of the South American republics. European commerce could only lose from this change, and civilization would probably gain nothing."[28] Later, in reporting the nomination of McClellan, Boilleau indicated his strong doubt that McClellan's candidacy, or even his election, would in any way contribute to peace.[29] In the face of these reports, and of Sherman's victories in Georgia, Emperor Napoleon in late September seized an occasion at the races in the Bois de Boulogne to discuss affairs with Slidell. According to the Southerner's account, Napoleon was warm and friendly. He asked questions about Atlanta and listened politely as Slidell minimized the effect of its fall upon the Confederacy and predicted a Lee victory over Grant; but there is no indication that the emperor agreed with Slidell's analysis. Napoleon then turned to politics, and especially to McClellan's letter concerning the maintenance of the Union. That letter, accepting the Democratic nomination, had "greatly disappointed him," he said, "for he had entertained strong hopes that the terrible conflict would soon be ended."[30]

In his dispatches from Richmond, French Consul Paul reported that, although they knew it would not mean peace, the South preferred McClellan to Lincoln if for no other reason than they knew he would be different, and "the South is willing to take a chance with the unknown rather than the known of Lincoln."[31]

By the beginning of October, then, the French officials were well informed on matters in the North and in the South. Drawing a realistic conclusion, they determined to make no move until the elections were over; but regardless of the victor in the political campaign, they were sure that the North would carry the war to a military conclusion. Sherman's position in Georgia and Grant's posture before Richmond and Petersburg indicated to them that the military victory would not be long delayed. These feelings were confirmed by the news contained in a long dispatch from Paul, written before the elections but arriving in Paris at about the same time as the election results. Paul wrote that despite the "strong hand" of the Richmond government, the "general weariness of the people" was beginning to be manifest. It showed itself in the actions of the state legislatures, and he cited at length Governor Watts' inability to control the Alabama legislators and of the resolution there to enter into negotiations for peace on the basis of McClellan's stand. He spoke of the South's realization that slavery was an institution of the past, regardless of the outcome of the war. And he freely predicted the victory of Lincoln, which would mean war to the end, with no chance for compromise.[32]

Involved as deeply as they were in Mexico and with European events attracting their attention more and more, the French now had to face the certainty of a Union victory in America. The only questions which remained were how soon that victory would come, how great would be the Federal strength in victory, and how quickly the French could settle their affairs in Mexico. The cessation of hostilities between the North and the South increasingly became more critical to French interests in the Western Hemisphere and in Europe. The French attitude now changed, definitely, from one of sympathy and concern to one of vital self-interest. The policy of strict neutrality, which Drouyn de Lhuys had begun to advocate and to execute as early as the previous year was emerging as a truly wise and sane policy for the self-interest of France. From this time onward, he would have a free hand in executing that policy. The matter of the ships at Bordeaux and Nantes had only to be worked out in detail; the policy toward the "Rappahannock" had only to be maintained; the question of belligerent rights was already settled. Drouyn needed only to deal deftly with the results of the election, the Hampton Roads Peace Conference, the fall of Richmond, the death of Lincoln, and the formalities of the cessation of hostilities; and he must do all this with one eye on events in Mexico, hoping that Maximilian would consolidate his position there before the full power of America should be free to challenge him.

Lincoln's Reelection and Confederate Peace Overtures

Although the emperor had expressed disappointment in McClellan's stand on the Union, he nonetheless followed the election results with much interest. He seems to have expected a McClellan victory to increase the chances of a negotiated peace in America and a Lincoln victory to prolong the war to a military decision. Earlier in the campaign French press opinion had reflected the same thought, but on the eve of the election it became more moderate. The *Constitutionnel*, analyzing the relative power of the two candidates, concluded that Lincoln would undoubtedly be reelected, and the *Journal des Débats* surmised that the question of war or peace would not be decided by the outcome of the election because McClellan would never consent to secession.[33] The *Débats*, however, named Lincoln as the representative of "the courageous party" which sought the elimination of slavery as an objective of the war, and McClellan's as the party which sought reestablishment of the Union through any sacrifice necessary. Since the Democrats were regarded as the party of peace at any price, the French liberals had more respect for McClellan than they did for his party, and they feared the possible results of a Democratic victory. The *Revue des deux mondes* considered that "the election of a Democratic candidate is the last chance upon which the Confederates count; the reelection of Lincoln would take away all hope from them."[34] Public opinion seems to have followed much the same line. As early as April 1864, the dominant view in Mulhouse expected the desire for peace during the year to be accomplished "either by the exhaustion of the South or by a change of policy in the North, or by the replacement of Lincoln by a president more favorable to the ideas of conciliation." As the election date neared, opinion crystallized. Wherever reported, public opinion saw the best hope for peace in McClellan's election but anticipated Lincoln's reelection which would prolong the war.[35] The emperor, public opinion, and the liberal French press, then, took the same view as to the outcome of the elections, but they all had different feelings about it.

Lincoln's victory brought surprisingly little comment from French officials. No reference to it is made in the diplomatic documents; about a month later Napoleon obliquely referred to it in a conversation with Lord Cowley when he agreed that it was wise for both England and France to retain a policy of "strict neutrality" towards the war.[36]   But the French press was quite outspoken.   The *Journal des Débats* openly praised the "very remarkable proof of intelligence and patriotism" of American universal suffrage in pronouncing so decisively in favor of the continuation of the war.[37]   Such favorable response lifted Dayton's spirits because this show of strength, he felt, would prevent any further foreign mediation efforts which had been based upon the presumed weakness of the Lincoln administration; "the conduct of foreign affairs shall be easier now these next four years."[38]

The conservative press in France, however, tried to rationalize the Lincoln victory.   The *Patrie*, on November 24, propounded the unlikely theory that Lincoln's presidency could be valid only in those states casting ballots in the election, and the Confederacy should be recognized as a separate, sovereign nation since the people in the South had no chance to vote for or against Lincoln.[39]   The liberal press immediately attacked this view as "casuistry and chicanery"; the provincial *Phare de la Loire* hit a sore point with the government by pointing out that the same notion, applied to Mexico, would make Juarez sovereign in those areas of Mexico not controlled by Maximilian.   Finally, the *Opinion Nationale* more seriously showed that all the electoral votes of the Southern states still would not have defeated Lincoln.[40]   Dayton, assuming that the *Patrie* accurately reflected the official views, launched into a tirade against both the English and the French press which he accused of conducting a joint effort to "encourage the South to hold out in the hope of recognition."[41]   Even Seward, as late as January 1865, blamed the *Patrie*'s theory for encouraging the "insurgent confidence at home and abroad."[42]

The press debate reflected the divided public opinion on Lincoln's reelection.   Republicans and those opposed to slavery applauded the victory.[43]   But most of the reactions, as shown in the procureur reports, were more prosaically economic than ideological.   In Amiens, where the cotton cloth manufacturers had adjusted to fibres from other parts of the world, the people were indifferent to the election results specifically because they had found other sources of raw cotton. In Besançon, Lyons, and Nancy, where the loss of the American market had hurt the industries, the public regretted Lincoln's victory because they believed it would delay peace by hardening Northern attitudes against conciliation. In Mulhouse, where the costly cloth had been produced despite the high cost of cotton, the industrialists were happy with the election results, despite their general pro-Southern feelings, because they did not want a sudden peace to catch them with a large inventory of high-priced cotton. They were confident Lincoln's reelection meant a prolonged war to a military decision, by which time they could adjust to a sudden drop in cotton prices.[44] Thus while the reaction varied, most Frenchmen felt the election results assured a delayed peace which could result only from a military victory.

The contemporary evaluation of the effect of Lincoln's victory on the war, then, was almost unanimous: in both France and the United States it was believed that the South would have to capitulate eventually to all of the Northern demands. But when the Confederates refused to lay down their arms, indeed when they continued their staunch defense of Richmond in the face of Sherman's practically uncontested advances, confidence turned to perplexity. As the weeks, then months slipped by without decisive military action, new peace overtures began to take shape. As it turned out, the Confederates were able to negotiate with the reelected Lincoln much as they would have with McClellan. Whatever historical hindsight has read into the campaign and election of 1864,[45] Davis' government did choose to seek a compromise with Lincoln while it still had arms in the field and thus had something to trade, and it also sought foreign recognition by giving up slavery.

But before either the Hampton Roads Conference or the Kenner Mission could reach the diplomatic level, tragedy struck the Federal establishment in Paris. William L. Dayton, the Minister of the United States, died unexpectedly on December 1, 1864.[46] After eating a heavy meal, he went for a walk. Feeling ill, he stopped to see a certain Mrs. Eckels, but died almost immediately of an apparent stroke. His health had been bad for some time and had been reflected in the attitudes expressed in his private as well as public correspondence. There are traces of a persecution complex in his private letters during the last few months of his life. As early as the previous April, he had written: "If we have difficulty with this country it will grow directly or indirectly out of complications in Mexico. I am sick and tired of the question of *recognition*. I am kept in a state of constant annoyance by this question. . . . the Emperor and his entire court are against us, and I never know when I am safe. . . ." And again: "I am sick, heartsick of our useless, abortive efforts." In September he expressed his despondency just before the elections: "I am very tired of France and will be happy when *my tenure is up*."[47] His elation over Lincoln's election had been replaced by depression resulting from the *Patrie* theory and by the indecisiveness of events since the election. Dayton's illness apparently was of long standing and accounts for the moody pessimism which Seward occasionally attempted to relieve.

The sad story of Dayton's death is enlivened by the tragicomedy surrounding the removal of his body from the apartment of Mrs. Eckels. The American doctor, who answered Mrs. Eckels' summons, perceived that should an official inquest into the death be held on the premises it would cause "many inconveniences." He therefore sent a message to Dayton's son to bring a carriage to Mrs. Eckels' address. After "an altercation with the proprietor of the hotel . . . they got the body in the carriage and took it home." But the precautions were taken in vain, for Mrs. Eckels insisted on riding with the body to the legation. When the doctor tried to discourage her, she exclaimed: "What will Mrs. Dayton think? My reputation is involved. I must go at once!"[48] And so the distinguished diplomatic career of Dayton was ended in the parlor of one whom history does not deny to have been a courtesan.[49]

Dayton had been an effective representative during the trying war years. He had reached a comprehension of Drouyn de Lhuys and of Napoleon which, except during the last months, had enabled him to interpret their moves with a high degree of accuracy. From the time the French suggested tripartite mediation of 1862, he and Drouyn had had no serious misunderstanding. His successor was John Bigelow, who had been in Paris as consul general since the middle of September 1861. His primary task in that office had been to present the Union cause in a favorable light to the French public, and he had worked hard and with some success.[50] By the time of Dayton's death, Bigelow was well known in Paris, particularly among the more liberal press officials. He had had some dealings with Drouyn de Lhuys so that the two men were not strangers. For the few remaining months of the war Bigelow served as an effective representative of the United States, working well with the French officials. He was more optimistic than the ill Dayton had recently been, could see the various sides of diplomatic questions, and contributed to the maintenance of friendly relations between the two countries.

These friendly relations shortly underwent the most serious trial of the entire war. The trial was of short duration, but it was intense and real; for the first time it created a thorough French study on the feasibility of a war against the United States in Mexico. But reassurances from Washington and the rapid movement of military events in the South prevented the crisis from developing beyond the alert stage; it never really reached the diplomatic stage.

The precipitating event was the Hampton Roads peace conference between Confederate commissioners and Secretary of State Seward and President Lincoln.[51] Amidst widespread rumors, the men met on February 3, 1865, on board the "River Queen" where Lincoln insisted, as conditions of peace, on the reunion of the states, the abolition of slavery, and the disbanding of all confederate forces. The Southern leaders, seeking an armistice, suggested a suspension of hostilities with "a postponement of the question of separation upon which the war is waged, and a mutual direction of the efforts of the Government as well as those of the insurgents, to some extrinsic policy or scheme for a season," during which passions would subside and trade be resumed.[52] This event led to the inevitable rumors which were reported to Paris more nearly as fact. The New York consul reported that the South's determination became stronger with each military defeat,[53] and the French chargé in Washington, Geofroy, sent two detailed accounts. Just before the meeting he reported that part of the agreement would be that "the army of the South would be retained in its present organization and used beside that of the North in a great foreign war." If the Conference succeeds, he continued, "the alliance against a foreign power will be the pivot of reconciliation; and we would, within the next six months, see the war transplanted to the borders of Mexico and Canada." Geofroy noted, finally, that Seward "continues to cast a skeptical eye on all of this."[54]

The references to a joint foreign war were underlined for special attention in the French foreign office, and undoubtedly caused much discussion. The implications of Geofroy's comments were obvious to Drouyn de Lhuys. Lincoln's desire to end the civil strife could easily lead him into a war with France in Mexico; the best hope to avoid such a conflict rested on Seward's skepticism of the South's sincerity. Drouyn awaited further reports. Geofroy's account of the meeting was soon forthcoming: but, except for the actual conversation aboard the "River Queen," it was filled with errors concerning friction between the president and his secretaries of war and the treasury, and between the president and Seward. But most important to Paris was Geofroy's evaluation of Lincoln and Seward in their reaction to the meeting. While their comments about the meeting have "been identical in form, they are obviously different in principle." Seward says the meeting failed, and that is the end of it; "Lincoln has not been as definitive by far in his assertions." Geofroy said that since his reelection Lincoln "affects a great independence from the members of his cabinet and would be perfectly capable of making some great decision without consulting his advisors."[55] It is paradoxical that Geofroy's report was so accurate about the actual exchanges during the conference and so misleading about the events surrounding it and about the attitudes of Lincoln and Seward.[56] In Paris, Geofroy's reports aroused real fear of a North-South coalition against the French position in Mexico, a danger all the more real because of Lincoln's desire to establish peace even against Seward's advice.[57] That Geofroy, in this respect, was wrong is beside the point; the French had to act on the assumption that he was correct.

Drouyn initiated action which led to a long conversation between Seward and Geofroy. Seeking to elicit a clear statement of United States policy toward Mexico, Drouyn, through Geofroy, first raised the question of the hostile attitudes towards France which were manifest in the Northern press. These attitudes had "even forced the government of the emperor . . . to ask ourselves seriously if, after the submission of the South, we would not have war with the United States over Mexico." Seward, still retaining his caution towards France, answered that the United States had no bad disposition against the French. "As for throwing ourselves into Mexico," he said, "we are a people too practical to undertake a costly affair which would increase our debt immeasurably without leading to any clearly defined gain." After a slight hesitation, he continued: "Only in a case where our national honor would be engaged, would we be so determined; but I believe that with circumspection on both our parts, this can be avoided." Geofroy was convinced that Seward was sincere; but such guarantees depended on Seward's health and power in the government. Given the differences between the president and the secretary of state, which Geofroy was sure existed, he warned Drouyn: "If Seward were a sovereign and could be counted on for ten years of life, assuredly the best could be accepted from his words; but who will be talking to us tomorrow?" [58] Drouyn, too, felt uneasy; he took care to remind the ministers of war and of the navy that French forces must maintain the strictest neutrality along the Mexican-Texas border. [59]

Seward, fearful France might undertake some drastic preventive action in Mexico, seized the occasion to send further assurances to Paris. "In regard to the apprehensions of aggression by the United States on the restoration of peace, you are authorized to say that no such policy is entertained by this government." [60] With Geofroy's evaluation clearly before him, and apprehensive that Seward might not long be in government, Drouyn responded with a detailed outline of French policy since 1861. He assured Seward that the French had always followed a policy of careful neutrality and had maintained "a friendly character in its relations with the United States." Saying that he rejected the suppositions existing in Europe that the United States would end the war by throwing itself against the French in Mexico, he professed to accept the assurances extended by Seward. "The high intelligence of the statesman frees him, we are sure, from prejudgement and prejudice, which events in Mexico could evoke in persons less elevated." Drouyn returned Seward's assurances with some of his own: French actions in Mexico did not conflict with United States' interests, and the French troops would be withdrawn as soon as possible.[61] Thus by reciprocal promises, the two chief diplomats tried to reassure each other; but as they did so, they inadvertently made the peace hang upon their personal words. Should either leave office for any reason, the mutual declarations could easily be voided.

Bigelow did not fully appreciate this, and he did surprisingly little to mitigate the impressions which Geofroy had created or to support Seward's assurances. Once when the minister of finance blurted out that "he feared that the greatest cause of war between France and the United States was Mexico," Bigelow did try to calm him by saying that the United States would find it impossible, once peace was concluded, to maintain 500,000 troops in its army.[62] And he did attempt to alleviate Napoleon's expressed fears about the Hampton Roads Conference by quoting Seward's account of the meeting.[63] But these were minor and responsive statements and they had little effect. Indeed, rumors spread in Paris that no alliance between the North and the South would be permitted by Europe and that Napoleon III would "punish any attempt on the part of the United States to pursue the Monroe Doctrine."[64] So thoroughly did Bigelow misunderstand the French mood that he failed to get intelligence of a most significant French move which resulted from the Hampton Roads Conference and its complications.

The emperor, as a responsible chief of state who saw the real possibility of a war, consulted his military authorities. Captain Hore, the British naval attaché in Paris, reported to Earl Russell:

I had a conversation yesterday with Admiral Page, the president of the "Conseil des travaux de la Marine," in the course of which in speaking of Mexico and the United States, he told me that the Emperor *some short time ago* desired the Minister of Marine to report on the means of conveying 100,000 troops to

Mexico, and of carrying on naval warfare single-handed against the United States.

A commission of officers drew up a report on these subjects which was far from satisfactory to His Majesty. It declared that the French navy was not competent to carry on a successful war at such a distance from France as the coasts of Mexico and the United States. The want of coal and the means of repairing machinery as well as the almost certain impossibility of keeping open their communications with France, would render such a war most hazardous.

The report ended by saying that if France and England were combined the case would be widely different, and they should look with confidence to the successful result of such a conflict.[65]

The difficulty of placing exactly the date of "some short time ago," is reduced by the flow of events. The French fear of the need for a war against the United States could not have materialized prior to the news of the Hampton Roads Conference (the 22nd of February) nor would it have arisen much after Appomattox. Indeed, there are indications that the officers' report was in the hands of the emperor by early March, for on the third of that month Bigelow noticed a change in the attitude of Drouyn de Lhuys:

> There was something in his manner if not in his words and in the whole tone of his conversation . . . that gave me the impression that the policy of his government towards the United States had recently undergone or was about to undergo a substantial change, provided nothing new occurred on our side to disturb the present tendency of events.[66]

Drouyn de Lhuys had long maintained a friendly and neutral attitude towards the United States; Bigelow spoke of a change of attitude of "his government," as if Drouyn had in some subtle fashion conveyed to him a French decision to ride out the storm of the Civil War without any intervention in the hopes that the Mexican question would not become more complicated. Such a decision would almost have to be based on a military evaluation of the course of action best fitting the needs and abilities of France. The Hampton Roads Conference had created, in the

French mind, a real possibility of war; the difficulty of carrying on such a war had determined the French to await events, pinning their hopes on Seward's personal assurances.

A final Confederate peace overture confirmed the French in the futility of intervention. Feeling the pressure of military necessity and the hostility of Europe towards slavery, the Confederate leaders reached the conclusion that both problems could be solved by freeing the slaves and inducting them into the army and at the same time using this act as an inducement to gain foreign recognition. On December 27, 1864, Benjamin wrote Slidell and Mason directing them to put the question to England and France: Would emancipation change their attitudes towards extending recognition to the Confederate States? He entrusted the letters to the care of Duncan Kenner, congressman from Louisiana. Thus was born the Kenner Mission.[67] On March 4, 1865, Slidell held an interview with Napoleon III on the subject. As usual, but now with added meaning, Napoleon told Slidell that he was "willing and anxious" to act with England but that he would do nothing without her. Furthermore, while he admitted that England might have been deterred by the question of slavery, that issue had never affected his own decisions concerning the South. He refused to approach England anew on the question of recognition because he had earlier "been so decidedly rejected" that he could not now expect the English to have changed.[68] The last desperate effort of the Confederacy revealed more than ever the wisdom of the officers' report, and Napoleon III must have been grateful that he had taken no action to ally himself with a crumbling government.

The reelection of Lincoln, the Hampton Roads Conference, and the Kenner Mission, then, forced the French to take a long, hard look at their position in Mexico vis-à-vis the United States and the prospects of peace. They had come to the conclusion that nothing could be done diplomatically nor militarily; they had to accept Seward's promises of continued neutrality towards events in Mexico, even when they were not sure of his ability to fulfill them. The success of Thouvenel's and Drouyn's policy of strict neutrality towards the American Civil War, now adopted without reservation by the emperor and other members of the government, hung on the thin thread of Seward's life. For the next two months the French would anxiously observe the unfolding of the tragic events which brought to a conclusion the bloodiest war of the nineteenth century.

Victory and Tragedy: the Fall of Richmond and the Death of Lincoln

On April 10, 1865, before the news of the evacuation of Richmond reached Europe, the legislative body debated an amendment to the emperor's address which demanded the recall of the French troops from Mexico. Offered and supported by the republican minority, it was defeated by an overwhelming vote. But during the debate, the republicans questioned the credibility of the government's reports on Mexico, tried to show that even the Mexican monarchists and clericals resented and rejected Maximilian, deplored the shedding of French blood for so hopeless a cause, and acclaimed the followers of Juarez as patriotic nationalists who really represented the sovereignty of the Mexican people. Finally, they questioned the endeavor especially as it affected relations with the United States. Jules Favre, a future leader of the Third Republic, reminded the chamber of his warnings in 1862; "may we not fear that at the termination of a terrible, a gigantic war . . . their armies, disbanded by peace, should rush into Mexico? Let our troops return then; let them return immediately!"[69] Five days later while debating another amendment to the address from the throne, this one designed to congratulate the United States for having abolished slavery, republican Eugène Pelletan expressed regret that the emperor had omitted all reference to the American question. Then he dramatically stated:

> Now, the American Question is sufficiently important to be treated with less reserve; besides, at the present time, all discussion is useless, for at this very moment while I am speaking the victorious sound of Grant and Sherman has decided the question. Richmond is taken! The slaveholding rebellion is striken to the earth, and the American Republic is reinstated in

its majestic unity. [Noise] Do not laugh, gentlemen; you may be heard on the other side of the Atlantic![70]

Events in America drowned the sound of French legislative laughter; but the connection between French danger in Mexico and the end of the war in America had been reported to the French public for all to ponder. The arrival of the news of the fall of Richmond preceded the news of Lincoln's assassination and the attack upon Seward by only ten days. The reaction to the first news was, generally, one of quiet resignation and expectancy; the reaction to the second was two-fold: shock and indignation by the public and fear by the government officials, for it appeared that their only guarantee against war, Secretary of State Seward, would be unable to guide the policies of the United States. In both acts, Frenchmen saw not only the end of a bloody war, but a challenge to their position in Mexico.

It was not until May 5 that Drouyn received a detailed account of the fall of Richmond.[71] The French consul in Richmond, Alfred Paul, had been summoned by Secretary of State Benjamin for a farewell talk and then had been busy arranging military protection for the tobacco of the Régie Impériale. By the time Drouyn received Paul's letter, he had also received further word of Lee's surrender at Appomattox and of the attacks upon Lincoln and Seward. There was little diplomatic reaction to the capture of the Confederate capital because there was little time before even more momentous events occurred.

The French press did express its opinions. The more conservative papers were cautious in their evaluation of the fall of Richmond. The *Constitutionnel* on April 19, 1865, concluded that the war was over, but maintained that occupying the South and dealing with the question of the freed Negro would present the United States with even more difficult problems. The *Pays*, on April 16, had refused to admit that the war was over; it predicted "guerrilla warfare—terrible, merciless, and of which at present it is impossible to see the end." Later the *Revue contemporaine* speculated on the political and constitutional implications of the Northern victory. The Republicans, it claimed, would try so to expand the powers of the central government over the states as to abolish the liberties of the people and to establish a military despotism; the Democrats, in opposing this tendency, would so weaken the bonds among the states that the slightest shock would destroy the republic. Either way, the *Revue* could see little hope for the success of a republic with such an enormous population under one government.[72]

The liberal press, on the other hand, hailed the fall of Richmond as the end of "one of the most cruel wars of modern times," praised the ending of slavery, and called for merciful and moderate treatment of the defeated.[73] In their efforts to interpret the implications of the evacuation of the Confederate capital, none of the papers mentioned the prospect of a conflict between the United States and France. And this possibility received little press notice in the publicity regarding ensuing events, yet it was ever present in the minds of the officials and of the general public.

The impact on general public opinion of the fall of Richmond, as an isolated event, is difficult to gauge because of the swift movement of events in America and because of the timing of the quarterly reports of the procureurs general. The second quarterly reports were made in late March or early April, frequently before the news of Richmond had reached France but included comments on the possibility of peace in America. The next reports, in July, included public reaction to the establishment of peace, not just to the fall of Richmond. Thus the fall of Richmond was considered together with the establishment of peace. In general, the French public applauded the end of such a long and bloody war; but they always associated this with the French industrial and commercial welfare. As the procureur general at Besançon put it: "The public is happy to see the end of this four-year war, so fatal to the cause of civilization and, at the same time, so disastrous for the European commercial interests."[74] They also related the end of the Civil War and the French position in Mexico and, unlike the press, expressed grave fear of an impending conflict between France and the United States. In Nancy although the people had supported the establishment of Maximilian and the suppression of the Juarist bandits, now "they are alarmed at the thought of a conflict with America, when the North, conqueror of the South, and disposing all of its forces, could direct them against the new empire." But at the same time, "they like to believe, and they rejoice in it, that the fall of Richmond will finally put an end to the fratricidal war which has lasted so long."[75] From Chambéry in the southeast, Douai in the north, and Paris came similar expressions of fear of a conflict with the United States.[76] Only in Riom, in south central France, was this fear not evident. There, the desire to resume exports of silks and laces to the American market apparently overshadowed even the fear of another war. Similar emphasis upon commerce and the American export markets appeared in Bordeaux and Nîmes.[77] The ideology of the war received some attention also. In Amiens the people were happy to see the cause of abolition prevail, but in Douai and Paris there remained a strong senti- ment for the South. This view turned less on slavery than on the prospect of the United States becoming a danger to the balance of power.[78] From all of these areas of France came the ex- pressed hope that the North would be moderate in victory. These reports reached the officials in Paris during the weeks of un- certainty which resulted from the Union military victories, and the assassination of Lincoln and the attack upon Seward. If the French officials were anxious because of the removal of these two men from the direction of American policy, their anxiety was increased by the French public's concern as to the effect of peace upon industry and commerce, and as to war between France and the United States. Drouyn de Lhuys had to tread lightly in his diplomatic maneuvers concerning the cessation of hostilities, and the dangers he faced were enhanced by events in Washington on April 14, 1865.

Those events were already part of history before the news reached France. An overcrowded city, illuminated by the im- minent conclusion of a four-year war, was dashed into the dark- ness of tragedy by the insane acts of a small band of men led by the brilliant and unbalanced John Wilkes Booth. But the activities of the day in no way portended the dreadful occur- rences of the night. Indeed, energies had been directed toward peaceful pursuits, for, although they were aware of the problems of transition, Lincoln and his officials were nevertheless boldly planning to return the society to a peace-time normality as rapidly as possible. General Grant had that day designated a number of military units to be disbanded. The draft law was suspended. On that Good Friday night, Lincoln reluctantly consented to attend the opening of a new play at Ford's Theater. He went there rather relaxed and lightheartedly.

The only cloud on the otherwise gay Washington scene was the incapacitation of Secretary of State Seward. Only nine days earlier he had been thrown from his carriage and suffered a broken jaw and a broken arm. His doctors and family were concerned that at the age of sixty-five he might not respond to treatment. But by April 14 he had regained strength and was out of danger. Even in his home on Lafayette Square, across from the White House, tension had eased and hearts were lighter and happier.

As Booth pulled the trigger that sent the fatal bullet into the president's head, a fellow conspirator by ruse entered Seward's home and mounted the stairs leading to the sickroom. Accosted by Acting Secretary of State Frederick Seward, the would-be assassin beat him over the head inflicting a near-fatal concussion. Before he had finished his five-minutes' work, he had wounded an older son, Major Augustus Seward, and a male army nurse, and had repeatedly stabbed the aged and bedridden Seward about the face and neck. Only the steel brace designed to support his broken jaw saved the secretary from death, turning the knife's blade away from the jugular. Even so, Seward's right cheek was slashed through, hanging loosely, and his chest was riddled with wounds. He bled profusely. But he lived.

Simultaneously another conspirator lost heart and in a drunken stupor failed to carry out his assignment to assassinate Vice President Johnson. But word quickly spread throughout the city that all the cabinet had been killed and that a general Confederate insurrection was under way. The early evening joy was turned into sorrow; crowds roamed aimlessly in the streets; Washington had become a city of fear and suspicion. Citizens spoke quietly to one another, wondering aloud: "What next?"[79]

United States Minister to France John Bigelow, late on the afternoon of April 26, 1865, entered a railway car in Brest to return to Paris after an official visit to the United States consulate at that port. He had concluded a day of hard work, but he felt revived by the recent news from Richmond and Appomattox. He expected further joyful news concerning Sherman's and Johnston's confrontation in North Carolina; but the message handed to him, just as the train began to move, read simply: "Telegram received at Paris Bourse from London at 2 o'clock. President Lincoln assassinated. An attempt against Seward failed." "It was like a clap of thunder from the sky!" Alone among the strangers in the car, Bigelow reflected upon the meaning of the news. The several hours trip, he wrote, "was depressing, and I am not sure that I entirely escaped a suspicion that the Lord's hand was shortened, not because it could not, but because it would not, save."[80]

The next morning, very early, an imperial aide-de-camp called upon Bigelow to convey "the horror and sorrow which His Majesty experienced on learning of the crime which had just deprived the United States of its President." Unable to credit the earlier reports, Napoleon had awaited confirming messages which arrived during the night; he sent his condolences as soon as possible.[81] The *Moniteur*, under a date line of April 27, carried the story of Lincoln's assassination, and added these paragraphs:

> The same evening the crime was committed, another assassin, said to be Booth's brother, entered the bedroom of Mr. Seward, where an illness kept him in bed, and stabbed him, as well as his son Frederick who tried to help his father. The young man is dead and little hope is held for Mr. Seward.
>
> In Europe as in America there is the same sense of horror against the wretches who put assassination at the service of political parties.[82]

That afternoon crowds began to gather in the street at Bigelow's residence; just as they had done in Washington on April 15, so they did now in Paris on April 27 and 28. So numerous were they that the police intervened, blocking the way. From his window Bigelow could count sixteen policemen. On the twenty-eighth, the second day of the news in Paris, three thousand mourners stood before his house. Messages began to pour in. Bigelow was surprised: "I had no idea," he wrote, "that

Mr. Lincoln had such a hold upon the hearts of the young men of France, or that his loss would be so properly appreciated." Many were surprised that Lincoln's martyrization was world-wide and immediate. All those who loved freedom felt the loss of Lincoln.[83] And no less so in imperial France.

Although the police prevented some from remaining in the streets or from speaking to Bigelow, their intent was apparently only to maintain order. Government officials sent strong and personal notes of condolence. Drouyn de Lhuys, on the very day he first heard the news, wrote to Bigelow: "The telegrams published in the evening papers inform me of the horrible crime of which Messrs. Lincoln and Seward have been victims. I would not delay a moment longer to express to you our profound sympathies."[84] Officially he wrote an appropriate letter for transmission to Washington and to the French senate and legislative body where it was unanimously adopted. In it Drouyn referred to Lincoln reverently as a man of "the most substantial qualities" and "elevation of principle." He especially regretted his untimely death:

> At the moment when an atrocious crime removed him from a mission which he fulfilled with a religious sentiment of duty, he was convinced that the triumph of his policy was definitively assured. His recent proclamations are stamped with sentiments of moderation in which he was inspired in resolutely proceeding to the task of reorganizing the Union and consolidating the peace. The supreme satisfaction of accomplishing this work has not been granted him; but in reviewing these testimonials of his exalted wisdom, as well as the examples of good sense, of courage, and of patriotism which he has given, history will not hesitate to place him in the rank of citizens who have most honored their country.[85]

The letter was published in the *Moniteur* of May 2. It expressed simply and with dignity the characteristics of a gentle and loving spirit, and it reflected the degree to which even the officials of imperial France had been touched by Lincoln's ordeals and career.

It remained to the people of France, however, fully to express the complete impact, political and social, which Lincoln had made. Of all the messages which arrived at the state department in Washington, only the people of Great Britain and her dominions sent more than did those of France. The close ethnic and linguistic ties with the English, their traditions of freedom, and their strong belief in the abolition of slavery explain their response. But for citizens of imperial France, with its restraints on republican activities, to respond in such large numbers requires explanation. Many individuals wrote letters; in nine provincial communities, collective letters were sent—signed only "Inhabitants"; by far the largest single group to testify were the Masonic lodges, thirty-seven of which wrote. With their tradition of the brotherhood of man, it is not surprising that the Masons would express their sorrow at Lincoln's death, nor is it surprising to find the Protestant clergy and theological students from all over France doing so. [It is, perhaps, strange that not one French Roman Catholic prelate expressed regrets to the American legation.] It is touching that a group of citizens in Tarare would sign themselves, simply, "the Working Classes," and that another in Tours would use the one word, "Democrats." But when the total is tallied the message is unmistakable: Frenchmen of all walks of life and in all parts of the country, although mainly republicans and liberal monarchists, felt that they had lost a friend and that freedom had suffered a severe blow when the life of Lincoln was snuffed out.

Many leading republicans, such as Edouard Laboulaye with whom Bigelow had conducted official legal business, wrote personal letters to Bigelow. The deputies of the opposition in the legislative chambers seized the occasion to act separately from the chambers, and jointly sent the following short address to Bigelow: "United from the bottom of our hearts with the American citizens, we desire to express to them our admiration of the great people who have destroyed the last vestiges of slavery, and for Lincoln, the glorious martyr to duty." It was adopted on April 30 and signed by seventy-four deputies, among them some of the great names of the Third Republic and of the Republican tradition in France: Jules Favre, Carnot, Garnier-Pagès, Ernest Picard, Jules Simon, Pelletan, Malespine, and Etienne Arago.[86]

Indeed, French republicanism spoke out loud and clear; not only from avowed political sources, but also from the business classes. Mr. Edward Talbot, a proprietor of Caen, sending a delayed address, wrote that America had given "to the Old World a grand and noble lesson." The successors of Lincoln, he said, will carry on his work:

> We thank them, we thank your president, and your noble American people for giving to us at this day the spectacle of the manly virtues of the bright days of the Roman Republic—to us people of the Latin race, who have now before our eyes only Octaviuses, without vigor, tottering in their buskins, while trying to play the part of worn out Caesars, amid the suppressed jeers of Europe.
>
> Hail, then, to Johnson, to Grant, to Sherman! Hail to all your citizens, and heaven grant that they may send back to France with the winds of the ocean—with its tempests if need be—those powerful blasts of liberty which it sent to them a century ago, at its first awakening.

The letter sent by Talbot, signed by the people of Caen, was more specifically concerned with Lincoln; even so, it held that America's "sorrow is the sorrow of all good men" because Lincoln had met his tasks and overcome them "without veiling the statue of liberty." To them, Lincoln should not be pitied because, by preventing the dismemberment of his country and by abolishing slavery, "He had lived enough, he could die."[87]

Sentiments of republicanism abound in the many letters from the Masonic lodges. Perhaps the Lodge of La Prévoyance, No. 88, Orient of Paris, expressed them as simply and as bravely as any. Citing those revolutionary words which Napoleon III had had chiseled from the public buildings of France, six members of that lodge wrote: "The guilty hand that struck Mr. Abraham Lincoln to glut the vengeance of an unrelenting fanaticism selected the noblest and most glorious defender of the three principles all humanity is endeavoring to realize, namely: liberty, equality, and fraternity."[88] Such militant republicanism, applied to all humanity, reflected the same dissatisfaction with the Bonapartist regime Talbot had expressed. Republicans and malcontents all over France were exploiting Lincoln's assassination to express the feelings which for so long had been censored. As Bigelow put it: "The Republicans here are taking advantage of this to keep the subject before the people as much as possible."[89]

One obvious effort to "keep the subject before the people" was a campaign in Nantes, if not initiated certainly supported by the newspaper *Phare de la Loire*, to raise by a popular subscription of two centimes each a fund for the purpose of striking a gold medal in honor of Lincoln. The medal would have borne, in part, the inscription "Liberty, Equality, and Fraternity." On May 24, the commissary of police of the commune of Chauvigny confiscated the list and the money. Bigelow's reaction was to pity the commune if it were endangered by such an expression of sympathy for Mrs. Lincoln. At any rate, nothing more was heard of such a medal until about eighteen months later when Bigelow forwarded one to Mrs. Lincoln through the department of state. This medal was accompanied by a note saying that it represented the sympathy of 40,000 French citizens, and adding that "if France had the freedom enjoyed by republican America, not thousands, but millions among us would be counted as admirers of Lincoln." On one side of the medallion, the words were printed around a profile bust: "Dedicated by the French Democracy to Lincoln, twice elected President of the United States." On the reverse side, which bore a replica of the Great Seal of the United States, this legend was printed: "Lincoln, an honest man; abolished slavery, saved the republic, and was assassinated the 15th of April, 1865." On the bottom circumference, enscrolled in bold letters was the Revolutionary motto: "Liberty, Equality, Fraternity!" The medal was designed by the sculptor Frank Magniadas and was struck in Switzerland. Whether it represents the culmination of the attempt at Nantes is not clear, but the signatures to the cover letter read like a French republican honor roll. Among them are Etienne Arago, brother of the minister in the Provisional Government and himself a future mayor of Paris: Jules Michelet, the historian; C. Thomas, the director of the National Workshops in 1848; Victor Schoelecher, responsible for the abolition of slavery in the French colonies as under-secretary of the marine in 1848 and a future life

senator of the Third Republic; Louis Blanc, the socialist leader
in 1848 and an historian; Victor Hugo, originator of the title
"Napoleon the Little"; and Eugène Pelletan, republican member
of the legislative body since 1863. Of the twenty signers, no less
than seven were still in exile in 1865. They must have signed the
letter in Switzerland and smuggled it into France, given it and
the medal to Bigelow, who then sent both by diplomatic pouch
to Washington.[90] This republican effort, then, "to keep the
subject before the people" lasted for some eighteen months, but
had to operate from the safety of republican Switzerland. Nonetheless, the death of Lincoln had been exploited by twenty leading French republicans, acting and speaking for a claimed 40,000
Frenchmen. The imperial government could not but take note.

The expressions which the imperial government was most likely
to resent, however, appeared in the French newspapers. Still
operating under strict control, certain of those organs seized the
opportunity in eulogizing Lincoln and in commenting upon the
meaning of the Northern victory, to attack the imperial system of
France. The *Journal des Débats*, in its first comments on the assassination, mistakenly included Secretary Seward and his son
among the victims of "a vast conspiracy against the principal
heads of" the U.S. government. The next day, in its April 29
issue, the *Débats* published a reflective article by Prévost Paradol.
He recalled that French opinion had been divided into roughly
four categories during the American war. The South was
favored, he said, by those who were patently antidemocratic, by
those who favored "a democracy disciplined, guided by a single
master," and by those who feared for the French position in
Mexico. But the fourth group favored the North; it consisted of
all "enlightened Frenchmen" who had "the desire to see a great
democratic state surmount terrible trials, and continue to give an
example of the most perfect liberty, united with the most absolute equality." These people favoring the North, he said, "were
jealous of maintaining the political traditions of France, and the
liberal spirit of our country."[91] Such implied criticisms of Napoleon III's regime followed the eulogies of Lincoln in all the republican papers. The *Avenir National* ran a long series of articles
which praised Lincoln and the Republic of the United States.

As late as May 4, it stressed that the widespread response to Lincoln's death showed "how extremely popular the ideas of liberty and equality have become." The example of the United States had earlier been cited in the same paper:

> The government of the United States is the freest, the mildest, and at the same time the strongest on the face of the earth, and what especially distinguishes the United States is not so much the courage with which they achieved their independence, as the wisdom with which they have constituted their liberty. That a people driven to extremities should overturn their oppressors is the most common thing in history; what is more rare is to see a people sufficiently energetic to assert their rights, vigilant and firm enough to preserve them. To conquer liberty, to lose it, to possess it and not know how to enjoy it—that is to say, to be ignorant of the way to be free—such has been the spectacle afforded more than once by European democracy.[92]

The open chastisement of the French people themselves was also a reflection on the origins of the Second Empire.

Even the conservative and imperial papers reported the events of the assassination and praised Lincoln as a man of humble origins who was twice elected to the highest office. But these papers played down the vitality of republicanism which was reflected in his career and in the Northern victory; instead they carefully distinguished between the dastardly assassins and the noble defenders of the South; they concentrated, too, on Lincoln's great "with malice toward none" speech and they called upon the Federal government to reconstitute the Union quickly and peacefully, with a spirit of forgiveness and not of vengeance.[93]

All the French papers praised Napoleon's and Drouyn's official letters as proper and correct; only the republican organs complained slightly that concurrence of the legislative bodies was late.

General public opinion, as reported by the procureurs general from all parts of France seemed unanimous in condemning the assassination as an act of horror and cowardice.[94] Paradoxically the same people who had opposed Lincoln's reelection some six months earlier because they felt Lincoln to be less moderate than McClellan on the question of peace, now lamented the loss of his moderation in victory. His "malice toward none" speech and the collapse of Southern arms had transformed the president into a humanitarian. The procureur reports do not reflect the outburst of republicanism which appeared in the liberal press and in tributes sent to the American legation. But they do show the universal respect in which the French people held Lincoln, and how they related events in America to French life. For example, in Caen, home of the ardent republican Talbot, the public was disturbed that Emperor Napoleon did not cancel his trip to Algeria. As the procureur expressed it: "Under the emotion of the detestable assassination of President Lincoln, our people look with alarm at His Majesty's departure for Algeria."[95] Lincoln's death, then, aroused a delicate sensitivity to political affairs among all French people.

What did all of this mean to the diplomats? Lincoln's removal from office was serious but, the French felt, not fatal as long as Seward remained at the department of state. They had never been confident of Lincoln's restraint on the Mexican question; they were hardly less certain with Johnson. But a new secretary of state would have forced the French seriously to examine their position in Mexico vis-à-vis the United States. Seward's constant objections to the presence of French troops in Mexico had, after all, always been accompanied by assurance of American neutrality. A new secretary could easily change that stand. More dangerous, the widespread and consistent expressions of republicanism within France warned of a real threat to the French emperor should he have to give in to republicanism either in Mexico or in the United States during the strong response to Lincoln's death. France's government, not only her posture in Mexico, very likely hung in the balance of the sixty-four-year-old Seward's struggle for life. If he lived, then Drouyn's policy of neutrality in the late war might be reciprocated; the French depended on Seward. His period of recovery provided a welcome moratorium in diplomatic activity; Drouyn successfully delayed even official recognition of the end of the Civil War until he was assured of Seward's recovery.

French Withdrawal of Rights of Belligerency
from the Confederacy

The relationship of a neutral to the belligerents during a war must be officially announced and defined at the beginning of the conflict; just so, the reestablishment of normal relations at the end of the war also must be announced officially. Until such announcement, the war is considered, legally, to be still in progress, regardless of the decisions of battles. Naturally the fortunes of arms will determine whether the diplomatic announcement will be made, but the exact timing of that announcement will often depend on many other factors. In the case of French neutrality and the American Civil War, the timing was affected by Lincoln's death, Seward's recovery, the coordination of the action with England's, the Mexican situation, and consideration for the maritime interests, both of the former belligerents and of France.

Because of the April 14 events, the diplomatic responsibility for negotiating the official ending of the war fell to John Bigelow in Paris. He opened the subject on his own initiative on March 17, even before Appomattox, in the form of a personal and unofficial conversation with Drouyn de Lhuys. He told Drouyn that for the sake of its friendship with the United States, France should "refuse belligerent rights or asylum to vessels built and equipped in violation of the municipal laws of the country from which they take their departure." Drouyn, sensing that this was the opening round of what could become the complicated negotiations surrounding the cessation of hostilities in America, answered carefully. "So long as the war lasts, that is so long as your government encounters serious resistance by land or water, France cannot be expected to treat your adversaries as merely disorderly persons." Acquiescing as to the military plight of the Confederates, he quickly added that as soon as the contest degenerated into a "small war," then France would withdraw all recognition of belligerent rights. The French foreign minister carefully reviewed his country's policy during the entire war, leaving little doubt that he considered France to have maintained a benevolent neutrality "to the United States as a whole."[96] A few days later Bigelow received Seward's opening salvo aimed at the withdrawal of the belligerent rights which had been extended to the Confederates.   Reviewing the devastation of Northern commerce by the Confederate cruisers, Seward blamed the loss on the British and French recognition of Southern belligerency and the corollary maritime rights.   Maintaining his protest against such recognition, he instructed Bigelow to "inform Mr. Drouyn de Lhuys that in the opinion of this government all previous justification of a continuance of that recognition has now failed by a practical reduction of all the ports heretofore temporarily held by the belligerents."[97]   Two days after Lee's surrender at Appomattox, Lincoln issued three declarations which Seward sent to Paris: the first closed several ports formerly held by the Confederates; the second announced the opening of the port of Key West; and the third demanded free access to foreign ports for United States naval vessels and threatened retaliatory treatment to foreign naval vessels in American ports.[98]   This last point challenged the French twenty-four-hour rule, which was an integral part of the French neutrality regulations.   But before Bigelow could act on Seward's letters news of Lincoln's assassination reached Paris, and he suspended all diplomatic activity temporarily.   Not until May 4 did he submit a copy of the proclamations, and not until May 10 did he officially request France to withdraw the belligerent rights which it had extended to the insurgents in 1861.   Stating that the "insurrectionary district of the United States" had no ports open to the sea, "no fixed seat for its pretended government, no coherent civil administration, no army that is not rapidly dissolving into fragments as the result of repeated defeats," and no ships save a few which were built in foreign lands, Bigelow asked for the withdrawal.[99]   He had described the "small war" which Drouyn had earlier promised would be the condition justifying the requested withdrawal; Bigelow had every right to expect prompt and decisive action.

Drouyn, however, was not yet ready to act.   After his "small war" promise he had initiated what proved to be a drawn-out exchange with England.   He believed the two governments "should continue to act in concert in questions relating to the

United States since he was convinced that so long as they held together, the United States Government could not provoke a contest with one or the other."[100] By the middle of April he and Earl Russell were in complete accord on their approach to the end of the Civil War. Both showed signs of respecting, if not fearing, the military might of the United States, and Drouyn now had the added worry of Seward's incapacitation.[101] Until he could be sure of Washington's policy towards Mexico, Drouyn wanted to avoid relinquishing the one restraint he had on the United States. He found a delaying tactic in his correspondence with Russell who pointed out that even a minor warfare continuing in the interior would justify the Union in exercising the right of search of neutral vessels entering former Confederate ports. Drouyn willingly agreed that before France or England should give up the neutral protection of their maritime interests afforded by the recognition of Southern belligerency, the United States would have to renounce this right of search.[102] Now even a "small war" would be sufficient to delay the acknowledgment of the end of hostilities; Drouyn had the diplomatic tool to survive the period of Seward's recovery.

When Bigelow submitted his official request for the withdrawal of belligerent rights, Drouyn drew up the response he intended to make; but instead of sending it to Washington, he sent it to London to assure complete agreement. Russell approved Drouyn's approach, adding only that England had decided to remove immediately the twenty-four-hour limitation on Federal naval vessels. He also stressed the benefits of joint action and insisted that the United States must first renounce its right of search.[103] Drouyn was happy to know that Russell saw the value of the joint approach because he was receiving distressing news from America. Dispatches described widespread recruiting in New York for Juarez's forces; they reported long conferences between President Johnson and Romero, Juarez's representative in Washington; they told of munitions manufacturers, caught by peace with large inventories, willing to sell to anyone, especially Spanish Americans; they described West Coast pride in the Northern victory and a desire to drive the French out of Mexico.[104] Drouyn, with Seward still absent from the state department, became ever more anxious over possible United States intervention in Mexico and he did not hide his feelings from Lord Cowley.[105] By early May, then, when Bigelow officially demanded France's recognition of the end of hostilities, Drouyn in coordinating his actions with Russell, definitely associated the end of the Civil War with the Mexican situation.   Furthermore, the whole picture was clouded by Lincoln's death and Seward's wounds.

On two different occasions when Bigelow tried to discuss the withdrawal of belligerent rights, Drouyn turned the conversation to Mexico.   Referring "to the interests of France in Mexico as the only apparent source of serious misunderstanding," Drouyn attempted to balance this by his diplomatic moves regarding the end of hostilities in America.   "France," he said, "is now involved in engagements with Mexico which must be respected; in adjusting differences among nations there is always a balancing of interests."   "The emperor," he continued, "was one of those men who when he received any favor always returned it double."[106]   Later, when Bigelow tried to get an answer to his May 10 note, Drouyn again dwelt on the Mexican problem.   "We received strong assurances about Mexico from Washington just prior to Lincoln's death," he said; "I cannot believe that President Johnson's administration will change its disposition so quickly."   "Yet," he continued, "the Northern press treats our support of Maximilian harshly and recruiting for Juarez goes on openly in New York."   He told Bigelow that French opinion and the closing of the ports to French commercial shipping tended to "render more difficult the response I proposed to make to the last communication [May 10] from the Washington cabinet."   Although Bigelow tried to reassure Drouyn on Mexico, he failed to elicit any answer to his demands;[107] the Frenchman obviously was biding his time pending some new sign of American intentions.

Drouyn had concentrated so exclusively on the Mexican prospects that he overlooked an important aspect of the question. The Lincoln proclamations of April 11 had demanded the lifting of the twenty-four-hour rule under threat of retaliation, and in mid-May, Earl Russell had indicated Britain's intention to remove the rule against United States naval vessels. But Drouyn had taken no action on that question—not a simple one because the twenty-four-hour rule was an integral part of the French system of neutrality. If that one rule were withdrawn, it should logically and legally vitiate the whole neutral position of France. Russell apparently did not let this deter him, for on May 19 Lord Cowley informed Drouyn that Great Britain had withdrawn its twenty-four-hour rule.[108] On the point of writing a delaying note to Bigelow, Drouyn suddenly realized that the solidarity which he wanted to maintain with England was about to be broken. Hastily, and without consulting his cabinet colleagues, he scribbled a telegram to the French consul in Liverpool, which should be sent by ship to Washington: "Announce that the French government revokes the disposition which limits to twenty-four hours the duration of the stay of United States warships in our ports." He immediately urged the minister of marine to issue the necessary orders to all French ports.[109] This hurried act, of doubtful legality, was most unlike Drouyn de Lhuys; it can be explained only by his strong desire to avoid any indication of a break in the Franco-British joint action.[110] Events, however, were moving swiftly and none of the diplomats noted the inconsistency; Drouyn accomplished his purpose without difficulty.

With the telegram written, Drouyn next set about answering Bigelow's notes. News reports indicated that Seward would recover, but the French foreign minister still sought to delay a definitive answer. In a note dated May 19, Drouyn acknowledged the Lincoln proclamations of April 11. While recognizing the changed military situation, he put it to Bigelow for the first time that the United States admitted that a state of war still existed by continuing to exercise its right of search and seizure. Having established this point, which Russell had first suggested, in one note, he wrote another dated May 20 in response to Bigelow's demands of May 10, and for the first time related the matter of search and seizure to the question of withdrawing the belligerent rights. Admitting that the situation which had necessitated the 1861 declaration had ceased to exist, Drouyn glibly wrote that "as soon as we are informed that the Federal Government relinquishes the right of search and capture in respect of neutral ships, there will no longer be any question of belligerency in respect to the United States for us to consider, and we will hasten to acknowledge it."[111]

Bigelow was disappointed in Drouyn's position. Noting the similarity between it and Russell's announced position, he complained that he labored "under the disadvantage of not knowing what view Mr. Adams had taken." The American diplomats obviously missed Seward's guiding hand. After nine days of deliberation, more than enough time to exchange several notes with Adams in London, on May 29 Bigelow submitted his reply to Drouyn. He protested that the Federal right to search and seizure was not at all related to the French recognition of Southern belligerency. Furthermore, since Jefferson Davis' capture the last symbol of Confederate sovereignty had disappeared, and France had no reason not to withdraw its declaration. But Bigelow was a practical diplomat, and despite his protests he also gave satisfaction to Drouyn: "The United States Government in applying for a repeal of the declaration of June 1861 abandoned any of the rights of a belligerent which it is presumed to have claimed and became directly responsible for anything it might do in the character of a belligerent."[112]

This response was exactly what Drouyn wanted, and it afforded him additional time to coordinate his actions with London. Furthermore, Seward was recovering at an unexpectedly rapid rate—Drouyn was happy to note that a cabinet meeting was held in the secretary's sick room on May 9—and news reports indicated the stabilization of the Mexican question. Drouyn felt secure enough to acknowledge the end of the war in America. After an exchange with Russell, in which he pointed out the necessity to provide for Confederate ships in port to denationalize themselves, Drouyn was satisfied that they were in perfect agreement.[113] He drew up the official French recognition of the end of the war. To Montholon, the new French minister in Washington, he wrote on May 30, that the Imperial government no longer considered a state of war to exist in the United States and therefore withdrew the recognition of belligerent rights accorded to the former Confederate states.[114] As to Bigelow, Drouyn formally replied to his note of May 29 and officially announced the withdrawal of the belligerent rights. He had read Bigelow's letter, he wrote, "with much satisfaction." Quoting those lines referring to the abandonment of any belligerent rights the United States was presumed to have claimed, Drouyn concluded:

> These declarations, Sir, respond exactly to what I have had the honor of requiring of you and bring us to agree upon the object we have in view. We have therefore no longer any objections to withdraw from the Confederates the quality of belligerents, and I am happy to congratulate you upon the opportunity which presents itself to revive the old sympathies of the two people whose interests and traditions constantly invite them to cultivate the most cordial friendships.[115]

Thus almost exactly six weeks after the collapse of the Confederate armies France officially recognized the end of the hostilities of the American Civil War.

Some diplomatic problems remained to be solved. Bigelow, for instance, wrote Drouyn denying that his statement concerning the United States' renunciation of the rights of search and seizure was in any way official. But Bigelow also pointed out that the actual suppression of the insurrection deprived such legal refinements of any practical value; Drouyn agreed and satisfied himself by simply thanking him "for having recalled to me the exact language of those declarations which you have had the goodness to make to me." Seward, also, carefully studied the language exchanged between Drouyn and Bigelow during the negotiations and saw no reason to dissent from any of the opinions expressed. Questions once practical, he wrote, "had now become to a great degree historical, and should be left alone." And so on behalf of the president and the United States, he accepted the French declaration and expressed the hope, along with Drouyn, that the two governments would "revive the old sympathies of the two nations whose interests and traditions constantly invite them to cultivate the most cordial friendship."[116] Both governments had finally acknowledged the end of a state of war the existence of which the United States government had at no time legally admitted.

Drouyn had a few formal acts to perform. He took his notice of the withdrawal of the Paris Declaration of Neutrality of 1861 and his orders to the French officials in all ports to a council meeting on the morning of June 3, 1865. Napoleon III was on an official visit to Algeria, and Eugénie presided. There all of Drouyn's acts were approved and ordered effectuated.[117] Ironically, the emperor, who had taken such a personal interest in the American war—who had encouraged the building of Confederate ships in France, who had twice offered to mediate the war, who had consulted with members of the English parliament concerning the war—was not even present when his government took the formal action which acknowledged the conclusion of the war. Drouyn had worked shrewdly with Bigelow and had carefully coordinated his actions with England to safeguard French interests involved in the cessation of hostilities. He had also attended closely to the American attitude toward affairs in Mexico.

That was the one remaining problem; but in June of 1865 it appeared to be one easily solved. The French army controlled the greatest extent of Mexican territory which it was ever to hold; most of the Mexican war lords had come over to the side of Maximilian; Juarez had no permanent seat of government. But most important, the Washington government and the American people seemed too involved with postwar problems to worry over much about Mexico. Consul Borg in New York wrote that the Mexican question had been pushed off the front pages by debates on what to do with the South, with the assassins of Lincoln, and with Jefferson Davis.[118]

Perhaps the best news Drouyn received relating to Mexico was the knowledge that Seward had returned to his office and was back on the job. Seward's first dispatch was to Bigelow, and in it he reasserted that the United States would maintain its neutrality towards Mexico "with diligence and energy" and that it would prevent recruitment for Juarez and anything else that might create "the least uneasiness to France or to Mexico."[119] A few days later, responding to a suggestion that France might undertake hostilities against the United States for the sake of Mexico, Seward stated flatly that he did not believe it would happen and that he would not allow the possibility to sway the

United States from its "strict line of forbearance and neutrality."[120] These strong assurances reconfirmed to Drouyn the wisdom of his own policy of neutrality and the confidence he had placed in the American secretary of state.

In the summer of 1865, after the four years of war in America with their many knotty diplomatic problems and near-war crises, the transatlantic area appeared calm to Drouyn. There were no problems of belligerent or neutral rights; no questions of recognition or intervention. France controlled most of the Mexican territory, and the American secretary of state as well as the New York press seemed willing to await events there; any clouds that might arise over the Mexican situation were still too far away to darken the clear summer skies. Furthermore, the emperor's system had survived, at least for the present, the strong outburst of republican sentiment which had followed Lincoln's death. Relations between imperial France and the newly strengthened American republic were cordial and friendly. Drouyn could relax and reflect on the merits as well as the problems of maintaining a strictly neutral policy during the trials of a foreign civil war.

For John Bigelow, too, the Paris skies were clear. The Civil War was over; the Union had been saved. Despite strong European opinion to the contrary, he and the other Federal diplomats had succeeded in their efforts to prevent diplomatic recognition of the "so-called" Confederate States of America. Lincoln's loss was tragic; but Bigelow nevertheless felt like celebrating. He would have, he decided, a typical American celebration of July the Fourth, and he would invite Americans from all over Europe as well as the leading French government officials.[121] When Drouyn de Lhuys received his invitation he quickly and graciously accepted. He was happy to share in the American republic's celebration.

July 4 dawned bright and sunny. Bigelow had rented a large area in the Bois de Boulogne. Tents were placed for eating, for dancing, and for speech making. Carpets were spread for the comfort of the guests. Band stands were spotted among the tents. And the whole was capped by a tall flag pole, atop which flew the stars and stripes. Guests began arriving at two in the afternoon. Americans from London and Rome, from Madrid and Berlin assembled. Drouyn de Lhuys, Chasseloup-Laubat, and most of the other cabinet ministers and their wives arrived. Foreign diplomats from Argentina and Turkey, from Holland and San Marino, and from all the republics joined the company.

Bigelow began the festivities with an appropriately short, but patriotic speech. He made the point clearly that "the American Union is safe; democratic-republican Government is no longer an experiment." And he proudly proclaimed that July the Fourth "has now acquired an importance in the eyes of mankind which it never possessed before." Bands played, speeches were made, children tumbled on the grass, ministers and diplomats danced. Over two hundred shared the food to which Bigelow had led Minister of Marine Chasseloup-Laubat, with whom he had contended when the Confederates tried to construct their ships at Bordeaux. The enthusiastic and joyous celebration was climaxed by gigantic fireworks displaying in brilliant colors an immense American eagle, under which appeared Daniel Webster's famous words: "The Union now and forever, one and inseparable!" Loud cheers greeted the American eagle over Paris, and the crowd dispersed.

Such a celebration was a fitting symbol for the end of the war and for the completion of a chapter of difficult relations between France and the United States. As Drouyn de Lhuys watched, recalling the real and imaginary problems between the two countries, could he but wonder at the meaning of it all? Could he have glimpsed the future, as he gazed at the eagle in the sky, and known in a moment of truth that but five short years hence, France too would be a republic? Perhaps he cast back in his mind to the four years of war and problems and understood that this celebration, far from marking the end of an epoch, opened instead a new era of friendly relations between the peoples of America and of France.

Chapter XVII

MEN AND ISSUES

Early French Public Attitudes

WHEN secession occurred and the war broke out in the United States, the French public in general regretted to see a country which France had helped to establish threatened by disunion. This feeling was enhanced by concern lest America's position as a helpful counterbalance to England would be weakened. The Northern and Southern arguments left Frenchmen cold, since they did not have any patriotic ardor for union and knew nothing about American constitutional law. However, they were in general hostile to slavery and disappointed that the North was putting union ahead of emancipation. As in the case of other wars in the 'sixties, the French impulse was toward neutrality. Since intervention would have been one in favor of the South and slavery, even the working classes would have opposed it, and the business classes were normally hostile to the economic disruption of war. This left only those businessmen likely to benefit by Southern trade and some of the aristocracy favorable to some form of intervention. Consequently there was widespread approval of the French declaration of neutrality.

As to the economic strangulation, there was fear of that in France even before any state had seceded, because exports to the United States declined, and Frenchmen's worst fears were substantiated as the Northern blockade and the Southern embargo began to take effect. From that time on, the general public (not including the cotton speculators) wanted an early end to the war, no matter what might be the outcome, and hoped French mediation or pressure might help to bring peace.

Policies of the French Government

From the evidence available it is safe to say that Napoleon III and Thouvenel felt as did the French public in regretting the division in the United States. They, too, counted on America as a powerful ally against Britain's naval preponderance, and they made unusual efforts to keep themselves informed. Nevertheless, as reports of Seward's warlike gestures began to arrive, the reaction of both the French and British governments was the policy of a common front and joint action in American affairs. This Anglo-French cooperation continued throughout the war, except in the cases of Mercier's visit to Richmond and France's unilateral offer of mediation.

The first instance of joint Anglo-French policy was their proclamations of neutrality. To Thouvenel and Russell this seemed a very natural move, since two belligerents appeared, one instituting a blockade and the other engaging privateers. But Seward soon brought them to realize that this inferential recognition of the Confederacy's belligerency was greatly resented by the United States. Seward's violent reaction to the neutrality proclamations marked the high point in his policy of threat and bluster. His unpredictability sobered Russell and Thouvenel and frightened Mercier and Lyons almost into silence. And yet, finally, we see Anglo-French cooperation on this issue—in the persons of Mercier and Lyons—march right up to the front door of the state department. The Federal secretary, always anxious to break up this two-power solidarity, deftly thwarted this move by separate interviews but also took the edge off his anger by a clever resort to the policy of the "averted glance." He would not react to the Anglo-French recognition of Southern belligerency if the two powers did not tell him of it officially and if they did nothing to raise the issue.

Yet, the United States was completely wrong on this question. By proclaiming a blockade "in pursuance of . . . the law of nations," it recognized the belligerency of the Confederacy before either Great Britain or France, and it reaffirmed this recognition by refraining from executing captured Confederate soldiers as traitors and by exchanging prisoners. The South's belligerent status was even recognized by a Federal court and eventually by the maritime states of Europe. Before the war was half over, Seward himself began to relax the fiction of the "averted glance."

On the question of privateers Seward outsmarted himself. France and England wanted him to acknowledge Articles II and III of the Declaration of Paris of 1856, which provided for immunity from capture of noncontraband neutral goods on enemy ships and enemy goods on neutral ships. The Federal secretary assured them that this immunity had always been practiced and advocated by the United States, but he offered to go further and adhere to the whole Paris declaration. This was an indirect way of trying to force England and France to treat Southern privateers as pirates and thus to violate their proclaimed neutrality. Having already received affirmative assurances from the North as to the immunity and blockade clauses, they deftly turned Seward's trick by rejecting his offer of adherence until after the war's end.

However, the most sensational crisis over international law concerning search and seizure came with the "Trent" affair. Seward was later proven innocent of ordering the removal of Mason and Slidell from the "Trent." His innocence was amply proven by the fact that he was the strongest advocate of release in Union governmental circles and set them free, however embarrassing it was for the North. On the contrary, evidence now seems to accumulate which indicates that the South may have staged the whole "Trent" affair in a deliberate attempt to precipitate a war between the North and Great Britain. These circumstances have not been brought out by previous historians.

Another oversight of historians has been to ignore France's role in the "Trent" affair. They exonerate Seward of starting the affair, and they exalt the prince consort for softening the British note, but they omit to mention the crucial part which the French note played in giving Seward a diplomatic and legal instrument for convincing the president, the cabinet, and the Northern people of the wisdom of releasing the two Confederate envoys. Here was another spectacular case of Anglo-French cooperation.

As far as the relations between France and the United States were concerned, the most serious threat to their amity was the economic impact of the war on France. The cotton famine hit

France nearly as severely as it did England. Cotton factories closed down; people were thrown out of work; and the prices of cotton clothing, worn so generally by the poorer classes, greatly increased. But this was not all of the suffering. French luxury exports—especially silks, gloves, china, watches, and wines—underwent a severe slump with unavoidable closings and unemployment. The French chambers of commerce and Rouher, the minister of commerce, brought great pressure to bear on Napoleon III and Thouvenel to challenge the effectiveness of the blockade and to undermine it by a recognition of Southern independence. Furthermore, the emperor was very much concerned over the possibilities of disorders and disaffection from his regime. By policies of vast public works and the modernization of France's farms and factories he tried to prevent discontent. The Civil War was counteracting all his efforts toward economic development and social pacification. Consequently, the entire four years of the Civil War found Napoleon III and his ministers thrashing around and grasping at any and every straw to end the war and its attendant economic depression.

First of all, the French inquired into the effectiveness of the blockade. In spite of the conflicting testimony from the two sides, the reports of the French and British naval commanders in American waters and those of Consul Paul in Richmond and Mure in New Orleans indicated a sufficiently enforced blockade. England accepted this view; and France, with some reservations, continued her common-front policy by deferring to the British opinion. As early as November 1861, before any Southern ports had been captured by the North, Consul Paul was describing the serious deprivations in the South in both military and civilian supplies. The Confederates could not obtain weapons, munitions, or army clothing. This situation became worse as the war wore on. To be sure, many small vessels and a few large ships were able to run the blockade, but these incidents are not considered in international law as proof of general ineffectiveness. Owsley, ignoring the fact that the blockade was proclaimed only against the larger ports—those engaged in international trade—and adopting a much too rigid definition of efficiency, claimed that "all evidence in the way of testimony indicates that the blockade was no more effective in the gulf than in the Atlantic," that "Old Abe sold America's birthright [an enforced blockade] for a mess of pottage."[1] Most historians since the war, however, accepting a broader interpretation of efficiency, tend to acknowledge that the blockade was effective.[2] Even Coulter, who doubted the blockade's efficiency during the first year, admitted that "without a doubt the blockade was one of the outstanding causes for the strangulation and ultimate collapse of the Confederacy."[3] In spite of the fact that a suspicion has been expressed that England accepted an unenforced blockade in order to have a precedent in support of later weak blockades, the Northern blockade appears to have been sufficiently enforced to be both legal and lethal.

The second French attempt to obtain cotton was a request in October 1861 for the relaxing of the blockade before a few Southern ports so that France might obtain cotton supplies. Seward implied that he wanted, in return, France's abandonment of belligerency recognition and of cooperation with England. After the settlement of the "Trent" affair, pressure was renewed for permission to export cotton. Then, besieged by Napoleon III, Thouvenel, Prince Napoleon, Morny, and Mercier, Seward conceded the opening of Beaufort, Port Royal, and New Orleans, all of which had fallen to the Federals in the meantime, and this without waiting for the withdrawal of belligerency recognition. But the French soon found that this Northern concession was a hollow one, because the Southern embargo effectively prevented the delivery of cotton to these ports. Now the lesson was brought home that it was the Southern embargo rather than the Northern blockade which caused the distress in the French cotton industries.

The embargo, therefore, brought French action to its third stage—that of intervention through mediation with an implied threat of full recognition of the South if mediation failed. Here, then, was the appearance in fact of the Southern theory that "Cotton is King"—that a cotton embargo would force Europe to recognition and the breaking of the blockade. In July 1862 Thouvenel was considering joint Anglo-French mediation, and Napoleon III, more than ever anxious about unemployment and labor unrest, was even contemplating the ultimate move of joint recognition, especially after the failure of the Lindsay visit. Here it was that military events showed their crucial influence in both directions. Southern victories in Virginia in June, July, and August—Seven Days, withdrawal from Harrison's Landing, and the Second Battle of Bull's Run—led Earl Russell to propose to Palmerston joint mediation with subsequent recognition; but, before the cabinet could return from vacation, the Antietam battle had been won, and emancipation had been announced. While the news of Antietam was more decisive than that of emancipation, the latter did also give reason for pause. The British government decided to wait for later developments, and France had to sit back and join the watch.

However, the emperor did not feel he could pause for long because of the worsening business situation and a rising demand by public opinion for mediation efforts toward a truce. Thus, soon after Thouvenel had been replaced by Drouyn de Lhuys, he instructed his new foreign minister to invite Great Britain and Russia to participate in a joint offer of mediation—both politely refused—while they awaited the results of the Union's congressional elections. The alacrity with which the French government published its proposal and the Anglo-Russian rejections indicated that the main purpose had been the satisfaction of public criticism. Napoleon III had his own legislative elections impending early in 1863, and the favorable public reaction to the mediation offer justified this premature and abortive effort.

Yet, in November the United States elections weakened the war faction in the congress, by January the economic depression was worsening, and the French elections were looming; in desperation the emperor ordered a unilateral effort by proposing to the North a North-South conference on a union or separation settlement while the fighting continued. Again Seward politely rejected the suggestion, and once more Napoleon III reaped popular favor for his attempt.

These empty gestures of diplomatic interposition did help to maintain public support, which, along with other factors, brought about a two-to-one French legislative victory for the regime in May 1863; but they did not solve the problem of economic distress in France by bringing about an early end to the war. From this point on, it appears that Napoleon III resorted to a scheme of helping the Confederates to do their own breaking of the blockade. In March 1863 he indirectly approved the sale of the Erlanger bonds and the construction of armed wooden clippers and ironclad rams.

But, by the time these ships were ready for delivery in the spring of 1864, military events here again impinged upon these do-it-yourself plans. In the previous year the turning-point battle of Gettysburg had been won by the North, and after the fall of Vicksburg "the Father of Waters [ran] unvexed to the sea"; in early 1864 Grant was slowly pounding his way into Virginia, and the Confederates had had to abandon Chattanooga. Not only was the Confederacy being strangled from the sea, but its very heart was being pierced. And, meanwhile, Mexico entered upon the scene as a new factor. While French forces had invaded Mexico and captured Mexico City in an effort first to collect debts and then to overthrow the Juarist republic in favor of a Maximilian empire, the United States had mildly protested but privately asserted a policy of neutrality. All these factors had their effects on French policy. A Northern victory seemed more plausible, and a need to match United States neutrality in Mexico with genuine French neutrality in the Civil War gave Drouyn de Lhuys his leverage to thwart the emperor and to prevent the constructed ships from falling into Confederate hands. If the "Stonewall" did eventually, and too late, come into the South's possession, it was not, under the circumstances, the fault of France.

The Mexican expedition by France had an influence on the French policy of neutrality, which has not been noticed by historians. Drouyn appreciated that the United States was in a position to be as unneutral or as neutral toward the Mexican expedition as France might be toward the Civil War. This interrelationship the French foreign minister did not fail to impress upon the emperor and his ministerial council. Thus, for France's part she refrained from recognizing the Confederacy and from breaking the blockade, and she strictly enforced her neutrality regulations regarding Southern ships in her ports and under construction in her yards.   In return Seward reassured France that the United States would not take action against the French expedition, nor permit the shipment of arms to the Juarez forces, nor allow recruitment in American cities of troops destined for the Mexican Republic.   Again, as the Civil War ground to a halt, and France hesitated to rescind her declaration of neutrality, Drouyn finally saw the utility of abrogating the twenty-four-hour limitation for belligerent ship refuge in French harbors lest the same rule be applied by the United States toward French warships on Atlantic or Gulf duty.   Yet, over and above these fine points, there hovered the danger of a victorious Northern army, swelled by amnestied ex-Confederate war-tested soldiers, eventually going to the aid of Juarez.   It was such sobering thoughts as these that restrained the French from any adventures in the last stages of the Civil War and in the end led them to withdraw from Mexico in 1867.

The Attitudes of Individuals

In examining the general policy of the French government, one has a chance, here and there, to sense the attitudes of the leading statesmen.   At this point it might be well to look a little more closely at their views and actions.

On the French side the most important and the most controversial figure was Napoleon III, who, under his imperial constitution, had full and final authority in foreign affairs.   Although he was a semi-dictator until 1867, he did adhere to certain democratic ideas, such as universal manhood suffrage, popular sovereignty, national referenda (plebiscites) for constitutional revisions, and representative government.   On the other hand he followed the repressive practices of exiling his more violent political opponents, of censoring the press, and of packing his elected house with "official" candidates.   Yet he indicated that he wanted eventually to move to a more liberal parliamentary regime as soon as Frenchmen were ready for it, a regime in which there would be freedom of expression and elections and a parliamentary sharing in executive responsibility.   This relaxation came about between 1867 and 1870, and in the meantime he kept in close touch with public opinion through the reports of his prefects and procureurs general.[4] He also tried to follow liberal social and economic policies by stimulating industrialization in support of the business classes, by promoting public works for the employment of the working classes, and by free trade treaties with France's immediate neighbors.

For him, then, the pre-war United States had many attractions and elicited much sympathy. It was democratic, representative, and vigorously progressive in the adoption of more and more industrialization. Up to 1861 it had also followed a low-tariff policy. Socially, too, America seemed to be a land of opportunity and of rewards to talent. As he had told Faulkner, while in the United States he had been so impressed with its energy, activity, and vitality that, on his return, Europe seemed to be asleep. Likewise, this solid block of growing power and naval strength on the western side of the Atlantic seemed to presage for France a balance against British preponderance. In the light of these sentiments one cannot but believe in the sincerity of his early protestations of sympathy for the preservation of the Union.

There were also reasons why the emperor eventually became more sympathetic toward the cause of the South as the war dragged on. Its stubborn and courageous resistance to the North's attempt to impose its will aroused a sense of fair play and pity for the underdog. More and more it seemed to him, as it did to liberal Gladstone, that Jefferson Davis had made a nation, and Napoleon III was known for his advocacy of national self-determination in Rumania, Italy, Savoy and Nice, Poland, and even in Germany. No doubt he thought that if one of his manhood-suffrage plebiscites could have been held in the South, the result would have been overwhelmingly for separation. He did not condone slavery, but the North itself was condoning it on its own territory and thus prevented him from considering it an issue.

Then, once the split had come, there were certain reasons for him to dislike the North. The United States in 1861 had introduced a high protective tariff, which not only offended the emperor's principles but hurt French exports. The South as an agricultural and importing area would continue to be favorable to freer trade. Furthermore, the North was generally brash, boastful, uncouth, and lower-middle-class in character and contrasted sharply with the well-mannered, well-educated, aristocratic Southern gentlemen. Nearly all the persons who surrounded Napoleon III—his court, his cabinet advisers, the accredited diplomats, the nobility, the upper bourgeoisie, and the clergy—were scornful of the democratic-republican North and well disposed toward the Southern way of life. Is there any wonder, then, when he received such Southerners or Southern sympathizers as Rost, Slidell, Lindsay, and Roebuck, he left with them the impression that he was on the side of the Confederacy?

But there were other more basic reasons for him to lean toward the South. As a Bonaparte with a Corsican-Italian background and French adoption, he was an advocate of a Latin revival of power and influence to counter the growing ascendancy of the Anglo-Saxon power of the British Empire and the United States. He was trying to balance off the British predominance in the Mediterranean by developing strong ties with the Latin countries of Rumania, Italy, and Spain and with such other countries as Greece, Turkey, and Egypt; he was building a stronger Mediterranean fleet, promoting his merchant marine, and maintaining a closer hold on Algeria. On the American side he was fearful of the expansion southward of the Anglo-Saxon United States at the expense of Latin peoples in Central and South America and in the Caribbean area. A separation of the North and South would reduce by half this "*Drang nach Süden.*" Furthermore, the South had furnished the main impetus to this expansion in their effort to find new potential slave states to balance the number of free states in the United States Senate. With separation, gone would be this motive and also the support of the Northern industrial complex for such expansionism. This would leave to France the opportunity to develop a Latin sphere of influence in Central America of which the Mexican Empire would be the entering wedge and French Louisiana would be a cultural tie in a somewhat toothless and complacent Anglo-Saxon Confederacy.[5] One is therefore not too surprised at the nature of the interrogation to which the emperor subjected Professor Maury in 1860.

However, Napoleon III was cautious enough to avoid, in public or in official documents, anything which might offend the North by its espousal of the Southern cause. Perhaps, he might be better described as acquiescing in the separation of the two warring sections, a position which was obviously that of the South. Above all he wanted peace in order to restore his flagging economy. He was irritated that the American quarrel should upset his domestic economic growth just at the moment when he anticipated so much commercial benefit from his new low-tariff treaty with England. So determined did the South seem, so successful militarily, and so unreconcilable toward the North, that he, along with most French and British leaders, felt that, right or wrong, separation was inevitable. If that was true, let it come and bring an end to the nuisance of the war— the sooner the better. When the battlefield determined that reunion was to be the outcome and that the restored United States might become a serious threat to the French presence in Mexico, he no longer flirted with interventionist schemes and welcomed the end of the war. In sum, the French emperor was pulled in two directions by the American struggle. If, in his precarious tight-rope walking, he leaned more often toward the South, it was more as a pro-separationist, because of separation's seeming inevitability, than as a convinced pro-Southerner.

In the case of Napoleon III's two foreign ministers, they were more impartial than he. Indeed, the evidence seems to indicate that Thouvenel was slightly and even consistently pro-Northern in sympathy. From the beginning, however, he favored the issuance of a declaration of neutrality, which implicitly recognized the South's belligerent status; yet that was no more than what the North had done unwittingly. In the "Trent" affair he actually lectured the North on the relevant international law, but that, too, helped Seward out of his embarrassing situation. Like the emperor, he became a believer in the inevitability of separation, but he retained his hope for some form of overall union. It was Thouvenel who even proposed a sort of dual republic for tariffs, defense, and foreign affairs—a scheme adopted five years later for the Austrian Empire. This would have given France the best of both worlds—that is, a quick end to the war by separation, a sufficient union to preserve the anti-British balance, and a large French market in the combined federations. Finally, he successfully fought the battle for strict neutrality against the pro-Southern proclivities of all his cabinet colleagues and against the wanderlust of his master.

Drouyn de Lhuys, as the successor of Thouvenel, was the same type of seasoned career diplomat who wanted to play by the rules of the game. If he differed from his predecessor, it was in degree and not in kind. He proceeded obediently to carry out the tripartite and unilateral peace proposals of the emperor, partly because the one had been concocted before he came into office and partly because he understood that both would be innocuous and rejected. The new foreign minister knew that the main reason for the proposal, like that for his own appointment, was to win votes in the coming election. Drouyn's complicity in these imperial initiatives was a harbinger of his subsequent toleration of irregularities regarding ship construction and the case of the "Rappahannock." He pretended to carry out his master's wishes, but at the same time his expertise in diplomacy found a way to thwart the policy. Thus, by playing upon the fear of United States' intervention in Mexico, he was able to steer as neutral a course as Thouvenel.

One other man of high position was also influential in his support of the Northern cause—Prince Napoleon, cousin of the emperor and second in the line of succession. He was the most democratic of all the Bonapartists, and by his supposed superior knowledge of the war because of his extended tour of the North and South in 1861 was listened to with respect. He invariably pleaded the cause of the North to the emperors and his ministers, was a great help to Dayton and Bigelow, and influenced public opinion through his newspaper, the *Opinion Nationale*.

The attitude of Mercier in Washington is a matter of controversy. He began his mission in the semi-secessionist atmosphere of the Buchanan administration. Many of his early political acquaintances were Southern leaders, such as Mason and Slidell, who plied him with the Southern viewpoint. The way

of life of his Southern friends was more attractive to him, an
aristocrat of lower rank, than that of the bustling, brash, middle-
class Northerners. Indeed, he had to make a great readjustment
upon the arrival of the Republican administration with its rough-
hewn president and its irascible and unpredictable secretary of
state. With the aid of Lord Lyons and the steadying hand of his
two foreign ministers he was able to weather the storm. In the
performance of his duties he came to understand better the views
and potentialities of both sides. He managed to keep on good
terms with Seward, to preserve the common front with Lord
Lyons, to defend French interests when endangered, and even to
visit the Confederate government in Richmond with the blessing of Seward. Mercier was greatly impressed with the vastness
and power of the North, especially after his cross-country tour
with Prince Napoleon. He therefore was greatly concerned to
keep the favor of the United States, truncated or reunited, as an
anti-British balance and as a theatre for future French trade. Yet
he, like pro-Northern Thouvenel, was convinced of the irreversi-
bility of separation and avowed it frankly to Seward's face. This
unrelenting secretary took such statements with equanimity and
did not seem to doubt Mercier's basic loyalty to the Northern
cause. How could he, when hundreds of thousands of loyal
Northerners harbored the same convictions? And this seemed
to represent the French envoy's basic position: an unwilling
separationist without being pro-Southern. Yet for his separationist views he was sometimes unjustly accused of being pro-
Southern.[6]

On the American side, President Lincoln was the official holding final authority in foreign affairs, and yet in this case he was a
sort of ancient Japanese emperor withdrawn into his Kyoto White
House, a shadowy figure in a distant retreat. Time and again
Shogun Seward would remark that he had spoken to the president or that he had shown a certain dispatch to him and that
the president had . . . etc., etc. Although Monahan has written
a book on Lincoln as *A diplomat in carpet slippers*, he was more
carpet slippers than diplomat. On rare occasions he did emerge
from his seclusion and play a role in foreign relations. During
his first month in office he scotched Seward's rash plan for a

foreign war. Later on he took a harder position than Seward on the "Trent" affair. Foreign intervention threats were no doubt part of his motive for the Preliminary Emancipation Proclamation, but even here Seward had to point out the poor timing of July 1862 as far as a predictable foreign reaction was concerned. In his reception of Prince Napoleon he presented a sorry appearance, and his realization of this, as well as his western unfamiliarity with foreigners, no doubt accounted for his desire to keep in the background. Scarcely ever did Mercier write and say that he had seen Lincoln or report a direct statement from him.

And yet, as the war went on, men abroad began to have an increasing respect for him. His state speeches showed a depth of sentiment and a breadth of vision and magnanimity; foreigners associated his name finally with emancipation; and his slow but steady conduct of the war toward success gave him a late aura of noble solidity. Thus, by the time of his assassination, France and England hesitated to do anything definite for a period of time because they had felt secure with Lincoln and Seward and for a while were uncertain about who might succeed them.

Usually Lincoln left diplomatic matters to his secretary of state, who did play a conspicuous role in Franco-Federal relations. A moderately well educated man, Seward had, nevertheless, in his career up to 1861, been limited to domestic politics: state legislator, governor, and senator. Twice the Republican Party had turned him down as its candidate for the presidency. Consequently he came to the state department with a good deal of experience in dealing with politicians and legislators but, like Lincoln, with no experience in international diplomacy. In the first few months of his secretaryship he proved to be very brash and belligerent. Being so preoccupied with domestic affairs and secession, he at first wanted to use foreign relations to thwart the secessionists by precipitating a war with France or any other European country. While Lincoln put a stop to this plan, Seward frightened Lyons and Mercier in Washington and their superiors, Russell and Thouvenel, in London and Paris, by his loud and violent threats of war and world revolution if they intervened or showed favor to the Confederacy. His sunjutified protests against foreign neutrality, his unmannerly lectures to Thouvenel on the latter's unofficial queries, and his menacing remarks over the unofficial interviews with Confederate agents and over Anglo-French joint approaches, all set him down in the eyes of foreign officialdom as a dangerous parvenu.

With hindsight one would almost gain the impression that Seward was deliberately utilizing his appearance of inexperience in order to do unorthodox things to fend off outside intervention. Foreigners may have smiled at his antics, but they also trembled at the thought that he was quite capable of becoming a bull in the china shop. So they held their breath and stayed their hand, a result which suggests considerable method in Seward's seeming madness. Having roared against French neutrality, he quietly struck the pose of the "averted glance"; having exploded against the reception of Rost, he sweetly expressed pleasure over the attitude of France; having shown anger over attempted joint Anglo-French interviews, he invited Mercier to dinner. At first reserved on the "Trent" affair, he welcomed the British and French notes with alacrity and released the captives; on Mexico he protested sadly over the French expedition and the Maximilian empire, but promised no interference. He promptly encouraged Mercier to go to Richmond with what he thought was a generous offer in return for reunion; and he urged foreign representatives to travel throughout the United States to witness the strength and determination in the North. Alarmed over the Roebuck attempt to win French recognition for the South, he went so far as to order a conditional threat of a diplomatic rupture, but a cautious French cabinet decision and the victories of Gettysburg and Vicksburg enabled Dayton to withhold this ultimate threat. By 1863 Europe began to have more confidence in the secretary, who was growing in stature as he remained in office; and confidence increased to respect, until, by the time of the assassination episode, European statesmen feared the prospect of his departure and hailed the news of his return to his duties. For four more years he occupied the state department post and has gone down in history as one of the more clever and distinguished secretaries.

Dayton, the minister to Paris, was just as inexperienced in

diplomacy as was his superior, Seward, and, in addition, knew scarcely any French. A former governor, he had had experience in dealing with men and conducted himself with a certain amount of dignity. Serious and diligent, he was able to satisfy Seward and gain the respect of Thouvenel and Drouyn de Lhuys. While Sanford and Bigelow sometimes felt that they had to lead him by the hand, he was quite capable of performing his own duties. In some instances, as in the questions of belligerency and adherence to the Declaration of Paris, he was more aware of the proper niceties and expectations than was Seward. Although not the model of an experienced diplomat, such as Charles Francis Adams, he learned his job and carried out his duties in a respectable fashion.

John Bigelow, who succeeded Dayton upon his sudden death, had several advantages over his predecessor. As a publisher and writer, he had a wider experience in worldly affairs, and he knew the French language. Furthermore, he lived to the unusual age of ninety-four, until forty-six years after the Civil War, and, as a writer, was able to give considerable favorable publicity to his role in his Paris posts. It was a wise choice when Seward sent him to Paris as a propaganda agent in the guise of consul general. Here his journalistic nose for news and his facile pen were able to serve the Union cause well for war intelligence and for a skillful manipulation of French opinion. He could also take upon his shoulders the shady deals which would have been beneath the dignity of our accredited minister. While somewhat more bustling and less dignified than Dayton, he also made a creditable record in the legation, combatting the Confederate ships in French ports and on the ways. His last wartime fight was for the abrogation of neutrality, and this was crowned not only with victory but also with the outpouring of adulation for the murdered president.

Vagaries of French Opinion

And what had been the French public opinion with which he had to deal? If press opinion was one aspect of general public opinion, it was a very unreliable representative during the

Second Empire because of governmental censorship and subtle pressures. Furthermore, the Civil War became largely an ideological football kicked about by the republican and Orleanist press on the one hand to attack the imperial regime by praising the North and by the imperialist press on the other to counter the liberals by sponsoring the Southern cause. With such ulterior motives one could not tell how sincere press opinion really was. Nor could studies of press opinion come to an agreement on which way it leaned. Owsley, who in his own treatment of the South's diplomacy seemed to be pro-Southern, still acknowledged that "public opinion [that is, press opinion] in France was almost solidly on the side of the United States," while West, in his study of the press, concluded, quite the contrary, that "the South received much sincere sympathy in France . . . shared, perhaps, in a passive way by the great masses of the supporters of Napoleon." Like West, but somewhat more cautiously, Julius Pratt concluded that the North's support was largely reduced to "the educated and intellectual French liberals."[7]

If the French press was unreliable and inconclusive regarding opinion on the war, there were other and better sources from which to estimate the broader and more solid opinion lurking beneath superficial journalistic expressions. Napoleon III, while he throttled the press, endeavored to learn about public opinion by receiving regular and secret opinion reports from his prefects and procureurs general (district attorneys). Although the prefect reports of this period have been lost, the procureur reports are full of detailed information on opinion from the provinces as well as Paris for the entire period of the Second Empire.[8]

From these reports we find that the first impulse of opinion was to be sympathetic toward the North, hostile toward England, but insistent upon the retention of French neutrality. As the war progressed, however, sentiment changed considerably. The economic distress in France became so acute that a large majority of opinion began to demand some form of intervention to end the war, and an abandonment of neutrality. Because the North persisted in the conquest of the South after all hopes of reunion seemed lost and minimized the slavery issue in favor of national integrity, opinion seemed to become more generally favorable to the South.   Even the Preliminary Emancipation Proclamation was not regarded as satisfactory because it guaranteed slavery wherever there were no insurrections.   There is little doubt that it was this pressure of public opinion which impelled Napoleon III to initiate his tripartite and his unilateral efforts at mediation.   So disappointed was opinion over the results of these steps that it tended to be more bitter toward England and Russia for their noncooperation than toward the United States for spurning France's suggestions.   After April 1863 Frenchmen seemed weary over the hopelessness of ending the war and confused by the alternation of Northern defeats and victories.   Late in 1864 there was some hope for peace if Lincoln should be defeated.   When he won, the resultant disappointment was again transformed into hope by the uninterrupted victories of the North, which in a different way might bring an end to the war. Thus, when the Southern forces did surrender, there were widespread expressions of relief because of the expectation that economic conditions would improve.   The North became more popular as the winner and as a more convincing emancipator. Yet, there was some apprehension that a victorious North might challenge the French presence in Mexico.   Lincoln's unpopularity changed to a general approval as Frenchmen saw his determination to enforce emancipation, his generous attitude toward the defeated South, and the unquestioned success of his war leadership.   There was still a lingering sympathy for the defeated South.   When the news arrived of Lincoln's assassination, there arose a genuine and extensive expression of horror and sorrow at his loss, which was especially effusive and prolonged among the Republicans.   Coupled with it was concern over a possible punitive policy by Lincoln's successor, Andrew Johnson.[9]

Northern opinion remained generally more pro-French than the French was pro-Northern.   The object of Northern resentment was obviously and continuously Great Britain.   Consequently, in comparison France usually seemed to be more a friend.   While there were at times criticism of Napoleon III and Mercier for what appeared to be their Southern sympathies, still there were not the same vituperative denunciations in the press and in congress with which Northerners assailed England. No doubt the visit and subsequent support of Prince Napoleon and the voluntary military service of the Orleans princes were associated with French sympathies. Complaint over the French recognition of Confederate belligerency was drowned out by the violence of protests against England; France's "Trent" note was welcomed while England was denounced. There was scarcely more than a whimper in response to the news of French mediation efforts; and whatever objection was voiced against the French expedition to Mexico, it was not so loud but that Seward, with his ear to the ground, could limit himself to mild protests and reassurances.

Indeed, looking back on this period of Franco-American history, one cannot but feel that the ordeal of the Civil War was in its totality beneficial to Franco-American relations. For the first time the common man in France became acquainted with America and its system of government. He also learned one of the early lessons of the industrial revolution—that the world was becoming economically interdependent. The Northern states, which for a time had appeared as crass and power-hungry conquerors and oppressors, again became credibly the emancipators of a downtrodden race and the preservers of democratic ideals and institutions. There is a clear connection between the victory of democracy in America in 1865 and the liberalization of the Empire between 1867 and 1870. Moreover, Frenchmen became impressed with the power and importance of the United States. More than ever the new ironclad American navy could be counted on to redress the balance of British power. A year later, in 1866, in an official circular issued by the emperor's government one reads these words:

> While the ancient peoples of the continent, in their restricted territories, are increasing only slowly, Russia and the United States of America may each by another century have a hundred million men. Although the growth of these two great empires may not be for us a matter of concern—on the contrary we ap-

plaud their generous efforts to help oppressed races—it is to the provident interest of the European center not to be split up into so many different states without strength or public spirit.[10]

As in so many other matters, the emperor's thoughts were far ahead of his times, and in less than eighty years his prophesy was to be more than fulfilled. It is therefore not surprising that, under cover of this awesome impression of American power, Napoleon III was able to withdraw his forces from Mexico with the general approbation of his people. With the removal of this last subject of discord between the French and American governments, their relations became friendlier and remained somewhat uneventful until the outbreak of World War I.

NOTES

Chapter I

Secession and the Union

1. *Moniteur*, Jan. 8, 1861.

2. Alexis de Tocqueville, *De la démocratie en Amérique* (Paris, 1835), part I, ch. xviii.

3. W. Reed West, *Contemporary French opinion on the American Civil War* (Baltimore, 1924), p. 9.

4. *Ibid*, p. 10.

5. Julius Froebel, *Amerika, Europa und die politischen Gesichtspunkte der Gegenwart* (Berlin, 1859), pp. 37–46. *See also* Henry Blumenthal, *A reappraisal of Franco-American relations, 1830–1871* (Chapel Hill, N.C., 1959), pp. 119–120.

6. Sartiges to Walewski, Washington, March 2, 1858, Archives du Ministère des Affaires étrangères, Paris, MSS, Correspondance politique (hereafter cited as AMAE CP), Etats-Unis, vol. 118; and Treilhard to Walewski, Washington, Jan. 16, 1861, *ibid.*, vol. 123. *See also* Blumenthal, p. 119.

7. See Lynn M. Case, "Thouvenel et la rupture des relations diplomatiques franco-sardes en 1860," *Revue d'histoire moderne et contemporaine*, VII (1960), 149–179.

8. On Syria see Pierre Renouvin, *Histoire des relations internationales*, V (Paris, 1954), 333–335.

9. John Bigelow, *Retrospections of an active life* (5 v. New York, 1903–1913), I, 601–602.

10. Faulkner to Cass, Paris, Oct. 8, 1860, National Archives, Washington, MSS, State Department Correspondence, France, Despatches (hereafter cited as SDC), volume 48, no. 55. Where conversations have been reported almost verbatim, the author has taken the liberty of putting the verbs in the present tense and the exchanges in dialogue to restore the original form and to enliven the narrative.

11. Beckles Willson, *Slidell in Paris* (New York, 1932), pp. 39–40.

12. Thouvenel to Belligny, Paris, Feb. 14, 1861, AMAE, Correspondance politique consulaire (hereafter cited as AMAE CPC), Etats-Unis, 8: 255–256. Thouvenel also complained to his consul in Philadelphia, de la Forest, and urged him to send fuller reports (Paris, May 16, 1861 [rcd. June 3], *ibid.*, fol. 192, no. 1).

13. Thouvenel to Mercier, Paris, Jan. 24, 1861, AMAE CP, Etats-Unis, 124: 37–38, no. 3.

14. Mercier to Thouvenel, Washington, Nov. 8, 16, and 26, and Dec. 7, 1860 (received on Nov. 25; and on Dec. 1, 11, and 25), AMAE CP, Etats-Unis, 123: 360–364, no. 9; 365–367, no. 10; 376–378, no. 11; 386–389, no. 14.

15. Faulkner to Cass, Paris, Jan. 2, 1861, SDC, France, 49: no. 86.

16. Mercier to Thouvenel, Washington, Dec. 17, 1860 (recd. Jan. 5, 1861), AMAE CP, Etats-Unis, 123: 398–401. no. 15.

17. Same to same, Dec. 31, 1860, *ibid.*, fol. 414–416, no. 17.

18. *New York Times*, Jan. 1, 1861.

19. Thouvenel to Mercier, Paris, Jan. 24, 1861, AMAE CP, Etats-Unis, 124: 37–38; no. 3. For marginal note see *ibid.*, 123: 414, no. 17.

20. Mercier to Thouvenel, Washington, Jan. 7, 1861 (rcd. Jan. 24), *ibid.*, 124: 8–11, no. 19.

21. Faulkner to Black, Paris, Jan. 24, 1861 (rcd. Feb. 21), SDC, France, Despatches, 49: no. 91.

22. Faulkner to Black, Paris, March 19, 1861, (rcd. April 16, 1861), SDC, France, Despatches, 49: no. 111.

23. Mercier to Thouvenel, Washington, Feb. 11, 1861 (rcd. Feb. 28), AMAE CP, Etats-Unis, 124: 53–60, no. 23.

24. Thouvenel to Mercier, Paris, March 4, 1861, *ibid.*, fol. 88.

25. *Moniteur*, March 18, 1861; Mercier to Thouvenel, Washington, March 7, 1861 (rcd. March 22), AMAE CP, Etats-Unis, 124: 90–95.

26. Jay Monaghan, *Diplomat in carpet slippers; Abraham Lincoln deals with foreign affairs* (New York, 1945), pp. 39–40.

27. Circular of Seward to all the ministers of the United States, Washington, March 9, 1861, *Executive documents of the Senate of the United States for the 2nd session of the 37th Congress, 1861–1862*, I (Washington, 1861), 32–33.

28. Thouvenel's younger son, Constantin, had attacks of convulsions from 7 to 9 April. "Absorbé par de douloureuses préoccupations j'ai [Thouvenel] un peu négligé les affaires" (Louis Thouvenel, ed., *Le secret de l'empereur, correspondance confidentielle et inédite échangée entre M. Thouvenel, le duc de Gramont, et le général comte de Flahault, 1860–1863* [2v. Paris, 1889], II, 54). On the 10th he cancelled his usual weekly diplomatic reception (*Moniteur*, 9 April 1861).

29. Faulkner to Seward, Paris April 15, 1861 (rcd. May 3), SDC, Despatches France, 49: no. 119.

30. Faulkner to Black, Paris, Jan. 14, 1861 (rcd. Feb. 21) *ibid.*, no. 90.

31. Faulkner to Seward, Paris, March 26, 1861, *ibid.*, no. 114.

32. Monaghan, p.32. Dayton had been the Republican vice-presidential candidate in 1856.

33. Lincoln to Seward, Washington, March 11, 1861, Roy P. Basher, ed., *The collected works of Abraham Lincoln* (9v., New Brunswick, N.J., 1953–55), IV, 281.

34. Same to same, Washington, March 18, 1861, *ibid.*, IV, 292–293.

35. Dayton to Seward, Trenton, March 22, 1861, Princeton University Library, Princeton, MSS, Dayton Papers, Box 2.

36. Thouvenel to Mercier, Paris, April 25, 1861, AMAE CP, Etats-Unis, 124: 161–163, no. 6.

37. Mercier to Thouvenel, Washington, March 25, 1861 (rcd. April 11), *ibid.*, fol. 119–120, no. 28.

38. Sanford to Seward, Paris, April 19, 1861 (rcd. May 11), SDC, Belgium, Despatches, V.

39. Thouvenel told Mercier: "... m'ayant lui-même [Faulkner] présenté M. Sanford, je ne pouvais avoir aucune difficulté à entrer en communications confidentielles avec un agent qui est appelé d'ailleurs à exercer dans un pays voisin des fonctions diplomatiques" (Paris, April, 25, 1861, AMAE CP, Etats-Unis, 124: 163, no. 6).

40. Same to same, Paris, April 25, 1861, *ibid.*, fol. 161–163, no. 6. It is curious that Sanford makes no mention of this part of the interview (Sanford to Seward, Paris, April 25, 1861 [rcd. May 11], SDC, Belgium, Despatches, V).

41. Sanford to Seward, *ibid.*

42. Thouvenel to Seward, Paris, April 25, 1861 (rcd. May 22), SDC, Notes from French Legation.

43. Sanford to Seward, Paris, May 12, 1861 (rcd. May 29), SDC, Belgium, Despatches, V, no. 2. *See also* Thouvenel to Mercier, May 16, 1861, AMAE CP, Etats-Unis, 124: 216–217, no. 8; and translation in SDC, Notes from the French Legation.

44. Same to same, Paris, May 7, 1861 (rcd. May 23, 1861), SDC, Belgium, Despatches, V.

45. Walsh to Seward, Paris, May 20, 1861 (rcd. June 21), *ibid.*, France, Despatches, volume 49. Sanford had strong misgivings about Dayton's ability. To Seward he reported: "Mr. Dayton is finally installed as minister—homesick I think and certainly finding himself uncomfortable here with ears and mouth closed to all around him. I have been doing all I could to help him comfortably into his place—presenting him around among the officials, telling him what to do, etc. He will be popular here—among those who speak English—but how little he will be able to do here actively or usefully in directing public, social, or official opinion!" (Sanford to Seward, Paris, May 21, 1861, SDC, Belgium, Despatches, V).

46. Dayton to Seward, Paris, May 22, 1861 (rcd. June 7), SDC, France, Despatches, 49: no. 5.

47. *Ibid.*

48. Frederic Bancroft, *The life of William H. Seward* (New York, 1900), II, 137 *See also* E. D. Adams, *Great Britain and the American Civil War* (New York, 1925), I, 117.

49. Bancroft, II, 120–121.

50. *Ibid.*, p. 132.

51. Lyons to Russell, Washington, March 26, 1861, private, British Public Record Office, London, MSS, Russell Papers (hereafter cited as PRO RP) 30/22/35: 24–34. For Republican reliance on Southern unionism see David M. Potter, *Lincoln and his party in the secession crisis* (New Haven, 1942), pp. 368–375.

52. Lyons to Russell, Washington, Jan. 7, 1861, private, PRO RP, 30/22/35: 1–4.

53. Schleiden to Bremen Senate, Washington, Jan. 26, 1861, in Ralph H. Lutz, ed., "Rudolf Schleiden and the visit to Richmond, April 25, 1861," *Annual report of the American Historical Association*, 1915, p. 210.

54. Mercier to Thouvenel, Washington, Feb. 1, 1861 (rcd. Feb. 18), AMAE CP, Etats-Unis, 124: 39–47, no. 20.

55. Lyons to Russell, Washington, Feb. 4, 1861, private, PRO RP, 30/22/35: 12–13.

56. Monaghan, pp. 51–52.

57. Mercier to Thouvenel, Washington, March 29, 1861 (rcd. April 18), AMAE CP, Etats-Unis, 124: 121–129, no. 29.

58. The above quotation is taken from Seward's draft rather than from the Lincoln manuscript and differs mainly in Seward's underlining of six words (University of Rochester Library, Special Collections, Seward Papers). For the Lincoln copy version see Nicolay and Hay, III, 439–441; Bancroft, II, 133.

59. Bancroft, II, 138. Since there is no copy of Lincoln's reply in the Seward Papers, a question arises whether Lincoln ever did give this written answer to Seward. He may have given an oral reply along these lines.

60. *Ibid.*, p. 159.

61. Mercier to Thouvenel, Washington, April 8, 1861 (rcd. April 23), AMAE CP, Etats-Unis, 124: 148–158, no. 31.

62. Seward to Dayton, Washington, May 4, 1861, SDC, France, Instructions, 15: 530–533, no. 7.

63. Both the Austrian and Russian envoys reported the publication to their home governments. The former, Hülsemann, remarked that "this publication no doubt came out at this very time to mark the decisive moment we're now in" (Hülsemann to Rechberg, New York, May 6, 1861, Haus-, Hof-, und Staatsarchiv, Vienna, MSS, PA [hereafter cited as HHSA PA], Vereinigte Staaten, 33/16: 241). See also Stoeckl to Gorchakov, Washington, May 1/13, 1861, Russian Central Archives, Foreign Affairs, United States, Instructions, no. 33, from Library of Congress, Washington, Division of Manuscripts, photostats (hereafter cited as RCA LC).

64. *New York Times*, May 6, 7, 1861.

65. Mercier to Thouvenel, Washington, May 12, 1861 (rcd. May 28), AMAE CP, Etats-Unis, 124: 207–214, no. 36.

66. Dayton to Seward, Paris, May 30, 1861 (rcd. June 14), SDC, France, Despatches, 49: no. 8. This dispatch and others from Dayton were published, but the part about Thouvenel's cold reprimand was deleted by Seward (*Executive documents, senate, 37th Congress, 2nd session, 1861–1862,* I, 216–218).

67. E. de Bellot des Minières to Thouvenel, Paris, May 7, 1861, "Lettre à M. le Ministre des Affaires étrangères sur la Question américaine. Lutte entre le Nord and le Sud," AMAE MD, Etats-Unis, 25: 187–188. This correspondent may have been one of the promoters of a canal project in Virginia in which the French were interested.

68. Thouvenel to Mejan, Paris, May 16, 1861, AMAE CPC, Etats-Unis, 9: 69–74, no. 2 bis.

69. Yancey and Rost to Hunter, Paris, Oct. 5, 1861, no. 8, Library of Congress, Washington, Manuscripts Division, MSS, Confederate States of America, State Department Papers (hereafter cited as CSDP).

70. Many of the evaluations of the French press are taken from W. Reed West's excellent study of *Contemporary French opinion on the American Civil War* (Baltimore, 1924). For these views of the *Débats* see West, pp. 11–12, 17–19, 25, 32.

71. West, pp. 20, 26, 32.

72. Faulkner to Cass, and enclosure, Paris, Dec. 4, 1860, SDC, France, Despatches, vol. 48.

73. West, pp. 13–14.

74. Quoted in the *New York Times*, April, 23, 1861.

75. Faulkner to Cass, Paris, Dec. 6, 1860, SDC, France, Despatches, 48: no. 74.

76. West, pp. 14–15.

77. Pierre de La Gorce, *Histoire de Second Empire* (7 v. Paris, 1894–1904), IV, 198.

78. Sanford to Seward, Paris, May 7, 1861 (rcd. May 23), SDC, Belgium, Despatches, V.

79. Same to same, Paris, April 25, 1861 (rcd. May 11), *ibid.*

80. West, pp. 10, 21, 26–29, 31, 33.

81. Pierre Rost, one of the Confederate agents, arrived in Paris on about May 12, 1861, and this argument appeared in the *Pays* on May 15, 1861 (West, p. 30). Sanford wrote: "Judge Rost and, I think, Dudley Mann are here" (Sanford to Seward, Paris, May 16, 1861, SDC, Belgium, Despatches, V).

82. West, pp. 12–13, 21, 30, 33.

83. West, pp. 21, 34.

84. On the unreliability of the press, see Lynn M. Case, *French opinion on war and diplomacy during the Second Empire* (Philadelphia, 1954), pp. 2–6.

85. On the survey reports on opinion, see *ibid.*, pp. 6–13.

86. Report from Nancy, July 6, 1861, Lynn M. Case, *French opinion on the United States and Mexico, 1860–1867* (New York, 1936), p. 245.

87. Report from Besançon, Oct. 22, 1861, *ibid.*

88. Report from Nîmes, Jan. 31, 1862, *ibid.*, p. 255.

89. *Ibid.*, pp. 244–255.

90. *Ibid*, pp. 245, 247, 252.

91. For early provincial opinions favorable to the North see *ibid.*, pp. 244–245, 249, 252.

92. For early sympathy for the South, see *ibid.*, pp. 247, 252.

93. On business concern or lack of concern over the war, see *ibid.*, pp. 246, 248, 251.

Chapter II

Recognition of Belligerency

1. Mercier to Thouvenel, Washington, Nov. 16, 1860, AMAE CP, E-U, 123: 365–367, no. 10.

2. Same to same, Washington, Feb. 11, 1861, *ibid.*, 124: 59–60, no. 23.

3. Stoeckl to Gorchakov, Washington, Jan. 31/Feb. 12, 1861, F. A. Golder, *Guide to the materials for American history in Russian archives* (2v. Washington, 1917, 1937), II, 25.

4. Circular to ministers abroad, Washington, March 9, 1861, *Papers relating to the foreign relations of the United States* (Washington, 1861–), I, 32–33 (hereafter cited as *FRUS*).

5. Confederate Secretary of State Robert M. T. Hunter to Yancey, Rost, and Mann, Montgomery, March 16, 1861, copy, Library of Congress, Washington, Division of Manuscripts, Eustis Papers.

6. Jay Monaghan, pp. 51–52.

7. Lyons to Russell, Washington, March 26, 1861, priv., PRO, Russell Papers, 30/22/35: 24–34.

8. Mercier to Thouvenel, Washington, March 29, 1861, AMAE CP, E-U, 124: 121–129, no. 29.

9. Stoeckl to Gorchakov, Washington, April 2/14, 1861, no. 863, RCA LC.

10. Mercier reported to Thouvenel: "Lord Lyons me dit avoir écrit à Lord John Russell au sujet de la reconnaissance . . . sur l'avantage . . . au commerce européen par une reconnaissance antérieure . . . et sur les inconvénients qu'il pourrait y avoir à ce que cette reconnaissance n'eut pas eu lieu simultanément de la part des puissances." In contradiction to Stoeckl's note to Gorchakov, the French minister wrote that "le ministre de Russie a écrit à son gouvernement exactement dans le même sens que moi" (Washington, April 8, 1861, AMAE CP, E-U, 124: 148–158, no. 31).

11. Washington, Feb. 12, 1861, priv., PRO, Russell Papers, 30/22/35: 17–18.

12. Washington, March 1, 1861, priv., AMAE MD, Papiers Thouvenel, XIII, 350–355.

13. ". . . et l'empêcher qu'elle n'y laisse des traces durables" (Washington, March 29, 1861, AMAE CP, E-U, 124: 121–129, no. 29).

14. Paris, Dec. 6, 1860, SDC, France, Despatches, 48: no. 74.

15. Jeremiah Black had succeeded Cass as secretary cf state in February 1861.

16. Faulkner to Black, Paris, March 19, 1861, SDC, France, Despatches, 48: no. 111.

17. Faulkner to Seward, Paris, April 15, 1861, *ibid.*, no. 119.

18. Flahault to Thouvenel, London, April 19, 1861 (rcd. April 20), AMAE CP, Angl., 719: 305–306, no. 29. Russell had confided to Lyons in Washington that "I shall see the Southerners when they come but not officially, and keep them at a proper distance" (London, April 6, 1861, PRO, Russell Papers, 30/22/96).

19. He appears to be following Russell's policy on recognition by tying it on with commercial interests.

20. Sanford to Seward, Paris, April 25, 1861, SDC, Belgium, Despatches, V. See also a more abbreviated version in Thouvenel to Mercier, Paris, April 25, 1861, AMAE CP, E-U, 124: 161–163, no. 6.

21. Russell to Cowley, London, March 30, 1861, no. 394. (See Cowley to Russell, Paris, April 2, 1861, PRO FO, 27/1389/505).

22. Cowley to Russell, *ibid.* It is quite likely that the two foreign ministers had in mind the Danish and Italian questions as well as the American, for Flahault had reported on March 28 that "Lord John Russell authorise l'envoyé d'Angleterre à seconder toute tentative de compromis à se mettre d'accord avec ses collègues de France et de Russie pour suivre une ligne de conduite identique et il considère que la conformité d'opinion des trois puissances, l'action commune de leurs représentants, peut être la chance la plus favorable qui reste de détourner les dangers dont la question des Duchés [Schleswig-Holstein] semble menacer chaque jour d'avantage la paix de l'Europe" (Flahault to Thouvenel, London, March 28, 1861, AMAE CP, Angl. 719: 227–229, no. 22).

23. Paris, April 17, 1861, *ibid.*, fol. 280, no. 56.

24. Flahault to Thouvenel, London, April 19, 1861, *ibid.*, fol. 305–306, no. 29.

25. Sanford to Seward, Paris, April 19, 1861, SDC, Belgium, Despatches, V.

26. Thouvenel to Mercier, Paris, April 25, 1861, AMAE CP, E-U, 124: 161–163. no. 6.

27. Sanford to Seward, Paris, April 25, 1861, SDC, Belgium, Despatches, V.

28. *Moniteur*, May 1, 1861.

29. Dallas to Seward, London, May 2, 1861, *FRUS* (1861), pp. 83–84, no. 333.

30. J. D. Richardson, *A compilation of the messages and papers of the presidents, 1789–1897* (10 v. Washington, 1896–1899), VI, 13–14.

31. Proclamation of April 17, 1861, Col. H. K. White, ed., *Official records of the Union and Confederate navies in the War of the Rebellion* (hereafter cited as *ORN*), 2nd ser., III, 96–97.

32. Richardson, *Presidents*, VI, 14–15.

33. In a decision on June 13, 1861 involving a British blockade-runner, the "Tropic Wind," the Federal judge, James Dunlap, declared: "A blockade, under the law of nations, must be the act of a belligerent. There must be a public war. . . . These facts set forth by the President, with the assertion of the right of blockade, amount to a declaration that civil war exists. Blockade itself is a belligerent right, and can only legally take place in a state of war . . ." (Circuit Court of the District of Columbia, *Reports*, II [1895], 375–382).

34. *Moniteur*, April 27, May 3, 1861.

35. E. D. Adams, I, 86.

36. London, May 6, 1861, PRO FO, 5/755/121. In a private letter to Lyons, Russell said further: "The Law Officers are of the opinion that we must consider the Civil War in America as a regular war—*justum bellum*—and apply to it all the rules respecting blockade [and] letters of marque which belong to neutrals during a war" (London, May 6, 1861, Newton, I, 37–38).

37. Russell to Cowley, London, May 6, 1861, PRO FO, 27/1375/553. The question of the Declaration of Paris will be separately discussed below.

38. Cowley to Russell, Paris, May 7, 1861, PRO FO, 27/1390/677. Thouvenel later wrote Flahault, in London: "Le Gouvernement de l'Empereur s'était déjà préoccupé lui-meme des questions dont Lord Cowley m'a entretenu, et après les avoir mûrement examinées, il était arrivé aux mêmes conclusions que le Cabinet Britannique" (Paris, May 11, 1861, AMAE, Fonds Divers, Guerre des Etats-Unis, Carton 1861).

39. Cowley to Russell, Paris, May 9, 1861, PRO FO, 27/1390/684.

40. Mercier told Stoeckl that he "a reçu un mémoire ou consultation, rédigé par un Comité du Ministère . . . à Paris, sur la conduite à tenir dans la crise actuelle" (Stoeckl to Gorchakov, Washington, May 29/June 10, 1861, RCA LC, Photostats, 49: 562, no. 41).

41. Thouvenel to Mercier, Paris, May 11, 1861, AMAE CP, E-U, 124: 194–206, nos. 7 and 7 bis.

42. The last three words were underlined by Seward in the report he read.

43. These words by Thouvenel resemble those of Gladstone's famous Newcastle speech a year and a half later (E. D. Adams, II, 47), only in this case they were uttered in a private conversation. Yet, in this instance too, Seward had to undergo the bitter experience of reading them.

44. Here, too, Sanford is anticipating C. F. Adams' protests to Russell six days later (May 18).

45. The dialogue has been restored to its original form in the present tense. Sanford to Seward, Paris, May 12, 1861, SDC, Belgium, Despatches, V, no. 2. On May 16 Thouvenel reassured Dayton that "the recognition of the Southern Confederates as possessing belligerent rights he did not consider at all as recognizing them as independent states" (Dayton to Seward, Paris, May 22, 1861 [rcd. June 7], SDC, France, Despatches, L, no. 5).

46. The British Proclamation of Neutrality, dated May 13, 1861, was published in the *London Gazette* of May 14. See also E. D. Adams, I, 94–95.

47. Lyons to Russell, Washington, June 14, 1861, PRO, Russell Papers, 30/22.

48. Thouvenel to Chasseloup-Laubat, Paris, May 18, 1861, Archives de la Marine, Paris, MSS, Series BB⁴/1345/I (hereafter cited as AM).

49. Russell to Cowley, London, May 21, 1861, PRO, Russell Papers, 30/22/104.

50. Thouvenel to Mejan (at New Orleans), Paris, May 16, 1861, AMAE, Correspondence politique consulaire (CPC), E-U, 9: 69–74, no. 2 bis; *New York Times*, May 28, 1861.

51. Thouvenel to Chasseloup-Laubat, Paris, May 18, 1861, AM, BB⁴/1345/I.

52. Same to same, Paris, May 24, 1861, with enclosures, *ibid.*

53. Chasseloup-Laubat to Thouvenel, Paris, June 1, 1861, AMAE, Fonds Divers, Guerre des Etats-Unis, Carton 1861, Droit Maritime.

54. Rouher to Thouvenel, Paris, June 5, 1861, *ibid.*, Pièces Diverses.

55. For the copy with the emperor's autograph signature see AMAE, Fonds Divers, Guerre des Etats-Unis, Carton 1861.

56. The Declaration of Neutrality was based upon art. 14 of the marine ordinance of Aug. 1681, art. 3 of the law of April 10, 1825, art. 84 and 85 of the Penal Code, art. 65 and following of the decree of March 24, 1852, art. 313 and following of the Maritime Penal Code, and art. 21 of the Napoleonic (Civil) Code.

57. Declaration of June 10, 1861, France, Ministère des Affaires étrangères, *Documents diplomatiques* (hereafter cited as *livre jaune*) (1861), pp. 97–98; AM, BB⁴/1345/I; *Bulletin de la Marine* (1861), no. 20, p. 413; *Moniteur*, June 11, 1861.

58. Thouvenel to Mercier, Paris, June 18, 1861, AMAE CP, E-U, 124: 319–320. no. 14.

59. *Ibid.*

60. Autograph unofficial note by Russell (recipient not indicated), June 13, 1861. AMAE, Fonds Divers, Guerre des Etats-Unis, Carton 1861, Communications anglaises.

61. Russell to Lyons, London, June 13, 1861, PRO FO, 5/755/177 (copy sent to Paris for the information of the French government).

62. Dayton to Seward, Paris, June 12, 1861 (rcd. June 28), SDC, France, Despatches, L, no. 10.

63. Russell to Cowley, London May 11, 1861, PRO FO, 27/1376/574.

64. Yancey and Mann to Toombs, London, May 21, 1861, *ORN*, 2nd ser., III, 215, no. 1. See original in Library of Congress, Washington, Division of Manuscripts, Confederate Dept. of State Papers (CSDP).

65. Thouvenel to Flahault, Paris, June 5, 1861, teleg., 10:00 A.M., AMAE CP, Angl. 720: 7; Flahault to Thouvenel, London, June 5, 1861, *ibid.*, fol. 18.

66. See above.

67. Seward to Mercier, Washington, May 23, 1861 (rcd. June 8), AMAE CP, E-U, 124: 229–230, enclosure with no. 37 bis (passage italicized by the author). Two days before, Seward had written his famous note instructing Adams to stop contacts with the British government if it received the Southern representatives (Seward to Adams, Washington, May 21, 1861, *FRUS* [1861], 87–88).

68. Enclosure with Mercier to Thouvenel, Washington, May 23, 1861 (rcd. June 8), AMAE CP, E-U, 124: 228, no. 37.

69. Thouvenel to Mercier, Paris, June 20, 1861, AMAE CP, E-U, 124: 346–349, no. 16.

70. Yancey and Mann to Toombs, London, July 15, 1861, no. 3, *ORN*, 2nd ser., III, 222. Thouvenel's reference to the sympathetic reports of the French consuls may have been an indirect way of encouraging the Confederate government to let the consuls function without new Confederate exequaturs.

71. *Patrie*, June 14, 1861; *Moniteur*, June 16, 1861.

72. This exchange of remarks has been restored to its original form in the present tense. Dayton to Seward, Paris, c. June 20, 1861, SDC, France, Despatches, L, no. 11. Only part of this dispatch was published in *FRUS* (1861), pp. 218–219.

73. About two weeks before this interview Thouvenel had received from England some summaries of Lyons' dispatches. In a dispatch of May 20, Lyons said that Seward's attitude was very violent on hearing that Russell would receive Yancey unofficially. It almost looked as if Seward and the American public wanted war with both France and England. Lyons says this must be countered by inflexibility of purpose and a calm warning that there is a limit to forbearance. The French minister may have decided to follow this advice in his conversation with Dayton (translations of summaries of Lyons' reports of May 20 and 23, 1861 [Thouvenel's autograph note: "Resumé des dernières dépêches de Lord Lyons"], AMAE, Fonds Divers, Guerre des Etats-Unis, Carton 1861, Communications anglaises).

74. Sanford to Seward, Paris, April 25, 1861 (rcd. May 11), SDC, Belgium, Despatches, V.

75. Dallas to Seward, London, May 2, 1861, E. D. Adams, I, 85.

76. *Ibid.*, pp. 90–91.

77. Lyons to Russell, Washington, May 23, 1861, *Sessional papers* (1862), LXII, 39.

78. Seward to Adams, Washington, May 21, 1861, *FRUS* (1861), p. 87, no. 10.

79. Clipping from the *New York Herald* in Mercier to Thouvenel, Washington, May 23, 1861, AMAE CP, E-U, 124: 231, no. 37. Mercier claimed that Seward read and corrected this editorial.

80. Mercier to Thouvenel, *ibid.*, fol. 225–227, no. 39 bis.

81. Schleiden to Bremen Senate, Washington, May 27, 1861, quoted in E. D. Adams, I, 130.

82. Seward to Mercier, Washington, May 23, 1861, in AMAE CP, E-U, 124: 229–230 (also found in SDC, Notes to the French Legation); Seward to Weed, Washington, May 23, 1861, quoted in E. D. Adams, I, 129.

83. Seward to Dayton, Washington, May 30, 1861, SDC, France, Instructions, XV, 535–538, no. 10.

84. Thouvenel to Mercier, Paris, May 16, 1861, AMAE CP, E-U, 124: 216–217. no. 8.

85. The Bunch mission will be taken up in Chapter III.

86. For Mercier's exploratory interview of June 6, see Mercier to Thouvenel, Washington, June 10, 1861, AMAE CP, E-U, 124: 301–308, no. 41. Lyons gave the following version of this interview: "M. Mercier . . . appears to be very frank and cordial with me. The instructions which he read to me insist very strongly upon his acting in entire concert with me. I think he may perhaps have received a confidential dispatch desiring him to proceed cautiously, for he is going at a much slower pace than his language a short time ago would have led one to expect. His giving Mr. Seward a copy of the Exposition of the French Jurists on the question of belligerent rights . . . seems to show a straightforward desire to make the government acquainted with the real sentiments and intentions of the Emperor" (Lyons to Russell, Washington, June 10, 1861, PRO FO, 30/22/35: 101–107). Stoeckl also gave Gorchakov an account of Mercier's June 6th interview and concluded that war with England and France seemed inevitable and that it would lead to a general European war. In the margin Gorchakov wrote "certes" (Washington, May 29/June 10, 1861, RCA LC photostats, 49: 562–564, no. 41).

87. Lyons to Russell, Washington, June 14, 1861, PRO FO, 30/22/35: 109–117.
88. *Ibid.*
89. Mercier to Thouvenel, Washington, June 14, 1861, AMAE CP, E-U, 124: 311–317, no. 42.

90. F. W. Seward, *Reminiscences of a war-time statesman and diplomat, 1830–1915* (New York, 1916), pp. 179–180. Lyons and Mercier never mentioned this separation incident and thus their reports sound as if their interview was a joint one throughout. Seward, in writing to Dayton, said: "As the fact of an understanding existing between them did not certainly imply an unfriendly spirit, we should not complain of it, but that it must be understood by the French and British Governments that we shall deal hereafter as heretofore in this case as in all others with each power separately, and that the agreement for concerted action between them would not at all influence the course we should pursue" (Washington, June 17, 1861, SDC, France, Instructions, XVI, 1–2, no. 19). In a private letter to Russell, Lyons gave a hint of an admission that there had been two separate interviews when he said: "M. Mercier and I have, by a course perhaps a little pusillanimous, prevented an explosion here on the subject of belligerent rights." While Lyons felt that England and France must persist in their concert approach, he added that "I do not think it necessary to annoy Mr. Seward by frequent identic or collective communications here" (Washington, June 18, 1861, PRO FO, 30/22/35: 119–124).

91. For the Seward-Lyons interview see Lyons to Russell, Washington, June 17, 1861, PRO FO, United States Despatches, 5/766/282; and a private letter to same, July, 18, 1861, PRO FO, 30/22/35: 119–124; and Seward to Adams, Washington, June 19, 1861, *FRUS* (1861–1862), pp. 106–109.

92. These instructions (Thouvenel to Mercier, Paris, May 11, 1861, no. 7) in English translation are found in SDC, Notes from the French Legation.

93. News of the French declaration did not arrive in the United States until June 23, 1861.

94. Russell had also presented arguments to Adams in defence of recognizing Southern belligerency. He could not believe that the North would hang Southern privateers, so how could they expect Britain to do so. The United States had not shot prisoners of war as traitors, so the United States themselves had in effect recognized Southern belligerency (Russell to Lyons, London, June 21, 1861, PRO FO, 5/755/185).

95. Washington, June 18, 1861, AMAE CP, E-U, 124: 338–345, no. 43.

96. Seward to Dayton, Washington, June 22, 1861, SDC, France, Instructions, XVI, no. 22; and see also same to same, June 17, 1861, *ibid.*, no. 19.

97. Same to same, July 1, 1861, *ibid.*, no. 24.

98. Thouvenel to Mercier, Paris, June 20, 1861, AMAE CP, E-U, 124: 346–349, no. 16.

99. Seward to Mercier, Washington, July 6, 1861, AMAE CP, E-U, 124: 378; copy also in SDC, Notes to French Legation.

100. Thouvenel to Mercier, Paris, July 4, 1861, AMAE CP, E-U, 124: 368–369, no. 18.

101. Richardson, *Presidents*, VI, 25–26.

Chapter III

The Declaration of Paris

1. Mercier may have learned this from his close association with Southern secessionists in congress and the Buchanan administration. Indeed, it may be wondered whether Trescott's position as assistant secretary of state may not have been responsible for Buchanan's dropping the negotiation, thus preserving privateering for the South in case of a future civil war.

2. Mercier to Thouvenel, Washington, March 1, 1861, AMAE MD, Papiers Thouvenel, XIII, 350–355.

3. First proclamation of the blockade, Washington, April 19, 1861, Richardson, *Presidents*, VI, 14–15.

4. Seward to Dayton, Washington, April 24, 1861, SDC, France, Instructions, XV, no. 4.

5. Same to same, Washington, Sept. 10, 1861, *FRUS*, (1861), p. 251.

6. Same to same, Washington, July 6, 1861, *ibid.*, p. 233.

7. On this point the author is in complete agreement with E. D. Adams (I, 153).

8. See note 4, above.

9. E. D. Adams, I, 90–91.

10. Russell to Lyons, London, May 4, 1861, PRO FO, 30/22/96.

11. This had been reiterated to Dallas, the American minister, on May 1. "He [Russell] told me . . . that there existed an understanding between this government and that of France which would lead both to take the same course as to recognition, whatever that course might be . . ." (Dallas to Seward, London, May 2, 1861, *FRUS*, [1861], p. 84, no. 333).

12. Russell to Cowley, London, May 6, 1861, PRO FO, 27/1375/553.

13. Stoeckl reported Mercier as saying that he "a reçu un mémoire ou consultation, rédigé per un Comité du Ministère des Affaires étrangères à Paris, sur la conduite à tenir dans la crise actuelle" (Stoeckl to Gorchakov, May 29/June 10, 1861, RCA LC, photocopies, 49: 562–564, no. 41). The two cabinet meetings with the emperor presiding were reported in *Moniteur*, May 5 and 9, 1861.

14. AMAE, Fonds Divers, Guerre des Etats-Unis, 1861, Pièces diverses.

15. Cowley to Russell, Paris, May 7, 1861, PRO FO, 27/1390/677.

16. The two versions of this conversation are found in Cowley to Russell, Paris, May 9, 1861, *Sessional papers*, 1862, LXII, 529; and in Thouvenel to Flahault, Paris, May 11, 1861, no. 71, AMAE, Fonds Divers, Guerre des Etats-Unis, 1861, Communications Anglaises.

17. Russell to Cowley, London, May 11, 1861, PRO FO, 27/1376/563.

18. Thouvenel to Mercier, Paris, May 11, 1861, AMAE CP, E-U, 124: 202–206, nos. 7 and 7 bis with enclosure (memorandum).

19. Sanford to Seward, Paris, May 12, 1861 (rcd. May 29), SDC, Despatches, Belgium, V, no. 2.

20 Thouvenel to Flahault, Paris, May 13, 1861, AMAE CP, Angl., 719: 377–379, no. 74.

21. Russell to Cowley, London, May 13, 1861, PRO FO, 27/1376/586.

22. Note by Thouvenel: "A communiquer à Sa Majesté" on Mercier's no. 33 of April 26, 1861, AMAE CP, E–U, 124: 164–175.

23. Thouvenel to Flahault, Paris, May 14, 1861, AMAE CP, Angl., 719: 383–384, no. 75.

24. *Ibid.*, fol. 385 (1:50 p.m.); Flahault to Thouvenel, London, May 16, 1861, *ibid.*, 386–387, no. 37.

25. Thouvenel to Mercier, Paris, May 16, 1861, *ibid.*, E–U, 124: 218, no. 9.

26. Russell to Lyons, London, May 18, 1861, PRO FO, 5/755/136. In an additional note of the same date Russell said he would not object to both sides agreeing to the whole declaration of 1856, but, he added, "You will clearly understand that Her Majesty's Government cannot accept the renunciation of privateering on the part of the Government of the United States if coupled with the condition that they should enforce its renunciation on the Confederate States . . ." (same to same, London, May 18, 1861, *Sessional papers*, LXII, 542).

27. Adams to Seward, London, May 21, 1861, *FRUS*, (1861), pp. 90–96, no. 2. Adams later came to feel that Russell had been deceitful because he thought that Russell had not sent the instructions until late that day and had implied that they dealt with the whole declaration rather than just Articles II and III. In defense of Russell (even beyond his defense by E. D. Adams, I, 147–148) it can be ascertained from the correspondence with France than Russell had been preparing Lyons' instructions for several days, and, being out of town as a result of his brother's death, may have thought the old instructions had been sent, dealing with the whole declaration. If he went in to London that evening and saw the unsigned instructions, he may have for the first time become fully aware of Palmerston's and the cabinet's changes. Thus he may have modified his instructions *after* seeing Adams and not deceitfully but obediently to cabinet insistence and French urging.

28. See above, ch. II.

29. Mercier to Thouvenel, Washington, June 2, 1861, AMAE MD, Papiers Thouvenel, XIII, 371–372.

30. Lyons to Russell, Washington, June 4, 1861, *Sessional papers*, 1862, LXII, 544.

31. Lyons to Russell, Washington, June 6, 1861, PRO FO, 5/765/253, teleg.; same to same, June 10, 1861, PRO RP, 30/22/35: 101–107; Hülsemann to Rechberg, Washington, June 8, 1861, HHSA PA, Vereinigte Staaten, LXXIII, 16: 287.

32. The italics are the author's. On this interview of June 6, 1861 and its immediate aftermath see Mercier to Thouvenel, Washington, June 10, 1861, AMAE CP, E–U, 124: 301–308, no. 41; enclosure with Thouvenel's instructions no. 7 bis, *ibid.*, fol. 203–206; and Seward to Lyons, Washington, June 8, 1861, *Sessional papers*, 1862, LXII, 53.

33. Mercier to Thouvenel, Washington, June 14, 1861, AMAE CP, E–U, 124: 311–317, no. 42.

34. See above, ch. II.

35. Mercier to Thouvenel, Washington, June 18, 1861, AMAE CP, E–U, 124: 338–345, no. 43. Thouvenel approved Mercier's cooperation with Seward's averted-glance policy: "Il m'a paru qu'il avait en cela sagement agi et je ne peux qu'approuver le soin qu'il a mis d'éviter tout ce qui aurait pu gratuitement blesser les susceptibilités du cabinet de Washington" (Thouvenel to Flahault, Paris, July 6, 1861, AMAE CP, Angl., 720: 63).

36. Lyons to Russell, Washington, June 17, 1861, *Sessional papers*, 1862, LXII, 546.

37. Seward was using the device of calling foreign countries *friendly* nations instead of *neutral* nations. He would do for friendly powers during insurrectionary hostilities what the United States would do for neutrals in time of war.

38. Seward to Dayton, Washington, June 17, 1861, SDC, France, Instructions, XVI, no. 19.

39. Seward to Adams, Washington, June 19, 1861, *FRUS*, (1861), pp. 106–109, no. 21.

40. Washington, June 18, 1861, PRO RP, 30/22/35: 119–124.

41. Dayton to Thouvenel, Paris, May 24, 1861, SDC, Paris Legation, Notes Sent; Thouvenel to Dayton, Paris, May 27, 1861, *ibid*, Notes Received.

42. Sanford to Dayton, Paris, Tuesday (May 28, 1861), Princeton University Library, Princeton, Manuscript Division, Dayton Papers, Box 3; Sanford to Seward, Paris, May 28, 1861, SDC, Belgium, Despatches, V.

43. This was the opinion of C. F. Adams, who accused Sanford of persuading Dayton to exceed his instructions, a step he himself refused to take (C. F. Adams' Diary, Roll 76, July 19, 1861).

44. Dayton to Seward, Paris, May 30, 1861, SDC, France, Despatches, L, no. 8.

45. Dayton to Thouvenel, Paris, May 31, 1861, SDC, France, Despatches, L, enclosure with no. 10 See also copies in *ibid*., Paris Legation Correspondence, Notes Sent; and in Dayton Papers, Box 2.

46. Dayton to Seward, Paris, June 7, 1861, SDC, France, Despatches, L, no. 9.

47. Thouvenel to Flahault, Paris, June 10, 1861, AMAE, Fonds Divers, Guerre des Etats-Unis, 1861, Communications Anglaises, no. 85.

48. Russell to Grey, London, June 12, 1861, PRO FO, 27/1376/57; Flahault to Thouvenel, London, June 12, 1861, AMAE, Fonds Divers, Guerre des Etats-Unis, 1861, Communications Anglaises, no. 44.

49. Flahault to Thouvenel, London, June 12, 1861, AMAE, Fonds Divers, Guerre des Etats-Unis, no. 44; Russell to Grey, London, June 12, 1861, PRO RP, 30/22/104. Russell also wrote to Lyons—for the benefit of Mercier: "I have to say that Her Majesty's Government desire to act in concert with the French Government upon the questions regarding America, and that hitherto there has been no difference of opinion between them" (PRO FO, 5/755/177). See also *Sessional papers*, 1862, LXII, 544, for note of June 21. Adams seemed to indicate that he interpreted his earliest instruction differently from Dayton and the other Northern envoys.

50. Grey reported to Russell: "M. Thouvenel expressed great satisfaction in finding how completely your Lordship's views co-incided with his own. His Excellency said that he was already aware that your Lordship entertained the same opinion as he himself did on this subject, but he had not yet heard it as decidedly expressed, and he desired me to convey his thanks to your Lordship for the communication" (Grey to Russell, Paris, June 14, 1861, *Sessional papers*, 1862, LXII, 543). That there was a general prevalence of apprehension over Seward's attempt at separation appears from Stoeckl's report when he told Gorchakov that Seward's transfer of the negotiations to Europe was an obvious attempt to separate the two powers. He added that it would not succeed, that France and England were working closely on belligerency and privateering (June 5/17, 1861, RCA LC, photocopies, 49: 565–568, no. 42).

51. Thouvenel to Dayton, Paris, June 20, 1861, SDC, France, Despatches, L, enclosure with no. 12; also *ibid*., Paris, Legation Corres., Notes Received.

52. Dayton to Seward, Paris, July 5, 1861, SDC, France, Despatches, L, no. 15.

53. Adams to Russell, London, July 11, 1861, *Sessional papers*, 1862, LXII, 547.

54. Russell to Adams, London, July 13, 1861, *ibid.*

55. Adams to Seward, London, July 19, 1861, *FRUS*, (1861), pp. 113–115.

56. Flahault to Thouvenel, London, July 9, 1861, AMAE CP, Angl., 720: 79–81, no. 50.

57. Same to same, July 15, 1861, *ibid.*, fol. 90, teleg.

58. Thouvenel to Flahault, Paris, July 16, 1861, *ibid.*, fol. 97–99, no. 103.

59. Same to same, May 14, 1861, *ibid.*, 719: 383–384, no. 75.

60. Flahault to Thouvenel, London, July 16, 1861, *ibid.*, 720: 100–105, teleg. and no. 54.

61. Thouvenel wrote Flahault: "Je n'ai pas manqué de faire connaître mon opinion à M. Billault. . . . Je crains qu'elle ne cache un piège et ne nous crée des embarras . . ." (July 19, 1861, Thouvenel, *Secrets*, II, 156).

62. Russell to Cowley, London, July 17, 1861, PRO FO, 27/1378/729.

63. Thouvenel to Flahault, Paris, July 18, 1861, AMAE CP, Angl., 720: 108, teleg. 5:00 P.M.

64. Russell to Adams, London, July 18, 1861, SDC, France, Despatches, L, enclosure with no. 22. See also AMAE, Fonds Divers, Droit Maritime. On hearing that Dayton had made no offer, Russell made a firm decision not to proceed any further with negotiations with Adams until Dayton had made the proposal to France and France had accepted it (Flahault to Thouvenel, London, July 19, 1861, AMAE CP, Angl., 720: 110, teleg. 12:30 P.M.).

65. Adams to Dayton, London, July 19, 1861, SDC, France, Despatches, L, enclosure with no. 22. See also C. F. Adams' Diary, July 20, 1861, Roll 76.

66. Dayton to Seward, Paris, June 12, 1861, SDC, France, Despatches, L, no. 10.

67. Lyons to Russell, Washington, July 8, 1861, (rcd. July 23), *Sessional papers*, 1862, LXII, 550.

68. Seward to Dayton, Washington, July 1, 1861, SDC, France, Instructions, XVI, no. 24.

69. Same to same, July 6, 1861, *ibid.*, no. 27.

70. Dayton to Seward, Paris, July 22, 1861, SDC, France, Despatches, L, no. 11.

71. For the Dayton-Adams conferences of July 24–25, 1861 see: C. F. Adams' Diary, July 23, 24, 25, 1861, Roll 76; Dayton to Adams, London, July 25, 1861, SDC, France, Despatches, L. enclosure B to no. 22; and a copy in Dayton Papers, Box 1.

72. Adams to Russell, London, July 29, 1861, *Sessional papers*, 1862, LXII, 551.

73. Russell to Adams, London July 31, 1861, *ibid.*, p. 552.

74. Adams to Seward, London, Aug. 2, 1861, *FRUS*, (1861), p. 124, no. 22.

75. Dayton to Seward, Paris, Aug. 2, 1861, SDC, France, Despatches, L, no. 24. Thouvenel said: "Dayton says he is soon going to present such a document" [draft convention] (Thouvenel to Flahault, Paris, Aug. 3, 1861, AMAE CP, Angl. 720: 135–136, no. 110).

76. Dayton to Adams, Paris, Aug. 5, 1861, SDC, France, Despatches, L, no. 44; copy in Dayton Papers, Box 1.

77. Dayton to Thouvenel, Paris, Aug. 2, 1861, SDC, France, Despatches, enclosure A with no. 24; *ibid*, Aug. 3, 1861, Paris Legation Correspondence, Notes Sent; AMAE, Fonds Divers, Guerre des Etats-Unis, Aug. 3, 1861. The note, as sent to Thouvenel, was obviously dated August 3 rather than the 2nd.

78. "M. Billault réclame sa liberté pour le 5 août. Je serai donc à Paris cinq jours plus tôt que je ne l'avais espéré . . ." (Thouvenel to Gramont, Paris, July 30, 1861, Thouvenel, *Secrets*, II, 157–158).

79. Thouvenel to Dayton, Paris, Aug. 13, 1861, SDC, Paris Legation Correspondence, Notes Received; AMAE, Fonds Divers, Guerre des Etats-Unis, 1861.

80. Dayton to Thouvenel, Paris, Aug. 16, 1861, SDC, Paris Legation Correspondence, Notes Sent.

81. Dayton to Adams, Paris, Aug. 16, 1861, Dayton Papers, Box. 1.

82. C. F. Adams' Diary, Aug. 18,1861, Roll 76.

83. Russell to Cowley, London, Aug. 13, 1861, teleg. 6:45 P.M., PRO FO, 27/1378/835.

84. The original and revised English versions appear on two separate sheets in AMAE, Fonds Divers, Guerre des Etats-Unis, 1861. The French text was an exact translation except for the names of ruler and government: "En apposant sa signature à la convention conclue en date de ce jour entre la France et les Etats-Unis, le soussigné déclare, en exécutant les ordres de l'Empereur, que le Gouvernement de Sa Majesté n'entend prendre, par la dite convention, aucun engagement de nature à l'impliquer, directement ou indirectement, dans le conflict intérieur existant aux Etats-Unis" (Thouvenel to Dayton, Paris, Aug. 20, 1861, SDC, France, Despatches, Paris Legation Correspondence, Notes Received).

85. Thouvenel to Flahault, Paris, Aug. 16, 1861, AMAE CP, Angl., 720: 158, no. 118.

86. Chateaurenard to Thouvenel, London, Aug. 21, 1861, AMAE CP, Angl. 720: 169–170, no. 68.

87. Cowley reported to Russell: "Knowing that Mr. Thouvenel was to see Mr. Dayton this morning, I sent His Excellency a copy of your Lordship's note and declaration to Mr. Adams with reference to the Convention respecting maritime law, as soon as they reached my hands" (Paris, Aug. 20, 1861, *Sessional papers*, 1862, LXII, 554).

88. The dialogue is verbatim but restored to its original form in the present tense. Dayton to Seward, Paris, Aug. 22, 1861, SDC, France, Despatches, L, no. 35. In this dispatch Dayton said: "My anticipations expressed in Despatch no. 10 are fully realized." Thouvenel's shorter account of the interview does not seem to vary from Dayton's (Thouvenel to Mercier, Paris, Aug. 29, 1861, AMAE CP, E–U, 125: 49–50, no 24). See also Cowley's account in his report to Russell of Aug. 20 (*Sessional papers*, 1862, LXII, 544).

89. Dayton to Seward, Aug. 22, 1861, *ibid.*; Dayton to Adams, Paris, Aug. 21, 1861, Dayton Papers, Box. 1.

90. Russell to Adams, London, Aug. 19, 1861, *Sessional papers*, 1862, LXII, 553; AMAE, Fonds Divers, Guerre des Etats-Unis, 1861. (For Adams' reaction see C. F. Adams' Diary, Aug. 19, 1861, Roll 76.)

91. This dialogue has been restored to its original form in the present tense. Webb to Lincoln, Southampton, Aug. 22, 1861, C. F. Adams, Jr., "The Declaration of Paris," *Proceedings of the Massachusetts Historical Society* (hereafter cited as *PMHS*), 46 (1912): 73–74, n. 2.

92. Adams to Russell, London, Aug. 23, 1861, *FRUS* (1861), pp. 136–139; *Sessional papers*, 1862, LXII, 554–556. A copy for Thouvenel in French translation is found in AMAE, Fonds Divers, Guerre des Etats-Unis, 1861. See also C. F. Adams' references in his diary for Aug. 23 and 24, 1861, Roll 76.

93. Dayton to Thouvenel, Paris, Aug. 26, 1861, SDC, Paris Legation Correspondence, Notes Sent; *ibid.*, France, Despatches, L, enclosure to no 37; original in AMAE, Fonds Divers, Guerre des Etats-Unis, 1861; original draft in Dayton Papers, Box 2. In a note to Adams, Dayton wrote: "Before receiving your reply to Lord John Russell in reference to the Treaty, I had stated my views to Mr. Thouvenel, and subsequently put them in writing substantially like your own" (Paris, Sept. 6, 1861, *ibid.*, Box 1).

94. Thouvenel to Dayton, Paris, Sept. 9, 1861, SDC, Paris Legation Correspondence, Notes Received; *ibid.*, France, Despatches, L, enclosure to no. 45; Dayton Papers, Box 3; AMAE, Fond Divers, Guerre des Etats-Unis, 1861.

95. Seward to Adams, Washington, Aug. 17, 1861, *FRUS*, (1861), pp. 128–130, no. 61; Seward to Dayton, Washington, Aug. 17, 1861, *ibid.*, p. 240, no. 41.

96. On Seward's break-off of the negotiations, *see* Seward to Dayton, Washington, Sept. 10, 1861, SDC, France, Instructions, XVI, no. 56; Seward to Adams, Washington, Sept. 7, 1861, *FRUS*, (1861), pp. 141–144, no. 83.

97. On Thouvenel's acquiescence in the break-off of negotiations, *see* Cowley to Russell, Paris, Sept. 24, 1861, *Sessional papers*, 1862, LXII, 564; Dayton to Seward, Paris, Oct. 14, 1861, SDC, France, Despatches, L, no. 59; Dayton to Thouvenel, Paris, Oct. 14, 1861, *ibid.*, Paris Legation Correspondence, Notes Sent; same in Dayton Papers, Box 2; Thouvenel to Dayton, Paris, Oct. 18, 1861, SDC, Paris Legation Correspondence, Notes Received.

98. Russell to Lyons, London, May 4, 1861, PRO RP, 30/22/96; Russell to Cowley, London, May 6, 1861, PRO FO, 27/1375/553.

99. Russell told Lyons: "But after communication with the French government it appeared best to limit our proposals in the manner proposed in my despatch" (London, May 18, 1861, *ibid.*, 5/755/139).

100. Cowley to Russell, Paris, May 9, 1861, *Sessional papers*, 1862, LXII, 539.

101. Thouvenel to Mercier, Paris, May 11, 1861, AMAE CP, E-U, 124: 194–201, no. 7. An English translation of this is found in the State Department files and is mute proof that Seward read of France's intentions to consult the Confederate government (SDC, Notes from the French Legation).

102. Russell to Cowley, London, May 11, 1861, PRO FO, 27/1376/563.

103. Thouvenel to Flahault, Paris, May 13, 1861, AMAE CP, Angl., 719: 377–379, no. 74. Russell expressed satisfaction with Thouvenel's cooperation on the Southern negotiation in his note to Cowley (PRO FO, 27/1376/586).

104. Thouvenel to Mercier, Paris, May 16, 1861, AMAE CP, E-U, 124: 218, no. 9.

105. Thouvenel to Mejan, Paris, May 16, 1861, AMAE CPC, E-U, 9: 69–74, no. 2 bis.

106. Russell to Lyons, London, May 18, 1861, PRO FO, 5/755/139.

107. Lyons to Russell, Washington, June 4 and 10, 1861, PRO RP, 30/22/35: 96–97, 101–107.

108. Mercier to Thouvenel, Washington, June 10, 1861, AMAE CP, E-U, 124: 301–308, no. 41.

109. Seward to Dayton, Washington, June 17, 1861, SDC, France, Instructions, XVI, no. 19. It was not read to Seward but handed to him, and he had it filed in the State Department files (SDC, Notes from the French Legation, May 11, 1861).

110. Dialogue restored to original present tense. Lyons to Russell, Washington, June 17, 1861, *Sessional papers*, 1862, LXII, 545–546.

111. Published in *FRUS*, (1861), pp. 224–228. Nor did England feel it necessary to keep this "averted-glance" agreement secret because she too published Lyons' account the next year (*Sessional papers*, 1862, LXII, 545–546).

112. Mercier to Thouvenel, Washington, June 18, 1861, AMAE CP, E–U, 124: 338–345, no. 43. Mercier's relation of the Lyons-Seward conversation stated: "He [Seward] seems to have said that we ought not to have spoken about this step and then he could have ignored it. Lord Lyons replied: 'Pretend we didn't say a word, as we have agreed.' This remark by Seward confirms me in my thought that, by proceeding as I indicated, we will avoid the inconveniences which could result from a direct communication with Mr. Jefferson Davis" (*ibid.*)

113. Mercier to French consul at Charleston, Washington, June 5, 1861, AMAE CP, E–U, 124: 390–391, enclosure 3 with no. 46. Lyons reported: "I drew up [my] instructions in concert with M. Mercier, and he sent by the same messenger similar instructions to M. Durand de St. André, the French acting consul at Charleston" (to Russell, Washington, July 8, 1861, *Sessional papers*, 1862, LXII, 549). Mercier thought that Belligny might have already gone home on leave, so he addressed his message merely to the "consul." For Lyons' instructions see *ibid.* Stoeckl said that the instructions left on July 3 but we know they were both dated the 5th (Stoeckl to Gorchakov, Washington, June 23/July 5, 1861, RCA LC, no. 47). Thouvenel approved these instructions (Thouvenel to Mercier, Paris, Aug. 8, 1861, AMAE CP, E–U, 125: 15–17, no. 22).

114. Bunch to Lyons, Charleston, July 28, 1861, AMAE MD, Papiers Thouvenel, XIII, 402, copy.

115. Same to same, July 31, 1861, *ibid.*

116. Bancroft, *Seward*, II, 198.

117. For the accounts of the Belligny-Bunch negotiations between Charleston and Richmond, see Bunch to Lyons, Charleston, Aug. 16, 1861, *Sessional papers*, 1862, LXII, 560–561; Belligny to Mercier, Charleston, Aug. 19, 1861, AMAE CP, E–U, 125; 56–61, enclosure 2 with no. 53; and Trescott to Hunter, Charleston, Aug. 3, 1861, *ORN*, 2nd ser., III, 230–232; E. D. Adams, I, 184–187.

118. For the Mure affair and the withdrawal of Bunch's exequatur see E. D. Adams, I, 187–195; C. F. Adams' Diary, Sept. 2–3, 1861, Roll 76; Seward to Adams, Washington, Aug. 17 and Oct. 23, 1861, and Adams to Seward with enclosures, London, Sept. 9 and 14, 1861, in *FRUS*, (1861), pp. 130–166, *passim*.

119. Russell to Cowley, London, Sept. 7, 1861, PRO FO, 27/1379/937.

120. Thouvenel to Mercier, Paris, Sept. 12, 1861, AMAE CP E–U, 125: 78–80; no. 25.

121. Cowley to Russell, Paris, Sept. 17, 1861, *Sessional papers*, 1862, LXII, 591.

122. Russell to Palmerston, London, Sept. 19, 1861, Palmerston Papers, cited in E. D. Adams, I, 191.

123. Lyons to Russell, Washington, Oct. 4, 1861, PRO RP, 30/22/35: 263–278.

124. Sept. 27, 1861, *ibid.*, fol. 257–258.

125. Mercier to Thouvenel, Washington, Oct. 8, 1861, AMAE CP, E–U, 125: 119–132, no. 63.

126. Lyons to Russell, Washington, Oct. 14, 1861, PRO RP, 30/22/35: 279–290; Mercier to Thouvenel, Washington, Oct. 14, 1861, AMAE CP, E–U, 125: 145–150, no. 65.

127. *Ibid.*

128. E. D. Adams says (I, 187) that "privately neither Lyons nor Russell were wholly convinced of the correctness of Bunch's actions."

129. Cowley to Russell, Paris, Sept. 10, 1861. PRO FO, 27/1396/112; same to same, private, Sept. 10, 1861, PRO RP, 30/22/35.

130. Flahault to Thouvenel, London, Nov. 10, 1861, AMAE CP, Angl., 720: 334-335.

131. Thouvenel to Flahault, Paris, Nov. 21, 1861, AMAE CP, Angl., 720: 338-339, no. 150.

132. Same to same, Paris, Nov. 28, 1861, *ibid.*, fol. 349-350, no. 153.

133. Flahault to Thouvenel, London, Nov. 29, 1861, AMAE CP, Angl., 720: 353-356, no. 91.

134. Cowley to Russell, Paris, Dec. 10, 1861, PRO FO, Cowley Papers, 519/229: 130-132.

135. Charles G. Fenwick, *International law* (New York, 1924), p. 109, n. 3.

Chapter IV

The Blockade and the Ports Bill

1. For England's dependence on Southern cotton see Frank L. Owsley, *King Cotton diplomacy* (1st. ed. Chicago, 1931), pp. 2-3.

2. For France's dependence on Southern cotton see Claude Fohlen, *L'industrie textile au temps du Second Empire* (Paris, 1956), p. 128.

3. John Chapman, *The cotton and commerce of India considered in relation to the interests of Great Britain* (London, 1851), pp. 1-3.

4. Lecture of Henry Ashworth before the Society of Arts, London, March 10, 1858 (cited in Owsley, p. 4).

5. Fohlen, p. 129.

6. Quoted in Owsley, p. 16.

7. Owsley, pp. 14-15.

8. Major W. H. Chase, "The secession of the Southern states," *De Bow's review*, O. S., XXX, no. 1 (Jan. 1861) (cited in Owsley, p. 17).

9. Mercier to Thouvenel, Washington, Jan. 20, 1861 (rcd. Feb. 6), AMAE CP, E-U, 124: 32-35, no. 21.

10. Monaghan, pp. 39-40.

11. *Ibid.*

12. Lyons to Russell, Washington, March 26, 1861, PRO RP, 30/22/35: 24-34.

13. When William Russell, the *Times* correspondent, had dinner with Seward, during the same week, the latter, a little in his cups, rather ungraciously threatened to break off relations with any country which received the Southern commissioners even unofficially (Monaghan, pp. 51-52).

14. Lyons to Russell, Washington, March 26, 1861, PRO RP, 30/22/35: 24-34.

15. Mercier to Thouvenel, Washington, March 29, 1961 (rcd. April 15), AMAE CP, E-U, 124: 121-129, no. 29.

16. Stoeckl to Gorchakov, Washington, March 28/April 9, 1861, RCA LC, photostats, 49: 809-812, no. 20.

17. On these valuable reports see L. M. Case, *French opinion on the United States and Mexico, 1860–1867. Extracts from the reports of the procureurs généraux* (New York, 1936), pp. xiii–xx.

18. Reports from Limoges (Jan. 12, 1861) and Lyons (Jan. 1 and Feb. 2, 1861) in *ibid.*, pp. 10–11.

19. Reports from Limoges (April 14, 1861), Lyons (April 4 and May 4, 1861), and Dijon (April 6, 1861) in *ibid.*, pp. 11–12.

20. Faulkner to Black, Paris, March 4, 1861, SDC, France, Despatches, XLIX: no. 108.

21. *Moniteur*, March 19, 1861.

22. Faulkner to Seward, Paris, April 15, 1861, SDC, France, Despatches, XLIX: no. 119.

23. Sanford to Seward, Paris, April 25, 1861, SDC, Belgium, Despatches, V.

24. *Ibid.*

25. Richardson, *Messages and papers of the presidents*, VI, 14–15.

26. For the initial diplomatic reaction to the blockade see Mercier to Thouvenel, Washington, April 26 and 27, 1861, AMAE CP, E–U, 124: 164–175, 180–187, nos. 33, 34; and Lyons to Russell, Washington, April 27, 1861, PRO FO, 30/22/35: 59–63. On Mercier's first dispatch Thouvenel had written: "A communiquer à Sa Majesté." Mercier was quite in line with international practice in insisting on the ships first being on station, for that was the positive evidence of effectiveness.

27. Ernest Baroche was the son of Jules Baroche, president of the council of state. He had been involved in a recent scandal in Paris and had been sent to America, supposedly on an economic mission, in order to get him conveniently out of the country for a safe period.

28. In criticism of young Baroche's plan Mercier said: "I do not see by what right we could prevent the Americans from acting toward their own ports as we would not think of preventing them from acting toward foreign ports. It even seems to me that if necessary they could claim to have even more right to act in the first instance than in the second and that from the moment they speak of establishing an effective blockade, we have nothing more we can legitimately ask of them. Besides I think it would be neither politic nor dignified for us to appear too hasty in treating them as a declining power (*puissance déchue*)" (Mercier to Thouvenel, Washington, May 6, 1861, AMAE MD, Papiers de Thouvenel, XIII, 362–365).

29. *Ibid.*

30. Lyons to Russell, Washington, May 6, 1861, PRO RP, 30/22/35: 73–79.

31. Published in *Moniteur*, May 3, 1861.

32. E. D. Adams, I, 90–91.

33. Russell to Cowley, London, May 6, 1861, PRO FO, 27/1375/553: Thouvenel to Flahault, Paris, May 11, 1861, AMAE, Fonds Divers, Guerre des Etats-Unis, 1861, Communications Anglaises, no. 71.

34. Sanford to Seward, Paris, May 7, 1861, SDC, Belgium, Despatches, V.

35. Thouvenel to Mercier, Paris, May 11, 1861, AMAE CP, E–U, 124: 194–201, no. 7.

36. Sanford to Seward, Paris, May 12, 1861, SDC, Belgium, Despatches, V, no. 2. In a later letter Sanford repeated Thouvenel's concern over the French ships already in Southern ports. "I told him—remembering a conversation we had before I left Washington—that I presumed such vessels would be allowed to go out" (May 21, 1861, *ibid.*).

37. Dayton to Seward, Paris, May 22, 1861, SDC, France, Despatches, L, no. 5; Dayton to Thouvenel, Paris, May 24, 1861, copy, *ibid.*, Paris Legation Correspondence, Notes Sent (with enclosures). See also originals in AMAE, Fonds Divers, Guerre des Etats-Unis, 1861.

38. Thouvenel to Mercier, Paris, June 7, 1861, AMAE CP, E-U, 124: 299–300; same to La Tour d'Auvergne, Paris, May 29, 1861, *ibid.*, Prusse, 339: 263–264, no. 55; and same in circular to consuls, Paris, June 7, 1861, AMAE MD, Circulaires politiques, 742: 283–284.

39. Thouvenel to Chasseloup-Laubat, Paris, May 30, 1861, AM, BB⁴/1345, I; Chasseloup-Laubat to Rear Admiral Reynaud, Paris, June 15, 1861, AMAE CP, E–U, 124: 324–330, enclosure to Mercier. These official statements seem to repudiate a statement attributed to Morny by Rost, the Confederate agent, who quoted the count as saying that "so long as we [the South] produced cotton for sale, France and England would see that their vessels reached the ports where it was to be had" (Yancey and Mann to Toombs, London, May 21, 1861, CSDP). Either Morny thought, in the middle of May, that the government's attitude would be defiant in its desperation to get cotton or else he was badly misquoted or misunderstood.

40. Fenwick, p. 538.

41. *Ibid.*, p. 539.

42. John R. Spears, *The history of our navy* (4 v. New York, 1897), IV, 28–32.

43. Spears admits (IV, 44) that "for several months after the President's proclamation nine-tenths of the 185 Southern harbors remained open." Soley confirms this when he says: "But for the first three months it was only a beginning; and at some points it cannot be said to have gone as far as that" (James Russell Soley, *The blockade and the cruisers* [New York, 1883], p. 84).

44. Owsley, pp. 281–282.

45. Soley, pp. 42–43.

46. *Ibid.*, p. 44.

47. Owsley, p. 285.

48. Spears, IV, 56.

49. E. Merton Coulter, *The Confederate States of America, 1861–1865* (Baton Rouge, Louisiana, 1950), p. 294.

50. Edward Channing, *A history of the United States*, VI (New York, 1927), 511–512.

51. J. H. Latané, *A history of American foreign policy* (New York, 1927), p. 361; Samuel F. Bemis, *Diplomatic history of the United States* (New York, 1936), pp. 375–376

52. Thouvenel to Rouher, Paris, Aug. 16, 1861, AMAE, Fonds Divers, Guerre des Etats-Unis, 1861.

53. St. André to Thouvenel, Charleston, Aug. 18, 1861, AMAE CPC, E-U, 8:. 260–261.

54. Sept. 4, 1861, *ibid.*, fol. 264; Bunch to Russell, Charleston, Sept. 4, 1861, *Sessional papers*, 1862, LXII, 784.

55. Seward to Dayton, Washington, Sept. 5, 1861, SDC, France, Instructions, XVI, no. 52.

56. Geoffroy to Thouvenel, Washington, Sept. 6, 1861 (rcd. Sept. 22), AMAE CP, E–U, 125: 64, no. 54. See also Montholon to Thouvenel, New York, Sept. 3, 1861, AMAE CPC, E–U, 8: 75–80, no. 9. The British consul at New Orleans seemed to confirm the French admiral's report on the Mississippi passes. "The blockade is rigidly enforced," he said (Mure to Russell, New Orleans, June 18, 1861, *Sessional papers*, 1862, LXII, 717).

57. Montholon to Thouvenel, New York, Sept. 17, 1861, AMAE CPC, E-U, 8: 90–97, no. 3; St. André to Thouvenel, Charleston, Sept. 30, 1861, *ibid.*, fol. 267–268, no. 6; Dayton to Seward, Paris, Sept. 30, 1861, SDC, France, Despatches, L, no. 55; Rost to Thouvenel, Paris, *c.* December 1, 1861, AMAE, Fonds Divers, Guerre des Etats-Unis, 1861; Commander Lyons to Rear-Admiral Milne, Dec. 19, 1861, *Sessional papers*, 1862, LXII, 820–821.

58. Paul to Thouvenel, Richmond, Nov. 2, 1861, AMAE, CPC, E-U. 9: 254–255, no. 40.

59. Lyons to Russell, Washington, Nov. 29, 1861, PRO RP, 30/22, cited in E. D. Adams, I, 254. E. D. Adams says that "this was a very fair description of the blockade situation."

60. See Bigelow's unpublished diary, Sept. 10, 1861, New York Public Library, New York City, Manuscript Room.

61. Webb to Seward, Fontainebleau, Aug. 1, 1861, Seward Papers; also memorandum of Webb to Napoleon III, Fontainebleau, Aug. 2, 1861, AMAE, Fonds Divers, Guerre des Etats-Unis, 1861. The emperor evidently gave the memorandum to Thouvenel and had it filed in the foreign ministry.

62. Thouvenel to Rouher, Paris, Aug. 16, 1861, AMAE, Fonds Divers, Guerre des Etats-Unis, 1861.

63. Yancey *et al.* to Hunter, Paris, Oct. 28, 1861, CSDP, A: 1, no. 9; *ORN*, 2nd series, III, 287–288.

64. While this privilege might exist for most sovereign states, there is some question whether the Union congress could do so. In Article I, Section IX, of the United States Constitution, listing the restrictions on congress, we read that "no preference shall be given by any regulation of commerce or revenue to the ports of one state over those of another...." The United States still insisted that South Carolina was in the Union, and thus Pennsylvania's ports would be given a preference over those of South Carolina, if Charleston was no longer allowed to be a port of entry.

65. Lyons to Russell, Washington, April 15, 1861, PRO RP, 30/22/35: 50–53.

66. Mercier to Thouvenel, Washington, April 26, 1861, AMAE CP, E-U, 124: 164–175, no. 33.

67. Lyons to Russell, Washington, May 23, 1861, AMAE, Fonds Divers, Guerre des Etats-Unis, 1861.

68. Seward to Adams, Washington, May 21, 1861, *FRUS*, (1861), p. 89. On Lincoln's addition see Nicolay and Hay, IV, 270.

69. Seward to Dayton, Washington, June 17, 1861, SDC, France, Instructions, XVI, no. 19.

70. Lyons to Russell, Washington, June 24, 1861, PRO RP, 30/22/35: 131–140. Mercier said in his dispatch: "Lord Lyons pense aussi que le Cabinet de Washington n'a pas entièrement abandonné l'idée ... de fermer par une loi les ports d'entrée ... ce qui serait plus économique qu'un blocus effectif; mais ... M. Seward ne saurait conserver la moindre illusion sur la manière dont cette mesure serait envisagée...." He adds at the end: "Je marche dans le plus parfait accord avec Lord Lyons" (Mercier to Thouvenel, Washington, June 14, 1861, AMAE CP, E-U, 124: 311–317, no. 42).

71. Dallas to Seward, London, May 2, 1861, *FRUS*, (1861), pp. 83–84, no. 333.

72. Adams to Seward, London, May 21, 1861, *FRUS*, (1861), pp. 94–95, no. 2.

73. French summaries of Lyons' reports are found in AMAE, Fonds Divers, Guerre des Etats-Unis, 1861, Communications Anglaises.

74. Adams to Seward, London, June 28, 1861, *FRUS*, (1861), p. 111, no. 10.

75. Thouvenel to Mercier, Paris, July 4, 1861, AMAE CP, E-U, 124: 368–369, no. 18.

76. Russell to Lyons, London, July 6, 1861, PRO FO, 5/756/211; *Sessional papers*, 1862, LXII, 55.

77. Billault (for Thouvenel) to Mercier, Paris, July 18, 1861, AMAE CP, E-U, 124: 451–452, no. 20.

78. Russell to Lyons, London, July 19, 1861, *Sessional papers*, 1862, LXII, 57.

79. Thouvenel to Flahault, Paris, July 16, 1861, AMAE CP, Angl., 720: 79–99, no. 103; Flahault to Thouvenel, London, July 17, 1861, *ibid.*, fol. 106; Thouvenel to Flahault, Paris, July 18, 1861, AMAE, Fonds Divers, Guerre des Etats-Unis, 1861, Communications Anglaises.

80. Only a month earlier the Federal Circuit Court of the District of Columbia handed down a decision in the case of the "Tropic Wind" that President Lincoln's proclamation of the blockade was proper and legal (Decision of Judge James Dunlap, June 13, 1861, *District of Columbia Reports*, II [1895], 375–382; *New York Times*, June 21 and 22, 1861).

81. Mercier to Thouvenel, Washington, July 15, 1861, AMAE CP, E-U, 124: 394–396.

82. Lyons to Russell, Washington, July 19, 1861, PRO RP, 30/22/35: 157–158.

83. On the conversations with Seward see same to same, July 20, 1861, *ibid.*, fol. 161–169; Mercier to Thouvenel, Washington, July 21, 1861, AMAE CP, E-U, 124: 453–459, no. 48; and Lyons to Russell, Washington, July 30, 1861, *Sessional papers*, 1862, LXII, 59–60.

84. Seward to Adams, Washington, July 21, 1861, *FRUS*, (1861), pp. 117–121, no. 42; Seward to Dayton, Washington, July 26, 1861, *ibid.*, pp. 235-236, no. 30.

85. Prince Napoleon, "Journal d'un voyage en Amérique," *Revue des deux mondes*, 1933, V, 266–267, Aug. 10, 1861; Mercier to Thouvenel, New York, Aug. 13, 1861, AMAE MD, Papiers de Thouvenel, XII, 398–401.

86. Russell to Cowley, London, July 26, 1861, PRO FO, 27/1378/761.

87. Thouvenel to Flahault, Paris, July 29, 1861, AMAE CP, Angl., 720: 126–128, no. 108.

88. Cowley to Russell, Paris, July 28, 1861, PRO RP, 30/22.

89. E. D. Adams, I, 247–248.

90. Russell to Law Commissioners of the Admiralty, London, July 27, 1861, copy sent to France, AMAE CP, Angl., 720: 121.

91. Billault (for Thouvenel) to Chasseloup-Laubat, Paris, Aug. 2, 1861, AMAE, Fonds Divers, Guerre des Etats-Unis, 1861, Droits Maritimes.

92. Thouvenel to Flahault, Paris, Aug. 3, 1861, AMAE CP, Angl., 720: 135–136, no. 110.

93. On their exchange and mutual approval see Russell to Cowley, Aug. 7, 1861, PRO FO, 27/1378/804; Thouvenel to Mercier, Paris, Aug. 8, 1861, AMAE CP, E-U, 125: 15–17, no. 22; Chateaurenard to Thouvenel, London, Aug. 15, 1861, *ibid.*, Angl., 720: 149–150, no. 63.

94. Thouvenel to Mercier, Paris, Aug. 8, 1861, AMAE CP, E-U, 125: 15–17, no. 22.

95. Russell to Lyons, London, Aug. 8 and 9, 1861, PRO FO, 5/756/269, 270; *Sessional papers*, 1862, LXII, 69–70.

96. Lyons to Russell, Washington, Aug. 16, 1861, PRO RP, 30/22/35: 195–198.

97. See Lyons to Russell, Washington, Aug. 27 and 30, and Sept. 2, 6 and 13, 1861, *Sessional papers*, 1862, LXII, 76; and PRO RP, 30/22/35: 211–214, 225–227 229–239, and 243–252.

98. Mercier to Thouvenel, Washington, Oct. 8, 1861, AMAE CP, E-U, 125: 119–132, no. 63.

Chapter V

First Year of Strangulation

1. Charleston *Mercury*, June 4, 1861, quoted on Owsley, pp. 25–26.

2. Owsley, p. 28

3. *Ibid.*, pp. 41–44.

4. Fohlen, pp. 284–286.

5. From the July 1861 reports of the procureurs general (Case, *U. S. and Mexico*, pp. 13–17).

6. From the October 1861 reports of the procureurs general (*ibid.* pp. 17–26).

7. From the January 1862 reports of the procureurs general (*ibid.*, pp. 26–45).

8. From the July, October, and January reports of the procureurs general (*ibid.*, pp. 13–45).

9. *Constitutionnel*, Oct. 7, 1861; *Journal des Débats*, Feb. 25, 1862 (cited in West, pp. 57–58).

10. Case, *U. S. and Mexico*, pp. 246, 250.

11. *Ibid.*, pp. 250–255.

12. Sanford to Seward, Paris, April 19, 1861, SDC, Belgium, Despatches, V.

13. Same to same, Paris, April 25, 1861, *ibid.*

14. Same to same, Paris, May 12, 1861, *ibid.*, no. 2.

15. Dayton to Seward, Paris, July 11, 1861, *ibid.*, France, Despatches, L, no. 17.

16. Same to same, Paris, Aug. 19, 1861, *ibid.*, no. 29.

17. A recapitulation of these complaints is found in Thouvenel to Rouher, Paris, Aug. 28, 1861, AMAE, Fonds Divers, Guerre des Etats-Unis, 1861.

18. Lyons to Russell, Washington, Oct. 4, 1861, PRO RP, 30/22/35: 263–278.

19. This person was very probably Lewis Cass, Buchanan's secretary of state, who was host to Prince Napoleon during his visit to Detroit. The prince, speaking of his host, said: "He [Cass] is sad, discouraged about the present war, almost despairs of the future of the Union" ("Journal du Prince Napoléon" [Aug. 20, 1861], *Revue de Paris* [1933], V, 554–555).

20. Mercier to Thouvenel, Niagara Falls, Sept. 9, 1861, AMAE MD, Papiers de Thouvenel, XIII, 385–392. *See also* a summary in Lyons to Russell, Washington, Oct. 4, 1861, PRO RP, 30/22/35: 263–278.

21. Thouvenel to Rouher, Paris, Aug. 28, 1861, AMAE, Fonds Divers, Guerre des Etats-Unis, 1861. Rouher followed his advice and sent a circular to the chambers of commerce (Paris, Sept. 10, 1861, *AD* [1861], III, 122–123).

22. Thouvenel to Flahault, Paris, Sept. 19, 1861, Thouvenel, *Secret*, II, 167–170.

23. Suzanne Desternes and Henriette Chandet, *Napoléon III, homme du XXe siècle* (Paris, 1861), pp. 183–243.

24. See margins of Mercier to Thouvenel, Niagara Falls, Sept. 9, 1861, AMAE MD, Papiers de Thouvenel, XIII, 385–392.

25. Thouvenel to Mercier, Paris, Oct. 3, 1861, AMAE CP, E-U, 125: 108–113, no. 27. The copy handed to Seward was misdated September 29 (SDC, Notes from the French Legation).

26. AMAE CP, Angl., 720: 221–230.

27. Lyons to Russell, Washington, Oct. 4, 1861, PRO RP, 30/22/35: 263–278.

28. *Ibid.*

29. Seward to Mercier, Washington, Oct. 4, 1861, SDC, Notes to the French Legation.

30. Mercier to Thouvenel, Washington, Oct. 14, 1861, AMAE CP, E-U, 125: 145–150, no. 65.

31. Stoeckl to Gorchakov, Washington, Oct. 9/21, 1861, RCA LC, photostats, 49: 884–887.

32. *Ibid.*

33. Mercier to Thouvenel, Washington, Oct. 22, 1861, AMAE CP, E-U, 125: 151–160, no. 66.

34. Lyons to Russell, Washington, Oct. 22, 1861, PRO RP, 30/22/35: 295–299.

35. Same to same, Oct. 25, 1861, *ibid.*, fol. 293.

36. Mercier to Thouvenel, Washington, Oct. 28, 1861, AMAE CP, E-U, 125: 167–180, no. 67.

37. Seward to Dayton, Washington, Oct. 26, 1861, SDC, France, Instructions, XVI.

38. Sanford to Seward, Paris, May 30, 1861, SDC, Belgium, Despatches, V. Dayton had also asked Seward for press help (May 22, 1861, *ibid.*, France, Despatches, L, no. 5).

39. Bigelow, *Retrospections*, I, 364–365.

40. F. Seward, *Seward in Washington*, II, 17–18.

41. Montholon to Thouvenel, New York, Nov. 5, 1861, AMAE CPC, E-U, 8: 125–136, no. 6. Montholon added that he had obtained good private information on this.

42. Seward to Dayton, Washington, Nov. 2, 1861, SDC, France, Despatches, XVI.

43. Seward to Hughes, Washington, *c.* Nov. 4, 1861, F. Seward, *Seward in Washington*, II, 19.

44. *Ibid.*, II, 18.

45. Weed to Seward, New York, Nov. 6, 1861, teleg. 6:00 P.M., Weed Papers, Rochester, microcard 54: 2875.

46. Seward to Weed, Washington, Nov. 7, 1861, teleg. 6:00 P.M., *ibid.*

47. Seward to Dayton, Washington, Nov. 7, 1861, draft, Seward Papers.

48. Seward to Russell, Washington, Nov. 7, 1861, draft, University of Rochester Library, Special Collections, Weed Papers; Seward to Prince Napoleon, Washington, *c.* Nov. 7, 1861, F. Seward, *Seward in Washington*, II, 19; and also *ibid*, p. 18.

49. Yancey and Rost to Hunter, Paris, Oct. 5, 1861, CSDP, file A: 1, no. 8; *ORN*, 2nd ser., III, 278–280, no. 8.

50. On the scarcity of wheat see *ibid.*; as well as Frederik Due to Manderström, Paris, Oct. 5, 1861, Riksarkivet (Sweden), Gallia, no. 119; and also "Malakoff" report in the *New York Times*, Oct. 19, 1861; Bigelow to Seward, Paris, Oct. 10, 1861, SDC, Consular Reports, Paris, XII.

51. Indeed, at this time when Thouvenel and the cabinet were in disagreement over the Civil War, there were rumors that he would be transferred to become ambassador in England (Dayton to Seward, Paris, Oct. 3, 1861, SDC, France, Despatches, L, no. 56).

52. *New York Times*, Nov. 2, 1861.

53. Bigelow to Seward, Paris, Oct. 25, 1861, Seward Papers.

54. London *Times*, Oct. 12, 1861; *New York Times*, Oct. 24 and 26, 1861.

55. Rouher to Thouvenel, Paris, Nov. 15, 1861, AMAE, Fonds Divers, Guerre des Etats-Unis, 1861.

56. Thouvenel to Rouher, Paris, Nov. 21, 1861, *ibid.*

57. *Morning Post*, Oct. 18, 1861; *New York Times*, Nov. 6, 1861.

58. On the French press and the question of intervention in October 1861, see Yancey and Rost to Hunter, Paris, Oct. 5, 1861, CSDP, A: 1, no. 8; Bigelow to Seward, Paris, Oct. 10 and 31, 1861, SDC, Consular Reports, Paris, XII; *New York Times*, Nov. 6, 1861.

59. On the attitude and influence of Prince Napoleon on his return from America, see *New York Times*, Oct. 28 and 30, and Nov. 6, 1861; Dayton to Seward, Paris, Oct. 21, 1861, SDC, France, Despatches, L, no. 68. Dayton to Everett, Paris, Oct. 24, 1861, Seward Papers, and Dayton Papers, Box 1; Bigelow to Seward, Paris, Oct. 31, 1861, SDC, Consular Reports, Paris, XII.

60. Hughes to Seward, Paris, Nov. 28, 1861, Seward Papers, Rochester Microcards, 54: 2876, pp. 60–62.

61. On Monday, April 25, Dayton did invite the archbishop to dinner and introduced him to a company of people (*ibid.*).

62. Dayton to Thouvenel, Paris, Nov. 23, 1861, SDC, Paris Legation, Notes Sent; Dayton Papers, Box 2.

63. Mercier to Thouvenel, Washington, Nov. 4, 1861, AMAE MD, Papiers de Thouvenel, XIII, 414–415; Montholon to Thouvenel, New York, Nov. 5, 1861, AMAE CPC, E–U, 8; 125–136, no. 6.

64. Seward to Dayton, Washington, Oct. 30, 1861, SDC, France, Instructions, XVI, no. 75.

65. Dayton to Seward, Paris, Nov. 25, 1861, SDC, France, Despatches, LI, no. 86.

66. Thouvenel to Mercier, Paris, Nov. 25, 1861, AMAE CP, E–U, 125: 215–218. no. 31.

67. See note no. 63, above.

68. Dayton to Seward, Paris, Nov. 30, 1861, SDC, France, Despatches, LI, no. 87. Five days later he was writing to Weed: "Mr. Thouvenel is not yet ready to see me. I do not believe they will say anything definite here at present—but my impression is they think more of the English alliance and American cotton than of our friendship—but we can't tell. This government is one of temporary expedients—it lives from hand to mouth. Hence its great reticence. It is easy to keep silent when there is nothing to say" (Dayton to Weed, Paris, Dec. 5, 1861, U. of Rochester, Weed Papers).

69. Dayton to Seward, Paris, Dec. 6, 1861, SDC, France, Despatches, LI, no. 91.

70. Seward to Dayton, Washington, Dec. 26, 1861, *ibid.*, France, Instructions, XVI, no. 94.

71. Dayton to Seward, Paris, Jan. 20, 1862, *ibid.*, France, Despatches, LI, no. 104.

72. From the evidence given above there is no doubt that the Civil War was the major cause of France's economic crisis. There was at one time a debate over whether the Anglo-French low-tariff commercial treaty of 1860 may have been the

cause of the cotton manufacturing crisis rather than the Civil War, but Claude Fohlen, in his *Industrie textile*, says that "Lancashire was then undergoing a more serious crisis than any region in France, had a genuine cotton scarcity, and could no longer dream of exporting" (p. 289) and that "the effects of the treaty, until 1865, were therefore favorable to [French] business and consequently to French cotton industries" (p. 292). Fohlen bases his positive conclusions on W. O. Henderson's *The Lancaster cotton famine* (Manchester, 1934) and on the testimony of Féray d'Essonnes and of William H. Waddington in the French *Enquête de 1870*. Féray said that "English competition only began to be felt by 1866, once the crisis had been weathered in England" (I, 630); and Waddington affirmed that "it was hardly earlier than 1866 that we began to notice English competition" (I, 359). Fohlen points out that some raw cotton was always available in France during the war but that the price was so high that French industries could not afford to buy it in large quantities and could not sell or make a profit on the finished product (pp. 253–254). Besides, the really serious factor in the French wartime depression was the reduction in exports to the United States (see above, pp. 128–132, 159–171, and Case, *French opinion on the United States and Mexico* [Part I, *passim*]).

Chapter VI

France and the "Trent" Affair

1. Davis to all concerned, Montgomery, March 16, 1861, *ORN*, ser. 2, III, 95–96,

2. For the ostensible reasons for the Mason and Slidell appointments, see Owsley, *King Cotton*, 77–78; E. D. Adams, II, 203–204; and E. M. Coulter, *The Confederate States of America, 1861–1865* (Baton Rouge, 1950), p. 186.

3. Davis to all concerned, Richmond, August 24, 1861, *ORN*, ser. 2, III, 113–114.

4. E. D. Adams, II, 203.

5. Mercier wrote from Washington: "M. Slidell doit être parti pour Paris, avec la mission d'y plaider la cause du Sud. Vous savez qu'il a été un des promoteurs les plus actifs de la sécession. Il passe pour un homme habile, très énergique, mais sans scrupule et d'un caractère peu estimable" (Mercier to Thouvenel, Washington, Sept. 29, 1861, AMAE MD, Papiers Thouvenel, XIII, 406–409). Mercier was well acquainted with these Southern senators from his association with them in the capital. See also Saint-André to Thouvenel, Charleston, Sept. 30, 1861, AMAE CPC, E-U, 8: 267–68, no. 6.

6. E. D. Adams, I, 206–207.

7. Edward Channing, *A history of the United States*, VI (New York, 1927), 352.

8. Mason to Hunter (Confederate secretary of state), Charleston, Oct. 5, 1861, *ORN*, ser. 2, III, 276–277.

9. E. D. Adams, I, 204.

10. Flahault to Thouvenel, London, Nov. 29, 1861, AMAE MD, Papiers Thouvenel, VII, 220–221. The "Trent's" purser gave this account: "Once arrived there [at Havana] they, of course, were perfectly free and safe from molestation, and therefore made no attempt to conceal their names, position, and intended movements" (*New York Times*, Dec. 13, 1861). Commander Williams' version (a

retired Royal Navy officer in charge of the mail on the "Trent") was: "Two of her [the 'San Jacinto's'] officers, passing themselves off as Southerners in their hearts, had lunched with Mr. Slidell and family, and extracted from them their intended movements" (*New York Times*, Dec. 30, 1861).

11. Bates's account quotes statements by Cameron in the cabinet meeting of Dec. 25: "Cameron said that his Assistant Mr. Scott had rec'd a letter from Mr. Smith [U. S. consul in Dundee] . . . to the effect . . . i.e. that Mr. Smith had rec'd information from respectable sources in London, that Commander Williams, the British mail agent on board the 'Trent' had declared that the whole matter, and the measures of the capture had been arranged at Havanna [*sic*] by Comns. Slidell and Mason themselves, and our Capt. Wilkes. This might seem incredible, if it stood alone, but that something of the sort was variously reported and believed, in well informed circles in England, is a fact, shown by other corroborative facts. For during the session, Senator Sumner was invited in, to read some letters. . . . One of these letters—Bright's I think—states as the news of the day, that at Havanna [*sic*], Slidell and Mason *dined with Capt Wilkes on board his ship* San Jacinto and then and there arranged for the capture, just as it was, in fact, done!" (H. K. Beale, ed., *The diary of Edward Bates, 1859–1866* [Washington, 1933], pp. 213–214).

12. Flahault to Thouvenel, London, Nov. 29, 1861, AMAE MD, Papiers de Thouvenel, VIII, 220–221. Commander Williams' account tells that "Miss Slidell branded one of the officers to his face with his infamy, having been her father's guest not ten days before" (*New York Times*, Dec. 30, 1861).

13. London *Times*, Nov. 28, 1861.

14. Mason to Mrs. Mason, aboard the U.S.S. "San Jacinto," Nov. 15, 1861, *ORN*, 2nd series, III, 296.

15. Weed to Seward, London, Dec. 5, 1861, 11:00 P.M., Seward Papers, University of Rochester Microcards, 54: 2877, p. 85.

16. "Malakoff" in the *New York Times*, Jan. 4, 1862.

17. Hülsemann to Rechberg, Washington, Nov. 29, 1861, HHSA PA, Vereinigte Staaten, XXXIII, 16: 420v, no. 76.

18. Paul to Thouvenel, Richmond, Jan. 22, 1862, AMAE CPC, Richmond, 5: 163, no. 287.

19. Slidell Memorandum, Paris, July 25, 1862, *ORN*, 2nd series, III, 484.

20. On receiving the news from Southampton, Russell sent a telegram to Cowley in Paris, recounting briefly the first report of the "Trent" affair (Foreign Office, Nov. 27, 1861, PRO FO, 27/1381/1299).

21. On the previous day Thouvenel had written to Benedetti: "Ja'i été plus fortement secoué par le fièvre que je ne le pensais d'abord. Quoi qu'il en soit, je suis mieux et puis me remettre un peu plus sérieusement à ma besogne" (Paris, Nov. 26, 1861, Thouvenel Family Papers).

22. On the affair of Bunch's exequatur see Thouvenel to Flahault, Paris, Nov. 28, 1861, AMAE CP, Angl., 720: 349–50, no. 153.

23. The next day Thouvenel wrote to Flahault: "Je suis revenue trop tard de Compiègne, hier, pour pouvoir joindre quelques lignes à mon expédition officielle" (Paris, Nov. 28, 1861, private, Thouvenel Family Papers).

24. Flahault to Thouvenel, London, Nov. 27, 1861, teleg., 6:20 P.M., AMAE CP, Angl., 720: 346.

25. On May 9, 1861, in a conversation with Cowley, Thouvenel had not only agreed on diplomatic co-operation with Great Britain in dealing with problems

arising from the American Civil War, but he had gone so far as to suggest the use of a common language and using prearranged methods of approach (Cowley to Russell, Paris, May 9, 1861, PRO FO, 27/1390/684; *Sessional papers*, 1862, LXII, 539).

26. *Moniteur*, Nov. 29, 1861.

27. Dayton was probably confusing the cabinet (or council of ministers) with another body called the council of state.

28. Dayton to Seward, Paris, Nov. 30, 1861, SDC, France, Despatches, 51 : no. 87.

29. Yancey, Rost, and Mann to Hunter, London, Dec. 2, 1861, CSDP, A; 1, no. 10.

30. Cowley to Russell, Paris, Dec. 2, 1861, private, PRO FO, 519/229: 120–21.

31. Thouvenel to Flahault, Paris, Nov. 28, 1861, private, copy, Thouvenel Family Papers. An extract of this letter was published in Thouvenel, *Secret*, II, 196–97.

32. Flahault to Thouvenel, London, Nov. 30, 1861, AMAE MD, Papier de Thouvenel, VIII, 234–35. See also same to same, London, Nov. 29, 1861, AMAE CP, Angleterre, 720: 353–56, no. 91. The law officers actually declared: ". . . We are of opinion that the conduct of the United States officer [Wilkes] . . . was illegal and unjustifiable by international law. The 'San Jacinto' assumed to act as a belligerent, but the 'Trent' was not captured or carried into a port of the United States for adjudication as prize, and, under the circumstances, cannot be considered as having acted in breach of international law. . . . Her Majesty's Government will, therefore, in our opinion, be justified in requiring reparation for the international wrong which has been on this occasion committed" (Law Officers of the Crown to Earl Russell, Doctors' Commons, Nov. 28, 1861, edited by James P. Baxter, III, in "Papers relating to belligerent and neutral rights," *American historical review*, XXXIV [Oct. 1928], 86–87).

33. Cowley to Russell, Paris, Dec. 3, 1861, PRO FO, 27/1399/1397. The British note of protest, after reviewing the facts of the "Trent" affair, described the seizure of Mason and Slidell as "an act of violence which was an affront to the British flag and a violation of international law" and demanded "the liberation of the four gentlemen [including two secretaries], and their delivery to your Lordship [Lord Lyons], in order that they may again be placed under British protection, and a suitable apology for the aggression which has been committed" (Russell to Lyons, Foreign Office, Nov. 30, 1861, *British and foreign state papers*, LV [1864–65], 605).

34. Dayton to Seward, Paris, Dec. 6, 1861, SDC, France, Despatches, LI, no. 91. In this letter Dayton reported that Thouvenel said "that all the Foreign maritime Powers with which he had conferred agreed that the act was a violation of public law."

35. The false rumors about Scott's supposed admission of Northern orders for the seizure of Mason and Slidell are found in the following: Palmerston to Victoria, London, Nov. 29, 1861; John Bigelow, *Retrospections*, I, 404–405; and in Cowley to Russell, Paris, Dec. 2, 1861, private, PRO FO, 519/229: 120–21.

36. London *Times*, Dec. 2, 1861; *Constitutionnel*, Dec. 3, 1861.

37. Bigelow, *Retrospections*, I, 384–86, 393; Weed to Seward, Paris, Dec. 4, 1861, Seward Papers.

38. Scott to a friend, Paris, Dec. 2, 1861, Bigelow, *Retrospections*, I, 387, 390; *Constitutionnel*, Dec. 4, 1861.

39. *Constitutionnel*, Nov. 29, 30 and Dec. 2, 1861. See also London *Times*, Nov. 29, 1861; and *New York Times*, Dec. 16, 19, 1861.

40. *Patrie*, Nov. 30, 1861. See also London *Times*, Dec. 2, 1861.

41. *Pays*, Nov. 28, 1861; *Presse*, Nov. 30, 1861. See also *New York Times*, Dec. 16, 1861.

42. *Débats*, Nov. 28, 29, Dec. 1, 2, 1861.

43. *Revue des deux mondes*, Dec. 1, 1861, Chronique politique.

44. P. Douhaire in the *Correspondant* (West, p. 52).

45. Weed to Seward, Paris, Nov. 29, 1861, rec. Dec. 19, 1861, Library of Congress, Washington, Division of Manuscripts, Lincoln Papers, microfilm roll, 29: 13165–66.

46. Bigelow, *Retrospections*, I, 384–85.

47. Cowley to Russell, Paris, Dec. 3, 1861, PRO FO 27/1399/1405.

48. It is quite likely that Laurent Basile Hautefeuille was one of his councillors on the "Trent" affair. Hautefeuille was an authority on international law highly respected in England and America as well as in France. What lends some plausibility to this assumption is the fact that, later in December 1861, Hautefeuille published a book on the question, entitled *Questions de droit international maritime; affaires du Trent et du Nashville*. In this study, issued before the publication of Thouvenel's note, he expressed in more detail many ideas similar to those of Thouvenel.

49. One can be sure of these consultations because Thouvenel was in the habit of holding them before any important decision involving international law, and he even hinted at it in his public statements by such phrases as "après mûre réflexion." In dealing with the questions of belligerency and neutrality, he had consulted a committee in the foreign ministry (see above). On another occasion he told Cowley he had been "looking for precedents" (Cowley to Russell, Paris, May 9, 1861, *Sessional papers*, 1862, LXII, 539). Two days later, to Flahault, Thouvenel said "après les avoir mûrement examinées" (Thouvenel to Flahault, Paris, May 11, 1861, AMAE, Fonds Divers, Guerre des Etats-Unis, Box 1861). A week later to the minister of marine he said, "Un examen réfléchi de ces questions m'a amené à penser . . ." (Thouvenel to Chasseloup-Laubat, Paris, May 18, 1861, Archives de la Marine BB^{14} 1345, I). And in the French note itself he used again one of these suggestive expressions "après mûre réflexion" (see below).

50. Cowley: "Monsieur Thouvenel having been in the country for the last few days . . ." (Cowley to Russell, Paris, 3 Dec. 1861, PRO FO, 27/1399/1397).

51. *Ibid.*

52. Cowley to Russell, Paris, Dec. 5, 1861, PRO FO, 27/1399/1409. The fact that the French delayed their note for six days after the dispatch of the British note caused a similar delay in its arrival in Washington, which very nearly had serious consequences (see below).

53. Same to same, Paris, Dec. 5, 1861, private, PRO FO, 519/229: 126.

54. The official note signed by Thouvenel and sent to Mercier was destroyed by fire when the French legation in Washington burned down in 1862, but the following copies were found in archives or printed collections: 1) the draft retained in the French foreign ministry (Thouvenel to Mercier, Paris, Dec. 3, 1861, AMAE CP, E–U, 125: 241–45, no. 32); 2) the copy furnished to Seward at his request (SDC, Notes from the French Legation, under date of Dec. 3, 1861); 3) *Livre jaune*, 1861, pp. 99–101; 4) also in Thouvenel, *Secret*, II, 197–203. On the same day when this note was sent (5 December), the French foreign minister also wrote to Montholon, French consul in New York, stating the same arguments (Paris, Dec. 5, 1861, AMAE CPC, E–U, 8: 178–79, no. 5).

55. Actually Thouvenel—and later Seward—were only trying to put into the mouths of the British the principles which France would have invoked in a similar incident against a French ship. Russell was wary about protesting on the same grounds the French would have relied on. In his protest, sent to Lyons, Russell merely said that international law had been violated without stating precisely what the violation had been. According to the law officers the violation was the failure to take the "Trent" into port for adjudication.

56. Thouvenel to Flahault, Paris, Dec. 4, 1861, *Livre jaune*, 1861, p. 102.

57. Flahault to Thouvenel, London, Dec. 6, 1861, AMAE CP, Angl., 720: 366–67, no. 95. To Cowley, Russell wrote: "I am very much pleased with Thouvenel's dispatch to Mercier" (Foreign Office, Dec. 6, 1861, private, PRO FO, 519/199).

58. Flahault to Thouvenel, London, Dec. 9, 1861, teleg. 3:20 P.M., AMAE CP, Angl., 720: 371. Three days later Thouvenel replied: "Je suis charmé du bon effet que ma dépêche à M. Mercier a produit sur Lord Palmerston et Lord Russell" (Paris, Dec. 12, 1861, Thouvenel, *Secret*, II, 206). Russell also told Brunnow, the Russian ambassador in London, how grateful he and Palmerston were for the French note. It was just the right degree of support, he said, because, if France had gone so far as to offer mediation, England would have had to reject it (Fournier, French chargé, to Thouvenel, St. Petersburg, Jan. 3, 1862, AMAE CP, Russie, 226: 4–9, no. 1).

59. London *Times*, Dec. 24, 1861; *Daily News*, Dec. 24, 1861; *Constitutionnel*, Dec. 25, 1861.

60. Weed to Seward, London, Dec. 25, 1861, F. Seward, *Seward in Washington*, II, 37.

61. David Urquhart to the *Free Press*, Dec. 25, 1861, in the *Free Press*, Jan. 1, 1862.

62. Adams to Seward, London, Jan. 10, 1862, C. F. Adams Letterbook, Microfilm Roll 166: 352, no. 99.

63. Circular of Dec. 10, 1861, AMAE MD, France, Circulaires politiques, 1859–62, 742: 321. See also Thouvenel to Montebello (in St. Petersburg), Paris, Dec. 10, 1861, AMAE CP, Russie, 225: 231, no. 115; and the London *Times*, Dec. 21, 1861. Three days later Cowley reported: "M. Thouvenel has sent a copy of his dispatch to M. Mercier relative to the affair of the Trent to all the principal governments of Europe. It does not appear as yet that any communication has been made to His Excellency by any of the Foreign Representatives here" (Paris, Dec. 13, 1861, PRO FO, 27/1400/1446). On this dispatch Russell noted: "Satisfactory to H. M. G." See also Russell to Cowley, London, Dec. 16, 1861, PRO FO, 27/1382/1395.

64. Rechberg to Hülsemann, Vienna, Dec. 18, 1861, rcd. Jan. 7, 1862, HHSA, PA, Vereinigte Staaten, XXXIII, 16: 480–81.

65. La Tour d'Auvergne to Thouvenel, Berlin, Dec. 24, 1861, AMAE CP, Prusse, 340: 351–52, no. 155. The Prussian note to the United States was read to Russell on January 2, 1862 (Russell to Lyons, London, Jan. 4, 1862, PRO FO, 5/817/6).

66. Ricasoli to D'Azeglio, Turin, Jan. 17–19, 1862, private, *I documenti diplomatici italiani*, edited by la Commissione per la Pubblicazione dei Documenti diplomatici of the Ministero degli Affari esteri, 1st series, II (Rome, 1959), 64, no. 39.

67. Fournier to Thouvenel, St. Petersburg, Dec. 27, 1861, AMAE, CP, Russie, 225: 269–73, no. 95.

68. Same to same, St. Petersburg, Dec. 31, 1861, *ibid.*, fol. 278–82, no. 97.

69. Thouvenel to Fournier, Paris, Jan. 6, 1862, AMAE CP, Russie, 226: 17–18, no. 4.

70. The London *Star* reporter said: "The note of M. Thouvenel . . . completely usurps the place in the papers of ordinary French news. . . . The tone . . . gives very general satisfaction here" (London *Star*, Dec. 25, 1861; *New York Times*, Jan. 11, 1862). "Malakoff" said that the note had "provoked an immense amount of discussion, and all on one side" (*New York Times*, Jan. 11, 1862).

71. Robert Mitchell in the *Pays* of Dec. 27, 1861. See also West, pp. 45–46.

72. J. Mahias in the *Presse*, Jan. 2, 1862. See also West, p. 52.

73. Louis Alloury and F. Camus in the *Débats*, Dec. 24, 1861. See also West, p. 49 and the *New York Times*, Jan. 11, 1862.

74. T. N. Bernard in the *Siècle*, Jan. 3, 1862. See also West, pp. 52–53.

75. Malakoff in the *New York Times*, Jan. 11, 1862.

76. Due to Manderström, Paris, Dec. 28, 1861, Riksarkivet, Stockholm, MSS., Diplomatica Gallia, no. 161.

77. Adams to Seward, London, Dec. 27, 1861, SDC, England, Despatches, 78: no. 95.

78. Fogg to Adams, Bern, Dec. 2, 1861, Adams Papers, roll 566/148/128.

79. C. F. Adams Diary, roll 76, Nov. 29, 1861.

80. Adams to Seward, London, Dec. 6, 1861, SDC, England, Despatches, 78, no. 84; Adams Papers, roll 556, draft copy.

81. Weed to Seward, Paris, Dec. 4, 1861, Seward Papers. Weed, however, was peeved at Seward and added: "But I do not know that you will read what I write or care to hear from me. You did not tell me what to do or say, and . . . I should wonder why I came."

82. Bigelow to Weed, Paris, Dec. 6, 1861, Weed Papers; same to James Bowen, Paris, Dec. 6, 1861, Seward Papers. "He [Napoleon III] will not arbitrate unless the Southern question is included I am quite sure."

83. A. Lomon in the *Pays*, Dec. 6, 1861, A. Vitu in the *Constitutionnel*, Dec. 15, 1861; and T. N. Bernard in the *Siècle*, Jan. 3, 1862. See also West, pp. 43–44, 52–53.

84. Talleyrand sized him up well when he said: ". . . sa mission s'étend bien au delà des frontières belges. Il réside peu à Bruxelles, se trouvant sans cesse appelé à Londres, à Paris, en Allemagne, et même à *Caprera*" [home of Garibaldi] (Talleyrand to Thouvenel, Brussels, Dec. 2, 1861, private, AMAE MD, Papiers Thouvenel, XVIII, 461–62).

85. Talleyrand, reading these arguments in the *Constitutionnel* of December 1, 1861 believed that Sanford did, indeed, influence the French press (*ibid*).

86. *Ibid.* See also Sanford to Seward, Brussels, Dec. 2, 1861, private, SDC, Belgium, Despatches, V.

87. Sanford claimed that the cabinet met on the afternoon of December 4, but the *Moniteur* reported the meeting to have been on the 5th (Sanford to Seward, Brussels, Dec. 5, 1861, private. SDC, Belgium, Despatches, V; *Moniteur*, Dec. 6, 1861).

88. Adelswärd to Manderström, Paris, Dec. 7, 1861, Riksarkivet, Diplomatica Gallia, no. 155.

89. Adelswärd had also said that "in his conversations M. Thouvenel says that the United States is in the wrong, but he feels authorized to say that the English government has not the slightest desire to precipitate a war" (*ibid.*).

90. As late as December 13, Sanford was writing that "Baron Talleyrand, who was in to see me today, said he had received nothing of note from his government" (Sanford to Seward, Brussels, Dec. 13, 1861, private, *ibid.*).

91. Hughes to Seward, Paris, Dec. 27, 1861, Seward Papers. Bigelow told Weed, "He wrote to the Emperor to solicit it" (Paris, Dec. 24, 1861, Weed Papers).

92. Hughes to Seward, Paris, Dec. 5, 1861, Seward Papers.

93. For Hughes's audience with Napoleon III *see* Hughes to Seward, Paris, Dec. 27, 1861, Seward Papers; and Hughes to Weed, Paris, Dec. 24, 1861, Weed Papers, microcards 54/2879/163.

94. Bright wrote to Sumner: "I think your government may fairly say that it is a question for impartial arbitration" (J. F. Rhodes, *History of the United States* [1850–1897] [8v. New York, 1920] III, 424–25, n. 2). Cowley said cautiously, "I suppose that in the case of national honour and international law, it would be impossible to offer, under the protocol of Paris, a reference to a third power" (Cowley to Russell, Paris, Dec. 9, 1861, PRO FO, Cowley Papers, 519/229: 129–30). For the Quaker petition see Adams Papers, roll 556/148/178A.

95. Russell told Brunnow that "should things go to the point where France thought, as a last resort, that she must offer her mediation, England would not be able to accept it" (Fournier to Thouvenel, St. Petersburg, Jan. 3, 1862, AMAE CP, Russie, 226: 4–9, no. 1).

96. London *Times*, Dec. 24, 1861, editorial.

97. Mercier to Thouvenel, Washington, Nov. 17, 1861, AMAE CP, E-U, 125: 204–212, no. 69.

98. William Howard Russell, *My diary North and South* (Boston, 1863), pp. 573–575.

99. Mercier to Thouvenel, Washington, Nov. 19, 1861, AMAE CP, E-U, 125: 204–212, no. 69.

100. *Ibid.*

101. Lyons to Russell, Washington, Nov. 19, 1861, Lord Newton, *Lord Lyons, a record of British diplomacy* (2 v. London, 1913), I, 55; Stoeckl to Gorchakov, Washington, Nov. 6/18, 1861, RCA LC, 49: 995, no. 68. After Stoeckl's remark about Seward's supposed order behind Lincoln's back Gorchakov wrote in the margin: "Charmant!"

102. Mercier to Thouvenel, Washington, Dec. 19, 1861, AMAE CP, E-U, 125: 291, no. 75.

103. Same to same, Washington, Nov. 25, 1861, *ibid.*, fol. 219–221, no. 70.

104. Seward to Adams, Washington, *c.* Nov. 27, 1861, private, F. Seward, *Seward in Washington*, II, 21.

105. Mercier to Thouvenel, Washington, Nov. 25, 1861, AMAE CP, E-U, 125: 219–221, no. 70.

106. Newton, I, 60.

107. Russell, *Diary*, pp. 587–588; Monaghan, pp. 186–187.

108. Mercier to Thouvenel, Washington, Dec. 18, 1861, private, AMAE MD, Papiers de Thouvenel, XIII, 416–418.

109. Same to same, Washington, Dec. 19, 1861, AMAE CP, E-U, 125: 288–295, no. 75.

110. Lyons wrote Russell, "I have kept M. Mercier *au courant* of all my communications, confidential as well as official with Mr. Seward, but I have given no information as to either to anyone else" (Dec. 23, 1861, Newton, I, 70).

111. Lyons to Russell, private, Washington, Dec. 19, 1861, *ibid.*, p. 66; same to

same, official, Washington, Dec. 19, 1861, *Sessional papers*, 1862, LXII, 628–629; Mercier to Thouvenel, Washington, Dec. 23, 1861, AMAE CP, E-U, 125; 308–317, no. 76. This "private and confidential" copy is found in the Lincoln Papers, Library of Congress, microfilms, reel 29: 13177–13183.

112. Russell to Lyons, Pembroke Lodge, Dec. 1, 1861, Newton, I, 63.

113. *Ibid.*, p. 66.

114. Mercier to Thouvenel, Washington, Dec. 23, 1861, AMAE CP, E-U, 125: 308–317, no. 76.

115. They were right in their surmise because Frederick Seward, the assistant secretary of state, said that Seward spent the day of the 21st writing his proposed note to England (F. Seward, *Seward in Washington*, II, 24–25).

116. "J'ai vu, par une conversation que j'ai eu avec lui [Seward], qu'il désirait aussi attendre la malle d'Europe, qui devrait être déjà arrivée, et qui lui apprendra comment le Gouvernement de l'Empereur est disposé à se prononcer dans la circonstance" (Mercier to Thouvenel, Washington, Dec. 23, 1861, AMAE CP, E–U, 125: 308–17, no. 76). See also Lyons to Russell, Washington, Dec. 23, 1861, private, Newton, I, 67–68.

117. Lyons to Russell, *ibid.*

118. Schleiden to Bremen senate, Washington, Dec. 23, 1861, E. D. Adams, I, 231, n. 2, quoting from Schleiden Papers, Library of Congress.

119. J. G. Nicolay and John Hay, *Abraham Lincoln: a history* (10 v. New York, 1890), V, 34–35.

120. Seward to Weed, Washington, Dec. 30, 1861, Seward Papers.

121. Lyons to Russell, private, Washington, Dec. 23, 1861, Newton, I, 67–68.

122. C. F. Adams to Seward, London, Dec. 6, 1861, Frederic Bancroft, *The Life of William H. Seward* (2 v. New York, 1900), II, 230.

123. Weed to Seward, Paris, Dec. 2, 1861, Seward Papers.

124. Bigelow to Seward, Paris, Dec. 5, 1861, Seward Papers, rcd. Dec. 25, 1861.

125. Dayton to Seward, Paris, Dec. 6, 1861, SDC, Despatches, France, 51 : no. 91. rcd. Dec. 25, 1861.

126. The delay of the French note was mainly due to the fact that it had been sent from Paris six days after the dispatch of the British note.

127. Mercier to Thouvenel, Washington, Dec. 27, 1861, AMAE CP, E-U, 125: 322–328, no. 77; Lyons to Russell, Washington, Dec. 27, 1861, *Sessional papers*, LXII, 1862, 630. Lyons and Bates, the U. S. attorney general, both say Thouvenel's note arrived on the 25th; Mercier in a dispatch of the 27th said the note arrived "hier," that is the 26th. It is likely, however, that Mercier started writing his report on the 26th and that "hier" referred to the 25th. Then, when he finished his report on the 27th, his copyist dated it the 27th.

128. Howard K. Beale, ed., *The diary of Edward Bates, 1859–1866* in *Annual Report* of the American Historical Association, 1930, IV, (Washington, 1933), 213–217.

129. F. Seward, *Seward in Washington*, II, 25.

130. Mercier to Thouvenel, Washington, Dec. 27, 1861, AMAE CP, E-U, 125: 323–324, no. 27.

131. The "San Jacinto" arrived at Fortress Monroe on Nov. 15, 1861 at 12:30 P.M. (*New York Times*, Nov. 17, 1861), and the news was no doubt telegraphed to the government in Washington. On the 15th Seward told Mercier the first news of Mason's and Slidell's capture without any other details (Mercier to Thouvenel, Washington, Nov. 17, 1861, AMAE CP, E-U, 125: 205, no. 69).

132. Thomas L. Harris, *The "Trent" affair* (New York, 1896), p. 125; Benson J. Lossing, *A pictorial history of the Civil War in the United States of America* (3 v. Philadelphia, 1866–1868), II, 156–157; Nicolay and Hay, V, 25–26. Stoeckl, the Russian minister, also heard that Lincoln was ready to surrender the Southern commissioners but that the cabinet and public opinion might change his mind (Stoeckl to Gorchakov, Washington, Nov. 6/18, 1861, RCA LC, photostats, 49: 995, no. 68).

133. J. D. Richardson, ed., *A compilation of the messages and papers of the presidents, 1789–1897* (10 v. Washington, 1896–99), VI, 45. He merely mentioned a policy of "prudence . . . toward foreign powers, averting causes of irritation."

134. *New York Times*, Dec. 9, 1861.

135. Law officers to Russell, London, Nov. 12, 1861, in James P. Baxter, III, "Papers relating to belligerent and neutral rights," *American historical review*, XXXIV (1928), 84–86.

136. Theodore C. Pease and James G. Randall, eds., *The diary of Orville Hickman Browning* ("Collections of the Illinois State Historical Library," vols. XX and XXII) (22 v. Springfield, Illinois, 1925–33), I, 513–14.

137. *Ibid.*, p. 515.

138. Russell, *Diary*, p. 587.

139. *Ibid.*, p. 588. *The New York Times* (Dec. 16, 1861) said that the news of the impending British demands was causing excitement and universal defiance in Washington.

140. *New York Times*, Dec. 18 and 19, 1861.

141. Library of Congress, Washington, Division of Manuscripts, microfilms of the Lincoln Papers, Russell to Lyons, London, F. O. Nov. 30, 1861, copy, envelope marked "Private and Confidential," reel 29: 13177–83.

142. *New York Times*, Dec. 16 and 19, 1861. These reports were not true, but of course Lincoln did not know it at the time.

143. See above under arbitration proposals.

144. Bright to Sumner, Dec. 5, 1861, in Rhodes, III, 424–425, n. 2. Rhodes feels that Bright not only inspired Lincoln's arbitration idea but also the very phraseology of his draft.

145. Memorandum of a draft dispatch unsigned, but in Lincoln's handwriting, Lincoln Papers, reel 30: 13623–13626. See also an early printing of it in Nicolay and Hay, V, 33–34.

146. *Diary of Browning*, I, 516–517.

147. F. Seward, *Seward in Washington*, II, 25–26.

148. See again Dayton to Seward, Paris, Dec. 6, 1861 (rcd. Dec. 25, 1861), SDC, France, Despatches, LI, no. 91; and Thouvenel to Mercier, Paris, Dec. 3, 1861, AMAE CP, E–U, 125: 241–245, no. 32.

149. *Diary of Browning*, I, 518.

150. Thouvenel held two law degrees from the Paris Ecole des Droits.

151. The notes of Austria and Prussia had not yet arrived, but Thouvenel had been positive about the attitudes of all the powers.

152. London *Times*, Dec. 24, 1861. This was the editorial on the Thouvenel note, which has already been referred to.

153. F. Seward, *Seward in Washington*, II, 26.

154. *New York Times*, Dec. 28, 1861.

155. *Diary of Browning*, I, 519.

156. Seward to Mercier, Washington, Dec. 27, 1861, annex to no. 1 to Mercier to Thouvenel, Dec. 27, 1861, AMAE CP, E–U, 125: 322–328, no. 77; SDC, Notes to the French Legation, Dec. 27, 1861. Seward also noted the differences in views on international law among the three powers and expressed the hope that this affair would lead to an agreement on neutral rights.

157. Mercier to Thouvenel, Washington, Dec. 27, 1861, AMAE CP, E–U, 125: 324, no. 77.

158. *Ibid.*

159. Mercier's reference to the financial situation represented another aspect of the softening Federal position. The Washington government was warned by George M. Barnard of Boston, George D. Morgan of New York, and Jay Cook of Philadelphia that financial support by Northern bankers probably would not be given in the case of a double war. Both Lyons and Mercier thought that these pressures also had a sobering effect on the cabinet, although there is no record of a mention of finance in the two days of cabinet discussions. See M. F. Clausen, "Peace factors in Anglo-American relations, 1861–1863," *Mississippi Valley historical review*, XXVI (1940), 512–516.

160. Mercier to Thouvenel, Washington, Dec. 31, 1861, AMAE CP, E–U, 125: fol. 339–40, no. 78.

161. Lyons to Russell, Washington, Feb. 3, 1862, private, Russell Papers, PRO FO, 30/22/36: 29–31.

162. *New York Times*, Dec. 29, 1861.

163. *Ibid.*

164. Mercier to Thouvenel, Washington, Dec. 31, 1861, AMAE CP, E–U, 125: 343, no. 78.

165. *National Intelligencer*, Dec. 28, 1861.

166. *New York Times*, Dec. 29, 1861.

167 *Congressional globe*, XXXII, 181, house debates, Dec. 30, 1861.

168. *Ibid.*, p. 230, house debates, Jan. 8, 1862.

169. *Ibid.*

170. *Ibid.*, p. 494, house debates, Jan. 27, 1862.

171. J. G. Randall, *Lincoln the president* (2 v. New York, 1945), II, 49–50.

172. *Congressional globe*, XXXII, 241–245, senate debates, Jan. 9, 1862. Mercier, in discussing Sumner's speech, said that "il n'a pas manqué de donner à la Dépêche de Votre Excellence la place qui lui revenait, en la louant au double point de vue du procédé envers le Cabinet de Washington, et des doctrines qu'elle soutient" (Mercier to Thouvenel, Washington, Jan. 14, 1862, AMAE CP, E–U, 126: 15–20, no. 80).

173. *Ibid.*

174. Randall, *Lincoln the president*, II, 50 and notes 24 and 25.

175. Mercier to Thouvenel, Washington, Dec. 30, 1861, private, AMAE MD, Papiers de Thouvenel, XIII, 420–421; same to same, Jan. 3, 1862, *ibid.*, fol. 427–428.

176. Same to same, Washington, Jan. 6, 1862, AMAE CP, E–U, 126: 10, no. 79.

177. Report of "Malakoff" on Jan. 9, 1862, in the *New York Times*, Jan. 30, 1862. Evidence of the spread of the rumor is found in the *Opinion Nationale*, *Patrie*, and the *Pays* of Jan. 7, 1862. On Jan. 10 the *Constitutionnel* said the news of the 7th had now been confirmed.

178. In a letter to Gramont of Jan. 7, Thouvenel was still saying that "je crains que la paix ne soit jouée à pile ou face" (Thouvenel, *Secret*, II, 218). Even on the

8th he wrote to Flahault that "le métier de prophète n'est pas bon à l'époque où nous vivons, et je préfère . . . attendre l'arrivée du prochain courrier d'Amérique" (*ibid.*, p. 220).

179 The identity of the American lady is not known, but the London *Star* correspondent related the incident in his news dispatch of January 10 (*New York Times*, Jan. 31, 1862). The lady also reported that the empress' words "were uttered in a voice that bespoke emotion and the deepest sympathy" (*ibid.*).

180. Private letter of Jan. 11, 1862, Wellesley and Sencourt, p. 192. To these spiteful remarks of the emperor, Cowley replied the next day: "Je partage en quelque sorte les regrets que V. M. me fait l'honneur de m'exprimer, parce que j'ai toujours eu la conviction que nous n'échapperons pas à la guerre avec les Etats-Unis, et je la crois encore. Mais enfin, il faut accepter la paix aussi longtemps qu'on veut bien nous laisser tranquilles. C'est le premier devoir d'un Gouvernement: V. M. qui a vu la guerre de si près, sait, mieux que personne, en redoubter les malheurs" (Chantilly, Jan. 12, 1862, PRO FO, 519/229: 154).

181. Thouvenel to Rouher, private, Paris, Jan. 9, 1862, Archives Nationales, Paris, MSS, Papiers de Rouher, 45 AP 3.

182. Thouvenel to Mercier, Paris, Jan. 9, 1862, AMAE CP, E-U, 126: 14–15, no. 1.

183. Cowley to Russell, Paris, Jan. 10, 1862, PRO FO, 27/1431/25.

184. Thouvenel to Mercier, Paris, Jan. 15, 1862, AMAE CP, E-U, 126: 45, no. 2. An English translation is found in SDC, Notes from the French Legation, XVIII (carrying an erroneous date of January 19).

185. Dayton to Seward, Paris, Jan. 14, 1862, private, SDC, France, Despatches, LI, near no. 102.

186. Hughes to Seward, Paris, Jan. 11, 1862, and Weed to Seward, Paris, Jan. 16, 1862, in Seward Papers.

187. "Malakoff" in the *New York Times*, Jan. 9 and 14, 1862.

188. *Siècle*, Jan. 10, 1862; *Journal des Débats*, Jan. 11 and 15, 1862. See also West, pp. 54–55.

189. *Revue des deux mondes*, Jan. 15, 1862, Chronique politique. See also West, pp. 54–55.

190. *New York Times*, Jan. 31, 1862, quoting the *Presse*, of Jan. 12, 1862.

191. As translated in the London *Times*, Jan. 14, 1862, from *Constitutionnel*, Jan. 12, 1862.

192. *Patrie*, Jan. 11, 1862. See also London *Times*, Jan. 13, 1862, and the *New York Times*, Jan. 31, 1862.

193. *New York Times*, Jan. 31 and Feb. 1, 1862.

194. Lyons to Russell, Washington, Dec. 27, 1861, *Sessional papers*, LXII (1862), 630.

195. Flahault to Thouvenel, London, Jan. 9, 1862, AMAE MD, Papiers Thouvenel, VIII, 266–67.

196. Russell to Cowley, London, Jan. 15, 1862, PRO FO, 27/1419/49, seen by Palmerston and the queen. See also his private letter to Cowley, London, Jan. 11, 1862, *ibid.*, 159/119.

197. Flahault to Thouvenel, London, Jan. 11, 1862, AMAE CP, Angl., 721: 6–7, no. 1; *Livre jaune*, 1861, p. 105.

198. Great Britain had strongly opposed the French annexation of Savoy in 1860.

199. Napoleon III to Cowley, Paris, Jan. 11, 1861 [1862], V. Wellesley and R.

Sencourt, *Conversations with Napoleon III* (London, 1934), p. 192. France had sided with Great Britain in the Crimean War.

200. Cowley to Napoleon III, Chantilly, Jan. 12, 1862, PRO FO, 519/229: 154. The British government expressed a restrained satisfaction over the attitudes of all the great powers in a note of Russell to Napier (London, Jan. 10, 1862, *Sessional papers*, LXII, [1862], 639).

201. London *Observer*, Jan. 12, 1862.

202. London *Times*, Jan. 9, 1862. On January 15 the *Times* in a leading editorial praised France for having taken the lead with the other great powers in tendering friendly advice to a power which was wrong in an international dispute. This, the *Times* thought, was in accord with the protocols of the Congress of Paris of 1856 and showed the world that France was not going to try to take advantage of a dispute for her own interest. Such an impartial act would create more confidence in France in future disputes.

203. Bertinatti to Ricasoli, Washington, Dec. 30, 1861, *DDI*, 1st ser., II, 70, no. 2.

204. *New York Times*, Jan. 30, 1862.

205. *La Presse*, Jan. 12, 1862 as quoted in the London *Times*, Jan. 14, 1862 and the *New York Times*, Jan. 31, 1862.

206. Report of Dubeux, Bordeaux, Jan. 17, 1862, in Case, *U. S. and Mexico*, p. 249. no. 302.

207. Thouvenel to Benedetti, Paris, Jan. 11, 1862, Thouvenel Family Papers.

208. Thouvenel to Flahault, Paris, Jan. 17, 1862, Thouvenel, *Secret*, II, 225–27.

209. *Moniteur*, Feb. 23, 1862.

210. Mercier to Thouvenel, private, Washington, Dec. 30, 1861, AMAE MD, Papiers Thouvenel, XIII, 420–21.

211. Same to same, Washington, Dec. 31, 1861, AMAE CP, E-U, 125: 339, no. 78.

212. Bigelow to Seward, Paris, Dec. 3, 1861 (rcd. Dec. 24), SDC, Consular Reports, Paris, XII.

213. *Constitutionnel*, Dec. 2, 1861.

214. Scott to a friend, Paris, Dec. 2, 1861, Bigelow, *Retrospections*, I, 387–90.

215. *Ibid.*, pp. 384–86, 393.

216. *Moniteur*, Dec. 6, 1861. Bigelow exulted over this in writing to James Bowen. "This is a great deal in that quarter [he exclaimed] and shows that if Mr. Seward chooses to press that view, he will be sure of aid in this quarter" (Paris, Dec. 6, 1861, copy in Seward Papers). Bigelow hastened to send a copy of the *Moniteur* to Seward and added: "It will be easy, I am persuaded, to put England on the defensive before Europe by offering to make the revision of the international code a condition of a peaceful settlement of the question provided we recognized such a result as much nearer our heart than the trifling gratification of national *amour-propre* by holding on to the captive emissaries" (Paris, Dec. 6, 1861 [rcd. Dec. 25], Seward Papers).

217. Bigelow told William Hargreaves that "the press here in Paris is quite disposed to have the rights of neutrals put upon a proper footing before the *Trent* affair is settled . . ." (Paris, Dec. 9, 1861, Bigelow, *Retrospections*, I, 413). C. F. Adams told Seward that "unquestionably the views of all other countries is that the opportunity is most fortunate for obtaining new and large modifications of International Law which will hereafter materially restrain the proverbial tendency of this country [England] on the ocean" (London, Dec. 27, 1861, SDC, England, Despatches, 78: no. 95).

218. Bigelow to Weed, Paris, *c.* Dec. 10, 1861, Weed Papers.

219. Metternich to Rechberg, Paris, Dec. 26, 1861, HHSA, PA, IX, Frankreich, 70: 606–7, no. 73.

220. Seward to Lyons, Washington, Dec. 26, 1861, *Sen. Ex. Docs.*, 37th Congress, 2nd Session, IV, Ex. Doc. no. 8, p. 12.

221. Seward to Mercier, Washington, Dec. 27, 1861, copy, AMAE CP, E-U, 125: 322–328, enclosure with no. 77. See also copy in SDC, Notes to the French Legation.

222. *Siècle*, Jan. 3, 1862; *Opinion Nationale*, Jan. 7, 1862.

223. *Journal de St. Pétersbourg*, Jan. 11, 1862.

224. *Moniteur, Presse, Journal du Havre, Journal des Débats*, all of Jan. 12, 1862.

225. "Malakoff" said: "Some papers praise the United States. Others say there should now be an international agreement on the point of law by the maritime powers" (*New York Times*, Jan. 30, 1862).

226. Dayton to Seward, Paris, Jan. 27, 1862, SDC, France, Despatches, LI, no. 109.

227. Russell to Lyons, London, Jan. 23, 1862, *FRUS*, (1862), pp. 249–250.

228. Russell to Cowley, London, Jan. 25, 1862, PRO FO, 27/1419/97.

229. Report in the *Moniteur*, Feb. 9, 1862. A month later Russell rejected the idea of a conference in his correspondence with the United States: "Her Majesty's Government have no present intention of inviting discussion upon amendments to be introduced into a recognized Law of Nations, as laid down in Treaties, Conventions, Judicial decisions, and works of eminent Jurists." There is no evidence that a copy of this was sent to France (Russell to Lyons, London, March 12, 1862, [seen by Palmerston and the queen], PRO FO, 5/818/108).

230. See the works of F. W. Seward, Nicolay and Hay, Bancroft, Rhodes, McMaster, Blumenthal, and Monaghan.

231. For other works not specifically mentioning the French note, see those of B. K. Hendrick, T. A. Bailey, S. F. Bemis, C. F. Adams, Jr., H. E. Allen, A. P. Newton in the *Cambridge history of British foreign policy*, and J. W. Pratt.

232. For the two French works which suggest in a brief way the influence of the French note on the "Trent" affair, see P. Renouvin, *Histoire des relations internationales* (7 v. Paris, 1954–1957), V, 342; and R. Korolewicz-Carlton, *Napoleon III, Thouvenel, et la Guerre de Sécession* (thèse de doctorat d'université, University of Paris 1951), pp. 61–74.

Chapter VII

Pendulum of Intervention Threats

1. Mercier to Thouvenel, Washington, Oct. 28, 1861, AMAE CP, E-U, 125: 167–180, no. 67.

2. Seward to Dayton, Washington, Jan. 2, 1862, SDC, France, Instructions, XVI, no. 97.

3. The discovery of subterranean petroleum by E. L. Drake at Titusville, Pa., in 1859 was fast substituting kerosene for whale-oil in domestic lighting resulting in an oversupply of obsolescent whalers.

4. Mercier to Thouvenel, Washington, Nov. 25, 1861, AMAE CP, E-U, 125: 223; Lyons to Russell, Washington, Nov. 29, 1861, *Sessional papers*, LXII, 1862, 112, no. 126.

5. Russell to Lyons, London, Dec. 20, 1861, PRO FO, 5/758/487; also in *Sessional papers*, LXII, 1862, 114, no. 127.

6. For French press and general opinion on the Stone Fleet see *New York Times*, Jan. 31, Feb. 1 and 6, 1862; London *Times*, Jan. 14, 1862; *Constitutionnel*, Jan. 12, 1862; *Moniteur*, Jan. 22, 1862. In a letter to Seward of February 4, George Bancroft reported: "A letter I have from Paris of January 10 is full of sorrow for the destruction of Charleston and Savannah harbors. Says it produced a violent sensation" (Seward Papers, Feb. 4, 1862).

7. *New York Times*, Feb. 1, 1862.

8. This referred to the impending speech of Napoleon III to the two houses of the legislature in which he was expected to hint at recognition or a breaking of the blockade. Dayton reported that "an impression for some days before [January 24] was almost universal among a certain class, both in England and here, that the Emperor would indicate a policy hostile to us in his speech today, opening the legislative chambers" (Dayton to Seward, Paris, Jan. 27, 1862, SDC, France, Despatches, LI, no. 109).

9. Weed to Seward, Paris, Jan. 20, 1862, Seward Papers.

10. Weed to Seward, Paris, Jan. 24, 1862, F. Seward, *Seward in Washington*, II, 56–57.

11. Dayton to Seward, Paris, Jan. 27, 1862, SDC, France, Despatches, LI, no. 109.

12. Thouvenel to Mercier, Paris, Jan. 23, 1862, AMAE CP, E-U, 126: 61–62, no. 4; and an English translation in SDC, Notes from the French Legation, under Jan. 23, 1862.

13. On Evans' conversation see Weed's later postscript in Weed to Seward, Paris, Jan. 20, [22], 1862 in Seward Papers; and the account of the London *Morning Star* (January 23, 1862) as reproduced in the *New York Times*, Feb. 12, 1862.

14. Seward to Dayton, Washington, Jan. 2, 1862, SDC, France, Instructions, XVI, no. 97.

15. Weed to Seward, Paris, Jan. 23, 1862, F. Seward, *Seward in Washington*, II, 55–56.

16. *Ibid.*

17. On the Bigelow public letter see *ibid.* and Weed to Seward of Jan. 24, 1862, *ibid.*, pp. 56–57. For the text see SDC, Consular Reports, Paris, XII, under Jan. 24, 1862. Four days later, after the emperor's speech, Bigelow decided against publication (Bigelow to Seward, Paris, Jan. 28, 1862, *ibid.*; and Bigelow to Weed, Paris, Jan. 29, 1862, Weed Papers).

18. For Dayton's long interview with Thouvenel see Dayton to Seward, Paris, Jan. 27, 1862, SDC, France, Despatches, LI, no. 109; and Weed to Seward, Paris, Jan. 24, 1862, F. Seward, *Seward in Washington*, II, 56–57.

19. Weed in F. Seward, *ibid.*

20. On the cabinet meeting see *ibid.*, pp. 55–57; and Dayton's dispatch no. 109 to Seward. In this report Dayton said: "I knew there was going to be a cabinet council, the emperor presiding, on Saturday at which I thought would be settled the character of the address . . . and I felt it important . . . to go as far as I rightly could upon the points hereinbefore stated" (Dayton to Seward, Paris, Jan. 27, 1862, SDC, France, Despatches, LI, no. 109).

21. *Moniteur*, Jan. 28, 1862.

22. For the first reactions to the speech see *New York Times*, Feb. 16, 1862; Bigelow to Seward, Paris, Jan. 28, 1862, SDC, Consular Reports, Paris, XII; and same to Weed, Paris, Jan. 28, 1862, Weed Papers.

23. *Exposé de la situation de l'Empire* in *Moniteur*, Jan. 30, 1862.

24. Dayton to Weed, Paris, Jan. 30, 1862, Weed Papers.

25. On Slidell's arrival and Rost's interview see Slidell to R. M. T. Hunter (Confederate secretary of state), Feb. 11, 1862, *ORN*, 2nd series, III, 336–338.

26. Slidell to Thouvenel, Paris, Feb. 3, 1862; and Berthémy to Slidell, Paris, Feb. 3, 1862, in *ibid.*, pp. 341–342.

27. Slidell's memorandum of his first interview with Thouvenel, *ibid.*, pp. 339–341.

28. Thouvenel to Flahault, Paris, Feb. 10, 1862, Thouvenel, *Secret*, II, 236–237.

29. Slidell's memorandum, *ORN*, 2nd series, III, 341; and Slidell to Hunter, Paris, Feb. 26, 1862, CSDC, D: 12, no. 2.

30. Willson, *Slidell*, pp. 72–76.

31. Russell to Lyons, London, Feb. 15, 1862, PRO FO, 5/817/71. A copy of this was also sent to France.

32. Palmerston to Victoria, London, March 7, 1862, *Victoria letters*, 2nd series, I, 22–23.

33. From report in *Moniteur*, March 13, 1862.

34. *Ibid.*, Feb. 17, 1862.

35. *Ibid.*, Feb. 25, 1862.

36. Paris, Feb. 27, 1862, AMAE CP, E–U, 126: 188–191, no. 6.

37. Paris, Feb. 27, 1862, SDC, France, Despatches, LI, no. 120.

38. Mason to Hunter, London, Feb. 28, 1862, *ORN*, 2nd series, III, 355–356.

39. Slidell to Mason, Paris, March 28, 1862, L. B. Sears, "The Confederate diplomats," *American historical review*, XXVI (1920), 257 (citing the Mason Papers).

40. For some time before the battle the "Monitor" had been called the "Erickson" after its designer. The "Merrimac" also had been rechristened the "Virginia."

41. For Captain Gautier's reports, maps, and designs see Gautier to Mercier, Hampton Roads, March 9, 1862, AMAE CP, E–U, 126: 213–214; same to same, March 11, 1862, *ibid.*, fol. 248–249; Gautier to the minister of marine, Hampton Roads, March 16, 1862, *ibid.*, fol. 280–291. This last report was considered very significant because it was not only detailed and professional but also because it was the only account by a foreign eyewitness. A copy was given to the Union authorities and partly published in English translation (*ORN*, 1st series, VII, 64–73) and another was given to the Russians through Stoeckl in Washington (Stoeckl to Gorchakov, Washington, March 28, 1862, no. 587, Golder, *Materials*, II, 28).

42. Mercier to Thouvenel, Washington, March 11, 1862 (rcd. March 30), AMAE CP, E–U, 126: 215–229.

43. *Moniteur*, March 26, 1862.

44. Bigelow to Seward, Paris, March 27, 1862, Seward Papers.

45. "Malakoff's" report of March 31, 1862 in *New York Times*, April 18, 1862.

46. Bigelow to Seward, Paris, April 4, 1862, SDC, Consular Reports, Paris, XII.

47. *Ibid.*

48. *New York Times*, April 24, May 6, 1862.

49. *Moniteur*, March 30, April 7, 1862.

50. *Ibid.*, April 17, 1862.

51. *Ibid.*, April 7, 1862.

52. *Ibid.*, April 2, 7, 16, 1862; and *New York Times*, May 8, 1862.

53. Dayton to Seward, Paris, April 17, 1862, SDC, France, Despatches, LI, no. 137.

54. For Lindsay's first interview with Napoleon III see E. D. Adams, I, 289–292; and Slidell memorandum in dispatch to Benjamin, Paris, April 14, 1862, *ORN*, 2nd series, III, 393–395.

55. Cowley to Russell, Paris, April 13, 1862, PRO RP, 30/22.

56. On the second interview cf April 12 see E. D. Adams, I, 289–292; and Slidell memorandum, Paris, April 14, 1862, *ORN*, 2nd series, III, 293–295.

57. Cowley to Russell, Paris, April 13, 1862, PRO RP, 30/22.

58. Same to same, April 15, 1862, PRO FO, 27/1437/497.

59. Thouvenel to Flahault, Paris, April 14, 1862, AMAE CP, Angl. 721:132–133, no. 35.

60. Russell to Cowley, London, April 15, 1862 (seen by Palmerston and the queen), PRO FO, 27/1422/402.

61. Slidell to Benjamin, Paris, April 18, 1862, *ORN*, 2nd series, III, 295–296, no. 6.

62. Flahault to Thouvenel, London, April 16, 1862, AMAE MD, Papiers de Thouvenel, VIII, 324–326.

63. Thouvenel to Flahault, Paris, April 23, 1862, Thouvenel, *Secret*, II, 278–280.

64. Napoleon III to Cowley, Paris, April 20, 1862, enclosure with Cowley to Russell, April 22, 1862, PRO RP, 30/22.

65. *Moniteur*, April 23, 24 and May 6, 1862.

66. Hotze to the [Confederate] secretary of state, London, April 25, 1862, *ORN*, 2nd series, III, 399–400.

67. Flahault to Thouvenel, London, May 11, 1862, teleg., 10:45 P.M., AMAE CP, Angl., 721: 187. See also Russell to Cowley, London, May 11, 1862, teleg., 7:45 P.M., PRO FO, 27/1423/528.

68. Flahault to Thouvenel, London, May 12, 1862, AMAE CP, Angl., 721: 188, no. 27.

69. Thouvenel to Mercier, Paris, May 15, 1862, *ibid.*, E-U, 127: 151–152, no. 13.

70. *New York Times*, June 2, 1862.

71. Slidell to Benjamin, Paris, May 15, 1862, *ORN*, 2nd series, III, 419.

72. Cowley to Russell, Paris, May 13, 1862, PRO RP, 30/22.

73. *Moniteur*, March 6, 1862.

74. Thouvenel to Mercier, Paris, March 6, 1862, AMAE CP, E-U, 126: 211–212, no. 7.

75. Same to same, Paris, March 13, 1862, Thouvenel, *Secret*, II, 247–249.

76. Dayton to Seward, Paris, March 4, 1862, SDC, France, Despatches, LI, no. 124.

77. Seward to Dayton, Washington, March 26, 1862, *ibid.*, Instructions, XVI, no. 133.

78. Mercier to Thouvenel, Washington, March 31, 1862, AMAE CP, E-U, 126: 297–309, no. 93.

79. For Mercier's plans for his trip to Richmond see same to same, Washington, April 13, 1862, *ibid.*, 127: 35–46, no. 96; and Lyons to Russell, Washington, April 14, 1862, PRO RP, 30/22. Lyons also took pains to tell Seward that Mercier's trip had his approval (*ibid.*).

80. On Mercier's Richmond visit see Mercier to Thouvenel, Washington, April 28, 1862, AMAE CP, E-U, 127: 50–78, no. 97; and Benjamin to Mason, Richmond,

July 17, 1862, in Virginia Mason. *The public life and diplomatic correspondence of James M. Mason* . . . (Roanoke, Virginia, 1903), pp. 297–303. Benjamin admitted to Mason that "the result of this conversation had been very fairly stated by him [Mercier]" (*ibid.*).

81. Mercier report above (*ibid.*).

82. Lyons to Russell, Washington, April 25, 1862, Newton, II, 82–85. A copy of this was also sent to Thouvenel by Russell because of France's delayed information (AMAE, Fonds Divers, Guerre des Etats-Unis, carton 1862).

83. *New York Times*, April 27, May 22, 1862.

84. Mercier report of April 28 (see above).

85. For the bombshell caused in London and Paris by news of the trip, see Reuter to Havas, London, April 29, 1862, teleg., 3:26 A.M., AMAE, Fonds Divers, Guerre des Etats-Unis, carton 1862; Russell to Cowley, London, April 29, 30, 1862, PRO FO, 27/1422/466, 472; Flahault to Thouvenel, London, April 30, 1862, AMAE MD, Papiers de Thouvenel, VIII, 337–338.

86. Thouvenel to Flahault, Paris, May 1, 1862, AMAE CP, Angl., 721: 163–164, no. 42.

87. Thouvenel to Mercier, Paris, May 1, 1862, *ibid.*, E-U, 127: 83–84, no. 12.

88. Thouvenel to Flahault, Paris, May 2, 1862, Thouvenel, *Secret*, II, 298–300. Billault also told Slidell that "the Emperor was far from satisfied with Mercier's visit to Richmond" (Slidell to Mason, Paris, May 16, 1862, Library of Congress, Washington, Division of Manuscripts, Mason Papers).

89. Flahault to Thouvenel, London, May 5, 1862, AMAE CP, Angl., 721: 178, no. 25.

90. *Ibid.*, fol. 179–180, no. 26, May 7, 1862.

91. Slidell to Benjamin, Paris, May 15, 1862, *ORN*, 2nd series, III, 419–421, no. 8.

92. Thouvenel to Mercier, Paris, May 15, 1862, AMAE CP, E-U, 127: 151–152, no. 13.

Chapter VIII

Opening Southern Ports

1. Thouvenel to Mercier, Paris, March 6, 1862, AMAE CP, E-U, 126: 211–212, no. 7; same to same, Paris, March 13, 1862, Thouvenel, *Secret*, II, 247–249.

2. Rost to Hunter, Madrid, March 21, 1862, *ORN*, 2nd series, III, 368, no. 1.

3. It was reported from Paris that the French public became convinced of an eventual Union victory as a result of the fall of Fort Donelson (*New York Times*, April 7, 1862).

4. Seward to Dayton, Washington, Feb. 27 and 28, 1862, SDC, France, Instructions, XVI, nos. 118 and 120.

5. Dayton to Seward, Paris, March 25, 1862, *ibid.*, Despatches, LI, no. 129. Weed reported that Napoleon III feared an outbreak in the manufacturing districts if cotton was not soon obtained (Weed to Seward, Paris, April 4, 1862, F. Seward, *Seward in Washington*, 11, 85).

6. Sanford to Seward, Paris, April 10, 1862 (rcd. April 25), Seward Papers. Four days later Thouvenel revealed his concern to Flahault. "On estime en effet [he wrote] que deux mois environ suffisent pour épuiser les ressources du marché français et le travail se ralentit déjà sensiblement. Ces mêmes appréhensions existent, à ce qu'il paraît dans les districts industriels de l'Angleterre . . ." (Paris, April 14, 1862, AMAE CP, Angl., 721: 132–133, no. 35).

7. Weed to Seward, Paris, April 15, 1862 (rcd. April 30), Seward Papers, Rochester Microcards, 54:2889, p. 554. See also F. Seward, *Seward in Washington*, II, 85–86.

8. Weed to Seward, Paris, April 18, 1862 (rcd. May 5), Seward Papers, Rochester Microcards, 54: 2889. See also F. Seward, *Seward in Washington*, II, 86.

9. Same to same, Paris, April 21, 1862 (rcd. May 7), *ibid.*, p. 567. See also F. Seward, *Seward in Washington*, II, 87.

10. See marginal note by Seward to Chase, April 1862, on Sanford to Seward, Paris, April 10, 1862, (rcd. April 25), Seward Papers.

11. Seward to Dayton, Washington, April 28, 1862, SDC, France, Instructions, XVI, 151–152.

12. May 1, 1862, *ibid.*, pp. 152–153, no. 148.

13. May 5, 1862, *ibid.*, pp. 154–155, no. 149.

14. Circular of May 2, 1862, *ibid.*, p. 154. See also Seward to Mercier, Washington, May 2, 1862, *Livre jaune*, 1862, p. 126.

15. Mercier to Thouvenel, Washington, May 5, 1862, private, AMAE MD, Papiers de Thouvenel, XIII, 448–451.

16. May 12, 1862, Richardson, *Presidents*, VI, 89–90.

17. "Mon collègue d'Angleterre [Lyons] a bien voulu se charger de faire parvenir sur le champ, au moyen du télégraphe de Halifax, cette nouvelle à Votre Excellence. Je pense qu'elle sera arrivée à Paris à peu près en même temps que ma dernière Dépêche" (Mercier to Thouvenel, Washington, May 6, 1862, AMAE CP, E–U, 127: 86, no. 98). It seems that most French communications to America, both telegraphic and courier, went through England and were therefore a day or two slower than English messages.

18. In Bigelow's Diary (Monday, May 11, 1862) we find this entry: "M. Laubat came in this afternoon to say that Thouvenel received a dispatch last evening removing all doubt of the occupation of New Orleans by Federal Arms. I called upon Mr. Dayton in the evening and he had received a dispatch transmitted to Mr. Adams by Mr. Seward to the same effect, adding that steps were being taken to open some of the blockaded ports at once to foreign commerce."

19. An unsigned, undated note on British embassy stationery. In the margin in pencil the notation "Communication Anglaise" (AMAE, Fonds Divers, Guerre des Etats-Unis, Box 1862).

20. Flahault to Thouvenel, London, May 12, 1862 (rcd. May 13), AMAE CP, Angl., 721: 188, no. 27.

21. Thouvenel to Mercier, Paris, May 15, 1862, AMAE CP, E–U, 127: 151–152, no. 13.

22. Slidell to Mason, Paris, May 14, 1862, *ORN*, 2nd series, III, 422-423.

23. On Dayton's unsatisfactory conversation with Thouvenel see Dayton to Seward, Paris, May 22 and 26, 1862, SDC, France, Despatches, LI, nos. 149 and 151; and Thouvenel to Mercier, Paris, May 21, 1862, AMAE CP, E–U, 127: 176–181, no. 14.

24. Mercier to Thouvenel, Washington, May 26, 1862, private, AMAE MD, Papiers de Thouvenel, XIII, 454–456.

25. Thouvenel to Mercier, Paris, June 12, 1862, AMAE CP, E-U, 127: 228–229, no. 15.

26. "Malakoff" report (June 13, 1862) in the *New York Times* of June 27, 1862.

27. Slidell saw Billault, the minister of state, on about June 16, 1862, and the minister told him that Persigny had gone to London to urge intervention but that France would do nothing without England (Slidell to Mason, Paris, June 17, 1862, Mason Papers).

28. Palmerston to Russell, June 13, 1862, H. L. Temperly and L. Penson, *Foundations of British foreign policy* (London, 1938), p. 294, cited from the Russell Papers.

29. E. D. Adams, I, 305. For references to Persigny's visit to London see "Malakoff" in the *New York Times* of June 27, 1862; and Bigelow to Seward, Paris, June 17, 1862, SDC, Consular Reports, Paris, XII.

30. *Moniteur*, June 15, 1862.

31. Mercier to Thouvenel, Washington, June 9, 1862 (rcd. June 25, 1862), AMAE CP, E-U, 127: 215–224, no. 103.

32. "Malakoff's" report of June 20, 1862 in the *New York Times*, July 2, 1862.

33. For Slidell's growing discouragement see Slidell to Mason, Paris, June 21, 1862, Sears, *loc. cit.*, pp. 261–262, cited from Mason Papers; and Bigelow to Seward, Paris, June 17, 1862, SDC, Consular Reports, Paris, XII.

34. *Moniteur*, July 15, 1862; London *Times*, July 14, 1862. Slidell said: "On Thursday, the 10th instant, we received the first intelligence of the battle of the 26th and 27th June . . ." (Slidell to Benjamin, Paris, July 25, 1862, *ORN*, 2nd series, III, 479, no. 10).

35. "I knew that the Emperor . . . was said not to dislike having the opportunity to converse in our language . . ." (Slidell in *ORN, ibid.*).

36. There was considerable speculation in French government circles on what solution should be offered and on the potential boundaries. Thouvenel had evidently asked for a study, which was submitted to him on July 4, 1862 ("Note pour le ministre. Question américaine" in AMAE, Fonds Divers, Guerre des Etats-Unis, carton 1862).

37. Slidell to Benjamin, Paris, July 25, 1862, *ORN*, 2nd series, III, 479, no. 10, enclosure, memorandum of conversation with Napoleon III.

38. To Gramont, Thouvenel wrote: "Je pars demain, et vous pouvez vous faire une idée du tohu-bohu dans lequel je suis" (Paris, July 8, 1862, Thouvenel, *Secret*, II, 331–332). See also Thouvenel to Cowley, Paris, July 7, 1862, PRO FO, 27/1442/940, enclosure.

39. London *Times*, July 12, 1862. On the Oxford trip see Flahault to Thouvenel, London, July 23, 1862, AMAE MD, Papiers de Thouvenel, VIII, 371–373.

40. Thouvenel denied the press rumors and steadfastly insisted in his private letters that he went to London solely for the distribution of the prizes (Thouvenel to Mercier, Paris, July 23, 1862, AMAE CP, E-U, 128: 53–55; same to Flahault, July 24, 1862, Thouvenel, *Secret*, II, 348–350).

41. E. D. Adams, II, 19–23.

42. Thouvenel to Flahault, Paris, July 26, 1862, Thouvenel, *Secret*, II, 351–352.

43. Thouvenel to Flahault, Paris, July 21, 1862, copy, AMAE, Fonds Divers, Guerre des Etats-Unis, carton 1862.

44. Thouvenel to Flahault, Paris, July 21, 1862, private, Thouvenel, *Secret*, II, 338–340.

45. Thouvenel said to Flahault: "Mon premier soin a donc été d'écrire à Sa Majesté dans le but de calmer son impatience, et je lui ai exposé en quelque sorte, au moment ou lord Palmerston parlait, les arguments qui ont décidé M. Lindsay à retirer sa motion" (Paris, July 21, 1862, *ibid.*).

46. Thouvenel to Fournier (in St. Petersburg), Paris, July 23, 1862, AMAE CP, Russie, 288: 151, no. 55. Knowing already Thouvenel's views favoring no mediation at this time, this note to Russia seems to denote an imperial inspiration.

47. Fournier to Thouvenel, St. Petersburg, July 29, 1862, *ibid.*, fol. 160–163, no. 90.

48. Slidell to Benjamin, Paris, July 25, 1862, *ORN*, 2nd series, III, 479–481, no. 10.

49. Slidell to Thouvenel, Paris, July 21, 1862, *ibid.*, pp. 467–479.

50. Thouvenel to Flahault, Paris, July 26, 1862, Thouvenel, *Secret*, II, 351–355.

51. For Mason's appeal to the British government, see Mason to Benjamin, London, July 30–Aug. 4, 1862, with enclosures, *ORN*, 2nd series, III, 490–504; and E. D. Adams, II, 25–29.

52. Slidell to Benjamin, Paris, Aug. 20, 1862, *ORN*, 2nd series, III, 518–520, no. 12.

53. Thouvenel to Mercier, Paris, Aug. 20, 1862, Thouvenel, *Secret*, II, 364–365. This scheme of a two-member confederation with a joint senate was not too "absurd." It was almost identical with the Austro-Hungarian *Ausgleich* arranged five years later.

54. This ministry reporter does not take into consideration the fact that the South had already paid its share for these Federal properties in its proportionate payment of pre-war taxes or the fact that the South would have lost its proportionate pre-war shares in Federal properties in the North, such as Washington, D. C., the naval bases, and the schools of West Point and Annapolis.

55. Note pour le Ministre, Paris, le 4 juillet 1862, Question américaine, AMAE, Fonds Divers, Guerre des Etats-Unis, carton 1862.

Chapter IX

Emancipation and Intervention Crisis

1. Channing, *United States*, VI, 529–534.

2. For the early partial steps toward emancipation see *ibid.*, pp. 524–536; and Richardson, *Presidents*, VI, 68–69, 93–96; and *Moniteur*, March 26, April 16, 1862.

3. Weed to Seward, Paris, Jan. 26, 1862, Seward Papers.

4. Bigelow, *Retrospections*, I, 568–569. Bigelow cites an anonymous informant for the details of this incident.

5. *Moniteur*, March 14, 1862.

6. On the news on compensated emancipation in the border states and the District of Columbia see the *Moniteur*, March 21, 22, 26; April 16, 18, 24, 1862.

7. On the French press reception of the news of compensated emancipation see the *New York Times*, April 13, 1862; and the *Moniteur*, March 22, 23, 1862.

8. Dayton to Seward, Paris, March 26, 1862, SDC, France, Despatches, LI, no. 130.

9. Slidell to Benjamin, Paris, April 14, 1862, *ORN*, 2nd series, III, 392–395, no. 5.

10. *Moniteur*, April 24, 1862.

11. *New York Times*, May 8, 1862.

12. *Moniteur*, April 19, 1862.

13. Mercier to Thouvenel, Washington, June 9, 1862, AMAE MD, Papiers de Thouvenel, XIII, 457–458.

14. Randall, *Lincoln*, II, 153–154.

15. *Ibid.*, pp. 155–156.

16. Sumner evidently learned of the cabinet session and the postponement and informed the British chargé, Stuart, who in turn informed Russell (Stuart to Russell, Washington, Aug. 22, 1862, E. D. Adams, II, 37).

17. Cited in Randall, II, 158.

18. For the details of the Battle of Antietam see James Ford Rhodes, *History of the Civil War, 1861–1865* (New York, 1917), pp. 159–170.

19. On the cabinet deliberations on the Emancipation Proclamation see Randall, II, 159–161.

20. Richardson, *Presidents*, VI, 97.

21. On Mercier's impression of the Emancipation proclamation and his plan for a mediated peace, see Mercier to Thouvenel, Washington, Sept. 23, 1862, AMAE CP, E-U, 128: 98–102, no. 116; same to same, Sept. 30, 1862, *ibid.*, fol. 107–113, no. 117; same to same, Washington, Sept. 25, 1862, private, AMAE MD, Papiers de Thouvenel, XIII, 502–509; same to same, Sept. 30, 1862, private, *ibid.*, fol. 510–513.

22. Stuart to Russell, Washington, Sept. 26, 1862, PRO RP, 30/22/36: 220–222. It is interesting to see that Count Edward Piper, the Swedish minister in Washington, noted that the Proclamation was probably intended to prevent European intervention and that now there would be no negotiated peace (Piper to Manderström, Washington, Sept. 26, 1862, [Swedish] Riksarkivet, Diplomatica Americana, no. 59). The Austrian minister also thought that the measure forestalled a negotiated peace and that Seward was opposed to the Proclamation for that reason (Hülsemann to Rechberg, Washington, Sept. 29, 1862, HHSA PA, Vereinigte Staaten, XXXIII, 17: 143–146, no. 45).

23. Dayton to Seward, Paris, Sept. 13, 1862, SDC, France, Despatches, LII, no. 195.

24. Bigelow Diary, Sunday, Oct. 5, 1862. The *Moniteur* (Oct. 6, 1862) just gave the facts of the news on the Proclamation without much comment.

25. Bigelow to Seward, Paris, Oct. 10, 1862, Bigelow Papers, Letters to Seward, p. 115. His hesitation was revealed in his remark that he did not know if publication was proper.

26. Seward's circular, Washington, Sept. 22, 1862, *FRUS*, (1862), p. 195.

27. Bigelow Papers, Letters to Seward, p. 115. However, Bigelow wrote to Seward that the Proclamation "had not produced the effect that it would have produced if issued earlier and less like an extortion" (SDC, Consular Reports, Paris XII, Oct. 7, 1862).

28. Sanford to Seward, Paris, Oct. 10, 1862, Seward Papers.

29. Dayton to Seward, Paris, Oct. 14, 1862, *FRUS*, (1862), p. 394.

30. West's translation of Auguste Vitu's article in the *Constitutionnel* of Oct. 8, 1862, West, p. 86. See also "Malakoff" in the *New York Times*, Oct. 27, 1862.

31. Translation by "Malakoff" in the *New York Times*, *ibid.*

32. *Ibid.*

33. West (p. 85), referring to the articles of Elias Regnault in the *Presse*, Oct. 8 and 15, 1862.

34. West (p. 86), referring to J. E. Horn's article in the *Revue contemporaine*, LXV (Dec. 31, 1862), 913–914.

35. Report of the procureur general of Dijon, Jan. 8, 1863, Case, *U. S. and Mexico*, p. 272.

36. *New York Times*, Oct. 27, 1862. See also West, p. 85.

37. West (p. 85), referring to J.-J. Weiss's article in the *Débats*, Oct. 9, 1862. See also Bigelow to Seward, Paris, Oct. 10, 1862, Bigelow Papers, Letters to Seward, p. 115.

38. West (p. 85), referring to Léon Plée's article in the *Siècle*, Oct. 12, 1862.

39. *Revue des deux mondes*, (Oct. 15, 1862), p. 249.

40. Procureur general report from Colmar, Jan. 24, 1863, Case, *U. S. and Mexico*, p. 272.

41. *Ibid.*

42. Report of Oct. 6, 1862, *ibid.*, p. 266.

43. Report of Jan. 13, 1863, *ibid.*, p. 269.

44. Report from Dijon, Jan. 8, 1863, *ibid.*, p. 272.

45. Report from Rouen, Oct. 12, 1862, *ibid.*, pp. 266–267.

46. Bigelow to Seward, Paris, Aug. 22, 1862, (rcd. Sept. 7, 1862), SDC, Consular Reports, Paris, XII.

47. Sanford to Seward, Brussels, Aug., 26, 1862 (rcd. Sept. 10, 1862), Seward Papers.

48. Dayton to Seward, Paris, Aug. 29, 1862, SDC, France, Despatches, LII, no. 185. It should be pointed out that in the 1840's both Thouvenel and the *Débats* had been Orleanist and that there no doubt remained a sympathy between them especially because of their mutual pro-Northern inclinations. Also Thouvenel's brother-in-law, Cuvillier-Fleury, had been literary critic on the staff of the *Débats*.

49. Same to same, Paris, Sept. 3, 1862, *ibid*, no. 189.

50. Bigelow to Seward, Paris, Aug. 29, 1862, (rcd. Sept. 12, 1862), SDC, Consular Reports, Paris, XII.

51. Russell to Palmerston, Aug. 6, 1862, Palmerston Papers, Russell File. See also E. D. Adams, II, 32, 36.

52. Same to same, Aug. 24, 1862, *ibid.*

53. For the British lull see also E. D. Adams, II, 35–37.

54. *Moniteur*, Sept. 10, 1862.

55. Thouvenel to Mercier, Paris, Sept. 11, 1862, Thouvenel, *Secret*, II, 387–388.

56. Dayton to Seward, Paris, Sept. 17, 1862, SDC, France, Despatches, LV.

57. For the press reports on the Second Battle of Bull Run see the *Moniteur*, Sept. 10, 12, 13, 15, 1862.

58. Russell to Cowley, London, Sept. 13, 1862, teleg. 4:20 P.M., PRO FO, 27/1427. See also E. D. Adams, II, 38.

59. Russell was probably referring to the 23rd or 30th of *October* because he had mentioned an October meeting in his earlier letter to Palmerston and because he was not thinking of interrupting the vacations of his colleagues. For this change

in Russell's and Palmerston's attitude see Russell to Palmerston, London, Sept. 14, 1862, Palmerston Papers, Russell File; Palmerston to Russell, Sept. 14, 1862, Walpole, *Russell*, II, 360; Russell to Palmerston, London, Sept. 17, 1862, *ibid.*, 361. For all this British reopening of the intervention question see also E. D. Adams, II, 37–59.

60. Cowley to Russell, Paris, Sept. 18, 1862, PRO RP, 30/22. See also E. D. Adams, II, 38–39.

61. Thouvenel to Mercier, Paris, Sept. 18, 1862, AMAE CP, E-U, 128: 93–95, no. 24.

62. *Moniteur*, Sept. 18, 1862.

63. *Ibid.*, Sept. 24, 1862.

64. Sanford to Bigelow, Brussels, Sept. 24, 1862, Bigelow, *Retrospections*, I, 550; and Cowley to Russell, Paris, Sept. 31, 1862, PRO RP, 30/22.

65. Russell to Gladstone, Sept. 26, 1862, British Museum, London, Additional Manuscripts, Gladstone Papers.

66. Russell to Palmerston, Sept. 22, 1862, Palmerston Papers, Russell File.

67. Palmerston to Russell, Broadlands, Sept. 23, 1862, Walpole, *Russell*, II, 350.

68. Chateaurenard to Thouvenel, London, Sept. 24, 1862, AMAE MD, Papiers de Thouvenel, VIII, 399–400.

69. *Moniteur*, Sept. 27, 30, 1862.

70. Seward to Dayton, Washington, Sept. 8, 1862, SDC, France, Instructions, XVI, no. 207, confidential.

71. Dayton heard of the Antietam victory on September 27 and on the 30th asked for an interview (Dayton to Thouvenel, Paris, Sept. 30, 1862, SDC, Notes from the Paris Legation, copy; also Dayton Papers, Box 2, copy).

72. This injection of the slavery issue even before the news of emancipation (arriving on October 6) lent force to the later news of the Proclamation. It also touched Thouvenel's antipathy for slavery, a sentiment which he shared with French liberals.

73. Dayton to Seward, Paris, Oct. 2, 1862, SDC, France, Despatches, LII, no. 202.

74. Thouvenel to Mercier, Paris, Oct. 2, 1862, Thouvenel, *Secret*, II, 414–416.

75. Palmerston to Russell, Oct. 2, 1862, Russell, *Later Correspondence*, II, 326–327.

76. Granville to Russell, Sept. 27, 1862; Granville to Stanley, Oct. 1, 1862, E. D. Adams, II, 42.

77. Russell memorandum, Oct. 13, 1862, Palmerston Papers, Russell File.

78. E. D. Adams, II, 50–51.

79. Clarendon to Palmerston, Oct. 16, 1862, Palmerston Papers, Clarendon File.

80. Lewis' countermemorandum quoted in part by C. F. Adams, Jr., "A crisis in Downing Street," in Mass. Hist. Society *Proceedings*, 2nd series, XLVII, 407.

81. Clarendon to Lewis, The Grove, Oct. 24–26, 1862, Maxwell, *Clarendon*, II, 265–266.

82. Palmerston to Russell, Oct. 22, 1862, Russell, *Later correspondence*, II, 327–328.

83. C. F. Adams, Jr., *loc. cit.*, 417.

84. Adams to Seward, London, Oct. 24, 1862, no. 248, *FRUS*, (1862), p. 224.

85. For elaborations of these considerations, see Henry Blumenthal, "Confederate diplomacy: popular notions and diplomatic realities," *Journal of Southern history*, XXXII (1966), 160, 166–167; and M. F. Claussen, "Peace factors in Anglo-American relations, 1861–1863," *Mississippi Valley historical review*, XXVI (1940), 516–522.

Chapter X

Joint Mediation, 1862

1. Count A de Hübner, *Neuf ans de souvenirs d'un ambassadeur d'Autriche à Paris sous le Second Empire (1851–1859)* (Paris, 1904), I, 147.

2. The most extensive biographical treatments are found in Hoeffer, *Nouvelle biographie générale* (Paris, 1868), VI, 803–806; A. Robert, E. Bourlaton, and G. Cougny, *Dictionnaire des parlementaires* (Paris, 1891), VI, 414; P. L. Pradier-Fodéré, *M. Drouyn de Lhuys* (Paris, 1881), *passim;* B. d'Harcourt, *Diplomatie et diplomates. Les quatres ministères de Drouyn de Lhuys* (Paris, 1882), *passim;* W. F. Spencer, *Edouard Drouyn de Lhuys and the foreign policy of the Second French Empire* (Unpublished dissertation, University of Pennsylvania, 1955).

3. A member of his staff, Baron de Courcel, in a dispatch to Drouyn's chief administrative assistant, Baron d'André, added these lines: "The minister has had a good trip and finds himself very well installed here" (*Origines diplomatiques de la guerre de 1870–71. Recueil de documents publiés par le ministère des affaires étrangères* [17 vols., Paris, 1910–1928], [hereafter cited as *Origines*], XI, 281). And Baron d'André, from his own knowledge of Drouyn, very pointedly warned Bigelow "that it would be most unfortunate" if Bigelow did not attend a dinner at Drouyn's (Bigelow, Diary, Jan. 2–Dec. 21, 1865, p. 108).

4. H. Soloman, *L'ambassade de Richard Metternich à Paris* (Paris, 1931), p. 51.

5. See for instance, Dayton to Seward, Paris, Feb. 26, 1863, SDC, France, Despatches, 53: no. 277.

6. Hübner, I, 152.

7. Except when otherwise noted, this biographical data is taken from the works cited in footnote number 2, above.

8. Drouyn de Lhuys to the mayor, Paris, Feb. 18, 1872, Bibliothèque de l'Institut (Paris) MS, 2596, no. 44.

9. Soloman, p. 40 and *passim;* A. Darimon, *L'opposition libérale sous l'Empire* (1861–63) (Paris, 1886), *passim.*

10. J. Maurain, *La politique ecclésiastique du Second Empire de 1852 à 1869* (Paris, 1931), p. 16, note 2; 34; 631.

11. Drouyn de Lhuys to Napoleon III, Paris, Aug. 16, 1867, as quoted in P. L. E. Pradier-Fodéré, *Documents pour l'histoire contemporaine* (Paris, 1871), pp. 42–44.

12. Dayton to Seward, Paris, Aug. 21, 1863, SDC, France, Despatches, 53: no. 336.

13. Bigelow, *Retrospections*, II, 73; Pradier-Fodéré, *Drouyn de Lhuys*, pp. 20–21.

14. Drouyn de Lhuys to Chasseloup-Laubat, Paris, Feb. 18, 1864, Archives de la Marine (Paris) (hereafter cited as AM), BB^4/1346/II. Also Bigelow to Seward, Paris, May 5, 1865, SDC, France, Despatches, 58: no. 88.

15. Slidell to Benjamin, Paris, July 6, 1863, as quoted in Bigelow, *Retrospections*, II, 27–28.

16. See for instance, Dayton to Seward, Paris, March 20, 1863, SDC, France, Despatches, 53: no. 288.

17. Hübner, I, 393–94.

18. Pradier-Fodéré, *Drouyn de Lhuys*, pp. 18–19.

19. The best account of this whole episode is to be found in Cowley to Russell, Paris, Oct. 17, 1862, most confidential, PRO FO 27/1446/1190 and same to same, Paris, Oct. 14, 1862, Private Russell Papers, PRO 30/22/58. See also: L. Thouvenel, *Le secret de l'empéreur* (Paris, 1889), II, 427–428; Ollivier, V, 505–510; Maurain, *La politique ecclésiastique*, pp. 618–625; Maurain, *Baroche*, pp. 236–242; Schnerb, pp. 128–129; Case, *Franco-Italian relations*, pp. 211–213; and Case, *War and diplomacy*, pp. 152–153.

20. Dayton to Seward, Paris, Dec. 12, 1862, SDC, France, Despatches, 52: no. 240.

21. Same to same, Paris, Oct. 17, 1862, *ibid.*, no. 211.

22. Seward to Dayton, Washington, Nov. 4, 1862, *ibid.*, Instructions, 16: 286, no. 247.

23. Dayton to Seward, Paris, Oct. 17, 1862, *ibid.*, Despatches, 52: no. 240.

24. The direct quote is taken from Dayton's despatch to Seward, Paris, Oct. 21, 1862, *ibid.*, no. 213. (Rcd. Nov. 9).

25. Seward to Dayton, Wash., Nov. 10, 1862, *ibid.*, Instructions, 16: 290, no. 248.

26. Drouyn de Lhuys to Mercier, Paris, Oct. 23, 1862, AMAE CP, E-U, 128: 142–43, no. 26.

27. The conversation has been taken from the despatch of Slidell to Drouyn de Lhuys (draft), Paris, Oct. 24, 1862, Eustis Papers; Slidell to Benjamin, Paris, Oct. 28, 1862, *ORN*, 2nd ser., III, 572–574.

28. Cowley to Russell, Paris, Oct. 27, 1862, Russell Papers, as quoted in Adams, *Great Britain and the Civil War*, II, 59.

29. Cowley's memorandum of conversation with M. Drouyn de Lhuys, Oct. 28, 1862, PRO FO 27/1446.

30. Memorandum of an interview of Mr. Slidell with the Emperor at St. Cloud on Tuesday, Oct. 28, 1862, Enclosure B in Slidell to Benjamin, Paris, Oct. 28, 1862, *ORN*, 2nd. ser., III, 574–578. Owsley (pp. 333–336) discusses this interview at length and bases his presentation on the same documents. With the following exception, Owsley's account is fair and thorough. Referring to King Leopold's letter, Owsley (p. 335) states: "Napoleon explained to Slidell . . . that Leopold had more influence with the Queen than any living man—in fact that he had assumed the role of chief advisor in the place of the late Prince Consort." Actually, Slidell wrote (p. 576): "It is universally believed that King Leopold's counsels have more influence with Queen Victoria than those of any other living man, that in this respect he has inherited the succession of the late Prince Consort," without even implying that Napoleon had told him this.

31. Cowley to Russell, Paris, Oct. 31, 1862, PRO FO 27/1446/1236; also quoted in Adams, *Great Britain and the Civil War*, II, 60.

32. Report of Brière-Valigny, Paris, Aug. 28, 1862, in Case, *U. S. and Mexico*, pp. 82–83. For the economic reports from the other twenty-eight judicial districts of France during the months of July and October 1862, preceding the inauguration of the mediation effort, see *ibid.*, pp. 70–100. This problem of unemployment and its impact upon government policy will be further analyzed in Chapter XI.

32a. Count Horace de Viel Castel, *Memoirs*, ed. by Charles Bousfield (2nd ed. London, 1888), II, 258. See also Case, *War and diplomacy*, p. 9.

33. Drouyn de Lhuys to French ambassadors in London and St. Petersburg, Paris, Oct. 30, 1862, as published in the *Moniteur* of Nov. 13, 1862; also in *Archives diplomatiques*, 1863, I, 288–290.

34. Russell to Lewis, London, Oct. 26, 1862, Gooch, *Later correspondence*, II, 328–329.

35. King Leopold to Russell, Brussels, Oct. 31, 1862, *ibid.*, p. 332.

36. Russell to Lyons, Woburn Abbey, Nov. 1, 1862, PRO FO 30/22/96 (copy), and Palmerston to Russell, Nov. 2, 1862, Gooch, *Later correspondence*, II, 333.

37. Russell to Palmerston, Nov. 3, 1862, as quoted in Adams, *Great Britain and the Civil War*, II, 61–62. For this question of the English response to the French proposal, see *ibid.*, pp. 60–74.

38. Russell to Lyons, Woburn Abbey, Nov. 8, 1862, PRO FO 30/22/96 (copy), and Adams, *Great Britain and the Civil War*, II, 63.

39. Maxwell, *Clarendon*, II, 268; and Morley, *Gladstone*, II, 85; both quoted in Adams, *Great Britain and the Civil War*, II, 64–65.

39a. See above, chapter IX and E. D. Adams, *Great Britain and the Civil War*, II, 37–74 for the British cabinet discussions on the Russell mediation plan. For further comments on British policy towards America, see: M. F. Claussen, "Peace factors in Anglo-American relations, 1861–1863," *Mississippi Valley Historical Review*, XXVI (1940), pp. 511–522; R. H. Jones, "Anglo-American relations, 1861–1865, reconsidered," *Mid-America*, XLV (1963); and Henry Blumenthal, "Confederate diplomacy: popular notions and international realities," *Journal of Southern History*, XXXII (1966), pp. 151–171.

40. Russell to Cowley, London, Nov. 13, 1862, PRO FO 27/1429/1128 (draft). The rough draft is in Russell's own hand, with notations by Palmerston. The letter also appears in *Archives diplomatiques*, 1863, IV, 68–70.

41. Cowley to Russell, Paris, Nov. 18, 1862, PRO FO 27/1447/1290.

42. Taylor to Seward, St. Petersburg, Oct. 29, 1862, quoted in Adamov, "Russia," *JMH*, II, 596–597.

43. Napier to Russell, St. Petersburg, Nov. 8, 1862, PRO FO 146/1047; Lyons to Cowley, Washington, Dec. 8, 1862, *ibid.*, 146/1051; Gorchakov to Stoeckl, St. Petersburg, Oct. 27/Nov. 7, 1862, Adams, *Great Britain and the Civil War*, II, 59, note 4, quoting the Russian Archives; Gorchakov to d'Oubril, St. Petersburg, Oct. 27/Nov. 7, 1862, *ibid.*

44. See the note as published in the *Moniteur*, Nov. 16, 1862.

45. Slidell to Benjamin, Paris, Oct. 31, 1862, *ORN*, 2nd series, III, 568.

46. Same to same, Paris, Nov. 11, 1862, *ibid.*, pp. 603–604.

47. Mason to Benjamin, London, Nov. 4, 1862, as quoted in Bigelow, "Shirt of Nessus," *Century Magazine*, XX, 115–116; same to same, London, Nov. 8, 1862, *ORN*, 2nd series, III, 602–603.

48. West (p. 87) referring to A. Grenier's article in the *Constitutionnel*, Nov. 10, 1862.

49. West (p. 88) referring to Gaiffe's article in *La Presse*, Nov. 11, 1862.

50. West (p. 88) summarizing articles in the *Journal des Débats* (Nov. 11) by J. J. Weiss, in the *Siècle* (Nov. 12) by *Bédollière*, and in the *Constitutionnel* by Limayrac.

51. The *Moniteur* of Nov. 13 and 16, 1862.

52. Cowley to Russell, Paris, Nov. 18, 1862, PRO FO 27/1447/1290. See Gladstone's note of Nov. 13, 1862 in Morley, *Gladstone*, II, 85, where he anticipated the French publication of Russell's despatch.

53. West (p. 89) quoting an article by Simon in the *Constitutionnel* of Nov. 14, 1862.

54. West (p. 89) quoting the Weiss article in the *Journal des Débats* of Nov. 14, 1862.

55. West (p. 90) quoting an article by Prévost-Paradol in the *Journal des Débats* of Nov. 14, 1862.

56. West (pp. 90–92) quoting Delord in the *Siècle* of Nov. 18, 1862 and Forcade in the *Revue des deux mondes* of Nov. 15, 1862.

56a. See the procureur reports in Case, *U. S. and Mexico*, pp. 257–258, 267–279.

57. Drouyn de Lhuys to Mercier, Paris, Oct. 30, 1862, AMAE CP, E-U, 128: 148–149, no. 27, confidential.

58. Drouyn de Lhuys to Mercier, Paris, Nov. 6, 1862, confidential, *Archives diplomatiques*, 9: 287.

59. Dayton to Seward, Paris, Nov. 6, 1862, SDC, France, Despatches, 52: no. 220. Rcd. Nov. 21, 1862.

60. Cowley to Russell, Paris, Nov. 7, 1862, PRO FO 27/1447.

61. Dayton to Seward, Paris, Nov. 10, 1862, SDC, France, Despatches, 52: no. 223. Rcd. Nov. 28, 1862.

62. Dayton to Seward, Paris, Nov. 12, 1862, *ibid.*, no. 224. Rcd. Nov. 24, 1862.

63. Drouyn de Lhuys to Mercier, Paris, Nov. 13, 1862, AMAE CP, E-U, 128: 156–157, no. 29; also in *Archives diplomatiques*, 1863, I, 290–291.

64. Dayton to Seward, Paris, Nov. 14, 1862, SDC, France, Despatches, 52: no. 226. Rcd. Nov. 30.

65. Dayton to Drouyn de Lhuys, Paris, Nov. 16, 1862, AMAE, Fonds Divers, Guerre des Etats-Unis, Box 1862. Drouyn de Lhuys responded to this note in a friendly and sympathetic manner, closing with almost the same words with which he announced to Mercier the failure of his overtures to England and Russia, cited above, fn. no. 58 (Drouyn de Lhuys to Dayton, Paris, Nov. 23, 1862, *Archives Diplomatiques*, 1863, I, 293).

66. See Seward's despatches to Dayton, Washington, Nov. 21, 28, 30, 1862, SDC, France, Instructions, 16: 294, 296, 297, 258, 261, 263; Dayton to Seward, Paris, Feb. 5, 1863, *ibid.*, Despatches, 53: no. 265; Lyons to Russell, Washington, Dec. 12, 1862, confidential, PRO FO 146/1051.

67. Drouyn de Lhuys to Mercier, Paris, Nov. 18, 1862, AMAE CP, E-U, 128: 181; also in *Documents Diplomatiques*, 1862, pp. 145–146; Cowley to Russell, Paris, Dec. 9, 1862, PRO FO 27/1448/1363.

68. Mercier to Drouyn de Lhuys, Washington, Dec. 1, 1862, AMAE CP, E-U, 128: 128.

69. Dayton to Seward, Paris, Nov. 21, 1862, SDC, France, Despatches, 52: no. 226.

70. Dayton to Seward, Paris, Nov. 21, 1862, *ibid.*, no. 228.

71. Dayton to Adams, Paris, Dec. 9, 1862, Dayton Papers, AM 15236, Correspondence, Box 1, Letters Sent A–C. On this same topic, see Bigelow to Seward, Paris, Nov. 21, 1862, Private and Confidential, Bigelow, *Retrospections*, I, 673–675.

72. Seward to Dayton, Washington, Dec. 21, 1862, SDC, France, Instructions, 16: 301–303, confidential.

73. See next chapter.

74. Dayton to Seward, Paris, Oct. 2, 1862, SDC, France, Despatches, 52: no. 202.

75. Adams, *Great Britain and the Civil War*, II, 74.

Chapter XI

Unilateral Mediation, 1863

1. Owsley, pp. 134–136.

2. Fohlen, pp. 253–254.

3. Report of the procureur general, Archives Nationales, BB^{30} 387, Rouen, Jan. 10, 1863, as quoted by Fohlen, p. 289.

4. Fohlen, p. 289.

5. The figures are taken from the U. S. Consular reports, as quoted in A. L. Dunham, *The Anglo-French Treaty of Commerce of 1860 and the progress of the industrial revolution in France* (Ann Arbor, 1930), p. 194. Experimentation with the cultivation in France of the long grain cotton of the Southern states was also contemplated. This perhaps reflects Drouyn's interest in agriculture because just a few weeks after he took office he asked the French consul general to send samples of Georgia long grain cotton seed. The request was "urgently" repeated in February of the next year. Unfortunately, the records do not indicate the outcome of this plan. See Drouyn de Lhuys to Montholon, Paris, February, 13, 1863, AMAE CC, E-U, New York, 21: 235, no. 156.

6. Owsley places the number at 275,000 (Owsley, p. 152), while Henderson estimates 379,700 (W. O. Henderson, *The Lancashire cotton famine, 1861–1865* [Manchester, 1934], p. 196). The most thorough analysis is given by Fohlen, pp. 161–249, but he does not give a grand total.

7. Henderson, p. 198.

8. *Ibid.*, pp. 196–197.

9. This and the following references to the Paris press in this paragraph are taken from West, p. 59.

10. See the January 1863 procureur reports from Amiens, Besançon, Caen, Grenoble, Nancy, and Rouen, in Case, *U. S. and Mexico*, pp. 101, 101–102, 103, 109, 111–113, and 119 respectively. It is considered sufficient to cite the page references only, since Case gives the full archival citations in his book.

11. Procureur reports from Grenoble, Colmar, Besançon, Colmar, and Nancy, respectively, as quoted in *ibid.*, pp. 126–127, 123, 121, 122, 128, respectively.

12. Fohlen, pp. 265–267.

13. *Ibid.*, p. 283.

14. *Ibid.*, p. 255

15. *Ibid.*, p. 269 ff., and Henderson, p. 197.

16. West, p. 60.

17. Fohlen, p. 272; West. p. 60.

18. Fohlen, p. 253.

19. West, p. 60.

20. Fohlen, p. 259.

21. *Ibid.*, p. 264, note 42.

22. Procureur reports from Nancy, Orléans, and Nîmes, as quoted in Case, *U.S. and Mexico*, pp. 79 and 81.

23. Dayton to Seward, Paris, Aug. 29, 1862, SDC, France, Despatches, 52: no. 186.

24. Slidell to Benjamin, Paris, Nov. 29, 1862, and Jan. 29, 1863, CSDP, D, nos. 21 and 25.

25. Mercier to Drouyn de Lhuys, Washington, Nov. 21, 1862, AMAE CP, E-U, 128: no. 126; and Lyons to Russell, Washington, Nov. 21, 1862, PRO FO 146/1049.

26. Drouyn de Lhuys to Mercier, Paris, Dec. 11, 1862, AMAE CP, E-U, 128: no. 34; and Cowley to Russell, Paris, Dec. 9, 1862, PRO FO 27/1448/1370.

27. Fauconnet to Drouyn de Lhuys, New Orleans, Aug. 14, 1863, AMAE CPC, E-U, 14: 255–259, no. 80.

28. Procureur reports from Bordeaux, October 1862 and April, 1863, as quoted in Case, *U. S. and Mexico*, pp. 86, 121.

29. See the procureur reports from Bourges, Grenoble, Nancy, Agen, Aix, Besançon, and Metz, respectively, as quoted in Case, *U. S. and Mexico*, pp. 121, 109, 111, 101, 139, respectively.

30. For this summary of the elections of 1862, see J. G. Randall and D. Donald, *The Civil War and Reconstruction* (Boston, 1961; 2nd ed.), pp. 458–459.

31. W. Gray, *The hidden Civil War: The story of the Copperheads* (New York, 1942), pp. 108–110.

32. *Ibid.*, p. 115, citing the Chicago *Times*, Dec. 16, 1862 and *The Crisis*, Dec. 17, 1862. For accounts of the peace movement and the Copperhead activity, see also F. L. Klement, *The Copperheads in the Middle West* (Chicago, 1960), *passim*, but especially Chapter IV.

33. *The congressional globe* 37th Cong., 3rd. sess., p. 314, appdx., pp. 52–60, as quoted in Gray, pp. 119–120.

34. Klement, pp. 107–168.

35. Forney to Drouyn de Lhuys, Philadelphia, Oct. 31, 1862 (rcd. Nov. 14, 1862), AMAE CPC, vol. 10.

36. See the reports from Montholon (New York) dated Oct. 21, Nov. 5 and 10, and Dec. 16, 1862 and from Baltimore dated Oct. 17, 1862, *ibid.*

37. Mercier to Drouyn de Lhuys, Washington, Nov. 10, 1862 (rcd. Nov. 25), AMAE CP, E-U, 128: 151–155, no. 124.

38. Paul to Drouyn de Lhuys, Richmond, Dec. 19, 1862, AMAE CPC, 12: 136–141, no. 67.

39. Russell to Cowley, London, Nov. 13, 1862, PRO FO 27/1129; also found in *Parliamentary papers*, 1863, Lords, Vol. XXIX, as quoted in Adams, *Great Britain and the American Civil War*, II, 67; and *Arch. Diplom.*, 1863, IV, 68–70.

40. Dayton to Seward, Paris, Nov. 25, 1862, SDC, France, Despatches, 52: no. 231.

41. Cowley's memorandum of conversation with Drouyn de Lhuys, Oct. 28, 1862, PRO FO 27/1446.

42. Cowley to Russell, Paris, Nov. 18, 1862, PRO FO 27/1447/1290.

43. Drouyn de Lhuys to Mercier, Paris, Nov. 18, 1862, AMAE CP, E-U, 128: no. 30.

44. Slidell to Benjamin, Paris, Jan. 21, 1863, CSDP, D, no. 24.

45. Drouyn de Lhuys to Mercier, Paris, Jan. 9, 1863, AMAE CP, E-U, 129: 15–18, no. 1. This dispatch is published in all essentials in: *Doc. dipl.*, 1863, pp. 109-110 and *Arch. diplom.*, 1863, I, 439–442. Dayton was later confused on the date of this dispatch, but he is the source of the information concerning its preparation (Dayton to Seward, Paris, Jan. 15, 1863, SDC, France, Despatches, 52: no. 355). Rhodes (IV, 348) implies that this note was inspired by Slidell's suggestion on January 8

that France alone extend recognition to the Confederate States. Such an implication is obviously erroneous. As to peace negotiations in the midst of battles Drouyn himself had met Russian diplomats at Vienna in 1855 during the Crimean War.

46. Dayton to Seward, Paris, Jan. 8, 1863, SDC, France, Despatches, 52: no. 251.

47. Same to same, Paris, Jan. 12, 1863, *ibid.*, no. 252. Dayton had requested an audience two days earlier (Dayton to Drouyn, Paris, Jan. 10, 1863, Dayton Papers, AM 15236, Correspondence sent to Drouyn de Lhuys) but there is no record that it was granted.

48. This conversation is reconstructed from Dayton's letter to Seward, Paris, Jan. 15, 1863, SDC, France, Despatches, 52: no. 255.

49. Paulin Limayrac in the *Constitutionnel* of Jan. 20, 1863, as quoted in West, p. 96. Slidell wrote that Persigny told him the article was inspired by Drouyn de Lhuys (Slidell to Benjamin, Paris, Jan. 21, 1863, CSDP, D, no. 24).

50. Dayton to Seward, Paris, Jan. 27, 1863, SDC, France, Despatches, 52: no. 262, confidential.

51. Same to same, Paris, Jan. 30, 1863, *ibid.*, no. 263.

52. Two letters from Cowley to Russell, Paris, Jan. 26 and 28, 1863, PRO FO, 27/1485.

53. The *Patrie* article appeared the same day that the legislative body approved a grant of five million francs for the relief of the unemployed (West, p. 60). In the dispatch cited in footnote 48, above, Dayton wrote: "This publication of a dispatch before it has reached its destination or been seen, even, by the party upon whom it is to operate, proves clearly that its first object was to operate at *home*, to satisfy the manufacturers and workmen of France."

54. Annual address of the emperor to the legislative chambers, Jan. 15, 1863, *Arch. dipl.*, 9: 175–177.

55. As quoted in West, p. 98.

56. *Ibid.*

57. West, p. 97. The following references to the press are taken from the same source.

58. Although this particular incident has received only scant treatment in historical literature, it has been related erroneously to the official act of January 9 (W. H. Hale, *Horace Greeley voice of the people* [New York, 1950; Collier Books Edition, 1961], p. 276; "Extracts from the Journal of Henry J. Raymond," in *Scribner's monthly*, XIX [March, 1880], p. 708). G. G. Van Deusen (*Horace Greeley nineteenth century crusader* [Philadelphia, 1953], pp. 294–295) does not relate Greeley's associations with Jewett and with Mercier, and thus fails to develop this incident. Furthermore, he attributes to Mercier the initiative for his statements, when in reality it belonged to the Americans. Rhodes (IV,222) discusses the January 9 dispatch and Greeley's correspondence with Mercier in the same paragraph; but he adds in a footnote that he has "no evidence to indicate that Greeley's intercourse with Mercier had any effect towards inducing this mediation offer from France," revealing his ignorance that the Greeley-Jewett-Mercier association began before the French dispatch was even put into final wording. Other American writers have overlooked this incident altogether. Biographical material on Jewett is in the *Dictionary of American biography* (New York, 1937), X, 73; for relevant material on Greeley, see *ibid.*, VII, 528–534, Hale, p. 276, and Van Deusen, pp. 294–295. The following narrative is based primarily upon a private letter from Mercier to Drouyn de Lhuys, Washington, January 19, 1863, AMAE CP, E-U, 129: 30–34. The quotes, unless

otherwise noted, are taken from this letter. The material is all corroborated by
Lord Lyons in a long dispatch to Earl Russell, Washington, Jan. 13, 1863, PRO FO
146/1077, copy.

59. New York *Tribune*, Dec. 4, 1862; Greeley to Jewett, New York, Jan. 2, 1863,
published in the *Tribune* of May 11, 1863. H. H. Horner, *Lincoln and Greeley* (University of Illinois Press, 1953), pp. 291–292, quotes the letter in full but fails to relate
it to this episode.

60. There is unfortunately no record of this Lincoln-Greeley encounter; Horner
makes no mention of it. See Jewett to Mercier, Washington, January 13, 1863,
attached as annex 2 to Mercier to Drouyn de Lhuys, Washington, Jan. 19, 1863,
cited above in footnote 58.

61. New York *Tribune*, Jan. 28 and 29, 1863.

62. "Extracts from the Journal of Henry J. Raymond," in *Scribner's monthly*, XIX
(March, 1880), 706, entry for Monday, Jan. 26, 1863.

63. *New York Times*, Jan. 29, 1863.

64. New York *Tribune*, Jan. 31, 1863.

65. Mercier to Drouyn de Lhuys, Washington, Feb. 2, 1863, AMAE CP, E-U,
129: 25–68, private.

66. Seward to Dayton, Washington, Feb. 6, 1863. SEC, France, Instructions, 16:
329 ff. The following quotes are also taken from this dispatch.

67. Dayton to Seward, Paris, Feb. 26, 1863, SDC, France, Despatches, 53: no.
277. Drouyn de Lhuys had received word of Seward's refusal on Feb. 24 (Mercier
to Drouyn de Lhuys, Washington, Feb. 10, 1863, AMAE CP, E-U, 129: 88–90,
no. 137). For Drouyn's acceptance of Seward's refusal as "reflecting the friendliness of the United States," see Drouyn de Lhuys to Mercier, Paris, Feb. 26, 1863,
ibid., fol. 155–156, no. 4.

Chapter XII

The "Awkward" Roebuck Affair

1. The Lindsay-Roebuck affair has been analyzed and evaluated by highly competent scholars. E. D. Adams in his *Great Britain and the Civil War* (II, 164-178) has
presented the story as it relates to his topic, and F. L. Owsley in his *King Cotton
Diplomacy* (pp. 179–183) has given an account of the incident as an anti-climax to the
question of the diplomatic recognition of the Confederacy. But neither author
has placed the controversy within the larger framework of 1863 mediation and
intervention, nor has either considered it purely from the Paris-Washington point
of view. This chapter will relate the incident to the broader tendencies of 1863
intervention and, with new archival material, to the specific topic of French-United
States diplomatic relations.

2. An account of the Polish insurrection in relation to French public opinion is to
be found in Case, *War and diplomacy*, pp. 179–183.

3. For the policy of Drouyn de Lhuys and of France in the diplomacy of the Polish
insurrection, see W. F. Spencer, *Edouard Drouyn de Lhuys and the foreign policy of the
Second French Empire* (Unpublished Ph.D. dissertation, the University of Pennsylvania, 1955), pp. 185-205.

4. Dayton to Seward, Paris, Feb. 23, 1863, SDC, France, Despatches, 53: no. 276,
and Slidell to Benjamin, Paris, March 4, 1863, CSDP, D, no. 28.

5. Seward to Dayton, Washington, May 11, 1863, SDC, France, Instructions, 16: 376–380, no. 342; and Dayton to Seward, Paris, May 29, 1863, *ibid.*, Despatches, 53: no. 310.

6. While crisis on the continent might drive American problems "out of view" in France, in England the situation was reversed. At least the Austrians believed that England's refusal to act with France was due to Lord Palmerston's fear of a war with the United States (Apponyi to Rechberg, London, April 25, 1863, HHSA, PA, VIII, 66: 358, no 29B). Most of the significant French correspondence on this question is published in *Archives diplomatiques*, 1863, II and 1864, I.

7. Dayton to Seward, Paris, Feb. 5, 1863, SDC, France, Despatches, 53: no. 265. The McDougall Resolution was against any French involvement in Mexico.

8. Shouchard to Drouyn de Lhuys, Boston, Feb. 17, 1863 (rcd. March 5) and April 14, 1863 (rcd. April 28), AMAE CPC, IX (Boston), 95–101, no. 28, and 104–107, no. 29.

9. Paul to Drouyn de Lhuys, Richmond, Feb. 3, 1863, (rcd. March 3), AMAE, CC, V (Richmond), 228–229, no. 327.

10. Same to same, Richmond, March 15, 1863, *ibid.*, 252–256, no. 333.

11. Same to same, Richmond, April 12, 1863, *ibid.*, 261–263, no. 336.

12. Cowley to Russell, Paris, April 10 and 28, 1863, PRO FO 30/22/59, confidential and private.

13. Slidell to Benjamin, Paris, May 3, 1863, CSDP, no. 34, quoted in Adams, *Great Britain and the Civil War*, II, 155 and quoted but not cited in Owsley, p. 442.

14. Same to same, Paris, Feb. 22, 1863, CSDP, D, no. 28.

15. Dayton to Seward, Paris, March 6, 1863, SDC, France, Despatches, 53: no. 283.

16. Slidell to Benjamin, Paris, April 20, 1863, Bigelow Papers, New York Public Library, CSA, 1861–65. Marginalia in Drouyn's handwriting, on Fauconnet to Drouyn de Lhuys, New Orleans, April 22, 1863 (rcd. May 18, 1863), AMAE, CC, IX (New Orleans), 194–200, no. 72.

17. Slidell to Benjamin, Paris, May 28, 1863, CSDP, D, no. 36; also in *ORN*, 2nd ser., III, 777–779. Owsley (p. 442) reports the incident to this point in its development.

18. Two letters from the Marquis of Miraflores (new Spanish foreign minister) to Isturitz, San Ildefonso, July 12 and 13, 1863, copies enclosed in Munay to Cowley, July 25, 1863, PRO FO 146/1095/937.

19. The story of the Erlanger loan is told by Owsley, pp. 369–382, and by Adams, *Great Britain and the Civil War*, II, 158–163. Both use the Pickett (CSDP) and Mason Papers extensively; most of these letters are published in *ORN*, 2nd ser., II and III. Since all three sources are readily available, only direct quotes and new material will be cited in this section.

20. Paul to Drouyn de Lhuys, Richmond, Feb. 8, 1863, AMAE CC, V (Richmond), 233–235, no. 328.

21. *Ibid.*, marginalia.

22. *Ibid.*, March 10, 1863, fol. 250–251, no. 332.

23. Dayton to Seward, Paris, Feb. 13 and March 13, 1863, SDC, France, Despatches, 53: nos. 269 and 286.

24. Slidell to Benjamin, Paris, March 4, 1863, CSDP, D, no. 28.

25. Dayton to Seward, Paris, March 20, 1863, SDC, France, Despatches, 53: no. 289.

26. *Ibid.*, March 27, 1863, no. 293.

27. See Owsley, p. 381.

28. Seward to Dayton, Washington, March 31 and April 15, 1863, SDC, France, Instructions, 16: 357–58 and 363.

29. Dayton to Seward, Paris, May 1, 1863, SDC, France, Despatches, 53: no. 303.

30. A small ripple did result from Seward's comment to the English minister in Washington, Lord Lyons. Seward implied that there might be a Federal retaliation by seizure of any neutral cotton purchased in the Southern states. Lord Lyons rejected such a possibility as a violation of the neutrals' rights to do business with either belligerent. Mercier and Drouyn strongly supported this view, though the question was never put to the French. See Mercier to Drouyn de Lhuys, Washington, April 23, 1863, and Drouyn de Lhuys to Mercier, Paris, May 14, 1863 and July 2, 1863, AMAE CP, E-U, 130; reprinted in *Doc. dipl.*, 1863, nos. 51, 53, 56, pp. 118, 119–120, 122. Adams (*Great Britain and the Civil War*) does not mention the exchange between Seward and Lyons.

31. This whole episode is presented in Adams and Owsley as cited above in footnote 1. A brief summary is presented here in order to give the setting for the new material and for evaluation of the effects of the affair upon Franco-American relations. Except as specifically cited, all information is based on Adams and Owsley.

32. This account of the interview is taken from Slidell's own memorandum (*ORN*, 2nd ser., III, 812–814) which Adams and Owsley both use. Unfortunately, no other account of the meeting could be located.

33. Note from "my friend at the affaires étrangères" to Slidell, Paris June 19, 1863, enclosed with dispatch from Slidell to Benjamin, Paris, June 21, 1863, CSDP, D, no. 18; *ORN*, 2nd ser., III, pp. 810–812. The editors of *ORN* attribute this note to Count de Persigny, but there is nothing in the Pickett Papers (CSDP) to justify this, and internal evidence, especially the last sentence, suggests the author to be an official of the foreign ministry and not a cabinet minister.

34. Mocquard to Slidell, Fontainebleau, June 21, 1863, copy enclosed in *ibid.*

35. Slidell to Benjamin, Paris, June 21, 1863, CSDP, D, no. 18; *ORN*, 2nd ser., III, 811.

36. Neither the French nor English correspondence reveals any such message until June 23.

37. In the Mason Papers and in the Pickett Papers (CSDP). A copy of the latter is in *ORN*, 2nd ser., III, 1047–55.

38. Owsley, p. 449.

39. T. W. Evans, *Memories*, I, 150–52.

40. Slidell to Benjamin, Paris, July 6, 1863, CSDP, D, no. 40; *ORN*, 2nd ser., III 833.

41. Metternich to Rechberg, Paris, July 1, 1863, HHSA, PA, Frankreich, as quoted in A. R. Tyrner-Tyrnauer, *Lincoln and the emperors* (New York, 1962), pp. 85–86.

42. Cowley to Russell, Paris, June 26, 1863, PRO FO 27/1493/736/, confidential.

43. Same to same, Paris, July 2, 1863, *ibid.*, no. 769, confidential.

44. Slidell to Benjamin, Paris, July 6, 1863, *ORN*, 2nd ser., III, 832–833. The French press had been strangely silent on the issue ever since Roebuck's speech of June 30 (West, p. 103).

45. *Moniteur*, July 5, 1863. This translation is the one enclosed in Slidell to Benjamin, Paris, July 6, 1863, *ORN*, 2nd ser., III, 833.

46. Mocquard to Slidell, as dictated by Napoleon III, Fontainebleau, July 6, 1863, copy enclosed in Slidell to Benjamin, Paris, July 6, 1863, CSDP, D, no. 40; *ORN*, 2nd ser., III, 835–836. Owsley (p. 458) quotes this memorandum, placing great stress on it as corroboration of Roebuck.

47. Napoleon III to Drouyn de Lhuys, Vichy, July 14, 1863, copy enclosed in Cowley to Russell, Paris, July 15, 1863, PRO FO 30/2259.

48. Cowley to Russell, Paris, July 2, 1863, PRO FO 27/1493/769, confidential; and Slidell to Benjamin, Paris, July 19, 1863, Bigelow Papers, CSA, 1861–65.

49. Owsley, pp. 460–61.

50. Cowley to Russell, Paris, June 26 and July 7, 1863, PRO FO 27/1493/736 and 793, confidential.

51. Both of these messages are quoted in English in "Cowley Memorandum on Correspondence Shown him by Drouyn de Lhuys," dated July 14, 1863, and enclosed in Cowley to Russell, Paris, July 14, 1863, PRO FO 30/22/59, private.

52. Drouyn de Lhuys to Gros, Paris, telegram, July 1, 1863 (sent at 2:45 P.M.), France, AMAE CP, Angleterre, 725.

53. Gros to Drouyn de Lhuys, London, July 1, 1863 (rcd. July 2), AMAE CP, 725: no. 86. This translation differs in detail from the one printed by Owsley (p. 461). Owsley omits Gros's words: "it is very likely" in the second section of the quote. While this does not materially affect Owsley's conclusion, it does indicate that Gros hedged on whether he had fulfilled Drouyn's mild first instructions.

54. Owsley, p. 462.

55. *Ibid.*, p. 460.

56. Dayton to Seward, Paris, May 29, 1863 and June 25, 1863, SDC, France, Despatches, 53: nos. 310 and 321, with enclosures.

57. Same to same, Paris, July 2, 1863, *ibid.*, no. 323.

58. Same to same, Paris, July 10, 1863, *ibid.*, no. 325.

59. Seward to Dayton, Washington, July 8, 1863, *ibid.*, Instructions, 16: 399–400. Italics are the present author's.

60. Same to same, Washington, July 10, 1863, *ibid.*, fol. 401–402.

61. Dayton to Seward, Paris, July 30, 1863, *ibid.*, Despatches, 53: no. 329.

62. Seward to Dayton, Washington, July 11, 1863, *ibid.*, Instructions, 16: 403–404; Drouyn de Lhuys to Mercier, Paris, July 8, 1863, AMAE CP, E-U, 130: 147–148, no. 17. See also Seward's letters to Dayton of July 13 and 17, SDC, France, Despatches, 16: 404, 406–408.

63. Seward to Dayton, Washington, July 29, 1863, *ibid.*, Instructions, 16: 412–413; Dayton to Seward, Paris, August 5 and 20, 1863, *ibid.*, 53: nos. 333 and 334.

64. Seward to Dayton, Washington, Aug. 31 and Sept. 8, 1863, *ibid.*, Instructions, 16: 434–440, 442.

65. Paul to Drouyn, Richmond, Aug. 24, 1863, AMAE CC, V (Richmond) 303–304 and *ibid.*, CPC, 15: 62–72, no. 79.

Chapter XIII

Confederate Naval Construction

1. Mallory to the president, Richmond, Feb. 27, 1862, *ORN*, 2nd ser., II, 151. This document was a report covering navy department activities since Nov. 18, 1861 and actually summarizing Mallory's decisions and actions since April 1861. For

fuller accounts of the South's deficiency in naval construction facilities and personnel, see Bulloch, I, 20–22, 46.

2. Mallory to North, Montgomery, May 17, 1861, *ORN*, 2nd ser., II, pp. 70–71. Permission and funds were obtained from the Act of the Congress of the Confederate States of America, approved May 10, 1861 (*ORN*, 2nd ser., II, 66–67).

3. See *ibid.*, pp. 87–88, 95, 122, 131, 151–152, which reflect also North's resentment over Bulloch's rank in the Confederate navy. North proved to be of little value to the Southern cause.

4. For a biographical sketch of Bulloch and a summary of his activities, see Philip Van Doren Stern's introduction to the 1959 edition of Bulloch's *Secret Service*, I, ix–xix.

5. For material regarding the British Foreign Enlistments Act as it applied to Bulloch's activities, see Bulloch, I, 67; Owsley, pp. 398–410; W. D. Jones, *The Confederate rams at Birkenhead: a chapter in Anglo-American relations* (Tuscaloosa, Ala., 1961), pp. 52–58; E. D. Adams, *Great Britain and the Civil War*, II, 117–122.

6. Bulloch to Mallory, Liverpool, Jan. 23 and Feb. 3, 1863, *ORN*, 2nd ser., II, 346, 351–352.

7. While many of these ideas were expressed in correspondence of the day, Bulloch summarized them in his *Secret Service*, II, 12, 22–23.

8. See above, chapter X, for Napoleon's plan for joint mediation. For the internal conditions which led him in Dec. 1862 and Jan. 1863 unilaterally to offer French good offices, see chapter XI.

9. Memorandum of an interview of Mr. Slidell with the emperor at St. Cloud on Tuesday, Oct. 28, 1862, enclosed in Slidell to Benjamin, Paris, Oct. 28, 1862, *ORN*, 2nd. ser., III, 574–578. The Conversation is taken from pp. 576–577.

10. Jan. 11, 1863, *ibid.*, pp. 638–639. Mocquard's note was dated Jan. 4, 1863.

11. *Ibid.*, p. 639. Conversation interpolated.

12. See above, chapter XI.

13. In addition to Slidell's letter of Jan. 11, 1863, cited above, see Benjamin to Slidell, Richmond, March 24, 1863, *ORN*, 2nd ser., III, 722; Benjamin to Mason, March 27, 1863, *ibid.*, p. 728; Mallory to Bulloch, Richmond, March 19, 1863, *ibid.*, II, 375–376; Mallory to Slidell, Richmond, March 27, 1863, *ibid.*, pp. 395–396 and Bulloch, I, 398–399. For evidence of direct correspondence between Slidell and Bulloch, see Bulloch, I, 399.

14. Bulloch's narrative account of this preliminary meeting with Arman is the best (II, 25–27). The general tone is confirmed in the various documents cited below.

15. Slidell to Benjamin, Paris, March 4, 1863, *ORN*, 2nd ser., III, 705–707. The conversation is taken from p. 706. The dispatch is also in Bigelow, *Retrospections*, I, 633–635.

16. *Ibid.*

17. Bulloch, II, 28. Bulloch ordered the wooden vessels on Mallory's insistence (*ibid.*, pp. 24–25).

18. Slidell to Benjamin, Paris, April 11, 1863, *ORN*, 2nd ser., III, 738–739.

19. April 20, 1863, *ibid.*, p. 742.

20. Bulloch, II, 28–29.

21. Arman to Chasseloup-Laubat, Bordeaux, June 1, 1863. Archives de la Marine (hereafter cited as AM), BB⁴/1345/I, dossier marked "Voruz et Arman concernant les navies construits à Nantes et Bordeaux." A translation appears in *ORN*, 2nd ser., II, 431–432.

22. Chasseloup-Laubat to Arman, Paris, June 6, 1863, AM, BB^4/1345/I; translation in *ORN*, 2nd ser., II, 433.

23. Slidell to Arman and Voruz, Paris, June 6, 1863, *ORN*, 2nd ser., II, 432. Owsley (p. 416 and fn. 8) cites a letter from Bulloch to Mallory (Liverpool, Nov. 26, 1863, *ORN*, 2nd ser., II, 524–527) as evidence that the emperor "after considerable delay . . . agreed to the contract which called for the building of four corvettes— two at Nantes and two at Bordeaux." But Bulloch does *not* imply any delay nor does he say that the emperor had approved the contract. Here are Bulloch's words: "When the construction of the corvettes was in progress of negotiation [i.e., middle of March] a draft of the proposed contract was shown to the highest person in the Empire, and it received his sanction—*at least I was so informed at the time.*" Bulloch was obviously referring to Arman's mid-March assurances, which Slidell had felt to be insufficient.

24. Memorandum of an interview with the emperor at the Tuileries, Thursday, 18th June, 1863, enclosure C, Slidell to Benjamin, Paris, June 21, 1863. *ORN*, 2nd ser., III, 814.

25. Bulloch, II, 35.

26. Voruz to Chasseloup-Laubat, Paris, July 29, 1863, and the response dated August 1, 1863, AM,BB^4/1345/I; translation in *ORN*, 2nd ser., II, 472, 473–474 respectively. For a description of the ships, see Bulloch to Mallory, Liverpool, Nov. 26, 1863, *ORN*, 2nd ser., II, 524.

27. Bulloch to Mallory, Liverpool, Nov. 26, 1863, *ORN*, 2nd ser., II, 525. For a more detailed description of the Bordeaux rams, see Bulloch, II, 33. The technical details concerning these ships are abstracted from *ORN*, and Bulloch in Maurice Melton, *The Confederate ironclads* (New York and London, 1968), pp. 267–268. This work, unfortunately, is limited in scope and sources and provides no insight into the diplomatic problems concerning the ships.

28. Bulloch to Mallory, Liverpool, Feb. 18, 1864, *ORN*, 2nd ser., II, 589.

29. Captain Hore to William Grey, Paris, Sept. 9, 1863, PRO FO 27/1496/ confidential, no. 1.

30. Sept. 19, 1863, *ibid.*, no. 3.

31. Bigelow, *Retrospections*, II, 56.

32. This man is referred to by the name Trémont in the correspondence of all the Americans, Northern and Southern; but Arman's lawyer during the trial brought by the United States government in 1868, called him Pesterman (*Plaidoirie de M. Lacan pour M. Arman Contre les Etats-Unis d'Amérique* [Paris, 1868], [hereafter referred to as *Plaidoirie*], p. 19).

33. Dayton to Seward, Paris, Sept. 11, 1863, SDC, France, Despatches, 53: no. 344, confidential.

34. *Ibid.*

35. Dayton to Bigelow, Paris, Sept. 9, 1863, Bigelow, *Retrospections*, II, 56. This Trémont episode and much of the subsequent events are variously presented in *ibid.*, pp. 56–64; Bigelow, *France and the Confederate Navy 1862–1868* (New York, 1888), chapter I; Bulloch, *Secret Service*, II, 38 ff., Owsley, pp. 422–426, and J. Thomas Scharf, *History of the Confederate States Navy from its organization to the surrender of its last vessel* (New York, 1887), pp. 804–806. The following account is based to some extent on material from all of these sources, but it relies principally on archival evidence as cited below.

36. This interview and the conversation are in Bigelow, *Retrospections*, II, 56–58. See also Bigelow Papers, New York City Public Library, Bigelow to Seward Letters, Confidential, 1862–66, especially the letter dated Sept. 14, 1863.

37. Bigelow to Dayton, Paris, Sept. 10, 1863, Bigelow, *Retrospections*, II, 63–64. The figure of 15,000 francs was finally agreed to (Dayton to Seward, Paris, Sept. 11, 1863, SDC, France, Despatches, 53: no. 344, confidential). Seward approved the arrangement and left the handling of the matter to Dayton (Seward to Dayton, Washington, Sept. 23, 1863, *ibid.*, Instructions, 16: 450, no. 405).

38. AM, BB⁴/1345/I, dossier marked "Voruz et Arman concernant les navires construits à Nantes et Bordeaux." While some of these documents have been published in *ORN* (as cited above) and by Bigelow in both *Retrospections* and *France and the Confederate Navy*, all of the exact documents originally procured from Trémont and submitted to the French government have nowhere else been itemized.

39. Bigelow, *Retrospections*, II, 62.

40. Dayton to Seward, Paris, Sept. 18, 1863, SDC, France, Despatches, 53: no. 349. Conversation interpolated.

41. *Ibid.*

42. *Ibid.*

43. Bulloch to Mallory, Liverpool, Nov. 26, 1863, *ORN*, 2nd ser., II, 524–527: also in Bulloch, II, 38–41.

44. Bigelow, *France and the Confederate Navy*, p. 195. This view is Bigelow's theme throughout the book. See, for instance, p. 18 for another statement of it. But his actions and correspondence at the time of the events reflect somewhat less certitude.

45. Dayton to Drouyn de Lhuys, Paris, Sept. 22, 1863, copy enclosed in Dayton to Seward, Paris, Sept. 24, 1863, SDC, France, Despatches, 53: no. 350. The original draft of the letter is in Dayton Papers, AM 15236, correspondence sent to Drouyn de Lhuys, Box 1, and a copy is in AM, BB⁴/1345/I.

46. Drouyn de Lhuys to Chasseloup-Laubat, Paris, Sept. 25, 1863 (recd. Sept. 26, 1863), AM, BB⁴/1345/I.

47. Dayton to Seward, Paris, Oct. 8, 1863, SDC, France, Despatches, 53: no. 360.

48. Seward to Dayton, Washington, Oct. 9, 1863, *ibid.*, Instructions, 16: 463; for the tobacco story, see below, chapter XV.

49. Drouyn de Lhuys to Chasseloup-Laubat, Paris, Oct. 12, 1863, AM, BB⁴/1345/I.

50. Chasseloup-Laubat to Drouyn de Lhuys, Paris, Oct. 12, 1863, draft, AN(M) BB² 419; translation from the copy enclosed in Dayton to Seward, Paris, Oct. 16, 1863, SDC, France, Despatches, 53: no. 364.

51. *Ibid.*

52. For Drouyn's attitude toward Chasseloup-Laubat's letter, see Drouyn de Lhuys to Dayton, Paris, Oct. 15, 1863, Dayton Papers, AM 15236, correspondence-Letters Received: Drouyn de Lhuys, Box 3; copy was enclosed in Dayton to Seward, Paris, Oct. 16, 1863, SDC, France, Despatches, 53: no. 364, from which the conversation was interpolated. For Arman's letter to Maury, see Dayton to Seward, Paris, Oct. 16, 1863, SDC, France, Despatches, 53: no. 363.

53. Drouyn de Lhuys to Chasseloup-Laubat, Paris, Oct. 16, 1863, AM, BB⁴/1345/I.

54. Arman to Chasseloup-Laubat, Bordeaux, Oct. 16, 1863, AM, BB⁴/1345/I; copy in AN(M), GG²42. Rcd., Oct. 18, 1863.

55. Voruz to Chasseloup-Laubat, Nantes, Oct. 16, 1863, AM, BB⁴/1345/I. Rcd., Oct. 20, 1863.

56. "Note au sujet de certains bâtiments en construction sur les chantiers de M. Arman," Oct. 19, 1863, AN(M), GG²42, filed with a copy of letter of Oct. 16. Internal evidence in Dayton to Seward, Paris, Oct. 22, 1863, SDC, France, Despatches, 54: no. 367, indicates that the "Note" was written by Drouyn de Lhuys, and it corroborates the content of the "Note."

57. Drouyn de Lhuys to Mercier, Paris, Oct. 22, 1863, AMAE CP, E-U, 130: 217–218, no. 22; Drouyn de Lhuys to Dayton, Paris, Oct. 22, 1863, copy enclosed in Dayton to Seward, Paris, Oct. 23, 1863, SDC, France, Despatches, 54: no. 368.

58. See Seward's dispatches to Dayton, Washington, Oct. 21, 24, Nov. 1, 1863, SDC, France, Instructions, 16: 466, no. 416; 472, no. 422; and 473, no. 425. For Seward's quote, see his dispatch of Nov. 10, 1863, *ibid.*, fol. 476, no. 429; for Mercier's quote, see his dispatch to Drouyn de Lhuys, Washington, Nov. 9, 1863, AMAE CP, E-U, 130: 223–224, no. 165.

59. Dayton to Seward, Paris, Nov. 13, 1863, SDC, France, Despatches, 54: no. 374.

60. Cowley to Russell, Paris, Nov. 3, 1863, PRO FO 27/1498/1051, confidential.

61. Slidell to Napoleon III, Paris, Nov. 6, 1863, copy in cypher enclosed in Slidell to Benjamin, Paris, Nov. 15, 1863, CSDP, D, no. 48; also in *ORN*, 2nd ser., III, 955-958 and Bigelow, *Retrospections*, II, 97–98.

62. Slidell to Benjamin, Paris, Nov. 15, 1863, CSDP, D, no. 48; also in *ORN*, 2nd ser., III, 955–958 and Bigelow, *Retrospections*, II, 97–98. Conversation interpolated.

63. Slidell to Benjamin, Paris, Feb. 16, 1864, CSDP, E, no. 56 (duplicate). Original in Bigelow Papers, CSA, 1861–65; see also *ORN*, 2nd ser., II, 1028–1030.

64. Bigelow to Seward, Paris, Sept. 18, 1863, Bigelow, *Retrospections*, II, 65–69. See also Bigelow to Seward, Paris, Nov. 20, 1863, Bigelow Papers, Bigelow to Seward letters, confidential, 1862–66, where the whole Berryer affair is detailed.

65. Dayton to Seward, Paris, Oct. 22, 1863, SDC, France, Despatches, 53: no. 367.

66. Nov. 27, 1863, no. 379, *ibid.*

67. *Ibid.*, and Dayton to Bigelow (in London), Paris, Dec. 7, 1863, *Retrospections*, II, 106–107.

68. Dayton to Seward, Paris, Dec. 31, 1863, SDC, France, Despatches, 54: no. 394.

69. Seward to Dayton, Washington, Dec. 20, 1863, SDC, France, Instructions, 16: 492–495, no. 447; Dayton to Seward, Paris, Jan. 8, 1864, *ibid.*, Despatches, 54: no. 397.

70. "Note presented to council meeting on January 26, 1864 by Drouyn de Lhuys," AM, BB⁴/1345/I.

71. Drouyn de Lhuys to Chasseloup-Laubat, Paris, Jan. 30, 1864, *ibid.*

72. The earliest estimate of the sailing dates was made on Nov. 24, 1863, by the United States consul at Bordeaux. He stated that one ship was due to sail on Feb. 28, 1864 and another on March 31, 1864 (Dayton to Drouyn de Lhuys, Paris, Nov. 27, 1863, Dayton Papers, Correspondence, AM 15236, Letters sent to Drouyn de Lhuys, Box. 1).

73. Slidell to Benjamin, Paris, Feb. 16, 1864, CSDP, E, no. 56; also in *ORN*, 2nd ser., III, 1028–1030 and in Bigelow, *Retrospections*, II, 150–152.

74. Bulloch to Arman, Paris, Feb. 8, 1864, *ORN*, 2nd ser., II, 590–591; also published in *Plaidoirie*, p. 26; Arman to Bulloch, Paris, Feb. 8, 1864, *Plaidoirie*, pp. 26–27.

75. *Plaidoirie*, p. 27.

76. Dayton to Seward, Paris, April 7, 1864, SDC, France, Despatches, 54: no. 448; Manderström (Swedish foreign minister) to Haldeman (U.S. minister to Sweden), Stockholm, March 15, 1864, copy enclosed in Dayton to Seward, Paris, April 22, 1864, *ibid.*, no. 456 and AM, BB^4/1345/I; Dayton to Drouyn de Lhuys, Paris, April 22, 1864, AM, BB^4/1345/I, copy in Dayton Papers, Letters sent to Drouyn de Lhuys, Box 1; Bulloch, II, 45.

77. Dayton to Seward, Paris, March 11, 1864, SDC, France, Despatches, 54: no. 433; see also Seward's expression of appreciation to Drouyn de Lhuys "for his action in regard to the ironclads building at Bordeaux and Nantes [*sic*]" (Seward to Dayton, March 26, 1864, *ibid.*, Instructions, 17: 34, no. 515).

78. Drouyn de Lhuys, Paris, Feb. 18, 1864, AM, BB^4/1346/II.

79. Mallory to Barron, Richmond, April 6, 1864, Whittle Papers, Folder III.

80. Evans (Lieutenant commanding the "Georgia") to Barron, aboard CSS "Georgia," Feb. 9, 1864, *ibid.*, Folder X, no. 1.

81. Dayton to Seward, Paris, April 22, 1864, SDC, France, Despatches, 54: no. 455.

82. Bulloch to Barron, Liverpool, April 29, 1864, Whittle Papers, Folder II, no. 9.

83. Drouyn de Lhuys to Chasseloup-Laubat, Paris, April 22, 1864, AM, BB^4/1345/I, with marginalia. This aspect of the Mexican question was noted by Kathryn Abbey Hanna when she wrote: "Actually the Mexican situation was one of the greatest handicaps to recognition faced by the South" ("The Roles of the South in the French Intervention in Mexico," *Journal of Southern History*, XV [Feb. 1954], 7). Citing Hanna's article, Henry Blumenthal made the same point ("Confederate Diplomacy: Popular Notions and Realities," *Journal of Southern History*, XXXII [1966], 167). Neither scholar, however, substantiates the statement by evidence from the French archives.

84. This plan is revealed in two dispatches from Dayton to Seward, Paris, Jan. 22 and Feb. 14, 1864, SDC, France, Despatches, 54: nos. 405 and 421, both marked confidential, and in Bigelow to Seward, Paris, Feb. 3, 1864, Seward Papers and Seward to Bigelow, Washington, Feb. 22, 1864, Seward Papers, private.

85. Bigelow to John de la Montagnie (U.S. consul at Nantes), Paris, May 2, 1863, Bigelow, *Retrospections*, II, 175–176.

86. Bigelow to Seward, Paris, May 3, 1863, *ibid.*, pp. 178–180 and a "Report of conversation at the Corps Législatif," Wednesday, 27th April [1864], *ibid.*, pp. 181–182.

87. Bigelow to Seward, Paris, May 3, 1862, *ibid.*, pp. 178–180.

88. Bigelow to Sanford (in Brussels), Paris, May 19, 1864, copy enclosed in Sanford to Seward, Brussels, June 4, 1864, Seward Papers.

89. Seward to Bigelow, Washington, May 21, 1864, private, unofficial, and confidential, Bigelow, *Retrospections*, II, 188–189.

90. Rouher to Chasseloup-Laubat, Paris, May 1, 1864, AM, BB^4/1345/I, and Chasseloup-Laubat's response, Paris, May 2, 1864, AN(M), GG^{2}42.

91. Slidell to Benjamin, Paris, May 21, 1864, *ORN*, 2nd ser., III, 1118–1119.

92. Dayton to Seward, Paris, May 2, 1864, SDC, France, Despatches, 54: no. 460. Conversation interpolated.

93. Slidell to Benjamin, Paris, May 2, 1864, CSDP, E, no. 60; also in *ORN*, 2nd ser., III, 1107–1110.

94. Chasseloup-Laubat to Arman, Paris, May 1, 1864, copy in Bigelow Papers, 1865, France and the Confederate Navy, Folder 3.

95. Comte du Châlons, Engineer de la Marine to Chasseloup-Laubat, Nantes, April 29, 1864 and two letters from the builders (Dubigeon and Jollet and Babin), Nantes, April 26, 1864, all in AM, BB⁴/1345/I.

96. Captain Pierre to Chasseloup-Laubat, Paris, May 5, 1864, *ibid.*

97. Chasseloup-Laubat to Arman, Paris, copy dated May 1, 1864, Bigelow Papers, 1865, France and the Confederate Navy, Folder 3; quotation taken from the translation in *ORN*, 2nd ser., II, 692, dated May 20, 1864. Evidence in Chasseloup-Laubat to Drouyn de Lhuys, Paris, May 13, 1864, AN(M), BB²426, indicates that the letter had not been sent as of that date, and Bulloch (II, 47) states that Arman did not inform him of this until early June.

98. Two letters from Chasseloup-Laubat, both dated May 20, 1864, to Jollet et Babin (builder of the "San Francisco") and to Dubigeon (builder of the "Shanghai"), Paris, AM, BB⁴/1345/I. A translation of the former appears in *ORN*, 2nd ser., II, 692–693, and the quote was taken from it.

99. As Arman described the scene to Bulloch through an intermediary (Bulloch, II, 47). For partial confirmation of this, see Bulloch to Barron, Liverpool, June 9, 1864, Whittle Papers, Folder II, no. 15.

100. Bulloch, II, 29–30.

101. For the initial contact, see Seward to Dayton, Washington, June 17, 1864, SDC, France, Instructions, 17: 99–100, unofficial and confidential; for confirmation of the purchase, see Pennington (secretary of legation) to Seward, Paris, Dec. 29, 1864, *ibid.*, Despatches, 56: no. 8. Chili had also been interested in the ships, and the activity of the Peruvian agents in Nantes had caused some consternation among the Federal agents (Seward to Dayton, Washington, Aug. 1, 1864, *ibid.*, Instructions, 17: 139, confidential and Seward to Bigelow, Washington, Dec. 29, 1864, *ibid.*, 17: 221, no. 9).

102. Dayton to Seward, Paris, May 16, 1864, SDC, France, Despatches, 54: no. 467 and *Plaidoirie*, p. 28.

103. Chief of service of marine, Bordeaux, to Chasseloup-Laubat, Bordeaux, June 1, 1864; Chasseloup-Laubat's negative response by telegram, Paris, June 2, 1864; and the confirmation of the detention by the marine chief of service, Bordeaux, June 2, 1864, all in AM, BB⁴/1345/I; Drouyn de Lhuys to Chasseloup-Laubat, Paris, June 6, 1864, *ibid.*, and marginalia.

104. See the exchange between the two men: from Dayton, June 4, 1864 and June 7, 1864; from Drouyn de Lhuys, June 6, 1864; all in Dayton Papers, correspondence, AM 15236, the first two in Box 1, Letters sent to Drouyn de Lhuys, the last one in Box 3. See also Dayton to Seward, Paris, June 8, 1864, SDC, France, Despatches, 54: no. 484, from which the quote is taken.

105. Drouyn de Lhuys to Geofroy, Paris, June 10, 1864, AMAE, CP, E-U, 131: 238–240, no. 8 and Seward to Dayton, Washington, June 28, 1864, SDC, France, Instructions, 17: 114, no. 595.

106. Chasseloup-Laubat to Drouyn de Lhuys, Paris, July 5, 1864, AN(M), BB² 426; Drouyn de Lhuys to Chasseloup-Laubat, Paris, July 26, 1864, AM, BB⁴/1345/I and the response, Paris, Aug. 1, 1864, AN(M), BB²426.

107. Seward to Dayton, Washington, July 11, 1864, SDC, France, Instructions, 17: 122–123, no. 603. The "Iroquois" and the "Niagara" had just joined the "Kearsarge" in European waters.

108. Drouyn de Lhuys to Chasseloup-Laubat, Paris, Sept. 5, 1864, AM, BB⁴/1345/I and Chasseloup-Laubat to Drouyn de Lhuys, Paris, Sept. 17, 1864, AN(M), BB⁴426. This is also published in *Plaidoirie*, pp. 37–38. Dayton refers to this episode in dispatches to Seward under dates of Sept. 15, 29, 30, 1864, all in SDC, France, Despatches, 55: nos. 540, 542, 543.

109. Copies of the exchanges were enclosed in Dayton's no. 542 of Sept. 29, 1864. Drouyn wrote to Washington explaining the exchange (Drouyn de Lhuys to Geofroy, Paris, Sept. 29, 1864, AMAE, CP, E-U, 132: 74–75, no. 17) and Seward approved Dayton's handling of the situation (two dispatches to Dayton, Washington, Oct. 4, 17, 1864, SDC, France, Instructions, 17: 175–176, 180, nos. 674, 681).

110. This is summarized in Drouyn de Lhuys to Chasseloup-Laubat, Paris, Oct. 3, 1864, AM,BB⁴/1345/I.

111. Slidell to Benjamin, Paris, Aug. 8, 1864, *ORN*, 2nd ser., III, 1187.

112. Nov. 19, 1864, *ibid.*, pp. 959–960; also in CSDP, D, no. 49 and Bigelow, *Retrospections*, II, 99. See also Slidell's dispatch of Dec. 13, 1864, CSDP, E, no. 76.

113. Bulloch, II, 74. While there is some indication that Arman knew of Denmark's reluctance to buy the ship once peace was established, there is no evidence that Arman had received a definitive rejection prior to Oct. 15, 1864.

114. Drouyn de Lhuys to Chasseloup-Laubat, Paris, Oct. 3, 1864, AM, BB⁴/1346/II, dossier marked "The Sphinx, Ster-Kodder, Stonewall Affair"; See also Lord Cowley's later summary of this aspect of the episode in Cowley to Russell, Paris, Feb. 17, 1865, PRO FO 30/22/61, private. There are many sources for the history of the episode: for the Confederate side, see *ORN*, 1st ser., III, 719–748 and Bulloch, II, 74–103; for the Federal side, see Bigelow, *France and the Confederate Navy, passim*, and *Retrospections*, II, 283 ff and 328 ff, *ORN*, 1st ser., III, 461–470, 518–545, and the Bigelow-Seward correspondence in the SDC. The most recent secondary accounts are Melton, pp. 271–284, based solely on Confederate sources and filled with errors of interpretation, fact, and spelling, and Lee Kennett, "The Strange Career of the 'Stonewall,' " *United States Naval Institute Proceedings*, February, 1968, no. 780, vol. 94, no. 2, pp. 74–85, a highly entertaining article, based upon sound research in Federal and Confederate sources, marred only by the journal's policy of omitting footnotes. The following section is based upon all of the above sources, including for the first time, French and British Archives and the unpublished letters of Bulloch in the Whittle Papers.

115. Chasseloup-Laubat to Chief of Marine Service at Bordeaux, Paris, Oct. 9, 1864, AM, BB⁴/1346/II.

116. Drouyn de Lhuys to Chasseloup-Laubat, Paris, Nov. 3, 1864, AN(M), GG²42.

117. Cowley to Russell, Paris, March 31, 1865, PRO FO 27/1569/393.

118. Bulloch, II, 74 and Bulloch to Mallory, London, Jan. 10, 1865, *ORN*, 1st ser., III, 720–721. The agreement with Henri A. de Rivière is in *ORN*, 1st ser, III, 721–724. This man's name is variously reported as H. Arman de Rivière and Arnous de Rivière. The difference could easily have originated from misreading his handwriting. To avoid confusion, and despite the usual French practice, he will hereinafter be referred to simply as Rivière.

119. *ORN*, 1st ser., 723. Rivière's role in this has been confused by a letter published by Bigelow in *Retrospections* (II, 452–455) from Major Caleb Huse, Confederate army purchasing agent in Europe. The letter, dated Oct. 11, 1888, was written in response to the publication of Bigelow's *France and the Confederate Navy*. In his letter, Huse tells a wild story about Rivière trying to get him to accept the ship because Bulloch refused to do so (thus before Dec. 14, 1864) and about Rivière opening a bilge-cock during a trial run and thus causing the Danes to reject the ship. But Huse gives no dates, and his account is hard to reconcile with the story that the Danes had notified Arman prior to October 1, that they no longer wanted the ship or with their telegram to Drouyn, dated Nov. 3, 1864. Despite this, Huse's bilge-cock story has been accepted by subsequent writers, including Stern (in Bulloch's *Secret Service*, II, 443, notes) who misleadingly presents it as coming from "*ORN*, I, 719 ff," and by Melton (p.273) who cites Bulloch, II, 443, as if Bulloch believed the story. It appears to be more Rivière's cock and bull bragadoccio than a true nautical account.

120. Barron to Page, Paris, Dec. 17, 1864, *ORN*, 1st ser., III, 719–720.

121. Bulloch to Barron, London, Jan. 9, 1865, Whittle Papers, Folder II, no. 36.

122. The best account of the ship movements and of the difficult trips is in Kennett, *loc. cit.*, pp. 78–85.

123. *Ibid.*, p. 79.

124. Davidson to Bulloch, aboard the "City of Richmond" off Funchal, Madeira, Feb. 6, 1865, *ORN*, 1st ser., III, 732.

125. Bulloch to Mallory, London, Jan 10, 1865, *ibid.*, p. 720.

126. Davidson to Bulloch, aboard the "City of Richmond" off Funchal, Madeira, Feb. 6, 1865, *ibid.*, p. 733.

127. Watch Officers of the "Stonewall" to Commodore Barron, Harbor of La Caruña, Spain, Feb. 4, 1865, Whittle Papers, Folder X. One of the signers was Barron's son, Lieutenant Samuel Barron, Jr.

128. Bigelow summarized his activities in a dispatch to Seward, dated Paris, January 30, 1864, SDC, France, Despatches, 56: no. 13: also in his *Retrospections*, II, 295–297.

129. Bigelow to Drouyn de Lhuys, Paris, Jan. 28, 1865, AM, BB4/1346/II; copy enclosed in Bigelow's Jan 30, 1865 dispatch to Seward, SDC, France, Despatches, 56; no 13, and printed in *Retrospections*, II, 285.

130. As reported by Bigelow in his Jan. 30, 1865, dispatch to Seward, cited above note no. 128.

131. These reports are all in AM, BB4/1346/II. Drouyn sent Bigelow's first note to Chasseloup-Laubat on Jan. 31, and asked for a report; the marine minister on the same day sent telegrams to St. Nazaire and to Belle Isle requesting information. He received answers from Belle Isle on Jan. 31; from Auray on Feb. 1; from Nantes on Feb. 2 and again on Feb. 7.

132. Bigelow to Seward, Paris, Jan. 31, 1865, SDC, France, Despatches, 56; no. 14; also in *Retrospections*, II, 297–298.

133. Bigelow to Drouyn de Lhuys, Paris, Feb. 2, 1865, AM, BB4/1346/II; two paragraphs quoted in *Retrospections*, II, 288–298; the interview was reported in Bigelow to Seward, Paris, Feb. 3, 1865, SDC, France, Despatches, 56: no. 17, which also enclosed a copy of the Feb. 2 note to Drouyn de Lhuys.

134. Bigelow to Seward, Paris, Feb. 6, 1865, SDC, France, Despatches, 56: no. 19; also in *Retrospections*, II, 320–322; Bigelow to Drouyn de Lhuys, Feb. 5, 1865, AM, BB⁴/1346/II.

135. Drouyn de Lhuys to Bigelow, Paris, Feb. 6, 1865, draft, AM, BB⁴/1346/II; copy in *Retrospections*, II, 290–293, dated Feb. 7, 1865.

136. For Perry's activities, see Kennett, *loc. cit.*, pp. 80–81. For the movements of the U.S. warships see Bigelow to Sanford, Paris, Feb. 5, 1865, *Retrospections*, II, 319–320, Craven to Bigelow, Feb. 20, 1865, *ibid.*, pp. 346–348, and *ORN*, lst series, III, 461–470. For Bigelow's evaluation of the situation, see Bigelow to Seward, Paris, Feb. 9, 1865, SDC, France, Despatches, 56: no. 23, not reproduced in *Retrospections*.

137. Two letters, Page to Barron, El Ferrol, Spain, Feb. 12, 1865 and Feb. 15, 1865, Whittle Papers, Folder X; three letters Bulloch to Barron, London, Feb. 10, 1865, and Liverpool, Feb. 15 and 16, 1865, *ibid.*, Folder II, nos. 38, 40 and unnumbered. In his *Secret Service*, Bulloch suppresses his severe criticism of Page.

138. Bigelow to Drouyn de Lhuys, Paris, Feb. 27, 1865, SDC, France, Despatches, 56: no. 40, enclosure and *Retrospections*, II, 348.

139. Cowley to Russell, Paris, Feb. 17, 1865, PRO FO 30/22/61, private, and March 31, 1865, *ibid.*, 27/1569/393.

140. Bigelow to Seward, Paris, Feb. 16, 1865, SDC, France, Despatches, 56: no. 34, also in *Retrospections*, II, 335–339. Bigelow does not reflect this satisfaction in his published writings; instead, he speaks of his "disgust" at the "obvious bad faith" of Drouyn (Bigelow, *France and the Confederate Navy*, p. 70).

141. Drouyn de Lhuys to Geofroy, Paris, Feb. 9, 1865, and Geofroy's response, Washington, Feb. 27, 1865, AMAE CP, E-U, 133: nos. 2 and 77, respectively. Seward's circular to Bigelow, Perry (in Madrid), Wood (in Copenhagen), and Adams (in London), Washington, March 11, 1865, SDC, France, Instructions, 17: 285 *bis*, no. 66.

142. For a narrative of the "Stonewall's" departure from El Ferrol, her entry into Lisbon, and voyage to Nassau (arrival May 6), and then to Havana (arr. May 11), see Melton, pp. 281–284 and Kennett, *loc. cit.*, pp. 82–84. For the documents, see *ORN*, 1st ser., III, 741–748, 463–466.

143. Acting Rear Admiral S. W. Godon to Welles, Havana, May 31, 1865, *ORN*, 1st ser., III, 536.

144. Kennett, *loc. cit.*, p. 85.

Chapter XIV

Neutrality: Ships and Harbors

1. Cowley to Russell, Paris, April 4, 1863, PRO FO 27/1089/395; Drouyn de Lhuys to Chasseloup-Laubat, Paris, April 6, 1863, Archives de la Marine (hereafter cited as AM), BB⁴/1345/I; Dayton to Seward, Paris, April 9, 1863, SDC, France, Despatches, 53: no. 297; Seward to Dayton, Washingto, April 24, 1863, *ibid.*, Instructions, 16: 365–367; Mercier to Drouyn de Lhuys, Washington, May 19, 1863, AMAE CP, E-U, 53: 49-63, no. 148.

2. Telegrams exchanged between the prefect of the marine at Brest and Chasseloup-Laubat, minister of the marine (Paris), Aug. 23, 1863, AM, BB⁴/1345/I, dossier marked: "Guerre de Sécession, Affaires de la Florida à Brest. Arrivée du Kearsarge. Divers mouvements de ces bâtiments."

3. Bulloch, I, 152–178.

4. See telegrams from Chasseloup-Laubat to the prefect at Brest, Paris, all dated between Aug. 24 and 27, 1863, AM, BB⁴/1345/I.

5. Dayton to Drouyn de Lhuys, Paris, Aug. 25, 1863, draft, Dayton Papers, Letters sent to Drouyn de Lhuys, Box 1, and Dayton to Seward, Paris, Aug. 25, 1863, SDC, France, Despatches, 53: no. 337. Dayton was in constant communication with the U. S. vice consul at Brest. (Dayton to Seward, Paris, Aug. 27, *ibid.*, no. 339.)

6. Drouyn de Lhuys to Chasseloup-Laubat, Paris, Sept. 3, 1863, AM, BB⁴/1345/I.

7. Maffitt to Bulloch, Brest, undated, quoted in Bulloch, I, 179.

8. Bulloch, I, 179. Evidence supporting Bulloch's statement is in two letters from the "Florida's" skipper, written just before departure and some nine days later; the skipper refers to a "Mr. L. E. Reisserton at N[Nantes?]," with whom he expects to make a rendezvous on Feb. 17, and he confirms the successful meeting on Feb. 19 when he has "all on board that was expected" (Morris to Barron, Brest, Feb. 9, 1864 and at sea, Feb. 18, 1864, *ORN*, 1st ser., II, 664–665).

9. Prefect of the marine at Brest to minister of the marine, Brest, Sept. 2, 1863, AM, BB⁴/1345/I, telegram; Eustis to Drouyn de Lhuys, Paris, Sept. 1863, copy enclosed in Slidell to Benjamin, Biarritz, Sept. 22, 1863, *ORN*. 2nd ser., III, 908; Paul Pecquet du Bellet, *The diplomacy of the Confederate cabinet of Richmond and its agents abroad: being memorandum notes taken in Paris during the rebellion of the Southern States from 1861 to 1865*, ed. by Wm. Stanley Hoole (Confederate Publishing Co., Inc.: Tuscaloosa, Ala., 1863), p. 77. Pecquet du Bellet's self-serving work is filled with errors, innuendos, and false impressions, but he does publish certain documents unavailable elsewhere. He claims to have been aboard the "Florida" when the first notice of Menier's suit was given to Maffitt and to have advised the latter to ignore the whole affair (Pecquet du Bellet, pp. 76–77).

10. Dayton to Seward, Paris, Sept. 3, 1863, SDC, France, Despatches, 53: no. 341.

11. Grey (British chargé d'affaires) to Russell, Paris, Sept. 14, 1863, PRO FO 27/1496/35.

12. Sept. 18, 1863, *ibid.*, no. 53. The records, unfortunately, do not reveal how Drouyn accomplished this.

13. *Moniteur*, Sept. 4, 1863. See also Eustis' letter to Drouyn de Lhuys, Paris, Sept. 1863, copy enclosed in Slidell to Benjamin, Biarritz, Sept. 22, 1863, *ORN*. 2nd ser., III, 908. While the word *corsaire* may mean either privateer or pirate, in this case it obviously meant privateer, for a pirate would not have been allowed within the port. The skipper of a privateer could be tried in a civil court as a private individual provided he was guilty of "conduct clearly amounting to 'Piracy of the Law of Nations,' " which in this case would be "the appropriation or destruction of property which [he] well knew was not the enemies' property, and which [he] did not intend or attempt to take before any prize court for adjudication" (J. P. Baxter, III, "Some British opinions as to neutral rights, 1861 to 1865," *American journal of international law*, XXIII [1929], 535, quoting Law Officers to Russell, Oct. 5, 1861, Admiralty Papers, 1/5768; for the distinction between pirates and privateers, see also C. J. Colombos, *The International law of the sea* [5th ed., London, 1962], p. 471).

14. Eustis to Drouyn de Lhuys, Sept. 1863, cited above.

15. *Moniteur*, Sept. 16, 1863. Grey considered this important enough to notify the British foreign office by telegraph (Grey to Russell, Paris, Sept. 16, 1863, PRO FO 27/1496/telegram).

16. Drouyn de Lhuys to Chasseloup-Laubat, Paris, Sept. 21, 1863, AM, BB⁴/1345/I.

17. Bulloch, I, 182–183. The dossier described in footnote no. 2 confirms Bulloch's complaint about the references to Paris; there are thirty-nine exchanges in the dossier between the prefect at Brest and the minister of the marine. These are principally telegrams covering every subject from actions of stevedores to ship movements and Menier's law case.

18. Prefect of the marine to the minister of the marine, Brest, Sept. 3, 1863, telegram and letter containing the affidavits, AM, BB⁴/1345/I. Bulloch (I, 180) confirms this, again without giving the compelling reason.

19. Belligerent recruitment in a neutral port was covered by international law for the first time in article 18 of the Hague Convention of 1907. This article prohibited belligerents "from enrolling sailors in a neutral port, with the exception of such few hands as are necessary to navigate the vessel safely to the nearest port of her home State" (Colombos, p. 615).

20. Dayton to Seward, Paris, Sept. 11, 1863, SDC, France, Despatches, 53: no. 355, confidential. The ironclads Dayton referred to were the Laird rams which were still under litigation in England (see Wilbur D. Jones, *The Confederate rams at Birkenhead: a chapter in Anglo-American relations* [Confederate Publishing Co., Inc.: Tuscaloosa, Ala., 1961]).

21. Dayton to Drouyn de Lhuys, Paris, Oct. 1, 1863, copy enclosed in Dayton to Seward, Paris, Oct. 2, 1863, SDC, France, Despatches, 53: no. 356. Dayton's actions were approved in Seward to Dayton, Washington, Oct. 24, 1863, *ibid.*, Instructions, 16: 469. Dayton was at least consistent in this question. Captain Winslow of the "Kearsarge" had mentioned that he needed more men and was contemplating signing them aboard in the port of Brest. Dayton, explaining that he was opposing a similar act by the "Florida" concluded: "Your act in shipping men for the Kearsarge' will be referred to as a full justification [for the 'Florida']. I would, prefer, therefore, to keep the question clear of any such act, that it may stand on its merits only" (Dayton to Winslow, Paris, Nov. 19, 1863, *ORN*, 1st ser., II, 498–499).

22. Dayton to Seward, Paris, Oct. 8, 1863, SDC, France, Despatches, 53: no. 359. Seward's approval is in Seward to Dayton, Washington, Oct. 24, 1863, *ibid.*, Instructions, 16: 470.

23. Prefect of the marine at Brest to minister of the marine, Brest, Oct. 15, 1863, AM, BB⁴/1345/I; Drouyn acknowledged receipt of this on Oct. 21 in a letter to Chasseloup-Laubat, Paris, *ibid.* The "Florida" had three skippers during her stay in Brest: J. N. Maffitt until Sept. 17, 1863; J. N. Barney, Sept. 17, 1863 to Jan. 9, 1864; and C. M. Morris after Jan. 9, 1864 (*ORN*, 1st ser., II, 680).

24. Chasseloup-Laubat to Drouyn de Lhuys, Paris, Oct. 19, 1863, Archives Nationales (Marine) [hereafter cited as AN(M)], BB² 419.

25. Dayton to Seward, Paris, Oct. 21, 1863, SDC, France, Despatches, 53: no. 365.

26. Bulloch, I, 182.

27. Slidell to Benjamin, Paris, Dec. 29, 1863, *ORN*, 2nd ser., III, 986; the original in the Pickett Papers (CDSP) (E, no. 52) shows the cited paragraph to have been sent in cypher.

28. Dayton to Seward Paris, Sept. 3, 1863, SDC, France, Despatches 53: no. 341; and Seward to Dayton, Washington, Sept. 19 and 23, 1863, *ibid.*, Instructions, 16: 445 and 455, nos. 399 and 404.

29. Prefect of the marine at Brest to minister of the marine, Brest, Sept. 18, 1863, AM, BB⁴/1345/I.

30. Dayton to Seward, Paris, Oct. 1, 1863, SDC, France, Despatches, 53: no. 354.

31. Prefect of the marine at Brest to minister of the marine, Brest, Nov. 19, 1863, AM, BB⁴/1345/I.

32. Prefect of the marine at Brest to minister of the marine, Brest, Oct. 15, 1863, with marginalia, and Drouyn de Lhuys to minister of the marine, Paris, Oct. 21, 1863, AM, BB⁴/1345/I; two letters from Dayton to Seward, Paris, Oct. 21 and 28, 1863, SDC, France, Despatches, 53 and 54: nos. 365 and 371.

33. Seven telegrams from the prefect of the marine at Brest to the minister of the marine, Brest, Oct. 31, Nov. 7, 11, Dec. 5, 11, 1863, Jan. 1, 16, 1864, AM, BB⁴/1345/I.

34. *Ibid.;* and Chasseloup-Laubat to Drouyn de Lhuys, Paris, copy undated but after Jan. 1 and before Jan. 16, 1864, *ibid.*

35. Prefect of the marine at Brest to minister of the marine, Brest, Feb. 18, 1864, *ibid.*

36. Chasseloup-Laubat to Drouyn de Lhuys, Paris, undated, *ibid.* This is the same letter cited above in footnote no. 34.

37. Prefect of the marine at Brest to minister of marine, Brest, Feb. 18, 1864, telegram, and minister to prefect, Paris, Feb. 19, 1864, *ibid.*

38. Dayton to Drouyn de Lhuys, Paris, Jan. 22, 1864, copy, and prefect of the marine to minister of the marine, Brest, Feb. 3, 1864, telegram, *ibid.* Seward approved Dayton's note of Jan. 22, and expressed "some anxiety here on this subject until the determination of the French Government can be known" (Seward to Dayton, Washington, Feb. 8, 1863, SDC, France, Instructions, 17: 1, no. 473). For the arrival of the "Georgia" see Dayton to Seward, October 29, 1863, SDC, France, Despatches, 54: no. 371. For the "Kearsarge's" three-way watch, see Winslow to Dayton, Brest, Dec. 4, 1863, *ORN*, 1st ser., II, 563.

39. U. S. Consul Kerros to Dayton, Brest, Feb. 11, 1864, copy enclosed in Dayton to Seward, Paris, Feb. 15, 1864, SDC, France, Despatches, 54: no. 422.

40. See Chapter III, above.

41. E. Drouyn de Lhuys, *Les neutres pendant la guerre d'Orient* (Paris, 1868), *passim:* and W. F. Spencer, *Edouard Drouyn de Lhuys and the foreign policy of the Second French Empire* (Unpublished Dissertation, University of Pennsylvania, 1955), pp. 58–60.

42. Cobden to Bigelow, Midhurst [England], Oct. 6, 1863, Bigelow, *Retrospections*, II, 79. Cobden confirmed the proper references in another letter of Oct. 10, 1863, *ibid.*, p. 82.

43. Bigelow to Cobden, Paris, Oct. 20, 1863, *ibid.*, p. 85.

44. Cobden to Bigelow, Midhurst, Oct. 29, 1863, *ibid.*, pp. 91–92.

45. Dayton to Drouyn de Lhuys, Paris, Nov. 6, 1863, copy enclosed in Dayton to Seward, Paris, Nov. 6, 1863, SDC, France, Despatches, 54: no. 372. Seward approved the note (Seward to Dayton, Washington, Nov. 21, 1863, *ibid.*, Instructions, 16: 478).

46. Dayton to Seward, Paris, two letters, Nov. 19 and 27, 1863, *ibid.*, nos. 378 and 380.

47. Same to same, Paris, Feb. 4, 1864, *ibid.*, no. 411.

48. Drouyn de Lhuys to Chasseloup-Laubat, Paris, Dec. 2, 1863, AM, BB⁴/1346/ II, and marginalia.

49. Conversation interpolated from Dayton to Seward, Paris, Dec. 4, 1863, SDC, France, Despatches, 54: no. 382.

50. Chasseloup-Laubat to Drouyn de Lhuys, Paris, Jan. 8, 1864, AN(M), GG² 42.

51. Note presented to council meeting on Jan. 26, 1864 by Drouyn de Lhuys, AM, BB⁴/1345/I; see also his letter to Chasseloup-Laubat on the same subject, Paris, Jan. 30, 1864, *ibid.*

52. Dayton to Seward, Paris, Jan. 29, 1864, SDC, France, Despatches, 54: no. 409. Conversation is interpolated.

53. Drouyn de Lhuys to Chasseloup-Laubat, Paris, Feb. 18, 1864, AM, BB⁴/ 1346/II.

54. Rules to observe towards belligerent ships, from Chasseloup-Laubat to all maritime officials in French and colonial ports, Paris, Feb. 5, 1864, copy enclosed in Drouyn de Lhuys to Dayton, Paris, March 2, 1864, as enclosed in Dayton to Seward, Paris, March 3, 1864, SDC, France, Despatches, 54: no. 427.

55. Drouyn de Lhuys to Chasseloup-Laubat, Paris, Feb. 4, 1864, AM, BB⁴/1345/I.

56. For the best accounts, see Bulloch, II, 265–269 and F. H. Morse to C. F. Adams, U. S. Consulate, London, Nov. 28, 1863, *ORN*, 1st ser., II, 505–507. The extent of the British government's concern as to the "Rappahannock" is reflected in a letter from the Law Officers to Earl Russell. They advised that if the Confederate government should refuse to disavow the act, the British government should close all of its ports to any Confederate ship which had been outfitted in England; and they further advised that should any vessel repeat the "Rappahannock's" offense, then British naval vessels should "pursue and capture such vessel on the high seas" (J. P. Baxter, III, "Papers relating to neutral rights, 1861–1865," *American historical review*, XXXIV (Oct. 1928), 88–91, quoting Law Officers of the Crown to Earl Russell, Lincolns Inn, Oct. 10, 1863, Admiralty Papers 1/5852). There is no indication that the French government was aware of this attitude.

57. Commandant de l'Inscription Maritime to Chasseloup-Laubat, Calais, Dec. 1, 1863, AM, BB⁴/1346/II.

58. Dayton to Drouyn de Lhuys, Paris, Dec. 4, 1863, copy, Dayton Papers, Letters sent to Drouyn de Lhuys, Box 1; copy also enclosed in Dayton to Seward, Paris, Dec. 4, 1863, SDC, France, Despatches, 54: no. 382.

59. Dayton to Drouyn de Lhuys, Paris, Dec. 12 and 28, 1863, Dayton Papers, Letters sent to Drouyn de Lhuys, Box 1.

60. Dayton to Drouyn de Lhuys, Paris, Dec. 19, 1863, copy enclosed in Dayton to Seward, Paris, Dec. 21, 1863, SDC, France, Despatches, 54: no. 387. Dayton's actions were approved by Seward (Seward to Dayton, Dec. 20, 1863 and Jan. 12, 1864, nos. 447 and 455, *ibid*, Instructions, 16: 492 and 503–504).

61. Dayton to Bigelow, Paris, Jan. 12, 1864, Dayton Papers, Letters sent, A-C, Box 1; Dayton to Seward, Paris, Jan. 15, 1864, SDC, France, Despatches, 54: no. 400.

62. Dayton to Drouyn de Lhuys, Paris, Feb. 2, 1864, Dayton Papers, Letters sent to Drouyn de Lhuys, Box 1; copy also enclosed in Dayton to Seward, Paris, Feb. 3, 1864, SDC, France, Despatches, 54: no. 408. Dayton's information that the "Rappahannock" would be armed by a ship from England was erroneous. The Confederates planned to arm her with the guns and munitions then aboard the "Georgia," and then to retire the "Georgia" (see correspondence in *ORN*, 1st ser., II, 810, 819; and in the Whittle Papers, Folder II).

63. Drouyn de Lhuys to Chasseloup-Laubat, Paris, Dec. 23, 1863, AM, BB⁴/1346/II, and marginalia.

64. Calais official to Chasseloup-Laubat, Calais, Jan. 4, 1864, and Drouyn de Lhuys to Dayton, Paris, Jan. 13, 1864, both enclosed in Dayton to Seward, Paris, Jan. 15, 1864, SDC, France, Despatches, 54: no. 400.

65. Drouyn de Lhuys to Chasseloup-Laubat, Paris, Jan. 15, 1864, AM, BB⁴/1345/II and marginalia.

66. Dayton to Seward, Paris, Feb. 5, 1863, SDC, France, Despatches, 54: no. 411.

67. Drouyn de Lhuys to Chasseloup-Laubat, Paris, Feb. 4, 1864, AM, BB⁴/1346/II.

68. Chasseloup-Laubat to Commissaire de l'Inscription Maritime (Calais), Paris, Feb. 15, 1864, *ibid.*

69. Slidell to Benjamin, Paris, March 5, 1864, CSDP, E, no. 57.

70. Chasseloup-Laubat to Commissaire de la Division Navale du Nord à Calais, Paris, March 7, 1864, telegram, AN(M), BB⁴ 836 and Commissaire de la Division Navale du Nord à Calais to Chasseloup-Laubat, March 7, 1864, telegram, AM, BB⁴/1346/II.

71. Slidell to Benjamin, Paris, March 5, 1864, CSDP, E, no. 57.

72. Slidell to Benjamin, Paris, March 25, 1864, CSDP, E, no. 58; and various letters from the two commanders to be found in the Whittle Papers, Folders I and II. Slidell attempted to reach the emperor at this time by submitting a long memorandum through Mocquard, the emperor's secretary. In it Slidell sought to prove that the "Rappahannock" had not violated the neutrality laws of France and that the detention was illegal (memorandum, dated March 15, 1864, *ORN*, 2nd ser., III, 1055–1056). See also his letters of complaint to Drouyn de Lhuys, dated March 14, and June 9, 1864, *ORN*, 2nd ser., III, 1056–1057 and 1151–1152. None of these was answered.

73. Bulloch to Barron, Liverpool, April 29, 1864, Whittle Papers, Folder II, no. 9.

74. See Slidell's strong letter of complaint to Persigny, Paris, June 17, 1864, enclosed in Slidell to Benjamin, Paris, July 11, 1864, CSDP, E, no. 67. In the face of this protest the general historical opinion has been that Slidell had frequent and easy access to Drouyn, based perhaps on the undocumented statement by Rhodes: ". . . the Emperor accorded three interviews to Slidell, and the Minister for Foreign Affairs and other members of the imperial ministry and household held with him unrestrained intercourse" (J. F. Rhodes, *History of the United States from the Compromise of 1850 to 1877* [New York, 1893–1906], IV. 389).

75. Slidell to Benjamin, Paris, May 2, 1864, CSDP, E, no. 60.

76. See the various correspondence in AM, BB⁴/1346/II, dated between March 7 and July 8, 1864.

77. Slidell to Benjamin, Paris, May 21 and June 11, 1864, CSDP, E, nos. 62 and 64.

78. Dayton to Seward, Paris, May 2, 1864, SDC, France, Despatches, 54: no. 460.

79. "List of Officers and Crew of the CS Steamer 'Rappahannock,' " submitted by Lieutenant C. M. Fauntleroy, Lieutenant-Commanding, May 16, 1864, Whittle Papers, Folder I.

80. Slidell to Benjamin, Paris, June 30, 1864, CSDP, E, no. 65.

81. Slidell to Persigny, Paris, June 17, 1864, enclosed in Slidell to Benjamin, Paris, June 30, 1864, CSDP, E, no. 65.

82. Slidell to Benjamin, Paris, July 11, 1864, *ibid.*, no. 67.

83. "Rapport à l'Empereur sur l'affaire du Rappahannock," dated July 10, 1864 and signed by Drouyn de Lhuys, AM, BB⁴/1346/II.

84. Slidell to Benjamin, Paris, Aug. 1, 1864, CSDP, E, no. 68.

85. Chasseloup-Laubat to Commissaire de l'Inscription Maritime à Calais, Paris, July 26, 1864, AN(M), GG² 42.

86. Slidell to Benjamin, Paris, Aug. 1, 1864, CSDP, E, no. 68.

87. Commissaire de la Marine, Calais, to le Contre-Amiral, Chef d'Etat-Major, Calais, Aug. 1, 1864, telegram, AN(M), GG² 42 and Slidell to Benjamin, Paris, Aug. 8, 1864, CSDP, E, no. 69.

88. Bigelow to Seward, Paris, March 3, 1864, SDC, France, Despatches, 56: no. 41.

89. Slidell to Benjamin, Paris, Aug. 1, 1864, CSDP, E, no. 68.

90. Dayton to Seward, Paris, Aug. 23, 1864, SDC, France, Despatches, 55: no. 527.

91. See Captain Winslow's own account in *ORN*, 1st ser., III, 59–60. For good secondary accounts, see W. Adolphe Roberts, *Semmes of the Alabama* (The Bobbs-Merrill Co.: New York, 1938), pp. 195–211; Edward Boykin, *Ghost ship of the Confederacy the story of the Alabama and her captain, Raphael Semmes* (Funk & Wagnalls Co.: New York, 1957), pp. 344–384. The best, most complete and impartial account still is in Bulloch, I, 277–290.

92. Barron to Semmes, Paris, June 14, 1864, draft, Whittle Papers, Folder X. These papers contain two descriptive letters from Captain George T. Sinclair to Barron. Sinclair, sent by Barron to do all he could to help Semmes, reported his conversations with Semmes aboard the "Alabama," his own eye-witness account of the battle, and the arrangements made for the burial of the dead and the care of the survivors. The "Alabama's" payroll for the dead and wounded, thus providing an accurate list of the killed, is also among these papers.

93. Dayton to Seward, Paris, June 13, 1863, SDC, France, Despatches, 55: no. 488. For Seward's approval, see his two letters to Dayton, Washington, July 2, 1864, *ibid.*, Instructions, 17: 116 and 117–118, nos. 597 and 599.

94. Chasseloup-Laubat to Drouyn de Lhuys, Paris, June 15, 1864, AM, BB⁴/1346/II.

95. Dayton to Seward, Paris, June 17, 1864, SDC, France, Despatches, 55: no. 491.

96. Chasseloup-Laubat to Drouyn de Lhuys, Paris, June 16, 1863, AM, BB⁴/1346/II.

97. Dayton to Seward, Paris, June 16, 1864, SDC, France, Despatches, 55: no. 491 and June 17, 1864, *ORN*, 1st ser., III, 57; maritime prefect at Cherbourg to Chasseloup-Laubat, Cherbourg, telegram, June 18, 1864, AM, BB⁴/1346/II.

98. Chasseloup-Laubat to maritime prefect at Cherbourg, Paris, telegram, June 18, 1864, AM, BB⁴/1346/II.

99. Slidell to Benjamin, Paris, June 30, 1864, *ORN*, 2nd ser., III, 1159–1160.

100. Napoleon III to Chasseloup-Laubat, Fontainebleau, telegram, June 19, 1864 (9:45 P.M.), AM, BB⁴/1346/II.

101. Two telegrams exchanged between the two men in the evening of June 19, 1864, *ibid.* Napoleon III's second telegram was sent at 11:55 P.M.

102. Letters are in *ibid.*

103. Slidell to Benjamin, Paris, June 30, 1864, CSDP, E, no. 65; and *ORN*, 2nd ser., III, 1160–1161.

Chapter XV

Neutrality: Movement of Goods

1. Drouyn de Lhuys to Chasseloup-Laubat, Paris, Jan. 8, 1863, AN(M), BB⁴ 810, f32.

2. Cowley to Russell, Paris, April 11, 1863, telegram, PRO FO 27/1489/428; and Russell to Cowley, London, April 11, 1863, telegram, PRO FO 146/1084/495.

3. Drouyn de Lhuys to Gros, Paris, April 8, 1863, coded telegram and the response, dated London, April 22, 1863, no. 55, both in AMAE CP, Angleterre, 724: 71–76.

4. Drouyn de Lhuys to Chasseloup-Laubat, Paris, April 17, 1863, AN(M) BB⁴ 810, 118–122. This letter enclosed a copy of the confidential and unsigned report, dated April 14, 1863, from Clifton, England.

5. This brief account is based upon two despatches: Gros to Drouyn de Lhuys, London, April 22, 1863, AMAE CP, Angleterre, 724; and Seward to Dayton, Washington, May 8, 1863, SDC, France, Instructions, 16: 370–375. See also Martin B. Duberman; *Charles Francis Adams 1807–1886* (Houghton Mifflin Co.: Boston, 1961), pp. 305, 308, for a discussion of this incident from the London-Washington point of view.

6. Gros to Drouyn de Lhuys, London, April 24, 1863, AMAE CP, Angleterre, 724: 80–82, no. 57.

7. Two notes from Cowley to Russell, Paris, April 21, 1863, PRO FO 27/1490; and April 26, 1863, PRO FO 30/22/59.

8. Dayton to Seward, Paris, April 24, 1863, SDC, France, Despatches, 53: no. 301, with translation of Drouyn's note enclosed. The draft translation is in Dayton Papers, Box 1, AM 15236. See also Drouyn's protest contained in Drouyn de Lhuys to Mercier, Paris, April 23, 1863, AMAE CP, E-U, 130: 38–40, no. 10; also published in *Documents diplomatiques*, 1863, 115–116, no. 50; and in *Archives diplomatiques*, 1863, IV, 278–281; and Seward's response through Mercier in Mercier to Drouyn de Lhuys, Washington, May 8, 1863, AMAE CP, E-U, 130: 45–48, no. 149; and published in *Archives diplomatiques*, 1863, IV, 284.

9. Drouyn de Lhuys to Gros, Paris, April 27, 1863, and the reply, London, May 2, 1863, AMAE CP, Angleterre, 724: 83 and 108–109, nos. 43 and 61.

10. Dayton to Seward, Paris, April 30, 1863, SDC, France, Despatches, 53: no. 303; and Drouyn's marginalia on Gros to Drouyn de Lhuys, London, May 2, 1863, AMAE CP, Angleterre, 724: 108–109, no. 61.

11. Seward to Dayton, Washington, May 8, 1863, SDC, France, Instructions, 16: 370–375, no. 341.

12. Dayton to Seward, Paris, May 29, 1863, *ibid.*, Despatches, 53: no. 309. Seward concurred in his acknowledgment on June 12, 1863, *ibid.*, Instructions, 16: 389.

13. Fauconnet to Drouyn de Lhuys, New Orleans, April 8, 1864, AMAE CPC, E-U, 19: 68–69, no. 96.

14. Drouyn de Lhuys to Geofroy (chargé d'affaires), Paris, May 4, 1864, AMAE CP, E-U, 131: 160–163, no. 5.

15. This information is contained in several dispatches: Fauconnet to Drouyn de Lhuys, New Orleans, June 17, 1864, AMAE CPC, E-U, 19: 90–98, no. 99; three letters from Geofroy to Drouyn de Lhuys, Washington, May 22, June 20, June 28, 1864, nos. 16, 24, 25; Seward to Geofroy, Washington, May 28, 1864 (containing

the quote); Drouyn de Lhuys to Geofroy, Paris, July 14, 1864, no. 13, all located in AMAE CP, E-U, 131. The New York *Herald* of June 20, 1864 reported the capture of the ships and the names of the transferred officers.

16. These incidents are reported in Cazotte to Drouyn de Lhuys, San Francisco, Aug. 22, 1864, April 21, 1865, May 2, 1865, Aug. 6, 1864, all in AMAE CPC, E-U, respectively: 19: no. 11; 23: no. 26; 23: no. 27; 19: no. 9.

17. Cazotte to Drouyn de Lhuys, April 6, 1864, San Francisco, *ibid.*, 19: 280–281, no. 4, and marginalia.

18. Cazotte to Drouyn de Lhuys, San Francisco, July 21, 1864, *ibid.*, 292, no. 8.

19. Drouyn de Lhuys to Cazotte, Paris, Oct. 27, 1864, *ibid.*, 207–308, no. 4; Drouyn de Lhuys to Chasseloup-Laubat, Paris, June 26, 1865, AN(M), BB³ 747, f332; Drouyn de Lhuys to Cazotte, Paris, May 2, 1865, AMAE CPC, E-U, 23: no. 27, marginalia entered June 9, 1865.

20. Stuart to Russell, Washington, Nov. 1, 1862, PRO FO 146/1047/328, confidential.

21. Dayton to Seward, Paris, Nov. 27, 1863, SDC, France, Despatches, 54: no. 380.

22. Borg to Drouyn de Lhuys, New York, May 8, 1865, AMAE CPC, E-U, 21: 3–10, no. 3.

23. See the letters to Drouyn de Lhuys from: Geofroy, Washington, May 8, 1865, no. 87 and Montholon (new minister), Washington, May 23 and 29, 1865, nos. 2 and 3, all in AMAE CP, E-U, 134; from Borg, New York, May 12 and Oct. 16, 1865, nos. 4 and 34, *ibid.*, CPC, 21; Cazotte, San Francisco, May 17, 1865, *ibid.*, 23: no. 30.

24. See the various reports in AMAE CPC, E-U, vols. 11–23 and in AMAE CC, E-U, vols. 5–7, 14, 15, 21, 22.

25. M. L. Bonham, Jr., "The French Consuls in the Confederate States," *Studies in Southern history and politics inscribed to William Archibald Dunning* (New York, 1914), pp. 81–104; Gordon Wright, in "Economic conditions in the Confederacy as seen by the French consuls," *Journal of Southern history*, VII (May 1941), 195–214, has presented a good survey of the French consuls' interest in, and observations on, economic conditions throughout the war.

26. See, for instance, Paul to Drouyn de Lhuys, Richmond, April 12, 1863, AMAE CC, E-U, Richmond 5: 261–263, no. 336.

27. For an excellent account of the role tobacco played in American-French relations prior to the Civil War, see Bingham Duncan, "Franco-American tobacco diplomacy, 1784–1860," *Maryland historical magazine*, LI (Dec. 1956), 273–301. Duncan shows the significance of the Régie Impériale to the French government both as a source of revenue and a means of control (*loc. cit.*, pp. 278, 279–280, 293–294, 300).

28. Paul to Drouyn de Lhuys, Richmond, Dec. 11, 1862, AMAE CC, E-U, Richmond 5: 201–203, no. 318; Bonham, *loc. cit.*, p. 87. For Slidell's verification of the Rothschild ownership, see Slidell to Hunter, Paris, Feb. 19, 1862, enclosure B in Slidell to Hunter, Paris, Feb. 26, 1862, *ORN*, 2nd ser., II, 350–351.

29. For an account of the court action and the issues raised, see W. F. Spencer, "French Tobacco in Richmond," *The Virginia Magazine of history and biography*, vol. 71 (April 1963), 187–188; also the Richmond *Examiner*, Nov. 26, 28, 1862; Robert D. Meade, *Judah P. Benjamin: Confederate statesman* (New York, 1943), *passim*, especially pp. 104–106, 108, 113; Louis Martin Sears, *John Slidell* (Durham, N.C., 1925), pp. 6, 87.

30. Drouyn de Lhuys to Paul, Paris, Jan. 30, 1863, AMAE CC, E-U, Richmond 5: 277, no. 105; and Paul to Drouyn de Lhuys, Richmond, March 21, 1863, *ibid.*, fol. 257, no. 334; Paul to Drouyn de Lhuys, Washington, June 19, 1863, AMAE CPC, E-U, Richmond 15: 60–61, no. 77.

31. Gideon Welles, *Diary of Gideon Welles* (New York, 1911), I, 339–340.

32. Paul to Drouyn de Lhuys, Washington, July 9, 1863, AMAE CC, E-U, Richmond 5: 291–292, no. 345.

33. Gros to Russell, London, July 28, 1863, copy, and Russell to Gros, London, July 31, 1863, copy, PRO FO, 146/1100 (unnumbered). But the British government double-checked in Washington and received Seward's assurance of his approval of the plan (Stuart to Russell, Washington, Sept. 14, 1863, *ibid.*).

34. Drouyn de Lhuys to Paul, Paris, Aug. 6, 1863, AMAE CC, E-U, Richmond 5: 294–295, no. 108.

35. Benjamin to Paul, Richmond, Aug. 4, 1863, *ORN*, 2nd ser., III, 851–852.

36. Benjamin to Slidell, Richmond, Aug 4, 1863, *ibid.*, pp. 853–854.

37. Paul to Drouyn de Lhuys, New York, Sept. 3, 1863, AMAE CC, E-U, Richmond 5: 305–308, no. 349.

38. Mercier to Drouyn de Lhuys, Washington, Sept. 14, 1863, AMAE CP, E-U, 130: 191–197, no. 162.

39. *Ibid.*

40. Paul to Drouyn de Lhuys, New York, Sept. 17, 1863, AMAE CC, E-U, Richmond 5: 311, no. 353.

41. Dayton to Seward, Paris, Aug. 25, 1863, SDC, France, Despatches, 53: no. 337.

42. Dayton to Seward, Paris, Sept. 11, 1863, SDC, France, Despatches, 53: no. 344, confidential. Rcd. Sept. 24, 1863.

43. Dayton to Seward, Paris, Oct. 20, 1863, *ibid.*, no. 366. Rcd. Nov. 5, 1863. As events turned out Drouyn was mistaken concerning the time of purchase.

44. Dayton to Seward, Paris, Oct. 22, 1863, *ibid.*, no. 367. Rcd. Nov. 5, 1863.

45. Mercier to Drouyn de Lhuys, Washington, Nov. 9, 1863, AMAE CP, E-U, 130: 223–224, no. 165.

46. Seward to Dayton, Washington, Nov. 10, 1863, SDC, France, Instructions, 16: 475–476, no. 429.

47. Seward to Dayton, Washington, Nov. 10, 1863, *ibid.*, 476, no. 428.

48. Copy enclosed in Seward to Dayton, Washington, Nov. 14, 1863, *ibid.*, 476, no. 430.

49. Dayton to Seward, Dec. 25, 1863, SDC, France, Despatches, 54: no. 390.

50. Slidell to Benjamin, Paris, Dec. 15, 1863, CSDP, E, no. 51.

51. A copy was enclosed in Benjamin to Slidell, Richmond, May 31, 1864, *ORN*, 2nd ser., III, 1128–1130, no. 38.

52. The entire paragraph is based upon Paul to Drouyn de Lhuys, New York, Dec. 15, 1863, AMAE CC, E-U, Richmond 5: 330–331, no. 359.

53. Paul to Drouyn de Lhuys, New York, Dec. 29, 1863, AMAE CC, E-U, Richmond 5: 339, no. 362.

54. Seward to Dayton, Washington, Jan. 4, 1864, SDC, France, Instructions, 16: 498–501, no. 452.

55. *Ibid.*

56. Dayton to Seward, Paris, Jan. 29, 1864, SDC, France, Despatches, 54: no. 408.

57. The ship was the "Tisaphone." Chasseloup-Laubat (minister of the marine) to Admiral Raynard (Commander in Chief of the Imperial Naval Forces of the Antilles and of North America), Paris, Jan. 16, 1864, AN(M), BB⁴ 836.

58. Paul to Drouyn de Lhuys, New York, Jan. 26, 1864, AMAE CC, E-U, Richmond 5: 347, no. 364.

59. Russell to La Tour d'Auvergne, London, Feb. 9, 1864, PRO FO 27/1548. La Tour d'Auvergne had requested this on Feb. 3, 1864 (*ibid.*).

60. Copy enclosed in Paul to Drouyn de Lhuys, March 14, 1864, AMAE CC, E-U, Richmond 5: 359, no. 367.

61. Dayton to Seward, Paris, March 18, 1864, SDC, France, Despatches, 54: no. 436.

62. Paul to Drouyn de Lhuys, New York, March 14, 1864, AMAE CC, E-U, Richmond 5: 357–359, no. 367.

63. Paul to Drouyn de Lhuys, New York, March 29, 1864, *ibid.*, pp. 363–364, no. 370.

64. The account of these operations can be found in various dispatches from Paul to Drouyn in *ibid.*, and between Paul and Benjamin in CSDP, E; but the most accessible account is in Bonham, "French Consuls," *Studies in Southern History*, pp. 88–91. The following account is based on all three sources.

65. Welles, *Diary*, II, 9–10.

66. Seward to Dayton, Washington, April 21, 1864, SDC, France, Instructions, 17: 49, no. 533.

67. Dayton to Seward, Paris, May 16, 1864, *ibid.*, Despatches, 54: no. 466.

68. Drouyn de Lhuys to Chasseloup-Laubat, Paris, June 2, 1864, AN(M), Paris, BB³ 740, Folio 228. He made the same statement to Slidell (French foreign office to Slidell, Paris, May 10, 1864, enclosed in Slidell to Benjamin, Paris, June 2, 1864, *ORN*, 2nd ser., III, 1141).

69. Paul to Drouyn de Lhuys, Aboard the "Tisaphone" off Fortress Monroe, April 29, 1864, AMAE CC, E-U, Richmond 5: 371–373, no. 372.

70. This section is based on five letters exchanged between Benjamin and Paul: from Benjamin, May 24, 1864; from Paul, May 26, 1864; from Benjamin, May 28, May 30, May 31, 1864, all enclosed in Benjamin to Slidell, Richmond, May 31, 1864, *ORN*, 2nd ser., III, 1125–1128, 1130–1135. Bonham (*loc. cit.*, pp. 89–91) presents an analysis of the exchange, but fails to mention Benjamin's plan to "force an abandonment of the blockade by the United States."

71. Grant to Stanton, City Point, Va., Feb. 21, 1865, *The War of the Rebellion: A compilation of the Official Records of the Union and Confederate Armies* (hereafter cited as *ORA*) (Washington, 1880–1901), 1st ser., XLVI, pt. II, 608.

72. Paul to Drouyn de Lhuys, Richmond, Feb. 28, 1865, AMAE CC, E-U, Richmond 6: 119–120.

73. Paul to Drouyn de Lhuys, New York, Nov. 7, 1864, AMAE CC, E-U, Richmond 6: 65, no. 397.

74. This and the following quotations and descriptions are all taken from Paul to Drouyn de Lhuys, New York, April 11, 1865, AMAE CPC, E-U, Richmond 23, 146–152.

75. The following scenes and quotations were reported in the Washington *National Intelligencer*, April 4, 1865.

Chapter XVI

The Cessation of Hostilities

1. Evans, I, 167.

2. Seward to Dayton, Washington, Sept. 12, 1862, SDC, France, Instructions, 16: no. 193, also quoted in Owsley, p. 513. Owsley (pp. 507–513) discusses this phase of the U. S.–French understanding over Mexico.

3. Slidell to Benjamin, Paris, Jan. 25, 1864, CSDP, E, no. 54.

4. Dayton to Corwin, Paris, Feb. 3, 1864, "confidential," Dayton Papers, Box 1, AM 15236.

5. Lyons to Russell, Feb. 23, 1864, copy PRO FO 146/1143.

6. Seward to Dayton, Washington, Feb. 13, 1864, confidential, SDC, France, Instructions, 17: no. 481, also quoted in Owsley, p. 517.

7. See Owsley, pp. 514–518.

8. See above, chapter X for Drouyn's general views on foreign policy and international affairs. See also Boilleau to Drouyn de Lhuys, New York, Feb. 2, 1864, AMAE, CPC, E-U, New York, 15: 193–198, where the possibility of a joint U.S.A.-C.S.A. invasion of Mexico is first discussed.

9. Bigelow to Seward, Paris, Sept. 14, 1863, Seward Papers, confidential.

10. Gramont to Drouyn de Lhuys, Vienna, Sept. 30, 1863, Archives Nationales, Paris, Gramont Papers (63 Mi 62, 448). Although these papers are fragmentary, they reveal much of the indecision in Vienna during the winter of 1863–64. Unfortunately, they throw little light on issues affecting Paris-Washington relations.

11. Slidell to Benjamin, Paris, Dec. 3, 1863, CSDP, E, no. 50.

12. La Tour d'Auvergne to Drouyn de Lhuys, London, Feb. 17, 1864, AMAE, CP, Angleterre, 728: no. 28.

13. Slidell to Benjamin, Paris, March 5, 1864, CSDP, E, no. 57; *ORN*, 2nd ser., III, 1046–47.

14. Same to same, Paris, March 16, 1864, CSDP, E, no. 58; *ORN*, 2nd ser., III, 1063. Although Owsley (p. 521) says that "Slidell was convinced that Napoleon had checked Maximilian's plans for recognition," there is nothing in this correspondence to confirm such a statement.

15. Two dispatches from Dayton to Seward, Paris, March 11 and 25, 1864, SDC, France, Despatches, 54: nos. 430 and 440.

16. Dayton to Seward, Paris, March 18, 1864, *ibid.*, no. 436, confidential.

17. *Ibid.*, March 24, 1864, no. 442.

18. Seward to Dayton, Washington, April 8, 1864, SDC, France, Instructions, 17: 41–42, no. 524.

19. See above, chapter XIV.

20. Paul to Drouyn de Lhuys, Aboard the "Tisaphone" at Fort Monroe, April 29, 1864 (rcd. May 20, 1864), AMAE, CPC, E-U, 19: 187–188, no. 88.

21. L. M. Case, *Franco-Italian relations, 1860–1865: the Roman question and the convention of September* (Philadelphia, 1932), *passim*.

22. Drouyn de Lhuys to La Tour d'Auvergne, Paris, June 10, 1864, *Origines*, III, 201–205. Ollivier (VII, 647) confirms this, quoting a letter from Drouyn de Lhuys to Gramont, Paris, June 26, 1877.

23. Slidell to Benjamin, Paris, June 2, 1864, CSDP, E, no. 63, also in *ORN*, 2nd ser., III, 1140; Dayton to Seward, Paris, June 10, 1864, SDC, France, Despatches, 55: no. 486.

24. Geofroy to Drouyn de Lhuys, Washington, July 26, 1864, confidential and reserved and Geofroy to Montholon, Washington, July 21, 1864, Private, AMAE, CP, E-U, 131; Drouyn de Lhuys to Geofroy, Paris, Aug. 11, 1864, *ibid.*, 132: no. 15.

25. Three dispatches, Seward to Dayton, Washington, June 27, July 16, July 30, 1864, SDC, France, Instructions, 17: nos. 592, 607, 621.

26. For a thorough account of the political activities among all factions, from January through the elections in November 1864, see William Frank Zornow, *Lincoln and the party divided* (Norman, Okla., 1954), *passim.*

27. For these peace efforts, see Edward Chase Kirkland, *The peacemakers of 1864* (New York, 1927), especially chapters II and III. See also Boilleau (French consul in New York) to Drouyn de Lhuys, New York, Sept. 2, 1864, AMAE, CPC, E-U, 17: no. 63.

28. Boilleau to Drouyn de Lhuys, New York, July 25, 1864, *ibid.*, no. 52 (bis.)

29. Sept. 1, 1864, *ibid.*, no. 62.

30. Slidell to Benjamin, Paris, Sept. 24, 1864, CSDP, E, no. 72; and *ORN*, 2nd ser., III, 1217–1219, where it is dated Sept. 26, 1864.

31. Paul to Drouyn de Lhuys, Richmond, Sept. 6, 1864, AMAE, CPC, E-U, 19: no. 95.

32. Washington, Oct. 31, 1864 (rcd. Nov. 15), *ibid.*, no. 96. For the events Paul described in Alabama, see Walter L. Fleming, *Civil War and Reconstruction in Alabama* (New York, 1905), pp. 97–98. The difficulties actually revolved around the Alabamian's resentment of the Confederate Conscript Bureau and were endemic throughout the year of 1864.

33. *Constitutionnel*, Nov. 21, 1864 (prior to election results reaching France) and *Journal des Débats*, Sept. 14, 1864, as cited in West, p. 141.

34. *Journal des Débats*, Sept. 16, 1864; quote from the *Revue des deux mondes*, Oct. 1, 1864, as quoted in West, p. 142.

35. See the procureur reports from Colmar (April 27, 1864), Amiens (Oct. 8, 1864), Colmar (Oct. 27, 1864), and Rouen (Oct. 11, 1864), in Case, *U.S. and Mexico*, pp. 286, 289, 290, 291, respectively.

36. Cowley to Russell, Paris, Dec. 18, 1864, PRO FO 30/22/60, private.

37. *Journal des Débats*, Nov. 27, 1864, as quoted in West, pp. 142–143. See also West's long quote from the *Revue des deux mondes* of Dec. 1, 1864.

38. Dayton to Seward, Paris, Nov. 21, 1864, Seward Papers.

39. *Patrie*, Nov. 24, 1864.

40. See West, p. 144, where he cites each of the papers.

41. Dayton to Seward, Paris, Nov. 25, 1864, SDC, France, Despatches, 55: no. 567.

42. Seward to Dayton, Washington, January 24, 1865, SDC, France, Instructions, 17: 230–231, no. 24, confidential.

43. Procureur report, Amiens, Jan. 7, 1865, as quoted in Case, *U.S. and Mexico*, p. 292.

44. See the procureur reports from Amiens (Jan. 7, 1865), Besançon (Jan. 11, 1865), Lyons (Dec. 28, 1864), Nancy (Jan. 15, 1865), and Colmar (Jan. 19, 1865), as quoted in *ibid.*, pp. 292, 294, 293.

45. See Zornow, *passim.*

46. For this account of Dayton's death, see Bigelow, *Retrospections*, II, 234–241.

47. Three letters from Dayton to George P. Marsh, Paris, April 13 and 5, Sept. 5, 1864, Library of the University of Vermont, Burlington, Vermont, MSS, George P. Marsh Papers. See also Bigelow's letter to Marsh, *ibid.*, dated Dec. 5, 1864, describing the circumstances of Dayton's death.

48. Bigelow, *Retrospections*, II, 235.

49. Bigelow's unpublished report of Dayton's death more strongly implies a not-so-innocent relationship with Mrs. Eckels (Bigelow Papers). There were many rumors about this lady, including accusations that she was a Confederate spy as well as a courtesan.

50. Bigelow, *Retrospections*, I, 365, 368.

51. See Kirkland, *Peacemakers of 1864*, pp. 141–258, particularly pp. 199–258; Bancroft, *Seward*, II, 410–414; Adams, II, 251–253. For a short, thorough account, see J. G. Randall and David Donald, *The Civil War and Reconstruction* (2nd ed., Boston, 1961), pp. 523–525.

52. Seward to Bigelow, Washington, Feb. 7, 1865, SDC, France, Instructions, 17: 251–257, no. 34. This dispatch is Seward's official account of the Hampton Roads Conference.

53. Boilleau to Drouyn de Lhuys, New York, Jan. 17, 1865 (rcd. Feb. 1, 1865), AMAE, CPC, E-U, 20: 35–39, no. 100.

54. Geofroy to Drouyn de Lhuys, Washington, Jan. 24, 1865 (rcd. Feb. 6, 1865), AMAE, CP, E-U, 133: 65–67, no. 63.

55. Feb. 7, 1865 (rcd. Feb. 21), *ibid.*, fol. 81–88, no. 67.

56. For the most accurate reconstruction of the Hampton Roads conference, see the carefully documented account of Kirkland, pp. 234–244. Seward's account is his dispatch to Bigelow of Feb. 7, 1865, cited above, no. 52.

57. Geofroy's account was reinforced by two letters from Boilleau, the French consul in New York, to Drouyn de Lhuys, New York, Feb. 7 and 10, 1865, AMAE, CPC, E-U, New York, 20: 88–93, 94, nos. 107 and 108.

58. Drouyn de Lhuys to Geofroy, Paris, Feb. 9, 1865, AMAE, CP, E-U, 133: no. 2; and the response, *ibid.*, no. 77.

59. Drouyn de Lhuys to Chasseloup-Laubat, Paris, March 18, 1865, AN(M), BB⁴ 810, fol. 244–245.

60. Seward to Bigelow, Washington, March 6 and March 11, 1865, SDC, France, Instructions, 17: 278 and 287. See also Seward's letter to Bigelow of March 17, 1865, where he reiterates the same policy, *ibid.*, fol. 300–303, no. 71.

61. Drouyn de Lhuys to Geofroy, Paris, March 23, 1865, AMAE, CP, E-U, 133: 176–179, no. 3.

62. Bigelow to Seward, Paris, Feb. 14, 1865, SDC, France, Despatches, 56: no. 30.

63. Bigelow to Seward, Paris, Feb. 22, 1865, SDC, France, Despatches, 56: no. 37 *bis;* Bigelow to Drouyn de Lhuys, Paris, Feb. 23, 1865, copy enclosed in *ibid.*

64. See enclosure of "a rebel emissary in Canada" to Jefferson Davis, Feb. 13, 1865, in Seward to Bigelow, Washington, March 1, 1865, SDC, France, Instructions, 17: 275–277, very confidential; and W. Hunter to Bigelow, Washington, May 6, 1865, *ibid.*, fol 353–354, no. 136.

65. Hore to Russell, Paris, June 30, 1865, enclosed in Cowley to Russell, Paris, June 30, 1865, PRO FO 30/22/61. Italics are the author's.

66. Bigelow to Seward, Paris, March 3, 1865, SDC, France, Despatches, 56: no. 42.

67. This account of the Kenner Mission is based upon Owsley, pp. 530–541, especially pp. 532, 537–538.

68. Slidell to Mason, Paris, March 6, 1865, Mason Papers, also quoted in Mason to Benjamin, London, March 31, 1865, *ORN*, 2nd ser., III, 1270–71, and cited in Owsley, p. 538.

69. *Moniteur*, April 11, 1865, reporting the debates of April 10, 1865. Translation is from Bigelow's enclosure to Seward, as published in Bigelow, *Retrospections*, II, 483–484.

70. *Moniteur*, April 16, 1865, reporting the debates of April 15, 1865. Translation is from Bigelow, *Retrospections*, II, 499–500.

71. Paul to Drouyn de Lhuys, New York, April 11, 1865, AMAE, CPC, E-U, Richmond, 23: 146–152; see W. F. Spencer, "A French View of the Fall of Richmond," *The Virginia magazine of history and biography*, LXXIII (1965), 178–188, for a detailed analysis of this report.

72. *Constitutionnel*, April 19, 1865; *Pays*, April 16, 1865; *Revue contemporaine*, April 30, 1865, all cited in West, pp. 145–146.

73. *Journal des Débats*, April 16, 1865; *Opinion Nationale*, April 16, 1865; *Temps*, April 16, 1865; *Revue des deux mondes*, March 15, 1865, all cited in West, pp. 146–147. For longer quotes, see Bigelow, *Retrospections*, II, 502–507.

74. Procureur General report from Besançon, July 8, 1865, as quoted in Case, *U.S. and Mexico*, p. 301.

75. Procureur General report from Nancy, April 24, 1865, as quoted in *ibid.*, p. 378.

76. See the procureur reports from those cities respectively in *ibid.*, pp. 299, 303.

77. Procureur reports, Riom (April 6, 1865), Bordeaux (July 13, 1865), and Nîmes (July 11, 1865), *ibid.*, pp. 300, 301, 303, respectively.

78. Procureur reports from Amiens (July 8, 1865), Douai (July 1, 1865), and Paris (August 4, 1865), *ibid.*, pp. 300, 302, 303 respectively.

79. Carl Sandburg, *Abraham Lincoln, the war years* (New York, 1939), IV, pp. 272–298 and Jim Bishop, *The Day Lincoln was shot* (New York, 1955), *passim*, are both exciting and detailed accounts of the day's events. See also Frederick Bancroft, *The life of William H. Seward* (New York, 1900), II, pp. 416–417.

80. Bigelow, *Retrospections*, II, 519.

81. Bigelow to Seward, Paris, April 28, 1865, *ibid.*, pp. 522–523.

82. *Moniteur*, April 27, 1865.

83. Bigelow to Seward, Paris, April 28, 1865, Bigelow, *Retrospections*, II, 523. See A. A. Woldman, *Lincoln and the Russians* (New York, 1952), pp. 261–276, for the Russian tributes to Lincoln, and especially pp. 272–273 for Count Tolstoy's account of a Circassian chieftain's tribute, deep in the Caucasian Mountains. United States State Department, *Appendix to diplomatic correspondence of 1865, the assassination of Abraham Lincoln* (Washington, 1866), Part 4, (hereafter referred to as *Dipl. corresp., 1865*, pt. 4), contains the messages of condolence from around the world.

84. *Dipl. corresp.*, pt. 4, 50. These notes of sympathy can be found in SDC, France, Despatches, 58, and some in Bigelow, *Retrospections*, II; but *Dipl. corresp.*, 1865, pt. 4, contains all of them in an easily located volume. It alone will hereafter be cited.

85. *Dipl. corresp.*, pt. 4, 50–51.

86. *Ibid.*, pp. 52–53.

87. *Ibid.*, p. 57. The phrase "Statue of liberty" was used figuratively because the actual statue was not placed in New York harbor until 1886. It is interesting that the phrase should have been used in connection with Lincoln's career by a Frenchman.

88. *Ibid.*, p. 74.

89. Bigelow to William Cullen Bryant, Paris, May 16, 1865, in Bigelow, *Retrospections*, II, 558.

90. A reproduction of the medal and letters concerning the suppression of the Nantes subscription effort, as well as the cover letter, are in a privately published pamphlet, *A French tribute to Lincoln and a three part poem: Abraham Lincoln* (Redlands, Calif., 1936), with an introduction by E. M. Freeman, M.D., and the article on the French tribute to Lincoln signed only by the initials "J.B.G." The pamphlet, including the poem, is ten pages long. The letters pertinent to this section, and which are reproduced in the pamphlet, are also in Bigelow, *Retrospections*, II, 596–597, III, 53–54, 57.

91. *Dipl. corresp., 1865, pt. 4*, pp. 124–126. West (pp. 150–151) cites these same paragraphs, but he fails to acknowledge the particular republican thrust; he also places the article in the *Courrier du Dimanche* of May 10, 1865, where it probably appeared as a reprint from the *Journal des Débats* of April 29, 1865.

92 *Avenir National*, April 28, 1865, article signed by A. Peyrat; the earlier quote was from the issue of May 4, 1865. Both are in *Dipl. corresp.*, 1865, pt. 4, pp. 113 and 110, respectively.

93. See the excerpts from *La France*, May 3, 1865, *Le Pays*, April 28, 1865, *Le Temps*, April 28, 1865, and a "Political Letter" appearing in the *Gazette de France*, April 30, 1865, all found in *Dipl. corresp.*, 1865, pt. 4, pp. 118, 135, 143, 121, respectively.

94. Procureur reports from Amiens (July 8, 1865), Besançon (July 8, 1865), Bordeaux (July 13, 1865), Caen (July 8, 1865), Nancy (July 18, 1865), and Paris (August 4, 1865), as quoted in Case, *U.S. and Mexico*, pp. 300, 301, 302, 303, and 304 respectively.

95. Report of procureur general in Caen (July 8, 1865), as quoted in *ibid.*, p. 302,

96. Quotes and interpolated conversation taken from Bigelow to Seward, Paris, March 17, 1865, SDC, France, Despatches, 56: no. 62; also in Bigelow, *Retrospections*, II, 421.

97. Seward to Bigelow, Washington, March 15, 1865, SDC, France, Instructions-17: 298–300, no. 70 *bis*.

98. Bigelow to Drouyn de Lhuys, Paris, May 4, 1865, AMAE, Mémoires et Documents, Etats-Unis, 1848–1865, XXV, 227–277. For a text of the proclamations, see R. P. Basler, ed., *The Collected Works of Abraham Lincoln* (New Brunswick, N. J., 1953), VII, 396–398.

99. Bigelow to Drouyn de Lhuys, Paris, May 10, 1865, AMAE, Mémoires et Documents, Etats-Unis, 1848–1865, XXV, 335–338; Bigelow to Seward, Paris, May 19, 1865, SDC, France, Despatches, 57: no. 91; Drouyn de Lhuys to Geofroy, Paris, May 18, 1865, AMAE, CP, E-U, 134: no. 11.

100. Cowley to Russell, Paris, April 22, 1865, PRO, FO 27/1570/495.

101. Drouyn de Lhuys to La Tour d'Auvergne, Paris, March 28, 1865, AMAE, CP, Angleterre, 732: no. 35; and La Tour d'Auvergne's responses from London, *ibid.*, March 31, 1865, no. 47 and April 15, 1865, no. 56; Drouyn de Lhuys to Geofroy, Paris, March 30, 1865, *ibid.*, CP, E-U, 133: no. 4; Cowley to Russell, Paris, March 30, 1865, PRO FO 27/1569/386.

102. Drouyn de Lhuys to La Tour d'Auvergne, Paris, April 28, 1865, no. 50, copy, AMAE, Mémoires et Documents XXV, Etats-Unis, 1848–1865; La Tour d'Auvergne to Drouyn de Lhuys, London, April 30, 1865, AMAE, CP, Angleterre, 732: no. 66.

103. Drouyn de Lhuys to La Tour d'Auvergne, May 15, 1865, no. 78, and the response, London May 17, 1865, both in AMAE, CP, Angleterre, 733.

104. Geofroy to Drouyn de Lhuys, Washington, Jan. 16, 1865, and May 2, 1865, AMAE, CP, E-U, 133: no. 60; and 134: no. 86, respectively; Cazotte to Drouyn de Lhuys, San Francisco, April 12, 1865, *ibid.*, CPC, 23: no. 24.

105. Cowley to Russell, Paris, May 23, 1865, PRO FO 27/1572/590. In referring to Drouyn's anxiety, Cowley used the verb tense "had been."

106. Bigelow to Seward, Paris, May 5, 1865, SDC, France, Despatches, 57: no. 88; also in Bigelow, *Retrospections*, II, 535–536. For Drouyn's account of this conversation, see Drouyn de Lhuys to Geofroy, Paris, May 2, 1865, AMAE, CP, E-U, 134: no. 10.

107. Drouyn de Lhuys to La Tour d'Auvergne, Paris, May 18, 1865, AMAE, CP, Angleterre, 733: no. 59.

108. Cowley to Drouyn de Lhuys, Paris, May 18, 1865, AMAE, Mémoires et Documents, Etats-Unis, 1848–1865. See Adams, *Great Britain and the Civil War*, II, 265–269, for Russell's actions on withdrawing the English recognition of belligerency.

109. Drouyn de Lhuys to French consul at Liverpool, Paris, May 19, 1865 (1:15 P.M.), AMAE, CP, E-U, unnumbered telegram. For the instructions to the minister of the marine, see Drouyn de Lhuys to Chasseloup-Laubat, Paris, May 20, 1865, and Chasseloup-Laubat's affirmative response, dated May 27, 1865, both in AMAE, Mémoires et Documents, Etats-Unis, 1848–1865. Actually the order was sent out on May 23 (directive from Chasseloup-Laubat's office, May 23, 1865, AM, BB⁴/ 1345/I).

110. Drouyn carefully notified Cowley of his actions and received Earl Russell's approval (Cowley to Russell, Paris, May 23, 1865, PRO FO 27/1572/589; and La Tour d'Auvergne to Drouyn de Lhuys, London, May 25, 1865, AMAE, CP, Angleterre, 733: no. 84).

111. Drouyn de Lhuys to Bigelow, Paris, May 19 and May 20, 1865, AMAE, Mémoires et Documents, Etats-Unis, 1848–1865. Copies of both letters enclosed in Bigelow to Seward, Paris, May 23, 1865, SDC, France, Despatches, 57: nos. 98 and 99.

112. Bigelow to Seward, Paris, May 23, 1863, SDC, France, Despatches, 57: no. 98; and Bigelow to Drouyn de Lhuys, Paris, May 29, 1865, AMAE, Mémoires et Documents, Etats-Unis, 1848–1865, with copies in Bigelow, *Retrospections*, III, 50–53 and enclosed in Bigelow to Seward, Paris, June 1, 1865, SDC, France, Despatches, 57: no. 111.

113. Drouyn de Lhuys to La Tour d'Auvergne, Paris, May 29, 1865, and the response, dated London, June 2, 1865, both found in AMAE, CP, Angleterre, 733, nos. 61 and 87. Bigelow was fully aware of this close coordination of policy (Bigelow to Seward, Paris, June 1, 1865, SDC, France, Despatches, 57: no. 111). The Cowley-Russell correspondence also reflects the close cooperation: see Russell to Cowley, London, May 30, 1865, PRO FO 27/1197, in which Russell submitted for Drouyn a draft of the proposed English proclamation; Cowley to Russell, Paris, May 31, (no. 631), June 3 (nos. 645 and 646), PRO FO 27/1572, which report agreement and concurrence as well as a mutual exchange of all the correspondence on the subject.

See also Drouyn's two letters to La Tour d'Auvergne of June 1 and 2, AMAE, CP, Angleterre, 733: nos. 64 and 66. Adams (*Great Britain and the Civil War*, II, 267) fails to acknowledge this close coordination between the two governments.

114. Drouyn de Lhuys to Montholon, Paris, May 30, 1865, AMAE, CP, E-U, 134: no. 14. Also published in *Doc. dipl.* 1866, pp. 92–93.

115. Drouyn de Lhuys to Bigelow, Paris, May 31, 1865, AMAE, Mémoires et Documents, Etats-Unis, 1848–1865. The original is in Drouyn's own handwriting. A copy is enclosed in Bigelow to Seward, Paris, June 1, 1865, SDC, France, Despatches, 57: no. 111.

116. Bigelow to Drouyn de Lhuys, Paris, June 12, 1865, AMAE, Mémoires et Documents, Etats-Unis, 1848–65; Bigelow to Seward, Paris, June 13, 1865, SDC, France, Despatches, 58, no. 117 (enclosing a copy of his letter to Drouyn); Drouyn de Lhuys to Bigelow, Paris, June 17, 1865, AMAE, Mémoires et Documents, Etats-Unis, 1848–65; Seward to Bigelow, Washington, June 17, 1865, SDC, France, Instructions, 17: 386–387, no. 176.

117. Drouyn de Lhuys to Chasseloup-Laubat, Paris, June 3, 1865, AN(M), BB³ 747, fol. 247–251. A copy of the circular issued to the French officials was sent to Bigelow on June 9 (enclosed in Bigelow to Seward, Paris, June 9, 1865, SDC, France, Despatches, 58: no. 116).

118. Borg to Drouyn de Lhuys, New York, May 29, 1865, AMAE, CPC, E-U, 21: no. 8.

119. Seward to Bigelow, Washington, June 3, 1865, SDC, France, Instructions, 17: 370–372. For Drouyn's reaction and comments, see Bigelow to Seward, Paris, June 29, 1865, Seward Papers; and Drouyn de Lhuys to Montholon, Paris, July 6, 1865, AMAE, CP, E-U, 134: no. 21.

120. Seward to Bigelow, Washington, June 12, 1865, SDC, France, Instructions, 17: 378–381, no. 167.

121. For the details of this fête, see Bigelow, *Retrospections*, III, 106–107.

Chapter XVII

Men and Issues

1. Owsley, pp. 281, 291.

2. See Chapter IV.

3. Coulter, *Confederate States*, p. 294.

4. For a discussion of these opinion reports and extracts from them on the United States and Mexico during these years, see L. M. Case, *United States and Mexico*, especially pp. vii–xx.

5. See Napoleon III's earlier idea of an isthmian canal separating the Latin and Anglo-Saxon spheres in America in Louis Napoleon Bonaparte, *Canal of Nicaragua: or, a project to connect the Atlantic and Pacific Oceans by means of a canal* (London, 1846). See also La Gorce, *Second Empire*, IV, 12–17.

6. For a recent thorough study on this French envoy, see Daniel B. Carroll's "Mercier in Washington" (a Ph. D. dissertation at the University of Pennsylvania, 1968).

7. On French press opinion, see W. R. West, *Contemporary French opinion of the American Civil War* (Baltimore, 1924), especially for this quotation, p. 152; Owsley, pp. 87, 183, 179, 196, 222–223; and D. Jordan and E. J. Pratt, *Europe and the American Civil War* (New York, 1931), pp. 218–219, 228. For a critique of French press opinion as a mirror of general opinion, see Case, *United States and Mexico*, pp. vii–xi, and the same author's *French opinion on war and diplomacy during the Second Empire* (Philadelphia, 1954), pp. 2–6.

8. For a discussion of the procureur reports, see Case, *United States and Mexico*, pp. xiii–xx; and his *French opinion on war*, pp. 6–10.

9. For this final survey of French opinion on the Civil War, see Case, *United States and Mexico*, pp. 244, 257–258, 281, 297–298.

10. See the La Valette Circular, Sept. 16, 1866, in the *Moniteur*, Sept. 17, 1866. For an English translation of the circular, see Case, *French opinion on war*, pp. 222–224.

BIBLIOGRAPHY

MANUSCRIPT SOURCES

OFFICIAL ARCHIVES.

Austria.

Haus-, Hof-, und Staatsarchiv (HHSA). Vienna. Politische Akten (PA). Vereinigte Staaten. Correspondence from Hülsemann, 1861–1862.

Bremen (Hansestadt Bremen).

Microfilm copies of Berichte des Minister Residents Schleidens, Correspondence with the Bremen Senate, 1861–1865. Library of Congress, Washington. Manuscripts Division.

France.

Archives de la Marine (AM). Paris. Fonds BB⁴ 1345, 1346.
Archives du Ministère des Affaires étrangères (AMAE). Paris.
Correspondance Politique (CP).
Angleterre, 1861–1865.
Etats-Unis, 1861–1865.
Correspondance Politique Consulaire (CPC)
Etats-Unis: Consulats de New York, Baltimore, Richmond, Charlestown, New Orleans, 1861–1865.
Fonds Divers.
Guerre des Etats-Unis, 1861–1865 (Etats Confédérés; Droit Maritime).
Archives Nationales (AN). Paris.
Ministère de la Justice. BB³⁰ Rapports périodiques des Procureurs Généraux, 1861–1865. Contain reports on economic conditions and public opinion in each of the twenty-eight judicial districts of France.

Ministère de la Marine (AN [M]). Fonds BB² 419; BB⁴ 810, 836; GG² 42.

Great Britain.

Public Record Office (PRO). London. Foreign Office Series (FO).
France. Despatches to and from Earl Cowley, 1861–1865.
United States. Despatches to and from Lord Lyons, 1861–1865.

Russia.

Russian Central Archives. Foreign Affairs. United States.
Library of Congress. Washington. Manuscripts Division.
Photostats of correspondence of Baron Stoeckl to Prince Gorchakov, 1861–1865.

Sweden.

Riksarkivet. Stockholm. Foreign Ministry Correspondence.
Diplomatica Gallica (France). Correspondence from Frederik Due, 1861–1865.
Diplomatica Americana (United States). Correspondence from Count Piper, 1861–1865.

United States.

Library of Congress. Washington. Manuscripts Division.
Confederate States of America. Department of State Papers (CSDP) (often referred to as the "Pickett Papers"). Slidell-Benjamin correspondence, 1862–1865.
National Archives (NA). Washington. Foreign Affairs Division. State Department Correspondence (SDC).
Belgium, Despatches, 1861–1862.
Belgium, Instructions, 1861–1862.
France, Despatches, 1861–1865.
France, Instructions, 1861–1865.

France, Notes to and from the French Legation, 1861–1865.

Great Britain, Despatches, 1861–1865.

Great Britain, Instructions, 1861–1865.

Great Britain, Notes to and from the British Legation.

Records of the Foreign Service Posts of the United States. Record Group 84. Dayton-Thouvenel correspondence, Paris, May 1861–October 1862.

PRIVATE PAPERS.

Adams Papers. Massachusetts Historical Society Microfilms. Boston.

Adams, Charles Francis. Diary. Massachusetts Historical Society Microfilms. Boston.

Bigelow, John. Papers. New York Public Library. New York City.

Billault, Adolphe. Fonds Adolphe Billault. Dossier Thouvenel (20 J 53). Archives Départementales de la Loire-Atlantique. Nantes.

Cowley, Henry Richard Charles Wellesley, First Earl. Public Record Office (PRO). Foreign Office Series (FO 519). London.

Dayton, William L. Papers. Princeton University Library. Princeton.

Eustis, George, Jr. Papers. Library of Congress. Washington. Manuscripts Division.

Gramont, Antoine Agénor Alfred, Duke of. Papiers. Archives Nationales (AN). Paris. Microfilms (63 Mi 62).

La Valette, Charles J. M. F., Marquis de. Papiers. Archives Nationales (AN). Fonds AB XIX 3038.

Lincoln, Abraham. Papers. Library of Congress. Washington. Manuscripts Division Microfilms.

Marsh, George P. Papers. University of Vermont Library. Burlington, Vermont.

Mason, James S. Papers. Library of Congress. Washington. Manuscripts Division.

Mercier de l'Ostende, Henri, Baron. Papiers de la Famille Le Cour Grandmaison. Château de Montaigne, par La Mothe-Montravel (Dordogne).

Palmerston, Henry John Temple, Viscount Letterbooks. British Museum (BM). London. Manuscripts Division.

Palmerston, Henry John Temple, Viscount. Papers. Historical Manuscripts Commission. National Register of Archives. London.

Pecquet de Bellet, Paul. The diplomacy of the Confederate cabinet at Richmond and its agents abroad. Memorandum notes taken in Paris during the rebellion of the Southern states from 1861–1865. Typed manuscript. Library of Congress. Washington. Manuscripts Division.

Rouher, Eugène. Papiers. Archives du Ministère des Affaires étrangères (AMAE). Paris. Mémoires et Documents (MD). 4 v. Vol. III, Pays Divers. Vol. IV, Mexique.

Rouher, Eugène. Papiers. Archives Nationales (AN). Paris. Fonds 45 AP 3.

Russell, John, First Earl. Papers. Public Record Office (PRO). London. Foreign Office Series (FO 30/22).

Sanford, Henry Shelton. Papers. General Sanford Memorial Library, Sanford, Florida.

Schleiden, Herr Minister Resident Rudolph. Privatbriefen, 1861–1862. Library of Congress. Washington. Manuscripts Division Microfilms.

Seward, William Henry. Papers. University of Rochester Rhees Library. Rochester, New York. Special Collections.

Thouvenel, Antoine Edouard. Papiers de Thouvenel. 20 v. Archives du Ministère des Affaires étrangères (AMAE). Paris. Mémoires et Documents (MD).

Thouvenel, Antoine Edouard. Papiers de la Famille Thouvenel. Archives Nationales. Paris. Microfilms MI 192.

Weed, Thurlow. Papers. University of Rochester Rhees Library. Rochester, New York. Special Collections.

Whittle Papers. Norfolk Public Library. Norfolk, Virginia. Correspondence of Commodore Barron and other Confederate naval officers with James D. Bulloch.

PUBLISHED SOURCES*

Adams Family. *A cycle of Adams letters, 1861–1865.* Ed. by C. Worthington Ford. 2 v. Boston, 1920.

Adams, Henry. *The letters of Henry Adams, 1858–1891.* Ed. by C. Worthington Ford. Boston, 1930.

Albert, Prince Consort. Theodore Martin, *The life of H. R. H. the Prince Consort.* 5 v. London, 1875–1880.

Bates, Edward. *The diary of Edward Bates, 1859–1866.* Ed. by Howard K. Beale, in the *Annual report of the American Historical Association,* IV (1930). Washington, 1933.

Baxter, James P., 3rd. "Papers relating to belligerent and neutral rights," *American historical review,* XXXIV (Oct. 1928), 77–91.

Beyens, Baron Eugène. *Le Second Empire vu par un diplomate belge.* Ed. by Baron Napoléon Beyens. 2 v. Paris, 1925.

Bigelow, John. *Retrospections of an active life.* 5 v. New York, 1909.

Browning, Senator Orville Hickman. *The Diary of Orville Hickman Browning.* Ed. by Theodore C. Pease and James G. Randall. ("Collections of the Illinois State Historical Library," vols. XX and XXII.) 2 v. Springfield, Illinois, 1925, 1933.

Bulloch, James Dunwoody. *The secret service of the Confederate States in Europe: or how the Confederate cruisers were equipped.* New York, 1884.

Butler, Major General Benjamin F. *Autobiography and personal reminiscences of Major General Benjamin F. Butler: Butler's book.* Boston, 1892.

——. *Private and official correspondance of General Benjamin F. Butler during the period of the Civil War.* 5 v. Norwood, Massachusetts, 1917.

Campbell, John A. "Papers of the Hon. John A. Campbell, 1861–1865," *Southern historical society papers,* XLI (Oct. 1917), 3–80.

*The printed papers or memoirs of private individuals are arranged alphabetically by their subject names rather than by those of the editors.

————. *Reminiscences and documents relating to the Civil War during the year 1865.* Baltimore, 1887.

Chase, Salmon P. *Inside Lincoln's cabinet: the Civil War diaries of Salmon P. Chase.* Ed. by David Donald. New York, 1954.

Clarendon, George William Frederick, Fourth Earl of. Sir Herbert Eustace Maxwell. *The Life and Letters of George William Frederick, Fourth Earl of Clarendon.* 2 v. London, 1913.

Claude, M. *Memoirs of M. Claude, chief of police under the Second Empire.* Tr. by Katherine Wormeley. London, 1908.

Confederate States. *Compilations of messages and papers of the Confederacy, including diplomatic correspondence, 1861–1865.* Ed. by James D. Richardson. Washington, 1905.

————. *Journal of the congress of the Confederate States of America, 1861–1865.* Senate Document, 58th Congress, 1st session, no. 234, vols. 25–31. Washington, 1904–1905.

Constitutionnel, 1861–1865.

Cowley, Henry Richard Charles, First Earl. *Conversations with Napoleon III: a collection of documents mostly unpublished and almost entirely diplomatic, selected and arranged with introductions.* Ed. by Victor Wellesley and Robert Sencourt. London, 1934.

————. *Secrets of the Second Empire: private letters from the Paris embassy during the Second Empire; selections from the papers of Henry Richard Charles Wellesley, 1st Earl of Cowley, ambassador to Paris, 1852–1867.* Ed. by F. A. Wellesley. London, 1928.

Davis, Jefferson. *Jefferson Davis, constitutionalist, his letters, papers, and speeches.* Ed. by Dunbar Roland. 10 v. Jackson, Mississippi, 1923.

————. *The rise and fall of the Confederate government.* 2 v. New York, 1881.

De Leon, Edwin. *Thirty years of my life on three continents.* London, 1890.

Dumond, Dwight L., ed. *Southern editorials on secession.* New York, 1931.

Evans, Dr. Thomas W. *Memoirs of Dr. Thomas W. Evans.* Ed. by Edward R. Crane M.D. 2nd impression. 2 v. London, 1906.

Examiner (Richmond), Nov. 1862.

Ferri-Pisani, Lieutenant Colonel Camille. *Lettres sur les Etats-Unis d'Amérique.* Paris, 1862.

————. *Prince Napoleon in America: letters from his aide-de-camp.* Tr. by Georges J. Joyaux. Bloomington, Indiana, 1959.

Fleury, General Emile Félix, comte de. *Memoirs of the Empress Eugénie by comte de Fleury: compiled from statements, private documents and personal letters of the Empress Eugénie, from conversations with Napoleon III and from family letters and papers of General Fleury, M. Franceschini Pietri, Prince Victor Napoleon and other members of the court of the Second Empire.* 2 v. New York, 1920.

France. *Archives diplomatiques, recueil de diplomatie et d'histoire.* Années 1861–1863. 12 v. Paris, 1862–1864.

————. *Exposé de la situation de l'empire présenté au sénat et au corps législatif.* 10 v. Paris, 1861–1869.

————. *French opinion on the United States and Mexico, 1861–1867. Reports of the procureurs généraux.* Ed. by Lynn M. Case. New York, 1936. Reprint. Archon Books, 1969.

————. Ministère des Affaires Etrangères. *Documents diplomatiques (Livres Jaunes).* Années 1861, 1862, 1863, 1866. Paris, 1861–1863, 1866.

————. Ministère des Affaires Etrangères. *Origines diplomatiques de la guerre de 1870–71. Recueil de documents publié par le ministère des affaires étrangères.* 17 v. Paris, 1910–1928.

Garcia, G. "La intervención francesa en México, segun el archivo del mariscal Bazaine." *Documentos . . . para la historia de México,* XXXIII. Mexico, 1910.

Gladstone, William E. *See* below under Palmerston.

Golder, Frank A., ed. *Guide to materials for American history in Russian archives.* 2 v. Washington, 1917, 1937.

Great Britain. *British and foreign state papers.* Years 1861–1865. London, 1862–1866.

————. *Foundations of British foreign policy from Pitt (1792) to Salisbury (1902) or documents old and new.* Ed. by Harold Temperley and Lillian Penson. Cambridge, 1938. Especially Ch. XV.

————. *Hansard's parliamentary debates.* 3rd series. Years 1861–1865. London, 1861–1865.

————. *Sessional papers.* 1861, Vol. LXV; 1862, Vol. LXII; 1863, Vol. LXXII; 1864, Vol. LXII; 1865, Vol. LVII. London, 1861–1865.

Gurowski, Adam. *Diary.* 3 v. Washington, 1862–1866.

Hay, John. *Lincoln and the Civil War in the diaries and letters of John Hay.* Ed. by Tyler Dennett. New York, 1939.

Hübner, Baron Joseph Alexandre de. *Neuf ans de souvenirs d'un ambassadeur d'Autriche à Paris sous le Second Empire (1851–1859).* Ed. by his son, comte Alexandre de Hübner. 2 v. Paris, 1904.

Hughes, Archbishop John. *Complete works of John Hughes.* Ed. by Lawrence L. Kehoe. 2nd ed. New York, 1865.

Italy. Ministero degli Affari Esteri. *I documenti diplomatici italiani.* Ed. by La Commissione per la Pubblicazione dei Documenti Diplomatici. 1st series: ed. by Walther Maturi, 1861–1870. Vol. I (1861); vol. II (Jan.–July 1862). Rome, 1952, 1959.

Journal des Débats, 1861–1865.

Lesseps, Ferdinand de. *Recollections of forty years.* Tr. by D. C. Pitman. 2 v. London, 1887.

Lieber, Francis. "Papers of Francis Lieber," ed. by C. B. Robson, *Huntington library bulletin,* no. 3 (1933), pp. 135–152.

Lincoln, Abraham. *Collected works of Abraham Lincoln.* Ed. by Roy P. Basler. 8 v. New Brunswick, New Jersey, 1953.

————. *Complete works of Abraham Lincoln.* Ed. by John G. Nicolay, John Hay, and F. D. Tandy. New ed. 12 v. New York, 1905.

Mexico. *Correspondencia de la legación mexicana en Washington durante la intervención extranjera, 1860–1868: collección de documentos para formar la historia de la intervención.* Ed. by Mathias Ramero. 10 v. Mexico City, 1870–1892.

Moniteur Universel, journal officiel de l'Empire Français, 1861–1865.

Moore, Frank, ed. *The Rebellion record: a diary of American events, with documents, narratives, illustrative incidents, etc.* 11 v. New York, 1861–1868.

Motley, John Lothrop. *The correspondence of John Lothrop Motley.* Ed. by G. W. Curtis. 2 v. New York, 1889.

Napoleon III. *Papiers sauvés des Tuileries.* Ed. by R. Halt. Paris, 1871.

―――. *Papiers secrets et correspondance du Second Empire* [retrouvés au Palais des Tuileries]. 2 v. Paris, 1873.

―――. *See also* Prince Napoleon, Cowley.

Napoleon, Prince Jerome. *The Second Empire and its downfall: the correspondence of the Emperor Napoleon III and his cousin Prince Napoleon.* Ed. by Ernest d'Hauterive. Tr. by H. Wilson. New York, 1925.

―――. Ernest d'Hauterive, "Voyage du Prince Napoleon aux Etats-Unis, 1861." *Revue de Paris,* XL (1933), 241–272, 549–587.

―――. See also Ferri-Pisani.

National Intelligencer (Washington), 1861–1865.

New York Herald, 1861–1865.

New York Times, 1861–1865.

Ollivier, Emile. *L'Empire libéral: études, récits, souvenirs.* 18 v. Paris, 1895–1918.

―――. *Journal, 1846–1869.* Ed. by Theodore Zeldin. 2 v. Paris, 1961.

Palmerston, Henry John Temple, Viscount. *Gladstone and Palmerston, being the correspondence of Lord Palmerston with Mr. Gladstone, 1851–1865.* Ed. by Philip Guedalla. London, 1928.

―――. *The life and correspondence of Henry John Temple Viscount Palmerston.* Author and Editor, Evelyn Ashley. 2 v. London, 1879.

Pecquet de Bellet, Paul. *The diplomacy of the Confederate cabinet of Richmond and its agents abroad: being memorandum notes taken in Paris during the rebellion of the Southern States from 1861 to 1863.* Ed. by William Stanley Hoole. Tuscaloosa, Alabama, 1963.

Perkins, Howard C., ed. *Northern editorials on secession.* 2 v. New York, 1942.

Pradier-Fodéré, P. L. E., ed. *Documents pour l'histoire contemporaine.* Paris, 1871.

Prim, Marshal Juan, Count of Reus. Louis Savinhiac, "L'Espagne et l'expédition du Mexique. Une lettre inédite du maréchal Prim (1862)," *Revue historique,* XXXVI (1888), 335–353.

Raymond, Henry J. "Extracts from the journal of Henry J. Raymond," *Scribner's monthly*, XIX (March 1880), 708–713; XX (June 1880), 275–280.

Revue de deux mondes (Paris). *Chronique politique*, 1861–1865.

Rothschild, Salomon de. *The home letters of Salomon de Rothschild, 1859–1861*. Ed. by Sigmund Diamond. Stanford, California, 1961.

Russell, John, First Earl. *The later correspondence of Lord John Russell, 1840–1878*. Ed. by G. P. Gooch. 2 v. London, 1925.

Russell, William H. "The London Times' American correspondent in 1861; unpublished letters of W. H. Russell," ed. by Louis Sears, *Historical outlook*, XVI (1925), 251–257.

————. *My diary North and South*. New York, 1863.

Russia. E. A. Adamov, ed., "Documents relating to Russian policy during the American Civil War," *Journal of modern history*, II (1930), 603–611.

Sand, Maurice. *Six milles lieues à toute vapeur* Paris, 1862.

Seward, Frederick William. *Reminiscencess of a war-time statesman and diplomat, 1830–1915*. New York, 1915.

Seward William H. *The diplomatic history of the war for the Union, being the fifth volume of the works of William H. Seward*. Boston, 1884.

————. *Seward at Washington as senator and secretary of state: a memoir of his life with selections from his letters*. Ed. by Frederick W. Seward. 2 v. New York, 1891.

————. *The works of William H. Seward*. Ed. by G. E. Baker. New ed. 5 v. Boston, 1890.

Siècle, Le (Paris), 1861–1865.

Sumner, Senator Charles. "Bright-Sumner letters, 1861–1872," ed. by Edward L. Pierce, *Proceedings* of the Massachusetts Historical Society, XLVI (Oct. 1912), 93–164.

————. "Letters of the Duke and Duchess of Argyll to Charles Sumner," ed. by M. Pearson, *Proceedings* of the Massachusetts Historical Society, XLVII (Dec. 1913), 66–107.

————. "Letters of Richard Cobden to Charles Sumner, 1862–1865," ed. by Edward L. Pierce, *American historical review*, II (1897), 306–319.

———. *Memoirs and letters of Charles Sumner*. Ed. by Edward L. Pierce. 4 v. Boston, 1877-1893.

———. *Speech on maritime rights, January 9, 1862.* Washington, 1862.

———. *Works of Charles Sumner.* 15 v. Boston, 1870–1883.

Thouvenel, Antoine Edouard. *Pages d'histoire du Second Empire d'après les papiers de M. Thouvenel, ancien ministre des affaires étrangères.* Ed. by Louis Thouvenel. Paris, 1903.

———. *Le secret de l'empereur: correspondance confidentielle et inédite échangée entra M. Thouvenel, le duc de Gramont, et le général comte de Flahault, 1860–1863* Ed. by Louis Thouvenel. 2. v. Paris, 1889.

Times, The (London), 1861–1865.

Tribune (New York), 1861–1865.

United States. *A compilation of the messages and papers of the presidents, 1789–1897.* Ed. by James D. Richardson. 10 v. Washington, 1896–1899.

———. *Congressional globe,* 1861–1865. Washington, 1862–1866.

———. *District of Columbia reports. Reports of cases civil and criminal argued and adjudged in the Circuit Court of the District of Columbia.* Washington, 1895. Vol. II, pp. 275–282, deals with the case of the "Tropic Wind" and the blockade.

———. Department of the Navy. *Official records of the Union and Confederate navies in the War of the Rebellion (ORN).* 1st series, v. 1–27; 2nd series, v. 1–3. 30 v. and Index. Washington, 1894–1927.

———. Department of State. *Exposé de la situation politique et militaire aux Etats-Unis; circulaire adressée par M. W. -H. Seward aux consuls des Etats-Unis en Europe.* Paris, 1863.

———. Department of State. *Papers relating to the foreign affairs [relations] of the United States, 1861–1865 (FRUS).* 10 v. Washington, 1862–1866.

———. Department of State. *Appendix to diplomatic correspondence of 1865, the assassination of Abraham Lincoln.* Part 4 of *Diplomatic correspondence, 1865.* Washington, 1866.

———. *Treaties, conventions, international acts, protocols, and agreements between the United States of America and the other powers, 1776–1923.* Ed. by William M. Malloy. 3 v. Washington, 1910, 1923.

————. *United States ministers to the Papal States, instructions and despatches, 1848–1868.* Ed. by Leo F. Stock. Baltimore, 1933.

————. War Department. *Official records of the Union and Confederate armies in the War of the Rebellion.* 128 v. Washington, 1880–1901.

Victoria, Queen. *Letters of Queen Victoria, a selection from Her Majesty's correspondence between the years 1837 and 1861, first series.* Ed. by Arthur C. Benson and Viscount Esher. New ed. 3 v. London, 1908.

————. *Letters of Queen Victoria, second series, a selection from Her Majesty's correspondence and journals, 1862–1885.* Ed. by George E. Buckle. 3 v. London, 1927.

Viel-Castel, Horace de. *Mémoires sur le régne de Napoléon III, 1851–1864, publiés d'après le manuscrit original.* 6 v. Paris, 1883–1884. English translation, ed. by Charles Bousfield, 2 v. London, 1888.

Walewski, Count Alexander Colonna. G. Raindre, ed., "Les papiers inédits du comte Walewski," *Revue de France,* XI (1925), 82–96.

Weed, Thurlow. *Life of Thurlow Weed.* Ed. by Harriet A. Weed and Thurlow Weed Barnes. I. Autobiography; II. Memoirs. 2 v. Boston, 1883–1884.

Welles, Gideon. *Diary of Gideon Welles Secretary of the Navy under Lincoln and Johnson.* Introduction by John T. Morse, Jr. 3 v. New York & Boston, 1911.

Published Historical Studies*

Adamov, E. A. "Russia and the United States at the time of the Civil War," *Journal of modern history,* II (Dec. 1930), 586–602.

Adams, Charles Francis. Martin B. Duberman, *Charles Francis Adams, 1807–1886.* Boston, 1961.

————. Charles Francis Adams, Jr., *Charles Francis Adams.* Boston, 1900.

*Biographies are listed alphabetically by biographee rather than by biographer.

————. *The struggle for neutrality in America: an address delivered before the New York Historical Society at their 66th anniversary, December 13, 1870.* New York, 1871.

Adams, Charles Francis, Jr. "The British proclamation of May 1861," *Proceedings* of the Massachusetts Historical Society, 2nd ser., XLVIII (1915), 190–241.

————. "A crisis in Downing Street," *Proceedings* of the Massachusetts Historical Society, 2nd ser., XLVII (1914), 372–424.

————. *The crisis of foreign intervention in the war of secession, September-November 1862.* Boston, 1914.

————. "The negotiations of 1861 relating to the Declaration of Paris of 1856," *Proceedings* of the Massachusetts Historical Society, XLVI (1912), 23–84.

————. "Seward and the Declaration of Paris," *Proceedings* of the Massachusetts Historical Society, 2nd ser., XLVI (1912), 23–81.

————. *Seward and the Declaration of Paris, a forgotten diplomatic episode, April-August, 1861.* Boston, 1912.

————. *Studies military and diplomatic, 1775–1865.* New York, 1911.

————. *Trans-Atlantic historical solidarity: lectures delivered before the University of Oxford in Easter and Trinity terms, 1913.* Oxford, 1913.

————. "The Trent Affair," *American historical review*, XVII (1912), 540-562.

————. "The Trent Affair," *Proceedings* of the Massachusetts Historical Society, 2nd ser., XLV (1912), 41 ff.

Adams, Ephraim Douglass. *Great Britain and the American Civil War.* 2 v. New York, 1925.

Allen, H. C. *Great Britain and the United States A history of Anglo-American relations (1783–1952).* New York, 1955.

Andreano, Ralph L., ed. *The economic impact of the American Civil War.* Cambridge, Massachusetts, 1962.

Bailey, Thomas A. *A diplomatic history of the American people.* New York, 1940.

Barker, Nancy Nichols. "France, Austria, and the Mexican venture," *French historical studies*, III (1963), 224–245.

Baroche, Jules. Jean Maurain, *Baroche, ministre de Napoléon III, d'après ses papiers inédits.* Paris, 1936.

Bates, Edward. Marvin R. Cain, *Lincoln's attorney general, Edward Bates of Missouri*. Columbia, Missouri, 1965.

Baxter, James Phinney, III. "The British government and neutral rights, 1861–1865," *American historical review*, XXXIV (Oct., 1928), 9–29.

———. *The introduction of the ironclad warship*. Cambridge, Massachusetts, 1933.

———. "Some British opinions as to neutral rights, 1861–1865," *American journal of international law*, XXIII (1929), 517–537.

Belliot des Minières, E. *La question américaine*. Paris, 1862.

Belloff, Max. "Great Britain and the American Civil War," *History*, XXXVII (1952), 40–48.

Belperron, Pierre. *La guerre de sécession, 1861–1865, ses causes et ses conséquences*. Paris, 1947.

Bemis, George. *Hasty recognition of rebel belligerency; and our right to complain of it*. Boston, 1865.

Bemis, Samuel F. *Diplomatic history of the United States*. New York, 1936.

Benjamin, Judah P. Robert D. Meade, *Judah P. Benjamin, Confederate statesman*. New York, 1943.

———. Robert D. Meade, "The relations between Judah P. Benjamin and Jefferson Davis," *Journal of Southern history*, V (1939), 468–478.

———. S. I. Neiman, *Judah P. Benjamin*, Indianapolis, Indiana, 1963.

Bernard, Montague. *A historial account of the neutrality of Great Britain during the American Civil War*. London, 1870.

Bernstein, S. "French diplomacy and the American Civil War," Chapter VIII in *Essays in political and intellectual history*. New York, 1955.

Bigelow, John. Margaret Clapp, *Forgotten citizen, John Bigelow*. Boston, 1947.

———. "The Confederate diplomats and their shirt of Nessus," *The Century magazine*, XX (May 1891), 113–116.

———. *France and the Confederate navy, 1862–1868. An international episode*. New York, 1888.

———. *Lest we forget: Gladstone, Morley and the Confederate loan of 1863*. New York, 1905.

Bigelow, Poultney. "John Bigelow and Napoleon III," *New York history*, XIII (1932), 154–165.

———. "John Bigelow and his relations with William H. Seward," *Proceedings* of the Ulster County Historical Society (1932), 32–42.

Black, Jeremiah S. Roy F. Nichols, "Jeremiah S. Black," in *American secretaries and their diplomacy*. Ed. by Samuel Flagg Bemis. New York, 1928. Vol. VI.

Blanchot, Charles. *L'intervention française au Mexique. Mémoires.* 3 v. Paris, 1911.

Blumenthal, Henry. *A reappraisal of Franco-American relations, 1830-1871.* Chapel Hill, North Carolina, 1959.

———. "Confederate diplomacy: popular notions and international realities," *Journal of Southern history*, XXXII (1966), 159–167.

Bock, Carl H. *Prelude to tragedy: negotiation and breakdown of the Tripartite Convention of London, October 31, 1861.* Philadelphia, 1966.

Bonham, Milledge L., Jr. *The British consuls in the Confederacy.* New York, 1911.

———. "The French consuls in the Confederate States," *Studies in Southern history and politics.* New York, 1915.

Bonnet, Victor. "L'enquête sur le crédit et la crise de 1863–1864," *Revue des deux mondes*, LIX (Nov. 15, 1865), 391–418.

Boykin, Edward. *Ghost ship of the Confederacy: the story of the "Alabama" and her captain, Raphael Semmes.* New York, 1957.

Buchanan, James. Philip G. Auchampaugh, *James Buchanan and his cabinet on the eve of secession.* Lancaster, Pennsylvania, 1926.

Butler, Major General Benjamin F. William D. Orentt, "Ben Butler and the 'stolen spoons,' " *North American review*, CVII (1918), 66–80.

———. James Parton, *General Butler in New Orleans.* New York, 1864.

———. Hans L. Trefousse, *Benjamin Butler, the South called him beast!* New York, 1957.

———. Richard S. West, *Lincoln's scapegoat general, a life of Benjamin F. Butler, 1818-1893.* Boston, 1965.

Callahan, James M. *American foreign policy in Mexican relations.* New York, 1932.

———. *The diplomatic history of the Southern Confederacy.* Baltimore, 1901.

———. "Diplomatic relations of the Confederate States with England, 1861–1865," *Annual report* of the American Historical Association, 1898. Washington, 1899.

———. *The evolution of Seward's Mexican policy.* Morgantown, West Virginia, 1909.

———. *Russo-American relations during the American Civil War.* ("West Virginia University studies in American history," series I. Diplomatic history no 1). Morgantown, West Virginia, 1908.

Case, Lynn M. "La France et l'affaire du 'Trent,'" *Revue historique* (July–September, 1961), 57–86.

———. "La France et la restitution de Mason et Slidell," *Bulletin* de la Société d'Histoire moderne, 59 (1961): 17–19.

———. "La question de la reconnaissance française au début de la Guerre de Sécession," *Bulletin* de la Société d'Histoire moderne, 61 (1963): 3–5.

———. "La sécession aux Etats-Unis, problème diplomatique français," *Revue d'histoire diplomatique,* LXXVII (1963), 290–313.

Casper, H. W. *American attitudes toward Napoleon III.* New York, 1947.

Cass, Lewis. Frank B. Woodford, *Lewis Cass, the last Jeffersonian.* New Brunswick, New Jersey, 1950.

Channing, Edward. *A history of the United States.* Vol. VI, *The War for Southern Independence.* New York, 1927.

Chapman, John. *The cotton and commerce of India considered in relation to the interests of Great Britain.* London, 1951.

Chase, Major W. H. "The secession of the Southern states," *De Bow's review,* O. S. XXX (Jan. 1861), no. 1.

Chevalier, Michel. *France, Mexico, and the Confederate States.* Tr. by William Henry Hulbert. New York, 1863.

Claussen, M. P. "Peace factors in Anglo-American relations," *Mississippi Valley historical review,* XXVI (1940), 511–522.

Colombos, C. John. *The international law of the sea.* London, 1943.

Copans, Simon J. "French opinion of American democracy, 1852–1860." Doctoral dissertation at Brown University, 1942.

Coulter, E. Merton. *The Confederate States of America, 1861–1865.* ("A history of the South," vol. VII.) Baton Rouge, Louisiana, 1950.

Cowell, John. *La France et les Etats-Confédérés.* Paris, 1865.

Crook, Cauland Elaine. "Benjamin Theron and the French designs in Texas during the Civil War," *Southerwestern historical quarterly,* LXVIII (1965), 432–454.

Curtis, Eugene N. "American opinion of French nineteenth-century revolutions," *American historical review,* XXIX (1924), 249–270.

Dana, Richard Henry. "The Trent Affair," *Proceedings* of the Massachusetts Historical Society, XLV (1913), 509–522.

Darimon, A. *L'opposition libérale sous l'Empire, 1861–1863.* Paris, 1886.

Davis, Jefferson. Hudson Strode, *Jefferson Davis.* 2 v. New York, 1955–1959.

Dayton, William. W. L. Whittlesey, "William Dayton, 1825, senator, presidential candidate, Civil War minister to France, a forgotten Princetonian who served his country well," *Princeton alumni weekly,* XXX (no. 30, May 9, 1930), 797.

Delesalle, Emile. *L'industrie linière dans le nord de la France.* Lille, 1865.

Dommartin, H. Du Pasquier de. *Les Etats-Unis et le Mexique— l'intérêt européen dans l'Amérique du Nord.* Paris, 1852.

Drouyn de Lhuys, Edouard. *Les neutres pendant la guerre d'orient.* Paris, 1868.

——. Bernard d'Harcourt. *Diplomatie et diplomates. Les quatres ministères de M. Drouyn de Lhuys.* Paris, 1882.

——. P. L. E. Pradier-Fodéré, *M. Drouyn de Lhuys.* Paris, 1881.

——. Warren F. Spencer, "Edouard Drouyn de Lhuys and the foreign policy of the Second French Empire." Unpublished Ph. D. dissertation, the University of Pennsylvania, 1955.

————. Warren F. Spencer, "Drouyn de Lhuys et les navires confédérés en France: l'affaires des navires d'Arman, 1863–1865," *Revue d'histoire diplomatique*, LXXVII (1963), 314–334.

Du Bose, J. W. "Confederate Diplomacy," *Southern Historical Society Papers*, XXXII. Richmond, Virginia, 1904.

Duncan, Bingham. "Franco-American tobacco diplomacy," *Maryland historical magazine*, LI (Dec. 1956), 273–301.

Dunham, Arthur L. *The Anglo-French Treaty of Commerce of 1860 and the progress of the industrial revolution in France.* Ann Arbor, Michigan, 1930.

Eaton, Clement. *A history of the Southern Confederacy.* New York, 1958.

Enduran, Lodoix. *France et Mexique. Histoire de l'expédition des Français au Mexique.* Limoges, 1868.

Eugénie, Empress. Nancy Nichols Barker, *Distaff diplomacy: the Empress Eugénie and the foreign policy of the Second Empire.* Austin, Texas, 1967.

————. Nancy Nichols Barker, "Empress Eugénie and the origins of the Mexican venture," *The historian*, XXII, 9–23.

————. Elisabet Esslinger, *Der Einfluss der Kaiserin Eugenie auf der äusseren Politik des Zweiten Kaiserreichs.* Stuttgart, 1932.

Evangeline, Sister. "Seward and the maritime question." Master's thesis at St. John's University, 1941.

Evans, Elliott A. P. "Napoleon III and the American Civil War." Stanford University dissertation, 1940.

Fairfax, Rear-Admiral D. McNeill. "Captain Wilkes's seizure of Mason and Slidell," in *Battles and leaders of the Civil War.* Ed. by R. U. Johnson and C. C. Buel. 4 v. New York, 1956.

Faulkner, Charles James. Donald R. McVeigh, "Charles James Faulkner in the Civil War," *West Virginia history*, XII (1951), 129–141.

Fenwick, Charles G. *International law.* New York, 1924.

Fite, E. D. *Social and industrial conditions in the North during the Civil War.* New York, 1910.

Fleming, Walter L. *Civil War and Reconstruction in Alabama.* New York, 1905.

Fohlen, Claude. *L'Amérique anglo-saxonne de 1815 à nos jours.* Paris, 1965.

——. "Crise textile et troubles sociaux: le Nord à la fin du Second Empire," *Revue du Nord* (1953), 107–123.

——. *L'industrie textile au temps du Second Empire* Paris, 1956.

Forcade, E. "Appel en faveur des chomeurs de Rouen," *Revue des deux mondes,* XLIII (1863), 228–234, 496–502.

——. Louis M. Sears, "A neglected critic of our Civil War," *Mississippi Valley historical review,* I (1915), 523–545.

France. *Enquête industrielle sur le traité de commerce avec l'Angleterre.* 8 v. Paris, 1860.

Fröbel, Julius. *Amerika, Europa und die politischen Gesichtspunkte der Gegenwart.* Berlin, 1859.

Gasparin, A. de. *Une parole de paix—sur le différend entre l'Angleterre et les Etats-Unis.* Paris, 1862.

Gaulot, Paul. *L'empire de Maximilien.* 2 v. Paris, 1889–1890.

——. *La verité sur l'expédition du Mexique, d'après les documents inédits d'Ernest Lavet, payeur en chef du corps expéditionairen.* 3 v. Paris, 1889–1890.

Gavronsky, Serge. "American slavery and the French liberals: an interpretation of the role of slavery in French politics during the Second Empire," *Journal of Negro history,* LI (1966), 36–52.

——. *The French liberal opposition and the American Civil War.* New York, 1968.

Garrity, Francis Xavier. "American editorial opinion of French intervention in Mexico, 1861–1867." Doctoral dissertation at Georgetown University, 1952.

Ginzberg, Eli. "The economics of British neutrality," *Agricultural history,* X (1936), 147 ff.

Gipson, Lawrence H. "The collapse of the Confederacy," *Mississippi Valley historical review,* IV (1917–1918), 437–458.

Gladstone, William E. John Morley, *Life of William Ewart Gladstone.* 3 v. New York, 1903.

Golder, Frank A. "The Russian fleet and the Civil War," *American historical review,* XX (1915), 801–812.

Goebel, Julius. *The recognition policy of the United States.* New York, 1915.

Gray, Wood. *The hidden Civil War: the story of the Copperheads.* New York, 1942.

Greeley, Horace. William Harlan Hale, *Horace Greely: voice of the people.* New York, 1950.

————. Glyndon Garlock Van Deusen, *Horace Greeley: nineteenth century crusader.* Philadelphia, 1953.

Gwin, William McKendree. "Memoir on the history of the United States, Mexico and California." Manuscript dictated by Dr. Gwin to H. H. Bancroft. Berkeley, California.

Hallberg, Charles W. *Franz Joseph and Napoleon III, 1852–1864: a study of Austro-French relations.* New York, 1955.

Hanna, K. A. "The role of the South in the French intervention in Mexico," *Journal of Southern history,* XX (1954), 3–21.

Harrington, Fred H. "A peace mission of 1863," *American historical review,* XLVI (1940), 76–86.

Harris, Thomas L. *The Trent Affair.* Indianapolis, Indiana, 1896.

Haut, Marc d'. *La crise américaine.* Paris, 1862.

Hautefeuille, Laurent Basile. *Quelques questions de droit international maritime à propos de la guerre d'Amérique.* Paris, 1861.

Henderson, William O. "The cotton famine on the Continent, 1861–1865," *Economic historical review,* IV (1933), 195–207.

————. *The Lancashire cotton famine, 1860–1865.* Manchester, 1934.

Hendrick, Burton J. *Lincoln's war cabinet.* Boston, 1945.

————. *Statesmen of the lost cause: Jefferson Davis and his cabinet.* Boston, 1939.

Herzog, Antoine. *L'Algérie et la crise cotonnière.* Colmar, 1864.

Horner, Harlan Hoyt. *Lincoln and Greeley.* Urbana, Illinois, 1953.

Hughes, Archbishop John. Rena Mazyck Andrews, *Archbishop Hughes and the Civil War.* Chicago, 1935.

————. Henry A. Brann, *Most Reverend John Hughes, First Archbishop of New York.* New York, 1912.

————. John R. G. Hassard, *Life of the Most Reverend John Hughes, D. D.* New York, 1866.

————. G. McGuire, "The mission of Archbishop Hughes to Europe, 1861–1862." M. A. Thesis. Columbia University, 1946.

————. Victor F. O'Daniel, "Archbishop John Hughes—American envoy to France, 1861," *Catholic historical review*, III (1917), 336–339.

Hunter, Robert M. T. Henry H. Simms, *Life of Robert M. T. Hunter*. Richmond, Virginia, 1935.

Huntley, Stephen McQueen. *Les rapports de la France et la Confédération pendant la guerre de sécession*. Toulouse, 1932.

Joinville, Prince de. *The Army of the Potomac, its organization, its commander, and its campaign*. New York, 1862.

Jones, Robert Huhn. "Anglo-American relations, 1861–1865, reconsidered," *Mid-America*, XLV (1963), 38–49.

Jones, Robert Owen. "British pseudo-neutrality during the American Civil War." Master's thesis at Georgetown University, 1952.

Jones, Wilbur D. *The Confederate rams at Birkenhead: a chapter in Anglo-American relations*. Tuscaloosa, Alabama, 1961.

Jordan, Donaldson, and Edwin J. Pratt. *Europe and the American Civil War*. Boston, 1931.

Juglar, Clément. *Des crises commerciales*. Paris, 1864.

Kennett, Lee. "The strange career of the 'Stonewall,' " *United States Naval Institute Proceedings* (Feb. 1968), XCIV (no. 2), 74–85.

Kiger, J. J. "Federal government propaganda in Great Britain during the American Civil War," *Historical outlook*, XIX (1928), 204–209.

Kirkland, Edward Chase, *The peacemakers of 1864*. New York, 1927.

Klement, Frank L. *The Copperheads in the Middle West*. Chicago, 1960.

Korolewicz-Carlton, R. "Napoléon III, Thouvenel, et la guerre de Sécession." Thèse de doctorat d'université, University of Paris, 1951.

Laboulaye, Edouard. *De la constititution américaine*. Paris, 1850.
————. *Upon whom rests the guilt of the war?* New York, 1863.

Lacan, A. J. B. *Plaidoirie . . . pour M. Arman contre las Etats-Unis d'Amérique*. Paris, 1868.

Lacour-Gayet, Jacques, ed. *Histoire du commerce*. 6 v. Paris, 1950–1955.

La Gorce, Pierre de. *Histoire du Second Empire.* 7 v. Paris, 1894–1905.

Lally, Frank E. *French opposition to the Mexican policy of the Second Empire.* Baltimore, 1931.

Lambelin, R. "L'intervention française au Mexique," *Revue des questions historiques*, XLIX (1891), 262–273.

Landry, Harral E. "Slavery and the slave trade in Atlantic diplomacy, 1850–1861," *Journal of Southern history*, XXVII (1961), 184–207.

Latané, J. H. *A history of American foreign policy.* New York, 1927.

Lavelaye, Emile de. *Le marché monétaire et ses crises depuis cinquante ans.* Paris, 1865.

———. "Les crises commerciales," *Revue des deux mondes*, LV (Jan. 1865), 207–233.

Lebleu. "Notes statistiques sur l'industrie textile du Haut-Rhin et des Vosges au 1ᵉʳ janvier 1864," *Bulletin* de la Société des Industries et des Manufactures, XXXIV (1864), 252–257.

Legoyt, A. "De la crises cotonnière," *Journal des économistes*, (March, 1863), 425–449.

Lemonnier, Léon. *La guerre de sécession.* Paris, 1942.

Levasseur, Emile. *Histoire des classes ouvrière et de l'industrie en France de 1789 à 1870.* 2nd ed. 2 v. Paris, 1903–1904.

———. *Histoire du commerce de la France.* 2 v. Paris, 1912.

Lincoln, Abraham. Jean Daridan, *Abraham Lincoln.* Paris, 1962.

———. Jay Monaghan, *Diplomat in carpet slippers. Abraham Lincoln deals with foreign affairs.* New York, 1945.

———. Reinhart H. Luthin, "Abraham Lincoln and the tariff," *American historical review*, XLIX (1944), 609–629.

———. John G. Nicolay and John Hay, *Abraham Lincoln, a history.* 10 v. New York, 1890.

———. Thomas H. O'Connor, "Lincoln and the cotton trade," *Civil War history*, VII (1961), 20–35.

———. J. G. Randall, *Lincoln the president.* 4 v. New York, 1945–1955.

———. Louis de Villefosse, *Abraham Lincoln.* Paris, 1956.

Lonn, Ella. *Foreigners in the Confederacy.* Chapel Hill, North Carolina, 1940.

————. *Foreigners in the Union army and navy.* Baton Rouge, Louisiana, 1951.

Lossing, Benson J. *Pictorial history of the Civil War in the United States of America.* 3v . Philadelphia, 1866–1868.

Lutz, Ralph H. *Die Beziehungen zwischen Deutschland und Vereinigten Staaten während des Sezessionskrieges.* Heidelberg, 1911.

Lyons, Richard Bickerton Pemell Lyons, First Earl. Thomas W. Legh, Baron Newton, *Lord Lyons; a record of British diplomacy.* 2 v. London, 1913.

Marcy, William L. R. L. Scribner, "The diplomacy of William L. Marcy." Doctorial dissertation at the University of Virginia, 1949.

McMaster, John Bach. *A history of the people of the United States during Lincoln's administration.* New York, 1927.

Malet, A. "L'expédition du Mexique," *Revue bleue, revue politique et littéraire,* XLV (1890), 124–125.

Mason, James M. Walter M. Case, "James M. Mason, Confederate Diplomat." Unpublished master's thesis in Stanford University Library, 1915.

————. Virginia Mason, *The public life and diplomatic correspondence of James M. Mason, with some personal history by his daughter.* Roanoke, Virginia, 1903.

Maximilian, Emperor. Comte Egon Corti, *Maximilien et Charlotte du Mexique, d'après las archives secrètes de l'empereur Maximilien.* French edition. Paris, 1927. English translation, 2 v. New York, 1928. German new edition, Vienna, 1949.

————. P. E. Martin, *Maximilian in Mexico.*, London, 1914.

Melton, Maurice. *The Confederate ironclads.* New York, 1968.

Mercier, Dr. Alfred. *Du panlatinisme: nécessité d'une alliance entre la France et la Confédération du Sud.* Paris, 1863.

Mercier de l'Ostende, Baron Henri. Daniel B. Carroll, "Henri Mercier in Washington, 1860–1863." Doctoral dissertation at the University of Pennsylvania, 1968.

Metternich-Winneburg, Prince Richard de. Henry Soloman, *L'ambassade de Richard Metternich à Paris.* Paris, 1931.

Moore, John Bassett. *Digest of international law,* VII, 568–573.

Moreau, Henri. *La politique française en Amérique, 1861–1864.* Paris, 1864.

Mowat, Robert B. *The diplomoatic relations of Great Britain and the United States.* London, 1925.

Nanette-Delorme, Emile. *Les Etats-Unis et l'Europe.* Paris, 1863.

Napoleon III. O. F. Aldis, "Louis Napoleon and the Southern Confederacy," *North American review,* CXXIX (Oct. 1879).

———. Lewis Einstein, *Napoleon III and American democracy at the outbreak of the Civil War.* London, 1905.

———. Lewis Einstein, "Napoléon III et les préliminaires diplomatiques de la guerre civile aux Etats-Unis," *Revue d'histoire diplomatique,* XIX (1905), 336–348.

Néré, Jacques. *La Guerre de Sécession.* Paris, 1961.

Nevins, Allen. *The War for the Union.* New York, 1959.

Newton, A. P. "Anglo-American relations during the Civil War, 1861–1865," *Cambridge history of British foreign policy,* II, 488–521.

Nichols, Roy F. *The disruption of American democracy.* New York, 1948.

———. *The stakes of power, 1845–1877.* New York, 1961.

Niox, G. *Expédition du Mexique, 1861–1867. Récit politique et militaire.* Paris, 1874.

Noël, Octave. *Histoire du commerce extérieur de la France.* Paris, 1879.

Owsley, Frank L. "America and the freedom of the seas, 1861–1865," in *Essays in honor of William E. Dodd.* Ed. by Avery Craven. Chicago, 1935.

———. *The CSS "Florida": her building and operation.* Philadelphia, 1965.

———. *King cotton diplomacy: foreign relations of the Confederate States of America.* 2nd edition. Chicago, 1959.

Palmerston, Henry John Temple, Viscount. H. C. F. Bell, *Lord Palmerston.* 2 v. London, 1936.

Paris, Count of. *History of the Civil War in America.* 4 v. Philadelphia, 1875–1888.

Patrick, Rembert W. *Jefferson Davis and his cabinet.* Baton Rouge, Louisiana, 1944.

Pelletan, Eugène. *Adresse au Roi Coton.* Paris, 1863.

Pérez de Acevedo, Javier. *Europa y México, 1861–1862.* Havana, 1935.

Perkins, Dexter. *Hands off! A history of the Monroe Doctrine.* Boston, 1946.

Piggot, F. *The Declaration of Paris, 1856.* London, 1919.

Pohly, Claire. *Les exportations de la France vers les nouveaux pays industriels, 1860–1935.* Geneva, 1935.

Pomeroy, Earl S. "French substitutes for American cotton, 1861-1865," *Journal of Southern history*, IX (1943), 555–560.

Potter, David M. *Lincoln and his party in the secession crisis.* New Haven, Connecticut, 1942.

Pouyer-Quertier, Augustin. *Crédit de cinq millions en faveur des ouvriers sans travail de l'industrie cotonnière. Rapport au corps législatif, 26 janvier 1863.* Rouen, 1863.

Pratt, Julius W. *History of United States foreign policy.* New York, 1939.

Prévost, F. and P. Pecquet. *Le blocus américain—droit des neutres.* Paris, 1862.

Prim, General Don Juan. Genaro Estrada, ed. *Don Juan Prim y su labor diplomática en México.* Mexico City, 1928.

Randall, John G. and David Donald. *The Civil War and Reconstruction.* 2nd edition. Boston, 1961.

Raymond, Henry J. *Raymond of the Times.* New York, 1951.

Reclus, Elisée. "Le coton et la crise américaine," *Revue des deux mondes*, XXXVII (Jan. 1862), 176–208.

Rémond, René. *Les Etats-Unis devant l'opinion française, 1815–1852.* 2 v. Paris, 1962.

Renouvin, Pierre. *Histoire des relations internationales.* Vol. V. *Le XIXe siècle.* I. *De 1815 à 1871. L'Europe des nationalités et l'éveil de nouveaux mondes.* Paris, 1954.

——. *La politique extérieure de Second Empire.* Paris, 1940.

Reybaud, Louis. *Le coton, son régime, ses problèmes, son influence en Europe.* Paris, 1863.

——. "La guerre d'Amérique et le marché du coton." *Revue des deux mondes*, LVI (Jan. 1864), 189 ff.

——. *La laine. Nouvelle série des études sur le régime des manufactures.* Paris, 1867.

Rhodes, James Ford. *History of the Civil War, 1861-1865.* New York, 1917.

————. *History of the United States from the Compromise of 1850 to 1877*. 8 v. New York, 1893–1906.

Rice, Allen Thorndike. "A famous diplomatic dispatch," *North American review*, CXLII (1886), 402–410.

Rippy, F. F. *The United States and Mexico*. New York, 1926.

Roebuck, John Arthur. R. E. Leader, *Life of John Arthur Roebuck*. London, 1879.

Romero, Matías. Robert R. Miller, "Matías Romero, Mexican minister to the United States during the Juarez-Maximilian era," *Hispanic American historical review*, LXV (1965), 228–245.

Rouher, Eugène. Robert Schnerb, *Rouher et le Second Empire*. Paris, 1949.

Russell, John, First Earl. Spencer Walpole, *The life of Lord John Russell*. 2 v. London, 1889.

Savage, C. *Policy of the United States towards maritime commerce in war*. Washington, 1934.

Scharf, J. Thomas. *History of the Confederate States Navy from its organization to the surrender of its last vessel*. New York, 1887.

Schefer, Christian. *La grande pensée de Napoléon III. Les origines de l'expédition du Mexique, 1858–1862*. Paris, 1939.

Schleiden, Rudolph. Ralph H. Lutz, "Rudolph Schleiden and the visit to Richmond, April 25, 1861," *Annual report* of the American Historical Association (1915). Washington, 1917.

Schmidt, L. B. "Influence of wheat and cotton on Anglo-American relations," *Iowa journal of history and politics*, XVI (1918), 400 ff.

Semmes, Raphael. W. Adolphe Roberts, *Semmes of the "Alabama."* New York, 1938.

Seward, William H. Frederick Bancroft, *The life of William H. Seward*. 2 v. New York, 1900.

————. Sister M. M. O'Rourke, "The diplomacy of William H. Seward during the Civil War: his policies as related to international law." Doctoral dissertation of the University of California, 1963.

————. Patrick Sowle, "A reappraisal of Seward's memorandum of April 1, 1861, to Lincoln," *Journal of Southern history*, XXXIII (1967), 234–239.

————. Henry W. Temple, "William H. Seward," in Samuel F. Bemis, ed., *American secretaries of state and their diplomacy.* 10 v. New York, 1927–1929. Vol. VII, pp. 3–115.

————. Glyndon G. Van Deusen, *William Henry Seward.* New York, 1967.

Seymour, Horatio. Stewart Mitchell, *Horatio Seymour of New York.* Cambridge, Massachusetts, 1938.

Slidell, John. Ethel Dugan, "John Slidell, Confederate diplomat to France." Unpublished master's thesis, Stanford University Library, 1915.

————. Louis M. Sears, "A Confederate diplomat [John Slidell] at the court of Napoleon III," *American historical review*, XXVI (1920–1921), 255–281.

————. Louis M. Sears, *John Slidell.* Durham, North Carolina, 1925.

————. Beckles Willson, *John Slidell and the Confederates in Paris, 1862–1865.* New York, 1932.

Soley, James Russell. *The blockade and the cruisers.* New York, 1883.

Spears, John R. *The history of our navy.* 4 v. New York, 1897.

Spencer, Warren F. "A French view of the fall of Richmond," *The Virginia magazine of history and biography*, LXXIII (1965), 178–188.

Stern, Philip Van Doren. *When the guns roared, world aspects of the American Civil War.* New York, 1965.

Stock, Leo F. "Catholic participation in the diplomacy of the Southern Confederacy," *Catholic historical review*, XVI (1930), 1–18.

————. "American consuls to the Papal States," *Catholic historical review*, IX (1929), 233–251.

Stoeckl, Baron Edouard de. F. A. Golder, "The American Civil War in the eyes of a Russian diplomat," *American historical review*, XXVI (1921), 454–463.

St. Paul, H. *Our home and foreign policy, November 1863.* Mobile, Alabama, 1863.

Sumner, Senator Charles. V. H. Cohen, "Charles Sumner and foreign relations." Doctoral dissertation at the University of Oklahoma, 1951.

————. David Donald, *Charles Sumner and the coming of the Civil War*. New York, 1960.

————. G. H. Haynes, *Charles Sumner*. Philadelphia, 1909.

————. Carl Schurz, *Charles Sumner*. Ed. by A. R. Hogue. Urbana, Illinois, 1951.

————. Walter G. Shotwell, *Life of Charles Sumner*. New York, 1910.

Teichmann, W. C. *Englands und Frankreichs Stellung zum Bürgerkriege in den Vereinigten Staaten von Amerika, 1861–1865*. Munich, 1885.

Thompson, Samuel B. *Confederate purchasing operations abroad*. Chapel Hill, North Carolina, 1935.

Tocqueville, Alexis de. *De la démocratie en Amérique*. 2 v. Paris, 1835. An English translation, 4 v. London, 1835.

Todd, H. H. "The building of the Confederate States navy in Europe." Dissertation at Vanderbilt University, 1941.

"Die Trent Angelegenheit, 1861–1862," *Preussische Jahrbücher*, VIII (1862), 630–636.

Tunc, André et Suzanne Tunc. *Le système constitutionnel des Etats-Unis d'Amérique*. 2 v. Paris, 1954.

Turgan, Julien. *Les grandes usines, études industrielles en France et à l'étranger*. 10 v. Paris, 1860–1874.

Tyrner-Tyrnauer, A. R. *Lincoln and the emperors*. New York, 1962.

Véron, Eugène. "Dissolution de l'union américaine, ses causes et ses conséquences," *Revue nationale et étrangère* (Feb. 1861), 321–345.

Victoria, Queen. Charles Francis Adams, Jr., "Queen Victoria and the Civil War," *Proceedings* of the Massachusetts Historical Society, 2nd series, XVII (1903), 439–448; XVIII (1905), 123–154; XX (1907), 453–474.

Vierne, Henri. "L'industrie du coton, son passé et la crise actuelle," *Revue contemporaine*, XXXI (1863), 691–713; XXXII (1863), 322–343.

Ward, Sir A. A. and G. P. Gooch, eds. *The Cambridge history of British foreign policy, 1783–1919*. 3 v. London, 1922–1923.

Watts, J. *Facts of the cotton famine*. London, 1866.

Weed, Thurlow. T. W. Barnes, *Memoir of Thurlow Weed*. Boston, 1884.

————. Glyndon G. Van Deusen, *Thurlow Weed, wizard of the lobby*. Boston, 1947.

Welles, Gideon. "The capture and release of Mason and Slidell," *Galaxy*, XV (1873), 640–651.

————. *Lincoln and Seward*. New York, 1874.

Wesley, Charles H. *The collapse of the Confederacy*. Washington, 1937.

West, Warren R. *Contemporary French opinion on the American Civil War*. Baltimore, 1924.

Wheeler-Bennett, Sir John. "The Trent Affair: how the Prince Consort saved the United States," *History today*, XI (1961), 805–816.

White, Elizabeth B. *American opinion of France from Lafayette to Poincaré*. New York, 1927.

Willson, Beckles. *American ambassadors to France, 1777–1927*. New York, 1928.

Winters, John D. *The Civil War in Louisiana*. Baton Rouge, Louisiana, 1963.

Woldman, Albert A. *Lincoln and the Russians*. New York, 1952.

Wright, Gordon. "Economic conditions in the Confederacy as seen by the French consuls," *Journal of Southern history*, VII (May 1941), 195–214.

Yancey, William Lowndes. John W. Du Bose, *The life and times of William Lowndes Yancey. A history of political parties in the United States, from 1834 to 1864, especially as to the origins of the Confederate States*. Birmingham, Alabama, 1892.

Zornow, Frank, *Lincoln and the party divided*. Norman, Oklahoma, 1954.

INDEX

Drouyn de Lhuys, Edouard, French foreign minister, iii, 13; character and ideas, 347–353; appointment of, 346–348, 353; and Dayton, 348, 354, 367–369, 371, 389, 402–404; and neutrality, 350–351, 381, 497, 565; and Napoleon III, 352, 413–414, 507–509; and Persigny, 352–353; and mediation note of 1862, 353–371; and slavery, 368–369; and peace commission plan, 385–397; and Polish insurrection, 399–400; and Roebuck affair, 402, 410, 414–426; and recognition of CSA, 402, 410–426, 549; and Slidell, 402–403, 413–414; and Erlanger loans, 405–407; and Arman ships, 431–432, 440–467, 472–477, 480, 532; and belligerent ships in French ports, 482–515; and tobacco shipments, 528, 531–534, 539; and Mexican expedition, 516–525, 527, 547–555, 561–564; and Lincoln's assassination, 572; and war's end, 561, 564, 567, 578; and withdrawing recognition of CSA belligerency, 579–586; and cooperation with UK, 355, 580–584; evaluation of, 600; writings on, 711–712

Dual republic idea, 313–314, 327, 336, 340, 599–600

Due, Frederik, Swedish minister in Paris, 179, 209

Dunlap, Judge James, of US Circuit Court of DC, 615 n. 33, 630 n. 80

Dupont, Rear-Admiral Samuel Francis, USN, 518

Eckels, Mrs., 558–559, 689 n. 49

Economic crisis, in France, 6–7, 132, 142, 146, 158–189, 252, 257–258, 276–277, 291, 304, 319, 358, 371, 374–381, 395, 591–592, 651 n. 6; in UK, 304, 643 n. 72; in CSA, 144, 401, 424–425, 526, 551

Egyptian cotton, 376

El Ferrol (Spain), 472, 474–475, 477–478

Elsinore (Denmark), 470

Elswick Works, UK munition firm, 435

Emancipation of slaves, 3, 14, 42, 316–333, 344; and France, 328–332, 343, 654 n. 27; Preliminary Proclamation of, 323–328, 343, 344, 382, 654 n. 16, n. 22; Final Proclamation of, 382. *See also* Slavery

Embargo in CSA, 1, 12, 14, 158–160, 172, 262, 280–281, 287, 295–296, 315, 333–334, 381, 593–594 *See also* "King Cotton"

Erlanger & Co., French banking house, 403–408

Erlanger, Emile, French banker, 406

Erlanger loan, 403–408, 420, 431, 433, 595; Seward on, 666 n. 30

Eugenie, Empress of France, 212, 235, 508, 586, 644 n. 179, 712

Eustis, George, Jr., secretary to John Slidell, 11, 487; papers of, 11, 697

Evans, Elliott, US historian, 6

Evans, Dr. Thomas W., dentist to Napoleon III, 9, 136, 253, 256, 412–413, 415, 700

Everett, Edward, US scholar and elder statesman, 175

Ewell, General Richard S., CSA, 542

"Expéditif," French collier, 470–471, 473

Export trade, 106; in France, 2, 13, 18, 42–43, 50, 55–57, 128–132, 136–137, 142, 158–189, 222, 252, 291, 319, 358, 374–381, 393, 569; in UK, 2, 47, 50, 129, 346

Exposé de la situation de l'Empire, and French economic crisis, 257–258

Fairfax, Lieutenant, USN, and the "Trent" affair, 192, 635 n. 12

Fair Oaks (VA), battle of, 297–298, 309, 311, 323

Falaise, economic conditions in, 161

Fauconnet, French consul in New Orleans, 521–522

Faulkner, Charles J., US minister in Paris, 7, 27–28, 40, 48–49; and Napoleon III, 18–24; and Thouvenel, 25–26, 29, 35, 37, 49, 610 n. 39; and Sanford, 27–31, 610 n. 39

Fauntleroy, Lieutenant, CSA navy, commander of the CSS "Rappahannock," 504–505, 508

Favre, Jules, French deputy, 460, 566, 573

Fenwick, Charles G., US professor of international law, 122, 139, 140

Féray d'Essonnes, on effects of the Cobden Treaty, 634 n. 72

Ferguson, Sir James, UK traveler, 173

Ferri-Pisani, Colonel, 9

Ferté-Macé, economic conditions in, 161